China's Regional Development

China is a large developing economy and it has been deeply involved in globalization since its economic reform and opening-up. Simultaneously, China has seen a significant change in the spatial distribution of economic resources, especially capital and labor. In the past 10 years, economists have made significant progress in both theoretical and empirical studies on related topics.

The book provides an overview of the existing literature and current policy debates on what we have known and what we have misunderstood. It includes an analytical framework of the *New Economic Geography* with political economy to help us understand China's regional development issues. The book of 10 chapters is organized into four thematic sections. Part One is a theoretical discussion on the relationship between economic agglomeration and interregional balanced development. Part Two is a political economy analysis on regional and urban–rural development. Part Three provides a summary on empirical literatures concerning market segmentation and institutional barriers that constrain production factors, including capital, labor, and land use rights, from being reallocated across regions. Part Four consists of four empirical chapters on the relationship between agglomeration and balance, which is the core of relevant policy debates.

The book is a valuable reference for readers who are interested in spatial economics and the Chinese economy, especially China's regional and urban development.

Ming Lu is Professor of Economics Shanghai Jiao Tong University and at Fudan University, China. He is also a Research Fellow of Peking University-Lincoln Institute and Hitotsubashi University. He has consulted for the World Bank and Asian Development Bank. He has a Ph.D. in Economics from Fudan University. His recent research covers labor economics (income distribution and migration), regional and urban economics (urbanization and regional development), and social economics (social network and economic development).

Zhao Chen is Professor of Economics and Deputy Director of the China Centre for Economic Studies at Fudan University, China. His recent research covers development economics (urbanization, migration, income inequality), industrial economics (industry policy, FDI, outward FDI), and political economy (political connections).

Xiwei Zhu is Associate Professor of Economics at the Center for Research of Private Economy, Zhejiang University, China. He obtained his Ph.D. in economics from Zhejiang University in 2005. Currently, his main research interests are new economic geography, industrial organization, and international trade.

Xianxiang Xu is Professor of Economics and Chair of the Economics Department at Sun Yat-sen University, China. His recent research covers economic growth and the political elite.

China's Regional Development

Review and prospect

Edited by
Ming Lu, Zhao Chen, Xiwei Zhu, and Xianxiang Xu

Routledge
Taylor & Francis Group
LONDON AND NEW YORK

First published 2013
by Routledge
2 Park Square, Milton Park, Abingdon, Oxfordshire OX14 4RN

Simultaneously published in the USA and Canada
by Routledge
711 Third Avenue, New York, NY 10017

First issued in paperback 2014

Routledge is an imprint of the Taylor and Francis Group, an informa business

Translated from the Chinese version

British Library Cataloguing in Publication Data
A catalogue record for this book is available from the British Library

Library of Congress Cataloging in Publication Data
[Zhongguo qu yu jing ji fa zhan. English] China's regional development : review and prospect / edited by Ming Lu, Zhao Chen, Xiwei Zhu, and Xianxiang Xu.
pages cm
Translation of: Zhongguo qu yu jing ji fa zhan. Shanghai : Ge zhi chu ban she : Shanghai ren min chu ban she, 2011.
Includes bibliographical references and index.
1. China—Economic conditions—1976-2000. 2. China—Economic conditions—2000- 3. China—Economic conditions—1976-2000—Regional disparities. 4. China—Economic conditions—2000—Regional disparities.
I. Lu, Ming, editor of compilation.
HC427.92.Z47844813 2013
338.951—dc23 2012051467

ISBN 978-0-415-52470-4 (hbk)
ISBN 978-1-138-91481-0 (pbk)
ISBN 978-0-203-75810-6 (ebk)

Typeset in Times New Roman
by Cenveo Publisher Services

Contents

Figures

Tables

Contributors

Zhao Chen is Professor of Economics and Deputy Director of the China Center for Economic Studies at Fudan University, China. His recent research covers development economics (urbanization, migration, income inequality), industrial economics (industry policy, FDI, outward FDI), and political economy (political connections).

Jianyong Fan is Professor of Economics and Director of the Center for Industrial and Regional Economic Studies at Fudan University, China. His recent research covers regional and urban economics (urbanization, regional development, and New Economic Geography).

Ziying Fan is Associate Professor of Economics at Huazhong University of Science and Technology, Wuhan, China. His recent research covers public finance (intergovernmental transfer and tax policies) and development economics (the Chinese Great Famine).

Yuanhua Gao is a Ph.D. candidate at Sun Yat-sen University, China.

Canfei He is Professor of Economic Geography and Deputy Director of Peking University-Lincoln Institute Center for Urban Development and Land Policy at Peking University, China. His recent research includes industrial agglomeration, multinational corporations, and regional and urban development.

Jiuli Huang is Associate Professor of Nankai University, China. His fields of interest include international trade (foreign trade of China, especially) and regional economics (regional development and industrial agglomeration).

Fangwen Li is a research fellow at the Center for Industrial and Regional Economic Studies at Fudan University, China. His recent research focuses on urbanization and regional development.

Zhigang Li graduated from University of California, San Diego, with a Ph.D. in Economics. He is now the Senior Economist of BBVA (Banco Bilbao Vizcaya Argentaria). His research area covers the taxation system, infrastructure investment, and real estate markets of China.

Ming Lu is Professor of Economics and Director of the Center for China Development Studies at Shanghai Jiaotong University, and Professor at Fudan University, China. His recent research covers labor economics (income distribution and migration), regional and urban economics (urbanization and regional development), and social economics (social interaction and economic development).

Fenghua Pan is Assistant Professor of Economic Geography at Beijing Normal University, China. His recent research includes industrial agglomeration, finance geography, and regional development.

Yongliang Tao is a Ph.D. candidate in School of Economics, Zhejiang University, China. His research focuses on provincial protectionism and industrial agglomeration in China.

Xianbing Wang is Assistant Professor of Economics at Guangdong University of Foreign Studies, China. His recent research covers economic growth, and the political elite.

Xianxiang Xu is Professor of Economics and the Chair of the Economics Department at Sun Yat-sen University, China. His recent research covers economic growth and the political elite.

Siqi Zheng is Associate Professor at the Hang Lung Center for Real Estate, and the Deputy Head of the Department of Construction Management at Tsinghua University, China. Her fields of specialization are urban economics, and the housing market. Her research interests include urban spatial structure, green cities, housing supply and demand, housing price dynamics, and low-income housing policies.

Xiwei Zhu is Associate Professor of Economics at the Center for Research of Private Economy, Zhejiang University, China. He obtained a Ph.D. in economics from Zhejiang University in 2005. Currently, his main research interests are New Economic Geography, industrial organization, and international trade.

Foreword

Economic activities are not concentrated on the head of a pin, nor are they spread evenly over a featureless plane. On the contrary, economic activities are concentrated in a fairly limited number of cities and regions that account for a sizeable share of the wealth produced in developed and emerging countries. Contrary to widespread belief, we do not live in a world where distance and location no longer matter. Recent empirical and theoretical work in the new economic geography and urban economics shows a very different reality. New forces, hitherto outweighed by natural factors, are shaping an economic landscape that, with its many barriers and large inequalities, is anything but flat. The aim of the new economic geography is to identify the main channels that generate peaks and troughs in the spatial distribution of wealth and people. Unlike earlier contributions in spatial economics, the acting centripetal and centrifugal forces are market-based and endogenous.

The conclusions of Krugman's ground-breaking paper are well known and have given rise to controversy. Unlike new trade theories that do not consider factor mobility, allowing for the migration of workers may lead to the emergence of large economic agglomerations and regional imbalance. In view of the political and social implications of this conclusion, it is important to assess its robustness. Indeed, the core-periphery model disregards several major factors that lead to less pessimistic conclusions. Above all, the high housing and commuting costs households must bear for living in large cities deter the continuing concentration of activities in a few giant cities. Thus, if economic integration can indeed initially foster a more intensive agglomeration of economic activities, its continuation is liable to generate a redeployment of activities that could lead to a kind of geographical evening-out. In short, one may expect the process of spatial development to unfold according to a bell-shaped curve.

The new economic geography appears to be especially well suited to the study of a fast-growing and large economy, such as China. China experiences widening regional disparities—with 67.9 percent of its GDP being produced by 42.8 percent of its population over 13.5 percent of its area in 2007, as well as a rapid urbanization—its rate of urbanization now slightly exceeds 50 percent. Both processes have, and will continue to have, a major impact on the way economic activities unfold across the Chinese space-economy, with immense social and political consequences. The research agenda involves an impressive list of key questions. Are Chinese cities too small or too big? Are internal trade borders still high within China? Will the development of large transportation infrastructures promote convergence or divergence across Chinese provinces? Will the West of China catch up with the East? These are just a few examples of issues that should be explored by Chinese scientists in cooperation with their foreign colleagues.

This book, written by leading young Chinese economists, is a very important contribution that will help both Chinese and international readers to understand what is going on in China's regional and urban development.

Jacques Thisse
CORE
Université catholique de Louvain
2013

Part I

Economic agglomeration and interregional development

1 Agglomeration and regional coordination

Xiwei Zhu and Yongliang Tao

1.1 Introduction

Spatial agglomeration of economic activity is a prominent fact with modern economic growth: (1) From a time dimension perspective, economic output grows continuously (Romer, 1986); (2) from a spatial dimension perspective, economic activity constantly agglomerates toward a few regions (Krugman, 1991a). Mainstream economists have studied the former for a long time, while research into the latter has only gradually formed and developed since the 1990s. As a matter of fact, spatial agglomeration of economic activities is a very widespread phenomenon in the real world, which can be observed at various levels. At the global level, in the 30 years since the 1980s, the aggregate economic output of NAFTA countries, 27 EU countries, and East Asian countries has always stayed above 70 percent of world output.[1] At the national level, on the one hand, the economic activity of developed nations such as the US and Japan shows a distinct trend toward spatial agglomeration. Take Japan as an example. In 2001, three megalopolis economic rims that occupy only 10.4 percent of Japan's land mass accounted for 48.6 percent of Japan's population, 66.2 percent of its GNP and 68.9 percent of its industry (Liu, 2006). On the other hand, according to our calculations, as the world's largest developing country, the spatial agglomeration of economic activities in China has constantly increased in the 30 years since reform and opening up. Using the Herfindahl–Hirschman Index (henceforth, HHI) of mainland China's interprovincial industrial output as an example, in 1978, the HHI of 31 provinces (excluding Taiwan, Hong Kong, and Macau; although this refers to provinces, directly administered municipalities and autonomous regions, the short version "province" will be used here) was 557.31; in 2009 it rose to 729.44, an increase of 30.89 percent.[2] In 2009, Jiangsu, Zhejiang, and Shanghai, which are located around the Yangtze Delta and occupy less than 3 percent of land mass, produced 22.14 percent of the industrial output; realized 40.87 percent of exports and 43.06 percent of imports; and generated 21.29 percent of GDP in China. These empirical facts indicate that economic agglomeration is a common phenomenon that occurs during economic development worldwide, and not only is this reflected at the global level, but also at the regional level within the world's major economies.

However, when it comes to mainland China after reform and opening-up, accompanying spatial agglomeration of economic activities is the significant expansion of regional disparities. Especially since the early 1990s, the trend of increasing regional disparities is very evident and becomes an important reason for the increase in regional income disparity (see, e.g. Chen and Xu, 2004; Guan et al., 2006; Wan et al., 2007; Wan et al., 2005; Wang and Fan, 2004; Wei and Sun, 2004; Xu and Li, 2006).[3] After entering the twenty-first century, in order to promote coordinated economic development among regions and decrease regional disparity, the central government successively implemented regional development strategies such as the "Grand Western Development Program"; "Revitalization of Northeast-China Old Industrial Bases" and "Rise of Central China", etc., slowing down the expansion rate of regional disparity compared to the 1990s (Wei and Sun, 2004; Xu and Li, 2006). Furthermore, Liu et al. (2009) stated that, after 2004, regional disparity measured by the ratio between the *per capita* income of Eastern regions and Central and Western regions demonstrated a slightly downward slope.

With regard to the debate on economic agglomeration and regional coordination in China, we believe the first question that needs to be answered is: Is the degree of spatial agglomeration in China's economy too high? Moreover, as far as China is concerned, is agglomeration of economic activities in coastal areas mainly responsible for increasing the *per capita* income gap between regions? What effects have a series of regional development strategies represented by the "Grand Western Development Program" had on reshaping China's regional economic geography? Finally, is there a proper way to realize both economic growth and regional coordination? To this end, the next section of this chapter will systematically review New Economic Geography's (NEGs) theoretical research on the spatial agglomeration of economic activities and regional coordinated development; section 1.3 will reply to, and comment on, the above questions in view of international experience, and proposes policy implications for the future development of China's regional economy; the final section will summarize the main conclusions of this chapter. We will point out institutional barriers in China that cause inefficient allocation of production factors; these not only restrict the spatial agglomeration of economic activities, but also are not conducive to reducing regional disparities, and may even hinder China's long-term economic growth.

1.2 Industrial agglomeration and regional disparity: a theoretical review

NEG's theoretical roots can be traced back to research on agricultural locations by nineteenth-century classical economists. *The Isolated State*, published by Von Thünen in 1826, explores the agricultural location issues within an isolated state composed of a city and surrounding agricultural regions. It is regrettable that until the 1990s, research regarding economic geography had always been at the periphery of mainstream economics (Krugman, 1991b). Krugman believes that mainstream economics neglects the location decisions of economic activities due to a key technical problem: How to consider the market structure? Essentially, discussions on the location decisions of economic activities must deviate from the neoclassical paradigm, i.e., constant returns to scale and perfect competition. As long as economists lacked analytic instruments to rigorously portray increasing returns and imperfect competition, research on economic geography will be excluded from the mainstream. Fortunately, Dixit and Stiglitz (1977) used an ingenious simplification to successfully incorporate increasing returns and imperfectly competitive markets into the general equilibrium analytic framework, clearing the technical barrier for the emergence of NEG. Based on the D-S setup, Krugman (1991a,b) took economies of scale, monopolistic competition and transport costs as keystones to construct a theoretical model; he successfully explained the spatial agglomeration of economic activities, marking the birth of NEG. Differing from the traditional research on location decision, NEG puts more emphasis on describing the microeconomic basis of individual choice and market clearing: The location choice of the economic agent—the firm—relies on the relative strength of agglomeration forces and dispersion forces, thus making spatial agglomeration of economic activities endogenously determined in the model. This section will review the classic theories of NEG and comment on the issues of industrial agglomeration and regional coordination.

1.2.1 Re-thinking of the core-periphery model

The initial core-periphery model, established by Krugman, studies an economic system including two regions with symmetric endowments; two sectors (the monopolistically competitive manufacturing sector and the perfectly competitive agricultural sector), and two production factors (mobile skilled labor and immobile unskilled labor). A static core-periphery model does not have capital accumulation and the number of differentiated manufactured goods are constant. Geographic distribution of firms in equilibrium is determined by the relative strength of agglomeration and dispersion forces.

Agglomeration forces usually have the following two sources:

1. Home market effect: Due to the existence of transport costs,[4] firms tend to locate in a region where market demand is large, and export products to the region where market demand is small, in order to lower transport costs. That is to say, in equilibrium, firms that locate in the region with the larger demand take up a larger proportion of total firms nationwide than the share the region's demand does. In other words, the region with larger market demand has a magnification effect, which means the share of firms it attracts is a more than proportional share of the demand.
2. Price index effect: Due to the existence of transport costs, the consumer price index (CPI) is lower in the region with a high share of firms. Thus, under

equal nominal wage rates in both regions, skilled labor in that region could obtain a higher real-wage rate, causing mobile skilled labor to shift towards it. In other words, the region with a high share of firms can pay a relatively low nominal wage rate to attract skilled labor, thereby obtaining relatively high profits; this further encourages firms to concentrate in the region with more firms. The former agglomeration force is called backward linkage, while the latter is called forward linkage.

Dispersion forces generally have the following two sources:

1. Market crowding effect: All other conditions being equal, on the one hand, the region with a high share of firms has tougher competition, causing firms in that region to face lower demand in the local market than firms in the other region; on the other hand, transport costs have a "protection effect," which causes the impact of foreign demand on firms' profits to be "discounted" compared with local demand.[5] Therefore, firms in the region with a high share of firms have low profits, encouraging firms to shift towards the region with fewer firms.
2. Immobile factors:[6] Unskilled labor employed in agricultural sector is tied to land and becomes an immobile factor. But unskilled labor also consumes manufactured goods, therefore the larger the relative quantity of symmetrically distributed immobile factor compared to the mobile factor (skilled labor), the smaller the difference between the quantities demanded for manufactured goods in the two regions, and the more likely it is for firms to be equally dispersed.

The relative strength of agglomeration and dispersion forces, which are usually determined by transport costs, will determine the spatial equilibrium distribution of firms. Specifically, when transport costs in an economy are high, which means the dispersion forces in the system are larger than the agglomeration forces, the agricultural and manufacturing sectors maintain a steady symmetric distribution in the two regions. As transport costs fall (in other words, as regional integration increases), agglomeration and dispersion forces both decrease. However, dispersion forces are more sensitive to a decrease in transport costs than agglomeration forces, so that dispersion forces decrease at a faster rate. There exists a certain critical level for transport costs (let ϕ_B be known as the break point). If transport costs are lower than the break point ($\phi > \phi_B$), agglomeration forces are larger than dispersion forces (Figure 1.1), and the symmetric equilibrium becomes unstable. As the transport costs continue to decline, firms gradually move to one region and the number of firms in each region is no longer equal. Furthermore, there exists another critical level for transport costs (let ϕ_S be known as the sustain point).[7] If transport costs are lower than the sustain point ($\phi > \phi_S$), all firms will be concentrated in one region and the other region will only be left with an agricultural sector. Such an equilibrium is stable and the economic system forms a core-periphery structure.

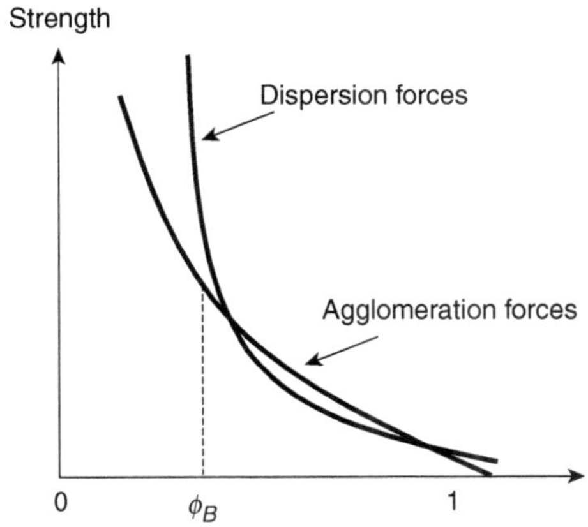

Figure 1.1 Dispersion forces, agglomeration forces, and transportation costs.

For welfare consideration, since the shipment of manufactured goods requires transport costs, the CPI of the core is lower than that of the periphery. Thus, consumers in the core (skilled and unskilled labor) enjoy greater well-being than those in the periphery (unskilled labor). When transport costs are very high, both regions maintain the initial symmetric distribution, with the welfare of skilled labor and unskilled labor being equal for both regions, though the welfare of skilled labor is higher than that of unskilled labor. As transport costs fall below the break point, the symmetric equilibrium becomes unstable. There are differences in the two regions' CPI due to some firms shifting from one region to the other, which causes the well-being of unskilled labor in the two regions to become unequal. As transport costs fall below the sustain point, the two regions form a core-periphery structure, with all skilled labor agglomerated in the core. Now the welfare of consumers in the two regions successively is: the well-being of skilled labor living in the core is greater than that of unskilled labor in the core, which is greater than that of unskilled labor in the periphery. When transport costs decline to near zero, CPI of the core and the periphery tend to converge, and the welfare of the unskilled labor in both regions eventually equalizes.[8] Thus, during the process where transport costs decline from infinite to zero, the real income differential of residents in the two regions displays an inverted U-shaped curve, initially increasing and then decreasing (Figure 1.2). The inverted U-shape of the real income gap between regions demonstrates the fact that during the process of government-facilitated regional economic integration, it is inevitable that "a few people get rich first," and the income gap between the regions that got rich first and those left behind will constantly increase for a prolonged period of time. Only when economic integration deepens does the social welfare increase simultaneously with a continuous decrease in the relative well-being gap between regions. That is to say, regarding the government, regional integration policies need to be

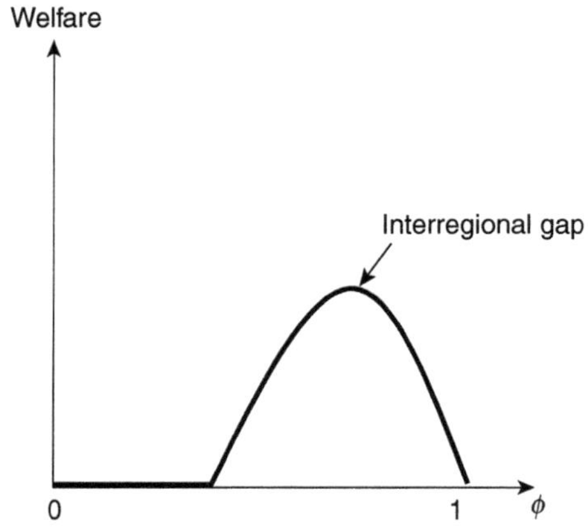

Figure 1.2 Regional gap and transportation costs.

pushed faster in order to prevent the economy from lingering in the "pain period" for a long time; and regarding the public, enough confidence and patience is required in the government's regional integration policies to narrow down regional income disparities, and quick results should not be expected.[9] What also needs to be noted, is that attaining the above-mentioned "inverted-U" trend is dependent upon a sufficient mobility of factors. Once factor mobility is restricted, delay and difficulty in attaining the final convergence is inevitable.

The original NEG model relied to a great extent on certain strong assumptions, such as two regions, two sectors, two factors, and zero transport costs for agricultural goods. The extension of the theory lies in gradually relaxing these assumptions, testing the robustness of the conclusions and improving the elaboration of the theory. Once these rigorous assumptions are relaxed, not only is redispersion of the firm possible, but even if the firm continues to agglomerate towards developed regions, the region left behind can still see an increase in *per capita* income, and may even exceed the developed region. This is to say, theoretically, the agglomeration of economic activities is not necessarily accompanied by magnification in interregional income differentials. Below, we will illustrate this point with a few examples.

1.2.1.1 Multi-region model and regional disparities

Ago et al. (2006) constructed an asymmetric multi-region model to explore the impact of location advantage on spatial distribution of economic activities and welfare. Specifically, suppose a region lies at the midpoint of a linear country, and two other regions lie at the endpoint, then the core region is endowed with location advantage. Ago et al. (2006) show that under Krugman's (1991a) CES utility function and iceberg transport costs, a decrease in transport costs can attract more manufacturing firms to the core region. Under Ottaviano et al.'s (2002) model, quadratic quasi-linear utility function and linear transport costs, due to the existence of the pro-competitive effect, the competition effect (caused by a decrease in transport costs attracting firms to the core region) exceeds location advantage, which instead causes firms to flee the core and move to the periphery, leading to a decrease in the well-being of consumers in the core.

1.2.1.2 Transport costs of agricultural goods and industrial redispersion

Early NEG literature usually neglected the function of the agricultural sector when studying industrial agglomeration. It is well known that agriculture plays a very important role in most developing countries. Picard and Zeng (2005) introduce diversified agricultural goods and transport costs into Ottaviano et al.'s (2002) model, and found that transport costs of the agricultural sector are significant in determining the spatial distribution of the manufacturing sector. Specifically, when transport costs for agricultural goods are above a certain level, agglomeration of firms will never occur; when transport costs for agricultural goods are below a certain level, as transport costs for manufactured goods decline, spatial distribution of manufacturing firms will display a process of dispersed to agglomerated then from agglomerated to dispersed again. This seems to indicate, that when economic integration deepens, the difference in the size of manufacturing sector across regions, as well as the income gap, will start converging.

1.2.1.3 Non-tradable goods and regional disparity

Zeng and Zhu (2011) explored the effect of the non-tradable goods sector's expansion in a large open economy on industrial agglomeration and its welfare implications by developing a model with two regions, three sectors and three factors. Their study shows, as a non-tradable good, the development of the tourism industry will have an income effect and resource movement effect on domestic industrial development. The income effect refers to a positive effect on the development of the manufacturing sector derived from an increased demand for manufactured goods with income improving by the development of the service industry (tourism). The resource movement effect refers to the competition for resources with the manufacturing sector that development of tourism will bring, causing a portion of resources to be diverted from the manufacturing sector to the tourism industry, forming a negative "crowding-out" effect on industrial agglomeration. However, whether the development of tourism promotes industrial agglomeration or hinders it, depends on the parameters. From the perspective of social welfare, if the residents of two countries both consume domestic and foreign tourism services, then as the proportion of their expenditure on tourism services increases, the well-being of the residents of the small country will increase, eventually exceeding that of the large country's residents. This is because the large country's demand for the small country's tourism services will exceed the small country's demand for the large country's tourism services. When the ratio of tourism goods expenditure is high, the income effect of a tourism boom on the small country exceeds the resource movement effect, and vice versa for the large country. This has important policy implications for coordinating regional development. Peripheral regions have smaller local demand and can increase their residents' income by developing such non-tradable goods as tourism services, thereby contributing to the realization of coordinated regional development. On the other hand, as the income of peripheral-region residents increases, the market demand of peripheral regions also increases. Thus, industries with increasing returns will relocate to peripheral regions, which is conducive to interregional convergence of *per capita* income.

1.2.2 Agglomeration and convergence in the open economy

The two-region core-periphery model for the closed economy has undoubtedly provided us with a theoretical benchmark and basic concepts for understanding industrial agglomeration. But reality is much more complicated than the environment specified by the core-periphery model. It is well known that globalization is a fundamental trend in today's world, and the spatial distribution of economic activity in every country is inevitably influenced by economic globalization. Behrens et al. (2007) show that with the deepening of EU integration, some EU member countries gained from the integration process, while others lost. Such unequal distribution of benefits from EU integration may induce unnecessary political turbulence and social turmoil that might shake the very foundations of the EU. As far as China is concerned, the policy of opening up not only boosted rapid economic growth, but also profoundly changed its economic geography. Fujita and Hu (2001) found that the Chinese government's policy of opening up was an important factor in the agglomeration of the economy to its Eastern coastal regions. Ever since Krugman (1991a), many subsequent studies have explored the impact of global economic integration in the open economy on the spatial distribution of industry and the welfare of multiple countries or regions (Behrens et al., 2007; Deng, 2009; Furusawa and Konishi, 2007; Krugman and Venables, 1995; Song et al., 2010; Tabuchi et al., 2005; Zeng and Zhao, 2010). The issue we are concerned with is whether an increase in the openness of a country increases or decreases regional disparities (including both industry size differences and *per capita* income gap) and the conditions that have to be met. Below, we review relevant recent literature according to this stream of thought.

By studying a two-country, four-region model without location or resource endowment advantage, Behrens et al. (2007) found that when a country has high internal trade costs, high international trade costs will magnify its regional disparities. If international trade costs are low, a country's high internal trade costs would be conducive to its interregional balanced development. Subsequent literature has introduced location and size differences to further explore the impact on a country's domestic regional disparities from an increase in openness. Based on size differences of a country's domestic regions, Song et al. (2010) found that when the home country's openness gradually increases, its interregional industry size differences first increases and then decreases, therefore a low or high level of openness is conducive for the home country's balanced interregional development, and industry size differences are larger under any level of openness, than when the economy is closed. Zeng and Zhao (2010) constructed a two-country, four-region model based on the "footloose capital" assumption, namely that capital can flow freely between countries and regions. Their research first showed that a country's domestic regional disparities are not only determined by its domestic infrastructure (i.e. internal trade costs), but also by the condition of other country's domestic infrastructure (i.e. internal trade costs). Second, for the large country, as openness increases, their domestic regional disparities assume an "inverted U" shape. This is because on the one hand, agglomeration forces mainly come from increasing returns to scale in the industry sector, a decline in external trade costs also implies that each country faces a larger international demand. This is conducive to the industrial sector obtaining profits from increasing returns to scale and causing capital and industry to cluster in the large country and the most advantageous region in the large country. On the other hand, due to the existence of the home market effect, a decline in external trade costs will cause firms to shift from the small country to the large country. This will weaken the positive impact of international demand on the development of the large country's industrial sector and cause spatial distribution of industry in the large country to trend towards dispersion. When openness is low, the former effect will predominate, which will cause regional disparities to increase. As openness increases, however, the latter effect will gradually strengthen and finally exceed the former, thereby causing regional disparities to trend towards convergence.

Since the above models all assume a country's different regions have the same external trade costs, this simplification is obviously not very suitable in the case of China. China's eastern region is next to the sea and its external trade costs are much lower than the central and western regions, i.e., the eastern region has a large international trade advantage. To weaken this advantage, the Chinese government has incrementally raised the openness of central and western regions, which will definitely have an important impact on the spatial distribution of China's industries. Deng (2009), using China as a context, constructed a two-sector, three-factor, and three-region open economy model, and specified different external trade costs for eastern and western regions. The study showed that if the eastern regions' external trade advantage is large enough, even if China's interregional trade costs are high, it will still cause capital and industry to cluster in the eastern region. As the western regions' external trade costs decrease and the eastern regions' external trade cost advantage gradually fades, capital and industry in China will tend towards a dispersed distribution. But if western regions' external trade costs decline simultaneously with China's interregional trade costs, domestic integration will negate, or even exceed, the negative impact on the eastern regions brought by the inland region's participation in the process of global integration. It will allow the eastern regions to maintain industrial agglomeration and raise income levels, which tends to enlarge China's interregional income and industrial size. Song et al. (2010) also found that the enhancement of a country's domestic integration will cause its interregional industrial size gap to continuously increase. Governments of underdeveloped regions will usually try to set up barriers to regional trade, in order to protect local firms and prevent industries from migrating to developed regions, thereby creating local employment opportunities, and opportunities for raising income levels. Therefore, when exploring globalization's reshaping effect on China's economic geography, other than the natural distinctions between coastal and inland regions, the imperfections in China's market economy system such as institutional arrangements require special attention. Zhu et al. (2005) set out from China's empirical evidence and introduce market segmentation and regional protectionism into a NEG model to find that firms with low efficiency will enter the local market, those with medium efficiency enter the local and foreign market, and those with high efficiency simultaneously enter the local, foreign, and domestic nonlocal market, if the entry cost of foreign markets is between that of local markets and domestic nonlocal markets. Furthermore, if domestic market segmentation is severe enough to make the entry cost for foreign markets lower than that of local markets, then in equilibrium, firms with low efficiency will enter the foreign markets, those with medium efficiency will enter the local and foreign markets, and those with high efficiency will simultaneously enter the local, foreign, and domestic nonlocal markets. This can explain the aberration of why China currently has many private enterprises that export products via the original equipment manufacturer (OEM), but those exported products are not sold in the domestic market. Also, as China continues to deepen its openness, the gaps between regional turnover of international trade continue to expand and have become an important factor for disparity of regional economic development (Li and Chen, 2007). Jin et al. (2008) introduced the assumption of heterogeneous local firms under the condition of market segmentation and established a two-country, three-region monopolistically competitive open economy model to explore the effect of disparities in the quality of local institutions on enterprise productivity and export. They find that after controlling for the differences in a region's technology, geographical factors, labor, foreign direct investment (FDI), etc., institutional arrangements as legal and property rights have a significant effect on regional export differences. Its sensitivity shows an upward slope, and exceeds that of geographical and foreign capital distribution disparities. Therefore, improving the institutional environment under which firms operate will contribute to easing interregional export disparities and reduce the imbalance in interregional economic development.

1.2.3 Dynamic efficiency and spatial equality

NEG's static core-periphery models show that as transport costs decline, regional income disparities display an inverted U-shaped curve. On the one hand, this depicts a bright vision for the government's promotion of regional economic integration policies, on the other hand, it also warns that during the process of regional integration, there is a stage when income disparities increase and this may trigger social disturbance. This encourages researchers to seek possibilities from a dynamic perspective to avoid such a "pain period" during regional integration. Since growth issues and spatial issues are both very complicated, placing them under a unified analytical framework is very difficult and requires sophisticated technical tricks. Fortunately, NEG and the new economic growth theory were both developed on the foundation of the D-S model, which makes it possible for the two research fields to be crossed and coalesced. As a result of introducing the research and development (R&D) sector's introduction into dynamic NEG models, the variety of industrial goods continuously increases and thus raises consumers' well-being, making it possible to improve the relative welfare of residents in the backward regions. It is well known that R&D activities (knowledge creation) often have a "spillover effect", which is reflected in its "standing on the shoulders of giants." At the same time, with the increase of spatial distance, such a "spillover effect" diminishes (Glaeser et al., 1992; Henderson et al., 1995; Jaffe et al., 1993). Specifically, each variety of manufactured goods represents a type of "patent" or "knowledge," and the R&D sector can be fully aware of the local manufactured goods' "patents" or "knowledge," but only partially aware of that of non-local ones. In other words, the spillover effect from non-local "patents" or "knowledge" needs to be discounted on local R&D activities. However, the spillover from local "patents" or "knowledge" does not require discounting. The "standing on the shoulders of giants" characteristic of R&D allows for new products to be developed faster at a lower cost, the more types of manufactured goods are there. Under the condition of a fixed number of firms, the "diminishing spillover from distance" characteristic causes the spatial distribution of firms to impact the R&D efficiency of the economic system. If firms are all clustered in one region, the economic system could attain maximum R&D efficiency and bring about the fastest growth in the types of goods, causing the CPI to fall at the fastest rate and social welfare to increase at the fastest rate. However, if industrial firms are entirely clustered in one region, this will make the CPI in the periphery higher than that of the core and cause unskilled labor's well-being in the periphery to be lower than that of the core. In short, spatial agglomeration of industrial firms can attain maximum dynamic efficiency, but spatial inequality of individual welfare is also high. Meanwhile, complete dispersion of industrial firms (i.e., symmetric distribution) has the minimum "dynamic efficiency" due to "diminishing spillover from distance," but individual welfare is spatially equal. Therefore, the dynamic NEG model is faced with a trade-off between "dynamic efficiency" and "spatial inequality."

Current theoretical research has found complicated channels that connect spatial agglomeration of economic activities and changes in regional income gaps based on knowledge spillover. Martin and Ottaviano (1999) study a two-region dynamic general equilibrium model with different endowments, i.e., the developed region has a higher initial wealth *per capita* than the underdeveloped region.

The study showed that there are three channels which agglomeration of firms and changes in regional income gaps affect each other:

1. Growth effect: Firms clustering in the developed region can facilitate the R&D sector to attain maximum efficiency. This brings about the fastest growth in the types of manufactured goods, which will lower the CPI in every region and allow residents of both regions to share equally in the positive impact of growth on real income.
2. Wealth effect: Clustering of firms in the developed region facilitates an augmentation in capital stock by increasing efficiency, which decrease the value of all capital. Since the initial wealth *per capita* in the developed region is larger than that of the underdeveloped region, the negative impact of capital depreciation is relatively more serious to residents in the developed region, and therefore helps to reduce regional income gaps.
3. Transport cost effect: Since the trade of manufactured goods incurs transport costs, firms clustering in the developed region enables the CPI in the developed region to be lower than that of the underdeveloped region, which means agglomeration has a positive transport cost effect on the real income of developed region residents and a negative transport cost effect on that of underdeveloped region residents. Thus, it will increase the income gap between residents of the two regions. The positive transport cost effect on developed region residents' real income has a lower absolute value than the negative transport cost effect on real income of the underdeveloped region residents. Therefore, the positive aggregated effect brought about by the agglomeration of industrial firms in the developed region provides the basis for welfare improvement of residents in all regions. But due to the difference in initial wealth *per capita* (endowment difference) or residents' region difference (location difference), the wealth and transport cost effect during the process of agglomeration on residents of different regions varies in direction and magnitude, though both effects are negative on residents of the underdeveloped region. Thus, only when the positive effect on the underdeveloped region by boosting efficiency of R&D due to clustering is strong enough to negate the effects of negative wealth and transport costs, can the welfare of residents in the underdeveloped region increase. As for regional income gaps, only if the gap between the two regions' initial wealth *per capita* is large enough, will it eventually decrease. The reason for this is that residents in the developed region suffer so deeply from the negative effect induced by the "devaluation" of initial wealth due to growth, the magnitude of the negative effect surpasses that of positive growth effect and transport costs effect, generated by more efficient R&D activities due to agglomeration.

If the starting point of the economic system is two regions with identical initial circumstances, and not two regions with comparative advantages, as studied by Martin and Ottaviano (1999), then what are the development prospects of the long-term stable equilibrium? Fujita and Thisse's (2003) study was based on the assumption of two regions with identical initial circumstances; two factors (mobile skilled labor and immobile unskilled labor) and "diminishing spillover with distance;" and found that there are only two situations when a steady-state is reached:

1. Agglomeration equilibrium: All the manufacturing firms and R&D firms are concentrated in one region (the core); the other region (the periphery) only has unskilled labor and an agricultural sector.
2. Symmetric equilibrium: Both regions have the same number of manufacturing firms and R&D firms. Stability analysis finds that the symmetric equilibrium is unstable, while the agglomeration equilibrium is stable. It is noteworthy that from the perspective of absolute welfare, if agglomeration has a large enough pro-growth effect, whether it is the core region's skilled and unskilled labor, or the peripheral region's unskilled labor, they can all enjoy higher welfare from the agglomeration equilibrium than they could from the dispersion equilibrium.

From the perspective of relative welfare, the core region's skilled labor has the highest well-being; unskilled labor in the peripheral regions has lower well-being than that in the core region and the relative well-being of the two regions' unskilled labor maintains a certain constant ratio in the long run. In short, the condition of the poor is continuously improved in the dynamic process but could never catch up to that of the rich.

Thus, whether regions have identical endowments or have significant disparities in endowments, consumers in all regions can share in the gains brought by growth. However, residents of different regions will eventually attain different levels of real income due to disparities in *per capita* endowment or differences in location. Furthermore, if the growth effect is not large enough, the real income gap between residents of different regions will be chronic and enduring. To break through potential development predicaments, and effectively resolve the dilemma between "dynamic efficiency" and "spatial inequality," the intervention of public policy is necessary. Of course, under many circumstances, problems that the market cannot work out may not necessarily be effectively settled by the government, who may in fact make it worse. Fortunately, the existence of the R&D spillover effect and pecuniary externalities[10] provide room for public policy to solve the above dilemma.

1.2.4 Public policy and regional coordination

Following the discourse in the previous section, this section will concentrate on the impact of government policy on industrial agglomeration and the possibilities for regional coordinated development. It should be mentioned that, despite the NEG's very complex depiction of increasing returns, imperfect competition and transport costs, the real world economy is much more intricate than the environment specified by the NEG models. Many public policies that attempt to facilitate regional coordinated development may very well have the opposite effect, thus policymakers need to tread especially carefully.

1.2.4.1 Subsidies for the backward regions

Dupont and Martin (2006) discover that different methods of subsidizing backward regions can cause significant disparities between the actual result and the policy objective. Specifically: (a) subsidies for firms' investment in backward regions, including free grants or below market price sales of land to firms, etc., equivalent to subsidizing firms' fixed costs. Since the developed region has higher initial income when implementing such a policy, it appears to be a redistribution measure that takes from the developed region and gives to the backward region, to increase the income of the latter and narrow regional income gaps. But in fact, under the condition of mobile capital, subsidizing firms' profits in the backward region will simultaneously increase profit rates for capital in both regions, and thus intensify the income gap between owners of capital and the average worker. Due to the fact that the developed region has more initial capital than the backward region, this will eventually cause the income gap between the two regions to increase. (b) Subsidies based on the number of jobs created by firms in backward regions. Different from the investment subsidy, directly subsidizing workers increases their real income, and is conducive to decreasing regional disparities. What is noteworthy, is Dupont and Martin's (2006) comparison of the US and Europe. They found that, despite the fact that the US and EU both implemented policies to support backward regions, EU's aid for backward regions is much stronger. They believe an important reason is that the labor mobility in the US is much higher than in the EU. Although economic activity in the US has a higher degree of agglomeration than in the EU, the high mobility of the American labor market enables there to be no prolonged increase in the *per capita* income gap between US states. The above study has important policy implications for China. On the one hand, the Chinese government should adamantly push forward reforms in such aspects as the Hukou system, social security system, land policy, etc., to lower the cost of interregional labor mobility and enable the migrants to enjoy the public goods of the area they relocate to. On the other hand, when supporting backward regions, the priority for allocating funds should be on people rather than attracting investment through means such as preferential tax treatment on capital, suppressing land prices, etc. The latter is not only detrimental to the long-term development of backward regions, but also causes regional disparities to increase.

1.2.4.2 Accelerating regional integration

Regional integration can usually be examined from two aspects: the degree of freedom of interregional trade of goods and services, and the degree of freedom of interregional labor mobility. Baldwin and Forslid (2000) find that public policies that promote exchange of ideas or increasing knowledge spillover can drive the dispersion of economic activities, while integration policies that lower the costs of trade in goods will increase the agglomeration of economic activities. Economic agglomeration has an enduring change on the capital–labor ratio between regions, thereby making it impossible to eliminate the difference between regional real-capital gain with the process of trade integration. China in the twenty-first century begins to enter the "high-speed railway era"; as of March 2010, there are 277 key railway projects under construction, including the Beijing–Shanghai high-speed railway. Over 40 dedicated passenger lines and intercity railway projects have begun construction, and the total length under construction will exceed 10,000 kilometers. High-speed railway construction in China not only forms an effective stimulus to China's economy through the expansion of government expenditures and domestic demand, and more importantly, for the long-term, aimed at serving passengers, it also narrows the spatial distance between residents of various cities and accelerates the flow of people and exchange of ideas between them, which facilitates R&D activities and knowledge spillover. In this respect, it will not only promote China's long-term economic development, but also be conducive to all regions better sharing in the benefits of growth and facilitating the convergence of regional income gaps.[11]

1.2.4.3 Dynamic effect of policies

From a dynamic perspective, Martin (1999) found that backward regions not only had low levels of *per capita* wealth, but also infrastructure that lagged behind. Therefore, the different policies the central government enacts to coordinate regional development do not just have different policy impacts, many policies seemingly beneficial to the development of backward regions may very well have the opposite effect.

1. Transfer payment policies: Transferring a portion of wealth from developed regions to underdeveloped regions may lower the real income gap between the two regions. However, such a transfer "artificially" increases the demand in underdeveloped regions and makes some firms move from developed regions to underdeveloped regions, which will lower the R&D sector's efficiency and cause low economic growth. It could also be said that transfer payment policies facilitate the narrowing of regional income gaps by sacrificing long-term economic growth.
2. Infrastructure policies: First of all, if the central government endeavors to improve the infrastructure in underdeveloped regions in order to lower their internal transport costs, this will cause a portion of firms to shift from developed regions to underdeveloped regions and result in lower economic growth. On the one hand, this will cause the CPI of underdeveloped regions to fall relative to that of developed regions. On the other hand, the slower growth rate will decrease the capital depreciation rate and the loss of capital gains incurred by residents of developed regions, which make the eventual impact on the real income gap between residents indefinite. This policy not only slows the rate of economic growth, but also increases the earnings of capital

relative to labor, and benefits the capital owners through slack competition between firms and lower capital depreciation rates caused by a decrease in the growth rate. Second, If the central government endeavors to improve the infrastructure that connects developed and underdeveloped regions (e.g. build interprovincial highways), then a portion of firms will move from underdeveloped regions to developed regions, resulting in an increase in R&D efficiency and boosting economic growth, i.e., the spatial distribution of firms will change and economic growth will be accelerated.

3. R&D subsidy policies: The central government subsidizes R&D activities to lower R&D costs for firms, which boosts economic growth and narrows the regional income gap through decreasing consumer expenditure disparities between the two regions by capital depreciation and therefore attracting a portion of industrial firms to relocate from developed region to underdeveloped region. Thus, compared with transfer payment policies and infrastructure policies, R&D subsidy policies can both narrow regional disparities and obtain high economic growth, which is a good solution for the dilemma between "dynamic efficiency" and "spatial inequality." The implications of the research by Baldwin and Forslid (2000), Dupont and Martin (2006), Martin (1999), etc. are as follows: when formulating policies that support industrial and economic development in central and western regions, the Chinese government needs to change its traditional way of emphasizing allocation of funds on "physical objects" (e.g. improving infrastructure), and instead emphasize allocating funds towards "people" (e.g. improving health care and education). The policymakers should greatly increase the budget for health care and education in the central and western regions, especially for basic education, to substantially enhance the quantity and quality of human capital in those regions. At the same time, the government needs to carry out more policies supporting firms' R&D activities regardless of their location, in order to give firms a stimulus to increase R&D outlay, facilitate development of new products, enhance innovative capabilities, and enable the whole nation to share in the benefits brought by economic growth.

We will first look at the impact of accelerated economic growth on *per capita* income in both regions. There are two channels through which this effect can be transmitted: (1) speeding up economic growth can equally increase the income level of residents in both regions, but not change the relative income gap between residents of the two regions; (2) accelerating economic growth will also accelerate capital depreciation, which is detrimental to the developed regions' residents who have a higher wealth *per capita* and thus will narrow the relative gap between the incomes of the two regions. Next, we will examine the impact of spatial distribution shift on *per capita* income in both regions. It is easy to see that the CPI in developed regions experiences a sharp decline due to the rapid increase of local firms. However, the CPI in underdeveloped regions is indefinite, as there is both the negative impact of a decrease in local firms, and the positive impact of a reduction in transport costs for "importing" manufactured goods from developed regions. What we can be sure of is that the magnitude of CPI's decline in developed regions will exceed that of underdeveloped regions. The cumulative impact of the above-mentioned effects on the *per capita* income gap between the two regions is hard to predict. It is noteworthy that if a country's initial infrastructure is complete, further improvement of the infrastructure that connects developed and undeveloped regions will narrow the real income gap between the two regions. The reason behind this is that the change in the relative CPI of the two regions will be small, and the capital depreciation effect brought by accelerated economic growth will exceed the CPI effect brought by an adjustment in the spatial distribution.[12]

1.3 China's practice and international experience

1.3.1 Economic agglomeration: high or low?

A commonly held opinion states that the degree of economic agglomeration in China is already very high, and a high degree of agglomeration in manufacturing will allow the core regions' economic development to enter a virtuous cycle, but the core regions' diffusion effect on other regions may not be effective due to many conditions, which would cause regional disparities to increase continuously. So, is China's current degree of economic agglomeration excessive or inadequate? We need to closely examine the current status of China's economic agglomeration, understand the current stage it is at, and its future trend of development in light of international experience, and provide a reference for the central government's regional policy.

Through calculating the HHI of China's 31 provinces' gross regional product and industrial output, we discover the spatial agglomeration trend of mainland China's gross regional product and industrial output by province has continuously strengthened overall (see Figure 1.3). The HHI of mainland China's gross regional product by province has risen from 471.10 in 1978 to 549.28 in 2009; an increase of 16.60 percent; the HHI of industrial output by province has risen from 557.31 in 1978 to 729.44 in 2009; an increase of 30.89 percent. Data shows the spatial agglomeration trend of industrial output by province reached a peak of 768.91 in 2004, with a small decline afterwards; while the spatial agglomeration trend of gross regional product reached a high of 563.97 in 2006, also with a small decline afterwards. It is worth mentioning that the small decline in the two indicators are not just the outcome of market forces, but have their roots in the proposals made by the Chinese government since 2000, such as the "Grand Western Development Program;" "Revitalization of Northeast-China Old Industrial Bases;" "Rise of Central China," etc., regional development strategies, and the subsequent large government expenditures made in the central and western regions. Take the Grand Western Development Program as an example—from 2000 to 2007, the state arranged various fiscal transfer payments to western regions of nearly 1.5 trillion yuan cumulatively, as well as arranged government bonds, on-budget construction funds, and departmental construction funds to

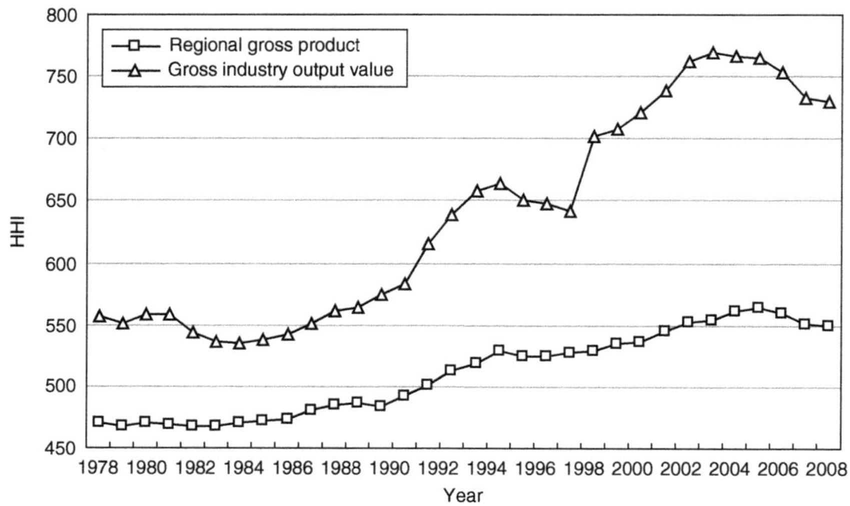

Figure 1.3 The HHI for mainland China regional gross product and gross industry output value by province (1978–2009).

Note: Data on Chongqing municipality are merged into Sichuan province.

Data source: 1978–1998 figures are from *New China 50 Years*; 1998–2008 figures are from the respective *China Statistical Yearbook*.

western regions totalling over 730 billion yuan cumulatively. From this could be seen that the implementation of these policies undoubtedly had a certain impact on the spatial redistribution of Chinese industry—what the actual effect was will be explored later. In addition, an important piece of information which Figure 1.3 conveys is the degree of spatial agglomeration of China's economy measured by the industrial output: HHI is higher than that measured by the gross regional product HHI. This coincides with the fundamental idea behind the home market effect, namely, the number of firms that regions with large market demands attract, is disproportionate to their demand.

As to specific industries, their uneven spatial distribution is often described as geographic, or spatial concentration. We calculated the spatial Gini coefficient of 18 major industries' output of China's 31 provinces from 1988–2006, using the *China Industrial Economics Statistics Yearbook*.[13] We found that during the near 20-year period from 1988 to 2008, all 18 industries displayed a trend towards becoming more spatially concentrated (see Appendix below). There are three industries that are highly spatially concentrated (spatial Gini coefficient above 0.70); six industries that are relatively spatially concentrated (spatial Gini coefficient from 0.55–0.70); five industries that are relatively dispersed (spatial Gini coefficient from 0.40–0.55); one industry that is highly dispersed (spatial Gini coefficient below 0.40) and three industries that turned from relatively spatially

Table 1.1 Spatial Gini coefficient distribution of 18 major industries in mainland China

Distribution type	*Industries*	*Industry name*
Highly concentrated	3	Textiles, Synthetic fiber, Electronics and communications equipment
Relatively concentrated	6	Ferrous metals mining, Fabricated metal product manufacturing, Coal mining, Tobacco processing, Electrical equipment and machinery, Instruments and office supplies
Relatively dispersed	5	Ferrous metals smelting and refining, Food manufacturing, Pharmaceuticals, Beverages, Transportation equipment manufacturing
Highly dispersed	1	Utilities
From Highly dispersed to Highly concentrated	3	Non-metallic mineral product manufacturing, Chemicals, Paper and paper products manufacturing

Note: Chongqing's data is merged into Sichuan Province.
Data source: *China Industry Economics Statistical Yearbook*, over the years.

dispersed to relatively spatially concentrated (see Table 1.1). Further analysis shows industries that have a high level of spatial concentration are mostly capital and technology intensive, have significant economies of scale, and are relatively mobile spatially, which is in accordance with Krugman's (1993) so-called second nature. At the same time, the ferrous metal mining, coal mining, and tobacco processing industries, which are relatively spatially concentrated, rely on mining deposits, land, climate, and natural conditions, so their spatial concentration is also high, which corresponds with Krugman's (1993) so-called first nature. On the contrary, the electricity, steam and hot water generation, and supply industries (i.e. utilities) mainly serve local needs, and transmitting them across long distances would be costly, which gives them a high level of spatial dispersion.

The above Gini coefficient calculations did not take into consideration the impact of differences in firm size for firms in the same industry, but in different provinces. When firm sizes in an industry vary widely among provinces, this indicator cannot objectively reflect the level of spatial concentration in that industry. Taking the impact of firm size into account, Ellison and Glaeser constructed the EG index, using the γ-coefficient to measure and eliminate the effects of firm size on the degree of industry spatial concentration.[14] Through international comparisons, it is not hard to find that the spatial Gini coefficient shows an upward trend in the degree of spatial concentration in all Chinese industries since reform and opening, but compared with developed countries, the levels of spatial concentration in China's industries are still relatively low (Table 1.2).

Another indicator to examine the degree of agglomeration in economic activity is city size. Economic models with the number of cities being endogenous all presume there exists an "inverted U" relationship between real *per capita* income and city size, i.e., when city size is at a low level, the expansion of city size brings more agglomeration benefits (e.g., diversification of goods, etc.) than

Table 1.2 Chinese industry spatial concentration comparison with developed countries

Literature	*Country studied*	*Year of data*	*Industry*	*Region*	*Ratio of low concentration (%)*	*Ratio of medium concentration (%)*	*Ratio of high concentration (%)*
Ellison and Glaeser (1997)	US	1987	459 4-digit codes	3,000 counties	10.00	65.00	25.00
Devereux et al. (2004)	UK	1992	211 4-digit codes	477 zip code areas	65.00	19.00	16.00
Maurel and Sedillot (1999)	France	1993	273 4-digit codes	95 counties	50.00	23.00	27.00
Lu and Tao (2006)	China	2003	539 4-digit codes	2,861 counties/districts	79.96	13.73	6.31

Note: Low, medium, and high degree of spatial concentration refer to $\gamma_i < 0.02$, $0.02 \leq \gamma_i < 0.05$, and $\gamma_i \geq 0.05$ respectively.
Data source: Lu and Tao (2006), p. 110.

costs (e.g., crowding, etc.), allowing real *per capita* income to increase as the city size expands; when city size is at a high level, expansion brings a faster rate of increase in agglomeration costs than that of agglomeration benefits, causing agglomeration benefits to be lower than agglomeration costs, eventually lowering real *per capita* income as the city's size expands (Black and Henderson, 1999; Duranton and Puga, 2001; Fujita et al., 1999; Helsley and Strange, 1990; Henderson, 1974). Through the perspective of city size, Au and Henderson (2006) used data from over 200 Chinese cities in the time period between 1990–1997 to estimate the "inverted U" relationship between real *per capita* income and city size. The study found that in the 205-city sample, at least 51 percent of cities were significantly smaller than optimal, and cities that were larger than optimal did not exceed 6 percent. Their research further shows, due to constraints from aspects such as the Hukou system, etc., that most Chinese cities are below their optimal size, thereby causing net *per capita* output to incur a 30 percent loss on average. Fujita et al. (2004) found that the size of Chinese cities were not just smaller than optimal, equalization in city size was also very evident, and pointed out that Shanghai's population and its growth rate was lower than that of the world's ten largest cities.[15] Henderson and Wang's (2007) statistical study of 2,684 cities in 142 countries with over 100,000 in population found that there were 94 cities with over 3 million in population in the 2,684 sample cities in 2000; 324 cities with 1–3 million in population, and the ratio between the two equalled 0.29 (see Table 1.3); there were nine Chinese cities with over 3 million in population, 125 cities with 1–3 million in population and the ratio between the two equalled 0.072. Through international comparisons of the spatial Gini coefficient of the city sample, they found that the spatial Gini coefficient of the entire sample of cities worldwide was 0.5619, while among China, India, the US, Indonesia, Brazil, Russia, and Japan (the seven countries with the largest population), Japan had the highest spatial Gini coefficient with 0.6579, whereas China's spatial Gini coefficient was lowest at 0.4234. It is thus clear that China's cities are not smaller than optimal, but also display a size equalization phenomenon in which "big cities are not big and small cities are not small."

It is worth mentioning that the latest international comparison studies show that the degree of China's economic agglomeration is still at a low level relative to developed countries. The World Bank (2009) discovered that from 2000–2005, the urban population grew at about 3 percent, 1.3 percent and 0.9 percent annually for low income, medium income and high income countries, respectively. Before *per capita* GDP reaches US$10,000, urbanization and economic development has a significant positive correlation, which is reflected in the early stages of urbanization where large numbers of the rural population move into the cities; when *per capita* GDP exceeds US$10,000 and the economic agglomeration index exceeds 0.6, the rate of urbanization clearly slows down; only a few outliers have a *per capita* GDP exceeding US$25,000 and the economic agglomeration index is above 0.7 (see Figure 1.4). Thus, we can see that whether it is *per capita* GDP, or the agglomeration index, China's

Table 1.3 Population distribution of cities with over 100,000 population in 142 countries in 2000

City population (10,000 people)	*Number of cities*	*Percentage of cities in group (%)*	*Cumulative percentage of cities (%)*	*Percentage of population in group (%)*	*Cumulative percentage of pop. (%)*
≥1700	4	0.15	0.15	4.5	4.5
1200–1700	7	0.26	0.41	5.2	9.7
800–1200	13	0.48	0.89	7.5	17.2
400–800	29	1.08	1.97	8.8	26.0
300–400	41	1.53	3.50	7.8	33.8
200–300	75	2.79	6.29	10.1	43.9
100–200	249	9.28	15.57	18.9	62.8
50–100	355	13.23	28.80	13.8	76.6
25–50	644	23.99	52.79	12.5	89.1
10–50	1267	47.21	100.00	11.0	100.1
Total	2684	100	–	100.1	–

Data source: Henderson and Wang (2007), p. 288.

ranking among world countries is rather low; even if it is compared to countries with the similar level of development (such as "BRIC countries," Brazil and India). That is to say, from the perspective of China's current distribution of economic activity, agglomeration has not reached an adequate degree and is still not sufficient.

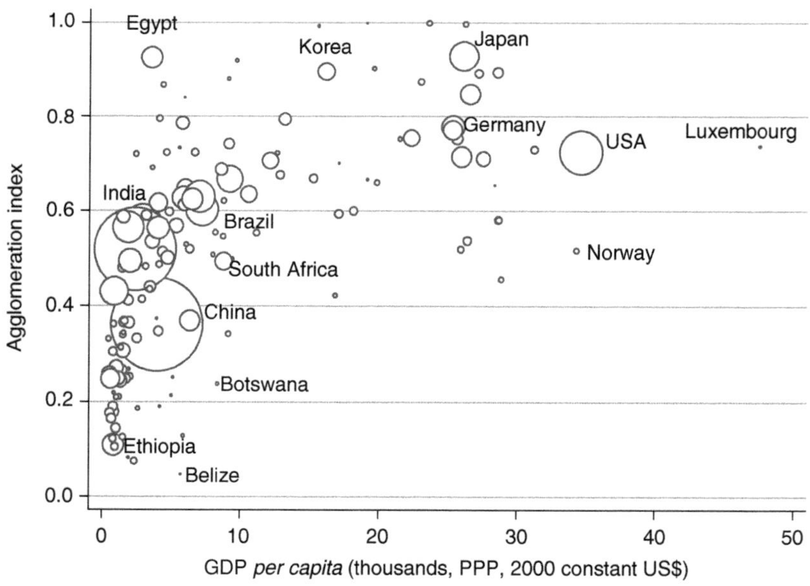

Figure 1.4 Cross-country comparisons of *per capita* GDP and degree of economic agglomeration.

Note: The circles represent population size.

Data source: World Bank (2009), p. 60.

1.3.2 *Agglomeration, growth, and gaps: what impacts on what?*

Spatial agglomeration of economic activity is conducive to economic growth (Martin and Ottaviano, 2001; Fujita and Thisse, 2003). Ciccone and Hall (1996) use American data to conduct an empirical test of the relationship between agglomeration and growth through two different models and find there to be a positive correlation between employment density and productivity: doubling employment density increases productivity by around 6 percent, and over half of the *per capita* disparity between states in the US can be explained by the density of economic activity. Braunerhjelm and Borgman (2004) use Swedish data to reach a conclusion similar to that of Ciccone and Hall (1996). Braunerhjelm and Borgman (2006) go further to examine the effect of different types of agglomeration on economic growth from a more specific angle. Their study classifies agglomeration into mono-industrial agglomeration, poly-industrial agglomeration, which respectively correspond to Marshall-Arrow-Romer externalities[16] and Jacobian inter-industry externalities.[17] The study finds Jacobian inter-industry externalities had a stronger effect on facilitating growth than Marshall-Arrow-Romer externalities.

Geographic factors also play an important role in explaining the regional growth rate disparities between Chinese provinces. Ying (2000) proved the existence of the spillover effect in China's spatial economy from the perspective of core-periphery theory. Afterwards, Ying (2003) conducted further studies on Chinese economic growth by province in 1978–1998. As a result, he found that Chinese GDP growth rate by province had some correlation spatially with neighboring regions; problems with inappropriate model specification may exist in previous research due to neglect of spatial factors. The estimator coefficient shows that the Chinese economy is currently undergoing polarization spatially. Wu and Xu (2004) use the Moran exponential method to analyze the economic growth of mainland China's 31 provincial districts. As a result, it was found that the agglomeration phenomenon exists for China's provincial economic growth on a geographic dimension. Correlation spatially and the degree of intensity in external and internal trade, as well as foreign capital and such economic activities, to a large extent leads to spatial imbalances among the economic growth of the 31 provincial districts. Geographic distinctions provide strong explanatory power concerning the "core-periphery" model of China's provincial district economic growth; the agglomeration of economic activity drastically lowers the spatial costs of economic activity. It is worth mentioning that in China's current situation, restrictions on the interregional migration of productive factors such as land and labor will distort the prices of factors such as land in the eastern regions, thereby restraining economic activity from agglomerating to the east. Lu (2011) found that from 1990–2006, the farther a city is distanced from a major port (Hong Kong, Shanghai, and Tianjin), the larger the negative impact on land use efficiency. In 2006, land use efficiency of cities that are around 500 kilometers from major ports was about 50 percent lower than that of areas near major ports. Within a range of 450 kilometers from major ports, the expansion of urban areas facilitates an increase in land use efficiency. However, for inland regions the, expansion of urban areas has the effect of lowering the average land use efficiency. This is to say, if construction land quotas are tradable across regions, then by trading western regions' construction land quotas with those of the eastern regions, the overall land use efficiency will increase, which is beneficial to economic growth. Xu et al. (2010) further verify the "∽" type non-linear relationship between geography and urban economic growth. Their study finds that as a city's distance to a major port narrows from afar, the effect on urban economic growth undergoes a process that is encouraging, discouraging and then encouraging again, and on the whole, the further the distance from a major port, the more disadvantageous to economic growth it is.

Whether from the perspective of China's current degree of economic agglomeration or from the perspective of agglomeration facilitating growth, it is necessary for China to encourage economic activity that is more agglomerated, not more dispersed. As the only possible reason for controlling economic agglomeration in China is the need to balance regional development, should the increase in regional gaps in China be blamed on economic agglomeration? It is worth mentioning that an important discrepancy between China's reality and classical New Economic Geography models is that many factors, which are freely mobile in the theoretical model, still face severe restrictions on mobility in China, and these artificial barriers to mobility may, at least to some extent be responsible for China's ever-increasing regional disparities. From the perspective of empirical research, the interregional migration and agglomeration of productive factors in China are not the reasons for the formation of regional gaps. Wang (2003) separates the wage differential caused by a series of personal characteristics of rural migrant labor and urban local labor from the wage determinants; estimates the degree labor discrimination affects the wage differential, and finds that labor discrimination could explain 76 percent of the above-mentioned types of labor wage differentials. Yao and Lai (2004) used survey data from firms and migrant workers in Zhejiang province to analyze the income differential between urban and migrant workers and found that the income differential could basically be summarized into two aspects: first, the difference in the level of human capital and employer; second, the Hukou discrimination the migrant worker faces. The former can explain around 70 percent of the income differential of the two types of workers; around 30 percent of the income differential is caused by Hukou discrimination. Démurger et al. (2009) used China's 2002 nationwide sample data to find that the annual earnings of urban residents are 1.3 times that of the long-term mobile population from the countryside. Fan and Yin (2009) used China's interregional input–output table's flow data and nationwide migrant worker survey tables, to analyze, in detail, the internal logical relationship and actual degree of impact between the migration of low-skilled labor and interregional income levels. They found that the elasticity coefficient of market access[18] in the coastal regions to income is 1.7–2.7 percent lower than that of non-coastal regions, which shows that an increase in the market access capability of coastal regions has a smaller impact on increasing earnings than non-coastal regions. This is also means that agglomeration of economic activity in the coastal regions, which causes low-skilled labor to migrate towards coastal regions, will not significantly magnify regional income gaps. In terms of theoretical research, Zhu (2004) found that the existence of the Hukou system causes potential industrial labor in the central and western regions to face a comparison between migration costs and technical skill deficiency when making a decision to move to the eastern region. That is to say, a population migration cost that is too high will inhibit industrial labor from the central and western regions to migrate towards the eastern region, and achieve the relatively high technical efficiency of the eastern region. At the same time, if the goods produced by the potential industrial labor from the central and western regions that migrate to the eastern region have little substitutability with those produced by the original workers in the eastern region, then relaxing restricting on population migration would not only allow mobile potential industrial labor to obtain a higher real level of well-being, it would also allow original workers in the eastern region to obtain a higher real level of well-being. This is because, although potential industrial labor that enters the eastern region may compete in the labor market with original workers in the eastern region, it will lower the nominal wage rate of the eastern region, if the goods produced by the potential industrial labor have substantial differences (i.e. little substitutability) with those produced by the original workers in the eastern region. This will cause the CPI of the eastern region to fall faster than the nominal wage rate by increasing the types of consumer goods available, thereby increasing the real well-being of the original eastern region's workers. Song et al. (2012) further verified the above conclusions through an endogenous population migration framework.

We hereby propose a theoretical hypothesis regarding the impact on regional income gap changes of the relaxing of population migration restraints and the enabling of interprovincial construction land quotas reallocation.[19] The core idea of the hypothesis, under the current Hukou and land policies agglomeration of economic activity towards developed regions is being restrained, therefore agglomeration is unable to exert its scale and growth effect, which is not only disadvantageous to increasing the absolute well-being of the entire society, but also restricts the profit-seeking actions of underdeveloped regions' residents and this will magnify regional income gaps. Therefore, the above-mentioned policy restraints have the effect, depicted in Figure 1.5, of increasing the income gap between developed and underdeveloped regions in the short term, thereby intensifying the "pain" in the long term; it will postpone the turning point on the "inverted U" curve of regional income gaps, thereby lengthening the pain period. These are all unconducive to narrowing regional income gaps. Of course, whether this hypothesis can be formally proven is a question worth deeper research.

1.3.3 Regional policy: reshaping the economic geography?

Domestically and internationally, there have been endless policies to support backward regions. Our concern is: to what extent have regional policies changed

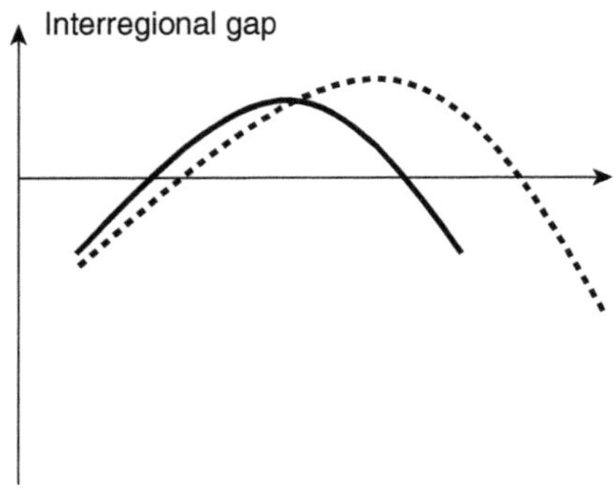

Figure 1.5 Policy regulations and changes in the interregional gap.

the economic geography? What inspiration can regional developmental policy research and experience at home and abroad provide for China's formulation of regional policy?

Balanced regional development has always troubled the EU. If we look at the EU's budget, around one-third of the money is spent on various regional policies. For example, in the six years between 2000 and 2006, around €213 billion (euros) were spent on this type of expenditure. Governments of EU member countries also spent large amounts on narrowing regional gaps (Dupont and Martin, 2006). However, even in the EU, policies endeavoring to narrow regional gaps have always had little effect (Brakman et al., 2005). Many empirical studies find that EU is a complex system composed of a series of "core-periphery" structures. Compared with the centripetal forces dominated by the market, the centrifugal forces brought by regional policies that endeavor to develop the peripheral regions always seem to be weak. This can partially explain why regional economic geography has not changed as policymakers thought it would. In EU, policymakers have already noticed this and are gradually changing their policy concepts. For example, the two reports: "Pieken in de Delta" (Ministerie van Economische Zaken, 2004) and "Third Report on Economic and Social Cohesion" (European Commission, 2004) show that policy focus has shifted from regional equality to enhancing overall efficiency. On the whole, past policies that attempted to boost backward regions are being gradually replaced by more flexible policies. In the concepts of these policies, the market is playing an increasingly important role (Brakman et al., 2005). In Asia, post-war Japan gradually attained economic recovery and endeavored to achieve balanced regional growth in the 1960s. As a series of environmental, transportation, housing, etc., problems became more prominent, along with Tokyo's expansion, the "Fourth Capital Circle Basic Plan" formulated by the Japanese government in 1986, explicitly stated that functions concentrated in the downtown area would also be dispersed to nearby areas; the "Fifth Capital Circle Basic Plan" formulated by the Japanese government in 1999 explicitly related to perfecting Tokyo's "dispersed network structure"

(Zhang and Lu, 2009). These policies caused Tokyo's population to stagnate and decline, which was accompanied by a decline in Tokyo's rate of development and international standing, and may have even affected Japan's economic growth to a certain extent (Chen and Lu, 2009). But since 2000, the population of Tokyo has been increasing again after years of stagnation and decline, and a "return to downtown" has emerged. Japan's "Dispersion of Capital Functions Plan" did not bring about the expected policy effect.[20]

Since reform and opening-up, the continuous increase in regional disparities in China is not just an economic issue, it is also a social issue, and has slowly become a source of social unrest in China. Based on the above considerations, since 2000, the Chinese government has proposed and implemented the "Grand Western Development Program;" "Revitalization of Northeast-China Old Industrial Bases;" "Rise of Central China," etc. regional development strategies, and made a series of policy measures, including quickening the pace of infrastructure construction in central and western regions, enhancing environmental protection, actively adjusting industrial structure and strengthening reform and opening, etc. From 2000 to September 2009, the central government cumulatively invested 550.7 billion yuan in central government construction projects in the central and western regions and raised subsidies for western region projects to an appropriate ratio, which caused the amount of on-budget central basic construction funds and government bond account funds allocated toward the construction of western regions' infrastructure to consistently increase. Yet it is still uncertain whether the Chinese government's efforts to balance regional development through regional policy will be able to remodel China's regional economic geography and enable backward regions to achieve sustained economic growth. If we look at the situation of regional industrial transfer, current research shows, "industrial transfer on a large scale did not occur," "the signs of industrial transfer are not evident" (Chen, 2002; Chen, 2007; Che and Xu, 2008; Zhao and Zhang, 2009). However, to those sub-industries that are in the process of dispersion, Chen and Xu (2008) further state that the dispersion process which occurred during 1996–2005 contributed greatly to regional industry structure conflicts,[21] with the dispersion process intensifying the regional industry structure conflicts. On the other hand, from the perspective of regional *per capita* income gaps, there is already research that states that before 2004, although regional *per capita* GDP and consumption gaps were increasing, the slope was more gradual; after 2004, the trend of increasing regional income gaps reversed (Liu et al., 2009; Wei and Sun, 2004; Xu and Li, 2006). The fact that the decline in regional development disparities happened after a series of regional balanced development policies such as the Grand Western Development Program were introduced should not be a coincidence. Liu et al. (2009) conducted tests on the effectiveness of the implementation of Grand Western Development Program. The study finds the implementation of the Grand Western Development Program caused the average annual growth rate of western regions to increase by around 1.15 percent since 2000, facilitating China's regional economy shift from divergence to convergence; but the mechanism through which the Grand Western Development

Program facilitates growth in the western regions is mainly realized through large amounts of physical capital, especially infrastructure investment, and the development of education; advancement of technology, as well as the soft environment, did not achieve significant improvements due to the Grand Western Development Program. Thus, whether the short-term economic growth brought about by the Grand Western Development Program can be transformed into endogenous long-term growth remains to be seen. In fact, after comparing the US and EU's developmental experience, we can see that, although the degree of economic agglomeration in the US is very high, since mobility of American labor is high, regional planning policy has never been as important an issue as it has been in EU.

1.4 Conclusion

Economic agglomeration is a commonly seen phenomenon during the process of economic development in all countries. International experience shows that whether from the perspective of the degree of economic spatial concentration, or city size, the degree of China's economic agglomeration cannot be considered high, and therefore controlling the degree of economic agglomeration in China is inefficient. If the government tries to control movement of factors in order to control the degree of economic agglomeration, this may even be disadvantageous to the convergence of regional income gaps. Theoretical and empirical studies show that agglomeration is beneficial to growth, while an enhanced degree of economic agglomeration accompanies economic growth. Since an increase in regional gaps (including *per capita* gaps and aggregate gaps) often accompanies economic agglomeration, high hopes are often placed on regional policies to reshape the economic geographic geography. It is regrettable that these hopes to achieve balance through regional policies have mostly ended in failure. In EU, policymakers gradually realized that the forces which agglomerate the economy towards the core regions are so strong that policies which endeavor to develop backwards regions have been costly but ineffective. In China, since the Grand Western Development Program, the trend towards increasing regional disparities has been alleviated. But if amelioration in regional disparities is only due to massive government expenditures, or preferential policies from central government toward the central and western regions, then industrial transfer from the eastern regions to the western regions on a large scale will not occur, unless factors that impact long-term economic growth, such as the accumulation of human capital, etc., see a fundamental improvement in the western regions. On the other hand, the rate of return on capital and the land use efficiency of eastern regions is higher than that of the central and western regions. The current market-dominated factor movement trends toward further agglomeration in the eastern regions, so regional policies that attempt to disperse economic activity to the central and western regions may very well have only short-term effects, and are eventually likely to be "costly" and even "twice the work with half the result."

Judging from China's current economic geographic disposition and phase of economic development, controlling the degree of economic agglomeration is unnecessary, unadvisable, and may even be impossible. The objectives pursued by regional policies should not be balanced on an aggregate basis, but should instead stress balance on a *per capita* basis. International experience shows, under the condition of a labor force freely mobile across regions, *per capita* income gaps will not display an extended trend towards increasing. China's current most urgent task is to achieve freely mobile labor across regions, which is achieved by gradually eliminating any institutional barriers unconducive to labor mobility. In this sense, the central government's regional policies towards balanced development and the various supportive measures provided for the central and western regions should invest their money in people (including healthcare and education) instead of physical objects, in order to promote the accumulation of human capital in the western regions and increase labor mobility.[22]

Notes

1 Calculated with international data published by National Bureau of Statistics, http://www.stats.gov.cn/tjsj/qtsj/gjsj/.

2 When calculating HHI for industrial output of mainland China's 31 provinces, municipalities, and autonomous regions, we merged Chongqing and Sichuan.

3 In the above-mentioned research, other than Wan et al. (2007) and Wan et al. (2005), most studies did not make a rigorous distinction between regional income gap and *per capita* GDP gap. Strictly speaking, the income gap and the *per capita* GDP gap are two different concepts. As far as this text is concerned, a detailed discussion of the difference between the two is beyond this chapter's scope, and from the perspective of the theme this text aims to discuss changes in the *per capita* GDP already provide enough information. Therefore, in the discussions henceforth, this chapter will not make a rigorous distinction between *per capita* GDP gap and *per capita* income gap.

4 New economic geography models often use the Samuelsson "iceberg form" of transport costs, namely, for 1 unit of the manufactured good to arrive at destination, $\tau > 1$ units of this good must be sent from the region of origin. Define $\phi \equiv \tau^{1-\sigma} \in (0,1)$, where $\sigma > 1$ represents the elasticity of substitution across varieties. Then ϕ represents the degree of trade liberalization or economic integration, a larger ϕ reflects a higher degree of trade liberalization or economic integration.

5 The existence of transport costs puts foreign markets out of reach for local firms. In the eyes of local firms, local potential demand could be 100 percent converted into real demand and produce profits, while foreign potential demand's conversion rate to real demand is less than 100 percent. Therefore, local and foreign potential demand of the same size have different impacts on the revenue and profits of local firms, the former being larger and the latter smaller. The difference comes from transport costs, and the size of the difference (or the magnitude of the "discount") is determined by the level of the transport costs.

6 Immobile factors here mostly refer to the portion of the labor displaying immobile characteristics due to the reliance of agriculture and resource-based industries on land and local resources.

7 In New Economic Geography models, the break point and sustain point is often unequal. The difference of the two points will form different bifurcations. When $\phi_B > \phi_S$, a tomahawk bifurcation is formed (e.g., Krugman, 1991a; Fujita et al., 1999); when $\phi_B < \phi_S$, a pitchfork bifurcation is formed (Pflüger, 2004); when $\phi_B = \phi_S$, the asymmetric interior equilibrium does not exist (e.g., Ottaviano et al., 2002).

8 Whether the nominal wage rate of skilled workers is equal to that of unskilled workers is determined by the parameters defined in the model. Under the Cobb-Douglas utility function assumption, the ratio of consumer expenditures on manufactured goods is equal to the ratio of skilled workers to the entire workforce (e.g., Krugman, 1991b), then skilled and unskilled workers would receive the same nominal wage rate under zero transport costs, which would allow all consumers have the same well-being. Refer to Song et al. (2012) for further discussions on the nominal wage rate of skilled and unskilled workers under zero transport costs.

9 Combes et al. (2011) use statistical data from 1860–2000 on 87 area units (similar to China's "province") in France on agriculture, manufacturing, and services. Their study discovers that the spatial distribution of French manufacturing, and services displayed a continuous trend towards concentration from 1860 to 1930, but trended towards spatial dispersion from 1930 to 2000. Their study believes that the enduring decline in transport costs is the main reason that spatial concentration of manufacturing and services displayed an "inverted-U" process. They also find that when spatial concentration of manufacturing and services underwent an "inverted-U" type process, regional labor productivity gaps in France displayed a trend towards convergence.

10 Pecuniary externalities refer to market participants exerting positive or negative influences on other participants through price mechanism. It differs from pure technical externalities (e.g., R&D spillover effect). In NEG literature, pecuniary externalities mainly refer to externalities caused by the linkages between demand and supply (i.e., backward linkages and forward linkages). For example, an increase in the number of firms in region A will increase the income in region A, attracting more workers to move there; the workers that move towards region A will increase the local demand, thereby increasing the profit of firms in region A, encouraging a further increase in the number of firms in region A. During the above process, any activity of participating agent influences other participants through price mechanism. Such an influence is called "pecuniary externalities".

11 It should be mentioned that we have not analyzed the investment returns for high speed railways. Whether the scale and speed of high speed railway construction corresponds to the current economic development phase is a topic worth researching on its own. We are more concerned here with the long-term effect high speed railways bring.

12 The central government's efforts to improve the internal infrastructure of developed regions has similar effects as efforts to improve the infrastructure between developed and underdeveloped regions. The details will not be addressed herein.

13 We thank Chen Yao, Yin Zhiqiang, Zhang Huan and Xie Songzhi of Zhejiang University for doing massive amounts of intricate and cumbersome data processing work in order to calculate the relevant indicators.

14 As micro-level figures are not obtainable, we did not estimate the γ coefficient for Chinese sub-industries. Fortunately, Lu and Tao (2006) provide sufficient information for our analysis.

15 Li and Fan (2003) discovered through international comparisons of production and population spatial concentration that relative to the spatial agglomeration of productive activities, the spatial agglomeration of China's population is clearly insignificant. For example, in 1997, Tokyo, Osaka, and Kanagawa took up 1.75 percent of Japan's total land mass, while the regional gross product took up 31.21 percent of Japan's GDP, and the population took up 22.94 percent of Japan's total population; whereas in 2000, in China's Jing-jin-tang region, Hu-ning-hang region, and Pearl Delta (excluding Nanjing, Huzhou, Shaoxing, and Jiangmen) took up 1.67 percent of the total land mass, 26.22 percent of the national GDP, and only 9.03 percent of the national population. It is worth noting that, Shanghai's area (6,300 square kilometers) is equivalent to the total of Japan's Tokyo, Osaka and Kanagawa (6,400 square kilometers), but Shanghai's population is 16.74 million (2000), while the latter's is 28.94 million (1997).

16 This mainly refers to the impact on productivity of the clustering of one specialized industry, e.g., the reduction of redundant R&D and cost savings at the industry level brought by the enhancement of vertical specialization and employment of economies of scale.

17 Compared with the Marshall-Arrow-Romer externalities, when it comes to Jacobian inter-industry externalities, since many industries are clustered, therefore more various types of knowledge can be provided for creativity; diversified production structures can reduce the sensitivities of one region to outer shocks (Braunerhjelm and Borgman, 2006).

18 Fan and Yin (2009) translated the phrase market access and we believe their translation is inappropriate and is easily misunderstood. The phrase is used to depict the ability of firms in one region to accommodate demand from all regions and its size usually depends on: (1) the income level in the area with demand; (2) the level of competition in the area with demand; (3) the trade costs between the region where the firm is located and the area with demand.

19 We benefited from discussions with Lu Ming and hereby express our appreciation.

20 In 1985, Tokyo's population was 11.829 million. By 1999, when the "Fifth Capital Circle Basic Plan" was published and implemented, the population changed to 11.973 million. During this period, the population fluctuated slightly. But after 2000, Tokyo's population rose. Up to 2005, Tokyo's population rose to 12.577 million (Lu et al., 2010).

21 This indicator is mainly used to measure how reasonable regional division of labor is: $E_{ij} = R_{ij} * r_{ij}$, R_{ij} represents the industry structure similarity coefficient between region i and region j, r_{ij} represents the situation where each industry in both regions show low efficiency and market denial, namely simultaneous industry weakness.

22 The March 12 2011 edition of "*The Economist*" published "Regional Disparities: Gaponomics". The article was based on the fact that the *per capita* income gap between the richest and poorest regions in the UK constantly increased over the past 20 years, criticized the policy that attempted to narrow regional gaps by providing subsidies to the poor regions from rich regions and proposed two policy measures to narrow UK regional gaps: one is to make it easier for people to move, the second is to increase the educational levels of poor regions. This is also the main policy implications this chapter attempts to enunciate.

References

In English

Ago, T., I. Isono and T. Tabuchi, 2006, "Locational Disadvantage of the Hub," *Annals of Regional Science*, 40(4), pp. 819–848.

Au, C. C. and J. V. Henderson, 2006, "Are Chinese Cities Too Small?," *Review of Economic Studies*, 73(3), pp. 549–576.

Baldwin, R. and R. Forslid, 2000, "The Core-Periphery Model and Endogenous Growth: Stabilizing and Destabilizing Integration," *Economica*, 67, pp. 307–324.

Behrens, K., C. Gaigné, G. I. P. Ottaviano and J.-F. Thisse, 2007, "Countries, Regions and Trade: On the Welfare Impacts of Economic Integration," *European Economic Review*, 51(5), pp. 1277–1301.

Black, D. and J. V. Henderson, 1999, "A Theory of Urban Growth," *Journal of Political Economy*, 107, pp. 252–284.

Brakman, S., H. Garretsen, J. Gorter, A. Horst and M. Schramm, 2005, *New Economic Geography, Empirics, and Regional Policy*, ERSA conference papers [ersa05p236], European Regional Science Association.

Braunerhjelm, P. and B. Borgman, 2004, "Geographical Concentration, Entrepreneurship and Regional Growth: Evidence from Regional Data in Sweden, 1975–1999," *Regional Studies*, 38(8), pp. 929–947.

Braunerhjelm, P. and B. Borgman, 2006, "Agglomeration, Diversity and Regional Growth," *CESIS Electronic Working Paper Series*, No. 71.

Ciccone, A. and R. E. Hall, 1996, "Productivity and the Density of Economic Activity," *The American Economic Review*, 86(1), pp. 54–70.

Combes, P.-P., M. Lafourcade, J.-F. Thisse and J.-C. Toutain, 2011, "The Rise and Fall of Spatial Inequalities in France: A Long-Run Perspective," *Explorations in Economic History*, 48(2), pp. 243–271.

Démurger, S., M. Gurgand, S. Li and X. Yue, 2009, "Migrants as Second-Class Workers in Urban China? A Decomposition Analysis," *Journal of Comparative Economics*, 37(4), pp. 610–628.

Devereux, M., P. R. Griffith, and H. Simpson, 2004, "The Geographic Distribution of Production Activity in the UK," *Regional Science and Urban Economics*, 34(5), pp. 533–564.

Dixit, A. K. and J. E. Stiglitz, 1977, "Monopolistic Competition and Optimum Product Diversity," *American Economic Review*, 67(3), pp. 297–308.

Dupont, V. and P. Martin, 2006, "Subsidies to Poor Regions and Inequalities: Some Unpleasant Arithmetic," *Journal of Economic Geography*, 6(2), pp. 223–240.

Duranton, G. and D. Puga, 2001, "Nursery Cities," *American Economic Review*, 91, pp. 1454–1463.

Ellison, G. and E. L. Glaeser, 1997, "Geographic Concentration in U.S. Manufacturing Industries: A Dartboard Approach," *Journal of Political Economy*, 105(5), pp. 889–927.

European Commission, 2004, Third Report on Economic and Social Cohesion: A New Partnership for Cohesion, http://ec.europa.eu/regional_policy/sources/docoffic/official/reports/cohesion3/cohesion3_en.htm.

Fujita, M. and D. Hu, 2001, "Regional Disparity in China 1985–1994: The Effects of Globalization and Economic Liberalization," *Annals of Regional Science*, 35(1), pp. 3–37.

Fujita, M. and J.-F. Thisse, 2003, "Does Geographical Agglomeration Foster Economic Growth? And Who Gains and Loses from It?," *Japanese Economic Review*, 54(2), pp. 121–145.

Fujita, M., P. Krugman, and A. J. Venables, 1999, *The Spatial Economy: Cities, Regions and International Trade*. Cambridge, MA: MIT Press.

Fujita, M., T. Mori, J. V. Henderson and Y. Kanemoto, 2004, "Spatial Distribution of Economic Activities in Japan and China," In *Handbook of Regional and Urban Economics*, ed. J. V. Henderson and T. Jacques-François. Oxford: Elsevier.

Furusawa, T. and H. Konishi, 2007, "Free Trade Networks," *Journal of International Economics*, 72(2), pp. 310–335.

Glaeser, E., H. D. Kallal, J. A. Sheinkman and A. Shleifer, 1992, "Growth in cities," *Journal of Political Economy*, 100(6), pp. 1126–1152.

Helsley, R. and W. Strange, 1990, "Matching and Agglomeration Economies in a System of Cities," *Journal of Urban Economics*, 20, pp. 189–212.

Henderson, J. V., 1974, "The Size and Types of Cities," *American Economic Review*, 64, pp. 640–656.

Henderson, J. V., A. Kuncoro and M. Turner, 1995, "Industrial Development in Cities," *Journal of Political Economy*, 103(5), pp. 1067–1090.

Henderson, J. V. and H. G. Wang, 2007, "Urbanization and City Growth: the Role of Institutions," *Regional Science and Urban Economics*, 37, pp. 283–313.

Jaffe, A. B., M. Trajtenberg and R. Henderson, 1993, "Geographic Localization of Knowledge Spillovers as Evidenced by Patent Citations," *Quarterly Journal of Economics*, 108(3), pp. 577–598.

Krugman, P., 1991a, "Increasing Returns and Economic Geography," *Journal of Political Economy*, 99(3), p. 483.

Krugman, P., 1991b, *Geography and Trade*, MA: MIT Press.

Krugman, P., 1993, "First Nature, Second Nature, and Metropolitan Location," *Journal of Regional Science*, 33(2), pp. 129–144.

Krugman, P. and A. J. Venables, 1995, "Globalization and the Inequality of Nations," *Quarterly Journal of Economics*, 110(4), pp. 857–880.

Martin, P. 1999, "Public Policies, Regional Inequalities and Growth," *Journal of Public Economics*, 73(1), pp. 85–105.

Martin, P. and Ottaviano, G. I. P., 1999, "Growing Locations: Industry Location in A Model of Endogenous Growth," *European Economic Review*, 43, pp. 281–302.

Martin, P. and Ottaviano, G. I. P., 2001, "Growth and Agglomeration," *International Economic Review*, 42(4), pp. 947–968.

Maurel, F. and B. Sedillot, 1999, "A Measure of the Geographic Concentration in French Manufacturing Industries," *Regional Science and Urban Economics*, 29(5), pp. 575–604.

Ministerie van Economische Zaken, 2004, Pieken in de Delta, http://archief.brainport.nl/Brainport_C01/Default.asp?CustID=354&ComID=1&ModID=940&ItemID=403&SessionID=-1&bottest=.

Ottaviano, G. I. P., T. Tabuchi and J.-F. Thisse, 2002, "Agglomeration and Trade Revisited," *International Economic Review,* 43(2), pp. 409–435.

Pflüger, M., 2004, "A Simple, Analytically Solvable, Chamberlinian Agglomeration Model," *Regional Science and Urban Economics*, 83, pp. 429–456.

Picard, P. M. and D. Z. Zeng, 2005, "Agricultural Sector and Industrial Agglomeration," *Journal of Development Economics*, 77(1), pp. 75–106.

Romer, P. M., 1986, "Increasing Return and Long-Run Growth," *Journal of Political Economy*, 94, pp. 1002–1037.

Song, H., J.-F. Thisse and X. Zhu, 2012, "Urbanization and/or Rural Industrialization in China," *Regional Science and Urban Economics*, 42(1–2), pp. 126–134.

Tabuchi, T., J.-F. Thisse and D. Z. Zeng, 2005, "On the Number and Size of Cities," *Journal of Economic Geography*, 5(4), pp. 423–448.

The Economist, 2011, "Regional Disparities: Gaponomics," March 12, pp. 13–14.

Wan, G., M. Lu and Z. Chen, 2007, "Globalization and Regional Income Inequality: Empirical Evidence from within China," *Review of Income and Wealth*, 53(1), pp. 35–59.

World Bank, 2009, *World Development Report 2009: Reshaping Economic Geography*. New York: Oxford University Press.

Ying, L. G., 2000, "Measuring the Spillover Effects: Some Chinese Evidence," *Regional Science*, 79(1), pp. 75–89.

Ying, L. G., 2003, "Understanding China's Recent Growth Experience: A Spatial Econometric Perspective," *Annals of Regional Science*, 37(4), pp. 613–628.

Zeng, D.-Z. and L. Zhao, 2010, "Globalization, Interregional and International Inequalities," *Journal of Urban Economics*, 67(3), pp. 352–361.

Zeng, D.-Z. and X. Zhu, 2011, "Tourism and Industrial Agglomeration," *Japanese Economic Review*, 62(4), pp. 537–561.

In Chinese

Chen, Jianjun, 2002, "Interregional Industry Transfer in China: An Analysis Based on 105 Manufacturing Firms in Zhejiang Province," *Management World*, 6, pp. 64–74.

Chen, Jiwang, 2007, "Main Factors Affecting Industrial Transfer of Eastern Region in China," *Productivity Research*, 5, pp. 99–101.

Chen, X. and Y. Xu, 2004, "Factors Affecting China's Regional Gap: An Empirical Study," *Economic Research Journal*, 5, pp. 117–129.

Chen, X. and Y. Xu, 2008, "Changes in the Spatial Structure of China Manufacturing Industries and Its Influence on Regional Specialization," *Economic Research Journal*, 10, pp. 104–116.

Chen, Z. and M. Lu, 2009, *Balance Through Agglomeration*. Beijing: Peking University Press.

Deng, H., 2009, "Trade Accessibility, Factor Distribution and Agglomeration: A Case of China," *Economic Research Journal*, 11, pp. 118–129.

Fan, J. and W. Yin, 2009, "Industrial Agglomeration, Labor Mobility and Coordinated Development of Regional Economy," Working paper, Fudan University.

Guan, W., Z. Lin and C. Gu, 2006, "Multi-Scale Analysis on China's Regional Economical Diversity and Reasons," *Economic Research Journal*, 7, pp. 117–125.

Jin, X., Y. Ru and H. Wu, 2008, "Institution, Production Efficiency and Chinese Regional Unbalanced Export," *Management World*, 11, pp. 65–77.

Li, B. and K. Chen, 2007, "Foreign Trade and the Change of Regional Disparity in China," *Journal of World Economy*, 5, pp. 25–32.

Li, G. and H. Fan, 2003, "The Distribution of Production and Regional Inequality," *Economic Research Journal*, 11, pp. 79–86.

Liu, G., 2006, "Influence of City Group Evolution From Japan on the development of Chinese City Group," *Contemporary Economic Research*, 5, pp. 40–43.

Liu, S., Y. Wang and A. Hu, 2009, "The Effect of Western Development Program and Regional Economic Convergence in China," *Economic Research Journal*, 9, pp. 94–105.

Lu, J. and Z. Tao, 2006, "Industrial Agglomeration and Co-agglomeration in China's Manufacturing Industries: with International Comparison," *Economic Research Journal*, 3, pp. 103–114.

Lu, J., W. Wang and J. Song, 2010, "Population Size Evolution in New York, Tokyo and London," *Urban Problems*, 9, pp. 84–90.

Lu, M., 2011, "Interregional Reallocation of Non-Agricultural Land Use Rights: A New Engine of Chinese Economic Growth," *Journal of World Economy*, 1, pp. 107–125.

Song, H., L. He and X. Zhu, 2010, "Dual Integration, Agglomeration and Regional Coordination," *Journal of Zhejiang University (Humanities and Social Science)*, 40(5), pp. 104–115.

von Thünen, J. H., 1826, *Der Isolierte Staat in Beziehung auf Landwirtschaft und Nationalökonomie*, Hamburg: Perthes. English translation: *The Isolated State*, Oxford: Pergamon Press (1966).

Wan, G., M. Lu and Z. Chen, 2005, "Globalization and Regional Inequality: Chinese Evidence," *Social Science in China*, 3, pp. 17–26.

Wang, M., 2003, "Wages Differential in the Transition Period: Econometric Analysis on Discrimination," *Journal of Quantitative & Technical Economics*, 20(5), pp. 94–98.

Wang, X. and G. Fan, 2004, "Income Inequality in China and Its Influential Factors," *Economic Research Journal*, 10, pp. 24–36.

Wei, H. and C. Sun, 2004, "The Evaluation of Actual Effect of Western Development Strategy in China," *Research on Development*, 3, pp. 21–25.

Wu, Y. and J. Xu, 2004, "A Spatial Analysis on China's Regional Economic Growth Clustering," *Scientia Geographica Sinica*, 6, pp. 654–659.

Xu, Z., Z. Chen and M. Lu, 2010, "Core-Periphery Model of Urban Economic Growth: Empirical Evidence from Chinese City-Level Data," *Journal of World Economy*, 7, pp. 114–160.

Xu, Z. and S. Li, 2006, "Analysis on the Trend of Regional Income Disparity in China," *Economic Research Journal*, 7, pp. 106–116.

Yao, X. and P. Lai, 2004, "Urban-rural Huji Differentials in Chinese Labor Relations," *Economic Research Journal*, 7, pp. 82–90.

Zhang, L. and B. Lu, 2009, "The Main Course of Tokyo Megalopofis Planning and its Revelation to Chia," *Urban Studies*, 12, pp. 5–11.

Zhao, W. and C. Zhang, 2009, "Market Integration and the Trend of Manufacturing Agglomeration in China," *Journal of Quantitative & Technical Economics*, 2, pp. 18–32.

Zhu, X., 2004, "Preference, Technology and Industrialization," *Economic Research Journal*, 11, pp. 96–106.

Zhu, X., X. Jin and D. Luo, 2005, "Market segmentation and the Expansion of China's Export," *Economic Research Journal*, 12, pp. 68–76.

Appendix: change of spatial Gini coefficient of 18 major industries

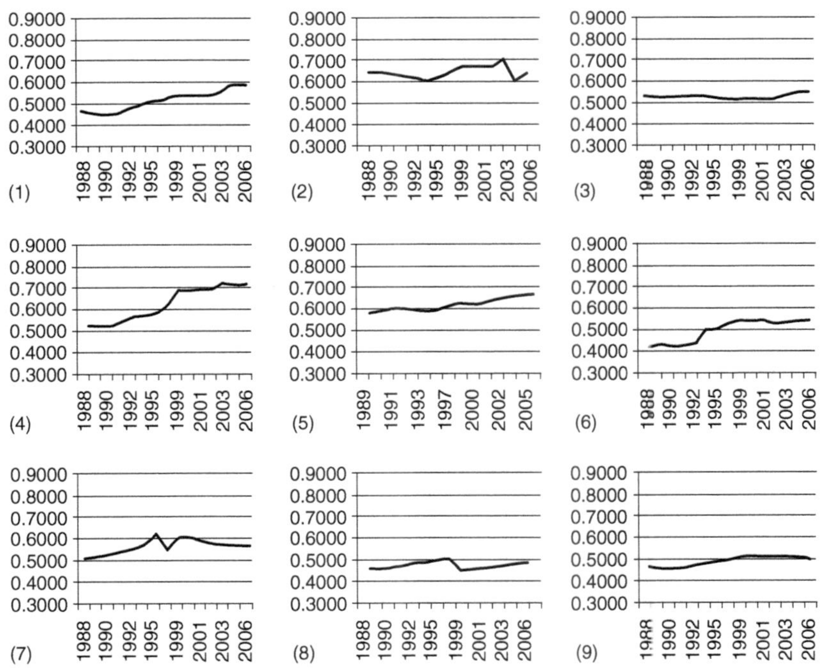

(Continued)

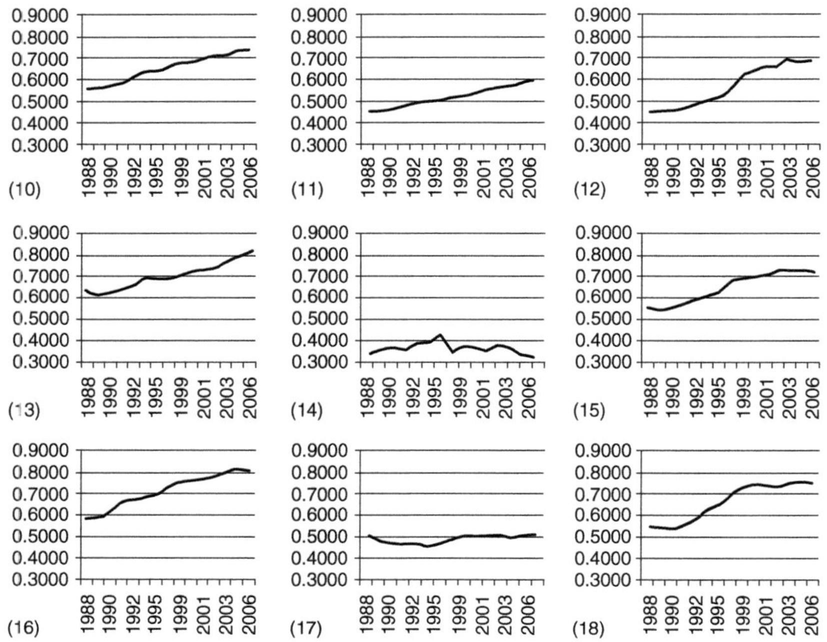

The horizontal axis in the chart represents year, the vertical axis represents spatial Gini coefficient. Each chart represents an industry: 1. Non-metallic mineral product manufacturing; 2. Ferrous metals mining; 3. Ferrous metals smelting and refining; 4. Fabricated metal product manufacturing; 5. Coal mining; 6. Food manufacturing; 7. Tobacco processing; 8. Pharmaceuticals; 9. Beverages; 10. Textiles; 11. Chemicals; 12. Paper and paper products manufacturing; 13. Synthetic fiber; 14. Utilities; 15. Electrical equipment and machinery; 16. Electronics and communications equipment; 17. Transportation equipment manufacturing; 18. Instruments and office supplies.

Data source: Authors' calculations based on *China Industry Economics Statistical Yearbook*.

Part II

Political economy and analysis

2 The political economy of regional development in China

Xianxiang Xu, Xianbin Wang, and Yuanhua Gao

2.1 Introduction

Since "reform and opening," China has always emphasized that "development is of overriding importance" and has caught the attention of the world with a 9.8 percent annualized growth rate from 1978 to 2008. National development is undoubtedly realized through regional development, and China's regional development is just as widely followed, with a considerable amount of relevant literature recently accumulated. Figure 2.1 displays the amount of literature in Chinese concerned with China's regional development.[1] In the early 1980s, the number of relevant papers published every year was in single digits. After entering the new millennium, the number of papers published annually exceeded 500, and the number has reached over 2,000 per year since 2007. Therefore, it is necessary to systematically review the development of over 30 years of research on Chinese regional development, based on the huge amount of literature accumulated up to the present.[2]

Before systematically examining literature on Chinese regional development, a question that needs to be clarified first is: what is regional development? The question seems to be an obvious one, but from the literature we possess, there is no clear definition. In this chapter, we examine Chinese regional development through the three dimensions of intraregional development, interregional gaps and interregional connections. We have consequently discovered, since 30 years of "reform and opening," Chinese regional development could be summarized as rapid intraregional growth and prominent interregional conflicts. Rapid intraregional growth refers to the fact that from the perspective of a vertical comparison, every region achieved rapid economic growth. Prominent interregional conflicts manifest themselves, from the perspective of a horizontal comparison, as the issues of regional development gaps and interregional economic integration, which have always been hot spots for attention.

There exists an inherently logically consistent political economy explanation for China's regional development model, in which there is rapid intraregional growth and prominent interregional conflicts. The reason why the explanation is one of political economy is that politics and economics are linked in China, and local officials are responsible for the development of their jurisdiction. Specifically speaking, after "reform and opening," the central government began to regard

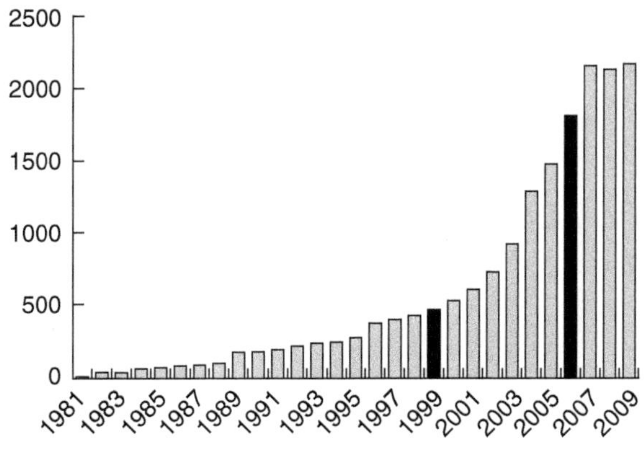

Figure 2.1 Number of papers concerning regional development.
Data source: Search results from CNKI.

economic development as its foremost objective, emphasizing "development is of overriding importance," binding local officials' careers, their jurisdiction's fiscal revenue and development together through institutional reforms in public finance and personnel administration system. Local officials reacted to the incentives and gradually became market preserving or market augmenting local officials.[3] Local officials endeavor to implement market-oriented economic reforms and develop their jurisdiction, while also actively or passively participating in yardstick competition between jurisdictions, endeavoring to attain better economic performance than other jurisdictions, in order to come out on top. The behavior of local officials, endeavoring to develop the economy in their jurisdiction while also endeavoring to widen regional gaps, is reflected on the macro-scale as rapid intraregional growth and prominent interregional conflicts.

The structure of the rest of the chapter is as follows: the second and third sections introduce the background and facts of China's regional development; the fourth and fifth sections respectively examine the reasons behind China's regional development and how regional disparities accompany such development; the sixth section concludes with the political economy logic of China's regional development and provide possible directions for further research.

2.2 The background of regional development

2.2.1 Opening up to the outside world is spatially gradual

China's opening to the outside world was gradually implemented. In 1979, under the advocacy of Comrade Deng Xiaoping, the central government decided to set up special economic zones in Shenzhen, Zhuhai, Shantou and Xiamen as an experiment, in order to attract overseas Chinese capital, investment from Hong Kong, Macau and Taiwan and foreign investment through preferential policies, to allow factories to be established through direct and joint investment.[4] As an extension of the special economic zone policy, in 1984, the central government expanded the "opening up" policy to 14 coastal cities,[5] and formulated special policies for the special economic zones and open coastal cities. In 1988, the central government implemented the "Coastal Regions Development Strategy", expanding the Yangtze Delta, Pearl River Delta, and Minnan Delta into a "Greater Delta," while enlisting the Liaodong Peninsula, Jiaodong Peninsula, Bohai Gulf Rim of Heibei Province and some cities close to the Beibu Gulf in Guangxi as coastal open regions.[6]

In 1992, after Deng toured the southern special economic zones, the central government decided to pursue the special economic zones and development and opening of coastal regions policies more extensively and began to implement all-around opening of areas close to seas, rivers, borders and roads. By 1993, it had established five special economic zones with 23 counties and county-level municipalities; 14 coastal open cities; 260 coastal open counties and county-level municipalities, the government approved the establishment of five open cities along the river; 18 provincial capital open cities; 13 border open cities and towns; and 13 border economic cooperation zones. "Reform and opening" was not just limited to coastal regions but had become national policy and practice.

2.2.2 The key to regional development is progressing spatially

The emphasis of China's regional development also experienced a process from east to west, from south to north and from coastal to inland. At the start of the reforms, which began in the 1980s in accordance with Deng's, "Let a few people and regions get rich first, those that get rich first will bring along those left behind, eventually realizing common prosperity" ideal, China implemented the "eastern coastal development strategy," during which development of the Pearl River Delta was given priority in the 1980s. Pudong was opened in the early 1990s followed by development of the Yangtze Delta. As the eastern coastal development strategy was implemented, in the mid- to late-1990s, regional development gaps began to surface.[7] China gradually bade farewell to shortages and began to show signs of inadequate effective demand.[8] Due to increased demand, fostering and expanding the market became the only choice for China.[9] At the turn of the century, to accommodate the proactive fiscal policy to increase domestic demand under national macro-control, by the end of 1999, the Grand Western Development Program began to be fully implemented; by the end of 2003, the "Revitalization of Northeast-China Old Industrial Bases Strategy" began to be implemented; in 2004 the "Rise of Central China" was the subject of a great deal of attention by the state. Doubtlessly, this type of spatial progression in regional development priorities is the result of constant adjustment to the state's regional development strategy.

2.2.3 Politically centralized and economically decentralized

After the founding of New China, China formed a centralized administrative apparatus and the relationship between the central and local government was constantly adjusted. After "reform and opening", in order to motivate the local government to participate in reforms and development, the central government adjusted relations with the local government, shifting from a highly centralized model to a structure where the central government centralizes political powers and moderately decentralizes economic powers to the local government.[10]

Concentration of political powers mainly refers to personnel appointments. After 1949, the most fundamental principle of China's personnel management system is "the party manages the cadres," while implementing administration according to "different departments and levels". The appointment system operates as the political mechanism, in which the promotion of a local official is decided by superiors and not subordinates or the electorate in his or her jurisdiction.[11] In China, the head of the local government at every level is appointed by the government of the next higher level. For example, the leading official of the provinces is appointed by the central government, the leading official of the prefectures is appointed by the provincial government and so on.

Decentralization of economic powers mainly refers to a higher level of government delegating powers to the next lower level, for example, the central government delegating fiscal powers to the local government. From the perspective of international comparison, the degree of economic decentralization in China is high. Xu (2009a) discovered that the ratio of local government expenditures to national fiscal expenditures in China is around 70 percent, while the figures for the US and Germany are, respectively, around 46 percent and 40 percent. This implies that China has delegated more powers to local government than federalist countries. Perhaps it is from this fact that second generation fiscal decentralization theory views China as a fiscal federation (Qian and Weingast, 1997).

Decentralization of power over resources refers to the fact that local government not only has "decentralized powers" granted by the upper level, but also has resources.[12] In the process of delegating powers, the form of property rights in China changed dramatically, gradually forming the so-called localization of property rights with local government controlling large amounts of resources (Zheng and Wu, 1995). Localization of property rights formed during the process of the local government's intervention in local economic activity, which forged close connections between the local government and economy. In fact, local government controlling large amounts of resources is not just something that happened after "reform and opening;" it may have been the case since ancient times (Xu, 2009b). Moreover, under the appointment system, the local government controls the appointments for the head of the next lower level of government, and the local government's will can be exercised through control over the immediate lower level's personnel, which is also a very important resource.

2.2.4 Market supply and demand condition shift from shortage to surplus

A characteristic of the traditional socialist economic system is "shortages" (Kornai, 1986) and a corresponding system of rationing through coupons developed.[13] In 1953, the center implemented a policy of planned purchase and marketing by the state toward agricultural goods.[14] Beijing and other medium and large cities began to issue, e.g., "flour purchase warrants," in accordance with urban household registers. In 1954, the center carried out the planned purchase and marketing of cotton and cotton cloth, regions such as Jiangxi began to issue "cotton cloth purchase warrants." In 1955, China issued its first edition of nationwide general food coupons, and every region issued vegetable oil coupons. In September 1955, a system of four warrants and three coupons was put into practice nationwide.[15] Henceforth, coupons became an integral part of economic life in China. After "reform and opening", the emergence and development of the chemical fiber industry ameliorated the tight supply of cotton cloth with cloth coupons no longer being collected after December 1983 and no longer printed or distributed after 1984, ending the planned supply of cotton cloth. Entering the 1990s, goods gradually became abundant and coupons of all sorts were no longer required. In 1993, the food warrant also known as the "First Coupon of China" disappeared from the stages of history. Since then, coupons have begun to fade out of daily life. There is no doubt that the evolution of coupons directly reflects the gradual emergence of Chinese markets from "shortage".

Moreover, we found data that systematically reflects changes in the market's supply and demand. According to the data on queues for 601 main goods provided by the Ministry of Internal Trade (Kong, 1998), in the 1980s, the proportion of goods in shortage was about 40 percent. After Deng's South Tour Speech, China's reform and opening entered a new historical phase, with the proportion of major goods in shortage falling rapidly to around 10 percent. In 1998, Chinese markets achieved an historical transformation from shortage to surplus. The supply- and demand-situation for agricultural goods and their byproducts all shifted to equilibrium or surplus following industrial consumer goods. Specifically speaking, 446 types of goods basically achieved equilibrium between supply and demand, 74.2 percent of total; 155 types of goods had a surplus, 25.8 percent of total; 0 types of goods were in shortage. Henceforth, the Chinese economy began to enter the era of surplus economy.

The Chinese economy's shift from shortage to surplus has strong policy implications. In the era of shortages, the fundamental orientation of economic policy is nurturing and enhancing productive capability and increasing supply in order to "meet the ever-increasing material and cultural needs of the people;" heading into the era of surplus, nurturing and developing the market, creating effective demand became the new fundamental orientation of China's economic policy.

2.3 The facts of regional development

2.3.1 Rapid economic growth in each province and region

From the perspective of vertical comparisons, after "reform and opening," China's economy developed rapidly, with each province and region showing fast economic growth. Speaking in nationwide terms, between 1978 and 2008, GDP grew at an average annual rate of 9.8 percent, while *per capita* gross regional product grew at an average annual rate of 8.6 percent. Speaking in terms of provinces (*Note*: In terms of Chinese administrative units, there are actually provinces, autonomous regions and directly administered municipalities but provinces will be used henceforth), between 1979 and 2008, the average annual gross regional production growth rate for every province exceeded 8 percent. Heilongjiang had the slowest growth rate with 8.4 percent; Guangdong had the fastest growth rate with 13.5 percent,[16] the difference between the two reaching around 5 percentage points percent. From a *per capita* perspective, between 1979 and 2008, *per capita* regional gross product for every province exceeded 7 percent. Heilongjiang again had the slowest growth rate with 7.7 percent; Zhejiang had the highest growth rate with 12.1 percent–the difference between the two is also around 5 percentage points. It is due to the rapid economic growth during the past 30 years that the size of the economy and *per capita* output increased dramatically in every province, as is shown in Figure 2.2.[17]

From a global perspective, the economic growth of China's provinces is very astounding. As Figure 2.3 shows, if the growth rates of the 31 provinces (Taiwan not included) are placed in the global context for comparison, whether in terms of gross product or *per capita* gross product, the record they have set over the past 30 years all rank at the forefront of the world development.[18]

2.3.2 Gaps between provinces show a trend toward "decreasing–increasing–decreasing"

Regional economic growth after "reform and opening" was rapid, but development among regions was unbalanced. As evidenced by Figure 2.4, economic disparities between provinces show a trend toward "decreasing–increasing–decreasing."

From the perspective of the Gini coefficient, between 1978 and 2008, economic disparities between China's provinces displayed a trend toward "decreasing-increasing-decreasing." In the 1980s, economic disparities between China's provinces, as measured by the Gini coefficient displayed a trend toward decreasing, but such economic disparities swiftly expanded in the 1990s. Only after 2005 did they again display a decreasing trend. However, judging from the current level of economic disparities measured by the Gini coefficient, it is close to the level before "reform and opening." If the coefficient of variation is used to measure the change in trend of *per capita* GDP differentials,[19] the direction of change is mostly consistent with that of the Gini coefficient. The turning points in each developmental stage and the magnitude of change are both very similar and verify each other.

2.3.3 Ratio of interprovincial trade becomes larger and larger

Xu and Li (2010) employed the interprovincial railway cargo database to calculate the ratio of intraprovincial and interprovincial trade for 29 Chinese provinces between 1985 and 2009.

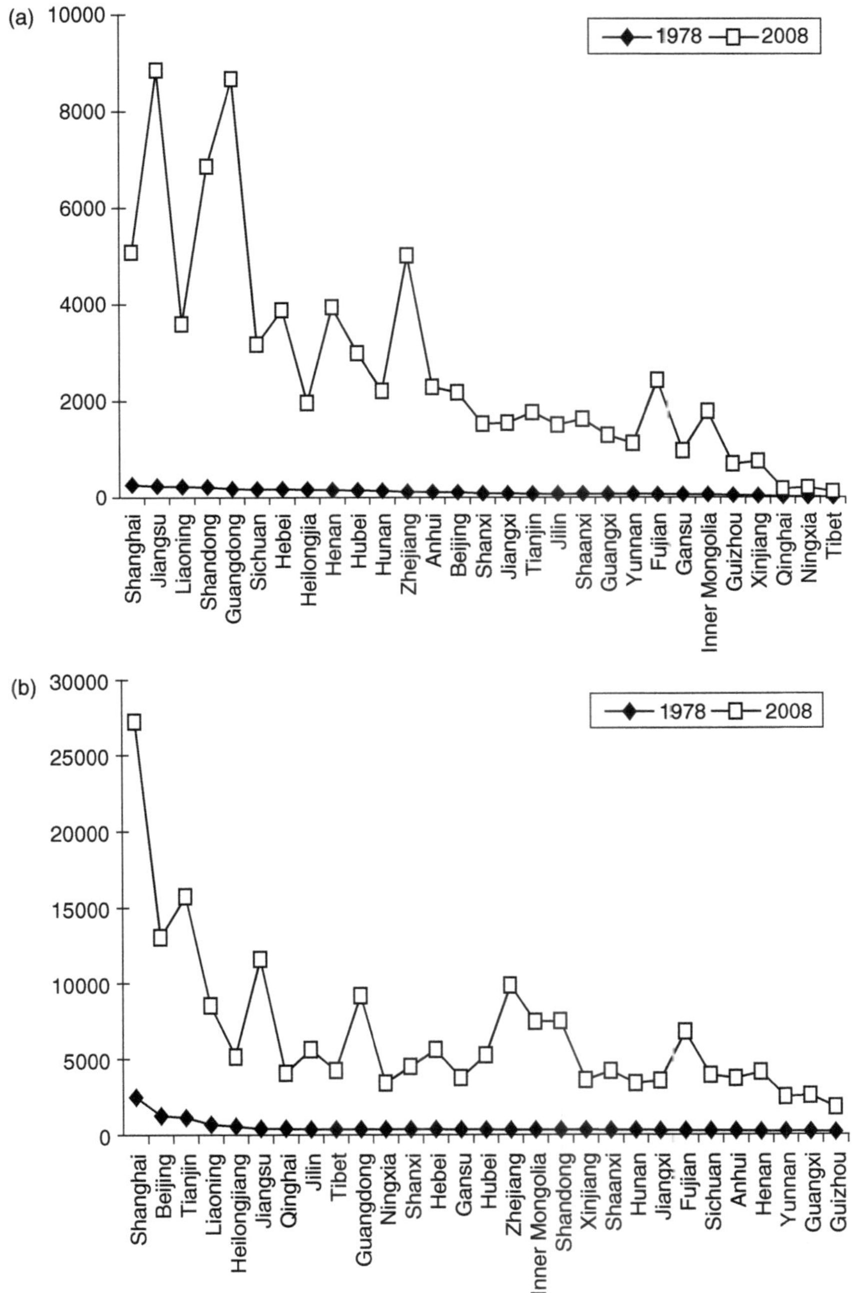

Figure 2.2 Economic growth of the 29 Chinese provinces, autonomous regions and municipalities from 1978 to 2008; (a) Real GDP (hundred million yuan). (b) Real GDP *per capita* (yuan).

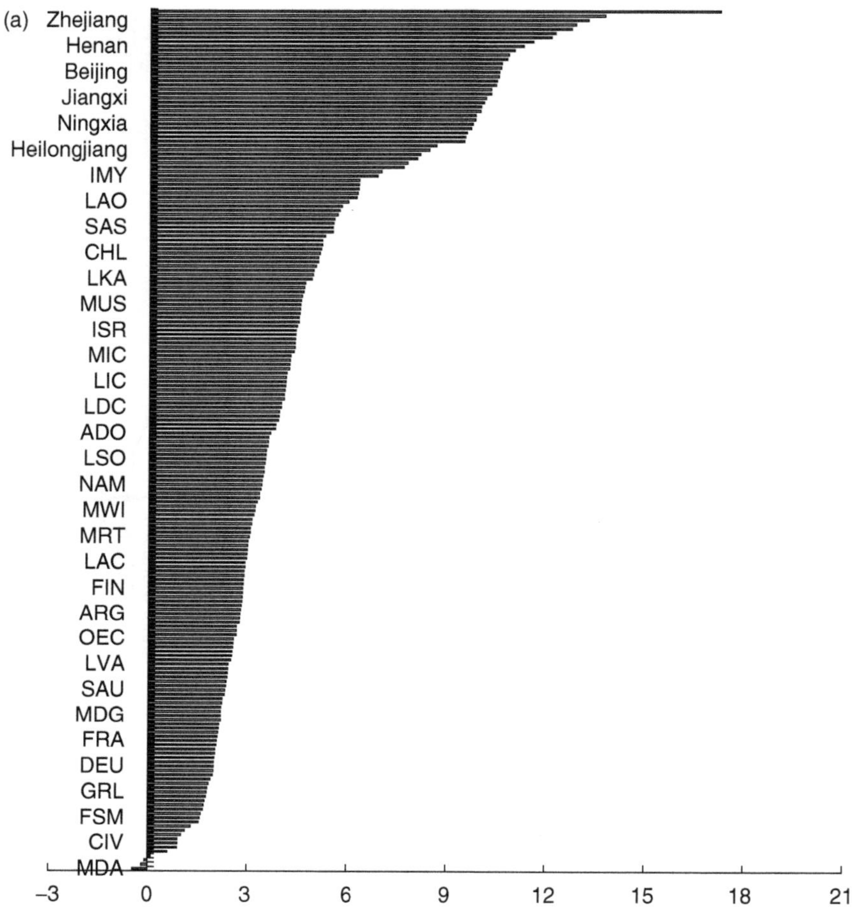

Figure 2.3 Economic growth of Chinese provinces in global context: (a) 1979–2008 average annual gross product growth rate (b) 1979–2008 average annual *per capita* gross product growth rate.

Note: Other than the data on Chinese provinces, all data on countries and regions comes from Penn World Table (PWT 6.2). (a) Chosen from 170 countries and regions between 1979 and 2008 with mostly complete data and (b) chosen from 180 countries and regions with mostly complete data. Since the data table used to generate the figure is rather large, only a portion is shown here.

Figure 2.5 displays the ratio of interprovincial trade of 29 Chinese provinces between 1985 and 2007. Looking from the chart, the ratio of interprovincial trade rose for most provinces, with some even rising year after year. Specifically speaking, in the 29 provinces, Zhejiang's interprovincial trade ratio rose and then fell; Shanghai, Zhejiang, Gansu, Qinghai, Xinjiang and Chongqing's interprovincial

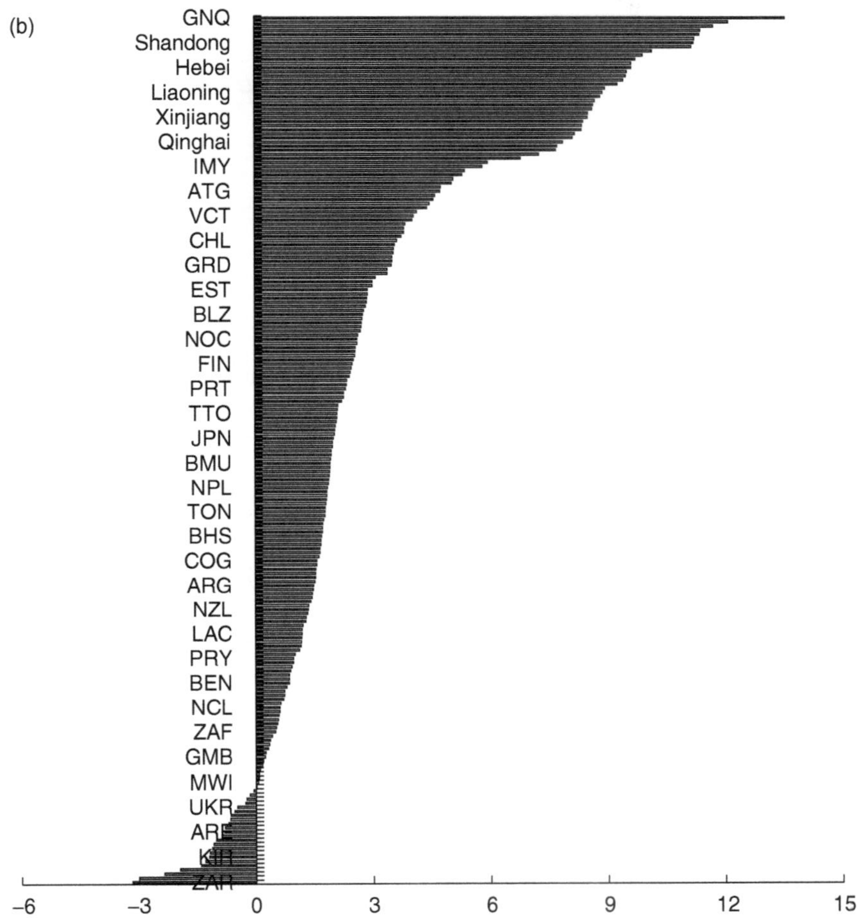

Figure 2.3 Continued

trade ratio ascended while fluctuating; the other 22 provinces saw a gradual rise in the ratio. This implies that over 96 percent of China's provinces experienced an increasing interprovincial trade ratio.[20] As the sum of the interprovincial and intraprovincial trade ratios equal 1, Figure 2.5 thus shows that between 1985 and 2007, for the ratio of intraprovincial trade decreased and the ratio of interprovincial trade increased 96 percent of Chinese provinces.[21]

Xu and Li (2010) also calculated the mean of the intraprovincial and interprovincial ratios for 29 Chinese provinces and discovered that the mean of the interprovincial trade ratio increased year after year, increasing by about 50 percent from 1985 to 2007; while the intraprovincial trade ratio correspondingly declined year after year, falling by about 50 percent from 1985 to 2007.

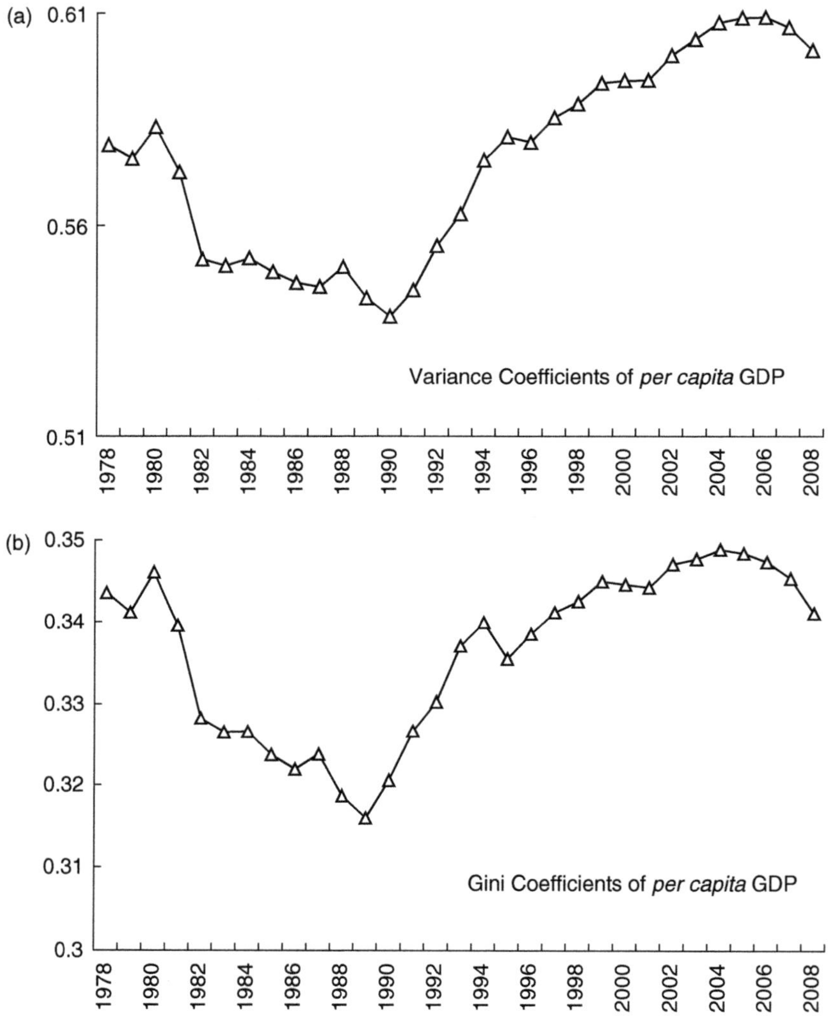

Figure 2.4 Economic disparities of Chinese provinces (1978–2008).

We can summarize the basic facts regarding Chinese regional development thus: in the 30 years since "reform and opening," regional development has been rapid, though there are prominent problems across jurisdictions. Rapid development within jurisdictions is manifested by, from the perspective of vertical comparison, the fact that each province achieved swift growth; prominent problems across jurisdictions are manifested by, from the perspective of horizontal comparison, by the fact that issues such as regional development gaps and interregional economic interaction are widely followed.

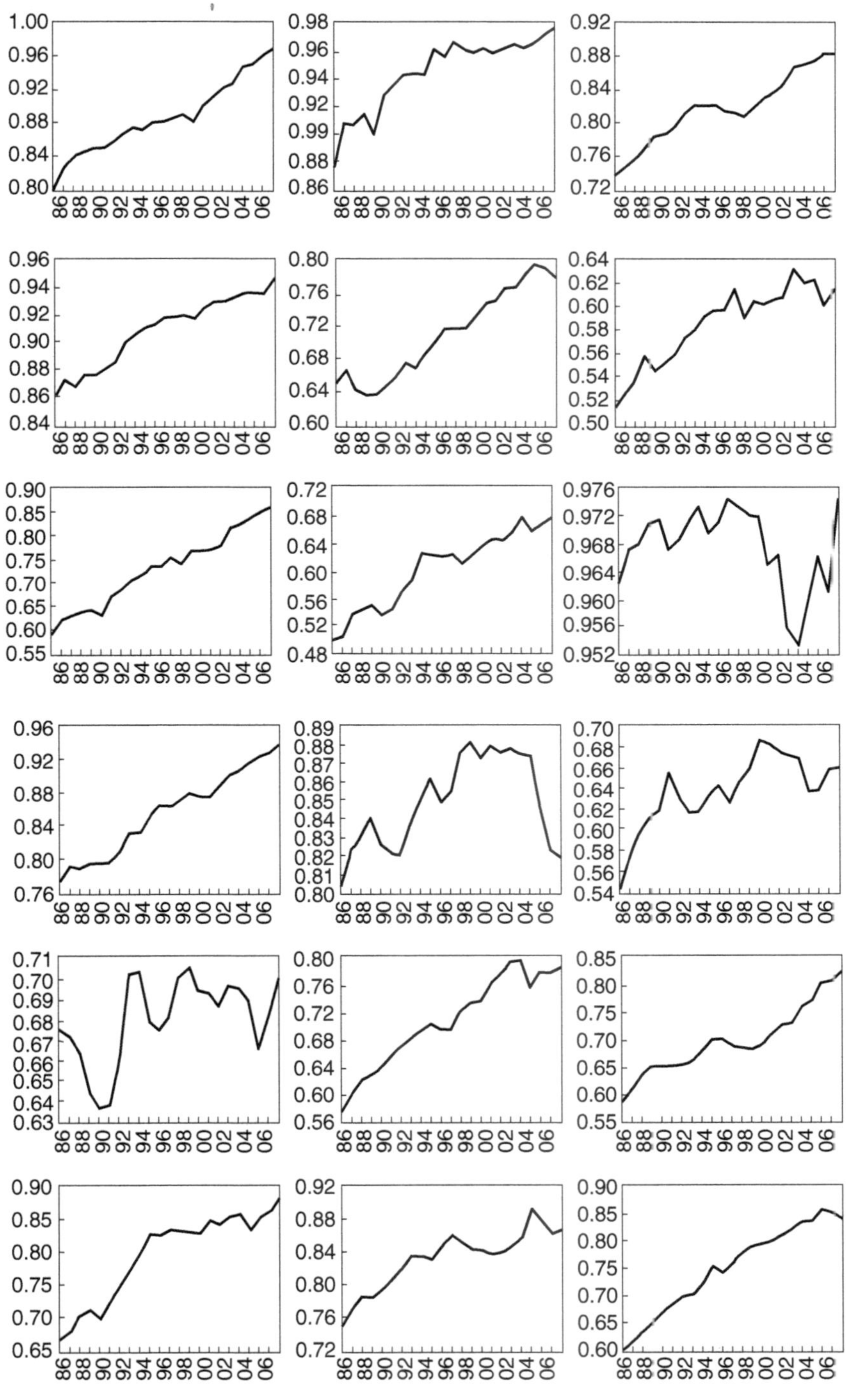

Figure 2.5 Each province's ratio of interprovincial trade (1985–2007).

Note: The 29 provinces left to right are Beijing, Tianjin, Hebei, Shanxi, Neimenggu, Liaoning, Jilin, Heilongjiang, Shanghai, Jiangsu, Zhejiang, Anhui, Fujian, Jiangxi, Shandong, Henan, Hubei, Hunan, Guangdong, Guangxi, Sichuan, Guizhou, Yunnan, Shaanxi, Gansu, Qinghai, Ningxia, Xinjiang, and Chongqing.

Data source: The original figure comes from Xu and Li (2010, Figure 2.3).

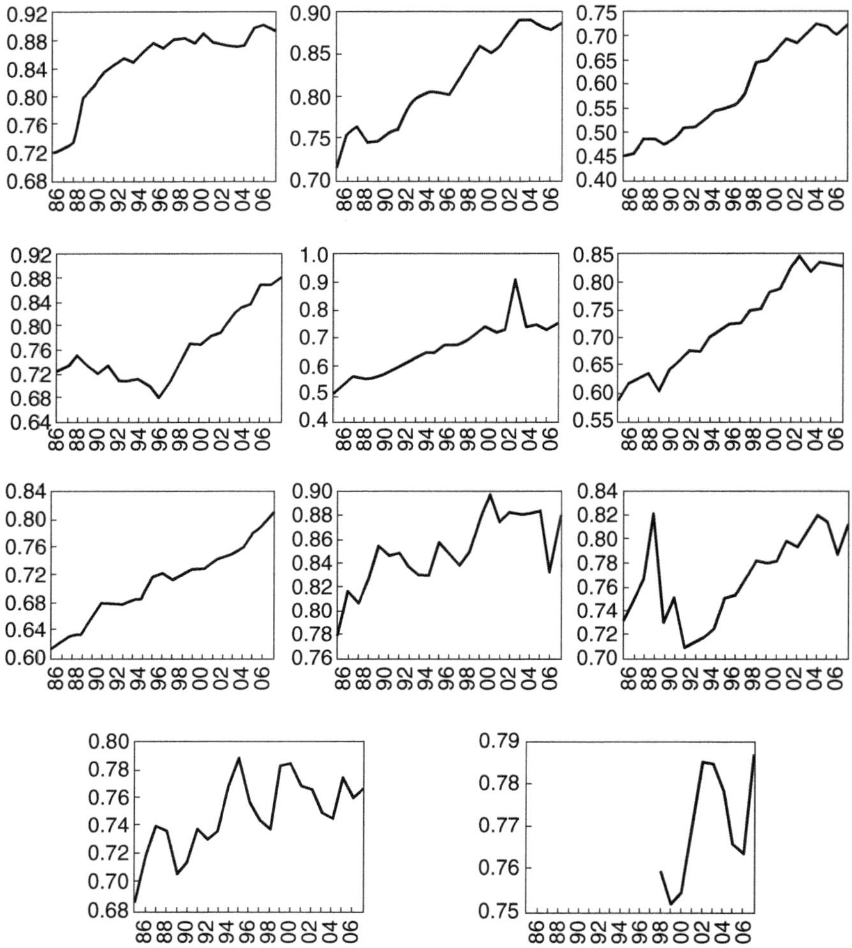

Figure 2.5 Continued

2.4 Why does regional development occur?

Based on China's gradual opening spatially and the center's spatial expansion policy regarding regional development, over the past 30 years, the Pearl Delta, the Yangtze Delta, and such regions have taken the lead in development and achieved an economic take-off.[22] Therefore, Chinese regional development took a path of "a few regions get rich first."

2.4.1 *A few regions get rich first*

Many studies have been carried out concerning the Pearl Delta, the Yangtze Delta and the regions that took the lead in development, while Guangdong and Zhejiang gives a strong feeling of "rags to riches." Before "reform and opening," these two provinces' proportion of the national economic aggregate ranked among the bottom. But during 1978–2008, they ranked among China's fastest growing economic bodies, with their long-term rank of first and fourth, respectively. Therefore, this section examines Guangdong and Zhejiang's economic take-off in depth.

2.4.1.1 Guangdong and Zhenjiang's economic take-off

As a pioneer in China's "reform and opening," Guangdong achieved spectacular achievements in development. Its economic aggregate grew 46.9 times between 1978 and 2008, making it the fastest-growing economy, with an average annual growth rate of 13.7 percent; its proportion of the national economic output rose from 5.4 percent in 1978 to 11.2 percent in 2008. As of 2008, Guangdong's economic aggregate has been ranked number one nationwide for a number of years.

Zhejiang grew 40.4 times between 1978 and 2008, with an average annual growth rate of 13.1 percent, second only to Guangdong, and its proportion of the national economic aggregate increased from 3.6 percent in 1978 to 6.6 percent in 2008. As of 2008, Zhejiang's GDP has been ranked number four nationwide for a number of years.[23]

Figure 2.6 puts Guangdong and Zhejiang's economic take-off in the international context.[24] Data is sourced from PWT 6.2,[25] which provides comparable international macroeconomic data from 1950 to 2004 for 188 economic bodies including China.[26] Figure 2.6 shows that Japan's *per capita* GDP in 1950 was US$371, and its economy took off first, though economic growth slowed entering the 1990s. South Korea's economy began to take off after the 1960s, though its growth rate showed a marked decline after the Asian financial crisis. However, the gap between South Korea and Japan's *per capita* GDP decreased significantly. In 1978, according to PWT 6.2's figures, China's *per capita* GDP was US$324, Guangdong and Zhejiang's *per capita* GDP were, respectively, US$313 and US$281, and took off thereafter. After 20 years of development, Guangdong and Zhejiang reduced their income gap with Japan and South Korea, and their rate of growth still shows no sign of significant deceleration.

It needs to be made clear that on a global scale, economic take-offs are common. From the growth experience of economies worldwide post-Second World War, other than in a few developed countries,[27] most economies experienced violent fluctuations. Such a phenomenon was first discovered by Easterly et al. (1993), and later emphasized by Pritchett (2000) and Hausmann et al. (2004). Jones and Olken (2008) discovered after a detailed examination that among the 125 economies worldwide with relevant data, 90 percent experienced a decade where the average growth record was higher than the highest American growth rate; 94 percent experienced a decade where the growth record was lower than lowest American growth rate. Jones and Olken (2008) dub such a phenomenon "Start–Stop Growth." The "start" phase corresponds with economic take-off,

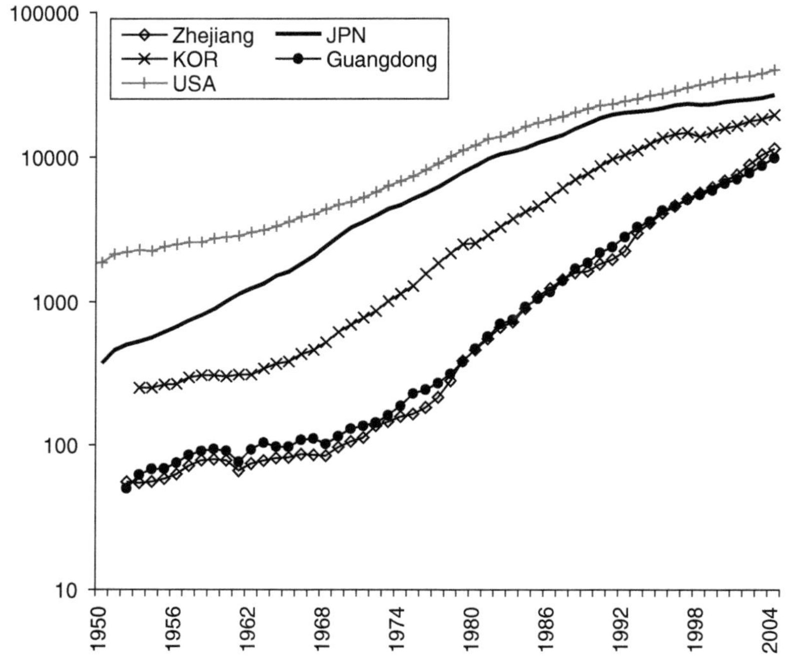

Figure 2.6 International comparisons of Guangdong and Zhejiang's economic take-off.
Note: The vertical axis is in logarithmic scale in dollar units; the horizontal axis is year.

while the "stop" phase is often vividly depicted as "the lost decade," implying that an economy may easily "fall" after take-off.

2.4.1.2 Geography and policy open the gate to economic take-off

Although economic take-off is a common phenomenon, for an economic body to take off, the hand of fortune is needed to open the gate: at a certain point, the gate to economic take-off is opened and the economy henceforth begins to grow rapidly. When the economy's income level reaches a certain height, growth starts to slow and the economic take-off nears its end. Lucas (2000) emphasized the need for the hand of fortune to open the gate to economic take-off. However, most current literature ignores Lucas's proposition.[28]

How should the Pearl Delta region's economic take-off be viewed? Experts and academics in various fields, as well as government officials, have given different conclusions for example famous academic Professor Vogel (1990) from Harvard delved deeply into on-site investigations in Guangdong, systematically elaborating the reasons, processes, and characteristics of Guangdong's economic take-off from 1979 to 1988, concisely summarizing it in "One Step Ahead in China,"[29] summarizing Guangdong's explorations and experimentations in the first ten years of "reform and opening" as "one step ahead." If the first ten years are one step ahead, then what are the following 20 years? On the eve of the 30th anniversary of "reform and opening", Shu et al. (2008) systematically concluded the process of Guangdong's economic take-off.[30]

At the beginning of "reform and opening," the center gradually got the incentives for economic development right.[31] Not only was development's overriding importance emphasized, concrete efforts were also made at development: one is the fiscal decentralization reform, in which the local government could directly retain a larger portion of local fiscal revenues from regional economic growth, thus making them highly motivated to promote local economic development; another is changing promotion standards for local officials from mainly political conduct-based to mainly economic achievement-based. This implies that economic development not only brings economic benefits to the local government, but can also create political advantages.

Given the domestic and international situation, Guangdong responded actively and innovated boldly, leading the way in experimentation on promoting economic development through reform and opening and gradually arranging incentives toward economic development. Through formulating the boundaries of policy, delegating powers to the immediate lower level of government, and mobilizing all forces possible to develop the economy, the local government has sufficient motivation to innovate and break with convention. For example, the Special Economic Zones actively carried out "reform and opening" experiments, Dongguan, Zhongshan, Shunde, and other Pearl Delta regions actively explored a suitable development model cohesive with their own endowments, in which Guangdong's economic development entered the experimental phase. Consequently, productive factors from other regions domestically and internationally progressively shifted toward the Pearl Delta, which made it the area these factors were clustered in. This not only caused the rapid growth of Shenzhen and other Special Economic Zones, but also created the professionalized cities of the Pearl Delta region, causing the swift economic growth of Pearl Delta minor and Guangdong to provide goods nationwide and globally. Since then, Guangdong's economy opened the gate to economic take-off.

If the Pearl Delta opened the gate to economic take-off through geography and policy, then how did Zhejiang open the gate to economic take-off? Zhejiang is a resource-scarce province with only half a mu of land *per capita*,[32] yet despite no preferential policy from "reform and opening", no monopoly on geographical and locational conditions, and even less of an advantage in economic fundamentals, it still miraculously ascended to become an economically significant province. Such a rapid take-off in Zhejiang's economy still has its roots in policies encouraging development and expansion of the private sector. Liu (1996, 1997) vividly summarizes Zhejiang's economy as a "small enterprise, large market" model, namely a primitive market economy model with perfect competition characteristics, with households and small non-state-owned enterprises as business entities and the goods and private factors market as methods of resource allocation, and believes such a model provided the institutional basis for the sustained fast growth in Zhejiang's economy. Zheng (2001) believes that the funds and entrepreneurial resources required for the development of Zhejiang's economy mainly relies on intraregional accumulation, such a model of endogenous private forces promoting economic development proliferated from Wenzhou to most of Zhejiang, bringing rapid growth to Zhejiang's economy. In "Institutional Change and Economic Development: A Study of the Wenzhou Model," Shi et al. (2002) also stated that Zhejiang employed a regional economic institution change and regional economic development model where privatization and market liberalization propelled industrialization and urbanization, and it is exactly such a model that enabled Zhejiang to developed rapidly. Zhao (2005) further emphasizes that Zhejiang and other Yangtze Delta regions' economic opening differs from that of the Pearl Delta in that it first promoted interregional trade, and then entered the international goods and capital market, promoting international trade with interregional trade and interregional factor mobility as a fulcrum. Since then, private, endogenous, market forces opened the gates for Zhejiang's economic take-off.

2.4.2 The center's correct arrangement of incentives

"Getting the incentives right" is of utmost importance. In "The Elusive Quest for Growth," Easterly (2002/2005) clearly points out that only when agents in economic development face correct incentives will economic prosperity arrive. The fundamental way of "getting the incentives right" is to establish good rules of the game, and the government's influence on rules determines its core status in "getting the incentives right". China has always been a large country with the central government's administration of the country realized through the local government. The center formulates and establishes economic and social development goals and visions, and requires the local government to support, implement and execute, and eventually realizes the above through the efforts of the local government. Thus, getting the incentives right is of the utmost importance and the success of China's regional economic development can largely be attributed to getting the incentives for encouraging development right.

2.4.2.1 Fiscal incentives

The center and the local fiscal relationship has always been an integral part of center-local relations. Overall, over the past 30 years, the center has delegated fiscal powers to the local government, motivating local government to develop the local economy and increase fiscal revenues, which proved to be the most important method to solve the incentive issue for local governments.

In 1980, China began to implement a fiscal management system, where there was "separation of revenues and expenditures with each level responsible" and every local government implemented various forms of a fiscal contract system. The fiscal contract system continued until 1993, significantly increasing the local government's enthusiasm in developing the jurisdiction's economy and increasing the tax base, boosting local economic development, though it caused the center's fiscal revenue growth to lag behind that of China's economic growth, and the center's proportion of national fiscal revenue showed a large decline, from 40 percent in 1984 to 22 percent in 1993. In 1994, the center implemented a tax division reform, using a tax division system to replace the fiscal contract system, and the center's proportion of national fiscal revenue rose to over 50 percent that year, and maintained around 50 percent henceforth. This reform mainly adjusted the distribution of power over fiscal revenues between the center and the local, with local fiscal revenue autonomy relatively weakened, but the local government still retained power over fiscal expenditure allocation similar to what they had originally.[33]

The center's delegation of fiscal powers releases the local government's impetus to increase fiscal revenues, triggering sustaining actions from the local government to develop the economy. This has been studied in depth by fiscal decentralization theory. Qian and Xu's (1993) research on Chinese fiscal decentralization started the research on fiscal federalism. Since then, e.g., Qian and Weingast (1997), Qian and Xu (1993) and Qian and Roland (1998) have continued pioneering, making strong connections between fiscal decentralization, local government incentives, economic transition and economic growth, forming the second generation of fiscal decentralization theory,[34] which allowed it to become an important theory to explain economic transition.

2.4.2.2 Political incentives

The center's incentives to the local are both fiscal and political. Since 1978, China's personnel administration system has undergone a series of adjustments and reforms which means local officials' devotion to their jurisdiction's economic development will not only bring fiscal benefits to the region, but will also have significant and even decisive impacts on their career.

In 1980, Deng proposed that the ranks of cadres become more revolutionary, younger in average age, better educated and more professionally competent. In 1982, the CPC central committee officially published the "Decision Regarding Establishing the Retirement Process for Senior Cadres," providing that cadres over 65 cannot hold a post of a provincial rank, meanwhile formulating the process for senior cadres to retire and resign from a leading post. This decision abolished the system of lifelong tenure for cadres and promoted a fixed-term appointment system, which not only renews the human capital for the ranks of cadres, but also constantly optimizes it. Furthermore, and more importantly, the center's standards for reviewing cadre performance changed fundamentally. The cadre's performance, especially achievements in economic development became an important indicator for performance review. Differing from the trajectory of fiscal decentralization reform, the personnel administration system reform was implemented in accordance with the center's will from start to end. The basis of political incentives is the concentration of personnel administration power in the hands of the superiors and the center, and such a personnel administration system which is responsible to the upper levels ensures the center's will can reach the basic levels from the center.[35]

Over a long period of time, economics literature neglected the importance of political incentives. Not until the late 1990s through to the twenty-first century was the issue of political incentives in China's economic development taken seriously. Huang and Li are among the early academics that noted the importance of the personnel management system to economic transition and development. During the process of analyzing the issue of Chinese inflation and investment control, Huang (1996) emphasized the importance of local officials' economic and political role. He believed that local officials played a critical role during the investment process since "reform and opening" and employed provincial data on local officials to perform statistical and econometric analysis. Li (1998) analyzed in detail the shift in incentive mechanisms within the Chinese government since "reform and opening" and believes that a reasonable change in and positioning of the government's role is a key factor in successful transition countries. Subsequently, economists gradually discovered evidence that political incentives exist in China, namely the political career of local officials is positively correlated with the economic growth achievements of their jurisdiction (Maskin et al., 2000; Bo, 2002; Li and Zhou, 2005). Based on these empirical findings, many academics believe that the political promotion tournament with GDP as the core indicator is the political economy's basis for understanding China's sustained economic growth.[36]

2.4.2.3 Incentive combinations

Fiscal incentives and political incentives both differ and are closely connected. Only if the two are combined can it be understood how the center got incentives for the local right. Fiscal incentives are a type of incentive directed toward the entire local government organization, yet they are highly relevant to every local official. For example, for those local officials that have promotion ambitions, fiscal power is an important method and instrument to realize their promotion goals; for those local officials that pursue economic interests, fiscal power is obviously a way and channel for increasing their own economic benefits. Political incentives are directed toward each individual local official, but they widely pervade the inner workings of the political organization. After all, retaining political power is the basis for officials' pursuits of other goals and interests, which makes it the fundamental incentive for officials. No matter if the incentives are fiscal or political, they are all blended into the decision-making and behavior of local officials.

Other than fiscal incentives and political incentives, the center gradually delegated administration and economic management powers to the local government, thereby the "vertical" characteristic of the administrative apparatus is continuously weakened, whereas the "horizontal" characteristic is continuously strengthened as the local level obtains ever-increasing autonomy. Such a decentralization reform was also advanced gradually in terms of time and space. Initially only certain special economic zones obtained more authority, but afterwards, open coastal cities, cities specifically designated in state plans, and comprehensive complementary reform experimental zones, etc., also obtained more authority. Administrative decentralization of power went through a process of partial experimentation to widespread implementation, gradually forming a "combining vertical and horizontal dimensions, with horizontal dimensions as the main part" situation. Up until the mid- and late-1990s, a few weakened vertically administered departments such as financial regulation, industry and commerce administration, land management etc. saw their power concentrated and enhanced again. Such a change in the administrative apparatus reform reflects the center's adjustment of center-local relations as developmental needs arise, maintaining incentives and control over the local.

The decentralization reform pushed by the center is multi-faceted, forming an incentive combo, giving the local a set of powers. In this set of powers, there are administration powers, economic management powers, fiscal powers and personnel powers, while the core of the incentive combo is composed of fiscal incentives and political incentives.

2.4.3 Local officials' reaction to incentives

Rational people respond to incentives. Chinese local officials control this set of powers and react to the incentive combo mentioned above.

2.4.3.1 Market preserving fiscal federalism

The 1980s fiscal contract system enabled the local government to become a residual claimant, while obtaining powers such as administrative and economic management, giving them motivation, capability and resources to devote themselves to their jurisdiction's development. Therefore, the local governments successively endeavor to develop local township enterprises, enhancing the local economic aggregate, and increasing local fiscal revenues. Qian and Xu (1993) summarized this as "market preserving fiscal federalism" and their political economy explanation of China's economic reforms is based on the course of China's economic growth in the 1980s, giving a high evaluation of township enterprises as well as giving prominence to the role of the local government, especially the basic level of government. On the other hand, since the Chinese economy was still in the shortage era, the local government's ability to expand local production was constrained by the economic resources it possessed, especially local resources, where all sorts of regional protectionist materials wars were continuously waged (Young, 2000) and even vassal economies emerged (Shen and Dai, 1990). Such a phenomenon is incongruous with the market preserving fiscal federalism theory proposed by Qian and Weingast (1997): the local government plays the role of advancing local economic development, creating market segmentation.

In empirical literature, the reaction of local officials toward fiscal incentives is specified as whether or not fiscal decentralization is conducive to growth. It is more or less regrettable that empirical literature has not fully reached a consensus on this. Zhang and Zou (1998) employed provincial data from 1978–1992 and gave a negative answer. Lin and Liu (2000) employed panel data from 28 provinces and cities during 1970–1993 and discovered that fiscal decentralization promoted economic growth. Afterwards, Jin et al. (2005) employed data from 1982–1992 to prove fiscal decentralization's positive effect on economic growth. Zhang and Gong (2005) elongated the sample to after the tax-sharing reform, employing 1986–2002 data to discover that fiscal decentralization and growth has obvious intertemporal disparities: significantly positive after the tax-sharing reform; negative before the tax-sharing reform. Chen et al. (2002) believe that the tax-sharing reform enhanced the center's budgetary fiscal revenues and the local government's action shifted from being helping hands to becoming grabbing hands.[37] However, more studies have found that local governments were able to provide more public goods under fiscal decentralization, especially productive infrastructure, promoting their jurisdiction's economic growth (Zhang et al., 2007; Chen, 2010). The reason why different studies have reached varying conclusions is an issue worth exploring in depth.

2.4.3.2 Competing for growth

The reaction of local officials toward political incentives is often dubbed "competing for growth" (Zhang and Zhou, 2008). Since political incentives have stronger personal features, the analytic unit used in literature in this aspect is usually the local official himself and no longer the jurisdiction he is within. Research on this aspect emerged in the mid-1990s, but only gradually bloomed after 2004. Currently, it is mainly unfolding in the following three directions:

1. *Exploring the relationship between political mobility and economic performance of the jurisdiction in order to prove the existence of political incentives.*[38] In this aspect, Li and Zhou's (2005) work is widely followed, as they found the faster the growth record of a provincial governor or party secretary's jurisdiction, the higher the probability of promotion. This discovery coincided with rather fragmentary observations and quickly became widely accepted. However, Bo's (2002) study may be the most systematic review of the political mobility of Chinese provincial leaders. He systematically collected data on party and government leaders and deputy leaders of provinces between 1949 and 1998 and discovered that since "reform and opening", the economic growth rate of jurisdictions and contribution toward the center's revenues has a significant correlation with the promotion of party and government leaders of provincial rank.[39] Tao et al. (2010) adopted data on provincial official promotion to empirically evaluate the local officials' promotion tournament and discovered economic growth rate at the provincial level had no significant impact on the promotion of local officials. Wang et al. (2011) discovered through empirical evidence that the strength of local officials' economic performance review mechanism differs between

provincial party secretaries and governors, and is more important on the governor's side but less important on the party secretary's side. The unending appearance of this type of literature allows us to gain a deeper understanding of the relationship between the career development of Chinese officials and economic development.

2. *Exploring the economic growth performance of local officials. Research on this aspect has just begun.* Xu, Wang and Shu (2007) and Zhang and Gao (2007) were among the early ones to discover significant effects on economic growth by local officials on their jurisdictions based on provincial level samples. This discovery coincides with the often-observed phenomenon of local officials busying with the development of their jurisdiction, thereby leading to further research constantly appearing. However, quantitative analysis of local officials' impact on their jurisdiction's economic development is not simple, since officials are often intertwined in positions; singling out the impact of officials themselves generally requires a specific sample, such as officials' exchange across regions (Xu, Wang and Shu, 2007; Zhang and Gao, 2007); change in the positions of officials (Wang et al., 2009); officials with industry backgrounds (Zhang, 2010), etc. It also needs clarifying that, when faced with the same incentives, the actions local officials take to develop their jurisdiction's economy may vary widely, as some local officials who have no prospects for promotion may rationally drop out of "competing for growth" (Cai and Treisman, 2005; Xu and Wang, 2010a). Yin (2010) employed methods of contract theory to construct a theoretical model and discovered that a system that rotated officials is more effective at incentivizing local officials to develop the economy than a system that retains officials in their posts, leading to faster economic growth and providing theoretical support for empirical research on exchange of officials promoting economic growth.
3. *Identifying the methods or channels with which local officials compete for growth. Local officials devoted to the development of their jurisdiction have rather many methods to accomplish their goals.* For example, within the province, they can endeavor to attract capital and business (Xu and Wang, 2010b), construction of infrastructure (Wang and Zhang, 2008), vigorously develop secondary industries (Xu, Wang and Shu, 2007), legally or illegally providing land (Zhang et al., 2010) as well as relaxing environmental regulations; beyond the province, they can attempt market segmentation (Zhou, 2004) or regional market integration (Xu, Li and Wang, 2007; Pi, 2008).

On the whole, literature on this aspect is in its nascence and has two characteristics: one is that it is heavy on empirical analysis and light on theoretical models; another is that many empirical analyses use provincial official samples, whereas few employ prefectural or county level official samples. Although current relevant research easily attracts attention, much research still needs to be further developed, on topics such as the behavior mechanism of local officials devoted to the development of their jurisdiction as well as a systematic study of prefectural and county level leaders.

2.4.3.3 Yardstick competition

Another way local government officials react to fiscal and political incentives is expressed in competition between local governments. Literature dubs this "yardstick competition." Since the 1990s, yardstick competition began to emerge in a wide range and lasted, currently becoming a normal state of affairs. This is consistent with the evolution process of fiscal and political incentives, as well as with the process of China's "reform and opening."

In the 1980s, fiscal decentralization was in the phase of differentiated implementation, and the form of fiscal contract was separately negotiated by the center and the local at that time. Meanwhile, the personnel administration system was undergoing a period of adjustment and China's economy had not yet exited shortage, so each region mainly "worked hard" and concentrated on local economic development. The local governments began to compete for economic resources to develop the economy in their jurisdiction, leading to regional protectionism. Enter the 1990s, with the implementation of the tax-sharing system and gradual improvement of the personnel system, the fiscal decentralization and political incentives in converged every region and local authorities discovered that in order to develop the local economy and attain promotions, they had to compete with other governments of the same level. Yang et al. (2010) employed data on officials of the provincial level and spatial econometric methods to discover that since "reform and opening," there has existed competing for economic growth between local officials, providing direct evidence for the existence of yardstick competitions.

Local governments engage in yardstick competitions through various means and in many fields. Literature has currently identified the following: a race to the bottom through attracting business and capital with preferential tax treatment as well as attracting investment by depressing the price of land (Li and Shen, 2008); distorting the structure of fiscal expenditures by being "heavy on infrastructure and light on human capital investment and public services" (Zhang et al., 2007; Wang and Zhang, 2008; Fu and Zhang, 2007); distorting regional interaction, with even the background of local officials influencing their choice of regional market strategy (Bai et al., 2008). On the whole, the yardstick competition produced a sustained devotion to economic growth by local governments, but also caused many distortions.

2.4.4 Coordinated development: a new goal for regional development

The center currently stresses coordinated regional development. To subordinate local officials, the task they face is shifting from a single goal to a dual goal: not only devotion to the development within their jurisdiction, but also paying attention to the balance between jurisdictions. When there are multiple goals, the first question we have to answer is: are the two goals of intrajurisdictional development and interjurisdictional balance conflicting? Recent empirical literature suggests a conflict may exist between the two. Market segmentation is a reflection of imbalance between jurisdictions, and as Lu and Chen (2009) discovered, market segmentation has an inverted U shape influence on a region's current and future economic growth and for over 96 percent of observation points, market segmentation is beneficial to local economic growth. Chinese economic growth may very well be entrapped in a prisoners' dilemma of interprovincial market segmentation. Though from the perspective of the overall situation, coordination between jurisdictions and an integrated domestic market is conducive for bringing into play the economies of scale from economic growth, choosing policies that produce imbalance between jurisdictions and segmented markets may be a dominant strategy for interprovincial competitions.

If the two goals of development within jurisdictions and coordination between jurisdictions are conflicting, then the next question is, under the current system: Can local officials simultaneously achieve these two conflicting goals? If the answer is "yes", then the conflict between the two is naturally inconsequential. Regrettably, current literature tends to give a negative reply.

The current system can solve the incentive issue for local officials' developing their jurisdiction rather well, but does not provide much incentive on the issue of interjurisdictional coordination. Zhou (2004) points out "the source of difficulty in cooperation among local officials mainly does not lie in the local officials' fiscal incentives and the nature of the economic competition they are engaged in, but lies in the nature of the political promotion competition they are engaged in". Specifically speaking, the number of posts provided for promotion is limited, as one person's promotion directly decreases the opportunity for another person's advancement. The participants face a zero-sum game, which gives local officials engaged in political and economic competition very many fields to compete in, but with very little room to cooperate. Xu, Li and Wang (2007) and Pi (2008) discovered that when the effort of local government officials has a positive externality or spillover, they will rationally choose to coordinate between jurisdictions, in order to internalize the positive spillover and obtain faster economic growth and a higher probability for promotion; on the contrary, if there exists a negative externality or spillover, local officials will rationally choose not to coordinate between jurisdictions, in order to externalize negative spillovers, to prevent negative impacts on their jurisdiction's economic growth and the corresponding likelihood of promotion. From an even more general perspective, development within jurisdictions is more of a private good to local government officials and is relatively controllable; but coordination between jurisdictions obviously cannot be achieved with only one entity.

To sum up, the current system solves the incentive issues of local officials' devotion to development of their jurisdiction but does not include incentive issues devoting local officials to regional coordination. From Tinbergen's Rule we know that when the goal that local officials face turns from one to two conflicting ones, the original policy instruments often find it hard to "kill two birds with one stone" and new policy instruments are needed.

2.5 Accompanying regional disparities

From a perspective of horizontal comparisons, intraregional development evolves into interregional gaps. Since 1978, as China has gradually opened and developed spatially, the issue of regional disparities began to attract attention. As the relevant data was progressively more accessible,[40] entering the early 1990s, people began to quantitatively study regional economic disparities more systematically.

2.5.1 Measurements and discoveries

2.5.1.1 Indicators that measure regional disparities

There does not appear to be any unified standard for instruments measuring regional disparities.[41] Literature that studies Chinese regional disparities is mainly based on *per capita* (or per worker) GNP; *per capita* (or per worker) GDP; *per capita* income; *per capita* consumption, etc. A few studies will also adopt other development indicators, such as average years of education; *per capita* health expenditures, etc. Different indicators convey differing information. For example, using *per capita* GDP reflects disparities in regional economic development, using per-worker GDP reflects disparities between regional productivity, using *per capita* income reflects disparities between income and living standards of interregional residents, and using *per capita* consumption reflects disparities in consumption and the corresponding level of well-being between interregional residents. Of course, it should be clarified that these indicators differ, yet are usually highly correlated.

Which indicator is employed is highly relevant with the accessibility of Chinese regional data. From an historical perspective, before 1993, the Chinese national economic accounts system was mainly based on the System of Material Product Balance (MPS), therefore *per capita* GNP became the first choice. For example, the earliest literature that quantitatively studies Chinese interregional gaps, such as Yang (1992), Wei (1992) and Song (1996), etc., all use *per capita* GNP. Yuan (1996) used *per capita* GDP to analyze interregional economic disparities and subsequent literature all used this indicator as well. From the perspective of international comparison, academia internationally generally uses *per capita* personal income or dispensable income to measure regional income gaps. Official Chinese data usually reports income and expenditures of urban and rural residents and early data has many imperfections. Such statistical urban and rural duality caused some literature to separately study urban and rural resident income gaps, for example Lin et al. (1998) employed peasant income per household and urban resident income per household to describe the trend of change in Chinese regional disparities post "reform and opening." But Wan, Lu and Chen (2005, 2007) were the first to calculate provincial *per capita* figures based on *per capita* income of urban and rural residents weighted in accordance with nonagricultural and agricultural population data, and then calculate interregional *per capita* income gaps and dissect such gaps. However, as some microeconomic individual survey data becomes accessible, current literature tends to use large samples and continuously followed microeconomic individual survey data to analyze income gap issues.[42]

2.5.1.2 Measurements of regional disparity

China's administrative regions are divided into provinces, prefectures, counties, and townships. Due to the significance of the province and especially the completeness of its data, most literature uses it as the analytic unit. Chinese provinces encompass a large area and population and using provinces as analytic units neglects the circumstances within provinces, which makes it necessary to adopt a smaller and more specific geographical analytic unit. Xu and Li (2004) studied the gaps between China's prefectural level municipalities and their convergence model, and discovered that there exists absolute convergence between prefectural level municipalities. Tsui (1993) was rather early to employ county-level data to dissect regional gaps, namely decomposing regional gaps into intraprovincial gaps, interprovincial gaps, gaps within rural areas, gaps within urban areas and gaps between rural and urban areas and reached the conclusion that urban–rural gaps have a significant impact on interregional product gaps. As to the disparities and gaps between urban and rural areas, Chen Zhao will give a detailed review in later chapters and this chapter will not delve into the matter.

2.5.1.3 Methods of analyzing regional disparity

Literature that studies Chinese regional economic disparities is gradually becoming more in line with international literature in terms of research methodology. In the early 1990s, scholars began to quantitatively study the issue of Chinese regional disparities, though they mainly used some static indicators. For example, Yang (1992) used the Gini coefficient, coefficient of variation etc. indicators to study regional disparities; Wei (1996) used the Theil index to dissect Chinese aggregate regional disparities. These internationally generally used methods of analysis and research approach were adhered to by later literature.

In the late 1990s, regional disparities turned into a hot issue for domestic economic analysis and the methods and research paradigms in international literature were referenced and employed more fully, of which the most important progress was changing cross-country analysis of growth convergence literature into interprovincial convergence analysis exploring Chinese regional disparities. Song (1996) introduced the neoclassical growth theory's absolute convergence analysis method early on; Cai and Du (2000) introduced the concept and method of conditional convergence and club convergence; Zhang (2004) introduced the dynamic panel regression technique, employing the SGMM method to estimate the enhanced Solow model. This caused the method for researching the issue of Chinese regional disparities to change from one variable regression to multivariable regression and finally, to dynamic panel regression.

In the mid-2010s, regional disparities almost became an experimental field for all sorts of econometric instruments, introducing spatial and time factors into traditional methods; employing random and times series testing methods; employing semi-parametric and non-parametric methods, quantile regressions, etc.[43]

2.5.1.4 Discoveries

The discoveries of current literature are mostly consistent with the information transmitted in Figure 2.5. In the early 1990s, literature mainly studied regional disparities in the 1980s, and all found that regional income gaps displayed a trend toward decreasing.[44] Yang (1992) used provinces as the analytic unit and discovered regional income gaps displayed a trend toward decreasing in the 1980s. Wei (1992) reached a similar conclusion and attributed the reason to the relatively lower economic growth shown by Shanghai, Liaoning, Tianjin, Heilongjiang and such old industrial regions which have higher *per capita* incomes compared with Zhejiang, Jiangsu, Guangdong and such newly industrialized regions which had relatively faster economic growth. Reduction of regional gaps implies convergence in regional growth. This is proven by relevant literature. For example, Song (1996) discovered that there existed absolute convergence between provinces from 1978–1992; Jian et al. (1996) and Chen and Fleisher (1996) also, respectively, found that there exists absolute convergence and conditional convergence in Chinese interprovincial *per capita* income growth from 1978–1993.

From the late 1990s to the early 2000s, the basic conclusion from literature is: regional income gaps decreased in the 1980s and increased in the 1990s. Lin et al. (1998) discovered, through calculating the Gini coefficient, that regional disparities displayed a trend toward gradual decline from the beginning of "reform and opening" to the mid-1980s and displayed an ascending trend afterwards. The expansion of regional disparities implies the disappearance of absolute convergence, which is proved by loads of literature. Meanwhile, it is also acknowledged that the reduction of regional gaps is conditional. Furthermore, interprovincial convergence is conditional as well, which caused conditional convergence and club convergence to become focal points for literature. Cai and Du (2000, 2001), Shen and Ma (2002). Wang and Ge (2002) discovered that there existed conditional convergence across provinces from 1978–1998/1999, and there existed absolute convergence within the three major areas, especially the eastern and central regions, which is to say, club convergence exists across China's provinces. Zhang (2004) expanded the sample to the period 1981–2001 and proved this as well. Through further expansion of samples, or introducing all sorts of new testing methods, more meticulous research has reached similar conclusions, for example Xu and Shu (2004, 2005) discovered that entering the 1990s, the distribution of provincial economic growth rates gradually displayed a twin peak shape; Xu and Li (2006) discovered that compared to the 1990s, Chinese regional gaps are still constantly growing larger, though at a slower rate since 2000. He (2008) discovered three convergence clubs nationwide during 1978–2006, with Shanghai and Guizhou not belonging to any convergence club. Overall, the literature for this period mainly focused on convergence testing and discovered that there exists conditional convergence across Chinese provinces; regional gaps are constantly increasing and absolute convergence is disappearing, though reduction of gaps and convergence exists within regions, which leads to the emergence of club convergence.

Generally speaking, current literature is mainly directed toward the descending and ascending phase of regional gaps, as displayed in Figure 2.5, and unfolds under the framework of convergence analysis, increasing the understanding of regional developmental gaps. However, it is regrettable that there has been little literature to this day that studies the current downtrend in provincial gaps,[45] and there has been none that systematically examine the mechanism of change the "decline-increase-decline" displayed by provincial gaps. More importantly, it should be noted that Chinese regional economic development is occurring under the existence of institutional barriers to the interregional redistribution of productive factors, of which institutional barriers to interregional mobility of labor is especially important. Meanwhile, since the early 2000s, China has implemented regionally balanced development programs on a large scale and many resources have been committed to supporting the development of underdeveloped regions. Under such circumstances, to what degree a change in Chinese regional disparities can be pinned on policy intervention and to what extent it is caused by the free flow of factors is an issue that demands careful treatment. It also pertains to what degree neoclassical growth theory and convergence analysis framework can be used to study Chinese regional disparities.

2.5.2 The causes of regional disparities

People pay attention not only to the measurement of regional disparities, but also to their cause, thereby finding the key to reducing regional disparities. Frankly speaking, searching for the causes of regional disparities is a tempting task, but it is also a very difficult and challenging one. Current literature provides many explanations but is still far from providing a consistent analytic framework or consensus. Below are the most common hypotheses.

2.5.2.1. Factor determinism

According to neoclassical economic growth theory, the amount of productive factors directly determines the level of economic development and even the rate of development. Factor determinism mainly attributes regional disparities to physical capital, human capital and technological level measured by total factor productivity (TFP). Shu and Xu (2002) emphasized that the specification of Chinese economic growth models are mainly AK types, namely Chinese economy growth mainly relies on the accumulation of physical capital. Wang and Ge (2002) discovered that the differential in the investment rate between provinces is the main reason for regional disparities. Xu and Shu (2004) attributed Chinese provincial growth to physical capital, human capital and technological progress and transfer, and discovered that physical capital dominates the polarizing of the distribution of Chinese provincial economic growth. Chen and Xu (2004) as well as

Wan et al. (2005) also stressed that capital is the foremost and most important factor that leads to regional income gaps.

Literature soon afterwards began underlining the impact of technology measured by TFP's impact on Chinese regional disparities. Peng (2005) estimated the TFP for each province from 1982 to 2002 and discovered that TFP explains a major portion of China's provincial income gaps. Li et al. (2006) also stressed that TFP gaps are the chief factor that explains Chinese regional disparities. However, Fu and Wu (2006a,b) believe that Peng (2005) and Li et al. (2006) overestimated TFP's effect. Based on provincial level data from 1978 to 2004, they discovered that economic disparities mainly arise from factor inputs and not TFP, but TFP's effect increased continuously and will become a critical factor in determining regional disparities from now on.

As North (1981) and Acemoglu et al. (2005) emphasized, factor input is only the approximate cause of economic growth, the more important task is to seek the fundamentals. After all, if productive factors determine regional disparities, then what determines the regional disparities of productive factors?

2.5.2.2 Structure determinism

What are the determinants of regional disparities? Structure determinism's reply is economic structure. Since "reform and opening", the Chinese economy experienced the process of marketization, industrialization, urbanization and internationalization. More importantly, these processes did not progress uniformly across Chinese regions, but instead progressed gradually.[46] This type of gradual implementation spatially inevitably leads to structural economic differences in industry structure, the degree of state ownership, marketization, urbanization, openness and so on. Such structural economic differences inevitably influence the allocation, direction and flow of productive factors in regions nationwide leading to the natural emergence of regional disparities.

Zhou (2000) emphasized the change in ownership structure, especially the effect of differences in aspects such as the development of the non-state-owned economy, the degree of market growth etc. on regional disparities. Wan et al. (2005) discovered that economic reforms with the characteristics of privatization have significant effects on regional income gaps, and the contribution of globalization to regional income gaps is significantly positive and strengthens with the passage of time. He and Liang (2004) also stress the degree of participation in globalization, marketization and urbanization etc. as significant causes of spatial and temporal changes in Chinese regional economic disparities.

The process of Chinese industrialization was gradually advanced across regions and this is inevitably reflected in the unequal spatial distribution of the industry-dominated secondary industry. Fan and Zhu (2002) elaborated on the fundamental reason for continuously increasing regional disparities since "reform and opening" being the unequal spatial distribution of the share of high output secondary industries and nonagricultural industries. Peng (2005) analyzed the source of Chinese provincial economic growth and disparities from 1990 to 2002, with a sectoral approach and discovered that provincial economic growth rates display significant divergence, with the divergence mainly coming from industry.

Economic structure determinism grasped certain key characteristics of China's gradual spatial economic transition, such as marketization, industrialization, internationalization, etc., but a very difficult issue it faces is that the formation and change of these economic structures themselves are doubtlessly endogenous, for example, the conditions of their formation and the factors which they change with. Therefore, understanding the mechanism by which these economic structures form and function is the deeper level issue that economic structure determinism has yet to solve.

2.5.2.3 Geographical determinism

Geography may be a deeper level determinant that affects regional disparities. In the process of Chinese economic reforms, the reforms were gradual or, to be more precise, spatially gradual and most went through the spatial process of experimentation-diffusion-convergence (Xu and Chen, 2008); opening up was spatially gradual; the center's regional development strategy was gradually pushed spatially as well. This implies that Chinese marketization, industrialization and internationalization policies appear to be related to geographical factors. Démurger et al. (2002) quantitatively studied the influence of geographical location and regional preferential policies on regional development. The empirical results show that the impact of preferential policies were significant and rather stable; the effect of geographical location was even more significant and sustaining, and the rapid growth of coastal provinces cannot be mainly attributed to the coastal regions obtaining more preferential policies than other regions.

If geographical factors are important in regional development, then an issue that draws even more curiosity is how geographical factors influence regional development. One explanation is that "market forces progressively caused differences in regional geographical and natural conditions to transform into regional economic development and income disparities" and became a determinant for regional development and their disparities. This is directly reflected in the agglomeration of industry in the southern and eastern coastal regions; meanwhile it determines the differences in each region's degree of openness, which in return impacts the marketization and industrialization of each region.[47] Démurger et al. (2002) stated that geographical factors mainly contribute to economic growth through the two channels of foreign direct investment and township industrial enterprises, namely the advantage of a coastal geographical location is realized through attracting FDI and agglomerating industry while conducting foreign export trade.[48] A second explanation is that the force of increasing returns to scale causes geographical factors to become determinants of regional development and their disparities. The development of New Economic Geography led to unprecedented focus by the academic community on the important role played by geography in economic development, which may have arisen from its grasp on the fundamental force that causes economic agglomeration—increasing returns to scale.

Geographical factors or other incidental factors led to industry clustering in a certain area and is self-enforcing under the effect of increasing returns to scale (Krugman, 1991). A third explanation is that geographical location also signifies the scale and potential of a regional economy's market. Much literature has emerged over the past few years, exploring the impact of market scope and potential on economic growth and economic disparities on the basis of New Economic Geography. Huang and Li (2006) discovered that the scale of regional markets and the openness of exports significantly influenced the growth rate in *per capita* income of each province during 1970–2000, while geographical location is an important factor that influences market scale and export openness. Xu, Chen and Lu (2010) carefully examined the mechanisms through which geographical factors take effect instead of simply using geography as a control variable, and discovered as a result that the distance to China's major coastal ports is a critical factor that influences a city's economic growth. Generally speaking, the smaller the distance to major ports, the rate of economic growth first declines, then increases, and declines thereafter. Moreover, after controlling for the distance to major ports, other explanatory factors of economic growth are not very significant, which illustrates certain orthodox economic growth "explanatory variables" are, to a large extent, endogenous to geographical factors.

No one can flatly deny the importance of geographical factors in regional development, but regional disparities generally change, e.g., the development gap in Chinese provinces as displayed in Figure 2.5, whereas geographical location is spatially constant. Therefore, geographical determinism usually needs to introduce "variables of other characteristics" in order to explain how geography influences regional development and how geography's effect changes with time and change in the economic system (Xu et al., 2010). This can rather persuasively illustrate the importance of geographical factors; however, this is also its drawback as such a method only measures the comprehensive impact of geographical factors along with variables of other characteristics but not the independent impact of geographical factors, since the "comprehensive impact" could also be attributed to variables of other characteristics.

2.5.2.4 Institution determinism

In recent years, much literature has quantitatively analyzed the role of institutions in economic development. Frankly speaking, the importance of institutions in economic development is hard to deny. The critical problem current literature attempts to solve is finding historical and geographical instrument variables, revising possible estimation bias caused by endogenous problems that may exist in institutional variables and identifying the real impact of institutions on economic development.[49] Of course, there are academics that hold different opinions, with the main point of contention being the sense in which institutions are important.[50]

It is difficult to generalize by directly applying the importance of institutions in international economic disparities to explain the regional disparities within an economy. There are differences in institutions in different countries while institutions within a country are usually thought of as identical. Therefore, if institutions are to be thought of as deeper factors in regional disparities, then they must be clarified conceptually as well as why they differ across regions.

In China, institutions change constantly, especially since 1978, institutional change bears the characteristics of spatially gradual. The most typical example is the experimentation-diffusion-convergence process experienced by old and new special economic zones when China was working on how "reform and opening" would be achieved (Xu and Chen, 2008; Xu, 2010). During the process of spatially gradual reforms, every successful institutional change has both an exemplifying effect and also a lock-in effect (Xu, 2006). The exemplifying effect mainly refers to a region that takes the lead in one institutional change that brings the growth and level effect to the region during the reform period, which imperceptibly gives other regions a clear signal that such reforms could increase output and improve well-being, thereby leading other regions to form expectations of reform, pushing forward an identical or similar institutional change. The lock-in effect refers to the active or passive interruption of the process of spatially gradual reforms, where other regions cannot achieve economic results equal to those attained by the reforms that took the lead in reforms. Therefore, during the process of spatially gradual institutional change, regional development will polarize, which would be a temporary phenomenon if the lock-in effect does not exist; otherwise it would be a long-term phenomenon. Empirically, just as international literature reveals, it is necessary to find an instrument variable for Chinese institutions. Xu and Li (2005) used the circumstances of private industry development before the Three Great Transformations as a variable instrument to verify that different institutional change in different regions has a significant explanatory ability for the development disparity in different regions.[51] When human capital, geographical factors and such factors as the process of marketization constructed by Fan et al. (Fan and Wang, 2001) are further introduced, institutional changes still have significant explanatory ability. Li Ming and Li Huizhong (2010) employed data for 30 provinces from 1998 to 2002, to empirically test the impact of political capital on Chinese regional income gaps and discovered that political capital has significant impact on Chinese regional income gaps, the result of which stands after controlling for geographical factors. On the issue of endogenous political capital, the text adopted the geographical distribution of the members of the 8th CPC Central Committee to process as the instrument variable.

The strategy adopted by Lu and Chen (2006) is not discriminating between the pair of concepts, namely institutions and policy, viewing change in institutions as a series of policy adjustments. On economic policy, the center treats each region differently by employing policies that are biased toward certain regions, for example, economic policies biased toward coastal regions and cities and so on. Of course, the most familiar of all are the various preferential policies. Démurger et al. (2002) emphasize the importance of economic policies with a regional bias in regional development. Lu and Chen (2006) mainly studied the influence of the two specific policies of openness and government participation in economic activity on industrial agglomeration and discovered that openness has significantly positive impacts on industrial agglomeration, which reveals the facilitation effect of industrial agglomeration by export-oriented economic development policy whereas the higher the level of government participation in economic activity, the more disadvantageous it is for regional industrial agglomeration.

As to China, which is in a transition period, no one will easily deny the importance of institutional change for economic development. Currently, viewing institutions as the deeper determinant of Chinese regional development disparities grasps the two dimensions of institutional change: spatially gradual and regional bias. Evidently, spatially gradual reform and regional bias policies themselves are endogenous and require further research into their causes.

2.5.3 The political economy of regional disparities

Consistent with the path taken by international literature in seeking for the determinants of international development disparities, the journey to finding the determinants of Chinese regional disparities began with productive factors and gradually traced back to geography and institutions. Such a painstaking investigation is an intellectual challenge, but it appears to be inadequate for studying the issue of China's domestic regional disparities.

From a straightforward economic perspective, it is difficult for geography and institutions to be the source of China's domestic regional disparities. Geographical and institutional factors are relatively stable but China's regional disparities change constantly, as is shown in Figure 2.4, during 30 years of "reform and opening", economic disparities between Chinese provinces displayed a trend toward "decreasing–increasing–decreasing." Employing relatively stable geographical and institutional factors to explain the constantly changing Chinese provincial disparities obviously requires the assistance of other factors, such as local government behavior (Lu and Chen, 2006; Xu, 2006).

From an analytic framework perspective, almost all current analyses simply apply across-country analytic framework. It is undeniable that, in terms of absolute size, Chinese provinces could entirely be analogous to the samples used in cross-country analysis. However, the resource constraints faced by Chinese provinces during economic development is essentially different from those of country samples: when countries develop their domestic economies, it is very difficult for them to obtain free resources from other countries or the UN and the resource constraints they face are hard; whereas when Chinese provinces develop their local economy, local officials often go to the center government and obtain preferential policies, subsidies, etc. and the resource constraints they face may be soft instead of hard. Therefore, directly applying a across-country analytic framework neglects the resource constraint issue rooted in the behavior of local officials.

The fact that local officials are responsible for the development of their jurisdiction, inevitably impacts regional disparities. The center correctly arranged local officials' incentives for developing their jurisdiction, but the ability of local officials to develop their jurisdiction's economy differs. So when local officials compete for growth, they may choose different economic growth behaviors, while faced with the same political incentives. Specifically speaking, when the policies conferred by the center on the local as well as the local officials' capability differ, a symmetric equilibrium will not exist in an economy with mobile productive factors such as capital. Suppose in one region, the center confers relatively unfavorable policies and the officials are relatively less capable, then during the competition for economic growth, the local officials of that region are definitely "disadvantaged". Since the odds of success in the growth tournament are low, they will tend to spend a larger portion of fiscal revenues on occupational expenditures to increase personal well-being rather than invest in productive social infrastructure, improving business environment, providing better services, etc., resulting in partial, perhaps even the majority, outflow of the region's capital when the economy reaches equilibrium. In contrast, if a region's policies conferred by the center are advantageous and its officials are capable, then in the competition for economic growth, local officials are definitely "advantaged" and will choose to allocate a larger portion of fiscal expenditures toward investing in social infrastructure, improving business environment, providing better services, thereby attracting capital from other regions, eventually increasing economic growth in their jurisdiction, which increases the probability of success in the growth tournament. In short, in the competition for economic growth, competition itself does not necessarily impel local officials to devote themselves to the economic development of their jurisdiction. Rational and heterogeneous local officials may react differently to the same incentives, thus producing different economic results.

The source of heterogeneous growth behavior in local officials is central appointment. Xu and Wang (2010a) proved that under a politically centralized, fiscally decentralized economy, when the center allocates officials in order to maximize the jurisdiction's output, the policies conferred onto the local by the center and the capability of the local officials complement each other: the more capable the appropriate local official appointed by the center is, the more favorable the policies conferred by the center on that region are. This implies that in a politically centralized, fiscally decentralized economy, differentiation in policies conferred by the center to the local corresponds to the differentiation in the capability of local officials appointed. Since the heterogeneous growth behavior of local officials is rooted in the center's appointment of local officials and the corresponding policy resources conferred, then the center can achieve the goal of coordinating or polarizing regional development through managing the appointment of local officials and regional development strategies.

2.6 What do we know? What else do we need to know?

2.6.1 The political economical logic behind Chinese regional development

Since "reform and opening", Chinese regional development could be summarized as rapid intraregional growth and prominent interregional conflicts. Currently, to serve as a correction for the latter, coordinated regional development becomes a rational demand.

There exists a political economy explanation for Chinese regional development that is inherently logically consistent. It is a political economy explanation because in China, politics and economics are linked and local officials are responsible for the development of their jurisdiction. The mechanism by which Chinese politics operates is the appointment system. The promotion of local officials is decided by the superiors and not the lower levels or electorate in their jurisdiction, which originally wasn't conducive to motivating local officials to devote themselves to economic development in their jurisdiction. But after "reform and opening", the central government slowly became a neutral government (He and Yao, 2009) and began to treat economic development as the first priority, emphasizing "growth is of overriding importance." Development nationwide comes from the contribution of each region, and since the central government is devoted to economic development, it naturally demands economic growth in each region. Thus, the center tied the career development and income of local officials with the development of their jurisdiction through fiscal and political incentives, and jurisdictional development became the encompassing interest between local officials and their jurisdictions, which led to local government officials becoming market preserving officials, or in other words market augmenting officials, devoted to market-oriented economic reforms and sparing no effort in promoting their jurisdiction's development. As a result, with the advancement of China's "reform and opening," the gate to rapid economic growth in each region was opened, and the economic take-off began.

On the other hand, from a horizontal perspective, faced with the fiscal incentives, and especially the political incentives, local officials actively or passively engage in a yardstick competition or political tournament based on the development performance of their own jurisdiction. Obtaining better economic development performance than their peers increases the probability that the local official can win in the yardstick competition or political tournament. This means that local officials not only don't have to be responsible for interjurisdictional disparities, expanding interjurisdictional economic performance gaps are actually beneficial to the development of one's professional career. More critically, China's opening to the outer world is spatially gradual and the focal point of regional development is spatially gradual too. When the center appoints local officials, highly capable market augmenting local officials can always win over more central policy support, softening the resource constraints faced during development of their jurisdiction's economy. Evidently, such a spatially gradual characteristic and appointment mechanism unintentionally aided local officials in widening the gap in economic performance between jurisdictions, thereby coming out on top in the political tournament.

To summarize, under the fiscal and political incentives given by the center, Chinese local officials became market augmenting local officials, devoting themselves to market-oriented economic reforms and development in their jurisdiction, while actively or passively participating in the interjurisdictional yardstick competition, endeavoring to achieve better economic development performance than other jurisdictions, in the hope of winning the competition. Such behavior of local officials, endeavoring to develop their jurisdiction's economy while endeavoring to widen the gap between jurisdictions, is reflected on the macro-scale as rapid intraregional growth and prominent interregional conflicts.

2.6.2 Further research directions

If we look forward to the future, in terms of the political economy perspective of Chinese regional development, there are at least the following aspects that are worth further attention:

First, constructing a model that explores Chinese regional development based on the practical experience from over 30 years of Chinese regional development. Current literature that explores Chinese regional development is almost all "copycats" that directly apply the paradigms of cross-country analysis. Such a research strategy neglects two points. The first point is the soft resource constraints faced by local officials when developing their jurisdiction's economy, that is, when a country developed its economy, it is hard to obtain free resources from other countries or the UN and the resource constraint it faces is hard, while when Chinese local officials develop their jurisdiction's economy, they often go to the central government and obtain policy, resources etc. and the resource constraint they face may be soft. Another is the fact that the economies studied by international political economy literature relating to economic growth have political systems based on elections while the basic characteristic of Chinese politics is appointments. Therefore, it is necessary to construct a new model for regional development according to the typical characteristics of China's regional development.

Second, how to coordinate the regional development? Since "reform and opening", the center emphasized development is of overriding importance, arranging the incentives correctly, resulting in rapid intraregional growth and prominent interregional conflicts. Currently, the center is trying to rectify the latter, stressing coordinated regional development. Under the current incentive mechanisms set by the center, local officials find it hard to achieve both the goals of intrajurisdictional development and interjurisdictional coordination. Even more disturbing is the fact that local officials that attempt to coordinate across regions spontaneously may face political risk. In terms of the two levels center and local, there is only one center, giving it a monopoly; whereas there are many locals, making them the monopolized. When local officials undertake interjurisdictional coordination, or even unite together, what used to be multiple competitive locals may possibly or *de facto* become "one", and center–local relations may shift from unilateral monopoly to bilateral monopoly. In such a transformation of market structure, the absolute authority of the center in the center–local relations will inevitably be damaged. Therefore, during the process of achieving coordinated regional development, whether the center should arrange correct incentives to devote officials to coordinate regional development, encouraging the local government to actively participate in coordinating regional development, or should it formulate new constraints to regulate the interregional actions of local officials will be a difficult issue.

Third, attention should be paid to start–stop growth. More than 30 years after "reform and opening", every region in China achieved rapid economic growth and began the economic take-off. Learning how to fly well means also involves learning how to descend well. Obvious systemic risks exist in economies that can only fly but cannot descend; judging from the international experience with economic growth, start–stop growth appears to be the norm. China is a large country composed of many regions. At the very least, from a probabilistic point of view, some regions may experience such start–stop growth in the near future. Therefore, taking preventive measures by systematically concluding the pattern of descent after economic take-off is necessary. Since start–stop growth is a type of international norm, systematically concluding the pattern of economic descent at least does not lack points of reference and should be viable.

Last but not least, a research direction that is even more challenging is how to effectively balance the market mechanism and local officials to promote regional development. Over the past 30 or so years, the center tied the career development and income of local officials to the development of their jurisdiction through fiscal, political, and other incentives and local officials propelled the economic development of their jurisdiction through market preserving and augmenting actions. The problem is, how should local officials be effectively restrained, in order to protect the market from being eroded by power? This is evidently worth further research.

Appendix

The swift growth in literature on Chinese regional growth benefits from the open publication of a series of relevant data. The accessibility of data is very important work.

Official data

First, there are data that reflect the economic aggregate of each region. Between 1949 and 1984, the core indicator for Chinese national economic accounting was the national income based on the System of Material Product Balance (MPS). In 1985, via the State Council's approval, the statistics departments put much effort in to establishing the Gross Domestic Product (GDP) accounts, while working on the national economy accounts. In 1993, the national income accounts were officially discontinued and the GDP became the core indicator of Chinese national economic accounting.[52] The problem is how should the GDP before 1993 and the economic aggregate for every region be accounted for? This is a troublesome issue. According to Xu's (2002) introduction, the National Bureau of Statistics carried out two major supplements to historical GDP data: one supplementing data between 1978 and 1984, and another supplementing data between 1952 and 1977. The former task was completed during 1986 and 1988, and the latter was accomplished during 1988 and 1997. Detailed data after adding the supplements were first published in "Historical Data on Chinese Gross Domestic Product Accounts (1952–1995)".[53] Thus far, the Chinese National Bureau of Statistics provided "continuous and comparable" data that reflected the economic aggregate in each region.[54] Afterwards, the "Data of Gross Domestic Product of China (1996–2002)" extended the base data that reflects each region's economic aggregate to the year 2002.

After the 2004 economic census, the National Bureau of Statistics carried out major adjustments in the historical data between 1993 and 2003 based on the results of the census, and provided data reflecting each region's adjusted economic aggregate for the first time in "Data of Gross Domestic Product of China (1952–2004)". Even more gratifying is the fact that this "latest" piece of historical data comes with a CD, providing an electronic version of the data, making it easier for the reader to process data.

Next, there is systematic data that reflects the development in each region. When it comes to data in this respect, the first that comes to mind may be the "Comprehensive Statistical Data and Materials on 50 Years of New China," compiled and published by the National Bureau of Statistics Integrated National Economy Accounting Division. Although the *China Statistical Yearbook* (National Bureau of Statistics of China, 2010) reported basic data on each region nationwide as well, this book compiled data on the main statistical indicators for 31 provinces other than Hong Kong, Macau, and Taiwan for every year from 1949 to 1998 in 16 fields with nearly 200 indicators, fully reflecting the current situation of each region's economy and social development since New China's founding. In the editor's statement, the "China Compendium of Statistics 1949–1998" clearly pointed out "in order to make it easy for readers' usage, we standardized the indicator's coverage so that the data is more comparable horizontally and vertically".[55] This compendium provided a solid numerical base for systematically examining Chinese provincial economic development and has been widely accepted in academia.[56]

The National Bureau of Statistics also endeavor to make these types of compendiums "develop sustainably." The National Bureau of Statistics Integrated National Economy Accounting Division respectively edited and published "China Compendium of Statistics 1949–2004" and "China Compendium of Statistics 1949–2009" in 2005 and 2010. However, it is regrettable that these did not provide any electronic data.[57]

Finally, data on regional economic interactions should be mentioned. Since an institution similar to "customs" does not exist, obtaining data on Chinese regional economic interaction is itself a challenging a task. Up to now, current literature discovered two types of database. One type is based on the Golden Tax Project's interprovincial trade database. The data in this database comes from the amount of value-added tax invoices received every month for each province since June 2003 gathered by the State Administration of Taxation Golden Tax Project's Integrated Collection and Management System.[58] Xing and Li (2009) have already used this data to study the home bias and boundary effect in China's interprovincial economic interactions. Another type is the data on interprovincial railway freight traffic. This database is not new and has been employed before in literature on geology.[59] Recently, Xu and Li (2010) employed this data to study Chinese interprovincial trade.

In the above two types of databases, compared with the former, the latter has the characteristics of an openly published, long sample period and small coverage. The *Yearbook of China Transport and Communications* (Year Book Editorial Department of China Transportation and Communications, 2009) reported railway freight volume between provinces year-by-year since 1985. From the manner in which goods are transported, Chinese interprovincial economic activity can be divided into railway transportation, highway transportation, airway transportation, and waterway transportation. As long as trade conducted through the four types of transportation are taxed in accordance with the tax law, then the total volume of interprovincial trade can be calculated. However, when reporting on the four ways to conduct interprovincial trade for each province, China's statistics departments only report the interprovincial trade volume conducted via railway. The interprovincial trade volume calculated by adding up value-added tax special invoices has a larger coverage than that based on railway transportation. But, it is regrettable that the statistics departments currently do not regularly publish interprovincial figures by adding up value-added tax special invoices. Xing and Li (2009) have only gathered the data since June 2003.[60] Judging from the current situation, railway freight volumes might be the best proxy variable with which to study Chinese regional economic interaction.

Data estimated and collected by academics

Frankly speaking, the basic data provided by Chinese statistics departments are incomplete, or in other words, certain basic figures academia requires are not provided. In order to explore regional development and other issues, academia did some data collection with at least the following three types being representative.

The first type estimates data on capital stock.[61] The importance of capital stock in economic growth and development theory is self-evident, but the statistics departments of many economies including China only provide data on investment but not data on capital stock. Thus, estimating an economy's capital stock becomes a significant task. Who first estimated China's amount of capital stock? Chinese economic academia does not appear to have an answer. According to our studies, Shu's (1993) doctoral thesis may be the first study that systematically estimated China's capital stock.[62] However, these figures were mostly interim products or by-products of economic growth accounting. Such a tradition continued till the dawn of the new century, when Zhang et al. (2004) viewed estimating China's capital stock as an important task, and published the results of their estimation of capital stock nationwide and each province in "Economics Research," one after another (Zhang and Zhang, 2003; Zhang et al., 2004), and actively promoted their estimation results in academia. Afterwards, work on updating and expanding capital stock estimation unfolded bit by bit, e.g., Zhang and Sun (2009) updated the figures up to 2005 using Zhang Jun et al.'s (2004) methodology; Xu, Zhou, and Shu (2007) expanded the capital stock estimation to the three industries of every province, systematically estimating the physical capital stock for the three industries in every province from 1978 to 2002.

The second type estimates the progress of marketization. China is an economy undergoing transition, and estimating the progress of its marketization is itself an important fundamental task. However, as Fan and Wang (2001) stressed, since economic theory and practice has not given a model and paragon for a 100 percent transition to "the other side," using a "pure" market economy as a frame of reference to measure the absolute degree of China's marketization is unrealistic. Based on these considerations, Fan and Wang et al. began to report the relative marketization progress index for each province since 1997. More importantly, since the marketization of each province is a dynamic process, Fan et al. periodically tracked the marketization progress of each region and endeavored to maintain the vertical comparability of the estimated figures. Four marketization progress reports have been published in the last eight years, and the samples have been updated to 2007. It is due to such continuous work that Fan et al.'s estimation of the marketization process in Chinese provinces is widely followed in academia.

The third type systematically gathers and sorts out data on Chinese local officials. Officials are one of China's most important economic activity entities. Elite literature in political science gathered and sorted out data on Chinese local officials. But these tasks were mainly finished by foreign academics, of which a representative one would be like Bo (2002). After entering the new millennium, domestic economics academics, such as Li and Zhou (2005), Zhang et al. (2007) and Xu, Wang, and Shu (2007) also rather systematically sorted out data on Chinese local officials. Currently, this is mainly data on the party and government leaders in each province. Up to now, the sorted out data is mostly dispersed in the hands of the data collectors and are not openly published. However, Northwestern University's Victor Shih published data on Chinese provincial officials from 1978 to 2006 on his homepage.[63]

Notes

1 Namely, the number of papers with "regional development" in their titles in CNKI's database.

2 Taking into consideration the fact that XuChenggang (Xu, 2010) has already systematically summarized English literature relating to Chinese development, this chapter will mainly focus on Chinese literature. XuChenggang also touched upon some Chinese papers published in domestic Chinese journals.

3 "Market preserving" is a term used by "market preserving fiscal federalism" literature; "market augmenting" officially comes from Olson's (2000) proposal of a "market augmenting government".

4 In August 1980, the Standing Committee of the National People's Congress passed the "Regulations on Special Economic Zones in Guangdong", formally establishing China's special zone policy, and the area of special zones was subsequently enlarged multiple times. In 1988, it was decided to open up Hainan as another special economic zone. The total area of Hainan Island is 34,000 square kilometers, so this measure further increased the boundaries of China's special economic zones.

5 The 14 open coastal cities are: Dalian, Qinhuangdao, Tianjin, Yantai (including Weihai), Lianyungang, Nantong, Shanghai, Ningbo, Wenzhou, Fuzhou, Guangzhou, Zhanjiang, and Beihai.

6 In the 1990s, the central government continued to implement this strategy, successively approving the development and opening of Pudong New District in Shanghai, adding Pudong's Waigaoqiao, Tianjinggang, Shenzhen's Shatoujiao, and Futian as tax-protected zones, and establishing a bonded production material market in Shenzhen Special Economic Zone.

7 The details are in the typical facts discussed later.

8 The details are in the fourth part of this section.

9 In the past, the purpose of development in China was usually expressed as "to meet the ever-increasing material and cultural needs of the people." After leaving the era of shortage, creating "effective" demand became the new choice.

10 According to Ding's introduction (Pan and Ma, 2010, pp. 217–218), at the beginning of "reform and opening," there was no way out other than delegating powers as the centrally administrated planned economy had lost its ability to command. For one, there was the Third Front Construction. The Third Front Construction concentrated one-third of the nation's investments before "reform and opening," most of which were eventually uncompleted. The central government wasn't able to continue the construction and could only hand over the enterprises to local governments. Another was the return to cities of the Rusticated Youth; 24 million Rusticated Youth were not allocated jobs for ten years and all were in rural areas. They needed jobs after returning to the city, so in 1980, the State Council issued a document letting every local government think of ways to increase employment opportunities.

11 In 1982, the central government delegated the authority of cadre administration to lower levels of government and put into practice a cadre administration system in which every level manages a lower level.

12 Xu (2009) pointed out clearly that over the past 20-odd years, decentralization of powers to the local level has been very common internationally, but such attempts have almost all failed. An important reason is, merely that decentralizing powers is not enough, as the local government needs to control resources.

13 Readers who are interested in coupons can further refer to Lu (2008) and Luo (2008).

14 On October 16 1953, the Politburo held an enlarged session once more and approved documents such as the "Central Committee of the CPC's Resolution on the Planned Purchase and Marketing of Food" that were discussed by the National Food Meeting and revised by Comrade Deng. On November 19 1953, the 194th government administration meeting of the Government Administration Council passed the "Order Regarding Implementing Planned Purchase and Supply of Food." In early December 1953, other than in Tibet and Taiwan, urban and rural areas nationwide began to implement planned purchase and marketing of food.

15 The four warrants refers to the urban residents' food supply warrant, industrial usage food supply warrant, urban feed supply warrant, urban residents' food supply transfer warrant; the three coupons refer to the nationwide general food coupon, local food coupon, local materials coupon.

16 Data from the "China Compendium of Statistics 1949–2008." Hainan and Chongqing's data begins from the date they became provincial administrative districts. Without any special specifications, the domestic data used in this chapter all come from this compendium.

17 It needs to be clarified that the sum of the economic aggregate and its growth rate statistics published by the local governments often exceed the national data published by the National Bureau of Statistics.

18 It should be mentioned that, whether in terms of gross product growth rate or *per capita* gross product growth rate, the winner is Equatorial Guinea. Equatorial Guinea has been enlisted as one of the least developed countries around the world for quite some time, but after sizable oil deposits were discovered in its territorial waters, the country's economic growth took off. The oil industry became a pillar of the country's socioeconomic development. Oil revenues enabled the GDP growth rate to be above 26.5 percent for ten consecutive years. In recent years, though the pace of its economic

growth has slowed, it is still one of the better developed countries economically in Central Africa.

19 According to Barro and Sala-i-Martin's (1995) analysis, the standard deviation (coefficient of variation) can be connected with σ-convergence; σ-convergence refers to the tendency of *per capita* income differentials between economies (internationally or interregionally) to decrease as time passes.

20 96 percent = 28/29.

21 If the ratio of interprovincial trade is divided into interprovincial export ratio and interprovincial import ratio, then changes in the trends of both among each province will be more varied.

22 Economic take-off, a concept proposed by Rostow (1960) in *The Stages of Economic Growth*, refers to economic development shifting from a traditional economy to the high growth phase of a modernized economy, and employs the analogy of an airplane breaking through a stagnant state to achieve take-off to express the fact that decisive changes have occurred in an economy. Rostow believes that for an economy to take off, three interconnected and indispensible conditions must be present: first, the productive investment rate must be increased to above 10 percent; second, the establishment and development of one or more major manufacturing sectors; third, institutional reforms are undertaken so a political, social, and institutional structure that fuels expansion in modern sectors can swiftly emerge.

23 The above set of GDP growth figures are nominal GDP growth rates.

24 Xu (2009b) laid an emphasis on examining Guangdong's economic take-off process in a global context.

25 PWT is the acronym for Penn World Table and is a database established by a University of Pennsylvania's research center commissioned by UN's ICP (International Comparison Program). The current version is 6.2 and mainly consists of purchasing power parity GDP comparative data for 188 economic bodies, with a sample range from 1950 to 2004.

26 PWT 6.2 does not provide *per capita* GDP figures for Guangdong and Zhejiang, but provides data for China. We calculated Guangdong and Zhejiang's *per capita* GDP in terms of PWT 6.2's database using Guangdong and Zhejiang's ratios from national comparisons, furthermore comparing them with other economic bodies worldwide.

27 The growth trajectory of these countries is mostly stable. Economic growth literature dubs this the "balanced growth trajectory", namely the rate of growth is a constant.

28 There appears to be solid theoretical basis for take-offs approaching their end: Neoclassical economic growth theory always emphasized that every economy will eventually converge to its own steady state, namely when an economy converges from a low level to its own equilibrium, the pace of economic growth will slow down. Of course, literature on technological diffusion can also give a very good explanation.

29 The translator of "One Step Ahead in China" insists that this is the first book by a foreign academic researching and reporting on China's reforms.

30 Shu et al. (2008) examined this process in detail, and summarized Guangdong's development into the three stages of experimentation, diffusion and convergence. This section only selects a portion of the content pertaining to Guangdong's experimentations with reform.

31 We will scrutinize this in the following paragraph.

32 According to Fang et al. (2000), "Up to 1978, Zhejiang was still an agricultural province with weak industrial fundamentals, a semi-autarkic natural economy society."

33 Zhang et al. (2007) reviewed fiscal decentralization practice and theoretical research after New China was founded, especially since the "reform and opening" began, in detail and depth, recounting China's story on transition and growth.

34 This is relative to traditional fiscal decentralization theory (Tiebout, 1956; Musgrave, 1959; Oates, 1972). Traditional fiscal decentralization theory emphasizes the local government's informational advantage relative to the central government in terms of

information relating to its jurisdiction. Fiscal decentralization enables the local government to use its informational advantage better and provide public goods more effectively. If traditional fiscal decentralization theory or the first generation of fiscal decentralization theory is said to emphasize the local's informational advantage, then the second generation of fiscal decentralization theory places more emphasis on local government incentives.

35 In 1982, the center delegated personnel management authority to lower levels, implementing the "each level administers the immediate lower level" personnel management system. This reform gave the local government partial personnel management authority, which was conducive to local dynamism.

36 In political science literature, the factors that influence official position changes include factionalism, localism and performance. In economics literature, performance is mainly reflected in the promotion tournament hypothesis; factionalism is mainly reflected in the influence of personal relationships on promotion. Although Zhou (2007, 2008) rather systematically explored the promotion tournament model, it is hard to simply deny the influence of personal relationships on promotions.

37 They believe, the expansion of non-budgetary revenue represents the shift of local government from being "helping hands" to becoming "grabbing hands".

38 Recently, Xu and Wang (2010b) employed a sample of provincial governors who were promoted to party secretary of that province, directly measuring the conducive effect of political incentives on Chinese economic growth quantitatively, and found that this conducive effect differs based on the officials' age and term.

39 Bo (2002) also discovered that factionalism, which relies on personal relationships as its main dimension, significantly explains position changes of provincial government and party leaders.

40 This chapter examines in detail the circumstances regarding regional development data in the appendix.

41 Recently, some academics were still studying interregional technological gaps. Yan and Wang (2004), Peng (2005), Fu and Wu (2006a,b), etc., employed data envelopment analysis, the Solow residual method, stochastic frontier analysis and so on to measure the total productivity factor for China's provinces and autonomous regions as well as their gaps.

42 Li (2003) wrote a good review.

43 Almost all current literature in this field has borrowed from other areas: employing new methods in international literature, inputting data for Chinese regions and reaching new solutions for old problems of Chinese regional disparity. Doubtlessly, this narrowed the technical gap between domestic and international literature, but it has not greatly enhanced the understanding of Chinese regional disparity.

44 Strictly speaking, in the literature with *per capita* (or per worker) GDP as base figures, the issue under research would be more aptly expressed as regional development gaps and not income gaps. In fact, paying attention to *per capita* income gaps is meaningful, especially since the issue of the degree to which government-driven decreases in *per capita* GDP gaps can transform into decreases in *per capita* income gaps is well worth researching. The goal of equalization should be reducing income gaps; if too much emphasis is placed on *per capita* GDP gaps, then it may exaggerate the impact of government policy on reducing regional income gaps. However, since the trend and influencing factors of both gaps are not materially different, we will not make a rigorous distinction between them when introducing literature conclusions.

45 Liu and Zhang (2007) may be an exception. They discovered that from the perspective of the σ-coefficient, Chinese regional economic disparities began to show a new trend toward decreasing.

46 In the context of Chinese regional development, we have clarified that China's reforms and development were spatially gradual.

47 Lu and Chen (2006, p. 4).

48 Cai and Treisman (2005) proved, within a rather general framework, that when local governments compete for business and investment, if there are disparities in initial endowments including geographical factors, then under certain conditions, varying results of business and investment attraction will be an equilibrium result.

49 Hall and Jones (1999) employed distance to the equator and the proportion of population with a western European language as its mother tongue as the instrument variable for institutions. Acemoglu et al. (2001) employed the death rate of colonists during the colonial age as the instrument variable. These quantitative studies both believe institutions to be the cause of economic growth.

50 There are debates in academic literature. Glaeser et al. (2004) believe that Acemoglu et al. (2001) have logical inconsistencies, since European colonists not only brought with them institutions, but also the human capital they possessed. This implies that European colonists not only influenced economic growth in colonies through institutions, but also through human capital and other channels. McArthur and Sachs (2001) also rebutted Acemoglu et al.'s (2001) argument by testing data from the same source and discovered that geographical and institutional factors were equally important in explaining income gaps. Acemoglu et al. (2005) enunciated in their economic growth manual the framework for studying the influence of institutions and the relevant evidence they found.

51 From an intuitive perspective, if New China's economy is divided into the three development phases 1949–1956, 1957–1978 and after 1979, then the first two phases indeed have many similarities. The change in the ownership structure was: multiple forms of ownership under the dominance of the state-owned economy→singular public ownership→multiple forms of ownership with public ownership as the principal part; the change in the method of resource allocation: market economy and planned economy→singular planned economy→market economy and planned economy, displaying a return to the neo-democratic economy. On the other hand, from the perspective of entities involved in economic activity, the Three Great Transformations were finished in 1956, whereas "reform and opening" began in 1978. This means two great historical events occurred during one generation and were personally experienced by a sizable number of people. Wu (1999) clearly pointed out that theory relating to these two great historical events "were formed on one generation, with many party leaders such as Deng and Chen Yun who led and participated in the formation of the theory of socialism with Chinese characteristics being main participants of the formation of the theory of Neo-democratism".

52 Xu (2002) studied this period in detail.

53 The first supplementary data was concisely published in 1988's *China's Statistical Year Book*.

54 This compendium was published in 1997 by Dongbei University of Finance and Economics Press, though it does not appear to have received the interest it should have at that time.

55 National Bureau of Statistics Integrated National Economy Accounting Division (1999) p. 3.

56 Actually, this compendium's quality is not very high. Attentive academics found errors while using this compendium.

57 This inconvenience also brought about all sorts of databases that provided the data in the compendiums in an electronic format. As long as the data input was error-free, the database in an electronic format is obviously more useful than a paper only version for search and usage.

58 Xing and Li (2009, p. 1459) clearly pointed out, "Since value-added tax employs a system of tax deductions, the amount payable can be deducted from the amount receivable as long as the conditions for deduction are satisfied. Thus, when firms in one region export goods to firms in another region, it must simultaneously send VAT invoices to the firm in the other region (hence output invoice) for it to use for deductions;

when this region's firms import goods from firms in other regions, in order to carry out payable deductions, they are motivated to obtain VAT invoices from other regions. To the firms in every region, it is possible for them to receive input invoices from firms in another region as well as send output invoices to firms in other regions. Therefore, these invoices effectively record the situation of interregional trade."

59 Xu, Li and Wang (2007) employed this data when choosing instrument variables.

60 From the implementation of the Golden Tax Project, beginning on January 1 2003, all normal entities that pay value-added tax must issue special invoices through the Value-added Tax Anti-counterfeiting Control System, meanwhile handwritten version special invoices will be discontinued nationwide. Beginning on April 1 2003, handwritten version special invoices cannot be used as VAT credit documents.

61 Human capital is very important to research on growth. School enrollment rates are often used in literature as a measurement, but this indicator is not a good measurement. Based on this, Chen et al. (2004) calculated the average years of education for each province, forming a provincial panel database.

62 Shu published his doctoral thesis through Fudan University Press and reported the basic data he estimated as well as the results of the estimation in the book's appendix.

63 The current address is http://faculty.wcas.northwestern.edu/~vsh853/

References

Acemoglu, D., S. Johnson and J. A. Robinson, 2001, "The Colonial Origins of Comparative Development: An Empirical Investigation," *American Economic Review*, 91(5), pp. 1369–1401.

Acemoglu, D., S. Johnson and J. A. Robinson, 2005, "Institutions as a Fundamental Cause of Long-Run Growth," *Handbook of Economic Growth*, 1, pp. 385–472.

Bai, C., Z. Tao and S. Y. Tong, 2008, "Bureaucratic Integration and Regional Specialization in China," *China Economic Review*, 19(2), pp. 308–319.

Barro, R. and I. Sala-i-Martin, 1995, *Economic Growth*, New York: McGraw-Hill.

Bo, Z., 2002, *Chinese Provincial Leaders: Economic Performance and Political Mobility Since 1949*, New York: M. E. Sharpe.

Cai, F. and Y. Du, 2000, "Convergence and divergence of Regional Economic Growth in China," *Economic Research Journal*, 10, pp. 30–37.

Cai, F. and Y. Du, 2001, "Regional Disparities, Convergence, and the Development of Western China," *China Industrial Economy*, 2, pp. 48–54.

Cai, H., and D. Treisman, 2005, "Does Competition for Capital Discipline Governments? Decentralization, Globalization and Public Policy," *American Economic Review*, 95(3), pp. 817–830.

Chen, C. and B. M. Fleisher, 1996, "Regional Income Inequality and Economic Growth in China," *Journal of Comparative Economics*, 22(2), pp. 141–164.

Chen, K., A. L. Hillman and Q. Gu, 2002, "Fiscal Re-centralization and Behavioral Change of Local Governments: From the Helping Hand to the Grabbing Hand," *China Economic Quarterly*, 2(1), pp. 111–130.

Chen, S., 2010, "Tax-share Reform, Local Fiscal Autonomy, and Public Goods Provision," *China Economic Quarterly*, 9(4), pp. 1427–1446.

Chen, X. and Y. Xu, 2004, "Factors Affecting China's Regional Gap: An Empirical Study," *Social Sciences in China*, 5, pp. 117–129.

Chen, Z., M. Lu and Y. Jin, 2004, "Regional Differences of Human Capitals and Education Development in China: An Estimation of the Panel Data," *Journal of World Economy*, (12), pp. 25–31.

Démurger, S., J. Sachs, Y. Hu, S. Bao, and X. Zhang, 2002, "The Relative Contributions of Location and Preferential Policies in China's Regional Development," *Economic Research Journal*, 9, pp. 14–23.

Department of National Accounts, 1997, *Data of Gross Domestic Product of China (1952–1995)*, Dongbei University of Finance and Economics Press.

Department of National Accounts, 1999, *China Compendium of Statistics 1949–1998*, China Statistics Press.

Department of National Accounts, 2004, *Data of Gross Domestic Product of China (1996–2002)*, China Statistics Press.

Department of National Accounts, 2005, *China Compendium of Statistics 1949–2003*, China Statistics Press.

Department of National Accounts, 2007, *Data of Gross Domestic Product of China (1952–2004)*, China Statistics Press.

Department of National Accounts, 2010, *China Compendium of Statistics 1949–2008*, China Statistics Press.

Easterly, W., 2002, *The Elusive Quest for Growth: Economists' Adventures and Misadventures in the Tropics*, [Chinese version, 2005], China: CITIC Press.

Easterly, W., M. Kremer, L. Pritchett, and L. Summers, 1993, "Good Policy or Good Luck? Country Growth Performance and Temporary Shocks," *Journal of Monetary Economics*, 32(3), pp. 459–483.

Fan, G. and X. Wang, 2001, *NERI Index of Marketization of China's Provinces 2000 Report*, Beijing: Economic Science Press.

Fan, G. and X. Wang, 2005, *NERI Index of Marketization of China's Provinces 2004 Report*, Beijing: Economic Science Press.

Fan, G., X. Wang and H. Zhu, 2007, *NERI Index of Marketization of China's Provinces 2006 Report*, Beijing: Economic Science Press.

Fan, G., X. Wang and H. Zhu, 2010, *NERI Index of Marketization of China's Provinces 2009 Report*, Beijing: Economic Science Press.

Fan, J. and G. Zhu, 2002, "The Evolution of Regional Disparities in China and its Structural Decomposition," *Management World*, 7, pp. 37–44.

Fang, M., et al., 2000, *The Institutional Change and Development pattern in Zhejiang Province*, Zhejiang: Zhejiang People's Publishing House.

Fu, X. and L. Wu, 2006a, "Technical Efficiency, Capital Deepening and Regional Disparity," *Economic Research Journal*, 10, pp. 52–61.

Fu, X. and L. Wu, 2006b, "The Role of Total Factor Productivity in China's Regional Disparities," *Journal of World Economy*, 9, pp. 12–22.

Fu, Y. and Y. Zhang, 2007, "The Chinese-style Decentralization and the Structure Deviation of Fiscal Expenditure," *Management World*, 3, pp. 4–12.

Glaeser, E., R. La Porta, F. Lopez-de-Silanes, and A. Shleifer, 2004, "Do Institutions Cause Growth?", *Journal of Economic Growth*, 9(3), pp. 271–303.

Hall, R. and C. Jones, 1999, "Why Do Some Countries Produce So Much More Output Per Worker Than Others?", *The Quarterly Journal of Economics*, 114(1), pp. 83–116.

Hausmann, R., L. Pritchett, and D. Rodrik, 2004, "Growth Accelerations," *NBER Working Paper*, No. 10566.

He, C. and J. Liang, 2004, "The Temporal and Spatial Variation in Regional Economic Disparities," *Management World*, 8, pp. 8–17.

He, D. and Y. Yao, 2009, "Equality and Neutral Government," *World Economic Papers*, 1, pp. 103–120.

He, Y., 2008, "Economic Convergence in Transition Economy of China: An Empirical Study with a Nonlinear Time-varying Factor Model," *Economic Research Journal*, 7, pp. 39–51.

Huang, J. and K. Li, 2006, "Openness, Regional Market Size and Economic Growth," *Economic Research Journal*, 6, pp. 27–38.

Huang, Y., 1996, *Inflation and Investment Controls in China: The Political Economy of Center Local Relations during the Reform Era*, Cambridge: Cambridge University Press.

Jian, T., J. D. Sachs and A. M. Warner, 1996, "Trends in Regional Inequality in China," *NBER Working Paper* No. 5412.

Jin, H., Y. Qian and B. Weingast, 2005, "Regional Decentralization and Fiscal Incentives: Federalism, Chinese Style," *Journal of Public Economics*, 89(9–10), pp. 1719–1742.

Jones, B. F., and B. A., Olken, 2008, "The Anatomy of Start-Stop Growth," *Review of Economics and Statistics*, 90(3), pp. 582–587.

Kong, F., 1998, "The Formation of a Buyer's Market in China," *Surplus Economy? Surplus Economy!*, Beijing: Economic Science Press, pp. 56–63.

Kornai, J., 1980/1986, *Economics of Shortage*, [Chinese version, 1986], Beijing: Economic Science Press.

Krugman, P., 1991, "Increasing Returns and Economic Geography," *Journal of Political Economy*, 99(3), pp. 483–499.

Li, D. D., 1998, "Changing Incentives of the Chinese Bureaucracy," *American Economic Review*, 88(2), pp. 393–397.

Li, H., and L. Zhou, 2005, "Political Turnover and Economic Performance: The Incentive Role of Personnel Control in China," *Journal of Public Economics*, 89(9–10), pp. 1743–1762.

Li, J., L. Meng and F. Wu, 2006, "Reexamination of Regional Development Disparities in China," *Journal of World Economy*, 1, pp. 12–22.

Li, M. and H. Li, 2010, "Political Capital and Regional Income Differences in China," *World Economic Papers*, 5, pp. 38–57.

Li, S., 2003, "The evolution of Personal Income Distribution in China," *China Economic Quarterly*, 2(2), pp. 379–403.

Li, Y. and K. Shen, 2008, "Yardstick Competitions, Strategic Fiscal Policies, and Regional Characteristics of FDI's Growth Achievements," *Economic Research Journal*, 5, pp. 58–69.

Lin, J. Y., and Z. Liu, 2000, "Fiscal Decentralization and Economic Growth in China," *Economic Development and Cultural Change*, 49(1), pp. 1–21.

Lin, Y., F. Cai and Z. Li, 1998, "The Analysis of Regional Disparities during the Period of China's Economy Transition," *Economic Research Journal*, (6), pp. 3–10.

Liu, J., 1996, "Small Business, Big Market" (I): The Description of Operating Characteristics of Zhejiang Economic System, *Zhejiang Academic Journal*, (6), pp. 19–24.

Liu, J., 1997, "'Small Business, Big Market' (II): The Description of Operating Characteristics of Zhejiang Economic System," *Zhejiang Academic Journal*, 1, pp. 22–26.

Liu, S. and X. Zhang, 2007, The Features of China's Sustained High Growth and the Decline of Regional Economic Disparity, *Economic Research Journal*, 10, pp. 17–31.

Lu, K., 2008, *Life under Food Coupons*, Academy Press.

Lu, M. and Z. Chen, 2006, *Market Integration and Industrial Agglomeration in China's Regional Economic Development*, Shanghai: SDX Joint Publishing Company; People's Publishing House.

Lu, M. and Z. Chen, 2009, "Fragmented Growth: Why Economic Opening May Worsen Domestic Market Segmentation?" *Economic Research Journal*, 3, pp. 42–52.

Lucas, R., 2000, "Some Macroeconomics for the 21st Century," *Journal of Economic Perspective*, 14(1), pp. 159–168.

Luo, P., 2008, *The History of Food Coupons in China*, Fujian: Fujian People's Publishing House.

Maskin, E., Y. Qian and C. Xu, 2000, "Incentives, Scale Economies, and Organization Forms," *Review of Economic Studies*, 67(2), pp. 359–378.

McArthur, J. W. and J. D. Sachs, 2001, "Institutions and Geography: Comment on Acemoglu, Johnson, and Robinson (2000)," *NBER Working Paper*, No. 8114.

Musgrave, R., 1959, *The Theory of Public Finance*, New York: McGraw-Hill.

National Bureau of Statistics of China, 1999, *Comprehensive Statistical Data and Materials on 50 Years of New China*, Beijing: China Statistics Press.

National Bureau of Statistics of China, 2010, *China Statistical Yearbook*, Beijing: China Statistics Press.

North, D. C., 1981, *Structure and Change in Economic History*, [Chinese version, 1994], Shanghai: Shanghai SDX Joint Publishing Company, Shanghai People's Publishing House.

Oates, W., 1972, *Fiscal Federalism*, New York: Harcourt Brace Jovanovich, Inc.

Olson, M., 2000, *Power and Prosperity*, [Chinese version, 2005], Shanghai: Shanghai People's Publishing House.

Pan, W. and Y. Ma, 2010, *Sixty Years of PRC and the Chinese Pattern*, Shanghai: SDX Joint Publishing Company.

Peng, G., 2005, "The Disparity of Income, TFP and the Convergence Hypothesis in Chinese Provinces," *Economic Research Journal*, 9, pp. 19–29.

Pi, J., 2008, "Regional Market Integration under Yardstick Competition in China: On the Role of the Central Government in Regional Market Integration," *Economic Research Journal*, 3, pp. 115–124.

Pritchett, L., 2000, "Understanding Patterns of Economic Growth: Searching for Hills among Plateaus, Mountains, and Plains," *World Bank Economic Review*, 14(2), pp. 221–250.

Qian, Y. and B. Weingast, 1997, "Federalism as a Commitment to Preserving Market Incentives," *Journal of Economic Perspective*, 11(4), pp. 83–92.

Qian, Y. and C. Xu, 1993, "Why China's Economic Reforms Differ: the M-Form Hierarchy and Entry/Expansion of the Non-State Sector," *Economics of Transition*, 1(2), pp. 135–170.

Qian, Y. and G. Roland, 1998, "Federalism and the Soft Budget Constraint," *American Economic Review*, 88(5), pp. 1143–1162.

Rostow, W., 1960, *The Stages of Economic Growth: A Non-Communist Manifesto*, [Chinese version, 2001], Beijing: China Social Sciences Press.

Shen, K. and J. Ma, 2002, "The Characteristics of "Club Convergence" of China's Economic Growth and Its Cause," *Economic Research Journal*, 1, pp. 33–39.

Shen, L. and Y. Dai, 1990, "On the Fragmented China Economy," *Economic Research Journal*, 3, pp. 12–19.

Shi, J., X. Jin, W. Zhao and W. Luo, 2002, *Institutional Changes and Economic Development: Studies on Wenzhou Model*, Zhejiang: Zhejiang University Press.

Shu, Y. and X. Xu, 2002, "The Specification of China's Economic Growth Model: 1952–1998," *Economic Research Journal*, 11, pp. 3–11.

Shu, Y., 1989, "The Analysis of Economic Growth in China," Doctoral Dissertation, Fudan University.

Shu, Y., 1993, *The Analysis of Economic Growth in China*, Fudan University.

Shu, Y., X. Chu, X. Li, Y. Zhou and X. Xu, 2008, *The Economic Development Pattern in Guangdong: Thirty years of Economic Development in Guangdong*, Guangdong: Guangdong People's Publishing House.

Song, X., 1996, "The Regional Economic Development and Convergence," *Economic Research Journal*, 9, pp. 38–44.

Tao, R., F. Su, M. Lu, and Y. Zhu, 2010, "Is Promotion Based on Economic Growth?" *Management World*, 12, pp. 13–26.

Tiebout, C., 1956, "A Pure Theory of Local Expenditures," *Journal of Political Economy*, 64(5), pp. 416–424.

Tsui, K. Y., 1993, "Decomposition of China's Regional Inequalities," *Journal of Comparative Economics*, 17(3), pp. 600–627.

Vogel, E. F., 1990, *One Step Ahead in China: Guangdong under Reform*, [Chinese version, 1991], Guangdong: Guangdong People's Publishing House.

Wan, G., M. Lu and Z. Chen, 2005, "Globalization and Regional Income Disparities," *Social Sciences In China*, 3, pp. 17–26.

Wan, G., M. Lu and Z. Chen, 2007, "Globalization and Regional Income Inequality: Empirical Evidence from within China," *Review of Income and Wealth*, 53(1), pp. 35–59.

Wang, S. and J. Zhang, 2008, "Why Chinese Cadres Improve Physical Infrastructure: Modeling the Incentive Mechanism?" *China Economic Quarterly*, 7(2), pp. 383–398.

Wang, X., X. Xu and X. Li, 2009, "Provincial Governors Turnovers and Economic Growth: Evidence from China," *China Economic Quarterly*, 8(4), pp. 1301–1328.

Wang, X., L. Zhang and X. Xu, 2011, "Growth Performance and the Promotion of the Provincial Governor and Party Secretary," *Comparative Economic and Social Systems*, 1, pp. 110–122.

Wang, Z. and Z. Ge, 2002, "The Multiple Equilibrium States of China's Regional Economic Development and the Omen of Changes," *Social Sciences in China*, 4, pp. 31–39.

Wei, H., 1992, "The Developing Pattern of China's Regional Income Disparities," *Economic Research Journal*, 4, pp. 61–65.

Wei, H., 1996, "The Income Disparities in China and its Decomposition," *Economic Research Journal*, 11, pp. 66–73.

Wu, L., 1999, "The Analysis of Economic Growth and Institutional Change in PRC," *Contemporary China History Studies*, 5–6, pp. 54–69.

Xing, W. and S. Li, 2009, "Home Biases, Border Effects and Market Integration: An Empirical Study Based on Inter-provincial VAT Survey," *China Economic Quarterly*, 8(4), pp. 1455–1474.

Xu, C., 2009a, "The Institutional Foundation of Economic Reform in China," *World Economic Papers*, 4, pp. 105–116.

Xu, C., 2011, "The Fundamental Institutions of China's Reforms and Development," *Journal of Economic Literature*, 49(4), pp. 1076–1151.

Xu, X., 2002, "China's GDP Accounting," *China Economic Quarterly*, 2(1), pp. 23–36.

Xu, X., 2006, *Growth Dynamics in Chinese Provinces (1978–1998)*, Sun-Yatsen: Sun-Yatsen University Press.

Xu, X., 2009b, "The Dynamic Mechanism of Guangdong's Economy Take-off," *Journal of Sun Yat-sen University*, 2, pp. 198–204.

Xu, X. and X. Chen, 2008, "Special Economic Zone: The Starting-point of Gradual Reform and Opening-up in China," *World Economic Papers*, 1, pp. 14–26.

Xu, X. and X. Li, 2004, "Convergence in Chinese Cities," *Economic Research Journal*, 5, pp. 40–48.

Xu, X. and X. Li, 2005, "Endogenous Institutions and Provincial Disparity in China," *China Economic Quarterly*, 44, pp. s83-s100.

Xu, X. and X. Li, 2010, "Interprovincial Trade in China: 1985–2007," *IRE Working Paper*, No. 2011004.

Xu, X. and X. Wang, 2010a, "Growth Behavior in the Appointment Economy," *China Economic Quarterly*, 9(4), pp. 1447–1466.

Xu, X. and X. Wang, 2010b, "Promotion Incentives and Economic Growth: Evidence from Chinese Provincial Officials," *Journal of World Economy*, 2, pp. 15–36.

Xu, X. and Y. Shu, 2004, "Growth Dynamics in Chinese Provinces (1978–1998)," *China Economic Quarterly*, 3(3), pp. 619–638.

Xu, X. and Y. Shu, 2005, "The Coordinated Development: A New Analytical Framework," *Management World*, 2, pp. 27–35.

Xu, X., J. Zhou and Y. Shu, 2007, "Estimates of Fixed Capital Stock by Sector and Region: 1978–2002," *Statistical Research*, 5, pp. 6–13.

Xu, X., X. Li and M. Wang, 2007, "Regional Integration, Economic Growth and Political Promotion," *China Economic Quarterly*, 6(4), pp. 1075–1096.

Xu, X., X. Wang and Y. Shu, 2007, "Local Officials and Economic Growth," *Economic Research Journal*, 9, pp. 18–31.

Xu, Z. and S. Li, 2006, "Analysis on the Trend of Regional Income Disparity in China," *Economic Research Journal*, 7, pp. 106–116.

Xu, Z., Z. Chen and M. Lu, 2010, "Core-Periphery Model of Urban Economic Growth," *Journal of World Economy*, 7, pp. 144–160.

Yan, P. and B. Wang, 2004, "Technical Efficiency, Technical Progress and Productivity Growth: An Empirical Analysis Based on DEA," *Economic Research Journal*, 12, pp. 55–65.

Yang, H., D. Luo and S. Chen, 2010, "Resource Endowment, Official Rotation and Economic Growth," *Management World*, 5, pp. 17–26.

Yang, W., 1992, "The Empirical Analysis of Regional Income Disparities," *Economic Research Journal*, 1, pp. 70–74.

Year Book Editorial Department of China Transportation and Communications, 2009, *Year Book of China Transportation and Communications*, Year Book Press of China Transportation and Communications.

Yin, Z., 2010, "Official Rotation and Economic Growth," *Comparative Economic and Social Systems*, 4, pp. 23–29.

Young, A., 2000, "The Razor's Edge: Distortions and Incremental Reform in the People's Republic of China," *Quarterly Journal of Economics*, 115(4), pp. 1091–1135.

Yuan, G., 1996, "Regional Economic Differences and Macroeconomic Fluctuation," *Economic Research Journal*, 10, pp. 49–56.

Zhang, E., 2010, "Economic Growth and Local Governors' Entrepreneurial Background: Evidence from the Secretary of the CPC Provincial Committee and Provincial Governor," *China Industrial Economics*, 3, pp. 129–138.

Zhang, H., 2004, "The Application of the Augmented Solow Model: Diversities and Convergence among Chinese Provinces," *China Economic Quarterly*, 3(3), pp. 605–618.

Zhang, J. and L. Zhou, 2008, *Competition for Growth: The Political Economy of Growth in China*, Shanghai: Truth and Wisdom Press, Shanghai People's Publishing House.

Zhang, J. and Y. Gao, 2007, "Term Limits and Rotation of Chinese Governors: Do They Matter to Economic Growth?" *Economic Research Journal*, 11, pp. 91–103.

Zhang, J. and Y. Zhang, 2003, "Recalculating the Capital of China and a Review of Li and Tang s Article," *Economic Research Journal*, 7, pp. 35–43.

Zhang, J., G. Wu and J. Zhang, 2004, "The Estimation of China's provincial capital stock: 1952–2000," *Economic Research Journal*, 10, pp. 35–44.

Zhang, J., Y. Gao, Y. Fu, and H. Zhang, 2007, "Why Does China Enjoy So Much Better Physical Infrastructure?" *Economic Research Journal*, 3, pp. 4–19.

Zhang, L., X. Wang and X. Xu, 2010, "Investment-driven Land Supply," *IRE Working Paper*, No. 2011001.

Zhang, T., and H. Zou, 1998, "Fiscal Decentralization, Public Spending, and Economic Growth in China," *Journal of Public Economics*, 67(2), pp. 221–240.

Zhang, X. and H. Sun, 2009, "Which is the True Source of Economic Growth in the Yangtze River Delta: Capital Accumulation, Efficiency Improvement, or TFP Contribution," *China Industrial Economics*, 5, pp. 36–45.

Zhang, Y. and L. Gong, 2005, "The Fenshuizhi Reform, Fiscal Decentralization, and Economic Growth in China," *China Economic Quarterly*, 5(1), pp. 76–107.

Zhao, W., 2005, *The Openness Pattern and Trend of China's Regional Economy*, Beijing: Economic Science Press.

Zheng, Y. and G. Wu, 1995, *The Relationship of Central and Local Governments: The Key Problem in China's Institutional Transformation*, Oxford: Oxford University Press.

Zheng, Y., 2001, "The Endogenous Folk Power Driven Economic Growth: Zhejiang's Experience," *Zhejiang Social Sciences*, 2, pp. 35–40.

Zhou, L., 2004, "The Incentive and Cooperation of Government Officials in the Political Tournaments: An Interpretation of the Prolonged Local Protectionism and Duplicative Investments in China," *Economic Research Journal*, 6, pp. 33–40.

Zhou, L., 2007, "Governing China's Local Officials: An Analysis of Promotion Tournament Model," *Economic Research Journal*, 7, pp. 36–50.

Zhou, L., 2008, *Local Government in Transition: Officials' Incentive and Governance*, Shanghai: Truth and Wisdom Press, Shanghai People's Publishing House.

Zhou, M., 2000, "The Economic Center, Regional Disparities and Coordinated Development," *Social Sciences in China*, (2), pp. 42–53.

3 The political economy of urban and rural development in China

Zhao Chen

3.1 Introduction

Nobel Prize laureate Stiglitz asserted during a World Bank conference in 2001 that in the twenty-first century, the two things that will have the largest global impact will be America's high tech industry and China's urbanization. Judging from the current trend, where the proportion of total population with permanent urban residence increases by 1 percent a year, in another 20–30 years, 70 percent or more of China's population will live in the city. Looking at the progression of industrialization and urbanization, China's achievements over the 30 or more years after "reform and opening" have been tremendous. China went from a poor and backward agricultural country to a major industrial country, occupying a prominent role in the international manufacturing division of labor. Yet, it is difficult for the "dual economy theory" (Lewis, 1954), used by orthodox developmental economics to analyze labor reallocation from the backward agricultural sector to the modern advanced industrial sector, to fully match the important facts of Chinese urbanization. This precisely illustrates the uniqueness of China's urbanization, which we have summarized into three characteristics, namely: urbanization lagging behind industrialization, a "dual society" segmentation forming within the cities, and continuous increases in urban–rural disparities.[1]

This chapter attempts to show that China's urban–rural policies reflect the conflict between urban and rural areas as two groups. However, in this game, cities have more influence over the formulation of urban–rural policy, which results in China's urban-biased policies. Only through such a "political economy" perspective can we fully understand the development of China's urban–rural economy and urbanization process, can we truly give a scientific reply to what situations may arise during urbanization in China, and further propose policy recommendations for Chinese urbanization that can provide meaningful guidances.

According to current literature, this chapter will first review important stylized facts of China's urbanization and the process of urban–rural development, then conceptually analyze the evolution and relevant consequences of the urban–rural segmentation policies with the Hukou system as their core. On this basis, this chapter will then analyze Chinese urbanization from a political economy perspective, meanwhile explaining the aforementioned stylized facts, and provide policy recommendations to achieve harmonious urban–rural development. Specifically speaking, the second section of this chapter will conclude a few major stylized facts of Chinese urban–rural development; the third section will study the institutional reasons of the aforementioned stylized facts from a historical perspective—the formation of the Hukou system and the relevant evolution of the urban–rural segmentation; the fourth section will emphasize the political economy perspective in illustrating how urban–rural segmentation impacts Chinese urban–rural development as well as the potential evolution from urban–rural segmentation to urban–rural integration in the future. The final section concludes.

3.2 The stylized facts of Chinese urban–rural development

The economic development after "reform and opening" is accompanied by a sustained increase in the level of urbanization. There were even seemingly "labor shortages" and rapid increases in wages after 2004. In the "dual economy theory" proposed by Lewis, there existed a backward agricultural sector and modern industrial sector. As the level of capital accumulation in the urban industrial sector continuously increased, is attracted more rural labor and the level of industrialization and urbanization rose at the same time. In terms the phase of economic development, an initial increase in labor reallocation does not lead to distinct increases in wages, as reallocation of labor does not impact agricultural production due to the existence of surplus labor in the countryside with almost infinitely elastic supply. But when economic development reaches the second phase, the urban industrial sector's capital accumulation creates further labor demand, then the further reallocation of rural labor will impact agricultural production. Under the effect of the price mechanism, the competition between the agricultural and industrial sector for labor will push wages higher. This critical shift is known as the "Lewis turning point" (Lewis, 1954). In a superficial sense, China's labor shortages and increase in wages appear to match Lewis's dual economy theory, but, upon close examination, the orthodox "dual economy theory" finds it difficult to fully match the important facts of China's urbanization and may even conflict. This precisely illustrates that China's urbanization has unique facets, which we summarize as: urbanization lagging behind industrialization, a "dual society" segmentation forming within the cities, and continuous increases in urban–rural disparities.

3.2.1 Urbanization lagging behind industrialization

In a research report regarding Chinese urbanization policy, Henderson (2009) mentions the laggardness of the rate of urbanization as the first important characteristic in China's urban development: Chinese urban population increases at a 3.5 percent annualized rate, significantly lower than the 5–6 percent urban population growth rate seen by other developing countries during a rapid economic growth phase. When China's urbanization rate reached 46 percent, countries with similar *per capita* incomes to China have urbanization rates that reach 55 percent,

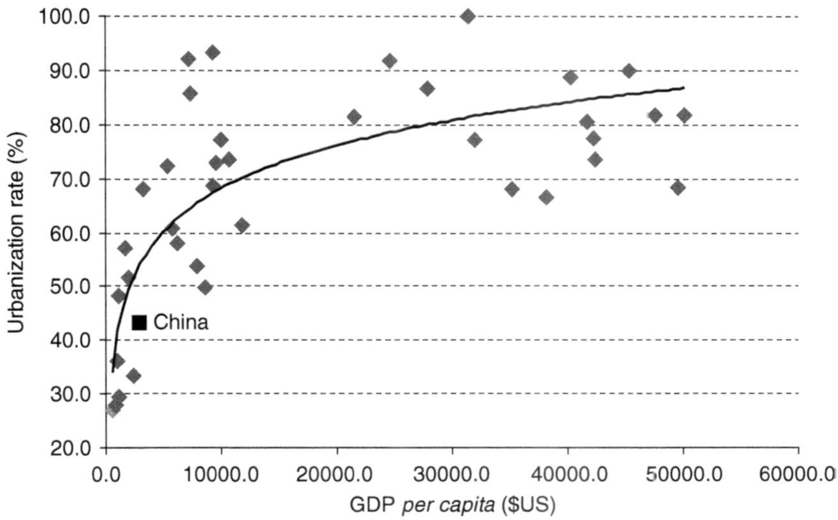

Figure 3.1 Cross-country comparisons of economic development and level of urbanization. Data source: Official site of Chinese National Bureau of Statistics.

and developed countries have urbanization rates of 70–85 percent. China's level of urbanization is significantly below average. Figure 3.1 displays the level of urbanization in various countries during different developmental phases, reflecting the fact that China's level of urbanization is at the low end. With the *per capita* GDP as the horizontal axis and the proportion of urban population (rate of urbanization) as the vertical axis, Figure 3.1 displays the relationship between the level of economic development and urbanization. It shows that China's level of urbanization is significantly lower than its *per capita* GDP suggests. The Figure's projection of China's urbanization rate based on *per capita* GDP was 50.5 percent, while the actual figure was 40.4 percent, a difference of nearly 10 percent. The laggardness of China's urbanization is consistent with Henderson's (2009) statement. If we take into consideration that in 2008, the Chinese RMB was still undervalued, then China's *per capita* GDP in terms of purchasing power parity should be even higher, and international comparisons suggest China's urbanization rates should be even higher.

How should China's below average urbanization rate be understood? If we compare China's urbanization and industrialization, we can discover that China's urbanization lags behind its industrialization, and this is precisely the crux to understanding China's below average urbanization rate.

Figure 3.2 shows the change in the level of Chinese industrialization and urbanization since "reform and opening," with the level of industrialization measured by the secondary industries' proportion of GDP and the level of urbanization measured by the proportion of urban residents. It shows the level of industrialization exceeded that of urbanization throughout the period, reflecting the

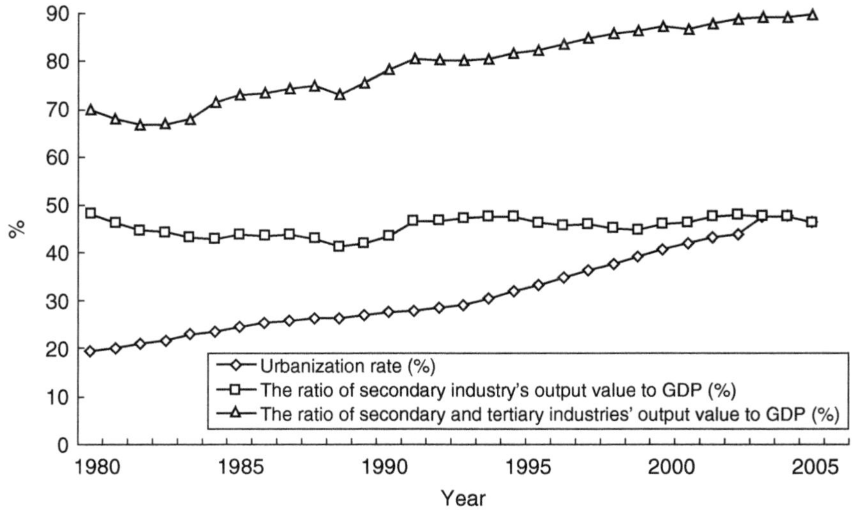

Figure 3.2 China's level of industrialization and urbanization (1980–2009). Data source: *China Statistical Yearbook*, 2010.[4]

characteristic of Chinese urbanization lagging behind industrialization for a prolonged period of time after "reform and opening." If the proportion of tertiary industries is included in the "industrialization indicator," then the gap between China's urbanization and industrialization will be even greater. As shown in Figure 3.2, the level of industrialization first gradually decreased after "reform and opening." This is, in fact, a structural correction to the legacy of over-emphasis on heavy industry, as the prioritized development of heavy industry during the planned economy era caused its proportion to be significantly too high. In 1978, when "reform and opening" was implemented, heavy industry's proportion of total industrial output was 56.9 percent.[2] Afterwards, due to the development of consumption-oriented light industry, the internal structure of industry experienced an adjustment. In the 1990s, under the industrial development model of consumption upgrades and government-guided export-orientation, the level of industrialization rose again, which is also reflected in Figure 3.2.

Next, we will examine China's process of urbanization according to urban population statistics published by the statistics departments. As shown in Figure 3.2, since "reform and opening," China's level of urbanization experienced a process of steady ascension, and the process of urbanization and industrialization were mostly consistent. The gap between levels of industrialization and urbanization seen in the data narrowed with the passing of time, but taking into consideration the fact that the development of urban service industries has the effect of attracting rural surplus labor, then if services are included in the "industrialization" indicator, the speed with which the gap between urbanization and industrialization narrows will decrease. The gap between the two was around 53.9 percent in 1978, and remains at 43.4 percent in 2009.[3]

Compared with industrialization, China's urbanization appears to be rather complicated. Due to the strict control imposed by the Hukou system, early official urban population figures mainly reflect the increase in population with urban Hukous from changes in administrative districts, namely causing locals to change from nonurban population to urban population by increasing the number of designated towns and changing counties to municipalities (districts). Also, the "from agricultural Hukou to nonagricultural Hukou" policy, immigrants caused by large-scale projects and so on, as well as becoming educated or joining the army and becoming a cadre are all important channels with which an urban Hukou could be gained. However, since "reform and opening," especially after the liberalization of the labor market, tremendous impacts on both industrialization and urbanization were caused by the reallocation of rural labor from the countryside to the cities, which is usually known as the large-scale emergence of the "new urban immigrant" group with "migrant workers" as its main body. Members of this group that have resided over half a year in the cities have already become permanent residents. Despite working in non-agricultural sectors in the city, due to the restrictions imposed by the current Hukou system, their status is still that of "peasant." The figures for urban population in the current officially published *China Statistical Yearbook* already include this portion of permanent residents, thereby more objectively reflecting the process of urbanization.[5] According to the sixth population census, the urbanization ratio was 49.68 percent.[6]

The characteristic of China's urbanization lagging behind industrialization could also be seen by comparisons with other countries. As shown in Figure 3.3(a),[7] the average level of urbanization in Russia, Brazil, Mexico, and South Korea far exceeds that of China. Bangladesh, as shown in Figure 3.3(b), has levels of urbanization and industrialization that are close, whereas India experienced a change in 1997, after which its level of urbanization exceeded that of its industrialization. In other words, compared with other countries, China has more people who cannot sufficiently share in the fruits of industrialization.

What implications does urbanization lagging behind industrialization have? It directly reflects the fact that reallocation of population to cities is not in sync with the development of urban industry. Obviously, this is not because the development of industry in China's cities did not adopt labor intensive production methods. The migrant workers that flooded into the cities beginning in the 1990s just happened to work in labor intensive industries. The key to the issue is that when cities are attracting rural surplus labor, they did not plan to let these people take root in the city as true "urban residents." Outsiders find it difficult to truly settle in the city, which necessarily makes mobility to urban areas insufficient. We will further discuss this in the section on "'dual society' segmentation in cities." At the same time, the natural growth of urban Hukou population is slow, and is even consecutively negative in Shanghai.

Correspondingly, Chinese urbanization is propelled not by population growth but through administrative district changes. This implies that each region's local government may cause the expansion of urban areas to become disjointed

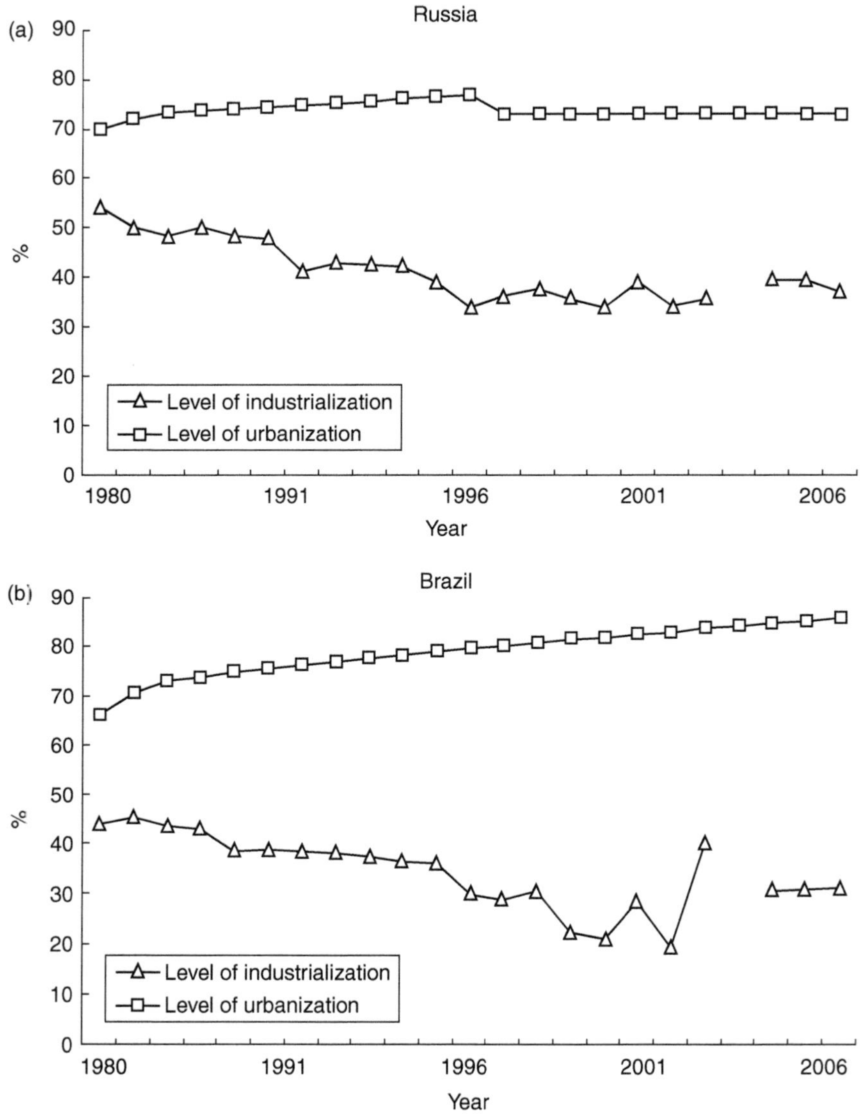

Figure 3.3 Historical industrialization and urbanization levels for various countries. (a) Russia, (b) Brazil, (c) Mexico, (d) South Korea, (e) Bangladesh, and (f) India.

Data source: Official site of Chinese National Bureau of Statistics.

with local population density and industrial development in pursuit of rapid urbanization. Data in the introduction of the National Bureau of Statistics' "Provisions Regarding Statistically Demarcating Urban and Rural Areas (1999 Trial Implementation)" shows that after the State Council approved the Ministry of Civil Affairs' "Report Regarding Adjustment of the Standard for Designating

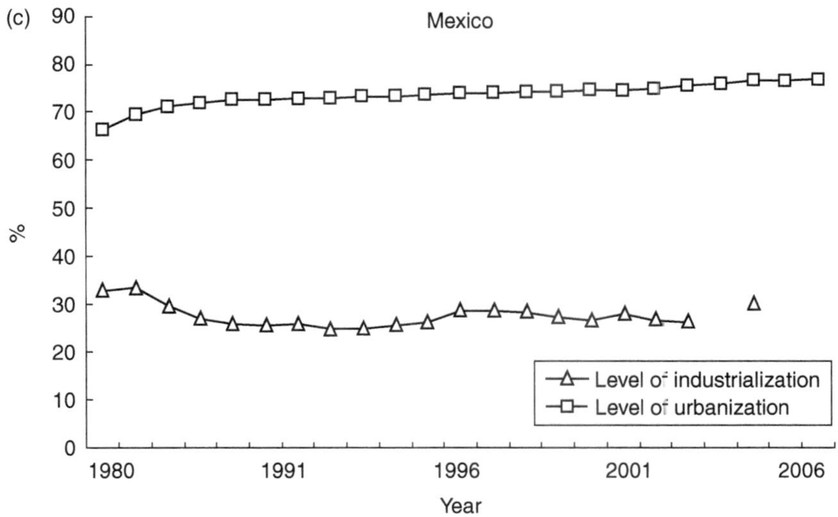

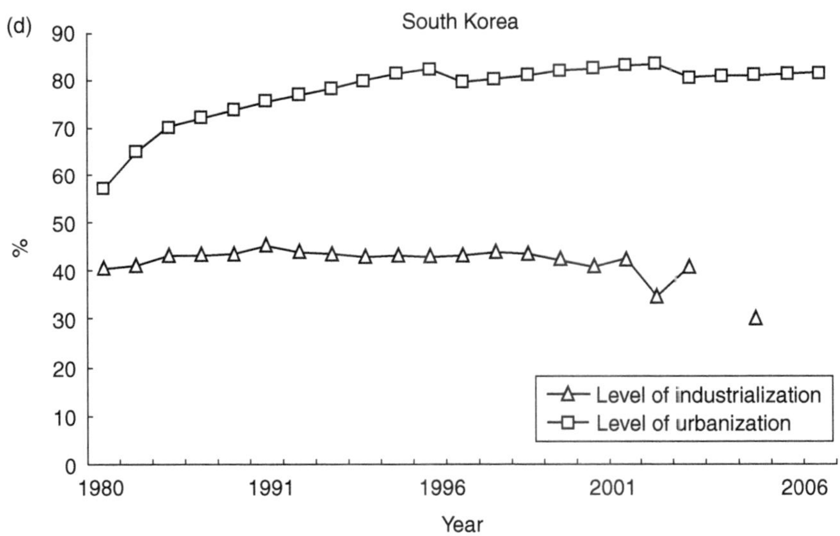

Figure 3.3 Continued

Townships" and "Report Regarding Adjustment of the Standards for Creating Municipalities and the Conditions for Municipalities Leading Counties" in November 1984 and April 1986, respectively, there was a widening of the former standards for designating municipalities and townships. Subsequently, actions to retract counties and designate municipalities, retract *xiang* and designate townships were pervasive everywhere, causing the number of municipalities and townships to see a large gain nationwide, which caused the urban population density to decline in the administrative district sense. According to statistics, in the only ten-plus years since the mid-1990s, the area of 338 municipalities nationwide of

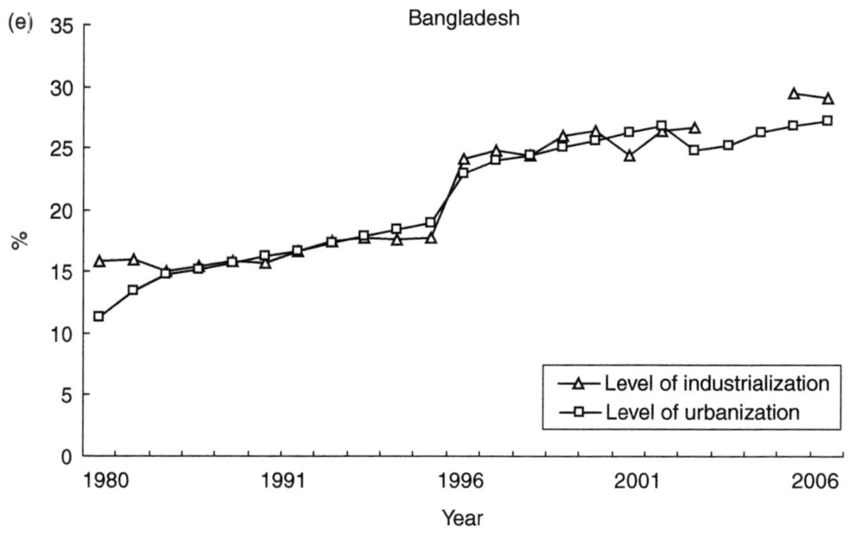

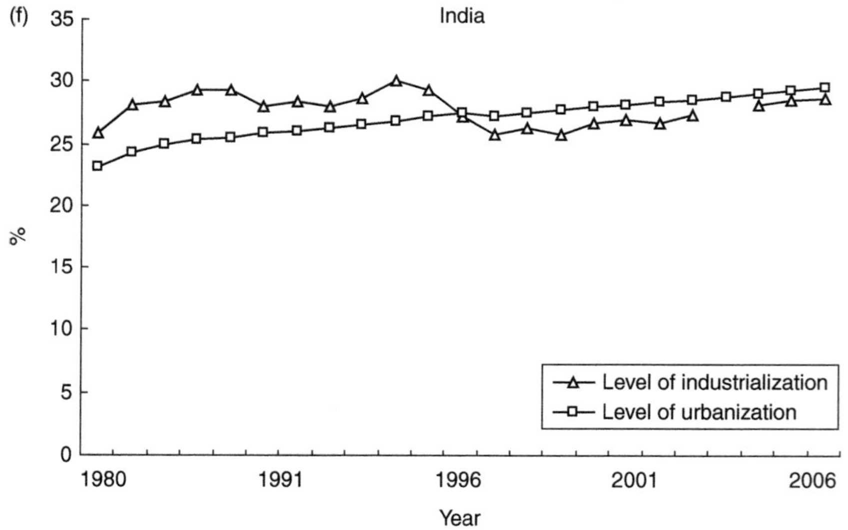

Figure 3.3 Continued

prefectural level and above grew from 16,000 sq km to 25,000 sq km, an increase of 60 percent. In the same time period, the urban district population (including migrant workers) of the abovementioned cities rose from 270 million to 300 million, an increase of only about 10 percent. The rate of increase in urban area is six times that of the rate of increase in urban district population (Yan and Jiang, 2007). This is a very thought-provoking phenomenon. On the one hand, Chinese urbanization is lagging behind. On the other hand, under an economically decentralized system, local governments pursue a larger urban area in an unbalanced manner and obtain revenue from land during the process of turning land used for agriculture-use land into land used for construction. The aggregate amount of construction-use land quotas is regulated in China, while the distribution of construction-use land quotas is relatively inclined toward the inland regions, therefore the phenomenon of the pace of expansion of constructed urban areas exceeding that of the expansion of the non-agricultural population is even more severe in the western regions, followed by the central regions, whereas the gap between the two figures is relatively small in the eastern provinces (Lu, 2011).

The laggardness in the level of urbanization is reflected in the relatively low proportion of urban population. Such an unbalanced pursuit of urbanization rates in an administrative district sense may increase urban population in a statistical sense, but the density of urban population decreases. Since there are many small cities without economies of scales that were created due to administrative district changes, the agglomeration effect of cities were not put to sufficient use. Au and Henderson's (2006a,b) empirical studies state that many Chinese cities suffer productivity losses due to their scale being too small and industrial agglomeration is still far from the level it should be. Their econometric analysis shows that, around 51–62 percent of Chinese cities are too small. Among rather typical cities, losses caused by cities that are too small take up about 17 percent of average employee output. The number of cities with average employee output losses as high as 25–70 percent account for at least a quarter of the sample cities. In addition, as their research also points out, as the proportion of the service sector increases, the optimal city size to maximize labor productivity becomes larger too, since the services sector has a greater need to benefit from economic agglomeration.

With the help of international comparisons to the Gini coefficient of city size, it was be discovered that the size difference between China's cities is smaller than average. According to Fujita et al.'s (2004) research, in 2000, the Gini coefficient of Chinese city size is 0.43, far lower than many large countries worldwide, including Brazil (0.65), Japan (0.65), Indonesia (0.61), Britain (0.60), Mexico (0.60), Nigeria (0.60), France (0.59), India (0.58), Germany (0.56), the US (0.54), and Spain (0.52). Only a few countries in the former Soviet Union have city size Gini coefficients close to China's, such as Russia (0.45) and Ukraine (0.40). Lu (2011) discovered that the GDP difference between Chinese cities, as measured by the Gini coefficient, has always been steadily ascending, while the population difference between cities changes very gradually, reflecting the fact that population agglomeration is not in sync with economic agglomeration.

We have already seen that the Hukou system restricts rural surplus labor from becoming urbanized, while being employed in the cities. This is the most important factor that causes China's level of urbanization to lag behind that of its industrialization. However, the Hukou system's impact on peasants that enter the city cannot just be summarized as "making it hard for them to become truly urbanized." In fact, the Hukou system has led to the formation of a "dual society" segmentation in cities. In recent years, government documents generally express such a phenomenon as the "new urban dual structure."

3.2.2 Formation of "dual society" segmentation in cities

Social segmentation of all dimensions also exists outside China. Becker (1957) included discrimination in economic analysis. But discrimination and the social segmentation it creates has always had some connection with innate differences, such as sex, race, etc. In a review, Arrow (1998) pointed out that racial discrimination may be reflected in various social relationships such as intermarriage and residential location, as well as income, prices, credit lines, and such economic dimensions. Schelling's (1971) research discovered that, even if an individual's preferences have a slight discriminative bias, provided that such bias is widely spread, then it can result in very severe social segmentation. What we discuss here is an acquired difference between people caused by institutional factors—the difference between people with urban Hukous and agricultural Hukous.

Since China's reforms began, rapid urban industrialization has attracted large numbers of workers from the countryside, with an increasing number of people with agricultural Hukous transforming into permanent urban residents. Acquired differences formed by such an institution gradually cause the former urban and rural difference to gradually evolve into the difference between people with two types of Hukou within a city. We might as well call this the new "dual society" segmentation in cities. Such a new "dual society" segmentation is pervasively seen in residential location within cities, in the labor market and even at a psychological level.

In terms of residential space, the dual society segmentation in cities is strongly reflected in the existence of the so-called "urban village." The "urban village" itself is the product of the urban–rural segmentation system. Due to the difference between land institutions in the countryside and in the city, when rapid urbanization produces large amounts of urban land through changing land usage, and such land begins to surround what used to be the countryside, the functionality of land in the countryside becomes close to that of urban land, while it is still, in fact, under the management of the former rural collective land institution. Therefore, urban villages begin to emerge. Dirty and messy urban villages with their densely packed, though cheap, housing naturally becomes the residential area of low income migrant workers. Thus, residential segregation between people with different Hukou in cities forms in a distinct manner.

Even without urban villages, the residential segregation of people with different Hukou in cities still exists. Since migrant workers belong to the low income group in cities, their residential location is often clustered in the margins of the urban area and low cost communities in the urban area where the environment is poor and the density of buildings is high. In time, residential segregation within a city will naturally intensify. Under such residential segregation, in low income communities, the interaction between residents may cause various social problems such as relatively severe unemployment, poverty and crime within the community, generating great difficulties for the city's administration. Such residential segregation has economic and socio-psychological reasons. The economic reason is that the high price of housing and services in high class communities has a squeezing effect on low income individuals, which means the average person cannot enter this market. Among the various amenities surrounding high class communities, the most important are expensive schools, hospitals and public security etc., and only high income individuals can afford the corresponding high costs. As for the sociopsychological aspect, being a resident in a high class community gives people a superior feeling and usually brings a more favorable social network. In fact, there have been negative effects from residential segregation during economic development in developed countries as well. During Chinese urban development, the higher the positioning of a community, the more a developer tends to choose locations where the environment is good and high income individuals are clustered. Meanwhile, the high price of housing forces low income individuals to migrate toward the margins of the urban area or the suburbs, and the rapid development of the property market accelerated the formation of residential segregation. In Shanghai, empirical analysis has discovered that there exists non-negligible residential segregation between people with and without local Hukou (Chen, Lu, and Chen, 2012).

Another manifestation of dual society segmentation in cities is the various segmentations or discriminations seen on the labor market. As Knight and Yueh (2004) discovered, job stability is worse for non-local people than the urban locals, and their job turnover is approximately six times that of urban locals. Even if only the urban locals that entered the labor market after the "iron rice bowl" system was smashed are taken into consideration, job turnover for non-locals is still twice that of urban locals. They also discovered that compared with urban locals, job changes for non-locals are more voluntary. In addition to that, education and job experience both increase job turnover, as an increase in human capital provides more employment opportunities for non-locals (Knight and Yueh, 2004). However, even so, the authors believe that it is hard to view the higher proportion of voluntary job changes for non-locals as evidence of any advantage they hold in the labor market. One explanation for this discovery is that urban locals don't want to give up a job they are satisfied with, unless enterprise reforms cause them to face unemployment. A study by Zhang (2010) on the job turnover of Beijing, Wuxi, and Zhuhai discovered that institutional discrimination reduces the job options of non-locals, increasing the cost of job hunting and unemployment. Other than that, compared with urban locals and the mobile population that has been long term urban resident, temporary migrants will work longer at a firm and experience shorter unemployment. Similarly, we should not view this as evidence of any advantage enjoyed by the mobile population that are temporary urban residents and should rather believe this to be caused by non-locals that have just arrived in an unfamiliar environment having to accept work even if the labor conditions are bad. Indeed, Zhang's (2010) study discovered that non-locals will switch jobs more often when they have accumulated enough assets after being in the city for a while.

Of course, migrant workers from rural areas are at a disadvantage even before they enter the urban labor market. In Démurger et al. (2009) decomposition analysis, annual income disparity between urban residents and non-locals who have been employed in the city for a long time, it was discovered that the population effect before entering the labor market was the most important and robust factor in explaining the income disparity between the two groups. Although this study believes that because of this, the source of the urban–rural worker income gap is mainly disparities in aspects such as education opportunities, etc. before entering the labor market, we also cannot deny that such human resource endowment disparity before entering the labor market is also a result of urban–rural segmentation, which we will discuss more in the next section.

More studies stress the discrimination non-local workers face in the cities. For example, Cai et al.'s study discovered that there exists discrimination in the labor market caused by differences in urban and rural identities. Specifically speaking, among the income disparity between rural migrant labor and urban local labor, only 24 percent is explained by the variation in personal characteristics. The remaining 76 percent is explained by discrimination (Cai, Du, and Wang, 2003). This implies that under the current system, increasing migrant workers' level of education cannot fully eliminate the income disparity between rural migrants and urban residents. On the contrary, due to the existence of segmentation in the labor market, the gap between labor with local Hukous and labor without local Hukous may continue to expand. As reported by Zhang (2004), beginning in the mid 1990s, during the next ten years when rural labor began to work in cities on a massive scale, wages for migrant workers in a few relatively developed regions did not change much, but within cities, from 1994 to 2004, the average urban employee's real average salary rose from 4,538 yuan to 11,902 yuan (1994 figures).[8] Meng and Bai (2007) employed payroll data from seven Guangdong enterprises between 2000 and 2004 and discovered that the gap between the wage for migrant workers and Guangdong province's average wage kept increasing, and during this period, migrant workers' wages did not see a significant increase. Yan (2007) employed data from four major surveys in Shanghai to discover that during 1995 and 2003, the pace at which the rate of return on human capital increased differed for non-local labor and local residents, and the gap between the two paces may even trend toward increasing. Zhang and Meng (2007) compared data from 1999 and 2002 and showed that the income gap between rural migrant workers and urban residents is increasing, mainly because of the relative decline in the educational return of migrant workers. These studies all illustrate the fact that the increase in the income gap between workers with different Hukou identities within a city is not just due to the gap in human capital, as it is also, to a certain extent, related to the increase in the gap between return on human capital. Cai and Du (2011) argue that there is some evidence indicating wage convergence between local and migrant workers based on a comparison between the wage growth rage of local and migrant workers. However, as Figure 2 in their paper shows, only migrant workers at the bottom of wage distribution have experienced faster wage growth, while migrant workers at the top of wage distribution have much lower wage growth than local workers. We would rather read this as the result of pro-agriculture policies, which increased the reservation wage of migrant workers, rather than as evidence of wage convergence.

Other than income gaps and gaps between the return on human capital, there also exists dual segmentation in professions, jobs, and industries in China's urban labor market. Labor market segmentation abroad is often related to factors such as sex, race, and union membership (Ashenfelter, 1997; Altonji and Blank, 1999), while dual segmentation in China's labor market is connected to Hukou. Meng and Zhang's (2001) study found that significant disparities in professional status and income levels exist between non-locals and urban residents, and these disparities mostly cannot be explained by the differences between the two types of labor relating to productivity. Employing data from the 5th population census as well as survey data from five cities, Wang's (2005) study classified jobs for urban residents and non-locals into five categories: "self-employed," "public sector worker," "public sector administrative and technical personnel," "non-public sector worker," and "non-public sector administrative and technical personnel." The results of relevant empirical studies show that among the income gap between non-local labor and urban local labor, 59 percent is caused by the income disparity between different jobs, and 41 percent is caused by the income disparity within the type of job. However, 43 percent of income disparity is caused by unexplainable factors such as discrimination. This reflects that non-locals enter into jobs that are relatively low-paid. Chen et al. (2009) have studied the effect of social networks on labor market entry into high income industries in Chinese cities, where *hukou* also plays a significant role as entry barrier. Zhang et al. (2008) and Zhang and Lu (2009) also provide some evidence about the role of social networks in Chinese labor market for migrant workers.

Accompanying dual society segmentation within cities may be difficulty in establishing new urban–rural integrated social networks for migrant workers, and this may even result in mutual distrust between urban and rural residents. Generally, migrant workers use kinship or geographical connections to choose their destination and obtain information regarding employment. Such a social network formed in the countryside is brought to the city and the individual ability of migrant workers to withstand risk is increased through mutual help. In comparison, the existence of the Hukou system often prevents the social organizations, social activities and social services of urban basic level communities from sufficiently digesting migrant workers. Trade unions have not covered migrant workers either. This causes the urban social capital of migrant workers to be limited to within the migrant worker community and no integration between urban residents and migrant workers is generated in terms of social capital. Other than that, the dual society segmentation in cities also fosters distrust among migrant workers toward urban residents and the municipal government, increasing the difficulty of city administration and implementation of public policy, creating immense social losses (Wang, Chen, and Lu, 2009).

Wang, Chen, and Lu (2009) analyzed the determinants of resident trust based on survey data from the Shanghai community with an emphasis on the impact of Hukou identity. The study found that, all other conditions being equal, residents without a local Hukou are more distrustful of their neighbors in the community and most people in society, and their trust in government is even lower. Also, Hukou segmentation's negative impact on trust levels won't decline or disappear with the

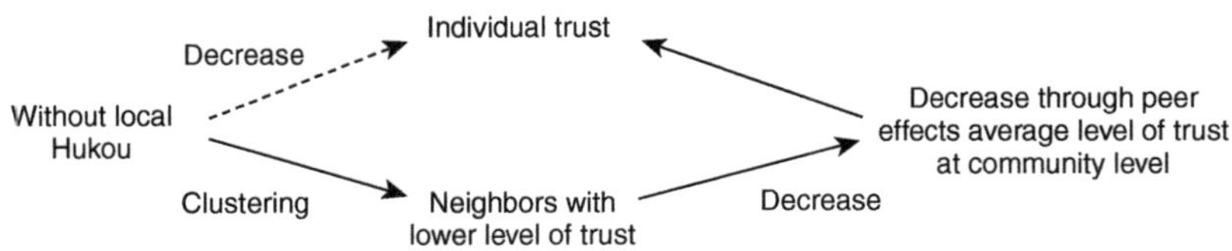

Figure 3.4 The impact mechanism of Hukou on individual trust.

non-local Hukou residents' increase in income or educational level. This is to say, we cannot think that, just by setting a certain threshold, enabling non-locals with relatively high educational level and technical skill to work in the cities, the problem of social discord that may emerge in cities can be solved. The fact is, even if non-locals can obtain higher incomes than local residents, if they are not given the same treatment as urban residents, then these people will still have a significantly lower trust level than urban locals with the same characteristics.

This study by Wang et al. (2009) also found that an individual's trust in society and government is also influenced by the trust of other residents in his or her community. In other words, there exists a peer effect in trust at the community level. Peer effects are produced through social interaction, thus the fact that there is interaction in trust at the community level is not at all surprising. Figure 3.4 depicts the direct and indirect impact of Hukou on individual trust. Hukou's direct impact on individual trust is shown by dotted lines. In addition to that, since there exists residential clustering of Hukous, individual trust is simultaneously indirectly impacted by Hukou, shown by a solid line. Clustering behavior causes communities where non-locals reside to have relatively low trust in other residents in the community as well, which lowers the average trust level of the community's residents. Thus, through the influence of the peer effect, individual trust levels will further decrease. There is current research that believes trust is conducive to increasing the execution efficiency of policy, the provision of public goods and social integration, and fostering cooperation and harmony, which is beneficial to increasing individual satisfaction with life (Delhey and Newton, 2003). Thus trust has a non-negligible effect on promoting harmony and sustainable development in cities. Using trust as an example, we can see the negative impact on the harmonious development of cities produced by dual segmentation in cities caused by Hukou.

But the impact of Hukou on urban harmonious development does not just stop there. Employing Chinese provincial level panel data, Chen's (2010) study discovered that, after controlling for the level of urbanization, non-locals without Hukou significantly increase crime rates. In other words, if there is not distinction between locals and non-locals caused by Hukou, then the level of urbanization itself does not significantly impact crime rates. This implies that abolishing Hukou's dual segmentation is also critical to urban harmony and stability from the perspective of crime prevention. Moreover, studies on individual satisfaction also found that non-local Hukou has a significant negative impact on individual satisfaction (Chen, Xu, and Liu, 2011; He and Pan, 2010). The dissatisfaction of the non-urban Hukou population mainly comes from income and education gaps between people with different Hukou identities. It is worth stressing that the income gap between people with different Hukou identities also has a negative impact on the satisfaction of urban residents with an advantaged status. The explanation is that, if identity-induced income gaps lead to problems such as conflict or crime, it will generate negative impacts on urban Hukou residents as well (Jiang, Lu, and Sato, 2012).

The reason why the "dual society" segmentation that has emerged in cities is so important now is that it is self-enforcing to a certain degree, which is to say, once "dual society" segmentation forms, it may persist and threaten future harmonious urban development. If one thinks about it, suppose non-local labor cannot equally share in the city's provision of such public goods as education and healthcare then such social stratification will be transmitted intergenerationally. The accumulation of human capital and "learn by doing effect" are becoming ever more important nowadays, and due to unequal educational opportunities, if most of the rural population is unable to reach the urban sector's high-skill labor requirements through human capital accumulation, then unequal opportunities to receive education, etc. at the starting point may very well have long-term effects. Simply put, when the children of migrant workers come with their parents to the city, if they are unable to obtain education opportunities equal with the children of urban locals, then they may very well be low income individuals when they grow up and intergenerational income mobility will decline.

Urban–rural segmentation and "dual society segmentation" in cities will also produce a series of Chinese economic structural conflicts on a macro-scale. When policy restricts the process of urbanization, rural labor supply increases relative to the free flow of labor, given rural land and capital, the marginal product of labor decreases, and rural labor's marginal product determines the reservation wage for migrant workers; on the urban labor market, despite receiving institutional discrimination, non-local labor still competes with urban labor, whereupon the low income of migrant workers restrains the urban sector's income growth.[9] Income (and its growth rate) is depressed under a distorted system, but the industrial sector persistently accumulates capital. In the industrial sector, high investment accelerates capital formation, while the industrial sector's absorption of labor is restrained along with urbanization. Thus, the capital–labor ratio constantly increases, pulling up labor productivity (product per unit of labor) swiftly, while in comparison, though *per capita* income is rising, it is dwarfed by the growth in labor productivity.

"Dual society segmentation" in cities also restricts the growth of personal consumption, aggravating China's problem with economic growth depending on investment and exports. Chen, Lu, and Zhong (2010) studied the Hukou system's impact on personal consumption behavior. Based on the Chinese Academy of Social Science's CHIPS (China Household Income Project Survey) data, the study discovered that the marginal propensity to consume of migrants is 14.6 percent lower than urban residents. If the general equilibrium effect of policy adjustments isn't considered, then a relaxation of Hukou restrictions can enable the *per capita* consumption level of 2002 migrant workers to increase by 20.8 percent and the total consumption level to increase by 2.2 percent. This can make up for 47.1 percent of the decline in China's personal consumption-to-GDP ratio between 2002 and 2003. If the same parameters are used in the period between 2000 and 2005, then migrant consumption restricted by the Hukou system is equivalent to 40.8–64.2 percent of the decline in the consumption-to-GDP ratio during this period.

3.2.3 Urban–rural income disparities continuously expand during urbanization

Since "reform and opening," the Chinese agricultural sector's market-oriented reforms have led agricultural development to attain great successes. These reforms mainly include reforms of rural land institutions and price reforms of relevant agricultural products. As Figure 3.5 shows, matching with the increase in food prices in 1994 and 1995, the full marketization of the national food purchase and sale system in April 2002 as well as the eight successive No. 1 Documents regarding the "Three Agricultures" from 2004 to 2011 by the central government, China's grain production and the value-added of the primary industries, all showed rather significant gains.

However, a marked contrast to the rapid growth in grain production or agricultural value-added is the fact that *per capita* income growth for peasants has been relatively slow. From Figure 3.6, it can be seen that urban *per capita* disposable income has always exceeded rural *per capita* pure income. In 1984, the aggregate urban–rural income gap dropped to its lowest point, mainly benefiting from

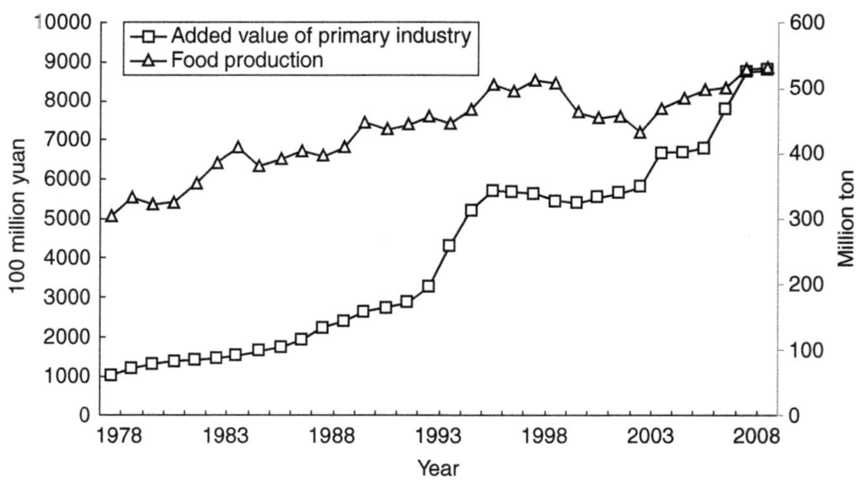

Figure 3.5 The change in food production and primary industries' value-added since "reform and opening".[10]

Data source: Various issues of *China Statistical Yearbook.*

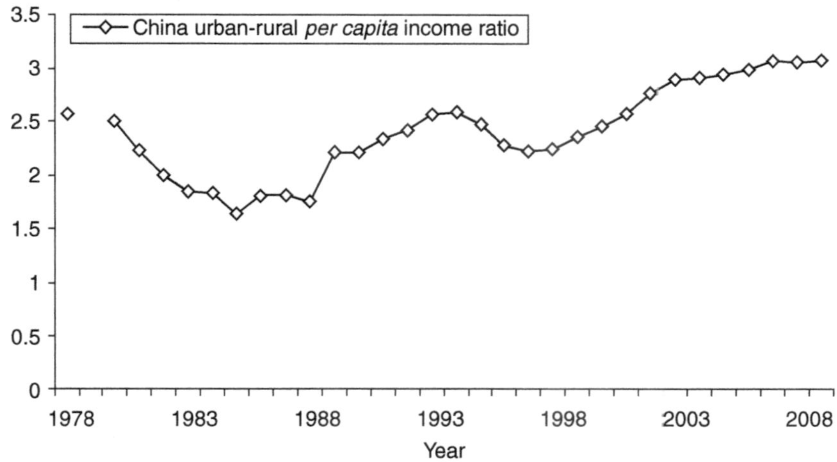

Figure 3.6 Chinese urban–rural *per capita* income ratio (1981–2009).

Data source: 1980–1987 data is from Ravallion and Chen (2007). Other data is calculated from relevant data from the *China Statistical Yearbook* over the years. Urban–rural *per capita* income is already deflated using the urban and rural CPI, respectively.

agricultural reforms that began in 1978 with the household contract responsibility system as its core. Subsequently, the urban–rural income gap continued to expand until 1994; only when the government increased the purchase price for agricultural products did it slightly decline. But after 1997, as the purchase price for agricultural products declined and the price for agricultural products was marketized, the urban–rural income gap expanded again. By 2009, the urban–rural *per capita* real income ratio has reached 3.07. If factors such as healthcare and education subsidies for urban residents are considered, the urban–rural gap would be even greater (Li, 2003).

It is a fact that the urban–rural income gap has already become the foremost reason for China's interregional income gaps, because the level of urbanization in China's relatively backward central and western regions is even lower than that of the eastern regions while the proportion of the rural residents there is higher. From a quantitative point of view, suppose we assume that each province is composed of a rural region and an urban region, then interregional inequality is composed of within-urban, within-rural, and urban–rural inequality. As Figure 3.7 shows, in the interregional income disparity composition expressed in the Theil index, the urban–rural income gap's contribution began to increase in the late 1990s and takes up 70–80 percent of the interregional income gap. This means that if the government can eliminate the urban–rural income gap, then interregional gaps will automatically fall by 70–80 percent. In the factors that lead to interregional development gaps, the importance of the urban–rural gap far exceeds that of the interregional gap between eastern, central, and western regions (Wan, 2007).

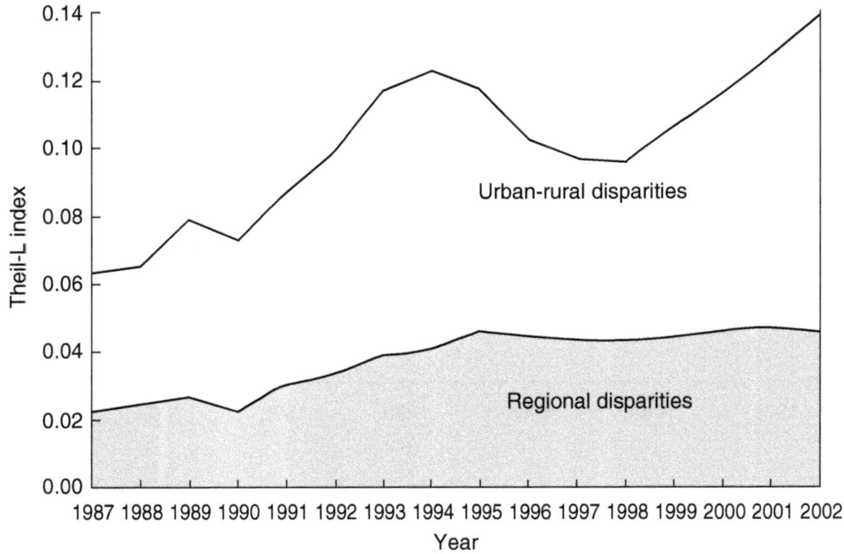

Figure 3.7 Contribution of urban–rural disparities to regional disparities.
Data source: Wan (2007).

Urban-biased economic policies are thought to be an important reason for the formation of urban–rural income gaps. Li (2003) believes the following aspects are non-negligible in the formation of huge urban–rural income gaps: (1) the government's control over the price of agricultural products; (2) the fact that rural residents bore unreasonable tax burdens; (3) the urban–rural labor market's segmentation and the urban labor market's inaccessibility; (4) discriminatory social welfare, and social security. Much literature points out that urban–rural income gaps are related to economic policies with an urban bias (e.g., Yang, 1999; Chen, 2002; Lu and Chen, 2004; Lu and Chen, 2006). In fact, the factors Li (2003) pointed out could all be viewed as the manifestation of economic policies with an urban bias in practice. Yang (1999) also believes that an important reason for the emergence of intensifying disparities accompanying rapid economic growth since the 1978 "reform and opening" in China is the Chinese government's implementation of policies and systems with an urban bias, including restrictions on labor mobility, welfare systems advantageous to urban residents and financial policies that are advantageous to urban residents including inflation subsidies and investment loans for the urban sector. Our research shows that a series of economic policies (such as opening up economically) since "reform and opening" have all enabled the urban sector to benefit more and possess the effect of increasing urban–rural income gaps. Among those policies, the proportion of fiscal expenditures that support agricultural production could significantly narrow urban–rural income gaps, but this proportion displayed a trend toward dramatic decreases in various provinces in the 1990s (Lu and Chen, 2006). Tian (2001) and Yang and Zhou's (1999) studies believe that one reason urban–rural income gaps expand after "reform and opening" is the urban bias of the financial system, as more financial resources were allocated to the cities. Knight and Song (1993) believe that urban-bias policies restrict rural labor from flowing to the cities, resulting in rural poverty being the main manifestation of the poverty issue. The Hukou system endowed housing, healthcare, retirement, and educational benefits to urban residents and these factors all led to urban–rural income gaps. Even if the Hukou system's restrictions on labor mobility are rescinded, these biased policies will cause rural residents that migrate to the city to face higher living costs. Thus labor migration still makes it difficult to alleviate urban-income gaps (Yang, 1999; Yao, 2000). In addition, Yang (1999) argues that implementation of urban-biased policies will not only distort the incentives of the workers in the sector that receives preferential income transfer, healthcare, housing, and educational expenses, but also impact the human capital investment of their children, further increasing urban–rural income gaps. These facts will all be detrimental to future economic growth. Indeed, since the main source of economic growth is the urban sector, then under a fiscal decentralization system, local governments have an incentive to prioritize urban development, give urban interests more consideration and implement urban-biased economic policies. This is supported by empirical research. Yao (2005) employed 2002 county level transfer payment data to study the current fiscal system's influence on interregional fiscal revenue disparities. The study discovered that under the current fiscal transfer system, equalization between interregional fiscal revenues does not exist. Actually, rural regions that have little fiscal revenue will instead decrease efforts to increase the tax base in order to obtain larger transfer payments, while rich urban regions will instead further increase their fiscal revenues since they obtained transfer payments from project support. The result of both actions is fiscal decentralization increasing urban–rural inequality. Carter's (1997) study believes that urban-biased policies generate negative impacts on agricultural production, while also distorting the agricultural products and productive factors market. These negative impacts on agricultural production also have the effect of expanding urban–rural disparities.

3.3 The formation of the Hukou system and the evolution of urban–rural segmentation

From the previous section's analysis, it can be seen that the three characteristics that impact urban–rural development during China's urbanization are all closely related to urban–rural segmentation and the Hukou system. Which is to say, in order to fully comprehend Chinese urban–rural development, we must start from the Hukou system, analyzing in depth the urban–rural segmentation formed therefrom, its consequences, and possible future institutional changes. Orthodox development economics theory on urbanization only analyzes the reallocation of labor from rural to urban, but does not pay sufficient attention to the fact that urbanization may progress under the condition of urban–rural segmentation, and neglects the fact that the meaning of "development" includes equal rights and social integration between migrants and "indigenous" urban residents. In fact, only urbanization that solves these issues can be said to have realized real development. Below, we will review the formation and transformation of the Hukou system from an historical perspective and conclude the evolution of urban–rural segmentation at different levels in order to provide lines of thought for necessary institutional improvements in the future.

There are historical reasons for the Hukou system's formation. However, once the implementation of the Hukou system gradually created two major social groups (urban and rural) with their own interests, the Hukou system becomes hard to dismantle in the short term. Even though the form of segmentation created by the Hukou system changed in different phases, what remained constant is the fact that urban-biased policies were implemented out of the cities' self-interest.

3.3.1 The formation of the Hukou system

Table 3.1 lists systematically the major events and changes of China's Hukou system. It can be seen that, from the founding of the People's Republic of China to year end 1957, there were no policies that placed special restrictions on migration, and the only requirements were the relevant paperwork, mainly out of consideration for population management and crime control. Correspondingly, the period from 1949 to 1958 had the highest frequency of Hukou migration after the founding of the country. One study then pointed out that the urban sector hired increasing amounts of temporary labor from the countryside: "Judging from the situation over the past few years, at least two million persons annually, reaching over three million in 1956. This is a large number. In the past, the procedures and paperwork regulations for hiring were not strict enough and produced many drawbacks. For example, some units or other units in the region already had surplus personnel but when they required temporary labor they didn't make internal adjustments from the personnel they had but hired more externally; some units often overhired, causing severe forced idleness…" (Ma, 1958). From Table 3.1, it can be seen that at year end 1957, the center began to control rural Hukou population migration. The "Order Regarding the Curbing of Blind Rural Population Outflow" policy promulgated in December 1957 clearly used the term "curb." The so-called "blind outflow" of rural population is not really a pointless, blind movement without destination, as they were actually mostly hired by urban units in the form of temporary labor. Therefore, to truly curb "blind movement", the employment system of urban units needed to be regulated. The "Temporary Provisions on Units Recruiting Temporary Workers from the Countryside" promulgated in December 1957 had this goal in mind, stipulating that each unit's recruitment must be centrally allocated by the labor departments. Closely following in January 1958, the center introduced the "People's Republic of China Rules on Household Registration." These rules officially established the Hukou migration approval system and certified settlement system, therefrom the resident and migration freedom endowed by the 1954 constitution was de facto restricted for

Table 3.1 Major events and changes in New China's Hukou system[1]

Date	*Event*
September 1954	1st National People's Congress passed China's first Constitution, provisioning that citizens have "freedom of residence and migration"
December 1954	Ministry of Interior, Ministry of Public Security, and National Bureau of Statistics issued a joint notification requesting that a rural Hukou registration system be established
March 1956	1st National Hukou Meeting requests the establishment of a rather strict Hukou administration system in a short period of time in order to "discover and guard against the activities of counterrevolutionary and various criminal activities"
December 1957	Central Committee of CPC, State Council published "Order Regarding the Curbing of Blind Rural Population Outflow", requiring enhanced Hukou management, controlling population movement
December 1957	"Temporary Provisions on Units Recruiting Temporary Workers from the Countryside" indicated that unit recruitment must be centrally allocated by the labor departments
January 1958	"People's Republic of China Rules on Household Registration" officially established the Hukou migration approval system and certified settlement system, rural population migration to cities was restricted by law for the first time
April 1962	Ministry of Public Security issued "Notification on dealing with Hukou transfer issues", pointing out that: "rural to urban transfers must be strictly controlled; urban to rural transfers should all be approved and not controlled"
January 1975	The "People's Republic of China Constitution" passed in the first session of 4th National People's Congress struck out the clause on "residents possess freedom of residence and migration"
November 1977	The State Council approved and forwarded "Ministry of Public Security Provisions on Handling Hukou Transfers," stressing that "rural migration to cities or towns can transfer agricultural households to nonagricultural households." From then on, "agricultural transfer to nonagricultural" became a buzzword
January 1984	"CPC Central Committee Notification on 1984 Rural Tasks" started the small city and town Hukou system reform, allowing peasants that work, do business or engage in services to be self-sustaining and settle their Hukou in market towns
July 1985	Ministry of Public Security decided to enforce "Temporary Residence Permit" and "Boarding Residence Permit" on the mobile population, enabling temporary residence in cities and towns
September 1985	NPC Standing Committee promulgated "People's Republic of China Resident Identity Card Rules," stipulating that PRC citizens 16 years old and above must get resident identity cards
August 1992	Ministry of Public Security issued "Notification on Implementing Locally Effective Urban Residence Hukou System," beginning to implement "blueprint Hukou"
October 2001	Ministry of Public Security stipulated non-locals with permanent residences and legitimate income in small cities and towns nationwide can all apply for local urban Hukou

Continued

Table 3.1 Continued

Date	*Event*
June 2003	Third Session of 10th NPC Standing Committee passed "PRC Resident Identity Card Law." China's Hukou management began to move toward informational management and identity card management
October 2008	The center proposed comprehensive urban–rural social management, pushing forward Hukou system reforms, relaxing conditions for settling in medium and small cities, enabling peasants who have stable employment and live in the city to orderly transform into urban residents

the first time by law, and was eliminated in the 1975 constitution. Rural population migrating to cities became ever more difficult thereafter.

Why did a Hukou-based urban–rural segmentation system emerge? Yang and Cai (2000) believe that, historically speaking, New China's catching-up strategy became an important reason for urban–rural segmentation policies. At the beginning of New China's founding, in order to demonstrate socialism's superiority and overtake western developed capitalist countries economically, developing industry, especially heavy industry, became a strategic means for the state. Actually, when faced with capital constraints, many governments of developing countries will attempt to employ economic and social policies advantageous to the urban sector in order to develop capital-intensive heavy industry by transferring agricultural profits to the industrial sector and accelerating the process of industrialization, thereby creating the conditions for economic takeoff (Krueger et al., 1992). China's economic fundamentals were still poor, so in order to enable more resources to be transferred from agriculture to industry, the scissors gap between the prices of agricultural and industrial goods maintained by the planned economy becomes a necessary means. Under the scissors gap, the industrial sector's profits are artificially inflated and may be transformed into industrial sector expansion through state investment. In fact, implementing "scissors gap between prices of agricultural and industrial goods" is precisely the policy instrument that forms urban-biased policies, namely, creating disadvantageous policies to agriculture, the countryside and peasants by distorting the prices of goods and productive factors, obtaining agriculture's surplus in order to subsidize industrialization (Schultz, 1978). Such a distorted price system requires the agricultural sector to make great sacrifices for the development of industry. According to Li's (1993) research, between 1955 and 1985, the government transferred 543 billion yuan's worth of agricultural surplus to the industrial sectors by depressing the price of agricultural goods. Since industry is mainly concentrated in the cities, relatively speaking, urban residents benefit more from industrial development. Therefore, the model of agriculture subsidizing industry is hard to maintain in the long term solely by relying on a distorted price system, it is also necessary to prevent free reallocation of labor factors from relatively deprived rural regions to the benefiting urban regions. Thus, a necessary measure is rigorous Hukou management, tying peasants to their land. The Hukou system is exactly the basis for urban–rural segmentation policies, and it was thus born.

Furthermore, the situation of high population, little rural land, and little urban capital also makes urban sectors hope for the implementation of urban–rural segmentation policies. Only through such policies, can large amounts of surplus rural labor not flood the cities, intensifying the already-existing unemployment or underemployment issue in cities. As mentioned before, as urban recruitment of temporary labor became pervasive, around 1956, the government felt the pressure to create employment in cities. The call to "Go to the mountains and countryside" (*Shangshan Xiaxiang*) precisely illustrates this point, as the government wished to decrease urban employment pressure. At the same time, the government enhanced restrictions on peasants' entry into cities. The measures taken against aimless city entrants ranged from the initial suasion to detainment and sending back. As "reform and opening" pushed forward, the aforementioned reasons that created the Hukou system appeared to no longer exist. For example, the People's Commune system has long been abolished, the price system is no longer controlled by the government, the catching-up strategy has mostly been rectified, the redundant labor issue in cities has mostly been solved due to the state-owned enterprise reform, and cities established a rather complete unemployment benefits system. However, the Hukou system did not disappear accordingly.

After "reform and opening," the Hukou system's continued existence is related to the de facto formation of urban and rural interests. The cities are beneficiaries and the countryside is the victim, and the cities hope to continue safeguarding their interests through the Hukou system. This explanation is consistent with the opinions of Lipton (1977) and Bates (1981). They point out that the political structure of most developing countries creates severe asymmetries between the negotiation status and policy influence of urban and rural residents. Yang and Cai (2000) also believe that after the government abandoned the catching-up strategy, the urban residents still pressured the government to maintain their relative well-being. For example, 1978 price subsidies to urban residents reached 1.1 billion yuan and rapidly rose to 7.9 billion in 1979. Starting in 1979, food subsidies to urban residents soared, and when meat prices were liberalized in 1985, these were subsidized. In 1985, the government's total price subsidies reached 26.2 billion yuan and rose to 71.2 billion yuan by 1998, accounting for 7.6 percent of the government's total budget (Yang and Cai, 2000). Moreover, the economic decentralization model implemented during "reform and opening" is also an important reason for the maintenance of urban–rural segmentation. First, under a decentralized system, local governments pursue economic growth with the GDP aggregate as its indicator, thereby showing more interest in industrial development that does better at propelling local economic growth, neglecting to support agriculture and construction in the countryside, and the proportion of agriculture in government expenditures displayed a trend toward dramatic decreases before the twenty-first century arrived (Lu and Chen, 2006). Second, under the current decentralized and municipality-managing-county system, local interests are more closely related to local economic development, thus the local government tends to take into account local interests more than overall interests. Thereby, policies of urban–rural segmentation that are believed to be beneficial to urban residents but detrimental to overall economic development are more easily adopted by local governments (Chen and Lu, 2008). Finally, under economic decentralization, the local government, with the objective of economic development in mind, is more inclined toward protecting the interests of investors, while neglecting the interests of the laborers (especially the migrant workers that do not have local Hukou).

Accordingly, we find that urban relaxations of the Hukou system are often made out of the requirements of urban development or the overall interests of urban residents. In this process, urban–rural segmentation is expressed in correspondingly different forms. For example, recently there have been innovative attempts in aspects such as letting peasants use land in exchange for security (urban resident identity) in Chongqing, etc. Although the exact handling of the issue is different in each area, they all reflect the fact that urban development is restricted by construction-use land quotes, and "purchasing" construction-use land quotas (mainly referring to construction-use land quotas that correspond with rural residential land) becomes the main measure with which to alleviate the urban development bottleneck.

Moreover, the duality of urban–rural land systems is connected to the Hukou system to a certain degree. Rural land is collectively owned and according to current law, all commercial development requires first turning the nature of land ownership into state-owned. Profits generated from such commercial development are often brought by the appreciation of rural land during urbanization. But since rural land cannot directly be commercialized, peasants cannot share in the benefits of land appreciation during commercialization. That is to say that such a dual land system makes peasants unable to share in the benefits from urbanization. This becomes a major institutional source of ever-expanding urban–rural gaps during urbanization. Empirical research discovered that urbanization itself is conducive to absorbing rural surplus labor and is thereby conducive to narrowing urban–rural income gaps. However, at the same time, due the evident decrease in agriculture's proportion of government expenditures, the government did not sufficiently enable peasants that have not been urbanized to share in the fruits of economic development, thereby leading to urban-biased economic policies expanding urban–rural income gaps (Lu and Chen, 2006).

3.3.2 The evolution of urban–rural segmentation

In Chen and Lu's (2008) analysis, urban–rural integration was divided into spatial, social, and political integration, that is, the urban–rural segmentation created by the Hukou policy has different manifestations in different stages. Similarly, we can distinguish between geographical segmentation, labor market segmentation, urban public services segmentation, and segmentation in say over policy.

Geographical urban–rural segmentation first refers to peasants being tied to their land, unable to work in cities for a prolonged period of time. When the Hukou system was first implemented, corresponding to the agriculture subsidizing industry policy and catching-up strategy, the rural population must provide food to the cities at low planned prices, meanwhile, the supply of consumption goods was also restricted by all sorts of coupon quotas in the cities, most important of which is the so-called "grain and oil rationing registration" (*Liangyou Guanxi*). People must change their grain and oil rationing registration when changing their Hukou. In cities, other than maintaining employment relations with employees, firms provided healthcare, housing, pensions and all sorts of other welfare. Due to the different welfare provided by firms of different nature, labor mobility between different firms in cities became highly difficult. Rural population that accounted for an overwhelming majority of the population was even more completely excluded from such a welfare and safety net system. Due to the existence of coupons allocating scarce resources in the cities, in comparison it was even more difficult for labor to move from the countryside to the city. If a peasant wanted to move into the city, he first had to obtain grain coupons. If moving out of the province, he needs to obtain nationwide grain coupons. Since he did not have grain and oil rationing registration in the city, he could not obtain housing, non-staple foods, energy supply, etc. welfare and benefits, so even if one entered the city, it was hard to stay long. It would be a Herculean task for peasants to enter the city and obtain urban Hukou. In the 1977, "Ministry of Public Security Provisions on Handling Hukou Transfers," it was clearly indicated that agricultural Hukou transfers to non-agricultural Hukou and migration to Beijing, Shanghai, and Tianjin from other cities were to be strictly controlled, whereas population migration from towns to cities, from small cities to large cities, from the average countryside to the suburbs also needed to be moderately controlled. Other than the Hukou system and the matching planned purchase and marketing program (*tong gou tong xiao*), the people's commune further extended the state's power to the countryside, enforcing organized rigorous control over rural society, completely tying peasants to their land.

With the rapid development of township enterprises in the 1980s, the non-agricultural proportion of the rural economy rose correspondingly, and the government began to advocate peasants "leaving the farmland but not the homeland, entering the factories but not the cities," and policies for peasants entering the cities, especially small cities and towns, were relaxed. The small city and town Hukou system reform beginning in 1984 allowed peasants that work, do business or engage in services bring their own food and settle their Hukou in market towns. Entering the 1990s, after experiencing three consecutive years in which grain was hard to sell, the government began to allow peasants to "bring their own food" and enter the city to do business and work. Around 1993, every region nationwide successively discontinued use of grain coupons, and the barriers to peasants entering the cities were further cleared. Thereafter, we see progressively larger waves of migrant workers every year. But we should also note that allowing migrant workers to enter cities was also in the cities' interests. Since the 1990s, China's urban economy and manufacturing developed rapidly which accordingly required large amounts of labor. Yet, most urban locals are unwilling to engage in certain types of work, at least they ask for a higher price, so migrant workers filled this gap. In fact, we can indeed see that many construction and factory workers at the construction site or production line are migrant workers from the countryside. The development of services such as restaurants also attracted large amounts of migrant workers.

However, after migrant workers enter the cities and become employed, the geographical urban–rural segmentation still has not fully disappeared. First, as mentioned above, the "village within city" is a distinct manifestation of the spatial urban–rural dual segmentation in cities under the current differing urban and rural land systems. Second, due to the choice in residential location, non-locals tend to choose communities with a high ratio of non-locals, which forms a certain degree of residential segmentation, another manifestation of geographical urban–rural segmentation in cities (Chen, Lu, and Chen, 2012).

As large numbers of migrant workers entered cities, urban–rural segmentation began to be reflected in the labor market. We have previously discussed this. Since non-locals do not have local Hukou, they are disadvantaged in income, employment opportunities, profession, type of work, etc. Such segmentation in the labor market may also take the form of local regulations. Early migrant workers that entered the city were strictly managed by urban departments. If they did not have a temporary residence permit, they were likely to be detained and deported by the urban administrative departments. Some big cities explicitly collected non-local population administration fees from employers that hired migrant workers, and such fees were used to support the local social security funds. Obviously, this is another piece of evidence that city governments formulate urban–rural policies out of the interests of the urban locals. In January 2003, the State Council promulgated the "Notification on Correctly Handling Management of and Services for Urban Employment of Migrant Workers," requiring each region to clean out and remove unreasonable restrictions on migrant employment. Subsequently, each region introduced relevant laws and regulations, requiring removal of administrative approval of migrant worker employment by all types of firms, removal of restrictions on types of migrant worker employment, removal of all approval, and registration programs specifically designed for migrant workers. Of course, as mentioned previously, income discrimination based on Hukou still exists. Though visible discrimination on the labor market disappears easily, invisible discrimination may continue to exist for a long time.

Urban–rural segmentation is also reflected in the connection between Hukou and the public services residents can enjoy. When migrant workers first entered the city, the city development plans did not take their housing, their children's education and social security needs into consideration at all when planning for the provision of urban public goods. In fact, a rather pervasive circumstance was the existence of institutional discrimination more or less in each region toward migrant workers' offspring education, maternity and child healthcare, social security, etc. Public schools in some areas still charge more temporary studying fees and donations from migrant workers' offspring of compulsory education age or simply push these children to market-oriented education institutions. Even though migrant workers often work in jobs with poor working conditions, much needed social security such as work injury and healthcare insurance only covers a minority of migrant workers. More importantly, due to the existence of the Hukou system, they cannot retire in the city. If the urban–rural segmented institutional arrangement is not changed, then in the foreseeable future, after dedicating their prime age to urban development, their retirement will have no guarantees. Although after the introduction of "Notification on Correctly Handling Management of and Services for Urban Employment of Migrant Workers" in 2003, provisions such as "employment and social security for migrant workers should be equal with urban residents," "many forms must be adopted to accept migrant workers' children into local full-time primary and secondary schools, entrance conditions must be equal with local students" began to appear in some local laws and regulations, de facto differences still exist. For example, in terms of social security, the actual circumstances are usually "same city but different program, incompatible across regions," which is to say, the level of social security for non-locals is lower than urban locals, and more importantly is the issue of incompatibility for social security across regions. As of the time of writing of this chapter, if a migrant worker has not paid endowment insurance for 15 years in one area, then when leaving that area, they cannot bring with them the accumulated funds paid by their employers and can only bring the portion paid by themselves. In the offspring education aspect, in recent years, governments in each region have gradually provided basic education for migrant worker offspring out of local fiscal expenditures, but if they want to enter public schools of high quality, non-locals still face huge difficulties from the Hukou issue, and hence may need to pay higher "donations" or use personal connections.

Despite the above facts indeed creating certain barriers to non-locals equally sharing in urban local public services, the most critical urban–rural segmentation in public services is reflected in the issue of university entrance examination (*Gaokao*). Differences in social security are, at most, some monetary losses, and limited offspring school entrance opportunities can often be remedied by money, but no matter how much money non-locals have, even if their children can go to the best local high school, when it comes to Gaokao, students without local Hukou have to return to where their Hukou is and participate in Gaokao there. We know that each university gives local students a larger admission quota, and China's best universities are concentrated in large cities, especially in the Yangtze Delta, Pearl Delta, Beijing, etc. where non-locals are rather concentrated, and these regions are exactly the main destination for non-local migrant population. Non-locals work, pay taxes and social security fees, but their offspring must go back to the province where their Hukou is to participate in the Gaokao, making it hard for them to enjoy the "preferential treatment" of easier admittance of local students to local universities.

We see that the various manifestations of urban–rural segmentation are all disadvantageous to migrant workers, and the reality thus reflected is, compared with the urban population, they relatively lack a say in policy. This is political urban–rural segmentation or segmentation in say over policy and is the most fundamental reason that leads to a series of other forms of urban–rural segmentation. Research by Lipton (1977) and Bates (1981), etc. state that there exists a severe asymmetry in political negotiation status and policy influence between urban and rural residents, which is the result of the political structure in most developing countries, leading to the government often enacting policies with an urban bias.

Under China's political system, a major channel through which the public influences policy is the people's congress system of all levels. However, in the people's congress system, peasants are severely underrepresented. Historically, it has been a long-term problem for peasants and the urban population to have "equal votes and rights." The 1995 revised "Election Law" gives provision that quotas are distributed in accordance to the principle that each rural representative represents four times the number of people than an urban representative. The 17th National Party Congress report proposed "recommending gradual implementation of people's congress elections with equal proportions between the urban and rural population." By 2010, this "equal votes and rights" transformation was finally realized. This reflects that China is currently taking the correct path toward political urban–rural integration. Of course, the path in practice is still long. After equal votes and rights are achieved, can representatives that truly represent the interests of the numerous peasants be chosen? This is the first step toward furthering urban–rural integration. More significant is the second step: are the representatives of the rural Hukous true peasants, or are they urban residents who have resided for a long time in the cities? Can they truly speak for migrant workers and peasants? Under the current approach to elections, migrant workers can only vote for the people's representative where their Hukou is. Representatives produced through such a process, unless they can rise to a rather high level, are otherwise unlikely to have a material impact on urban policy through participating and commenting on policy. An approach that can better realize political or say in policy urban–rural integration would be for the urban people's representative to be produced not by elections according to Hukou but according to all permanent residents, enabling migrant workers from other areas to exercise their political power in the area they live and work in. Only such an approach can truly reflect the city government serving all permanent residents of the city.

3.4 Comprehending China's urban–rural development: the political economy perspective

The first section of this chapter pointed out a unique phenomenon during Chinese urbanization: urbanization lagging behind industrialization, a "dual society" segmentation forming within the cities, and continuous increases in urban–rural disparities until recently. This is totally different from the description by orthodox development, which shows that economic development is the process of urbanization, industrialization, and narrowing income gaps (Lewis, 1954; Mas-Colell and Razin, 1973; Lucas, 2004). The key to solving this "puzzle" is to comprehend Chinese urbanization through a political economy perspective based on the actual background of Chinese urbanization. Below, we will first begin from this logical starting point, construct a theoretical framework to describe Chinese urbanization and correspondingly explain the stylized facts of Chinese urbanization. Then, we need to answer the question: can the transition from urban–rural segmentation to urban–rural integration be achieved spontaneously? Finally, we will demonstrate the importance of viewing Chinese urban–rural development through discussion of the "Lewis turning point."

3.4.1 The political economy context of Chinese urban–rural labor mobility

As mentioned previously, during the process of Chinese urbanization, urban–rural segmentation in say over policy existed from start to finish. This inevitably causes formulation of urban policy to only stem from the interests of urban locals. Song (2004) pointed out that Chinese policies on urban–rural labor mobility have always been policies of urban restrictions and management of rural labor mobility. Cai et al. (2003) concur and state that the urban bias of urban–rural labor mobility policy is formed under the mechanism in which urban residents influence government decisions out of their own interests. So, defining the goal of urban policies as maximizing the interests of urban locals is a reasonable starting point with which to analyze Chinese urban–rural policy. This makes Chinese urban–rural policy formulation take on a distinct shade of political economy – the urban and the rural become two different groups; the former can actively formulate policies advantageous to itself, while the latter, to a greater extent, has to passively accept given institutional arrangements. This is our basic starting point for the theoretical discussions on the urban–rural issue below.[12]

Suppose we assume that the cities only engage in industrial production, which employs labor and capital and there exists a dynamic process of capital accumulation. The countryside only engages in agricultural production, which only uses land and labor and factor accumulation does not exist. The question that follows is how to determine rural labor mobility. Simply put, peasants will choose between working in agriculture in the countryside and working in industrial production in the cities. Here, we make the further assumption that each peasant that works in agriculture can only obtain average agricultural production. This is the reservation wage when peasants migrate to the city to work. We assume that peasants can only obtain the reservation wage in the city, while the wages of urban locals equal their labor productivity. Thus, differentiated wages between the two emerge. This matches empirical findings regarding Hukou income discrimination. Perhaps one may wonder: wouldn't there be competition between firms to hire migrant workers? Won't such competition cause migrant workers' wages to increase to a higher level than their reservation wage? This could be explained with the two following aspects. First, discriminative provisions toward migrant workers' wages, such as the early migrant workers administrative fees, are overall enacted by the city government which is equivalent to depressing migrant worker wages with a monopolistic force. Second, we consider the impact of such income discrimination, then further examine what results would differences in public services lead to if income discrimination did not exist.

The next question is: how does the urban–rural policy formulated by cities manifest itself? We think of this question in the abstract sense of cities controlling the scale of rural to urban labor reallocation. No matter what kind of urban–rural policies are enacted, the eventual effect will be manifested as how many "benefits" migrant workers can receive by entering the city. So, such an urban–rural policy can be embodied in administrative controls such as a system of coupon (like *liangpiao*), rigorous Hukou management (e.g., deportation back home), etc. making costs for peasants entering the city to be high enough, thereby de facto completely prohibiting rural to urban labor mobility. Such an urban–rural policy can be assisted with economic measures, such as levying administration fees or implementing differentiated social security to change the real wage paid to migrant workers, etc. Current research on the Hukou discrimination of income has already provided evidences for this discrimination. In this section, we will temporarily limit the issue under discussion to urban differentiated payment of wages to labor with different Hukou. Below, we will further discuss Hukou discrimination not in the income sense, but also in terms of public services. Under this analytical framework, controlling the income gap between laborers of different Hukou in cities and controlling the scale of rural to urban labor reallocation are two sides of the same coin. The former is the method, while the latter is reflected in the result of the decisions taken on migrant worker mobility.

This urban–rural labor mobility analysis has another characteristic, namely we assume that people with different Hukou in cities have identity-based income gaps which generate social conflicts between the two groups, thereby consuming urban resources. Such unproductive loss is positively correlated with the size of the non-local population. Such resource consumption due to social conflict between urban locals and migrant non-locals is reflected in: (1) such conflicts may cause migrants to damage urban resources; (2) out of guarding against migrants, the existence of such conflicts may cause urban residents to allocate certain resources toward property protection. But such input is unproductive and is therefore wasteful. In the above two mechanisms, the former is the direct damage caused by criminal activity to urban property and although the latter may avoid criminal activity, it cannot avoid wasting resources. No matter which mechanism actually takes effect, the result will be transforming the conflict between urban locals and rural non-locals into output losses. In fact, our assumption holds easily. On the one hand, with the growth in the scale of migrant workers, the total amount of criminal activity may increase. Chen (2010) found that under the conditions of the existing Hukou system, an increase in the proportion of non-locals in urban population will increase crime, after controlling for the urbanization ratio including non-locals as a part of urban population, which does not impact crime. This means that non-locals will not increase crime by adding urban population, but they will do when treated as a discriminated group. On the other hand, even if the total amount of criminal activity does not increase with the number of migrants, as long as the media and city government provide "evidence" that makes urban residents believe unemployment, crime and environmental degradation are all caused by migrant workers, then the social conflict between urban local and rural migrant population will escalate and unproductive urban property protection as well as respective resource consumption will increase.

3.4.2 The decisions of the urban government and their consequences

Starting from the above background, we need to know how the urban government implements its policies on urban–rural labor mobility. This is a process which changes with urban capital accumulation and its basic story is as follows. At the beginning of the reforms, the cities had little capital and abundant labor. At this time, the cities did not lack labor. Therefore, an inevitable result is the cities prohibited rural labor from entering the cities just as they did during the planned system era. As urban capital accumulation increased, labor began to become scarce, in other words, the marginal product of labor significantly increased. At this juncture, allowing one rural laborer to enter the city, on the margin, improves the welfare of urban locals. This is because, on the one hand, agriculture has low *per capita* output due to the existence of massive amounts of surplus labor; thereby the reservation wage of migrant workers is very low and lower than that of the urban marginal labor product. Thus, even if the resource consumption produced by social conflicts in cities is calculated, allowing migrant workers to enter cities is, on the margin, in accordance with the interests of the urban locals.

As capital accumulates, increasing numbers of migrant workers will enter the city to engage in industrial production, which can explain why the scale of urban–rural labor went from non-existent to ever-increasing. However, the cities' policies on urban–rural labor mobility meanwhile also place restrictions on the scale of migrant workers. Of course, this is still out of consideration of the urban interests. The benefits of restricting the scale of migrant workers are mostly embodied in the following two aspects: (1) since more peasants will remain in the countryside, depressing the *per capita* income in agriculture, thereby lowering the reservation wage for migrant workers, enabling cities to obtain larger surpluses; (2) restricting the scale of migrant workers decreases cities' resource consumption from social conflict. The consequences of such institutional restrictions against migrant workers is obstructing urbanization, while urban industry is rapidly developing and the rural surplus labor is not sufficiently absorbed into urban industrialization. This is consistent with the fact which we proposed at the beginning, namely during the process of Chinese urbanization, urbanization lags behind industrialization. This analytical framework has another important conclusion, that is, the marginal labor product of the urban industrial sector increases faster than the growth in migrant workers' income, which explains expanding urban–rural income gaps during urbanization. The underlying reasons are precisely the various restrictions placed by cities on rural labor mobility.

From this we can see that, if we put Chinese urban–rural development under the political economy context of city governments formulating urban–rural policy out of their own interests, then the stylized facts of Chinese urban–rural development can be explained very well.

3.4.3 From segmentation to integration: the endogenous shift in urban–rural policy

Since entering the twenty-first century, faced with ever-increasing urban–rural disparities, the Chinese government has stressed rural development and urban–rural integration. Contemporary China is now at a crossroads. If urban–rural integration is not realized, then lagging urbanization will be disadvantageous to fully employing the urban agglomeration effect and more seriously, prolonged urban–rural segmentation will sow hidden perils for future urban development. Chinese city governments and residents face a test of wisdom today and we must understand that if urban–rural segmentation was once a method to prioritize development of urban industry and protect the interests of urban residents, then sustained urban–rural segmentation not only harms rural residents, but the interests of urban residents are also negatively impacted. Jiang, Lu and Sato's (2012) study has already provided evidence that the income gap between people in cities that have local Hukous and those that do not only makes the migrants unhappier, but also lowers the satisfaction of urban residents. Under the institutional context of urban–rural segmentation, labor reallocation from the traditional and backward agricultural sector to the modern and advanced industrial sector stressed by orthodox development economics does not envelop the entire meaning of all-round economic and social harmonious development.

But a realistic question is: can we realize the transformation from urban–rural segmentation to urban–rural integration? From the previous analyses, we can see that the requirements of urban development indeed become an impetus for urban–rural integration. From the perspective of geographical segmentation, at least partial urban–rural integration has been realized. Although urban–rural segmentation still exists in the labor market, change in labor demand and supply may be a future impetus for urban–rural integration. Suppose that rural surplus labor has been mostly absorbed by the urban sector, with the increase in agricultural production, the reservation wage for peasants will increase. At this time, the competition for labor will intensify between cities as well as between firms within cities and the system may shift toward a direction conducive to urban–rural integration.[13] For example, from 2004 to 2005 and after the 2008 international financial crisis, Chinese domestic media reported heavily on the appearance of "migrant worker shortages" in Guangdong, Fujian, etc., and the shortage phenomenon displayed a trend toward expanding inland. Despite different views on whether this "migrant worker shortage" phenomenon implies that the era of general shortage in Chinese rural labor has arrived, one thing is certain: there indeed exists competition for migrant workers between different regions and such competition will only intensify as urban employment of non-locals increases. In fact, the relative weakening of Pearl River Delta region's competitiveness to the Yangtze Delta region in terms of income level and social security is believed to be an important reason for more migrant workers moving toward the Yangtze River Delta region in recent years and the labor supply to be tight in the Pearl River Delta region.

The content earlier in this section is based on brief descriptions of Chen and Lu's (2008) theoretical model and discussed urban–rural economic development models under the premise of the existence of income discrimination. A question that this begets is: if urban–rural integration is realized in the future labor market, then what will the urban–rural economic development model be like? Liu, Chen and Lu (2010) further answered this question on the basis of Chen and Lu's (2008) theoretical model and we will give a brief description of the study below as well. Now, we will only consider urban–rural segmentation beyond the labor market in terms of public services for people with different Hukous in cities. Presently, although people with different Hukous within cities have equal wages, urban locals have higher *per capita* welfare levels since they can enjoy urban public services.[14] Similar to the assumption earlier in this section, the welfare gap between people with different Hukous will generate capital deterioration. We can further clarify it as: such capital deterioration will accelerate upwards as the number of migrants and the gap in *per capita* welfare levels increases. This is equivalent to saying expansion in urban–rural income (or welfare) gaps will hurt economic growth by decreasing capital accumulation. Theoretically speaking, income gaps can indeed impact economic growth through many mechanisms. For example, expansion in income gaps will produce social and political turmoil, worsening the social environment for investment, meanwhile, as mentioned above, more resources will be spent on protecting property rights and accumulation of productive physical capital will correspondingly decrease (e.g., Benhabib and Rustichini, 1996). The statement that urban–rural income gaps have a negative impact on investment and economic growth is also supported by empirical studies on Chinese data (Wan, Lu, and Chen, 2006).

Now we need to answer: if there is only differentiated treatment in public services, what would be the resulting evolution in the urban–rural economic development path? Since allowing fewer migrant workers to enter the cities is both conducive to lower capital deterioration and obtaining larger capital gains through depressing wages, therefore, similar to Chen and Lu's (2008) findings, we still reach the conclusion that city governments will lean toward using policies to restrain inflow of non-locals. Thus, we can still explain the aforementioned important stylized facts of Chinese urbanization.

The unique contribution of this theoretical model proposed by Liu, Chen, and Lu (2010) is its reply to whether urban–rural segmentation in public services can spontaneously transform into urban–rural integration. Since the above analyses all proceed under the premise of the city government only implementing urban–rural segmentation in the provision of public goods, a possible question would be: even if considerations out of the urban population's interests are taken, at a certain point, would it not be a better option to provide equal public goods and services to non-locals? This is a study of endogenous mechanisms through which urban–rural segmentation institutions transform into urban–rural integration. The results of this theory's research show that if urban–rural segmentation is implemented in the provision of public goods, then as a city's non-local population increases, capital deterioration or social discord induced by the *per capita* welfare gap between locals and non-locals will continuously increase up to a certain stage when the city government would find that allowing non-locals to equally enjoy urban public services actually enhances the interests of the locals. This is because, even if the direct impact of such an action is spreading across more people, the public services formerly enjoyed by the locals, the indirect benefits exceed the losses to the locals caused by the aforesaid effects. Here, the indirect benefits are two-fold. First, the equalization in public services totally eliminates the capital deterioration caused by the discord between the locals and non-locals. Second, increased living standards in the city attract more migrant workers to work in the cities, increasing urban economic growth accordingly, and the total amount of resources cities can commit to public services inevitably increases accordingly as well. This theoretically gives a possibility in which urban–rural segmentation can spontaneously evolve into urban–rural integration under the current institutional framework.

In practice, we can clearly perceive the central government's regard for the relevant interests of migrant workers through recent policy adjustments. In 2000, there were adjustments in the central government's policies toward migrant workers of a more proactive nature. In the "Outline of the Tenth Five-Year Plan for National Economic and Social Development", the government proposed "breaking through urban–rural segmentation institutions;" "reforming the urban and township Hukou system, forming mechanisms for orderly urban and rural population movement, discontinuing unreasonable restrictions on rural labor entering the cities to work." At the end of March 2001, the State Council approved and forwarded the Ministry of Public Security's "Opinions On Pushing Forward Hukou Management System Reform in Small Cities and Towns," which provisioned that in county-level municipalities, prefectural townships and designated towns, as long as "persons (or directly related kin that live together) with legitimate and fixed residences, stable jobs or income sources can all apply for city and township permanent Hukou according to the person's wish." At the same time, it provisions that persons settling their Hukou in small cities and towns "have equal rights and obligations as the original urban residents in terms of school entrance, military enlistment, employment etc., and discriminative policies may not be enacted toward them."

Of course, promoting the above mentioned proactive policy adjustments in practice will be more difficult in the big cities. Judging from Liu, Chen and Lu's (2010) theoretical model, it appears equalization in public services should first occur in big cities, though it has not played out this way in reality. Our explanation is that, in reality, more benefits will be shared due to equalization in public services in the big cities and locals may very well only pay attention to this obvious drawback, while not recognizing as much the potential benefits brought by city harmony and economic growth. However, some cities have indeed actively engaged in institutionally protecting the interests of migrant workers. For example, in December 2006, Shenzhen, one of the cities that has attracted the largest migrant worker population nationwide, implemented its first comprehensive document pushing forward work on migrant workers—"Shenzhen Municipality People's Government's Opinions on Further Enhancing Work on Migrant Workers", proposing the realization of the long-term goal of equal treatment toward locals and migrant workers in the fields of education, housing, rights, social security, training, etc. This "Opinion" requires: integrating migrant worker offspring education into the entire city's education plans and providing a comprehensive plan for their school entrance, unified student roll management, unified education administration, encouraging the solution of the migrant worker offspring education issue through multiple paths; quickening the establishment of the young children hospitalization insurance system and bringing the offspring of migrant workers that live and study in Shenzhen into the hospitalization healthcare program; solving the issue of major illness healthcare payments for migrant workers working in Shenzhen with employers paying the fees; improving the settlement of healthcare insurance, providing major illness treatment for migrant workers that voluntarily return to their original Hukou location with healthcare fee settlement services.[15] Similarly, in Shanghai, another city with massive migrant worker inflows, the first healthcare insurance designated hospital specially directed toward migrant workers from Xi County in Henan Xinyang, Shanghai Anguo Hospital, officially opened in April 2007. Within two months, nearly 200 migrant workers from Xi County entered into insurance programs and received medical treatment there, with some coming from other districts and counties.

Entering 2011, a rather significant change in pushing forward urban–rural integration is the opening of urban public rental housing to non-local Hukou persons. For example, Shanghai recently promulgated the "Implementing the Various Provisions of 'Opinions on the Implementation of Public Rental Housing in Shanghai'." This new policy states the admittance conditions of public rental housing as: "holding 'Shanghai Residence Permit' for over two years and consecutively paid social security fees (including urban social security) for over a year" and "when formulating each district (county)'s admittance conditions, different time lengths may be set for applicants signing labor or employment contracts with employers in this city, of which the time lengths for applicants with this city's permanent Hukou can be set according to the type of work, and the time lengths for applicants holding 'Shanghai Residence Permit' can be set according to the type of residence permit." At least this implies that non-locals have something to expect in terms of enjoying the housing support policy of urban low-income individuals.

3.4.4 Has the "Lewis turning point" emerged in China?

The "Lewis turning point," a term with academic connotations, has increasingly become widely discussed, with the discussions having gone beyond academia long ago. In Lewis's (1954) dual economy model on population mobility and economic development, large numbers of surplus labor are believed to exist in the countryside, thereby even if the urban industrial sector's labor demand further increases, rural labor will still endlessly flow toward the cities at the current unchanged wage level. Only when rural surplus labor with low productivity is totally reallocated will rural labor supply no longer be infinitely elastic. At this point, increase in labor demand will lead to higher incomes. Thus, a seeming "Lewis turning point" with rising incomes as its feature appears.

When we discuss the Lewis turning point, we should accept the assumptions and premises of Lewis's model. However, the facts of China's development have two key characteristics that are incompatible with Lewis's model. The first is Hukou segmentation in cities, and the second is a non-competitive labor market. These two facts precisely determine the characteristics of Chinese urban–rural labor mobility and wage level change. It is also due to this that rising incomes in recent years cannot simply be seen as a "Lewis turning point."

Let us first take a look at urban segmentation in cities. In Lewis's model, urban industrial workers do not have such identity differences as Hukou, whether original urban residents or new rural migrants, they all get industrial worker wages. According to this model, before the "Lewis turning point" appears, urban industrial sector wages are almost constant, and the industrial surplus is all converted into profits for capitalists. However, what actually happened in China is a non-stop increase in wages for urban locals whereas the income of migrant workers did not significantly increase and the gap between the two kept expanding (Meng and Bai, 2007; Zhang and Meng, 2007). Obviously, this phenomenon cannot be depicted merely using the Lewis dual economy model that features labor reallocation from orthodox agriculture to modern industry.

Then let us look at the non-competitive labor market. The Lewis model depicts a perfectly competitive labor market with wages entirely jointly determined by labor market supply and demand curves. Correspondingly, the scale of labor flowing into cities is also jointly determined by market supply and demand. Yet, China's reality is the urban government unilaterally formulating policies disadvantageous to the increase of migrant workers' incomes (e.g., collecting migrant worker administration fees, different social security systems in one city and incompatibility across regions, etc.) and the differentiated access of urban public services between people with different Hukous also restricted migrant worker inflow. Under restricted labor mobility, rural labor cannot sufficiently move outwards and rural marginal productivity is depressed, which further depresses the reservation wage of migrant workers. In the urban labor market, the low wage requirements of migrant workers impact urban labor wages (Liu and Zhao, 2009). That is to say, in the Chinese labor market, urban regions change the real wages non-locals receive through various policies and the wages are not entirely determined by market supply and demand.

The above two points imply that using the "Lewis turning point" to comprehend rising wages in China's labor market is inappropriate. If we change the assumptions of the Lewis model and consider urban–rural segmentation on different levels in dual labor mobility, then this will turn into a "Lewis + Marx" political economy model of a dual economy. By "Marx," we mean urban residents are like a privileged social class in China. In this model, the city government decreases the degree of urban–rural segmentation and labor further flows from the countryside, which will be reflected in an increase in wages. Such an increase in wages is essentially the consequence of policy adjustment and does not show that rural surplus labor has been entirely reallocated (Chen and Lu, 2008). More important is the fact that a few critical facts of the Chinese economy at the macro-level cannot be explained by the Lewis model, while they can be explained with political economy models. These facts mainly include the "three great gaps," namely: the gap between urbanization and industrialization, the gap between the growth rate in urban and rural resident incomes and the gap between the speed with which income and productivity rises (Chen and Lu, 2008).

The reason why the applicability of the Lewis theory needs to be re-thought is because drawing the conclusion that the "Lewis turning point" has arrived just because migrant workers' wages have increased may be misleading in practice. If the Lewis model is simply applied to China's economy, then of course China has entered the era of accelerated industrial upgrade. However, if it is viewed through political economy models, then what China presently needs is to achieve integration between residents of different Hukou in cities by promoting urbanization through changes in land, Hukou, etc. institutions. These policies can further create job opportunities for low-skilled individuals in the countryside, avoiding labor market distortions and even a disconnection between industrial upgrade and labor supply created by current policies.

3.5 Conclusion and direction of future research

For a long time, the orthodox "dual economy theory" has been used to comprehend Chinese urban–rural economic development. This theory states that industrialization is the basis of urbanization and that it is exactly the development of modern industry that enables labor to be liberated from traditional agricultural production, entering the city to engage in productive activities in manufacturing and services. However, this traditional "dual economy theory" can explain neither the "dual society" that is currently taking shape in Chinese cities nor the important stylized facts of Chinese urban–rural economic development such as urbanization lagging behind industrialization and continuous increases in urban–rural disparities.

Comprehending Chinese urbanization and urban–rural development requires the aid of the political economy perspective and requires starting from the context of China's urban–rural segmentation system. The Hukou system is the basis of China's urban–rural segmentation and its creation has special historical circumstances. But this system's long-term existence is due to the fact that cities already have a vested interest in it. Despite different manifestations of urban–rural segmentation, from the earliest geographical segmentation to the later labor market and urban public services segmentation, they all reflect the unilateral control over urban–rural policy by cities acting out of their own interests, of which the underlying fundamental fact is the unequal voice over policy by urban and rural residents.

Ever since the geographical urban–rural segmentation was broken, although the scale of China's urban–rural labor flow became greater and greater and China's labor market is often believed to be the most flexible and market-oriented, when cities formulate urban–rural policy unilaterally as a vested interest entity, a labor market that appears to be competitive is under the control of the cities in a certain sense. Due to the existence of the Hukou policy, rural surplus labor can enter cities to work but not truly settle down in the cities. Thus, a portion of rural surplus labor is still tied to the land, agricultural modernization is hindered, *per capita* agricultural output remains at a low level and artificial depression of the reservation wage of migrant workers is institutionalized. This is the crux in comprehending the relative backwardness in the level of urbanization, continuously increasing urban–rural income disparities and the existence of dual society segmentation in cities all along. Once we comprehend Chinese urban–rural economic development through a political economy lens, then we can find that only using a term such as the "Lewis turning point" to depict Chinese urban–rural development is not enough.

This chapter has theoretically explored the possibility that such an urban–rural segmented system may spontaneously transform into an urban–rural integrated system. Since ever-increasing urban–rural income disparities will generate negative impacts on the harmonious developments of cities, then there will eventually be a day when compared with the welfare loss of urban residents induced by such a system, discontinuing Hukou segmentation and allowing non-locals to equally share in urban public services lowers urban residents' welfare by a smaller extent, thereby an endogenous change in the system spontaneously occurs.

We might as well start from concrete policy objectives and attempt to propose four standards by which new urban migrants and original urban locals can construct a harmonious city together, namely: mechanisms for the appealing of interests, wider coverage of social security, no discrimination in public services and equalization of development opportunities. "Mechanisms for the appealing for interests" means disadvantaged groups should have spokespersons for their interests, allowing their will to directly influence government decisions and allowing them to have channels to express appeals when their interests are harmed or when they have received unfair treatment. "Wider coverage of social security" refers to the coverage of all permanent urban residents into the basic social security system, whether or not the resident has local Hukou or whether or not the resident has urban Hukou. "No discrimination in public services" requires the government to expand public fiscal expenditures and provide urban services in a nondiscriminatory fashion, especially in the aspect of offspring education. "Equalization of development opportunities" implies that even if there are status and income differences between individuals, each person's development opportunities (especially human capital investment and labor market treatment) should be equal institutionally.

Finally, it needs to be pointed out that Chinese urban–rural development still leaves much for us to research. We need more research in at least the following few aspects to provide answers. First, it is undeniable that early urban–rural segmentation policies had a positive impact on promoting urban growth, so can China's development path from urban–rural segmentation to urban–rural integration be an economically optimal developmental path? Second, this chapter sets out from a political economy perspective and discusses urbanization theory based on urban–rural segmentation. Although the context under discussion is a story on China, the interactive mechanisms between social integration and economic growth behind the story have general theoretical implications. Under this research direction, could there be an even more general theory in the future that can depict the process of urbanization, economic growth, urban–rural income disparity changes and transformation in urban–rural segmentation policy? This is a challenging research direction. Third, does the evolution from urban–rural segmentation to urban–rural integration provide evidence to the existence of the Kuznets curve based on Chinese experience? This chapter's analyses from the perspective of urbanization gave an affirmative answer to a certain degree and it is worth expecting further empirical research. Finally, urban–rural integration and a more mobile labor force is indeed beneficial to economic agglomeration, as on the one hand factor income equalizes across regions, and on the other hand, the scale economy effect will play a larger role in cities. What impact will this change have on interregional development? Especially, how does such impact take place, what impact does it generate on such different dimensions as economic aggregates and *per capita* levels, and which policy conditions are relevant to these impacts? These questions require further answers.

Notes

1 The urban–rural income gap has declined in recent years, but whether this is sustainable is still in question.

2 *Data source*: *Comprehensive Statistical Data and Materials on 50 Years of New China*, published by China Statistics Press in 2000, p. 38.

3 *Data source*: "China Statistical Abstract 2007" (China Statistics Press).

4 In the diagram, the basis for urbanization rate calculations is urban population. 1980 figures are Hukou statistics. 1985, 1988–1989 figures are based on adjusted 1990 Census data; 1990–2000 figures are based on adjusted 2000 Census figures; 2001–2004 figures are extrapolations based on population change surveys. 2005 figures are based on national 1 percent population sample survey data. National Bureau of Statistics 2005 National 1 percent population sample survey form fill-in instructions provide that the surveyed subject is: all persons in the neighborhood drawn to participate in the survey. It is further indicated that this refers to persons residing in the survey neighborhood in the evening of October 31 2005, no matter where their Hukou was registered, including Hukous in the local xiang, township or neighborhood as well as all non-local population, in other words, current population. It could be seen that in the 2005 proportion of urban population, non-local urban population was already included. It could be inferred that figures according to the Census or adjusted sample population survey data, proportion of urban population already includes non-local population without local Hukous.

5 For a detailed explanation, see the previous footnote. But there also exists some research that states statistics on urban population may possibly overestimate the level of urbanization. For example, Tao and Xu (2005) pointed out that the official statistics of population urbanization include rural migrant population that resides in cities for over six months. However, we know that such migrant population often only temporarily resides in the city. Other than that, they also point out that a portion of landless peasants that saw their land requisitioned did not actually obtain urban Hukous, and there exists a portion of peasants that were included in the urban population due to statistical discrepancies.

6 *Data source*: State Statistical Bureau of China: "The First Report on the Main Statistics of the Sixth Population Census," www.stats.gov.cn/tjfx/jdfx/t20110428_402722253.htm
7 The level of industrialization shown does not include the proportion of services.
8 Data comes from the *China Statistical Yearbook* 2005.
9 Liu and Zhao (2009) employed census data on 1 percent of the population in 2005 and discovered that the impact of non-local labor on urban sector wages is larger than the impact on the employment rate, which demonstrates the reaction of urban labor to non-local labor is limited and is mainly reflected in a lower reservation wage and not giving up job opportunities. Many people simply believe that the existence of rural surplus labor causes the rural sector's marginal product to be depressed and this determines the low income of migrant workers in the city. This is only half true, as it should be noted that in an economy where there are policies restrictions on the size of labor flows, the quantity of rural surplus labor is not just determined by the factors in textbook theories, such as total rural labor, urban capital accumulation, etc. It should be understood that in China, the degree of restraint institutions such as Hukou has on urbanization directly impacts the quantity of labor that can be reallocated to the city. Of course, it in turn impacts a series of variables such as the quantity of rural surplus labor, the reservation wage of migrant workers, etc. (For theoretical research refer to Chen and Lu, 2008).
10 The value-added of the primary industries is deflated to 1978 comparable prices with the primary industries' domestic product index.
11 Most of the content in the table comes from "Qiushi Forum," at: http://bbs.qstheory.cn/action-model-name-bianti-itemid-8.html
12 This theoretical framework is based on Chen and Lu (2008).
13 However, it needs to be pointed out that if urban–rural segmentation policies are unhelpful in enhancing the educational level of the rural population and urban development's requirements for human capital becomes ever higher, especially when industries that require cheap labor transfer toward other developing countries than China, then the transformations conducive to achieving urban-rural integration on the labor market may be severely delayed or even unlikely to appear.
14 Assuming urban capital gains are fully converted into public services for urban locals.
15 "Shenzhen: Migrant workers will become equal with local Hukou residents," "China Youth Daily," December 8 2006.

References

In English

Altonji, Joseph G. and Rebecca Blank, 1999, "Race and Gender in the Labor Market," *Handbook of Labor Economics*, ed. Orley Ashenfelter and David Card, Vol. 3C, 3143–3260. Amsterdam: Elsevier Science, North-Holland.

Arrow, Kenneth J., 1998, "What Has Economics to Say About Racial Discrimination?" *Journal of Economic Perspectives*, 12(2), pp. 91–100.

Ashenfelter, Orley, 1997, "Union Relative Wage Effects: New Evidence and A Survey of Their Implications for Wage Inflation," *Employment, Labor Unions and Wages. The Collected Essays of Orley Ashenfelter,* Volume 1, ed. Kevin F. Hallock, 79–108. Cheltenham: Edward Elgar.

Au, Chun-Chung and J. Vernon Henderson, 2006a, "Are Chinese Cities Too Small?" *Review of Economic Studies*, 73(3), pp. 549–576.

Au, Chun-Chung and J. Vernon Henderson, 2006b, "How Migration Restrictions Limit Agglomeration and Productivity in China," *Journal of Development Economics*, 80(2), pp. 350–388.

Bates, Roberts, 1981, *Markets and States in Tropical Africa*, Berkeley, CA: University of California Press.

Becker, Gary, 1957, *The Economics of Discrimination*, Chicago: University of Chicago Press.

Benhabib, J. and A. Rustichini, 1996, "Social Conflict and Growth," *Journal of Economic Growth*, 1(1), pp. 129–146.

Cai, Fang and Yang Du, 2011, "Wage increases, wage convergence, and the Lewis turning point in China," *China Economic Review*, 22, pp. 601–610.

Cai, Fang, Yang Du, and Meiyan Wang, 2003, *The Political Economy of Labor Mobility*, Shanghai: Shanghai Sanlian Press, Shanghai People's Press.

Carter, Conlin A., 1997, "The Urban-Rural Income Gap in China: Implications for Global Food Market," *American Journal of Agricultural Economics*, 79(5), pp. 1410–1418.

Chen, Aimin, 2002, "Urbanization and Disparities in China: Challenges of Growth and Development," *China Economic Review*, 13, pp. 407–411.

Chen, Shuo, 2010, "Judicial Inputs and Crime Prevention in Transitional China," *Working Paper*, Division of Social Science, The Hong Kong University of Science and Technology.

Delhey, Jan and Newton, Kenneth, 2003, "Who Trusts? The Origins of Social Trust in Seven Nations," *European Societies*, 5(2), pp. 93–137.

Démurger, Sylvie, Marc Gurgand, Shi Li and Ximing Yue, 2009, "Migrants as Second-class Workers in Urban China? A Decomposition Analysis," *Journal of Comparative Economics*, 37, pp. 610–628.

Fujita, Masahisa, J. Vernon Henderson, Yoshitsugu Kanemoto and Tomoya Mori, 2004, "Spatial Distribution of Economic Activities in Japan and China," *Handbook of Regional and Urban Economics*, ed. J. V. Henderson and T. Jacques-François, 2911–2977. Oxford: Elsevier.

Henderson, J. Vernon, 2009, "Urbanization in China: Policy Issues and Options," Report for China Economic Research and Advisory Programme.

Jiang, Shiqing, Ming Lu and Hiroshi Sato, 2012, "Identity, Inequality, and Happiness: Evidence from Urban China," *World Development*, 40(6), pp. 1190–1200.

Knight, John and Lina Song, 1993, "The Spatial Contribution to Income Inequality in Rural China," *Cambridge Journal of Economics*, 17, pp. 195–213.

Knight, John and Linda Yueh, 2004, "Job Mobility of Residents and Migrants in Urban China," *Journal of Comparative Economics*, 32, pp. 637–660.

Krueger, Anne, Maurice Schiff, and Alberto Valdes, eds, 1992, *The Political Economy of Agricultural Pricing Policy*, Volume 5, Baltimore, MD: Johns Hopkins University Press.

Lewis, W. A., 1954, "Economic Development with Unlimited Supplies of Labour," *The Manchester School*, 22(2), pp. 139–191.

Li, Wei, 1993, *Agricultural Missing Surplus and Industrialization Capital Accumulation*, Yunan: Yunan People's Publishing House, December, 1st edn.

Lipton, M., 1977, *Why Poor People Stay Poor: Urban Bias in World Development*, Cambridge, MA: Harvard University Press.

Lucas, R.E., 2004, "Life Earnings and Rural-Urban Migration," *Journal of Political Economy*, 112(1), pp. 29–59.

Ma, Wenrui, 1958, "An Illustration about 'the Sate Council's Temporary Rule on Each Departments' Recruiting Jobbers from Country'," *Shan Xi Zheng Bao*, 1, pp. 21–22.

Mas-Colell, A. and A. Razin, 1973, "A Model of Intersectoral Migration and Growth," *Oxford Economic Papers*, 25(1), pp. 72–79.

Meng, Xin and Junsen Zhang, 2001, "The Two-Tier Labor Market in Urban China Occupational Segregation and Wage Differentials between Urban Residents and Rural Migrants in Shanghai," *Journal of Comparative Economics*, 29, pp. 485–504.

Meng, Xin and Nansheng Bai, 2007, "How Much Have the Wages of Unskilled Workers in China Increased?: Data from Seven Factories in Guangdong," *China: Linking Markets for Growth*, ed. Ross Garnaut and Ligang Song, Canberra: ANU E Press and Asia Pacific Press, 151–175.

Schelling, Thomas, 1971, "Dynamic Models of Segregation," *Journal of Mathematical Sociology*, 1, pp. 143–186.

Schultz, T. W., 1978, *Distortions of Agricultural Incentives*, Bloomington: Indiana University Press.

Song, Hongyuan, 2004, "Policy Issues Analysis on Rural Labor Mobility," *Equity and Social Equality in Transitional China*, ed. Yang Yao, 307–335. Beijing: China Renmin University Press.

Tian, Qunjian, 2001, "China's New Urban–rural Divide and Pitfalls for the Chinese Economy," *Canadian Journal of Development Studies*, 22(1), pp. 165–190.

Wan, Guanghua, 2007, "Understanding Regional Poverty and Inequality Trends in China: Methodological Issues and Empirical Finding," *Review of Income and Wealth*, 53(1), pp. 25–34.

Wan, Guanghua, Ming Lu and Zhao Chen, 2006, "The Inequality–Growth Nexus in the Short and Long Runs: Empirical Evidence from China," *Journal of Comparative Economics*, 34(4), pp. 654–667.

Yan, Wei and Jiang Nan, 2007, Land Usage Must be Strictly Saved in Accelerating the Process of Urbanization, *Social Science Weekly*, August 9.

Yang, Dennis Tao, 1999, "Urban-Biased Policies and Rising Income Inequality in China," *American Economic Review*, 89(2), pp. 306–310.

Yang, Dennis Tao and Fang Cai, 2000, "The Political Economy of China's Rural-Urban Divide," Working Paper No. 62 of Center for Research on Economic Development and Policy Reform, Stanford University.

Yang, Dennis Tao and Hao Zhou, 1999, "Rural-Urban Disparity and Sectoral Labor Allocation in China," *Journal of Development Studies*, 35(3), pp. 105–133.

Yao, Shujie, 2000, "Economic Development and Poverty Reduction in China over 20 Years of Reform," *Economic Development and Cultural Change*, 43, pp. 447–474.

Yao, Yi, 2005, "Equalizing or Not? Assessing the Intergovernmental Grants and Their Incentive Effects in China's Fiscal Reform," working paper accepted by Far Eastern Meeting of the Econometric Society, July 9–12, Tsinghua University, Beijing, China.

Zhang, Dandan and Xin Meng, 2007, "Assimilation or Disassimilation? – The Labour Market Performance of Rural Migrants in Chinese Cities," paper presented at the 6th Conference on Chinese Economy, October 18–19, CERDI-IDREC, Clermont-Ferrand, France.

Zhang, Huafeng, 2010, "The Hukou System's Constraints on Migrant Workers' Job Mobility in Chinese Cities," *China Economic Review*, 21, pp. 51–64.

Zhang, Xiaohui, 2004, "The Supply of Cheap Labor isn't Unlimited: An Investigation into the Truth of Labor Shortage in the Pearl River Delta Region," *China Business Times*, October 20.

In Chinese

Cai, Fang, and Justin Yifu Lin, 2003, *Chinese Economy*, Beijing: China Financial & Economic Publishing House.

Chen, Binkai, Ming Lu and Ninghua Zhong, 2010, "Household Consumption Constrained by Hukou System," *Economic Research Journal*, S1, pp. 62–71.

Chen, Zhao and Ming Lu, 2008, "From Segmentation to Integration, the Political Economy of Urban–rural Economic Growth and Social Harmony," *Economic Research Journal*, 1, pp. 21–32.

Chen, Zhao, Ming Lu and Hiroshi Sato, 2009, "Who Entered Higher Wage Industries? The Role of Social Network, Hukou and Labor Productivities," *Economic Research Journal*, 10, pp. 121–132.

Chen, Zhao, Ming Lu and Jingmin Chen, 2012, "Hukou and Residential Segmentation: A New Challenge to Public Management in Urban China," *Fudan Journal* (Philosophy and Social Sciences), 5, pp. 77–86.

Chen, Zhao, Tong Xu and Xiaofeng Liu, 2011, "Hukou Identity, Urban Labor Market Segmentation and Citizens' Subjective Well-being: Micro-Evidence from Communities of Shanghai," *World Economy*, 4, pp. 79–101.

He, Lixin and Chunyang Pan, 2010, "Explaining China's 'Easterlin Paradox': Income Difference, Opportunity Inequality and Citizens' Subjective Well-being," *Management World*, 8, pp. 11–22.

Li, Shi, 2003, "Reviews and Prospects on the Studies of China's Personal Income Distribution," *China Economic Quarterly*, 2(2), pp. 379–403.

Liu, Xiaofeng, Zhao Chen and Ming Lu, 2010, "Social Integration and Economic Growth: Endogenous Policy Transition Theory of Urbanization and Urban Development," *World Economy*, 6, pp. 60–80.

Liu, Xuejun and Yaohui Zhao, 2009, "The Impact of Labor Migration on Urban Labor Markets in China," *China Economic Quarterly*, 2, pp. 693–710.

Lu, Ming, 2011, "Reallocation of Rights of Construction Land Usage Across Areas: New Engines of China's Economic Growth," *World Economy*, 1, pp. 107–125.

Lu, Ming and Zhao Chen, 2004, "Urbanization, Urban-Biased Policy and Urban–rural Inequality," *Economic Research Journal*, 6, pp. 50–58.

Lu, Ming and Zhao Chen, 2006, "Urbanization, Urban-Biased Policies and Urban–rural Inequality in China: 1987–2001," *Chinese Economy*, 39(3), pp. 42–63.

Tao, Ran and Zhigang Xu, 2005, "Urbanization, Rural Land System and Migrant's Social Security," *Economic Research Journal*, 15, pp. 45–56.

Wang, Hui, Zhao Chen and Ming Lu, 2009, "Hukou, Social Segmentation and Trust: Evidence from Shanghai," *World Economy*, 10, pp. 81–96.

Wang, Meiyan, 2005, "Employment Opportunities and Wage Gaps in the Urban Labor Market: A Study of the Employment and Wages of Migrant Laborers," *Social Science in China*, 5, pp. 36–46.

Yan, Shanping, 2007, "Human Capital, Systems and Differences in Wages: A Case Study on the Dual Labor-Markets in Large Cities," *Management World*, 6, pp. 4–13.

Zhang, Yuan and Ming Lu, 2009, "Is Social Network Helpful to Promoting Migrant Workers' Wages?" *Management World*, 3, pp. 45–54.

Zhang, Yuan, Rui Li, Hou Wang and Liang Chen, 2008, "Social Network and Wages: Positive Analysis Based on the Sample of Migrant Workers," *World Economic Papers*, 6, pp. 73–84.

Part III

Segmentation and integration

4 Labor mobility and laggard urbanization under institutional restrictions

Ming Lu

4.1 Introduction

Glass-curtain walls are invisible but existent. Institutional barriers to urban–rural and interregional labor mobility are like a glass-curtain wall situated between rural and urban residents.

Urban–rural and interregional labor mobility in China is a major event in the global economy that has occurred over the past 20 years. It pertains to the repositioning of the global economy, the take-off of the Chinese economy and its regional structural adjustments. The objective of this chapter is to review the background, facts and research progress of Chinese labor mobility. In order to focus on analyzing rural–urban labor mobility, we neither cover urban resident migration to the countryside nor do we cover inter-city migration of urban residents.[1] The interregional labor mobility referred to in this chapter is the cross-region migration of rural labor to cities. A cursory review of the facts of and empirical studies on Chinese labor mobility reveals that the discoveries of most studies are highly consistent with the classic theories on labor mobility and similar empirical studies. Economic theory views labor mobility as the result of rational decision-making, while the individuals (or households) that make these decisions face institutional constraints that differ. In recent empirical studies on Chinese labor mobility, some puzzles were discovered (see section 4.6 for details), and this chapter will indicate that if institutional constraints in Hukou, land, social security, etc. are cast aside when viewing the facts and conclusions of empirical studies, then economic phenomena occurring in China cannot be truly comprehended.

Given the above understanding, this chapter heavily emphasizes institutional constraints as the crucial link to comprehending Chinese labor mobility. Due to the existence of institutional constraints for labor mobility and asymmetric information in the labor market, which is related to the former, social interaction becomes an important factor that impacts labor mobility and provides explanations for some puzzles regarding Chinese labor mobility. This chapter believes that the phenomena in Chinese labor mobility that differ from other countries and regions should draw sufficient attention from researchers and policymakers. Only thus can we have a more accurate grasp on the present and future of Chinese labor mobility and the trend of global and Chinese economic development, and correctly formulate relevant policies related to labor mobility, urbanization and urban development.

The chapter will unfold as follows: in the second section, we will analyze the background of Chinese labor mobility through the perspective of globalization and domestic market segmentation. The third section will summarize the main facts of Chinese urban–rural and interregional labor migration. The fourth section is an analysis of the determinants of labor mobility based on classic theories and findings by empirical studies. The fifth section is an analysis of human capital externalities, economies of scale and migration. This theoretically determines the direction of labor migration, but corresponding empirical studies have only just begun. The sixth section will emphasize socioeconomic analysis of labor mobility and conclude the impact on labor mobility of such factors as social interaction, social networks etc. The final section concludes and discusses the policy implications of existing research. There have already been many literature reviews on Chinese labor mobility (e.g. Cai et al., 2003; Zhao, 2004; Sheng, 2008; Zhou, 2010). Compared with them, the second, third and fourth sections of this chapter somewhat overlap with existing literature reviews, thus the marginal contribution of this chapter is mainly the fifth and sixth sections, which stress the new directions of relevant research.

4.2 Globalization and domestic market segmentation: the background of Chinese labor mobility

Just like labor migration that took place all across the world, Chinese labor migration is also the result of rational decision-making by individuals or households after weighing the costs and benefits. Comprehending the background of this rational decision-making is the key to understanding relevant phenomenon and facts.

Before "reform and opening," in order to achieve capital accumulation in the industrial sector and rapid industrialization, China adopted a "scissors gap" system that depressed the relative price of agricultural goods and boosted the relative price of industrial goods. At the same time, the wages of the urban industrial sector were also artificially suppressed in order to increase the profit potential and capital accumulation of industrial sectors. In cities, accompanying low wages were a series of state-sponsored pension, healthcare, education, housing etc. welfare programs. The real income of urban residents is much higher than that of rural residents which created a huge incentive for rural residents to migrate to the cities. Meanwhile, the urban industrial sector's lean toward heavy industry caused the job-creation ability of industrial sectors to be low and since achieving full employment for urban residents was already difficult enough, the government rigorously restricted peasants from migrating to the cities through the Hukou system (household registration system), and even attempted to alleviate urban employment pressure through the "Go to the mountains and countryside" (*Shangshan Xiaxiang*) movement.

After "reform and opening," the Chinese economy began to gradually participate in the globalization process. The comparative advantage of relatively high quality and low cost labor enabled China to enter the labor intensive link of the global supply chain, especially export-processing manufacturing. Since situating export-processing manufacturing near the eastern and southern coastal regions can save transport costs, thus much foreign capital is concentrated in the coastal provinces. Accordingly, most newly created jobs in manufacturing are in the coastal provinces. This causes Chinese labor to migrate from the countryside to the cities while also migrating from inland to the coast (Duan et al., 2008).

In the 1980s, labor migration was still strictly constrained by the Hukou system. At that time, since the economy was still in a state of shortage, urban residents still purchased grain with grain coupons (*liangpiao*) and even if peasants entered the city to find work, they had to bring their own food or obtain grain coupons in the city, which made the costs of labor migration very high. On April 1 1993, the state increased the purchase and sale price for grain; on May 10, the control over prices of grain and cooking oil were relaxed in Beijing and grain coupons finally withdrew from the stage of history. Guangdong had already realized a stable transition after relaxing grain price controls a year earlier. "Grain and oil rationing registration" (*liang you guanxi*) was no longer a restraint on labor mobility and the scale of labor migration grew rapidly.[2] Duan et al. (2008) made an estimate according to the population censuses (or minor censuses) over the years, using persons separated from their Hukou location as a criteria,[3] and estimated the migrant population to be 6.57 million, 18.10 million, 21.35 million, 70.73 million, 102.29 million and 147.35 million in 1982, 1987, 1990, 1995, 2000 and 2005, respectively, among which the most evident acceleration in the migrant population growth rate appeared during 1990 and 1995.

Urban–rural and interregional labor migration in China provides much labor for the manufacturing industry, propels economic growth and is conducive to narrowing urban–rural income gaps. After computing relevant figures, Sun (2004) reached the conclusion that migrant workers made a great contribution to the economic development of coastal regions. The GDP created by migrant workers is equivalent to 32 percent of Beijing's economic aggregate; 31 percent of Shanghai's; 30 percent of Guangdong's; 11 percent of Jiangsu's; 17 percent of Zhejiang's; and 16.8 percent of Fujian's. One-sixth to one-third of the social wealth in these provinces was created by migrant workers. Urbanization and rural resident migration to cities is the key to narrowing urban–rural income gaps. Li (1999) was among the earliest to use data from sample surveys to study the income growth effect and income distribution effect of labor migration. He pointed out that rural labor migration to cities has a positive impact on income growth and income distribution within the countryside and can play a positive role in restraining increases in urban–rural, interregional and even intra-countryside income gaps that general income redistribution policies cannot replace. Correcting unequal income distribution that emerges during economic development through rural labor migration is undoubtedly an effective rational choice that meets the requirements of marketization. Besides, such a choice is not just harmonious with the whole point of market-oriented economic reforms, it is also consistent with the strategic goal of urban–rural economic development integration.

Migrant workers are believed to have given a shock to the urban labor market, especially during the mid to late 1990s. On the one hand, large numbers of migrant workers flooded the cities, on the other hand labor market reforms in cities rapidly progressed, and many enterprises fired redundant employees, which led many people to believe that migrant workers took the jobs from urban residents. It must be pointed out that the oft-held belief that migrant workers had a squeezing effect on the employment of urban residents is not supported by empirical studies, or if there was any impact, the main impact it had was on urban wages. Li's study (1997a) showed that rural labor migration's negative impact on the urban economy is infinitesimal and its employment substitution effect is only around 0.1. In the long run, it will depress the trend of urban employee wages rising too fast. Li (1997b) provided a theoretical model and policy simulation analysis showing that the entry of rural labor will increase the income gap between skilled and non-skilled laborers within cities, which is a correction of the traditional wage administration apparatus. Liu and Zhao (2009) employed 1 percent population census data from 2005 and discovered the impact of migrant workers on urban wages is larger than its impact on the employment rate, which means that there is a limited reaction of urban labor to migrant labor. This limited reaction is mainly reflected in reduction of reservation wages, but not giving up job opportunities.

Although the impact of migrant labor on urban employment is exaggerated, labor market segmentation policies according to Hukou were still formulated and implemented in cities. Such identity discrimination from Hukou policy still exists and the difficulty of obtaining urban Hukou varies in different regions. Wu et al. (2010) constructed a "Hukou Settlement Threshold Index," with four directly administered municipalities, 27 provincial capitals and 15 cities of other levels and found that cities with high Hukou Settlement Threshold Index readings are mainly situated in the eastern coastal regions, while the cities with low index readings are relatively concentrated in the central regions. One view is that China's present-day labor mobility appears to be very free and interregional labor mobility is especially uninhibited. In fact, without local urban Hukous, migrant locals face at least the following "three discriminations and one barrier" in Chinese cities, which increases the costs of labor migration, thereby restricting labor mobility and urbanization. Specifically speaking, the "three discriminations" are as follows:

1. *Employment*. At the beginning, city governments attempted to directly restrain firms from recruiting migrant labor through policy restraints, the main method of which was levying extra fees against firms that recruit migrant labor, while at the same time limiting migrant labor entrance to a few specific industries. Today, although most discriminative policies have been rescinded, it is almost impossible for people without local urban Hukous to enter the civil service and high income monopolistic industries. By employing quite recent China Health and Nutrition Survey (CHNS) data for 2006, it can still be observed that good jobs are almost all occupied by labor with

urban Hukous and, even in an inferior labor market, labor with urban Hukous are at an advantage (Qiao et al., 2009). Yao and Lai (2004) studied data from surveys on Zhejiang's firms and rural labor, and discovered that Hukou discrimination can explain 20–30 percent of the difference in labor and capital relations between urban and rural workers. Other than in terms of labor contracts, migrant workers face Hukou discrimination in aspects such as wages, pensions, healthcare, unemployment insurance and trade union participation. Zhou and He (2009) found that urban regions' attraction of rural migrant labor is closely related to the ownership structure of the urban economy. After the 1990s, rural labor that migrated to the cities tended to work outside the traditional system and few could squeeze into the state-owned enterprises. Démurger et al. (2009) employed 2002 nationwide sample data to find that in cities, the annual wage of local residents is 1.3 times that of the long-term rural migrant workers. Further decomposition of this differential shows that the migrant population has a comparative advantage in the private sector and entering the public sector cannot increase their average wage, vice versa for local residents; other than that, the population factor itself is very important, which reflects that the wage differentials between the two groups mainly come from differences before entrance into the labor market (e.g., education opportunities) but not the market itself. The Hukou system's discrimination is not only reflected in wage differentials, but also in discrimination toward job opportunities. Based on Beijing, Wuxi and Zhuhai survey data, Zhang (2010) discovered that Hukou discrimination reduced the job opportunities for the migrant population, and increased the costs they faced while job hunting and unemployed. Therefore, although short-term migrants might mainly work in jobs locals are unwilling to perform, they change jobs less often; only when they have stayed in the cities for a while and have accumulated enough assets, will they change jobs more frequently.[4]

2. *Social security*. China's current social security system operates independently on local fiscal support, thus each city's social security mainly serves its local residents. Even if some cities have social security provided especially for non-locals, the level provided is low and participation by migrant labor is not high.[5] It is especially worth mentioning that, although the Chinese government is endeavoring to make personal endowment insurance accounts transferrable across regions, this has still not been achieved. Under the current system, a non-local worker must pay for 15 years in the location where he works to enjoy pension insurance. For payments under 15 years, if a non-local worker leaves the location where he works, he can withdraw from the program, but can only take away the accumulated funds of his individual contribution in his personal account whereas only a small proportion of the comprehensive contribution paid by the firms can be taken away. This is not a small loss for non-local workers.
3. *Public services, especially education for offspring*. Some public services provided by the local government are not discriminatory and are hard to become discriminatory, e.g., greenery and public transportation. However, there are

> still some public services that are linked to Hukou, among which education is especially important. Beginning in kindergarten, without a local urban Hukou, one cannot attend a public kindergarten at the rate charged to local residents. In the compulsory education phase, under the former system, local public schools did not admit children of migrant workers, and even if they did, the fees would be higher, which produced many schools specifically for the children of migrant workers. Since these schools have limited funds, the educational quality provided was evidently poorer. Presently, compulsory education phase schools have already opened toward migrant workers' children, but the good schools do not offer migrant workers children equal treatment. Other than that, cities where higher education resources are concentrated often tend to allocate a much larger university admittance quota to local students and the children of migrant workers must return to their original Hukou location and participate in the higher education entrance examination there, making them face even more severe competition, which creates evident unequal opportunities for higher education and blocks intergenerational income and social mobility.[6] A connected result is high school education in cities (especially large cities) is, de facto, not equally accessible to the non-local population.[7]

Urban–rural and interregional labor mobility also faces barriers from the land system. In order to guarantee "food security," a certain amount of farmland must be maintained, thus a "construction-use land quota rationing system" was implemented with a total quota for construction-use land development every year that could not be exceeded. Though the allocation of this quota has to take into consideration the different economic development needs of every region, an approach that is inclined toward egalitarianism leads to the following situation: coastal regions that need construction-use land more, do not have enough quotas, whereas the inland regions have land quotas, but cannot make sufficient use of them and the efficiency of land use is low. Suppose a market exchange mechanism exists and regions with higher demand for land quotas can buy them from regions with relatively abundant land quotas, then more farmland can be converted into construction-use land, whereas the regions that have sold construction-use land quotas have to increase the reserves of agriculture-use land. In practice, this is called "the balance between occupation and compensation" of agriculture-use land. At the time of writing, cross-provincial "balance between occupation and compensation" of agriculture-use land is still prohibited. Moreover, peasants that enter the city have their own rural residential land, which naturally corresponds to the construction-use land quotas by demolishing their housing. In practice, peasants that enter the city are still prohibited from transferring the construction-use land quotas corresponding to their rural residential land at home. In other words, the rural residential land use rights peasants have at home cannot be traded as an asset.

The aforementioned institutional constraints increase the costs of labor migration and create barriers for the integration of migrant workers into the cities.

As time passes, the new generations of migrant workers have evidently stronger aspirations than the previous generation of becoming urbanized, therefore, the barriers placed by institutional constraints on their integration into the cities is even more significant (Liu and Cheng, 2008).

4.3 Mobility and migration: the basic facts of Chinese labor mobility

When discussing the issue of Chinese urban–rural and interregional labor mobility, the terms "mobility" and "migration" are used interchangeably. Strictly speaking, the two are different, as short-term "migration" is only "mobility," whereas only a long-term change of residence can be truly called "migration." The problem is, when a system is undergoing major changes, whether or not something is long-term migration is hard to judge from present circumstances, as a change in the system could turn short-term mobility into long-term migration. In international academia, at first it was hard to accept the interchangeable use of mobility and migration when discussing the topic of Chinese labor mobility, but now people are used to using the term "migrant" to refer to short-term migrants that have not obtained urban Hukou. Of course, this portion of the population mainly refers to permanent residents that reside in the cities for over half a year every year, thereby differentiating them from the truly short-term mobile population. In comparison, those non-locals that have already obtained local urban Hukous are no longer treated as "migrants."[8] In the discussion below, we will not make any distinction between mobility and migration.

Although all sorts of institutional urban–rural and interregional segmentations make Chinese labor migration far from free and sufficient, but in the process of industrialization, urbanization and globalization, labor migration has still developed on a large scale. If the most important characteristics of Chinese labor mobility are to be summarized, I believe there are mainly three points.

First, on a time dimension, the scale of Chinese labor migration is ever increasing. Up to the early 1990s, urban–rural and interregional labor migration was still on a very small scale, but today, the scale of Chinese labor migration is tremendous. The key turning point was the abolition of grain coupons in the early 1990s. The second nationwide agriculture census shows that migrant workers employed outside the countryside reached 132 million people in 2006, about 25 percent of aggregate rural labor. Add to this the 80–90 million rural laborers who are working in local non-agricultural industries, then the amount of rural labor reallocated to the non-agricultural sector is around 210–220 million, which exceeds 40 percent of aggregate rural labor.[9] Commonsense tells us such large-scale labor migration has already exceeded the entire population of Japan. Based on surveys by the National Bureau of Statistics, Sheng (2008) provided a time series estimate of the scale of labor migration, which can reflect the changes in the scale of labor migration more clearly (see Table 4.1).

Second, on a spatial dimension, the direction of labor migration is mainly from inland rural regions to eastern and southern coastal cities. The agglomeration of Chinese industry toward coastal regions accompanies the agglomeration of labor

Table 4.1 Scale of rural labor migration (1985–2005)

Year	*Aggregate rural labor (10,000)*	*Local rural non-agricultural labor (10,000)*	*Proportion of non-agricultural labor in countryside (%)*	*Rural migrant labor population (10,000)*	*Migrant labor proportion of rural labor (%)*	*Rural population migrated into cities (10,000)**	*Urbanization rate calculated according to Hukou population (%)*
1985	37,065	6,233	16.8	800	2.2	260	20.2
1986	37,990	6,682	17.6	900	2.4	248	20.9
1987	39,000	7,050	18.1	1,050	2.7	235	21.6
1988	40,076	7,361	18.4	1,250	3.1	290	21.9
1989	40,939	7,558	18.5	1,500	3.7	212	22.1
1990	42,010	7,694	18.3	1,800	4.3	198	21.6
1991	43,093	7,916	18.4	2,140	5	228	21.8
1992	43,802	8,380	19.1	2,592	5.9	221	22.2
1993	44,256	9,209	20.8	2,752	6.2	222	22.9
1994	44,654	9,798	21.9	2,888	6.5	223	23.6
1995	45,042	10,257	22.8	3,000	6.7	254	24.3
1996	45,288	10,378	22.9	3,400	7.5	257	24.9
1997	45,962	10,610	23.1	3,890	8.5	299	26
1998	46,432	10,804	23.3	4,936	10.6	339	26.3
1999	46,897	10,955	23.4	5,240	11.1	377	26.7
2000	47,962	11,224	23.4	7,600	15.8	507	26.8
2001	48,229	11,532	23.9	9,050	18.8	258	26.8
2002	48,472	11,873	24.5	10,470	21.6	780	27.2
2003	48,884	12,080	24.7	11,390	23.3	694	27.5
2004	49,676	12,753	25.6	11,823	23.8	520	27.5
2005	50,387	13,480	26.7	12,578	24.2	600	27.7

Note: *"Rural population migrated into cities" refers to the rural population that has obtained urban Hukou, since this number is far lower than the migrant labor population, therefore the urbanization rate calculated according to Hukou population is far lower than that calculated using permanent residents.
Data source: Sheng (2008, p. 9, Table 1–4 and p. 72, Table 4–1).

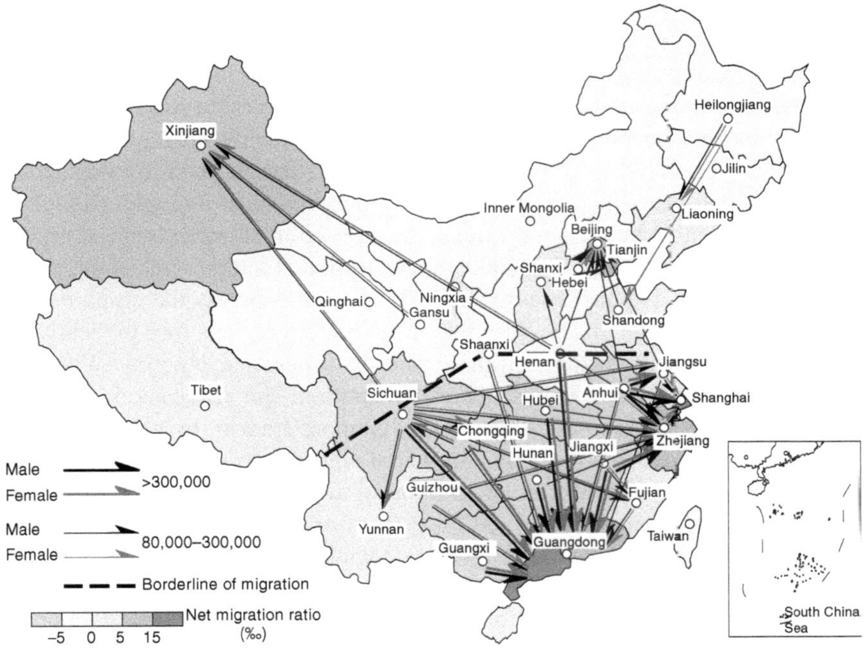

Figure 4.1 1995–2000 Main direction and flow of interprovincial migration.
Data source: Ding et al. (2005).

(mainly rural surplus labor). Analysis based on data from the 2000 population census shows the destination of labor migration is highly consistent with the provinces with the fastest industrial growth in 2001 (see Figure 4.1). Yangtze Delta's Jiangsu, Zhejiang and Shanghai and the Pearl Delta's Guangdong province became the main destinations for interregional labor migration. Wang and Liu (2007) employed 1 percent sample data from the Fifth Census and 1 percent sample data from the Fourth Census to compare the basic circumstances of interprovincial population migration between the Yangtze Delta and Pearl Delta region and found that the Pearl Delta region almost entirely exhibited economic attraction, whereas the Yangtze Delta not only exhibited economic attraction but also strong social attraction, as "marriage immigration" and "alongside migration of family relatives" with mainly females is also an important reason for interprovincial migration into the Yangtze Delta region.

So, is labor migration necessarily interprovincial? Zhu (2004) believes that there are two ways out for Chinese agricultural surplus labor: migrating to the cities (regional mobility) and working in non-agricultural productive activities locally (professional mobility). Compared with regional mobility, working in non-agricultural professions in rural areas is a more accessible and lower cost activity; in terms of participation in productive activities, the two types of mobility are substitutes; from a time dimension, the two types of mobility grow simultaneously and a "complementary" relationship exists between them. Cai and Wang's (2003) study points out that, due to the constraints of the Hukou system, once rural labor mobility exceeds regional boundaries, the costs increase dramatically. In 2000, 56.3 percent of the national migrant population went beyond their county, 42.7 percent went beyond their prefectural level municipality and region, and 26.4 percent went beyond their province. The 10 percent data for the Fifth Population Census of 2000 shows that the proportion of intraprovincial migration is high at 73.4 percent, but looking from the trend, the proportion of interprovincial migration is increasing. From 1987 to 2000, the proportion of interprovincial migration within the eastern regions rose by nearly 15 percent, whereas the proportion of migration from central and western regions to eastern regions rose by nearly 24 percent, the latter overshadowing the former by 9 percentage points. When we describe the direction of interprovincial migration, the tendency for eastern regions to be the migration destination is even more evident. In 2000, nearly 65 percent of interprovincial migration in eastern regions was concentrated in other eastern provinces, 84 percent of interprovincial migration in central regions was concentrated in eastern regions and 68 percent of interprovincial migration in western regions was concentrated in eastern regions.

Under what circumstances will interprovincial labor migration appear? Early research found that the tendency for labor to migrate outward is stronger for provinces with huge populations and relatively backward economies. Investment from abroad to local can directly create many employment opportunities and also indirectly create job opportunities through economic growth, which has a reducing effect on labor's tendency to flow outwards. Meanwhile, those who choose migration (especially short-term migrants) are more willing to choose those places that have attracted more foreign capital as their destination; moreover, the tendency of residents to leave their hometown is stronger for regions with better developed township enterprises, while it is the opposite for rural residents with higher levels of education, as they are more willing to stay in their hometown, whereas short-term migrant and poorly educated labor tends to migrate toward provinces that have better developed township enterprises (Liang and White, 1997). Xiao and Liu (2007) employed 9.5 percent sample data from the "Fifth Census" and regional data from the 2000 *Chinese Statistical Yearbook*, to study the factors that impact interprovincial labor migration. They consequently found that between the inflow and outflow provinces, labor tends to migrate to provinces that are richer, densely populated, more open, with more investment, more developed in secondary and tertiary industries, geographically closer, and within the same economic belt. Cai, Du, and Wang's (2003) research discovered that the scale of labor migration from central provinces to eastern provinces is larger than the scale of labor migration from western provinces to eastern provinces, which shows that distance apparently impacts interprovincial labor mobility.

Third, in terms of the mode of labor migration, China's rural to urban labor migration displays a "migratory bird type" characteristic of short-term migration and not family relocation. Li (2005) believes that China has two systems of social stratification, an urban society stratification system and a rural society stratification system. These two systems operate almost independently and do not intersect, even though large numbers of migrant workers migrate between cities and the countryside, as, due to a series of Hukou-related restrictions, they cannot become integrated into urban society. In the city, workers from the countryside do not possess equal rights with urban residents, as they cannot enjoy equal rights with urban residents in terms of employment, social security, offspring education, etc., which greatly increases the uncertainty for income from working out of town, lowering the real income of working. Meanwhile, since living expenses are high in the city, entire family relocation of rural migrant labor is restricted. Besides, migrant workers are not recognized by urban residents and cannot obtain comfort from family members, as they cannot bring their families with them, making it hard for them to fulfill their family obligations. Therefore, they face a difficult psychological adjustment in the city. This explains why the majority of migrant workers hope to return home in the future, why they strive to obtain local non-agricultural employment opportunities, and why relatively well educated people tend toward employment in local non-agricultural industries instead of going out (Zhao, 1997; Zhao, 1999a,b). However, if a man relocates his entire family, and the land in his countryside hometown becomes idle, then he may lose land contract rights, so, leaving the old and women in the hometown, thus preventing land from becoming totally idle, is a rational choice. According to estimates by Sheng (2008), labor that relocates their entire family only constitutes of about 5 percent of the total rural labor in 2005, whereas the proportion of migrant labor is 20 percent. However, there is also data that shows, as time passes, trends such as the migrant population becoming more permanent, entire family relocations and more migrant females are gradually becoming more evident (Roberts, 2005; Duan et al., 2008; Hou, 2009).

In order to display the characteristics of migrant labor more directly, we can take a look at the comparison between the personal characteristics of rural migrant worker and non-migrant worker samples in CHIPS 2002 data.[10] From Table 4.2, it can be observed that, in terms of personal characteristics, migrants are more likely to be male and young, with the proportion of the married even lower and the health condition even better. In terms of household characteristics, migrant workers have more family members and less land *per capita*. In terms of population structure, migrants have families with fewer children aged six to 12 and more seniors aged 65 and above. Although the figures reported here are only descriptive statistics, if these variables are used as explanatory variables of labor migration tendency to conduct econometric analysis, then these explanatory variables all significantly impact labor migration tendency (Chen et al., 2013).

It is important out that China's urban–rural and interregional labor migration takes place under urban-biased economic policies. In the planned economy era before "reform and opening," urban-biased economic policies mainly employed the agricultural sector's surplus for the industrial sector's accumulation, thereby paving the way for rapid industrialization. After "reform and opening," urban-biased economic policies are the result of urban residents and governments

Table 4.2 Comparison between migrant and non-migrant samples

Variable	*Total samples 16,401 (average)*	*Migrant labor samples 2,675 (average)*	*Non-migrant labor samples 13,726 (average)*
Personal characteristics			
Female (Yes=1)	0.4459	0.3727	0.4602
Age (Years)	34.6344	27.1166	36.0995
Married (Yes=1)	0.6993	0.4501	0.7479
Good health (Yes=1)	0.8688	0.9458	0.8539
Bad health (Yes=1)	0.0328	0.012	0.0368
Household characteristics			
Number of laborers in household	2.7678	3.3544	2.6534
Land *per capita* in household (Mu)	2.0937	1.6258	2.1849
Children under 6	0.1818	0.2011	0.178
Children from 6–12	0.3354	0.2819	0.3458
Seniors above 65	0.1806	0.1966	0.1775

Note: If a variable in the table is a dummy variable (namely "Yes=1", "No=0"), then the average is the ratio, e.g., females account for 44.59 percent of the sample.
Data source: Chen et al. (2013).

maximizing their own interests, and its fundamental institutional background is the massive migrant worker population having almost no influence on urban–rural policies (Chen and Lu, 2008). This is reflected in the issue of urban–rural and interregional labor migration by the city government's setting up of urban–rural segmentation policies in employment, social security, education, etc., artificially increasing the costs of labor mobility and creating urban–rural income gaps. It is due to this that another phenomenon unique to China emerges, namely, while the scale of urban–rural and interregional labor migration has grown ever larger, China's urban–rural and interregional income gaps had not only not decreased, but also show a trend towards increasing until recent years. At the same time, if we look at the process of China's urbanization, we can discover that China's urbanization lags behind its industrialization.[11] In China, disparities in the size of GDP between cities are clearly increasing, whereas disparities between the size of cities as indicated by population, non-agricultural population, or constructed area lingers at a relatively low level. This illustrates that the trend toward agglomeration of economic activities is rather evident, while the trend of agglomeration in population and land is still limping along. From the perspective of urbanization, the process of urbanization as measured by area is clearly faster than that measured by the growth rate of the non-agricultural population. If we shift from the eastern regions to the central and western regions, the disparity between the two becomes even larger, which shows that in many inland cities, urbanization in terms of land has not brought about simultaneous urbanization in terms of population, illustrating the low efficiency with which land is used (Lu, 2011).

4.4 Determinants of labor migration: new migration economics

Starting from the fundamental logic of modern economics, decisions regarding labor migration are essentially an individual cost–benefit trade-off. An important path to increasing utility is increasing income and Zhu (2002) indeed discovered that the income disparity between agricultural and non-agricultural employment significantly impacts the probability of working out of town, which fits the Harris-Todaro model (Harris and Todaro, 1970). In the 1980s, new migration economics began to develop. This school of thought states that labor migration decisions are not only individual decisions, but also household decisions. In order to demonstrate this theoretical progress, we will review the empirical studies, summarize their conclusions, and compare the similarities and differences between the findings of existing studies and our own.

We will first begin with personal characteristics. If the return on education is higher in industry and services, then one theoretical inference is that education can increase the tendency for labor to migrate from the countryside to the city. In household decisions, better educated family members who have comparative advantages in industry and services will be sent to do migrant jobs. Empirical studies mostly support this theoretical inference, though there are some findings that differ. Early studies find that formal education's impact on increasing the probability of labor migration is insignificant, though it has a positive impact on increasing the probability of employment in local non-agricultural industries (Zhao, 1997; Zhao, 1999b); Zhao (2003) found that no educational level has a significant impact on labor migration. Nevertheless, many empirical studies provide evidence that education significantly impacts labor migration. Du and Park (2003) also found that the highest educational level of a household has a positive impact on migration; Zhu's (2002) research found that education only has a positive impact on the reallocation decisions of males, while there exists no such impact for females. We employed the CHIPS 2002 data in our study and found that, after controlling for other individual, household and village characteristics, different levels of education have different positive effects on migrant workers. If we use illiterates as a reference, then middle school education increases the probability that rural labor will work out of town most (7.13 percent or more), followed by primary education (5.25 percent). Compared with illiterates, the tendency for individuals with relatively higher education to work out of town actually shows small increase (the figures for technical schools or higher education schools is 4.75 percent; high school education is 4.9 percent). Of course, this could be due to the fact that rural residents with high school education and above find it easier to obtain urban Hukous and therefore are no longer classified as rural residents that "work out of town" (Chen et al., 2013).

Age is an important factor that influences labor migration. Wang and Liu's (2007) study discovered that, due to the strong constraints imposed by dual institutions such as the Hukou system on population migration, interprovincial population migration is, to a large extent, mainly reflected in young laborers working as migrant labor and the age distribution is highly concentrated in the 20–30 year bracket.

The impact of age on labor migration is both positive and negative. On the one hand, an increase in age brings experience, which enables higher returns to be gained; on the other hand, older migrants have higher psychological costs and the period in which they benefit from migration is short (Zhao, 1999b). At the same time, the lack of social security and public services that migrant workers face in the city will cause bigger problems as age increases. If we take these effects into account comprehensively, the impact of age on the probability of migration may be an inverted U, namely first ascending then descending. Zhu (2002) and Sheng's (2008) study discovered that age does, in fact, display an inverted U relationship with the probability of labor migration. We used the CHIPS 2002 data ourselves and found again this inverted U relationship. After controlling for other factors, 33-year-old labor has the highest probability of migration (Chen et al., 2013).

Empirical studies consistently find that the impact of gender and marriage on reallocation decisions is significant. Females and married people have higher migration costs (including monetary costs and psychological costs), at the same time, in household decision-making, males and singles obviously have a comparative advantage when it comes to working out of town. Zhao (1997) discovered that the migration probability for females is lower than that for males by 7 percent. Zhao (1999b) points out that compared with the average level, 37.6 percent of married rural labor are unwilling to relocate. Similarly, Zhu (2002) also discovered that married status has a significantly negative impact on labor migration. In our own study employing CHIPS 2002 data, we found that the migration probability for females is 4.45 percent lower than that for males, and compared with people of other marital status, the migration probability for the married group drops enormously by 11.76 percent (Chen et al., 2013). Since the data we employed is newer than Zhao (1997, 1999b) and Zhu (2002), by combining these studies, a point could be made that the effect of gender and marital status on labor migration is declining. This is consistent with the aforementioned trend that females and entire family relocation in labor migration is increasing.

From the perspective of land and population, all else being equal, more laborers and less land per household implies that the relationship between population and land is tenser, and the probability of labor migration will be increased. Studies by Zhao (1997, 1999b) and Zhu (2002) find that households with more land *per capita* have a lower probability of labor migration. Du and Park's (2003) study on labor migration of the poor also found that household land *per capita* has a negative impact on migration. In our own study employing CHIPS 2002 data, we found that for every additional laborer in a household, the individual labor migration probability decreases by 4.01 percent, meanwhile, for every *mu* increase in household land *per capita*, the individual tendency to migrate decreases by 1.25 percent (Chen et al., 2010).

Of course, government policy variables affect the relative gain between working in agricultural production at home and working outside and are important parameters that affect labor migration decisions. Zhao's (1997, 1999a) studies show that during one period in the 1990s, the burden of agricultural taxes lowered the real income of agricultural production, causing a portion of capable and strong labor to flow into non-agricultural industries, affecting agricultural production. In recent years, the Chinese government has placed heavy emphasis on the "Three Agricultural" issues (issues of agriculture, peasants and rural area) and has abolished agriculture taxes for the first time in thousands of years, with some grain farmers even receiving subsidies from the government. These policy measures conducive to increasing income from agricultural production brought back some migrant workers to growing crops again. Meng's (2010) study discovered that policy adjustments after 2004 indeed reduced the tendency for migrant workers to work out of town, though the strength of the policy is limited.

The impact on labor migration of factors such as personal characteristics, household land–person ratio and policy variables still cannot fully reflect the fact that labor migration is the result of household decisions. Even if labor migration is only the result of individual decisions, the aforementioned factors on labor migration will still make their impact felt. Differing from orthodox theory that assumes individuals as the decision-making entity, new economic migration theory emphasizes the importance of households as decision-making entities as households determine the relocation or migration of their members in accordance with the principles of maximizing expected income and minimizing risk (Stark and Bloom, 1985). This theory has three core concepts. One is "risk transfer." Household income is unstable in the hometown and in order to hedge risks and diversify income sources, households will decide to make some of its members work out of town or migrate, so as to reduce the dependence of the household on traditional or single income sources. Second is "economic constraints." Many households face monetary constraints in the hometown, for example, not having crop insurance, unemployment insurance or enough credit support. In order to break through these constraints to development, households will decide that some of its members should work out of town, in order to obtain the necessary money and technology. Third is "relative deprivation." When making migration decisions, households not only take into account the absolute expected income level, but also the income level relative to the reference group in the hometown. Even if a household's income level in their hometown sees a large increase, as long as the degree of the increase is below that of the reference group, the household will still feel relatively deprived and their tendency to migrate will increase.

In studies on Chinese labor migration, the fact that labor migration is the result of household decisions is critically reflected in two aspects: diversifying risks and remittances back home. Du (2001) employed agricultural household survey data and discovered that after inputting the "1996 household asset value" variable into the determinant model of labor's time supply for non-agricultural work, the coefficient of this variable is significantly positive. He believes that the greater the value of household assets, the higher the ability to withstand risk, and the time supply for non-agricultural work is higher. Since the rural labor market is underdeveloped in poor regions, further labor migration is often restricted, thus it is necessary to reduce welfare losses by effectively enhancing marginal labor productivity through cutting down barriers to labor mobility.

Remittances exhibit the fact that labor migration is the result of household decisions even more clearly.[12] Li (2001) observed the proportion of migrant workers remitting earnings is higher in China than in other countries and the ratio of urban migrant worker remittances to rural resident household income is rather high as well. Du and Park (2003) employed agricultural household survey data on poor countryside areas in China's western regions and discovered that income transfer of migrant labor is an important factor in alleviating poverty. The proportion of relatively poor households that have income transfer among households with migrant workers is higher than that of rich households, which shows that the altruistic nature of migrants has a positive impact on alleviating poverty. Ma et al. (2004) examined the trend of population migration and its impact on local labor and rural income growth and the results show that labor migration has already become a new source of rural income growth for undeveloped regions and is gradually playing the role of eliminating poverty and checking regional disparities. The remittances of migrant workers play a decisive role in rural life. The younger generation in rural areas increasingly yearns for a modernized way of life and most of their remittances are used on day-to-day consumption expenditures such as holding weddings and birthday parties similar to urban residents, renovating their homes, etc. To this end, they would undertake arduous and dangerous jobs in the cities for a long time. These jobs generally do not have labor contracts and wages are usually settled together at Spring Festival. Since most countryside areas did not have medical insurance until recently, many families become poor as a result of illness and remittances from migrant workers plays an immense role in paying for their household's medical expenses. Remittances become one of the most important economic activities that connect migrant workers with their household. In terms of lifestyle, remittances and the acceptance of such has already become an important element of migrant worker and rural household life. In a poor Sichuan township in the mid-1990s, the money posted back home by migrant workers every year was five times greater than that of the town government's fiscal revenue. Remittances are only a portion of the money they send back home; when they go home at Spring Festival or autumn harvest, they will bring a portion of the money home as well. Relatively speaking, among those that work out of town, those that work in sectors such as transportation, communications and industry send more money home while those that work in agriculture send the least home; the closer the location of work and residence from home, the greater the amount of money sent home; the higher the education level, the larger the remittances (Huang, 1997). Hu and Wang (2007) discovered that the larger the following variables, the larger the amount of remittances: migrant worker income, rural hometown non-remittance income, amount of rural hometown farmland and migrant worker age. Migrant workers with higher reallocation costs (transportation expenses), entire family working out of town together, unemployment experience and university education are associated with smaller remittances.

The two above-mentioned studies have different findings regarding the role of remittances. As time passes, remittance behavior changes as well. A recent small scale survey shows that, compared with first generation migrant workers, second generation migrant workers send less money home, and a smaller proportion of them do so. The survey shows that 30.3 percent of second generation migrant workers send back 100–300 yuan every month, 25.8 percent send 301–500 yuan, while 25.8 percent send no money at all or their family members back home do not need them to send money back. In that case, their income is entirely disposable for their own wishes (Liu and Cheng, 2008).

4.5 "Going higher": human capital externalities, economies of scale, and migration

Orthodox theory and empirical studies stress the impact of personal and household characteristics on labor migration, but these studies are not very clear on the implications of the direction of labor migration, and thus their connection with regional economics research and policy formulation is not strong enough. An ancient Chinese proverb is, "people strive to go higher." The migrant population generally pursues higher incomes, but the question is: where are the higher incomes? What are the characteristics of the regions that experience an inflow of migrants? From the perspective of policy formulation, if the question of what type of region is conducive to increasing migrant working income is not resolved, then this may lead to certain policy errors in practice, e.g., putting the emphasis of Hukou reform on small and medium sized cities.

In recent years, a new direction in theoretical and empirical research has involved human capital externalities and economies of scale in the urban labor market. "Human capital externality" is an important mechanism that forms "social return on education," which means that education not only increases personal incomes, but also increases the average educational level of a region (or the proportion of people who have received higher education) and can also increase personal incomes. If this is so, labor would, of course, tend to gravitate toward cities with higher average educational levels. The externalities of human capital in Chinese cities have only been estimated in recent empirical studies. Liu (2007) employed 1988 and 1995 CHIPS data to estimate the externalities for education in Chinese cities and consequently found that the external return of one-year education is between 4.9 percent and 6.7 percent. Li, Chen, and Zhang (2010) found that, as of 2006, for every percentage point increase in the proportion of the urban population that has received higher education, wages for workers increase by 1 percent. Our own recent study shows that individual hourly earnings increase by 12 percent with each year of schooling in the Chinese census district. Using university department relocation (*yuanxi tiaozheng*) in the 1950s as the instrument of city-level education, the impact of area years of schooling is 23 percent per year (Glaeser and Lu, 2013).

Then, is it a fact that people with different educational levels are all inclined to gravitate toward big cities to live and work? US data shows that over the past several decades, new university graduates tend to cluster in regions where the proportion of university graduates was already high, which fully reflects the agglomeration effect of high-skilled labor (Moretti, 2004). In China, it's the same.

First, Xiao and Liu (2007) found that regions with high population density have a larger inflow population, which is consistent with theoretical expectations, as a high population density is conducive to social interaction, thereby obtaining higher expected income.

Does Chinese urban development also exhibit a trend toward high-skilled persons agglomerating in the big cities? We analyzed aggregate data from the two population censuses in 1982 and 2000 and consequently found that in cities with high university graduate ratios in 1982, in the following 18 years, the magnitude of increase in the university graduate ratio was higher as well (see Figure 4.2). This result shows that an overall trend toward agglomeration of high-skilled labor has also appeared in China. But it needs to be specially noted that, under China's institutional context, it cannot be simply believed that population agglomerates to big cities only for higher labor productivity and income. China currently still enforces a rigorous Hukou system and residents with local Hukou enjoy better public services and welfare of all sorts. Under the constraint of the Hukou system, the Hukou settlement policy in each region (especially big cities) is more or less inclined toward highly-educated individuals, which motivates people to obtain big city Hukou and the corresponding welfare through over-pursuit of higher education.

Under the usual circumstances, when highly skilled workers agglomerate in the big cities, more demand for low-skilled workers will be created as well, since they are complementary within one production unit. At the same time, highly

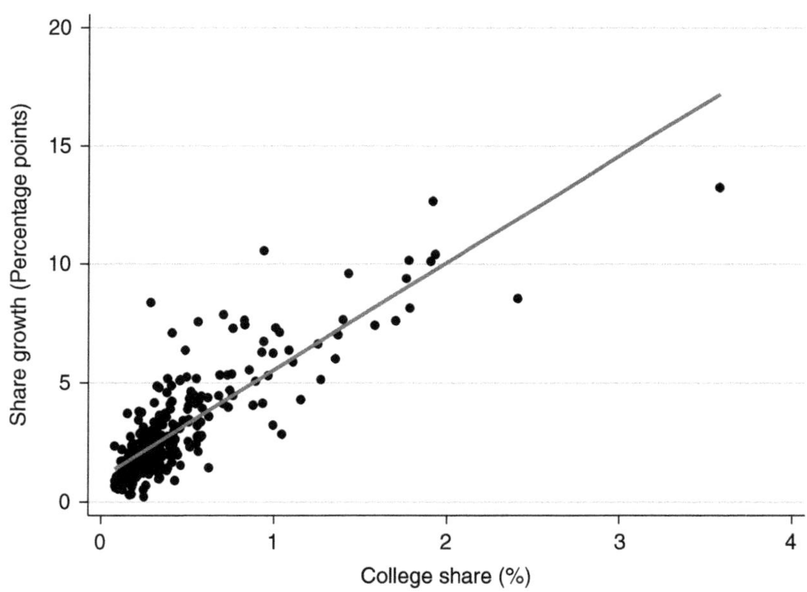

Figure 4.2 Growth of university graduate ratio (1982–2000). X-axis: 1982 university graduate ratio; Y-axis: 2000 university graduate ratio−1982 university graduate ratio.

skilled workers will create demand for the daily life services in which low-skilled workers are employed. Thus, under general circumstances, the agglomeration of highly skilled workers will bring faster population growth in big cities. Then, has such a situation occurred in China? We employed the aggregate data from the two population censuses in 1982 and 2000 and considered the 1982 university graduate ratio and the population growth 18 years later. We consequently found that there is still a positive correlation between the two (see Figure 4.3a). If we observe the relationship between the initial year's population and urban population growth, such a positive correlation still exists (see Figure 4.3b). However, it could be seen from the scatter plot that variance in the data is still large. In other words, although the agglomeration of highly skilled workers has the effect of promoting overall population agglomeration, such an effect is weaker than the agglomerative effect on highly skilled workers. We also compared 1990–2000 urban level migrant data,[13] tested the impact of urban educational levels and population size on the number of migrants and found that cities with higher *per capita* educational levels and population sizes indeed attract more migrants, but the variance of the data is quite high as well. Such a situation is understandable, as the current Hukou and corresponding public services system restricts the migration of population into big cities even more, especially restricting the migration of low-skilled workers, inhibiting the population agglomeration effect of cities with high educational levels and large populations.

The urban characteristics of the labor inflow regions are a topic worth further, deeper research. Labor in cities obtain knowledge by social interaction through spillover effects, while social interaction is often generated in social networks, thus, in this respect, urban labor economics touches upon labor economics, urban economies and social economics, and is a frontier research direction.[14]

4.6 The social economics of labor migration

Migration theory based on household decisions appears to be very suitable for explaining Chinese urban–rural and interregional labor migration. Human capital externalities and the urban economies of scale effect can also explain the direction of labor migration. Does this mean, then, that labor migration theory and empirical studies have reached their end? Here, we propose a few findings from empirical studies and attempt to demonstrate that the socioeconomic analysis of behavior must be introduced in order to study the issue of Chinese labor migration.

The first study relates to happiness. Knight and Gunatilaka (2010) studied the determinants of happiness for urban non-local labor. They found that the happiness of urban non-local labor is lower than that of rural residents and explained this finding as the migrants' erring in their expectations of future urban living conditions, aspirations and their future selves. Meanwhile, non-local labor will change their reference group from countryside companions to urban residents. One of our own studies uses urban and non-local samples in CHIPS data to conduct joint analysis and we found that when income gaps and educational gaps increase between labor with different Hukou identities within a city, happiness

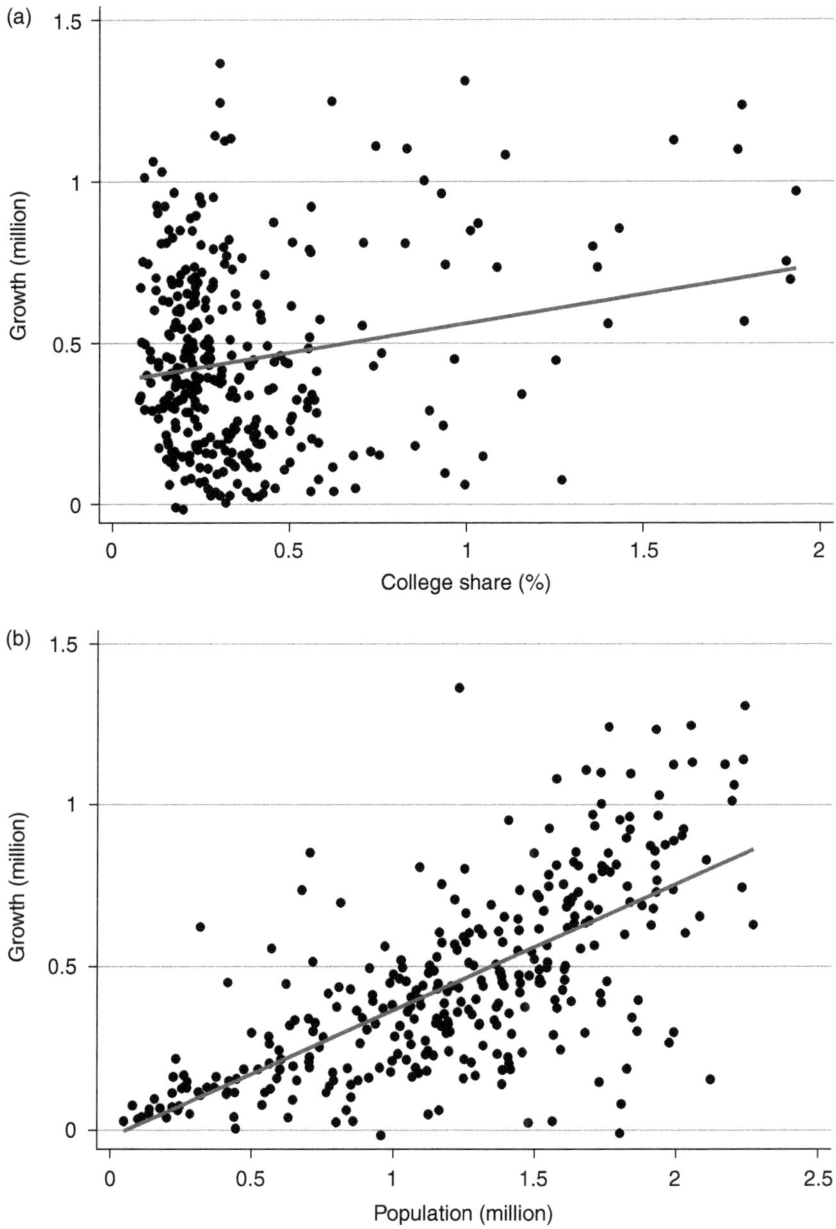

Figure 4.3 Urban population growth (1982–2000). X-axis: (a) 1982 urban university graduate ratio (%); (b) log (1982 population (in millions) +1); Y-axis: log (1982–2000 population growth (in millions) +1).

Note: The six largest and smallest points in population growth were removed as outliers from the figure.

will decline significantly for everyone, while compared to residents born in the city, happiness will decline even more for non-local labor (Jiang, Lu, and Sato, 2012). Evidently, non-local labor faces a relatively low income and educational level, which labor that has not left the countryside will not perceive. Therefore, the happiness of migrants will actually be lower. If the ex-post happiness is lower, why would rural labor still enter the city? This would require the assistance of ex ante asymmetric information to explain. To rural residents, the income and education gap one would face when working in the city is not a complete information variable that could be learned before the fact. Thus, during labor migration decisions, their considerations are more based on income growth and incomplete information on other factors may lead them to underestimate the negative impacts they face entering the city to work.

The second study relates to the impact of labor migration on public trust. Under normal circumstances, when labor migrates, their interaction and connection with their hometown's residents and government institutions decreases, and since trust is founded on the basis of repeated interaction, thus labor migration will reduce their trust in their original rural community's residents and government institutions. Miguel et al. (2006) studied the relationship between labor migration and social capital during Indonesian industrialization. They found that labor migration to other places will lower cooperation and trust between local residents, thereby weakening local informal institutions. Our own study examined the impact of labor migration on rural public trust and consequently found that households that have a higher proportion of migrant labor actually have a higher level of trust in their hometown. This is a different finding. Our explanation for this still proceeds from institutions and asymmetric information. It is precisely because labor that migrates from the countryside to the cities in China faces severe discrimination, the more they migrate, the more they trust their hometown's public institutions (Lu and Zhang, 2008). Our finding may illustrate that under China's urban–rural dual segmentation system, on the one hand, since China's rural labor migration is mainly short term, rural labor migration reduces their long-term interaction with local institutions by a limited extent, as every rural household still has some family members residing in the countryside; on the other hand, as rural migrant labor faces discrimination in the cities, negative evaluations of the city may be generated, which enhances their public trust in their former hometown community. When discrimination toward non-local population becomes a pervasive phenomenon in cities, the impact of this mechanism on public trust may exceed the other one in which the migrant population's interaction with their former rural community is reduced. Another study of ours relating to trust, found that, compared with local Shanghai residents, people in Shanghai without local Hukous are indeed less trustful of government institutions, the public, and community neighbors (Wang et al., 2009).

Certain slightly strange discoveries in studies on happiness and trust still require further research and explanation. For example, with regard to the same rural labor, one topic worth researching is, what are the differences between their trust in rural communities and public institutions and their trust in urban communities and public institutions? Before obtaining further research conclusions, a logically consistent explanation can be provided for the relevant findings of existing studies from the perspective of institutions and incomplete information.

Due to the institutional existence of social segmentation as well as incomplete information, the mutual effect of behavior between humans may become an observable result. Socioeconomic analysis believes that a person's behavior depends on the choices of others around him because, under incomplete information, people gather information by observing the behavior of others. Behaving in a way that converges with others is a choice that enables oneself to achieve maximum utility under the condition of incomplete information. Another explanation for behavior convergence is social psychology, which states that people just don't want to be different from others (Zanella, 2004).[15] If Chinese urban–rural and interregional labor migration is a decision made under institutionally existent social segmentation and incomplete information, then introducing socioeconomic analysis to labor migration becomes a necessary research path.

The core concept of socioeconomic analysis is social interaction and the interdependence of behavior between humans. The research is further divided into two aspects: First, direct analysis of the interdependence of behavior between humans, observing the correlation between individual behavior and the behavior of people around the individual (neighbors or other people of the same group); second, since social interaction takes place in social networks, how social networks influence human behavior can be observed. In terms of labor migration, research starts first from the influence of social networks.

In the process of labor migration, possessing social networks is important for rural migrant workers. A practical observation is that rural migrant workers are often introduced by their village peers and work together. The advantages of doing so are evident: peasants receive information directly from a fellow villager that he has high trust in, thus his probability of obtaining a job is high, and his expected income is raised. Meanwhile, working together not only makes the direct costs of migration low, more importantly, it lowers the psychological cost brought by the unfamiliarity of the city. In this process, possessing social networks may have positive impacts on population migration. Based on sample survey data from a questionnaire conducted in Jinan in 1995, Li (1996) consequently found that during the process of rural to urban migration, workers mainly rely on traditional kinship and geographical social networks. Such traditional social networks, as a type of informal institution, play the role of saving rural–urban labor migration costs, and efficiently allocating resources.

Moreover, on the urban side of the story, there are studies that find the size of migrant peasants' social support network not only smaller than that of urban residents, but also smaller than that of rural residents, with the degree of closeness lower than that of rural residents and close to that of urban residents (Wang and Tong, 2004). Zhang and Li (2003) discovered that having friends and relatives outside the village will increase the probability of non-agricultural employment for peasants and those that have "relations" will work longer in non-agricultural jobs. Bao et al. (2007) found that the "proportion of people from the same hometown" in the labor migration destination will significantly increase the probability of working out of town. Zhao (2003) found that the total number of people working out of town in a village will significantly impact the employment decisions of individuals. She explains this as the existence of migrant networks lowering the psychological costs and information-seeking costs of population migration. Sheng (2008) also discovered that a village's migration network significantly increases the migration probability of individual laborers. Our own study again found that households that have relatives and friends outside the village assist in increasing the probability of working outside (Chen et al., 2013). Studies on the impact of social networks on migrant worker wages consequently discovered only very weak evidence that possessing a larger social network can directly increase the income level of migrant workers on the urban labor market. The main effect of social networks in urban labor markets that are highly competitive is mainly allocating jobs, but almost none directly change the wages that migrant workers can obtain (Zhang et al., 2008; Zhang and Lu, 2009).

Social networks aid migrant workers in working out of town, but this conclusion cannot be generalized into saying that social capital aids migrant workers in working out of town. According to its nature, social capital could be divided into bridging social capital and bonding social capital. Social networks that are helpful to rural residents working out of town are often of a bridging nature, usually referring to whether or not a peasant household has relatives and friends outside the village or in the city or whether or not there are people from the same hometown in the migration destination. However, bonding social capital may restrain migrant labor. Bonding social capital increases the mutual trust and cooperation between residents within villages, reducing the income and consumption risks of rural residents,[16] so when bonding social capital is rather strong within a village, the opportunity costs for working outside rises and the probability of working outside falls accordingly. The mutual trust between villagers is a type of bonding social capital and Gao and Lu (2010) found that such social capital has the effect of lowering the probability of labor migration.

Research on social networks enriched our understanding of labor migration, but little research examines the interdependence in Chinese labor migration decision-making. The interdependence of human behavior is dubbed the peer effect or the neighborhood effect.[17] In fact, as Bauer et al. (2002) pointed out, even if we control for social capital, networks, etc. that affect labor migration, we cannot neglect the neighborhood effect's impact. Social capital and networks mainly provide information, thus diminishing marginal returns apply to them, while the neighborhood effect studies the interdependence of individual decisions within groups and mainly impacts human behavior through behavior emulation and decision-making under asymmetric information, thus diminishing marginal returns do not apply to it. More importantly, the existence of social interaction and the interdependence of behavior implies the existence of the multiple equilibria effect in economic processes (Moffitt, 2001; Zanella, 2004). Villagers might go out to work at the same time or could observe the choices of other villagers to not migrate and choose to not migrate at the same time, thereby leading to an

Table 4.3 Difference between network effect and neighborhood effect

	Network effect	*Neighborhood effect*
Cause	Information	Information, social psychology
Time	Past	Present
Definition	Intragroup and intergroup	Only intragroup

equilibria with a low migration rate, producing a negative impact on the sustained growth of the economy. This shows that the neighborhood effect has rich public policy implications.

Specifically speaking, this author believes that the network effect and neighborhood effect differs in three aspects (as illustrated in Table 4.3). First, the network effect stresses more the information transmission role, whereas in the neighborhood effect, members within a group affect each other because incomplete information makes emulation of others the best choice and because emulation of others has sociopsychological reasons, as people are unwilling to be different from others. Second, the occurrence of the network effect takes some time. For example, it takes time for a person from the same hometown to go out to work, relay relevant information and thereby impact a person, while the neighborhood effect does not take a period of time to take effect as it is manifested in the present interdependence of human behavior. Third, the occurrence of the network effect is determined by whether the network is within a group or across groups. Networks of different natures have different effects. Generally speaking, intergroup networks facilitate labor migration while intragroup networks may facilitate or restrain labor migration. But the neighborhood effect must occur between members within a group and is the interdependence of behavior between group members. Individual behavior is usually explained through the average behavior of group members.

Based on the above distinctions, we employed CHIPS 2002 data to study the neighborhood effect in labor migration. Of course, we controlled for the "number of relatives and friends outside the village" and "proportion of villagers who are working out of town," which are used to reflect the network effect. The results show that the neighborhood effect in labor migration decision-making among residents of the same village is significant. Social interaction with other villagers when exchanging information on employment and lending a helping hand during harvest season facilitates the neighborhood effect, unless helping out happens too often and takes up time for working outside. Since the neighborhood effect leads to multiple equilibria, our parameters based on empirical models simulated the equilibrium between individual probability of migration and village average migrant labor ratio and consequently, found that for a typical person whose other characteristics are all at the mean, the equilibrium propensity to labor migration is very low (Chen et al., 2013). This empirical result highly fits China's current circumstances. On the one hand, due to incomplete information on the labor market, interdependence exists between villagers in labor migration decision-making, so this is understandable. On the other hand, since labor migration is restricted under China's current system, under the interdependence of labor migration decision-making, a low equilibrium probability for labor migration is understandable as well, as this provides yet another explanation for China's urbanization lagging far behind its industrialization.

So far, we have traced the path of orthodox labor migration theory to socioeconomic analysis and rather completely—though inevitably leaving much to be desired—summarized the development of relevant research on labor migration. On the whole, the results of empirical research can confirm China's labor migration as indeed the result of household decision-making under institutional constraints and the impact of social networks and social interaction on labor migration reflects the impact of institutional constraints.

4.7 Policy discussion: why an institutional big-push is needed

Basic economic theory tells us that if, as a productive factor, labor's interregional mobility is restricted, then maximization of social welfare will not be attainable. The urban–rural dual segmentation and "new dual structure" segmentation in cities are only policies that maximize the utility of urban residents (especially residents of relatively developed regions) but restrict the urban–rural and interregional mobility of labor (Chen and Lu, 2008; Liu, Chen and Lu, 2010). The phenomenon of Chinese labor mobility being dominated by short-term migration concluded in the second section of this chapter is also the result of institutional restrictions. China's urbanization severely lags behind its industrialization; something that could be said to be unmatched worldwide, and this is actually also relevant to the constraints on labor migration.[18] Urban–rural segmentation policies blocked the free urban–rural and interregional flow of productive factors, with the result being not only impeded urbanization, insufficient development of big cities, and distortion of the urban system, but also the magnification of urban–rural and regional income gaps as well as social segmentation in cities (Lu, Xiang, and Chen, 2011). Meanwhile, the consequences of limiting labor's sufficient migration are also reflected in the development of the countryside and agriculture. Since labor cannot migrate sufficiently, migration is mostly short term without relocation of the whole family, thus the issues of ageing and retirement, children left behind on a large scale, low efficiency of agricultural land use, environmental degradation etc. formed in the countryside (Lu, 2010).[19]

Economic policies that eliminate urban–rural segmentation, facilitate the social integration of China's urban and rural labor and thereby promote labor mobility and urbanization are necessary measures to building a harmonious society and promoting sustainable economic growth. When the neighborhood effect exists for labor migration decision-making, the negative impact of urban–rural segmentation policies that are an external barrier to labor migration will be amplified through social interaction, causing the labor migration rate to be locked in at a low equilibrium level. Our empirical research provides support for three types of policies that promote urbanization. From the perspective of traditional economic policies, peasants can be encouraged to work outside by increasing their level of education, etc. From the perspective of social policies, peasants can be encouraged to work outside through promoting information exchange between villagers and using more complete market services to substitute for over-frequent mutual labor assistance between rural residents, which are more conducive for giving scope to interdependence in labor migration decision-making's propelling effect on urbanization. However, the results of policy simulation show that only adopting these two policies cannot immensely increase the rate of peasants working outside, nor can it change the low level equilibrium of the labor migration rate. To this end, a third type of policy needs to be implemented, namely institutional adjustments that facilitate urban–rural labor market integration, eliminating urban–rural segmentation policies and discrimination toward migrant workers through institutional reforms. Not only can this directly promote labor migration, under the neighborhood effect, it can also enable labor migration and urbanization to break away from a low level equilibrium (Chen et al., 2013).

Whether it is for urban development or for rural development and increasing peasant incomes, and whether it is to enable the next round of economic growth to have a stronger impetus, or to narrow interregional and urban–rural income gaps, urbanization founded on the basis of freer and more sufficient migration of labor is the best policy and a win-win policy. Currently, in order to realize balanced urban–rural and regional development, the crux of the issue is how to urbanize and integrate into the city non-local labor that has entered the city and will permanently reside there. For this purpose, current Hukou and land systems must receive corresponding reforms, in order to reduce their restrictions on the free urban–rural and interregional flow of labor. Among this, one feasible plan is "land and Hukou system linked reform," the core idea of which is allowing those peasants that already permanently reside and work in the city and do not want to return to the countryside to transfer, with compensation, the construction-use land quotas their hometown rural residential land corresponds with to the city they are in, as land quotas for urban expansion, while their hometown correspondingly increases the amount of reserved agricultural land. Thus, the policy must achieve a breakthrough in the interprovincial (municipality/autonomous region) "balance between occupation and compensation" of agriculture-use land (Lu and Chen, 2009; Lu, 2010, 2011).

Notes

1 Cai and Wang (2003) employed data from the Fifth Census and found that the proportion of rural–urban migration in total migration was 40.7 percent in 2000, the proportion of urban–urban migration was 37.2 percent, the proportion of rural–rural migration was rather low at only 18.2 percent, while the proportion of urban–rural migration was lowest at less than 1/25 of total migration.

2 Refer to Chan and Zhang (1999) for an early introduction and critique of the Hukou system.

3 The definition of migrant population slightly differed in each census but they are largely comparable. In the "Fifth Census," migrant population refers to people with two types of Hukou registration situations (survey item R6): "Has resided over half a year in this township's neighborhood, Hukou is in another area's neighborhood" and "Has resided less than half a year in this township's neighborhood, been away from Hukou registration area for over half a year," while eliminating people that live in a place different from their registered residence within a city; according to a 2005 1 percent sample survey project, migrant population refers to population whose "Residence at time of survey" (survey item R7) is at this area, but "Hukou registration residence" is beyond this township (neighborhood), while also eliminating people that live in a place different from their registered residence within a city. Refer to Duan et al. (2008).

4 Li's (1999) early studies discovered as well, the first occupational change by migrant workers achieves a rather large augmentation in occupational status, whereas the second occupational change is horizontal and status augmentation is not attained, mainly due to the lack of status accumulation, status inheritance and social resources.

5 Zhang, Gao and Hou (2007) found that urban-rural segmentation factors and regional segmentation systems all form a negative impact on nonlocal urban population's participation in social security.

6 There is no unanimous opinion on whether or not higher education is a public service. Recent research shows that higher education has strong externalities so the government input in higher education has certain public services properties.

7 For an early critique on the social segmentation between population with different Hukous within cities, refer to Wang and Zuo (1999). Cai, Dou and Wang (2001) studied the issue of Hukou system and labor market protection. Using "Living Standards of Migrant Workers is Worrisome" as a topic, Sheng (2008) summarized the condition of migrant workers into seven aspects: low compensation and benefits, poor residential conditions, lack of social security, difficulty in offspring education, heavy urban discrimination, and lack of spiritual life. As to the impact of such segmentation and its impact on the labor market, especially the impact on inequality between nonlocal labor and local urban labor, much empirical literature already exists. The critique of such literature is not a key point in this review. Please refer to the review by Zhao Chen's chapter in this book.

8 This is in contrast with international academia's definition of "migrant" when researching international "migrant" issues as people whose birthplace is not the current country they live in, even if that person has already obtained the nationality of the current country.

9 *Data source*: http://www.stats.gov.cn/tjgb/nypcgb/qgnypcgb/t20080227_402464718.htm, report on main figures from the Second National Agricultural Census (No. 5).

10 The Chinese Academy of Social Sciences 2002 Chinese Household Income Project Survey (CHIPS 2002) in all randomly selected 121 counties, 961 administrative villages, 9,200 households and 37,969 village individuals from the countryside nationwide. In CHIPS 2002 data, individually reported number of days away from home in 2002 is recorded. We define individuals away from home for over six months (180 days) in one year as migrant worker and eliminate students that are long-term residents in a place other than their hometown and peasants working in local township enterprises. The biggest reduction to the original data was dropping males younger than 16 or older than 60 and females younger than 16 or older than 55 from the sample (in all eliminating 11,404 observation values). This was done since, according to China's labor statistics, this portion of the population does not belong in the labor age. Finally, we also eliminated samples with missing variables and outliers. After the above processing, we finally obtained 16,401 effective observation values.

11 For a review of these issues, refer to *Urban–Rural Economic Development in Urbanization and Industrialization* written by Chen Zhao (Lu et al., 2008, Ch. Three). Another outstanding review and critique is Bai and Li (2008). The paper

comprehensively critiqued the labor migration and urbanization issues. However, the paper believed that China's gap between the rate of urbanization and the rate of industrialization is narrowing, which is a view that this author does not share, since when calculating the rate of industrialization, the development of services should be considered. If the proportion of services is included in "rate of industrialization," then since "reform and opening," the gap between rate of urbanization and rate of industrialization has not distinctly narrowed (refer to Chapter 3 in this book).

12 Dustmann and Mestres (2010) found that remittances are mostly made by short-term migrants, which matches China's situation of migrants mostly being short term.

13 The 1982 population census data do not include information on migrants. Our "migrant" figures come from the "migrant" population figures at the city level in the 2000 population census.

14 Moretti (2004, 2010) has two related literature reviews.

15 In empirical research, behavior convergence caused only by social psychology does not have enough evidence, while behavior convergence as a way of collecting information, also known as social learning, does have empirical evidence. Due to lack of space, we will not discuss this further.

16 Lu, Zhang, and Sato (2010) found that social capital in a village is conducive to households resisting the shock of natural disasters on consumption.

17 The interdependence of behavior is named different under different research themes. Zanella (2004) discussed this specifically and this chapter will not make further distinctions. Araujo et al. (2004) and Munshi's (2003) research found that peer effects exist for Mexico rural–urban migrants and immigrants to the US.

18 See Chen's *Urban-Rural Economic Development in Urbanization and Industrialization* (Lu et al., 2008, Ch. 3).

19 For more on the impact of mobility on rural economics, see Wang's (2006) review.

References

In English

Araujo, Caridad, Alain de Janvry, and Elisabeth Sadoulet, 2004, "Peer Effects in Employment: Results from Mexico's Poor Rural Communities," *Working Paper*, University of California at Berkeley.

Bao, Shuming, Örn B. Bodvarsson, Jack W. Hou and Yaohui Zhao, 2007, "Interprovincial Migration in China: The Effects of Investment and Migrant Networks," *IZA Discussion Paper* No. 2924.

Bauer, Thomas, Gil Epstein and Ira N. Gang, 2002, "Herd Effects or Migration Networks? The Location Choice of Mexican Immigrants in the U.S.," *IZA Discussion Paper* No. 551.

Cai, Fang and Dewen Wang, 2003, "Migration As Marketization: What Can We Learn from China's 2000 Census Data?" *China Review*, 3(2), pp. 73–93.

Chan, Kam Wing and Li Zhang, 1999, "The Hukou System and Rural-Urban Migration in China: Processes and Changes," *China Quarterly*, 160(Dec), pp. 818–855.

Chen, Zhao, Shiqing Jiang, Ming Lu, Hiroshi Sato, 2013, "China's Labour Market, Rural-Urban Migration and Growth Pattern: Future Prospect," in Jun Zhang (ed.) *Unfinished Reforms in the Chinese Economy*, Singapore: World Scienfitic Publishing, pp. 83–123.

Démurger, Sylvie, Marc Gurgand, Shi Li, and Ximing Yue, 2009, "Migrants as Second-Class Workers in Urban China? A Decomposition Analysis," *Journal of Comparative Economics*, 37(4), pp. 610–628.

Dustmann, Christian and Josep Mestres, 2010, "Remittances and Temporary Migration," *Journal of Development Economics*, 92, pp. 62–70.

Glaeser, Edward L. and Ming Lu, 2013, "Human Capital Externalities in China," *Working Paper*, Harvard University and Fudan University.

Harris, J. R. and M. Todaro, 1970, "Migration, Unemployment and Development: A Two-Sector Analysis," *American Economic Review*, 60(1), pp. 126–142.

Jayet, Hubert and Ming Lu, 2010, "Heterogeneous Human Capital Externality and Scale Economy in Wage Formation: Evidence from Urban China," *Working Paper*, Fudan University.

Jiang, Shiqing, Ming Lu and Hiroshi Sato, 2012, "Identity, Inequality, and Happiness: Evidence from Urban China," *World Development*, 40(6), pp. 1190–1200.

Knight, John and Ramani Gunatilaka, 2010, "Great Expectations? The Subjective Well-being of Rural Urban Migrants in China," *World Development*, 38(1), pp. 113–124.

Liang, Zai and Michael J. White, 1997, "Market Transition, Government Policies, and Interprovincial Migration in China: 1983–1988," *Economic Development and Cultural Change*, 45(2), pp. 321–339.

Liu, Z., 2007, "The External Returns to Education: Evidence from Chinese Cites," *Journal of Urban Economics*, 61(3), pp. 542–564.

Lu, Ming, Zhao Chen, Yongqin Wang, Yan Zhang, Yuan Zhang and Changyuan Luo, 2013, *China's Economic Development: Institutions, Growth and Imbalances*, Edward Elgar.

Meng, Lei, 2010, "Can Grain Subsidy Impede Rural-Urban Migration in Hinterland China? Evidence from Field Surveys," paper presented at 2010 International Workshop on Employment Dynamics and Social Security, June 12–14, Fudan University in Shanghai.

Miguel, E., P. Gertler and D. I. Levine, 2006, "Does Industrialization Build or Destroy Social Networks," *Economic Development and Culture Change*, 54(2), pp. 287–317.

Moffitt, Robert, 2001, "Policy Interventions, Low-Level Equilibria, and Social Interactions," In *Social Dynamics*, ed. Steven N. Durlauf, H. Peyton Young. Cambridge, MA: MIT Press.

Moretti, Enrico, 2004, "Human Capital Externalities in Cities," Vol. 4, Ch. 51, In *Handbook of Regional and Urban Economics*, ed. J. V. Henderson and J. F. Thisse. Amsterdam: Elsevier.

Moretti, Enrico, 2010, "Local Labor Markets," In *Handbook of Labor Economics*, http:// emlab.berkeley.edu/ moretti/handbook.pdf.

Munshi, Kaivan, 2003, "Networks in the Modern Economy: Mexican Migrants in the U.S. Labor Market," *Quarterly Journal of Economics*, 118(2), pp. 549–599.

Stark, Oded and David Bloom, 1985, "The New Economics of Labor Migration," *American Economic Review*, 75(2), pp. 173–178.

Wang, Feng and Xuejin Zuo, 1999, "Inside China's Cities: Institutional Barriers and Opportunities for Urban Migrants," *American Economic Review, Papers and Proceedings*, 89(2), pp. 276–280.

Zanella, Giulio, 2004, "Social Interactions and Economic Behavior," *Working Paper*, University of Siena.

Zhang, Huafeng, 2010, "The Hukou System's Constraints on Migrant Workers' Job Mobility in Chinese Cities," *China Economic Review*, 21, pp. 51–64.

Zhang, Xiaobo, and Guo Li, 2003, "Does *Guanxi* Matter to Nonfarm Employment?" *Journal of Comparative Economics*, 31, pp. 315–331.

Zhao, Yaohui, 1999a, "Leaving the Countryside: Rural-to-Urban Migration Decisions in China," *American Economic Review, AEA Papers and Proceedings*, May, 281–286.

Zhao, Yaohui, 1999b, "Labor Migration and Earnings Differences: The Case of China," *Economic Development and Cultural Change*, 47, pp. 767–782.

Zhao, Yaohui, 2003, "The Role of Migrant Networks in Labor Migration: The Case of China," *Contemporary Economic Policy*, 21(4), pp. 500–511.

Zhu, Nong, 2002, "The Impact of Income Gaps on Migration Decisions in China: A Verification of the Todaro Model," *China Economic Review*, 13(2–3), pp. 213–230.

In Chinese

Bai, Nansheng, and Jing Li, 2008, "Urbanization and Rural Labor Migration in China," *Chinese Journal of Population Science*, 4, pp. 2–19.

Cai, Fang, Yang Du, and Meiyan Wang, 2001, "Household Registration System and Labor Market Protection," *Economic Research Journal*, 12, pp. 41–49.

Cai, Fang, Yang Du, Meiyan Wang, 2003, "Research Review of Rural Labor Migration in China," the Appendix in *The Political Economy of Labor*, Shanghai: Shanghai Sanlian Press, Shanghai People's Publishing House.

Chen, Zhao and Ming Lu, 2008, "From Segmentation to Integration: Political Economy of Urban–rural Economic Growth and Social Harmony," *Economic Research Journal*, 1, pp. 21–32.

Ding, Jinhong, Zhenyu Liu, and Danming Cheng, 2005, "Regional Differentiation of Inter-provincial Migration in China and Characteristics of the Flow Field," *Geographic Sinica*, 60(1), pp. 106–114.

Du, Yang, 2001, "Risk Diversification and Supply of Non-agricultural Labor – Empirical Evidence from Countries of Poor Region," *Quantitative & Technical Economics*, 1, pp. 46–50.

Du, Yang, and Albert Park, 2003, "Migration and Poverty Reduction: Empirical Evidence from Farmer Survey," *Chinese Journal of Population Science*, 4, pp. 56–62.

Duan, Chengrong, Ge Yang, Fei Zhang, and Xuehe Lu, 2008, "Nine Trends of China's Population Flow since the Reform and Opening-up," *Population Research*, 32(6), pp. 30–48.

Gao, Hong, and Ming Lu, 2010, "The Impact of Social Trust on Labor Mobility," *Chinese Rural Economy*, 3, pp. 12–24.

Hou, Jiawei, 2009, "Whole-Family Population Flow and Individual Factors," *Population Research*, 33(1), pp. 55–61.

Hu, Feng, and Wang Qiwen, 2007, "An Analysis of Determinants of Remittances of China's Rural Migrants: an Application of Interval Regression Model," *Statistical Research*, 10, pp. 20–25.

Huang, Ping (eds.), 1997, *In Search for Survival: A Sociological Study of Rural-urban Migration*, Kunming: The People's Press of Yunnan.

Li, Peilin, 1996, "The Social Networks and Social Status of Migrant Workers," *Sociological Research*, 4, pp. 42–52.

Li, Qiang, 1999, "Migrant Workers' Occupation Flow in Urban Areas of Mainland China," *Sociological Research*, 3, pp. 93–101.

Li, Qiang, 2001, "Analysis of the Remittance of the Out-Migrant Workers in China," *Sociological Research*, 4, pp. 64–76.

Li, Qiang, 2005, "T-shaped Social Structure and Social Tension," *Sociological Research*, 2, pp. 55–73.

Li, Shi, 1997a, *China's Rural Labor Flow and Income Distribution Research Report*, Washington: Center for China Studies.

Li, Shi, 1997b, "The Model of Labor Mobility in China Economic Transition," *Economic Research Journal*, 1, pp. 23–30, 80.

Li, Shi, 1999, "Rural Labor Mobility and the Growth and Distribution of Income in China," *Social Sciences in China*, 2, pp. 16–33.

Li, Xiaoying, Guanghan Chen, and Yingwu Zhang, 2010, "Estimating the External Return of Higher Education in Urban China," *World Economic Papers*, 1, pp. 76–91.

Liu, Chuangjiang, and Jianlin Cheng, 2008, "The Second-generation Rural Migrants' Acquiring Citizenship: Analysis of Current Situation and Measure of Progress," *Population Research*, 32(5), pp. 48–57.

Liu, Xiaofeng, Zhao Chen, and Ming Lu, 2010, "Social Integration and Economic Growth – Theory of Endogenous Policy Changes of Urbanization and City Development," *Journal of World Economy*, 6, pp. 60–80.

Liu, Xuejun, and Yaohui Zhao, 2009, "The Impact of Labor Migration on Urban Labor Markets in China," *China Economic Quarterly*, 2, pp. 693–710.

Lu, Ming, 2010a, "Transfer of Land Quotas for Construction: a Breakthrough Point in China's Coordinated Rural-Urban and Regional Development," *International Economic Review*, 2, pp. 137–148.

Lu, Ming, 2011, "Cross-regional Reallocation of the Land-use Right: A New Engine of China's Economic Growth," *Journal of World Economy*, 1, pp. 107–125.

Lu, Ming, and Zhao Chen, 2009, "Why Land and Household Registration System Need Combining Reform: A Theoretical and Empirical Review on China's City and Regional Development," *Academic Monthly*, 9, pp. 78–84.

Lu, Ming, Kuanhu Xiang and Zhao Chen, 2011, "China's Urbanization and Urban System Adjustment: a Review Based on Literature," *Journal of World Economy*, 6, pp. 3–25.

Lu, Ming, Shuang Zhang and Hiroshi Sato, 2010, "Does Social Capital Help Households Cope with Natural Disaster during Marketization? Evidence from Rural China," *World Economic Papers*, 1, pp. 16–38.

Lu, Ming, Shuang Zhang, 2008, "The Effects of Labor Migration on Public Trust in Rural China," *World Economic Papers*, 4, pp. 77–87.

Lu, Ming, Zhao Chen, Yongqin Wang, Yuan Zhang, Yan Zhang, Changyuan Luo, 2008, *Economic Development Path of China as a Large Country*, Beijing: Encyclopedia of China Publishing House.

Ma, Zhongdong, Weimin Zhang, Zai Liang, and Hongyan Cui, 2004, "Labour Migration as A New Determinant of Income Growth in Rural China," *Population Research*, 3, pp. 2–10.

Qiao, Mingrui, Xueya Qian, and Xianguo Yao, 2009, "Labor Market Segmentation, Hukou and Urban–rural Difference in Employment," *Chinese Journal of Population Science*, 1, pp. 32–41.

Roberts, Kenneth, 2005, "The Trend and Change of China's Labor Mobility: the Implication of the Long-Lasting Migration," *Chinese Journal of Population Science*, 6, pp. 17–29.

Sheng, Laiyun, 2008, *Flow or Migration – Economic Analysis of the Progress of Rural Labor Mobility*, Shanghai: Shanghai Yuandong Publishing House.

Sun, Ziduo, 2004, "The Effect of Farmers' Cross-provincial Work on Regional Economic Development," *Chinese Rural Economy*, 3, pp. 28–33.

Wang, Guixin, and Jianbo Liu, 2007, "Inter-provincial Migrations to Yangtze River Delta and Pearl River Delta," *Chinese Journal of Population Science*, 2, pp. 87–94.

Wang, Hui, Zhao Chen and Ming Lu, 2009, "Hukou, Social Segmentation and Trust: Empirical Evidence from Shanghai," *Journal of World Economy*, 10, pp. 81–96.

Wang, Meiyan, 2006, "Review for Effect of Labor Migration on Rural Economy in China," *China Rural Observation*, 3, pp. 70–73, 79.

Wang, Yijie, and Xing Tong, 2004, "Analysis on the Social Supporting Network of the Rural Migrants," *Sociological Research*, 2, pp. 42–48.

Wu, Kaiya, Li Zhang, and Xiao Chen, 2010, "The Barrier of Hukou Reform: An Analysis of the Qualifications for the Urban Hukou," *Chinese Journal of Population Science*, 1, pp. 66–74, 112.

Xiao, Qunying, and Huijun Liu, 2007, "Retesting Dynamical Factor Theories on Inter-Provincial Labor Migration with QAP Algorithm," *Chinese Journal of Population Science*, 4, pp. 26–33.

Yao, Xianguo and Puqing Lai, 2004, "Urban–rural Hukou Differentials in Chinese Labor Relation," *Economic Research Journal*, 7, pp. 82–90.

Zhang, Yuan, and Ming Lu, 2009, "Does the Use of Social Network Raise the Wage of Rural Migrant," *Management World*, 3, pp. 45–54.

Zhang, Yuan, Rui Li, Hou Wang and Liang Chen, 2008, "Does the Use of Social Network Have a Positive Effect on a Rural Migrant's Wage? Evidence from China," *World Economic Papers*, 6, pp. 73–84.

Zhang, Zhanxin, Wenshu Gao, and Huili Hou, 2007, "Urban–rural Divide, Regional Segmentation and Insufficient Access of Urban Floating Population to Social Security: Evidence from Shanghai and Other Four Chinese Cities," *Chinese Journal of Population Science*, 6, pp. 33–41.

Zhao, Yaohui, 1997, "China's Rural Labor Flow and The Role of Education: Research Based on the Sichuan Province," *Economic Research Journal*, 2, pp. 37–42, 73.

Zhao, Zhong, 2004, "Rural-Urban Migration in China: What Do We Know and What Do We Need to Know?" *China Economic Quarterly*, 3(3), pp. 517–536.

Zhou, Jingxiang, 2010, "Research Progress of Rural Labor Mobility in China," *China Labor Economics*, 6(1), pp. 214–244.

Zhou, Jingxiang, and Yan He, 2009, "An Empirical Test of Rural Labor Force Employment in Cites and China's Regional Economic Growth: Ownership Transformation among China's Provinces (1990–2006)," *World Economic Papers*, 1, pp. 33–49, 93.

Zhu, Nong, 2004, "Leaving Land or Leaving Countryside: An Analysis on the Relationship between Interregional and Inter-Occupational Flow of Chinese Rural Labor," *World Economic Papers*, 1, pp. 53–63.

5 Foreign trade, interregional trade, and regional specialization

Jiuli Huang

5.1 Introduction

China is a developing country with a vast territory, in which each region varies a lot in its location, human atmosphere, and initial level. In 1978, China ended the enduring *Closed-Door* policy, and chose to reintegrate into the global economy. Since then, economic and trade ties between China and the outside world have been increasingly consolidated. Blessed with superior location and policy preferentials, the east coast regions enjoy more opportunities for globalization, in international trade especially, and thereby surpass the hinterland in many aspects, such as industrialization, urbanization, income *per capita*, etc. Moreover, the east gathers most of the national economic activities, and thus evolves increasingly into the core, while the hinterland the periphery.

In retrospect of history, the asymmetry between the coastal and hinterland is not unique to modern times. After the *Tang Dynasty*, the *Silk Road* connecting western China and mid-west Asia was gradually replaced by sea lanes because of wars which occurred in northwest China and Central Asia and of the development of seamanship. By the tenth century, in the *Song Dynasty*, the *Silk Road* was hardly used for foreign trade. Meanwhile, as foreign trade developed in the eastern region, the economy center gradually moved eastward, which made the coastal area far superior to the hinterland in economic prosperity. Driven jointly by the *Westernization Movement*, foreign investment and the development of national industry in modern times, most of Chinese modern industry agglomerated in the coastal region, whose social openness and economic development significantly surpassed that of the hinterland. By a series of preferential arrangements and deployments after the founding of the *People's Republic of China*, industries moved westwards on a large scale. The level of economic development in the hinterland once paralleled the east. However, during globalization and the market-oriented reform after 1978, regional development strategies formulated during the *Planned Economy* withered and the coastal-hinterland gap has widened once again.

Foreign trade intertwines with interregional trade in many dimensions. Foreign trade changes the economic landscape within China, alters each region's comparative advantage and economies of scale, and thereby reshapes the pattern of interregional trade and regional specialization. During this process, as spatial relationship adjusts, the interests of firms and the behaviors of local governments acclimatize themselves, which may promote or impede regional market integration and in return, change the motivation for foreign trade. What we attempt to summarize in this chapter is how foreign trade affects interregional trade. What we want to stress here, however, is the ever-changing regional and international markets in which each region is involved, and the interdependence between these two markets. Without these two aspects, we could not understand accurately the external environment and the internal impetus that jointly help to shape the development of the Chinese regional economy.

A great deal of literature has investigated the impact of foreign trade on interregional trade and regional specialization, and has put forward many valuable insights from different perspectives through different methods. These studies have reached a consensus on quite a few questions. Of course, controversy still lingers over many important topics, some of which need to be examined in more depth. This chapter is designed to summarize the existing consensuses, discuss the causes of controversies, and point out the directions for further investigation. Specifically, we attempt to answer the following four questions: First, what are the stylized facts about regional foreign trade, and what are the determinants and how do they function? Second, what are the stylized facts about interregional trade within China? Does foreign trade affect interregional trade directly? Are foreign and regional markets mutually substitutive or complementary with regard to regional economic development? Third, since specialization depicts trade ties in another way, how about the dynamics of regional specialization, and how does foreign trade impact on it? Fourth, now that local protectionism, one of the main sources of interregional trade cost, leads to market segmentation at the expense of efficiency, does foreign trade undermine or strengthen the local protectionism and segmentation (and vice versa)?

The remainder of this chapter is divided into five sections. Section 2 describes a set of stylized facts concerning regional foreign trade, and summarizes the existing explanations. Section 3 outlines the stylized facts about interregional trade, and analyzes the interrelationship between foreign trade and interregional trade. Section 4 reviews literature regarding the impact of foreign trade on internal economic geography and regional specialization both theoretically and empirically. Section 5 discusses the interaction between foreign trade and regional market integration, and Section 6 concludes and points out possible directions for future research.

5.2 Regional foreign trade within China: stylized facts and determinants

5.2.1 Regional foreign trade within China: stylized facts

China integrated into the global economy rapidly and witnessed explosive growth in foreign trade after the *Reform and Opening-up*. Products *Made in China* or *Processed in China* swept the world market with low prices and satisfactory quality.

However, we can find that foreign trade across Chinese regions varies a lot when we look back. Below, we successively illustrate the development of regional foreign trade from five aspects, i.e. growth rates, trade modes, product types, trade entities, and trade partners.

5.2.1.1 A few eastern provinces see supernormal growth in foreign trade

China's opening-up experienced two important time-points successively after 1978. One was the publication of *Deng Xiaoping's Southern Tour Speeches* in the spring of 1992, after which China set the clear-cut goal of market-orientation and determined to further the opening-up policy. The other is China's accession to the WTO at the end of 2001, which initiated the institutionalization of opening-up. Correspondingly, China's regional foreign trade experienced two growth phases. Figure 5.1 depicts separately the dynamics of export and import in the east, central and west from 1978 to 2008,[1] where exports are higher than imports with similar trends. Without loss of generality, we take exports as the example. In 1978, the exports of the east, central and west were 8.53 billion dollars, 0.54 billion dollars and 0.42 billion dollars, respectively. Then in 1992, exports of 11 provinces in the east rose to 68.596 billion dollars, and further soared to 1.28459 trillion dollars in 2008—18.7 times that of 1992 and 150.6 times that of 1978. In contrast, exports of the central and west were 84.35 billion dollars and 61.75 billion dollars, respectively in 2008, which were much smaller than that of the east despite high growth rates.

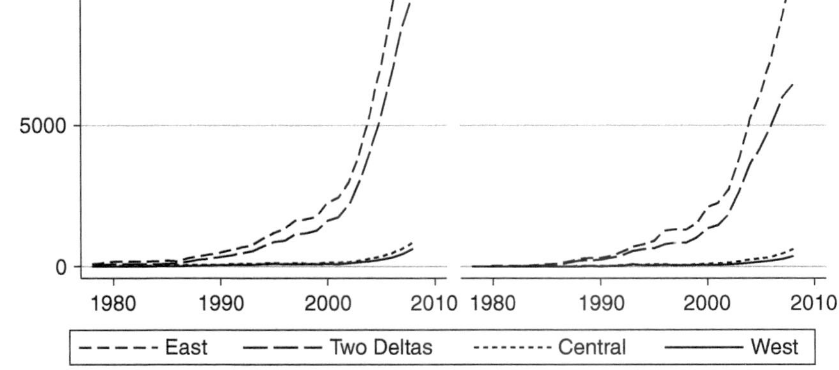

Figure 5.1 Foreign trade in China's three economic regions between 1978 and 2008, in 100 million US dollars ($US).[2]

Further examination reveals the imbalance of foreign trade even within the east, marked with the supernormal growth in the two deltas, namely, the *Pearl River Delta* (Guangdong) and *the Yangtze River Delta* (including Jiangsu, Zhejiang and Shanghai). In 1978, exports of the two Deltas combined were 4.75 billion dollars, accounting for 55.7 percent of the east and 50.1 percent of the nation. In 2008, total export of the two Deltas further rose to 967.14 billion dollars, accounting for 75.3 percent (roughly three-quarters) of the eastern regions' exports and 67.6 percent (roughly two-thirds) of national exports. In fact, since 1988, the export of Guangdong alone exceeded not only the total of five provinces in *Bohai Economic Rim* (including Shandong, Liaoning, Hebei, Beijing and Tianjin), but also the total of 20 central and western provinces. Such concentration in foreign trade leads to strong export-orientation in a few provinces. In 2008, the dependence on export and import in Guangdong were 78.9 percent and 54.3 percent, respectively, while Shanghai was even higher with 85.8 percent and 77.5 percent.

5.2.1.2 Process trade exceeds ordinary trade as the main form of regional foreign trade

In China, processing trade refers mainly to inward outsourcing, namely importing raw materials and intermediate inputs, then re-exporting after processing and assembling,[3] which includes *process and assembling* and *process with imported materials*.[4] Outward outsourcing is rare here. According to the statistics from China Custom, processing exports totaled $179.85 billion in 2002, exceeding ordinary export ($135.97 billion) and other export ($8.85 billion) and accounting for 55.4 percent of total exports. Processing exports rose to $675.28 billion in 2008. Although the growth slowed somewhat, the overall level was still higher than that of ordinary trade ($662.6 billion).

Figure 5.2 shows that, compared to ordinary trade, the agglomeration of processing trade is even higher, locating mostly in the east, especially in Guangdong and Jiangsu. For example, processing exports in the east reached $174.92 billion in 2002, accounting for 97 percent of the whole nation. Guangdong and Jiangsu totaled $115.32 billion ($93.47 billion and $21.84 billion, respectively), accounting for 65.9 percent of the exports of eastern regions and 64.1 percent exports of the nation.[5]

5.2.1.3 Mechanical and electrical products are the most important products in regional trade

Mechanical and electrical products (Section XVI in the Harmonized Code, M&E products for abbreviation hereafter), which include mechanical and electrical appliances, audio and video equipment, and their components and accessories, play an especially important role in China's foreign trade. According to Figure 5.3, income from China's M&E exports amounted to $410.8 billion in 2008,

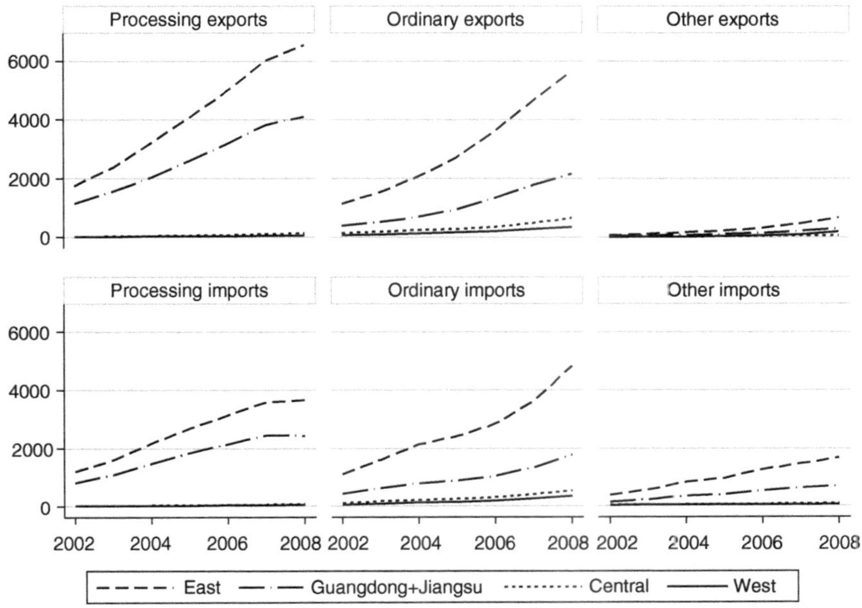

Figure 5.2 Regional trade of different types in China's three main regions between 2002 and 2008, in 100 million $US.[6]

Data source: Statistics of China Customs.

accounting for as much as 42.7 percent of total exports. The east's M&E export reached $588.59 billion, 96.3 percent of total national exports. In 2008, total national M&E products imports were $405.07 billion, 35.8 percent of total imports, among which the east contributed $379.48 billion, accounting for 93.7 percent of national imports on M&E products. Among other products, textiles (Section XI) and base metals (Section XV) exports are also high, accounting for over 10 percent of total exports. Imports for minerals (Section V) are also quite high, accounting for 23 percent of total imports.[7]

Such imbalanced distribution over products in China's exports can be partly attributed to the processing trade. M&E products are the largest product category in processing trade. In 2008, processing exports on this category in the east were $427.55 billion, accounting for 72.6 percent of this region's total exports on such products and 65.2 percent of its total processing exports. Guangdong's processing exports of M&E products totaled $177.58 billion, 43.2 percent of the province's total exports. Jiangsu's processing exports of M&E products were $102.74 billion, 41.9 percent of its total exports. M&E products are mostly high-tech and high value-added ones with a generally higher technological level. This causes China's exports to display an illusion of *high tech* and *high complexity* (Wang and

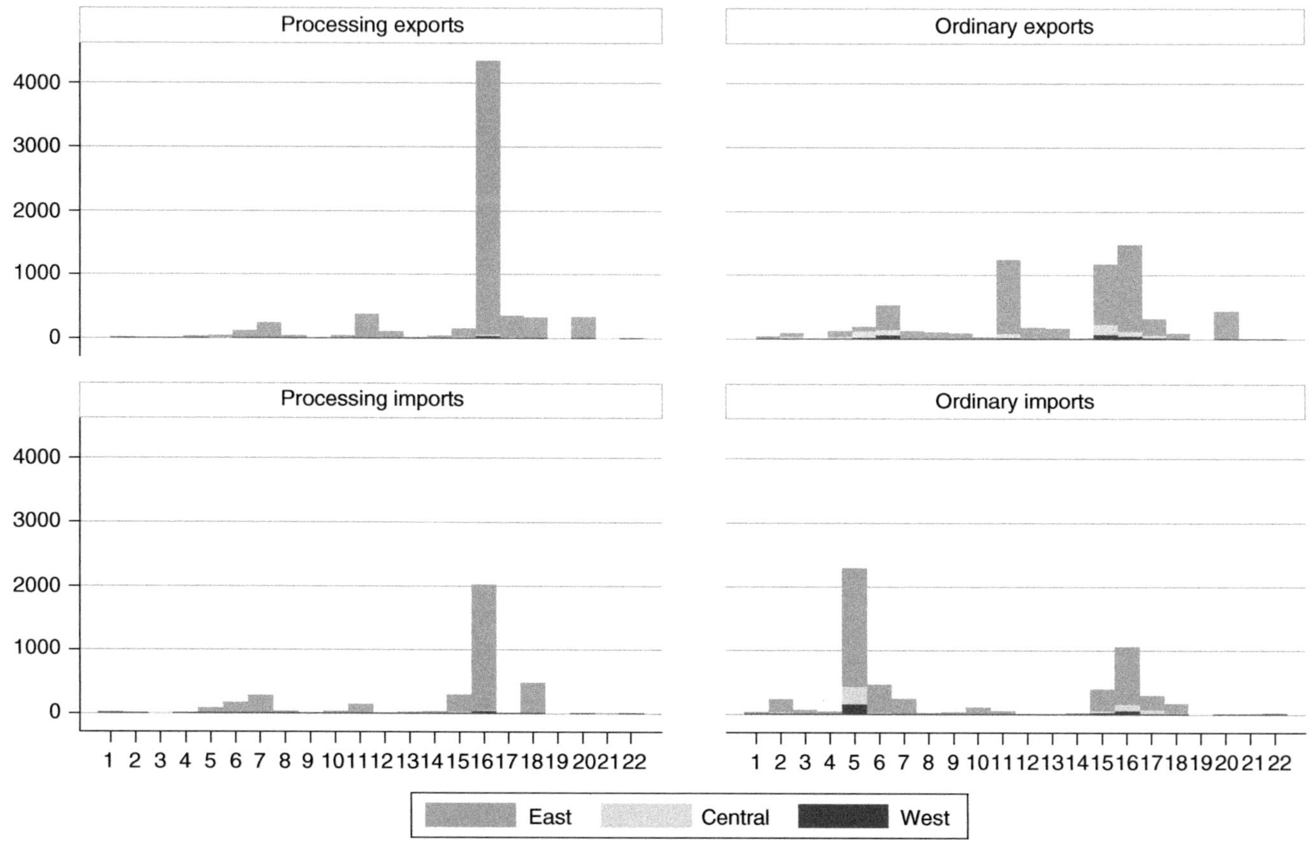

Figure 5.3 Exports of China's three regions over HS 2-digit products in 2008, in 100 million dollars.[7]
Data source: Statistics of China Customs.

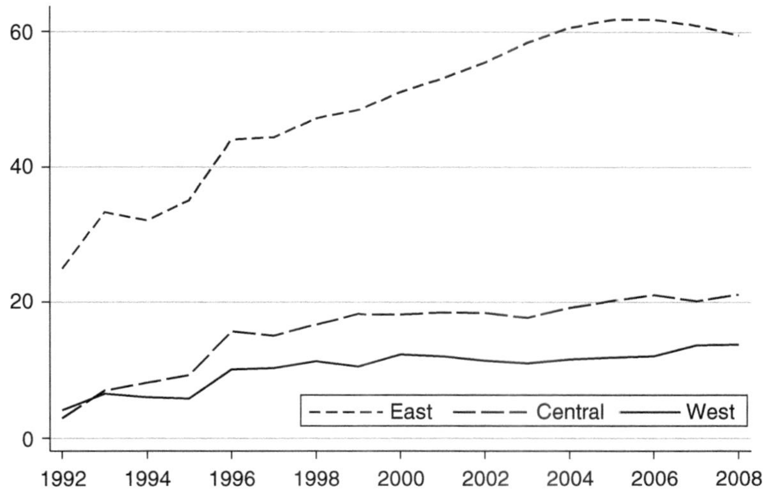

Figure 5.4 Export proportions of foreign enterprise in China's three economic regions from 1992 to 2008, in percentage.

Data source: Calculated with data from historical *China Statistical Yearbook*.

Wei, 2008). However, once the technology embedded in imported intermediate inputs is eliminated, the technological level of Chinese exports is not that high.[8]

5.2.1.4 Foreign enterprise contributions to regional foreign trade

As shown in Figure 5.4, in 1992, the exports of foreign enterprises in the east, central and west accounted for 24.9 percent, 3 percent and 4.1 percent of their regional exports, respectively.[9] Since then, the contribution of foreign enterprise to exports, in the east especially, has increased continually. By 2008, 59.5 percent, 21.2 percent and 13.8 percent of regional exports were realized by foreign enterprises in the east, center and west, respectively.

In the east, the propensities of foreign trade propelled by foreign enterprises are most obvious in Jiangsu, Shanghai and Tianjin, where foreign enterprise exports account for over 70 percent of total exports. In Beijing, Guangdong, Fujian and Shandong, over half of total exports can be attributed to foreign enterprises.

5.2.1.5 Regional trade partners are highly concentrated

The main export destinations for each Chinese region are the US, Japan, South Korea and Hong Kong. According to 2008 data (see Table 5.1), the US is the first export destination for 15 provinces, including Beijing, etc., and Japan is the first export destination for six provinces, including Inner Mongolia, etc. According to the frequencies of each country appearing in the top three export destinations of

Table 5.1 The top three trade partners of each China province and the proportion in 2008 (%)

	Export destination			*Import origin*		
	First	*Second*	*Third*	*First*	*Second*	*Third*
Beijing	USA 9.1	Japan 8.4	Hong Kong 6.0	Japan 15.1	Germany 13.2	USA 13.1
Tianjin	USA 19.2	South Korea 10.8	Japan 8.0	South Korea 21.3	Japan 16.4	USA 10.2
Hebei	South Korea 13.9	USA 10.4	Japan 4.6	Australia 19.5	India 17.8	Brazil 12.5
Shanxi	USA 15.6	Japan 14.7	South Korea 10.4	Australia 12.8	USA 10.1	Cuba 9.0
Inner Mongolia	Japan 16.6	South Korea 11.4	USA 8.1	Russia 49.7	Mongolia 13.7	Australia 8.3
Liaoning	Japan 21.9	South Korea 13.5	USA 11.3	Japan 12.7	Saudi Arabia 9.6	South Korea 7.4
Jilin	Japan 13.5	Russia 13.5	South Korea 12.2	Germany 42.4	Japan 18.9	Hungary 6.9
Heilongjiang	Russia 39.4	North Korea 5.4	USA 5.3	Russia 76.7	USA 4.3	Germany 3.6
Shanghai	USA 22.3	Japan 11.9	Hong Kong 7.7	Japan 17.7	USA 10.2	Taiwan 8.3
Jiangsu	USA 20.3	Japan 8.8	Hong Kong 7.3	South Korea 16.1	Japan 15.1	Taiwan 15.1
Zhejiang	USA 16.7	Japan 6.1	Germany 5.8	Japan 12.0	Iran 11.9	Taiwan 11.8
Anhui	USA 12.9	Japan 6.4	Hong Kong 4.6	Chile 16.4	Australia 15.3	Japan 13.1
Fujian	USA 21.0	Japan 11.9	Hong Kong 6.4	Taiwan 19.7	Japan 10.0	South Korea 10.0
Jiangxi	USA 11.7	Hong Kong 8.4	Germany 7.8	Brazil 11.0	USA 9.5	Chile 9.4
Shandong	USA 17.2	South Korea 14.1	Japan 12.6	South Korea 14.2	USA 7.7	Japan 7.1
Henan	USA 12.8	South Korea 9.9	Hong Kong 6.6	Australia 14.9	USA 11.2	India 10.0
Hubei	USA 11.7	South Korea 9.2	Hong Kong 7.9	Japan 20.9	Australia 9.5	Brazil 8.8
Hunan	USA 12.5	South Korea 11.4	Hong Kong 8.8	Australia 15.1	Japan 13.4	Germany 9.9
Guangdong	Hong Kong 32.6	USA 18.8	Japan 4.7	Hong Kong 20.6	Japan 14.0	Taiwan 13.2
Guangxi	Vietnam 13.3	USA 11.3	Japan 8.8	Brazil 14.9	Australia 10.9	Vietnam 10.1
Hainan	Hong Kong 33.4	USA 12.0	Japan 8.6	Amman 34.6	Saudi Arabia 13.1	Angola 10.9
Chongqing	USA 10.4	Japan 5.3	Brazil 5.0	Japan 20.4	USA 15.9	Germany 15.7
Sichuan	Hong Kong 19.3	USA 10.4	India 8.9	USA 28.9	Japan 15.9	Germany 8.2
Guizhou	Japan 10.7	USA 9.8	India 6.6	Canada 18.7	India 15.6	Australia 11.4
Yunnan	Vietnam 9.6	Japan 8.3	India 7.1	Burma 9.5	Canada 8.3	Australia 7.7
Tibet	Nepal 73.7	Kyrgyzstan 13.9	Singapore 6.5	Germany 21.4	USA 20.4	Nepal 18.6
Shaanxi	South Korea 12.6	Japan 11.6	USA 10.2	USA 23.7	Germany 14.0	Brazil 8.8
Gansu	USA 16.1	South Korea 13.0	Japan 10.5	Australia 25.2	Congo 11.6	Chile 9.5
Qinghai	Japan 49.1	South Korea 11.5	USA 7.7	Australia 39.7	South Africa 15.1	Germany 13.4
Ningxia	Japan 23.6	USA 11.1	South Korea 7.6	Australia 30.6	Germany 21.6	Japan 9.9
Xinjiang	Kyrgyzstan 42.3	Kazakhstan 37.4	Tajikistan 6.3	Kazakhstan 72.6	Russia 11.0	USA 3.7

Data source: Calculated with data from Chinese customs.

each Chinese province, the US shows up 27 times, Japan appears 23 times, and South Korea and Hong Kong emerge 14 and 12 times, respectively.

Compared with exports, imports are more dispersive, mainly originating from Australia and Japan. Australia is the number one import origin for seven provinces, while Japan is the number one import origin for six provinces. According to the frequencies of each country appearing in the top three import origins of each province in 2008, Japan appears 16 times, both Australia and the US appear 13, Germany appears 10 times, South Korea and Taiwan appear five, and India totals three.

The high concentration of import destinations for China's mainland regions is closely connected with processing trade too. Particularly, the coastal regions import components from Japan and South Korea, and primary products such as mineral ore, energy, etc. from Australia. After processing and assembling, the final goods are shipped to the US and European markets. Moreover, regional foreign trade demonstrates location advantage, for member states of the Commonwealth of Independent States (e.g. Russia), are the main trade partners of the three northwestern provinces in China, whereas Vietnam, Burma, India and other Southern Asian countries maintain close trade connections with southwestern provinces such as Guangxi, Yunnan and Guizhou, etc.

Above, we analyzed five important characteristics of China's regional foreign trade development. Of course, these five stylized facts are not isolated from each other. An obvious thread is that the rapid growth of Chinese processing trade (on M&E products in the east especially) results from the global production system dominated by foreign enterprises or multinationals, also leading to a high concentration of foreign trade partners for each region. Furthermore, it is noteworthy that due to limitations of spaces our summary above is rather rough and we have omitted many important aspects, such as the intensive and extensive margin and prices. Further research would be very helpful.[10]

5.2.2 The determinants of imbalanced regional foreign trade

From the above analysis, we learn that foreign trade across Chinese regions is highly imbalanced, with the east holding an overwhelming advantage. The next question is: what are the determinants or influencing factors behind such imbalanced development?

Undoubtedly, the east has innate geographical advantages that the central and west lack. From the perspective of trade costs, as ocean shipping is the main form of international transportation, so the east can save on transportation costs as it is either close to the coast or possesses ports or usually has a web of rivers.[11] By contrast, the west has many plateaus, mountains and deserts, which causes problems with transportation.[12] Also, after the reform, the east took the lead in giving up the *Overtake Strategy* that ran counter to their comparative advantage (Lin and Liu, 2003), and turned to developing industries that matched its own endowment advantages, which greatly strengthened the foundation of the east's trade with other countries in the world. One the country, economic transition in the central and west regions lagged behind, and the industrial development did not reflect their local endowment advantages, which made it difficult for these regions to be competitive in foreign trade. Regional disparities in foreign trade are so pronounced, however, that they go far beyond the explanatory adequacy of geographical and comparative advantage, which motivates us to seek further justifications and explanations. In summary, possible understandings, besides the reasons mentioned above, can be divided into the following five aspects.

5.2.2.1 Chinese regional foreign trade under the international division of labor system

Processing trade or undertaking international outsourcing, which is the result of international vertical specialization, is an important way in which China participates in international trade. Under such a system of labor division, a typical Chinese firm imports components and other intermediate inputs, and employs cheap labor domestically to conduct processing and assembling for exporting. Since such a form of trade has *both ends abroad*, it is more sensitive to transportation costs than ordinary trade. Therefore, it is mostly concentrated in the coastal regions and rarely extends to the hinterland, which thereby magnifies the east's geographical advantage (see Figure 5.2).[13] Moreover, processing trade cannot do without the support of the local industrial system, such as energy, materials, other components, and machinery, etc., which explains why processing trade is mostly concentrated in just a few coastal provinces such as Guangdong and Jiangsu. These provinces have strong industrial bases and a complete assortment of industries.[14]

However, we must realize that China's processing trade is mostly concentrated at the low ends of the value chain, which has both low technological content and low value added. Such pattern confines China's foreign trade largely to the global value chain dominated by multinationals. In the long run, it will not only cause the foundation of Chinese foreign trade to be fragile, but will also dominate the direction in which indigenous enterprises develop and eventually impair their export competitiveness. Liu and Zhang (2009) employed questionnaire data from 342 indigenous manufacturers located in Jiangsu, a typical processing trade province, and examined the determinants of enterprises' expanding exports. Their research proved that the supply-chain relation is an important factor in promoting indigenous manufacturer exports, while technological innovation, human and physical capital, as emphasized by classic trade theory, is irrelevant.[15] Besides, these processing trade enterprises are mostly small and medium-sized, ones which mainly adopted the *OEM* approach, and have little say on cooperation (Yan, 2009). This means that indigenous Chinese firms may be *locked in* at the low end of the global value chain and find it hard to develop further.

Compared with intermediate imports in the processing trade, Wu and Liu (2009) emphasized the importance of machinery imports for exports. They believe that the export growth miracle dominated by consumer goods in China's coastal regions is the result of *importing for exports* or *import-induced exports*, which is achieved through importing large amounts of advanced machinery from abroad. This is due to the fact that the international market has stricter demands on product quality, which cannot be met with the machinery manufactured by indigenous enterprises. Importing machinery enables the east to overcome this technical restriction.

5.2.2.2 The spatial consistency in the distribution of foreign direct investment (FDI) and foreign trade growth

As two important forms through which China participates in globalization, FDI inflow and foreign trade have internal consistency in their spatial distribution, as foreign investors give priority to the east with preferential policies, convenient transportation, complete supportive facilities and high purchasing power. Guangdong has a special advantage in attracting foreign investment due to its language, cultural and even blood connections with Hong Kong and Taiwan (Gao, 2003).

Regional FDI and regional foreign exports are interdependent and mutually promotive. On the one hand, foreign-invested enterprises have a strong export propensity and the ability to develop the international market, and they are closely connected with the multinationals' global production and sales system. For this reason, they can enhance the structure of exports, while expanding the scale of exports (Jiang, 2002).[16] On the other hand, the cost advantage implied by China's abundant labor resources is exactly the important determinant for attracting FDI inflow (vertical FDI inflow, especially). Export growth facilitates FDI inflow into China (Xian et al., 2003).

Liang and Su (2004) studied the dynamic relationship between regional foreign trade and FDI inflow from 1980 to 2001. They find that there exists a surprising consistency between provincial foreign trade and FDI, the complementary effects of which far surpass the substitution ones. If imports and exports are examined separately, bi-directional causality exists between FDI and manufacture exports; FDI can substitute for manufacture imports in the short run, but facilitate the imports in the long run. Similarly, Wang and Feng (2006) illustrate that FDI has significant *creation effect* and *substitution effect* on both imports and exports in the east, while the impact on the central and west is either insignificant or rather weak. Zhou (2009) also find that FDI inflows can facilitate export growth, and export can attract FDI inflows by a demonstration effect, which leads to a positive correlation between Chinese provincial FDI and exports.[17]

Logically, foreign enterprises can indirectly impact on or facilitate indigenous enterprises' exports through technological spillovers, vertical linkages, and market competition, etc. However, these effects have not gained strong support in the empirics. Yang and Chen (2005) find that FDI promotes only the exports by foreign enterprises themselves, the effect on indigenous enterprises is trivial, and the so-called *technological spillover* does not exist. They infer that this is mainly because of the fact that trade by foreign enterprises is mostly processing trade, in which the high value-added links in the chain are mostly located overseas. Chai (2006) also finds that although the export behavior of foreign enterprises can indirectly enhance indigenous firms' exports through export information spillover, they cannot induce significant competition. We believe that the reasoning based on processing trade cannot explain the logic of FDI inflow, as *domestic-market-seeking* FDI can not only enhance the industrial base and promote the quality and types of intermediate products in the host region, but also introduces new products and develops new fields, which undoubtedly enhances the comparative advantage and export competitiveness in the host region. Further research needs to examine FDI's impact on regional exports through forward and backward linkages and horizontal spillovers, with input and output relations in mind.

5.2.2.3 Policy and institutional factors that influence regional foreign trade

More economists have come to realize that policies and institutions shape the expectations and incentives of economic agents, and thus impact on regional economic development and openness. Differential regional policies include general preferential policies by the central government as well as a multitude of special arrangements (e.g. *development zone*, *bonded zone*, *export processing zone*, etc.).[18] Up to now, China's three fundamental strategic policy arrangements were all biased toward the coastal regions. The opening of the *Shenzhen Special Economic Zone* in the 1980s, the development of *Shanghai Pudong New Area* in the early 1990s, and the development and opening of the *Tianjin Binhai New District* proposed early in this century were situated in three core coastal areas of China, namely the *Pearl Delta*, *Yangtze Delta* and *Bohai Rim*, respectively. Under the impetus of a series of policies, these regions became the national demonstration regions in development and openness, where foreign trade expanded rapidly. Here, we can easily find that the choice of differential regional policies is not random but endogenous to the historical starting points, location advantages and regional gaps.[19] Of course, this also implies that the east's location advantage is not absolute, and can be adjusted or reversed entirely through policy measures (such as subsidies on the hinterland's foreign trade).

Institution is another source of regional comparative advantage. Compared to policies, the impact of institutions is more profound and more persistent. Judging from China's actualities, though different Chinese regions share almost the same social system and legal framework, their institutional environments vary due to the vast territory and difference in both human society and economic development. In view of the fact that institutional environment shapes regional incentives to participate in foreign trade, several papers have examined its impact on regional export (Wang et al., 2009; Jin et al., 2008; Zhang et al., 2010a; Li and Wang, 2010). These studies confirmed that institutions are surely an important source of regional comparative advantages of foreign trade. Of course, the word *institution* covers a wide range of things, and different researchers emphasize the different aspects. Jin et al. (2008) emphasized the importance of legal systems and property right protection. They discovered that legal systems and property rights protection both have a significant impact on regional export,[20] and the sensitivity of such an impact continuously increases, and even exceeds that, of geography and FDI distribution. Wang et al. (2009) and Li and Wang (2010) emphasized that the process of production and exporting are a set of bundled contracts, thus the efficiency of transactions and contract enforcement will impact on regional comparative advantage. Wang et al. (2009) argued that since most contracts are incomplete, the supplier may face the risk of hold-up if the two sides of a transaction are distant from one another. Agglomeration can solve this issue, thereby causing contract-intensive industries (namely, industry that is sensitive to, or dependent on, the efficiency of contract enforcement) to have a comparative advantage in regions with high agglomeration. Li and Wang (2010) find that regions with efficient contract enforcement tend to specialize in industries with high contract intensity, high specific physical asset, and low specific human capital, and that difference in firm integration is critical to reach these conclusions. Zhang et al. (2010a) consider the impact of regional marketization on exports and find that in provinces with better institutions, industries more reliant on institutions have a high proportion of exports.

It is to be noted that the effect of institutions on regional foreign trade is multilayered and multidimensional. First, the institutional environment will directly impact on interregional investment or FDI, which will impact on regional exports. Second, other than the fact that multidimensional institutions are worth studying, the reaction of different types of trade (processing or ordinary trade) toward institutions differs as well. Finally, the difference in institutional environment is not only manifested in the various local laws and regulations introduced based on local needs and interests, but also reflected in the overt and covert biases in the administration and enforcement of law of each region. The impact of these factors on regional foreign trade advantages requires further scrutiny.

5.2.2.4 Financial development and regional foreign trade

Financial market reform lagged during China's economic transition, and credit resources are still mainly concentrated in the four major state-owned commercial banks. Such a quasi-monopoly financial market is evidently detrimental to economic development, which causes the economy to exhibit obvious features of *financial repression*. Given the difference in regional financial markets, a few studies have examined its relationship with exports. Shen et al. (2006) discover that financial deepening is conducive to regional export openness, but rapid export growth in some regions largely benefited from informal finance rather than bank loans. Yang (2007) and Bao and Yang's (2008) studies, which are both based on Chinese provincial panel data, showed that financial development is surely one of the sources of regional foreign trade, and that financial efficiency indicators are more explanatory than financial scale indicators.

However, financial repression in China differs a lot from that in other developing countries due to obvious selectiveness or bias. It is reflected in the fact that banks allocate loans not according, to the potential profitability of projects, but to the applicant's institutional property or political pecking order, namely whether or not it is a state-owned enterprise (Huang, 2005).[21] Only the state-owned and state-controlled enterprises can obtain continuous and sufficient loans. By contrast, it is usually the case that vibrant private enterprises cannot obtain the necessary funding, causing *difficulty in obtaining loans* to become a significant bottleneck that restrains the development of the private sector.[22] Huang and Xian (2010a) discover that, although selective financial repression restrains the development of regional industry and its export advantage, FDI inflows de facto fill in the gap left by domestic enterprises due to lack of funding and contribute to the growth of industrial exports.

Trade financing (namely payables and receivables), derivative to the exchanges of goods, is also a substitutive form of formal bank financing. It can alleviate, to a certain extent, the credit restraints firms face, and enhance their export competitiveness. However, if the debt chain is too long, its negative effect is also obvious: once one firm has difficulty in repaying debt due to an export drop, other firms on the debt chain will then be affected. Moreover, the Yangtze and Pearl Delta are China's two richest regions; informal finance such as underground banks are relatively developed and private borrowing and lending is pervasive, which may help to enhance regional exports. But there exists no relevant empirical work in the current literature.

5.2.2.5 Economies of scale, productivity and regional exports

Other than factor endowment, new trade theory focuses on economies of scale and new-new trade theory emphasizes firm heterogeneity as important sources of export competitiveness. The former predicts that due to the existence of economies of scale and trade costs, countries with large domestic markets enable industries to make use of economies of scale sufficiently, and thus become net exporters, i.e. the existence of a *home market effect*. The latter believes that due to the existence of sunk costs and trade costs, only firms whose productivity surpasses a threshold can overcome these costs and become exporters, namely efficient firms self-select into the international market and not vice versa.

These theoretical predictions have already been preliminarily validated with Chinese samples. Yang (2008) found that the *home market effect* does exist among Chinese manufacturing exporters; the larger the relative domestic size and the better the future prospects of an industry, the faster its exports grow. ISGEP's (2008) study on Chinese firm data from 1998 to 2005 supports new-new trade theory's prediction about the relationship between productivity and exports. Zhang et al.'s study (2008) based on survey data on 342 firms from Jiangsu province also proved that firms' total factor productivity was conducive to exports, while the reverse does not hold.[23]

The above conclusions in existing literature are either based on the national samples or samples from a specific region (such as Jiangsu). If they are to be employed to explain the unevenness in China's regional foreign trade, we should still assume the regional disparities in economic (market) scale and firm productivity, namely the east's manufacturing has a larger economic (market) scale and higher average firm productivity. Although this assumption is intuitive, rigorous studies are necessary. Nowadays, research based on new-new trade theory is developing rapidly, which allows us to directly view through the firm the inner source of regional disparities on foreign trade.

5.3 Interregional trade and foreign trade

5.3.1 Notes on interregional trade data

Data is the prerequisite for empirical study, but there is no official interregional bilateral trade data, which causes difficulties for relevant research. Although literature based directly on interregional bilateral trade is scarce due to the lack of first-hand data, many researchers did lots of work with different methods from various perspectives. In this way, they have attempted to restore the logical relationship embedded in this process. To sum up, there are already four alternative proposals in the existing research.

The first one is to use provincial input–output data. Each province formulated an input–output table (referred to as the IO table hereafter) along with the national one every five years from 1982 onward. A basic transaction table in most provincial IO tables has two columns (*domestic inflow* and *domestic outflow*) that systematically report the interprovincial trade flow of each industry. However, since the inflow and outflow are summed up for all domestic regions as a whole, it cannot provide bilateral trade flows between two provinces. Therefore, the key in using this data is to view *other domestic regions combined* as one trade partner, and to deal with each variable accordingly (Naughton, 2003; Poncet, 2003). It should be noted that the quality of each province's IO table varies. For some provinces, the inflow and outflow data include exports and imports, while others only have a column of net outflows including net exports or net exports including net interprovincial outflows (Naughton, 2003; Xu and Li, 2009). For this reason, researchers have to sift through the samples according to their objective.

The second one is the use of interregional IO tables. National Information Center (2005) and Shinichi and Wang (2007) provided interregional IO tables for 1997 and 1987, respectively, which report both intraregional and interregional intermediate inputs and final use by sector. The data is valuable.[24] The table by the National Information Center (2005) disaggregates up to 30 sectors and is widely used. Taking the National Information Center's (2005) table as an example, this was established on the basis of each province's IO table with interregional bilateral trade coefficients determined by typical surveys (on the input structure of firms and the direction of product sales) and gravity model estimations. However, the common disadvantage for interregional IO tables is that the regional division is too broad to meet the needs of provincial level research. For example, the National Information Center (2005) divides the country into eight major regions according to location, economic development and industry structure.[25] Moreover, regional IO tables are only available for certain years so that comparisons cannot be made among successive years.

The third one is to resort to the aggregated transactions recorded by the VAT system of *Golden Tax Project* (VAT data in short).[26] Since VAT is levied only against the value-added part of goods and services, the purchaser has an incentive to ask for invoices (input invoices) in order to deduct the amount of taxes payable. For a specific firm located in a certain region, it could receive input invoices from firms in other regions and could also make out an output invoice for firms in other regions. In this way, according to the transaction recorded on the invoice and the information of locations, we can make an inference about interregional *imports* and *exports* (Xing and Li, 2009). Logically, this data can be disaggregated into county or even more refined administrative units, but existing research only uses the provincial level data. We believe that this data can provide the most credit-worthy information of bilateral trade, but it is regrettable that it is restricted and is not publicly available. Representative studies can be found in Research Group of DRC (2006a,b),[27] and Xing and Li (2009).

The fourth and final one is to use interprovincial railway freight exchange volume to approximately stand for trade flows. The *China Railway Yearbook* and *Yearbook of China Transportation & Communications* consecutively report inter-provincial exchange data on goods and coal which are transported by the national railways from 1998 to the present. Some researchers have used this data as a substitute for bilateral trade flows (Ye, 2000; Huang and Xian, 2010c; Xu and Li, 2010). In fact, this data was also an important basis for the National Information Center (2005) to estimate the coefficients of interregional bilateral trade. But rail-way transportation can only partially reflect interprovincial trade and the units are weight rather than value.[28] After careful examination, we are worried to find that the data may include information about goods that are re-exported abroad after reaching their destination. Despite its flaws, it is the only data which has provincial bilateral dimension and which is publicly available.

5.3.2 Stylized facts about interregional trade flows

Due to differences in data source, period of time and methodology, current literature arrives at different conclusions as to interregional trade flows. For example, Naughton (2003) believes that interprovincial trade flows in China are tremendous. After comparing 1987 and 1992 IO tables for each region, he discovered that interprovincial trade in this period grew much faster than provincial GDP and foreign trade: the ratio of total provincial outflows to GDP rose from 52 percent to 69 percent, and that of total provincial inflows to GDP rose from 53 percent to 68 percent. However, by just extending the period to 1997 with the same IO tables, Poncet (2002, 2003, 2005) reached a totally different conclusion. Her studies reveal that the average ratios of interprovincial trade flow to GDP in 1987, 1992, and 1997 were 54 percent, 50 percent, and 38 percent respectively, and that the proportions of interprovincial trade to total provincial trade were 88 percent, 80 percent, and 66 percent respectively. In other words, interprovincial trade declines relatively, rather than increases. Xu and Li (2009) found with regional IO tables that the ratio of interprovincial inflow (outflow) to GDP was 47 percent in 2002. We can nevertheless obtain following three basic consensuses, despite all these discrepancies.

5.3.2.1 The distribution of trade flows is asymmetrical

The trade volume of each region is positively proportional to its economic scale. The coastal provinces are more developed and therefore have larger interregional trade flows. In this sense, the *Yangtze Delta*, the *Pearl Delta* and the *Bohai Rim* are not only the economic centers but also the centers of interregional trade (Xu and Li, 2009). According to outflow proportions (see Table 5.2), Shanghai, Jiangsu and Zhejiang (in the Yangtze Delta) combined accounted for 33.04 percent of the total interregional trade volume, in which Shanghai ranked first nationwide with 14.04 percent. If Beijing, Guangdong and Shandong are further included, total trade flows of these six coastal provinces combined account for 54.27 percent of the national volume. On the contrary, goods exchanges of underdeveloped provinces with other provinces are much less. Interregional outflows in each of the three northwestern provinces (Qinghai, Ningxia, and Gansu) and the three southwestern provinces (Guizhou, Guangxi, and Hainan) amount to less than 1 percent of the total outflow, in which Qinghai's share is only 0.24 percent.

5.3.2.2 Trade flows display obvious gradient patterns

Coastal regions not only dominate interregional goods outflow, but also are important destinations for goods inflow. According to the interregional input–output table,[29] the gradient patterns can be easily identified for the interregional manufacturing flows, i.e. goods flow from the hinterland to coastal and from the west to central. The east coastal region is the most important destination for interregional flows, and takes up 8.71 percent, 8.04 percent, and 7.03 percent of the total outflows of the central, northern coastal, and southern coastal, respectively. Furthermore, several ratios of outflows are over 5 percent, which includes flows from the northwest to the central, those from northern coastal to the central, and those from the central the southern coastal regions. Of course, product nature and its usage also affect its spatial mobility. According to the interregional input–output information provided by the National Information Center (2005), we calculated the spatial characteristics of the mining, light industry, and heavy industry sector with regard to intermediate and final use. The spatial dimension is redivided into four major regions: northeastern, eastern, central, and western. According to Table 5.3, the interregional mobility of intermediate use is much higher than that of final use, but the *east-central-west* gradient pattern is still very obvious. Specifically, most mining products are for intermediate use and thus have the highest spatial mobility. In northeastern, central, and western regions, the ratios of mining output that flow to the eastern regions as intermediate use are 23.08 percent, 33.32 percent, and 14.27 percent, respectively. In the western region, 8.14 percent of the mining output flows into the central region as intermediate use. The reverse flow is much less. The output proportion of heavy industry

Table 5.2 The proportion of interregional trade of each province and their top three trading partners

Province	*Outflow proportion (%)*	*Top three trade partners*
Beijing	7.83	Shanghai, Guangdong, Hebei
Tianjin	4.38	Beijing, Hebei, Guangdong
Hebei	4.94	Beijing, Tianjin, Shandong
Shanxi	2.53	Hebei, Beijing, Shandong
Inner Mongolia	1.49	Beijing, Hebei, Liaoning
Liaoning	4.55	Shanghai, Beijing, Jilin
Jilin	1.8	Liaoning, Beijing, Guangdong
Heilongjiang	2.3	Liaoning, Jilin, Beijing
Shanghai	14.04	Jiangsu, Zhejiang, Guangdong
Jiangsu	11.84	Shanghai, Zhejiang, Guangdong
Zhejiang	7.16	Shanghai, Jiangsu, Guangdong
Anhui	2.42	Jiangsu, Shanghai, Zhejiang
Fujian	1.97	Guangdong, Shanghai, Zhejiang
Jiangxi	1.16	Guangdong, Shanghai, Zhejiang
Shandong	5.88	Jiangsu, Shanghai, Zhejiang
Henan	2.98	Jiangsu, Guangdong, Shandong
Hubei	2.84	Guangdong, Hunan, Shanghai
Hunan	1.61	Guangdong, Hubei, Zhejiang
Guangdong	7.52	Shanghai, Beijing, Jiangsu
Guangxi	0.95	Guangdong, Zhejiang, Yunnan
Hainan	0.48	Guangdong, Shanghai, Zhejiang
Chongqing	1.15	Sichuan, Guangdong, Jiangsu
Sichuan	2.03	Chongqing, Guangdong, Zhejiang
Guizhou	0.67	Guangdong, Guangxi, Chongqing
Yunnan	1.28	Guangdong, Sichuan, Jiangsu
Shaanxi	1.58	Gansu, Inner Mongolia, Beijing
Gansu	0.99	Sichuan, Shaanxi, Shanghai
Qinghai	0.24	Gansu, Guangdong, Shanghai
Ningxia	0.31	Inner Mongolia, Shaanxi, Shanghai
Xinjiang	1.1	Gansu, Shanghai, Jiangsu

Note: Tibet is excluded from the table.
Data source: Research Group of DRC (2006b, Tables 1 and 2).

for intermediate use is high as well and spatial mobility is only second to mining. The northeastern, central and western heavy industry sectors have 5.61 percent, 19.24 percent, and 8.91 percent respectively of their total output flow into the eastern region as intermediate input. Since the proportion for intermediate use is relatively small, the spatial mobility of light industry products is relatively low.

5.3.2.3 The bias toward intraregional trade is quite high

As shown in the National Information Center (2005) table, due to geographical and industry structure, intraregional trade accounts for most of the total trade volume for each region. In northwestern and central regions, intraregional trade has a proportion of over 75 percent, while the northeastern region has the

Table 5.3 Distribution of each region's "total output" flow direction by sector (1997)

Industry	*Region*	*Intermediate use*				*Final use*			
		Northeastern	*Eastern*	*Central*	*Western*	*Northeastern*	*Eastern*	*Central*	*Western*
Mining	Northeastern	74.09	23.08	1.73	1.19	0.57	–0.07	–0.01	0.01
	Eastern	3.66	112.36	7.95	2.51	0.1	1.62	0.07	0.08
	Central	4.07	33.32	76.33	5.16	0.13	0.45	2.36	0.13
	Western	3.06	14.27	8.14	83.21	0.09	0.14	–0.01	2.16
Light industry	Northeastern	40.35	1.98	0.33	0.52	49.83	1.36	0.42	0.72
	Eastern	0.88	52.23	1.48	1.22	0.95	23.35	1.75	1.93
	Central	0.9	7.99	44.9	2.07	1.06	4.74	44.09	2.77
	Western	0.49	3.47	1.1	38.25	0.56	2.3	1.31	44.09
Heavy industry	Northeastern	76.52	5.61	1.03	1.28	13.41	0.51	0.26	0.34
	Eastern	1.47	74.16	3.47	2.84	0.29	16.23	1.44	0.97
	Central	1.13	19.24	67.11	4.45	0.16	2.13	18.08	1.32
	Western	0.6	8.91	3.9	63.1	0.08	0.76	0.86	18.62

Notes: (1) Heavy industry in the table does not include utilities. Eastern region includes Jing-jin, northern coastal, eastern coastal and southern coastal regions. Western region includes northwestern and southwestern regions. (2) For example, the *74.09* in the first column and first row of the table means that, in terms of usage, 74.09 percent of the northwestern region's mining output is for the local region's intermediate use during production. Since imports and exports are excluded, the horizontal sum does not equal 100 percent.

Data source: Calculated from National Information Center (2005).

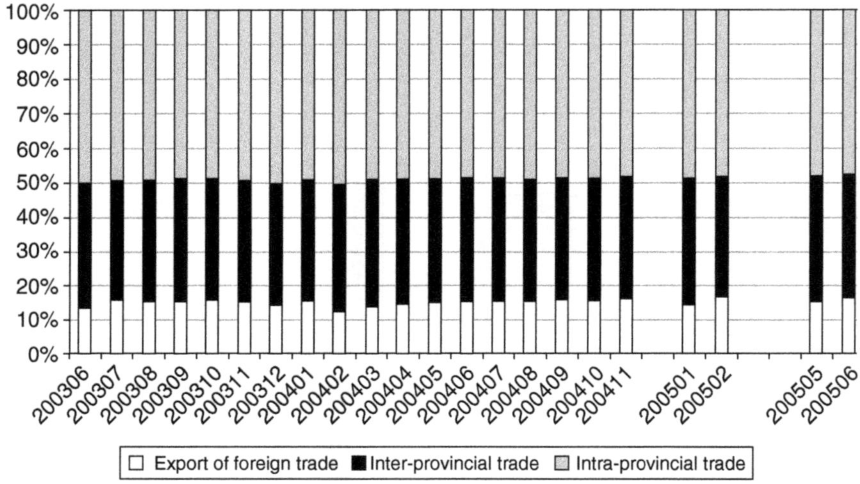

Figure 5.5 June 2003 to June 2005 Chinese exports, interprovincial trade and intraprovincial trade.

Data source: Research Group of DRC (2006a).

highest proportion of nearly 90 percent. Regions whose proportion exceeds 80 percent, are Beijing-Tianjin, eastern coastal, and southwestern regions, while those below 80 percent are northern coastal and southern coastal regions. Table 5.3 also shows that no matter for intermediate or final use, the proportion of intraregional trade is much higher than that of interregional trade.

Studies based on VAT data uncover the same regularities (see Figure 5.5). As showed in studies by the Research Group of DRC (2006a), from June 2003 to June 2005, foreign exports, interprovincial trade, and intraprovincial trade account for 14.93 percent, 36.12 percent, and 48.95 percent of provincial total exports, respectively. So the intraprovincial trade is 1.36 times that of interprovincial trade, and interprovincial and intraprovincial trade combined is 5.7 times that of foreign exports. It indicates that the existence of both a domestic trade bias and an intraregional trade bias.

5.3.3 Impact of foreign trade on interregional trade

Does foreign trade directly impact on interregional trade? The answer is affirmative. By the cluster analysis with trade volumes, the Research Group of DRC (2006b, p. 16) divided the country into four major trade regions: eastern, southern, northern, and northwestern. The southern trade region has Guangdong as its core, and the eastern trade region has Shanghai, Jiangsu, and Zhejiang as its core provinces. The northern trade region has Beijing as its core, and includes Tianjin, Hebei, and Liaoning. According to the analysis in Section 5.2, these three regions, especially the former two, are key areas in China's foreign trade, and thus foreign

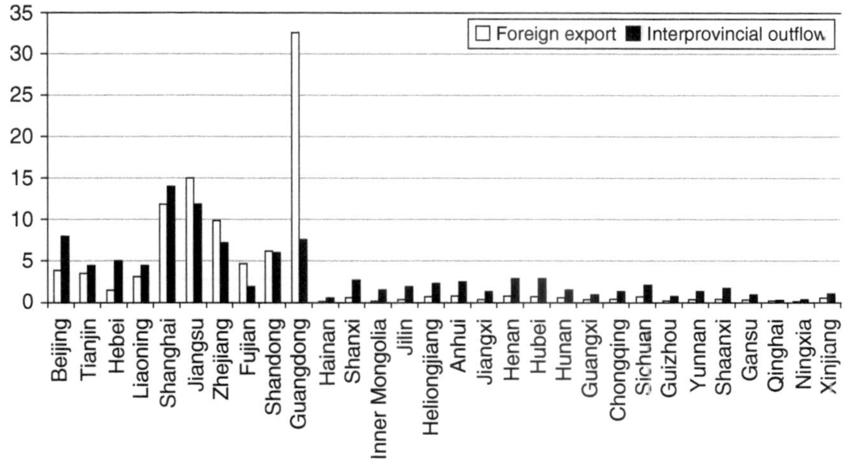

Figure 5.6 2003–2005 Foreign exports and interprovincial outflow proportion of Chinese regions in percentage.

Data source: Interprovincial outflow figures come from Table 1 in Research Group of DRC (2006a). Export data comes from the Guoyan website database (http://edu-data.drcnet.com.cn). Provincial data in the figure does not include Tibet, Hong Kong, Macau and Taiwan.

trade and interregional trade are consistent. More specifically, Figure 5.6 reports the share of each province's foreign exports and interregional outflow. The simple correlation coefficient between the two indicators is 0.691 and the rank correlation coefficient reaches 0.911.

Xing and Li (2009) add an *international trade* variable (defined as the total value of imports and exports) their gravity estimation about interregional trade. They find that after this variable is included, the *border effect* is slightly lessened, and the model's explanatory power increases significantly, which indicates that foreign trade impacts on interprovincial trade. More accurately, the coefficients of importer and exporter are both significantly positive, so foreign trade does promote the flows of interprovincial trade within China.

In Xing and Li's (2009) estimation, the *international trade* variable varies in only provincial dimension rather than in bilateral dimension, and thus cannot detect the impact of bilateral differences in regional foreign trade. In view of this, Huang and Xian (2010c) re-examine the impact of foreign trade with relative export dependence, i.e. export dependence of outflow province divided by that of inflow province. Huang and Xian (2010c) use the data of railway freight exchange flows between 1998 and 2006. They find that, relative to the outflow region, the higher the inflow region's export openness, the larger the influx of goods. To put it differently, goods tend to flow from provinces with relatively fewer exports to provinces with relatively greater exports, so foreign exports do induce domestic interregional trade flows.

Table 5.4 2002 Chinese surveyed firms export and domestic market entrance observation value distribution

Entrance or non-entrance		*Whether exporting to foreign market*		*Total*
		Export	*No export*	
Entrance	Sample size	4390	10985	15,375
	Proportion (%)	46.04	36.21	38.56
Non-entrance	Sample size	5146	19354	24,500
	Proportion (%)	53.96	63.79	61.44
Total		9536	30339	39,875

Data source: Author's calculations based on World Bank firm survey data.

In another study, Huang and Xian (2010b) examine the relationship between a firm's exports and its entry into markets in other regions with micro-level data.[30] The explained variable is a 0–1 dummy variable (with dimensions of both firm and provincial market) regarding whether or not a firm enters some other provinces. The proportion of *entrance* and *non-entrance* observations are 38.56 percent and 61.44 percent, respectively (see Table 5.4). For the subsamples of foreign-exporter and non-foreign-exporter, the proportions of *entrance* observation are 46.04 percent and 36.21 percent, respectively. After controlling for the bilateral trade costs and firm-specific factors such as productivity, economic scale, etc., they find that the higher a firm's proportion of foreign exports, the more likely it is to enter into a specific domestic market, but the marginal effect gradually declines. The reason why export's influence gradually diminishes lies in the fact that given the total amount of production, the higher the proportion of exports, the lower the amount of products can be sold domestically.

5.3.4 Regional and foreign markets: substitutes or complements

The relationship between foreign trade and interregional trade can be examined from another viewpoint, that is, regional economic growth. Economic theory confirms that market size is conducive to the division of labor, enhancing economies of scale, thereby facilitating economic growth. The famous hypothesis of the extent-of-the-market states that the bigger the market, the more elaborate society's division of labor and the higher the efficiency. The theory of Big Push in economic development argues that, due to increasing returns to scale characteristic of modern industry, the size of market demand plays a critical role for underdeveloped economies to escape from the *poverty trap*, as it determines whether it is attractive for large-scale investment and production.

Foreign and interregional trade correspond to foreign and regional markets, respectively. The eastern provinces have larger foreign markets than those of the hinterland, while the central provinces have larger domestic markets due to being situated in the center of the country. Theoretically, regional and foreign markets may substitute for each other and complement each other. If two markets are mutually substitutive, then the importance of foreign (domestic) markets for regional economic growth diminishes as the domestic (foreign) market expands. If the two markets are complementary, however, the impact of foreign (domestic) markets on regional economic growth will increase as domestic (foreign) markets expand.

Huang and Li (2006a) proxied foreign and regional market sizes with export dependence and market potential index in the *New Economic Geography*, respectively. They included these two variables and their interaction in a growth equation.[31] The estimation results show that the estimators for domestic markets and foreign markets are both significantly positive, while the estimators for the interaction are significantly negative. It shows that regional market size and export openness do impact on the rate of regional economic growth, in which foreign and regional markets are shown to substitute for each other. Based on data from 1995 to 2007, Ke and Guo (2010) found that internal and external openness significantly promoted provincial growth. However, the two factors are complementary rather than substitutive, which is pronounced in undeveloped provinces. The discrepancy between conclusions above lies in the fact that Huang and Li (2006a) paid attention on regional market size, while Ke and Guo (2010) focused on provincial trade openness calculated with the approach of relative price variance.

Based on Huang and Li (2006a), Huang and Huang (2008) further examined the channels through which different markets impact on regional economic growth. They further divided the domestic market into local markets and regional markets (that is, the domestic non-local market). Their estimation model has both regional and industry dimensions. They found that regions with a high proportion of exports (thereby having a large foreign market size) showed fast growth in industries dependent on foreign demand, and that regions with large local and regional market sizes showed fast growth in industries dependent on domestic demand.

5.4 The impact of foreign trade on regional specialization: theory and evidence

5.4.1 Foreign trade and internal geography: theoretical analyses

The essence of trade is exchanging goods and offsetting weaknesses with strengths. The larger the differences in industry structure across regions, the stronger the basis for interregional trade. Constrained by data availability, more researchers turn to the spatial economic connections from the viewpoint of specialization, which is usually treated as the substitute or equivalent of interregional trade or regional market integration.[32] How then, does foreign trade impact on China's regional specialization? Since regional specialization and industry agglomeration are two closely linked concepts which are used to measure the spatial distribution of industry,[33] this question can be expressed as how foreign trade has impacted China's industrial agglomeration.

The impact of foreign trade on domestic industry distribution is discussed in the early literature of *New Economic Geography*. Krugman and Livas Elizondo (1996) first used Mexico as the background to construct a two-country-three-region model. This model predicts that foreign trade liberalization will dissolve the economic centers formed during the closed economy (or import-substitution economy), thereby causing economic activity to be dispersed rather than concentrated. It is explained that the center of Mexico's domestic industry has drifted from Mexico City to the northern US-Mexico border since the integration of North American economies. Since then, theoretical models with similar spatial structures gradually increased,[34] among which Crozet and Koenig-Soubeyran (2002; 2004) examined geographical advantages in foreign trade. They believed that as long as competitive pressures from foreign firms are not too strong, trade liberalization will cause agglomeration forces to surpass dispersion ones, and industry will cluster in border regions close to foreign markets. Similar research in China came from Chen and Zhang (2007), whose simulation results illustrated that the difference among regional foreign trade costs facilitated the agglomeration of domestic manufacturing toward the coastal regions. This is quite close to the actual change seen in China's economic geography after the reform.

All of the above theoretical models are in the background of matured economies. As for China, why industry concentrates in the eastern coastal regions can be explained in two ways. On the one hand, it results from the relocation of footloose industry as described in the orthodox *New Economic Geography*.[35] On the other hand, it reflects the difference in industrialization among eastern, central, and western regions. The former and the latter refer to spatial adjustments in the *stock* and incremental sense, respectively. Theoretical models that accurately depict Chinese industry distribution and agglomeration should include the structural transformation across regions or regional industrialization.

Hu (2002) was the first to develop a two-country-three-region model, which includes rural industrialization, based on the case of China. In his model, the east becomes the initial region with the geographical advantage of international trade, and the advantage has been continuously strengthened due to the positive feedback mechanism by increasing returns to scale. This model assumes that interregional migration is prohibited due to policy restrictions, and that the extra labor supply required by manufacturing growth can only come from *rural–urban migration* in the local region. This depicts very well the impact of township enterprises (i.e., *leaving the farmland without leaving the hometown*) on the spatial distribution of Chinese industry in the 1980s.[36] However, since the 1990s, China's reform entered into a new phase and interregional labor migration has already been quite frequent. Labor required for industrial development is no longer limited to local supply, thus giving rise to the need for a theoretical model including *leaving both the farmland and the hometown*.

By relaxing the assumptions regarding consumer utility function and the labor market in Krugman (1991), Murata (2008) analyzed the process of structural transformation derived by transport-cost reducing.[37] Declining interregional transport costs will expand the extent of the market for manufactured goods while enhancing the real purchasing power of consumers, thereby increase wages in the industrial sector, which has increasing returns to scale. In this way, when transport costs fall below a certain threshold, industrialization and industrial agglomeration occur at the same time. On the basis of this model, Huang (2006) developed a two-country-three-region spatial model in order to examine the impact of foreign trade liberalization on regional industrialization and internal economic geography. The simulation results show that trade liberalization can both facilitate labor reallocation across regions and industrialization causing industries to concentrate in regions closer to foreign markets.

In all of the models described above, it is assumed that there are only two factors, namely labor and land, in which the land is immobile. Deng (2009) developed a two-country-three-region model that included three factors (worker, peasant, capital) and two sectors (agriculture, manufacturing), based on the modelling in Ihara (2005). The simulation results show that even if domestic interregional trade barriers are high, such barriers cannot stop industry from agglomerating in the east if its advantages in foreign trade are large enough. Moreover, although enhancing trade opening of the hinterland facilitates the dispersion of capital and manufacture sector, agglomeration forces produced by lower interregional trade barriers will compensate for the relatively weakened advantages in foreign trade so that the east can retain its growth trend.

5.4.2 The facts of China's regional specialization

The *Krugman* index and *Hoover* index are indicators often used to depict regional specialization in the literature. The former compares each region with all other regions combined, while the latter compares each region with the average.[38] There are many studies regarding the measurement of Chinese regional specialization (Young, 2000; Bai et al., 2004; Huang and Li, 2006b; Xian and We, 2006; Fan, 2007; Ma et al., 2010). Young (2000) was the first to study Chinese regional specialization. He found that Chinese regional specialization declined continuously rather than increasing after the reform. In addition to the rough classifications of three sectors, he also neglected the very important fact that regional specialization or diversification is related to the level of economic development.[39] During the time period studied by Young (which may even be extended to the present), China was still at the stage of industrialization. Besides the directly administered municipalities, all the other regions are endeavoring to develop secondary and tertiary industries. Therefore the specialization indicator calculated in this way is naturally gradually declining.[40] Du and Park (2006) revised this understanding and found that after controlling for the economic structure related to each province's economic growth, regional specialization has been increasing since the 1980s.

More research was conducted within industry and manufacturing. Huang and Li (2006b), Xian and Wen (2006), Ma et al. (2010) calculate the specialization for each province (the *Krugman Index*). It is shown in these studies that the average level of specialization slightly declined before the 1990s and constantly increased thereafter.[41] Table 5.5 reports the results for 28 Chinese provinces in the various years between 1980 and 2008. Compared with 1980, 20 out of 28 Chinese provinces in 1988 showed a decline in specialization to different extents, among which

Table 5.5 1980–2008 Specialization index of mainland Chinese provinces

Year		*1980*	*1985**	*1988*	*1992*	*1995**	*2000*	*2004**	*2008**
Eastern	Beijing	0.406	0.395	0.383	0.402	0.556	0.668	0.474	0.644
	Tianjin	0.211	0.206	0.263	0.315	0.448	0.422	0.453	0.483
	Hebei	0.302	0.305	0.227	0.276	0.389	0.484	0.648	0.674
	Liaoning	0.462	0.41	0.386	0.423	0.467	0.53	0.559	0.482
	Shanghai	0.377	0.335	0.332	0.367	0.442	0.397	0.386	0.442
	Jiangsu	0.357	0.336	0.307	0.388	0.419	0.379	0.38	0.409
	Zhejiang	0.244	0.292	0.366	0.411	0.473	0.492	0.608	0.532
	Fujian	0.55	0.48	0.47	0.49	0.516	0.45	0.488	0.489
	Shandong	0.249	0.299	0.296	0.307	0.358	0.474	0.476	0.42
	Guangdong	0.451	0.447	0.418	0.459	0.533	0.638	0.705	0.7
Central	Shanxi	0.288	0.389	0.432	0.449	0.609	0.78	0.979	1.03
	Inner Mongolia	0.582	0.554	0.427	0.497	0.57	0.845	0.797	0.766
	Jilin	0.483	0.483	0.457	0.556	0.725	0.952	1.067	0.936
	Heilongjiang	0.54	0.495	0.458	0.495	0.624	0.798	0.838	0.821
	Anhui	0.255	0.293	0.282	0.24	0.32	0.317	0.435	0.372
	Jiangxi	0.306	0.28	0.315	0.298	0.347	0.535	0.503	0.348
	Henan	0.346	0.288	0.299	0.314	0.413	0.49	0.522	0.518
	Hubei	0.36	0.353	0.31	0.303	0.321	0.389	0.432	0.412
	Hunan	0.314	0.304	0.312	0.343	0.455	0.496	0.493	0.451
Western	Guangxi	0.408	0.329	0.385	0.461	0.556	0.656	0.716	0.644
	Sichuan	0.305	0.311	0.273	0.32	0.427	0.536	0.543	0.436
	Guizhou	0.569	0.58	0.531	0.648	0.682	0.9	0.86	0.822
	Yunnan	0.472	0.528	0.643	0.754	0.966	1.006	1.036	0.928
	Shaanxi	0.443	0.366	0.377	0.357	0.414	0.417	0.535	0.602
	Gansu	0.57	0.468	0.335	0.398	0.603	0.789	0.827	0.949
	Qinghai	0.578	0.579	0.464	0.512	0.707	1.078	1.055	1.029
	Ningxia	0.606	0.6	0.451	0.584	0.798	0.821	0.725	0.72
	Xinjiang	0.457	0.472	0.545	0.55	0.682	0.897	0.922	0.858
Simple average		0.41	0.399	0.384	0.426	0.529	0.63	0.659	0.64

Note: This table reports the *Krugman Index* calculated for 25 manufacturing industries. For details see Huang and Li (2006b). 1980–1995 indexes come from that publication, and raw data for 2000–2008 indexes are from the industrial statistics database of the Guoyan website (http://edu-data.drcnet.com.cn). Indexes for 2000 are calculated with product sale revenue, while other years, the industrial output (valued at current prices). The asterisk (*) represents a census year. This table excludes indexes for Tibet, Hong Kong, Macau, and Taiwan. Indexes of Sichuan and Guangdong include Chongqing and Hainan, respectively.

Gansu, Inner Mongolia, and Ningxia saw the largest magnitude of decline. The mean of the specialization index declined from 0.41 in 1980 to 0.384 in 1988. However, entering the 1990s, regional difference in industry structure turned to expand rapidly. Compared with 1988, four provinces (such as Anhui, Shaanxi) saw a decline in the specialization index, and the other 24 provinces saw a rise in this index, of which Ningxia, Guizhou, and Yunnan experienced the largest magnitude. In 1992, the mean of the specialization was 0.426, exceeding that of 1980. Since then, it rose continually, reaching 0.659 in 2004 and experiencing a slight fall in 2008. Huang and Li (2006b) argue that the reason for slight drops in specialization index in the 1980s can possibly be the development of township enterprises, which can be found in nearly every region. During this mode of industrialization (that is, *leaving the farmland without leaving the hometown*), people tend to choose the low-technology and labor-intensive industries (such as food, textiles, etc.), which are closely related with the primary industry and can source raw materials locally. So the regional industry structure trends to convergence. Entering the 1990s, as the global specialization deepened, the coastal regions gradually shifted toward high-technology and capital-intensive industries (such as machinery, electronics, transportation etc.), and their industry structure gap with the hinterland regions rapidly expanded.

Spatially, the regional specialization index is negatively correlated with developmental phase, economic scale and *per capita* income. The specialization indexes of hinterland regions, especially the western underdeveloped provinces, are generally higher than those of the coastal regions. This is because the west evidently lags behind the rest of the country in many important industries, thus exhibiting sharp difference in industry structure. On the contrary, the east is more developed, and has more complete industry system. According to the 3-year specialization in the 1980s in Table 5.5, Guizhou, Ningxia, Yunnan and Qinghai, which locate in the west, are among the highest, while Tianjin, Anhui, Hebei, and Shandong are among the lowest. According to 3-year averages in the new millennium, Qinghua, Yunnan, Jilin, and Shanxi are among the highest, while Anhui, Jiangsu, Shanghai, and Hubei are among the lowest. This confirms Imbs and Wacziarg's (2003) statement on the relationship between developmental phase and specialization from another perspective.

5.4.3 The impact of foreign trade on regional specialization

The essence of a specialization indicator is to compare the difference in industry distribution structure between regions. So, factors that impact on industrial location naturally affect regional specialization. Many studies examined foreign trade's impact on the industrial location in China. Representative studies include Batisse and Poncet (2006), Huang and Li (2006b), Xian and Wen (2006), Ge (2009), Li and Peng (2010). The common estimation model used in these studies is developed by Midelfart-Knarvik et al. (2000). This model is a generalization of comparative advantage, that is, industries that are intensive in a certain *factor* are more likely to be located in regions abundant with this *factor*. The key explanatory variable of this model is a group of interaction terms (i.e., cross-products) between geographical and industry characteristics. In order to examine the impact of regional foreign trade, these studies included the interaction term of one province's distance to coast and the degree of industrial dependence on export (trade).[42] Although the measurement of distance to coast varies, the estimation results are quite similar in that industries dependent on foreign trade tend to be located in the coastal regions which close to foreign markets, and thus foreign trade contributes to regional specialization and industrial agglomeration in China. It is noteworthy that these studies emphasize the importance of export but do not pay due attention to import or trade liberalization (such as tariff-cutting). Since the mechanisms and effects on industry location differ a lot between export and import,[43] further research is necessary.

Batisse and Poncet (2006) as well as Huang and Li (2006b) also considered the impact of local protectionism or interregional trade costs on the spatial distribution of industry, but their methods are different.[44] Batisse and Poncet (2006) add in the model an interaction term of regional market potential and industry interprovincial trade barriers (calculated based on the border effect). Huang and Li (2006b) follow Bai et al.'s (2004) approach by including an interaction terms of the proportion of provincial fiscal revenue and industry output tax rate or industry proportion of SOEs. Batisse and Poncet (2006) discover that industries vulnerable to local protectionism are more likely to be located in regions with large market potential. It implies that interregional trade costs formed by local protectionism lead industry to locate in regions with more consumers and higher purchasing power, which goes against the principle of free trade. However, Huang and Li (2006b) discovered that industries which are locally protected (having high output tax rates or high proportion of SOEs) tend to be located in provinces dependent mostly on fiscal revenues (i.e., the proportion of fiscal revenue in regional GDP is high). However, such a result is confined to the hinterland regarding the 1990s sample.

More directly, Ma et al. (2010) estimated the effect of the opening-up and fiscal decentralization on regional specialization. They find that fiscal decentralization encourages local government to adopt protectionist policies, which defer specialization, but the opening-up will gradually weaken this incentive, which is conducive to reducing local protectionism.

5.5 The interaction between foreign trade and regional market integration

5.5.1 Interregional trade costs and composition in China

5.5.1.1 Trade costs and interregional trade

Trade costs that restrict the circulation of goods refer to all costs incurred in obtaining the goods over the marginal production cost, including transport costs (consisting of shipping costs and time value), tariff and non-tariff trade barriers, contract enforcement costs etc. (Anderson and van Wincoop, 2004). China's interregional trade costs come mainly from two sources: one is interregional transport costs, and the other is local protectionism. Interregional trade costs are the equivalent of international tariffs and non-tariff barriers.

According to the questionnaire survey conducted jointly by the World Bank and the DRC in 2003 (Table 5.6), overall, for firms that already have out-province businesses, transport costs rank second among the factors restricting firms from conducting sales, being next only to the lack of price competitiveness on products, while local protectionism and unfair competition ranks fourth, before product quality. For products that are closely related to local tax revenue and/or with low unit values, such as beverages, pharmaceuticals, tobacco, and lumber, transport costs and local protectionism both have a larger impact.

Table 5.6 Barriers of firms' sale of products

	For firms with out-province business			*For firms without out-province business*		
	Overall	*Beverages*	*Pharmaceuticals*	*Overall*	*Beverages*	*Pharmaceuticals*
The demand is inadequate	3	4	3	1	2	3
Product lacks of price competitiveness	1	3	2	2	4	4
Product quality should be improved	5	7	5	6	7	7
Product is unsuitable for long-distance sales	7	5	7	5	6	5
Transport cost is too high	2	1	4	3	3	2
The logistics are inconvenient	6	6	6	7	5	6
There exist local protectionism and unfair competition	4	2	1	4	1	1

Note: In the table, 1 stands for the most severe; 2 the second most, etc. and 7 the least severe.
Data source: The Research Group of DRC (2004, Tables 14 and 15).

Interregional trade costs inhibit trade flows, thereby hindering market integration, which has been confirmed in many studies. Huang and Xian's (2012) study firm's entry into domestic market and shows that, all else being equal, firms have a higher probability of entering into closer or adjacent provinces. For an average distance of 1,145 km, if the geographical distance is narrowed by 10 percent (to 1,030 km), then the probability of market entrance increases by 1.64 percent. In the aforementioned study by Huang and Xian (2010c), which is based on the freight exchange data, both geographical distance and whether being adjacent or not significantly impact on interprovincial trade flow. On average, every 1 percent narrowing of the bilateral distance causes freight flow to increase by 1.5 percent. This estimator is much higher than the result of 1.044 for the states of the US (Knaap, 2006). In addition, Huang and Xian (2010c) also discovered that the coefficient of adjacent variable is lower than the estimations about the states of US. It also reflects the fact that the degree of integration among Chinese provinces is significantly lower than that among US states.

5.5.1.2 Composition of interregional trade costs

5.5.1.2.1 TRANSPORT COSTS

On the one hand, transport costs depend on the development of infrastructure. Compared with developed economies, the construction of China's transportation infrastructure started late, and the density of transportation networks is rather low. In 2002, railway mileage under operation nationwide was only 71,900 km, and road and highway mileage was 1.7652 million km and 25,100 km, respectively. Large disparities in the density of transportation networks also existed between regions. In 2002, 12 western provinces combined, which account for 71.5 percent of national landmass, account for only 37.2 percent, 41.1 percent, and 22.9 percent of the national mileage of railway, road, and highway, respectively.[45]

On the other hand, transport costs are also related to the operation systems of infrastructure. Roads are an important means of transportation. In 2002, 75.1 percent of freight volume nationwide was transmitted through roads, which was 5.5 times that of railways.[46] However, the investment and operations system with regard to road construction is rather chaotic and its quality varies widely. It is especially pronounced that each region sets up a shocking number of toll stations on highways/roads to collect fees from vehicles passing through. According to news reports, China has 100,000 kilometers of toll roads, 70 percent of the world total, which is a world record.[47] The toll fees increase the transportation costs, which add to the burdens of firms. In addition, the vicious cycle caused by overweighting and arbitrary fining often creates traffic jams, which sometimes last for several days and severely impact on the efficiency of transportation. It is estimated that unit transport costs for 900 miles from Chengdu (a western capital city) to Shanghai (an eastern city) are equivalent to the shipping costs from Shanghai to Long Beach, California (Treece and Webb, 2004). In this sense, the interregional transportation costs cannot be entirely attributed to natural barriers.

5.5.1.2.2 LOCAL PROTECTIONISM

Local protectionism in domestic trade is a hidden equivalent of tariffs and non-tariff barriers in international trade. It is commonly known that local governments in China tend to use all sorts of means to protect industry in their jurisdiction from competitive pressures. However, literature has different understandings on the source and determinants of the protection motivation. Young (2000) believes that during the process of reform, each sector still retains large amounts of *rent* formed by distortions in the *planned economy*. In order to prevent these rents from dissipating due to competition, local governments tend to set up various kinds of barriers to hinder interregional circulation of goods. Domestic researchers tend to believe that local protectionism is the inevitable result of *fiscal responsibility system*, *delegation of power over investment and financing*, and *de facto ownership of many SOEs by local governments*, which are characteristic of administrative decentralization. Furthermore, the accountability and evaluation of local officials, bulkiness of administrative organs and industry location inherited from the traditional system further enhance the motivation to enact protectionism (Yin and Cai, 2001). Lin and Liu (2004) combine fiscal decentralization and the traditional system together in their explanation of local protectionism. They argue that local protectionism (and market segmentation) during the reform is the logical extension under a decentralized reform of the traditional *overtaking* strategy, which prioritizes heavy industry development. The reason is simple: since many SOEs cannot *be viable*, local governments who want to solidify their tax base have no other choice but to aid them.

In literature, transport costs can be approximately depicted through bilateral distances, the degree of remoteness or centrality, but it is not that easy to measure local protectionism. Compared with the protectionism of international trade, local protectionism involve broader content and more diversified forms, thus it is hard to make ex-ante evaluation. Another difficulty to accurately measure local protectionism lies in the fact that discrimination against non-local goods and factors is explicitly prohibited by the central government. In view of the brazen protectionism and market anomalies, in September of 1993, the Third Meeting of the Standing Committee of the 8th National People's Congress passed the *Law of the People's Republic of China Against Unfair Competition*, in which Article 7 provides that "*A local government and its subordinate departments shall not abuse their administrative power to restrict the entry of goods from other parts of the country into the local market or the flow of local goods to markets in other parts of the country.*" In 2001, the State Council promulgated the *State Council Provisions on Prohibiting Implementation of Regional Blockades in Market Economy Activities* (State Council Order No. 303), listing all sorts of protectionist actions more clearly. On August 30 2007, The Twenty-ninth Meeting of Standing Committee of the 10th National People's Congress passed the *Anti-monopoly Law of the People's Republic of China*, in which the Article 33 provides that "*No administrative organ or organization empowered by a law or administrative regulation to administer public affairs may abuse its administrative power to block the interregional free trade of goods.*"[48] Through such means, protectionism often exists in more hidden forms, so it is very hard for us to find direct evidence except for questionnaires. Currently, interregional market segmentation (or local protectionism) can mainly be measured through three methods, that is, the methods of *trade volume*, *production* and *price*. This is because of the fact that local protectionism restricts trade and aggravates market segmentation, so we can *ex-post* infer the degree of local protectionism through that of market segmentation.[49]

5.5.2 The impact of international trade on regional market integration

International trade alters each region's level of economic development and its growth rate, thus changing its comparative advantages and economies of scale in intraregional trade, which further impacts on its volume, direction, and structure. At the same time, the interests of stakeholders adjust accordingly, which will directly impact on domestic market integration or a region's openness toward other regions. Moreover, the influence of globalization on market segmentation is highly complicated; different features can be found among regions, across sectors, and over periods of time.

Joining the WTO is a landmark event in China's opening to the world and is also an important milestone in China's participation in the globalization. WTO requires member countries to reduce international trade barriers by phases, to eliminate overt and covert discriminative policies of all sorts, and to eliminate subsidies to domestic firms. This requirement undoubtedly increases the cost of local protectionism, and thereby promotes market integration. However, it is not impossible for local governments to adopt more covert protectionist measures against other domestic regions. The changes in local protectionism after accession to the WTO still depend on the trade-off between costs and benefits. Li et al. (2003) examined the impact of this event on interregional trade protectionism based on a monopolistic competition framework. They believe that high import tariffs after fiscal decentralization can shield competition from foreign firms, and reduce the misgivings of governments in protecting local firms. Therefore, interregional trade protectionism is the joint result of fiscal decentralization and international trade protectionism. By contrast, accession to the WTO is conducive to reducing interregional trade barriers. The empirical study of Li and Sun (2004) on integration of the beer market also finds that accession to the WTO is conducive to eliminating local protectionism. They explain that since accession to the WTO implies obligations to gradually trade liberalization (i.e., promise to lower tariffs every year), trade barriers sand the wheels of non-local firms rather than foreign firms. Thus, when local governments conduct protectionist actions, they have to trade-off between increasing firms' profits and decreasing consumers' welfare. If the former cannot compensate for the latter, then protectionist actions are worthless.

Poncet (2002) also includes the variable of *international border effect* in her estimation of interregional border effect. She finds that the international border effect constantly declines with the gradual rise of the interprovincial border effect, which indicates the coexistence of international integration with intra-national integration. Further estimates discover that coastal regions with higher openness have lower interprovincial border effects than the hinterland regions (the former is roughly half of the latter). She thereby infers that the international integration does not result in international market segmentation; foreign openness and domestic market integration facilitate each other. However, Poncet (2005) finds that openness expressed by foreign imports has no impact on the interprovincial border effect, but promotes the industrial border effect.

Furthermore, how does foreign trade impact on local government's incentives to undertake protection? The preceding parts about the substitution or complementariness between regional and foreign markets explain the incentive source of local protectionism from another view. If two markets are mutually substitutive, opening up could induce local governments to actively abandon the domestic market. If complementariness holds, opening up would then urge local governments to abandon protectionism and try to enhance market integration. Chen et al. (2007) use a market segmentation index by the price-based approach as the explained variable and conduct a panel data regression. They find that the coefficient of the variable *openness* was significantly positive, and the coefficient of its quadratic form was significantly negative, which implies that the impact of openness on market segmentation is non-linear. That is, when openness is low, opening up further will intensify segmentation, but when openness is high, further opening up will promote integration. Lu and Chen (2009) examined the impact of opening and market segmentation on economic growth with the market segmentation of neighboring provinces as subjects. Their study further proved Chen et al.'s (2007) study that market segmentation has an inverted *U*-type impact on the immediate and future local economic growth. For over 96 percent of the observations, segmenting markets is conducive to local economic growth. The situation is similar to *prisoner's dilemma*, and segmenting markets is conducive to its own economic growth as from the individual province's perspective, but this is under the condition that everyone takes actions to segment markets. On a macro-level, segmenting markets is obviously disadvantageous for us to make use of economies of scale and to achieve economic growth.

5.5.3 The reaction of regional market integration on international trade

International trade impacts on market segmentation, which, conversely impacts on each region's incentive to go global. The overall opinion in the current research is that market segmentation would force each region to conduct more foreign trade.

From the perspective of firm's sales, if barriers in domestic markets are high, then exporting might be more desirable. Zhong (2002) pointed out that regional trade barriers from market segmentation hinder both interregional specialization and domestic trade. Although this lowers the overall national competitiveness, it does create a preference for international trade in each region to a certain extent. Based on the model of firm heterogeneity, Zhu et al. (2005) examined the behaviors of exporting and domestic market entrance Chinese firms. They argue that, due to local protectionism, a manufacturing enterprise has to pay a certain entry cost (including costs for advertising, promotion and greasing the wheels) for each *fragmented* local market if it wants to sell its products there. These *fragmented* market entry costs amounts to a huge cost. For this reason, many small and medium-sized enterprises in the coastal regions are forced to turn to the foreign markets. In this sense, due to severe segmentation, firms are unable to utilize the economies of scale provided in such a large domestic market, so the strong trend of Chinese exports in fact the distorted growth with a *forced export* nature.[50] Zhang (2010) believes that local protectionism and duplicated construction *push* people to abandon domestic trade, whereas openness *pulls* them to participate in international trade by more positive incentives

Based on Chinese industrial firm-level data from 1998 to 2003, Zhang et al.'s (2010b) empirical study supported Zhu et al.'s (2005) hypothesis. They also find that domestic market barriers only impact on domestic firms and do not constitute a barrier to foreign-owned enterprise. Zhao and Cai's (2009) discovery is contrary to the common opinion. Their estimation found that the higher the *border effect* depicting domestic market barriers, the lower the amount of international trade (imports and exports), thus domestic market segmentation is not conducive to external market integration.[51] The explanation they offer is that import and export both depend on interregional division of labor, and breaking regional blockades and local protectionism can facilitate regional specialization and collaboration, thereby promote foreign openness. Similarly, Zhang and Zhang (2009) found that market segmentation hinders provincial foreign trade, and its obstruction against imports is stronger than that against exports. Market segmentation also contributes to China's long-term trade surplus by this way.

5.6 Concluding remarks

This chapter has reviewed the current literature regarding regional foreign trade and its impact on interregional trade. According to the sequence of the narrative, the main conclusions will be briefly outlined as follows.

First, China's regional foreign trade exhibits a high but imbalanced growth characteristic. On the one hand, China's foreign trade concentrates mostly in the eastern coastal regions, especially the *Yangtze Delta* and *Pearl Delta*, and foreign trade is relatively low in inland provinces. On the other hand, the partners for each region's foreign trade are highly concentrated; foreign firms are important entities in regional foreign trade, and processing trade, especially in M&E products, is the most important form of foreign trade, especially in the east. Apart from location and comparative advantage, the international specialization, FDI, policy preferential and institutions, financial development, economies of scale and firm productivity, all shown to be among the important factors that impact on imbalanced growth in regional foreign trade.

Second, China's interregional trade volumes are concentrated mostly in the coastal developed provinces and are proportional to their economic scale.

Directionally, the trade volumes flow mostly from west to east, exhibiting a gradient pattern, and there is an obvious bias toward intraregional trade. Foreign trade promotes the development of interregional trade, and impacts on both its volume and direction. As for firms, foreign exports and domestic sales are intrinsically consistent; as for regional economic growth, however, interregional trade and foreign trade substitute for each other.

Third, China's regional specialization returned to continuous increases after experiencing slight drops. Foreign trade promotes regional specialization, and thus becomes an important source of coastal–hinterland disparities. Under the mechanism of cumulative causation, foreign trade attracts labor and capital to flow unceasingly toward the coastal region, which becomes the winner in regional specialization and industrial agglomeration. Apart from the reallocation of *footloose* industries across the regions, the propelling effect of foreign trade is also reflected in differences in regional industrialization and industrial growth.

Fourth, the effect of regional foreign trade openness on market integration exhibits a *U-shaped* characteristic. That is, when openness is low, opening trade will hinder regional market integration, but further opening is conducive to the elimination of trade barriers. Conversely, market integration impacts on regional foreign trade, which is mainly demonstrated by the fact that market segmentation encourages regional exports.

Although the review has to end here, the topics covered in this chapter are only in its nascence and many issues require further exploration. I believe that, as the economy develops, theory advances, and data accessibility is improved, five topics in particular will require more attention.

The first aspect is the relationship between domestic and foreign demand. China is a big economy and the economic scale of each region is also increasing. Presently, the growth of China's manufactured exports depends mainly on quantitative expansion and on a limited number of markets, which may lead to the sustained worsening of terms of trade. It can be forecast that if this continues, China may sink into *immiserizing growth* where the faster exports grow, the slower the economy grows. So, how should we promote foreign openness and at the same time, take full advantage of domestic market?

The second aspect is about bilateral trade between each region and its foreign trade partners. Current research treats the world as one entity, and then considers the total trade for each region (or the sector-level trade for each region). However, some regions are over-reliant on some common markets, and compete fiercely on these international markets. So it is necessary to examine empirically the competition across China's regions on the international markets.

The third aspect relates to processing trade. First of all, as compared with ordinary trade firms, the input–output relationship of processing trade firms with domestic industry is quite different. Also, its pushing and pulling effect on interregional trade, as well as its impact on regional specialization is also obviously different from those of ordinary trade. Next, processing trade will affect a region's export competitiveness through wage levels and input prices. Processing trade that also conducts domestic sales will directly impact on interregional trade in goods. However, there has been no relevant theoretical and empirical research up to now. In fact, current literature regarding the impact of regional trade does not consider the role of processing trade. If this is taken into account, many conclusions may subsequently change.

The fourth aspect that we should consider is the indirect impact of foreign trade. Foreign trade can transcend the limitations of domestic market extent and those of development phases, realizing economies of scale while avoiding decreasing returns to the largest extent. This is conducive to factor accumulation in each region through *small steps but fast pacing*, and therefore enhances its endowment rapidly. However, existing studies only consider the direct impact of foreign trade, ignoring its indirect impact, such as the impact on interregional trade and regional specialization through regional factor endowment, economies of scale and productivity, etc.

The fifth and the last aspect regards data. Many conclusions in this chapter are based on province-level empirics. As more micro-level firm data becomes available, studies on finer dimensions need to be strengthened, at the spatial level as well as the industry level. Studies on finer dimensions not only allow us to get closer to the real world, but also help us to reach more practical and pertinent policy implications.

Notes

1 The *east*, *central* and *west* is the shorthand for the eastern, central and western regions of China, respectively. For the specification, see Table 5.5. The same applies hereafter.
2 *Data source*: Data for 1978–1996 and 1997–2008 are from *China compendium of statistics 1949–2004* and the Guoyan website database, respectively. For details of the latter, see http://edu-data.drcnet.com.cn/web/.These data are reported according to the locations of importer/exporter rather than those of consumer/producer. In the figure, data of two *Deltas* are also included in the east.
3 It causes the dynamics of import and export for processing trade to be similar.
4 *Process and assembling* includes process with provided materials and samples, or assembling with supplied parts, in which the client (foreign firm) provides materials or semi-finished products to the processer (domestic firm) who process according to the requirements. The client in *processing and assembling* is responsible for sales and the processer only charges processing fees, so the relationship between these two parties is one of consigned processing rather than those between buyer and seller. *Process with imported materials* refers to the activities such that the domestic producer imports materials and components and then exports the finished goods, both on his own. So importing and exporting are independent of each other.
5 Also, processing trade explains the bulk of China's trade surplus. In 2008, the whole nation's trade surplus was \$297.58 billion (\$267.84 billion for the east), in which processing trade was \$297.12 billion (\$289.46 billion for the east). Data in this section all come from the statistics of China Customs.
6 The figures of Guangdong and Zhejiang are also included in that of the east.
7 Numbers on the horizontal axis stand for the Harmonized System (HS) 2-digit product categories in the statistics of China Customs, and defined as follows: Section I (Animals), Section II (Vegetables), Section III (Fats and oils), Section IV (Foodstuff; beverages, spirits and vinegar; tobacco and tobacco products), Section V (Mineral products), Section VI (Products of the chemical and allied industries), Section VII (Plastics and

articles thereof; rubber and articles thereof), Section VIII (Leather, skin, fur and their products; containers and bags; catgut products), Section IX (Wood and wooden products; wood charcoal; cork; plaiting products), Section X (Wood pulp, etc.; recovered paper; paper and paperboard and their articles), Section XI (Textiles and textile articles), Section XII (Footwear, headgear, umbrellas, etc.; prepared feathers and articles made thereof, artificial flowers, articles of human hair), Section XIII (Articles of stone, plaster, cement, asbestos, mica or similar materials; ceramics; glass and glassware), Section XIV (Jewelry, precious metals and precious metals products; imitation jewelry; coins), Section XV (Base metals and their products), Section XVI (Mechanical and electrical appliances, audio and video equipment and their components and accessories), Section XVII (Vehicles, aircraft, vessels and associated transport equipment), Section XVIII (Optics, medical or surgical instruments; clocks and watches; musical instruments), Section XX (Miscellaneous), Section XXI (Art, collectibles and antiques), Section XXII (Special dealings and uncategorized goods). Data on Section XIX (Arms, ammunition and their components and accessories) is not available.

8 According to the estimation in Yao and Zhang (2008), after taking into consideration the imported intermediate inputs, the domestic technological content of national and Jiangsu's exports during 1997–2002 fell rapidly, and the overall technological content did not increase significantly either.

9 Foreign enterprises include two types, namely foreign invested enterprises and those funded by Hong Kong, Macau and Taiwan.

10 Amiti and Freund (2008) outlined the structural characteristics of China's overall export growth between 1992 and 2005 from multiple dimensions such as skill, intensive margin, and extensive margin, etc.

11 Huang and Xu (2012) investigate empirically the impact of inland transportation costs on regional export modes. They find that inland transportation costs significantly dampen the flow of regional exports, which is mostly along the extensive margin, along product category.

12 For example, in the 1,085-kilometer-long railway line that runs from Chengdu to Kunming, the total length of bridges (991) and tunnels (427) reaches 400 kilometers (Liang, 2004). High gradients and the complex geography not only lengthens the transportation distance, but also increases the technical difficulty of locomotive traction. In some locations, two locomotives for traction are needed, or the number of carriages has to been decreased.

13 Yi (2003) argues that it is vertical specialization that magnifies the effects of a reduction in trade barriers, which caused the abnormal growth of global trade during post-World War II.

14 The production chain of processing trade in China is short and mainly relies on cheap labor, which makes it more mobile than the ordinary trade. Once the wage advantage of the coastal changes, this kind of trade may gradually shift toward the hinterland within China, or even to neighboring countries such as Vietnam. It also implies that regional preferential policies are conducive to the location transfer of processing trade. The fact that the plants of the controversial Taiwanese enterprise *Foxconn,* which mainly engages in processing trade, relocated to hinterland cities (such as Zhengzhou, Henan Province), is a very good example.

15 Zhong (2007) also found that capital intensity, R&D and human capital are unimportant for China's exports in electronics.

16 In fact, *to earn foreign exchange through exporting* is just one of China's original intentions in attracting foreign investment.

17 Zhong (2007) found that FDI, especially those from Hong Kong, Macau and Taiwan, and the economies of scale both contribute to China's electronics exports.

18 Actually, preferential policies are mostly the removal of government regulations (Démurger et al., 2002).

19 Driven by the logic that *let a few get rich first and the rich then promote those left behind*, it is reasonable for preferential policies to be biased toward the advantageous coastal regions.

20 Here, the tendency toward property right protection is expressed as the ratio of regional GDP to penalty and confiscatory income, and the quality of the legal system is defined as the ratio of public security expenditures to regional GDP. The reasoning is that officials have a stronger incentive to increase fiscal revenues with fines in regions with weak property rights protection, and larger expenditures on law and order help to build up a more efficient legal system.

21 Undoubtedly, the disadvantages of China's non-state-owned enterprises in obtaining loans are partially innate due to the fact that they are relatively small and usually lack collateral and guarantees.

22 Huang (2005) believes that the selective repression characteristics of China's financial market leaves room for FDI inflow by blocking the development of many domestic firms. In this sense, the massive FDI inflows since the 1990s up until now is not a manifestation of an increase in China's global competitiveness, but instead the consequence of lagging financial reform and the distorted financing system, which leads to selective repression.

23 A few studies have identified a negative correlation between firm productivity and exporting. This is mainly attributed to the high ratio of processing trade (Li, 2010). Once processing trade is excluded, such a *productivity paradox* no longer exists. The underlying reasoning is as follows: processing trade firms in China lies at the bottom of global production chain, and the value-added is quite low. It makes firm-level productivity *per capita* or total factor productivity not only lower than ordinary trade firms, but also lower than firms with domestic sales only.

24 In addition, Japan's Institute of Developing Economies (IDE) and the Japan External Trade Organization (JETRO) jointly formulated in 2003 the Multiregional Input Output Model for China 2000. This model distinguishes up to 17 sectors (see www.ide.go.jp/English/Publish/Books/Sds/086.html).

25 These eight regions are, respectively, Northeast (Heilongjiang, Jilin and Liaoning); Jing-jin (Beijing and Tianjin); Northern Coastal (Shandong and Hebei); Eastern Coastal (Jiangsu, Shanghai, Zhejiang); Southern Coastal (Fujian, Guangdong, Hainan); Central (Shanxi, Henan, Anhui, Hubei, Hunan, Jiangxi); Northwest (Inner Mongolia, Shaanxi, Ningxia, Gansu, Qinghai, Xinjiang) and Southwest (Sichuan, Chongqing, Guangxi, Yunnan, Guizhou, Tibet). More details can be found in National Information Center (2005, p. 5–6).

26 The Golden Tax Project is the key project of the national e-government project, which aims to enhance the levying and administration of VAT. The whole process regarding VAT can be realized online, including the determination of eligibility as a general taxpayer, receiving and purchasing invoices, tax declaration and payment, etc. Output and input VATs refer to the VATs paid by the taxpayers when selling goods and purchasing materials, respectively.

27 The full title is the Research Group of Interregional Trade affiliated to the Research Department of Developmental Strategy and Regional Economics, an academic organization in State Council Research Center. DRC is the abbreviated form for Development Research Center of the State Council, and is used hereafter.

28 According to regional comparative advantages, raw materials and ore that have relatively low value to weight account for a large proportion of the goods transported from the central and western regions to the eastern regions, while manufactured goods that have relatively high value to weight take up a large proportion in the goods shipped from the eastern regions to the central and western regions.

29 To be more precise, we refer to the coefficients of interregional goods flows, which come from Table 14 of National Information Center (2005, p. 21).

30 Namely, World Bank 2003 questionnaire survey database on 2,400 firms in 18 Chinese cities. This survey selected 1,331 firms with outer-province sales records, of which 318 firms also sell goods overseas; 1,076 firms were from manufacturing and 255 were from services; 736 large firms employed over 100 while 595 small and mid-sized firms employed fewer than 100.

31 Similar modeling can be found in Sheng and Mao (2011) and Mao and Sheng (2011).

32 In fact, the relationship between regional specialization and interregional trade is not that simple, as it is not only dependent on the fineness of the demarcation of sectors, but also on many factors such as production scale, nature of product, etc. (e.g. high regional specialization will decrease the demand for intermediate products from other regions).

33 The former refers to the industry structure differences among regions; the latter refers to the spatial concentration or dispersion characteristic of industry among regions.

34 See Brülhart's (2010) latest review.

35 Footloose industry usually refers to manufacturing industries that do not strictly depend on local natural resources and local market demand.

36 Similarly, Zhu (2004) describes the industrialization typical of *leaving the farmland without leaving one's hometown*. In his model, differences between preferences and factor endowment will cause real income gaps between the industrial and agricultural sector, thereby attracting peasants in the countryside to become workers. But his model did not include outer driving forces such as foreign trade.

37 The structural transformation includes two aspects. From the perspective of demand, the increase in consumers' real purchasing power will increase the relative demand for non-agricultural goods. From the perspective of supply, the increase in wages in the industrial sector will attract labor to shift from the agriculture sector to the non-agriculture one.

38 Fan (2007) constructed a new specialization indicator that controlled for the scale factor.

39 Imbs and Wacziarg (2003) pointed out in the paper of *Stages of Diversification*, that in the early phase of economic development, a country initially exhibits diversification (equal distribution of economic activity in each sector), and specialization commences only when economic development reaches a certain stage.

40 Another explanation is that China's regional industry development was artificially over-specialized during the era of planned economy. So it is reasonable for specialization to experience a decline under the forces of market during the first phase of the reform.

41 Fan (2004) compared results of the two time points 1980 and 2001 and also discovered that each region's specialization index significantly increased.

42 This assumes implicitly that the tradability across industries or the dependency on foreign markets varies innately.

43 For processing trade, the effects of import and export coincide with each other. However, as to ordinary trade, competition brought by imports propels firms to move away from coastal regions where industries are highly agglomerated and competitive.

44 Huang and Li (2006b) and Xian and Wen (2006) also considered the important effects of FDI on the spatial distribution of industry. The former substitute the industry degree of export dependence in the interaction term for proportion of foreign investment, and the latter directly add an FDI variable with the two dimensions, i.e. FDI distribution over geography and industry.

45 These figures are calculated with the length of transportation routes in each region provided by *China Statistical Yearbook* 2003.

46 These figures are calculated using data provided by *China Statistical Abstract* 2003.

47 See the report of *China Economic Weekly*, August 6 in 2007.

48 The forbidden protectionist actions include: (1) Imposing discriminatory charge items, or implementing discriminatory charge rates or prices on non-local commodities;

(2) Imposing technical requirements or inspection standards on non-local goods as different from those on local counterparts, or taking discriminatory technical measures, such as repeated inspections or repeated certifications on non-local goods, so as to restrict the entry of non-local goods into the local market; (3) Adopting administrative licensing aimed at non-local goods so as to restrict the entry of non-local goods into the local market; (4) Setting up barriers or adopting any other means to block either the inflow of non-local goods or the outflow of local goods; (5) Other activities that may block the interregional free trade of goods.

49 For the literature review on the methodology, refer to Yu and Liu (2009). We omit the details here.

50 During the Three Kingdoms Era, "Besides developing the lands within China, foreign relations were expanded, especially for the states of Wei and Wu." The reason lies in the fact that "the economies were segmented within China and interregional trade was difficult to conduct, therefore foreign trade was preferred." See Hou (2008, p. 265).

51 Zhang et al. (2010) employed firm-level data, whereas Zhao and Cai (2009) employed provincial level data. Another source of disagreement came from the measurement of the border effect: Zhang et al. (2010) employed the price-based measure, while Zhao and Cai (2009) obtained the border effect based on the wage-to-market potential estimation equation.

References

In English

Amiti, M. and C. Freund, 2008, "The Anatomy of China's Export Growth," *World Bank Policy Research Working Paper*, No. 4628.

Anderson, J. E. and E. van Wincoop, 2004, "Trade Costs," *NBER Working Paper*, No. 10480.

Bai, C., Y. Du, Z. Tao and S. Y. Tong, 2004, "Local Protectionism and Regional Specialization: Evidence from China's Industries," *Journal of International Economics*, 63(2), pp. 397–418.

Brülhart, M., 2010, "The Spatial Effects of Trade Openness: A Survey," *University of Nottingham, GEP, Discussion Papers*, No. 10/10.

Crozet, M. and P. Koenig-Soubeyran, 2002, "Trade Liberalization and the Internal Geography of Countries," Center for Research in Economics and Statistics, *Discussion Paper*, No. 2002–2037.

Crozet, M. and P. Koenig-Soubeyran, 2004, "EU Enlargement and the Internal Geography of Countries," *Journal of Comparative Economics*, 32(2), pp. 265–279.

Démurger, S., J. D. Sachs, W. T. Woo et al., 2002, "The Relative Contributions of Location and Preferential Policies in China's Regional Development: Being in the Right Place and Having the Right Incentives," *China Economic Review*, 13(4), pp. 444–465.

Du, Y. and A. Park, 2006, "Blunting the Razor's Edge: Regional Development in Reform China," *China Journal of Economics*, 1(2), pp. 149–159.

Gao, T., 2003, "Ethnic Chinese Networks and International Investment: Evidence from Inward FDI in China," *Journal of Asian Economics*, 14(4), pp. 611–629.

Ge, Y., 2009, "Globalization and Industry Agglomeration in China," *World Development*, 37(3), pp. 550–559.

Hu, D., 2002, "Trade, Rural–Urban Migration, and Regional Income Disparity in Developing Countries: A Spatial General Equilibrium Model Inspired by the Case of China," *Regional Science and Urban Economics*, 32(3), pp. 311–338.

Huang, Y., 2005, *Selling China: Foreign Direct Investment during the Reform Era*, Cambridge, MA: Cambridge University Press.

Ihara, R., 2005, "Factor Distribution, Capital Intensity and Spatial Agglomeration," *Annals of Regional Science*, 39(1), pp. 107–120.

Imbs, J. and R. Wacziarg, 2003, "Stages of Diversification," *American Economic Review*, 93(1), pp. 63–86.

ISGEP (International Study Group on Exports and Productivity), 2008, "Understanding Cross-Country Differences in Exporter Premia: Comparable Evidence for 14 Countries," *Review of World Economics*, 144(4), pp. 596–635.

Knaap, T., 2006, "Trade, Location, and Wages in the United States," *Regional Science and Urban Economics*, 36(5), pp. 595–612.

Krugman, P., 1991, "Increasing Returns and Economic Geography," *Journal of Political Economy*, 99(3), pp. 483–499.

Krugman, P. and R. Livas Elizondo, 1996, "Trade Policy and Third World Metropolis," *Journal of Development Economics*, 49(1), pp. 137–150.

Li, J., L. D. Qiu and Q. Sun, 2003, "Interregional Protection: Implications of Fiscal Decentralization and Trade Liberalization," *China Economic Review*, 14(3), pp. 227–245.

Midelfart-Knarvik, K.H., H. G. Overman, S. J. Redding and A. J. Venables, 2000, "The Location of European Industry," *European Commission, Economic Papers,* No. 142.

Murata, Y., 2008, "Engel's Law, Petty's Law, and Agglomeration," *Journal of Development Economics*, 87(1), pp. 161–177.

Naughton, B., 2003, "How Much Can Regional Integration Do to Unify China's Markets?" In *How Far Across the River? Chinese Policy Reform at the Millennium,* ed. Nicholas C. Hope, Dennis Tao Yang, and Mu Yang Li, 204–232. Stanford, CA: Stanford University Press.

Poncet, S., 2003, "Measuring Chinese Domestic and International Integration?" *China Economic Review*, 14(1), pp. 1–22.

Poncet, S., 2005, "A Fragmented China: Measure and Determinants of Chinese Domestic Market Disintegration," *Review of International Economics*, 13(3), pp. 409–430.

Treece, J. B. and A. Webb, 2004, "Cheap China Parts are a Myth," *Automotive News Europe*, 6/28, 9(13).

Wang, Z. and S. Wei, 2008, "What Accounts for the Rising Sophistication of China's Exports?" *NBER Working Paper*, No. 13771.

Yi, K., 2003, "Can Vertical Specialization Explain the Growth of World Trade?" *Journal of Political Economy*, 111(1), pp. 52–102.

Young, A., 2000, "The Razor's Edge: Distortions and Incremental Reform in the People's Republic of China," *Quarterly Journal of Economics*, 115(4), pp. 1091–1135.

In Chinese

Bao, Q. and J. Yang, 2008, "Financial Development and Chinese Industrial Product's Competitiveness," *Journal of World Economy*, 3, pp. 21–33.

Batisse, C. and S. Poncet, 2006, "Determinants of Activities Location in China: Factor Endowments, Geography and Interventionism," *China Journal of Economics*, 1(2), pp. 160–178.

Chai, M., 2006, "The Effect of FDI on the Exporting of Domestic Firms in China: Empirical Analysis with Provincial Panel Data," *Management World*, 7, pp. 46–52.

Chen, M., Q. Gui, M. Lu, and Z. Chen, 2007, "How to Maintain China's High Growth Rate via Scale Economy: An Empirical Study of Economic Opening and Domestic Market Segmentation," *China Economic Quarterly*, 7(1), pp. 125–150.

Chen, X. and R. Zhang, 2007, "Openness, Cost of Trade, and Conglomeration of Chinese Manufacturing," *Economic Theory and Business Management*, 1, pp. 11–17.

Deng, H., 2009, "Trade Accessibility, Factor Distribution and Agglomeration: A Case of China," *Economic Research Journal*, 11, pp. 118–129.

Fan, F., 2007, "The Measurement of Regional Specialization," *Economic Research Journal*, 9, pp. 71–83.

Fan, J., 2004, "Market Integration, Regional Specialization and Tendency of Industrial Agglomeration: An Implication for Regional Disparity," *Social Sciences in China*, 6, pp. 39–51.

Hang, W. and S. Li, 2009, "Home Biases, Border Effects and Market Integration: An Empirical Study Based on Inter-provincial VAT Survey," *China Economic Quarterly*, 8(4), pp. 1455–1474.

Hou, J., 2008, *The History of China's Economy*, Vancouver: New Star Press.

Huang, J., 2006, "Trade, Regional difference: A Two Countries-Three Regions Model," *Forum for Economic Development Working Paper,* No. FC20060125.

Huang, J. and G. Xian, 2010a, "The Financial Development, the FDI and China's Regional Manufacturing Export," *Management World*, 7, pp. 8–17.

Huang, J. and G. Xian, 2010b, "Firm Heterogeneity, Trade Cost and Domestic Market Entry," Paper of the 10th China Economics Annual Conference, Zhengzhou.

Huang, J. and G. Xian, 2010c, "Export and Regional Trade – Study on Railway Transporting Data," *Working Paper*, Nankai University.

Huang, J. and J. Huang, 2008, "Market Size and Industrial Growth in Chinese Provinces," *China Economic Quarterly*, 7(4), pp. 1317–1334.

Huang, J. and K. Li, 2006a, "Export Openness, Regional Market Size and Economic Growth," *Economic Research Journal*, 6, pp. 27–38.

Huang, J. and K. Li, 2006b, "Foreign Trade, Local Protectionism and Industrial Location in China," *China Economic Quarterly*, 5(3), pp. 733–760.

Huang, J. and M. Xu, 2012, "Inland Transportation Costs and Regional Export Modes in China," *Journal of World Economy*, 4, pp. 58–77.

Jiang, X., 2002, "Growth in Export and the Change of Structure: Formation of Exporting Merchandise," *Nankai Economic Studies*, 2, pp. 30–34.

Jin, X., Y. Ru and H. Wu, 2008, "Institution, Production Efficiency and Chinese Regional Unbalanced Export," *Management World*, 11, pp. 65–77.

Ke, S. and S. Guo, 2010, "The Interaction of Market Integration and Regional Economic Growth in China: 1995–2007," *Journal of Quantitative & Technical Economics*, 5, pp. 62–72.

Li, C., 2010, "Do Chinese Export Firms Have 'Productivity Paradox'," *Journal of World Economy*, 7, pp. 64–81.

Li, J. and Q. Sun, 2004, "How Does China's WTO Entry Affect Interregional Protectionism: The Case of Beer Market Integration," *Journal of World Economy*, 6, pp. 37–45.

Li, J. and Y. Peng, 2010, "An Empirical Analysis to the Determinants of China's Manufacture Geographic Distribution," *South China Journal of Economics*, 7, pp. 28–40.

Li, K. and Y. Wang, 2010, "Contract Enforcement and Regional Export Performance: Empirical Analysis Based on Industry Characteristics," *China Economic Quarterly*, 9(3), pp. 1007–1028.

Liang, Q., 2004, *The Industry Agglomeration*, HK: Commercial Press.
Liang, Q. and X. Shi, 2004, "An Empirical Analysis of the Relationship between Trade and FDI in China," *China Economic Quarterly*, 3(4), pp. 839–858.
Lin, Y. and M. Liu, 2003, "Growth Convergence and Income Distribution in China," *Journal of World Economy*, 8, pp. 3–14.
Lin, Y. and P. Liu, 2004, "Regional Protection and Market Segmentation: In the View of Developing Strategy," *CCER Working Paper,* No.C2004015.
Liu, Z. and J. Zhang, 2009, "Determinants of Export in Chinese Local Manufacturing Firm," *Economic Research Journal*, 8, pp. 99–112.
Lu, M. and Z. Chen, 2009, "Fragmented Growth: Why Economic Opening May Worsen Domestic Market Segmentation?" *Economic Research Journal*, 3, pp. 42–52.
Ma, G., E. Yang and M. Zhou, 2010, "Fiscal Decentralization, Local Protectionism and China's Regional Specialization," *China Journal of Economics*, 1, pp. 15–27.
Mao, Q. and B. Sheng, 2011, "Economic Opening, Regional Market Integration and Total Factor Productivity," *China Economic Quarterly*, 11(1), pp. 181–210.
Poncet, S., 2002, "Is China's Market Approaching Disintegration: A Comparison on China's Intranational and International Market Integration," *Essays on World Economy*, 1, pp. 3–17.
Shen, N., F. Liu and J. Zhao, 2006, "Fiscal Decentralization and the Divergence of Regional Foreign Trade in China," *Finance & Trade Economics*, 1, pp. 41–45.
Sheng, B. and Q. Mao, 2011, "Trade Openness, Domestic Market Integration and China's Provincial Economic Growth: 1985–2008," *Journal of World Economy*, 11, pp. 44–66.
The Research Group of Development Research Center of the State Council, 2004, "The Report of China's Regional Protectionism – Based on the Analysis of Firm Sampling Survey," *Review of Economic Research*, 6, pp. 2–18.
The Research Group of Development Research Center of the State Council, 2006a, "The Contact Degree of China's Inter-provincial Trade – Based on 'Jinshui' Value-Added Tax Data," *Research Report of China's Development Research Center*, No. 19.
The Research Group of Development Research Center of the State Council, 2006b, "The Space Correlations of China's Inter-provincial Trade and Trade Areas – Based on the Analysis of 'Jinshui' Value-added Tax Data," *Research Report of China's Development Research Center*, No. 75.
The State Information Center, 2005, *China' s Regional Input–Output Table*, Beijing: Social Sciences Academic Press.
Wang, S. and F. Feng, 2006, "The Impact of FDI on China's Trade and Regional Difference," *Journal of World Economy*, 8, pp. 23–30.
Wang, Y., K. Li and D. Sheng, 2009, "Does Agglomeration Matter for Competitive Advantage – An Incomplete Contract Approach," *World Economics Paper*, 5, pp. 61–75.
Wu, Q. and Z. Liu, 2009, "Analysis on the Realization Mechanism of the Export Miracle in Chinese Coastal Regions," *Economic Research Journal*, 6, pp. 83–93.
Xian, G. and D. Wen, 2006, "FDI, Regional Specialization and Industry Agglomeration," *Management World*, 12, pp. 18–31.
Xian, G., B. Yan, A. Zhang, 2008, "Export from China and Foreign Direct Investment in China? The Study of the Data 1983–2000," *Nankai Economic Studies*, 1, pp. 45–48.
Xu, X. and X. Li, 2010, "China's Inter-Provincial Trade: 1985–2007," *Working Papers of Lingnan College*, Zhongshan University.
Xu, Z. and S. Li, 2009, "The Estimates of China's Inter-Provincial Trade in 2002," Paper of the 4th Management Annual Conference.

Yan, G., Q. Sun, H. Zhong, N. Zhao, and X. Jin, 2009, "Strategic Restructuring and Policy Adjustment of Chinese Processing Trade," *Economic Research Journal*, 5, pp. 66–78.

Yang, J., 2007, "Financial Development and Foreign Trade: Panel Data Evidence on Provincial Performance," *Economic Science*, 4, pp. 46–57.

Yang, Q. and P. Chen, 2005, "The Impacts of FDI on China's Export," *Management World*, 5, pp. 65–69.

Yang, R., 2008, "Factors Affecting the Growth of China's Industrial Products Export," *Journal of World Economy*, 8, pp. 32–41.

Yao, Y. and Y. Zhang, 2008, "Upgrading the Domestic Technological Contents of China's Exports: Evidence from Jiangsu and Guangdong Provinces and China as a Whole," *Social Sciences in China*, 2, pp. 67–82.

Ye, Y., 2000, "From Mechanism and Its Countermeasures of Trade Conflicts between Chinese Regions," *Economic Geography*, 20(6), pp. 13–16.

Yin, W. and W. Cai, 2001, "The Genesis of Regional Barriers in China's Local Market and Countermeasures," *Economic Research Journal*, 6, pp. 3–12.

Yu, D. and Y. Liu, 2009, "The Measurement and Identification of Local Protection and Market Segmentation: A Literature Review Based on the Methodology," *World Economic Papers*, 1, pp. 80–93.

Zhang, J., P. Zhang and T. Huang, 2010b, "Does Domestic Market Segmentation Push Chinese Firms' Exporting?" *Economic Research Journal*, 8, pp. 29–41.

Zhang, J., Y. Li and Z. Liu, 2008, "Export and Productivity of China's Domestic Enterprises," *Management World*, 11, pp. 50–64.

Zhang, J., Y. Li and Z. Liu, 2010a, "Institution and Chinese Regional Unbalanced Exports: Evidence from Four-digit Industries at Level of Province," *Journal of World Economy*, 2, pp. 83–103.

Zhang, R. and E. Zhang, 2009, "Market Segmentation, FDI and Trade Surplus: An Analysis based on Inter-provincial Data," *World Economy Study*, 2, pp. 3–6.

Zhang, S., 2010, "Research on the Intrinsic Mechanism Economy Open Up and the Formation of Regional Market Segmentation," *Study and Practice*, 2, pp. 19–25.

Zhao, Y. and G. Cai, 2009, "Border Effect of Market Potential and Inter-External Market Integration," *Economic Research Journal*, 7, pp. 119–130.

Zhen, S. and H. Wang, 2007, *China's Regional Input-output Table*, Beijing: Chemical Industry Press.

Zhong, C., 2002, "Domestic Regional Division of Labor and Trade at Home and International Competitiveness," *Social Sciences in China*, 1, pp. 94–100.

Zhong, C., 2007, "Determinants of Exports in Chinese Electronics Industry," *Economic Research Journal*, 9, pp. 62–70.

Zhou, J., 2009, "Study on China's FDI-inflow and its Endogenous Effect on Export Growth," *South China Journal of Economics*, 5, pp. 45–57.

Zhu, X., 2004, "Preference, Technology, and Industrialization," *Economic Research Journal*, 11, pp. 96–106.

Zhu, X., X. Jin and D. Luo, 2005, "Market Segmentation and the Expansion of China's Export," *Economic Research Journal*, 12, pp. 68–76.

6 Transportation infrastructure investment and economic development[1]

Zhigang Li

6.1 Introduction

There are different categories of infrastructure. According to Gramlich (1994), infrastructure is generally capital intensive, large-scale facilities with natural monopoly properties, e.g. facilities such as transportation, irrigation, communications, and water, electricity and gas, etc. They usually have strong externalities. Since studies that review domestic and foreign literature on infrastructure are quite abundant already, e.g. Gramlich (1994) and Gao (2005), this chapter will not attempt to provide a comprehensive literature collection. Its aim is to estimate the socioeconomic benefits from Chinese infrastructure investment in recent years through integrating credible results from relevant literature (especially Chinese literature) and further to make a judgment on investment efficiency. The chapter also intends to provide directional suggestions to future infrastructure investment.

Since research results by literature on transportation infrastructure is relatively more abundant, this chapter will mainly focus on its discussions on transportation infrastructure. This does not mean that transportation infrastructure is more important than other facilities. In fact, other infrastructure investments, such as communication networks, may have a greater impact on society. But since there is a lack of current research on that subject, this chapter cannot delve deeply into the matter.

On the whole, most of China's infrastructure is the result of contemporary construction. Especially since the 1990s, the scale of investment in infrastructure has increased significantly. Whether in terms of absolute scale or proportion of total economic output, the figures exceed those of other major countries. Even so, the current density of roads and railways in China is still lower than that of major developed countries (calculated by figures according to the *China Statistical Yearbook*). According to plan, in the foreseeable future, the scale of China's infrastructure investment will continue to grow.

The results from integrating literature and all types of research methods (including time series econometric models, panel data analysis and micro-level econometric estimation, etc.) consistently show that China's recent infrastructure investment enhanced economic output and production efficiency. More specifically, on the issue of transportation infrastructure investment, the enhancement of social productivity comes from the cost-savings and gains from interregional trade. First, since the major road and railway investments in the late 1990s drastically cut down on the jamming of interregional traffic, transport costs and time costs have been reduced. Next, there is evidence that proves the firm inventory levels benefit from road investment and fall, thereby increasing firm productivity. Third, transportation infrastructure investment has facilitated a change in the regional disposition of industry, causing production to agglomerate toward the developed regions, but the development of underdeveloped regions may be negatively impacted, even if overall economic efficiency may be enhanced.

Although infrastructure investment promotes economic growth, there is evidence that proves the efficiency of Chinese infrastructure investment is lower than developed countries and exhibits an obvious declining trend. One possible reason is that financing for infrastructure is becoming ever more dependent on local funds. Since much infrastructure, such as roads and railways, have strong interregional externalities, and local investments do not include such externalities in their deliberations, infrastructure projects with high returns may not be constructed. Other reasons, such as investment in advance, may exist, but empirical literature is lacking.

It should be mentioned that infrastructure investment not only has a direct impact on economic output, it might also have other consequences, such as environmental pollution. In addition, since most infrastructure investments are dominated by the government, corruption may increase (Fan, 2011). These negative effects will reduce the aforementioned positive effects. It is regrettable that due to the lack of research, this chapter cannot provide an estimate of the net benefit from infrastructure investment.

This chapter will be structured as follows: first, there will be a review of Chinese infrastructure construction; then, on the topic of the relationship between infrastructure and economic development, reviewing the findings of currently available literature on the mechanisms through which infrastructure affects economic development; finally, providing some policy recommendations based on these findings.

6.2 The development of Chinese transportation infrastructure

Transportation infrastructure mainly includes railways, roads, waterways, airways, and pipelines. Much has been written about the history of transportation infrastructure construction, and there will only be a brief review here. The objective here is to have some sense of which phase Chinese transportation infrastructure development is currently in.

Transportation infrastructure construction had reached a large scale in China, historically. For example, the Qin dynasty's imperial roads and military roads; the Han dynasty's roads leading to the Western Regions; the Sui dynasty's opening of the Grand Canal; the Tang dynasty's intricate national highway system and the "Silk Road", and the Qing dynasty's official roads. In the last years of the Qing

Table 6.1 The length and density of roads and railroads in each Chinese dynasty

Dynasty	*Highway length (km)*	*Railway length (km)*	*Road density (km/1,000 people)*	*Road density (km/1,000 square km)*	*Railway density (km/1,000 people)*	*Railway density (km/1,000 square km)*
Qin	12387	0	0.413	3.492	0	0
Tang	18169	0	0.363	2.042	0	0
Ming	20409	0	0.157	1.655	0	0
Qing	58556	9292	0.138	4.558	0.022	0.723

Data source: Mi Ru Cheng, *Imperialism and Chinese Railroads*, Shanghai People's Publishing House, 1980; *Bai Shouyi, History of Chinese Transportation*, Henan People's Publishing House, 1987; *Book of Tang*: "Chapter on Officials and Institutions," *History of Ming*: Chapter on Geography"; *Book of Han*.

dynasty, China de facto possessed a relatively developed road and railway network. According to data on road and railway history, we calculated the mileage of roads, railways and the density in proportion to population and area at major in history point.

Current Chinese transportation infrastructure is mostly the fruits of modern and contemporary construction. China underwent large scale road and railway construction from the end of the Qing dynasty to the Republic of China era. From 1922 to 1945, the length of Chinese railways more than doubled and the number of roads increased by nearly 16 times. From 1949 to 2010, railways grew about four times and roads grew about 47 times (calculated according to the *China Statistical Yearbook*).

The massive increase in contemporary China's transportation infrastructure mostly fits its economic development trajectory. China's *per capita* economic output grew slowly in the 2,000 years pre-1949, but post-Liberation (especially since "reform and opening"), it has grown rapidly (Maddison, 1998). This is why studying the relationship between post-Liberation infrastructure investment and the economy becomes an important topic. This is the time period upon which this chapter focuses.

The chapter will now further summarize the main features of recent Chinese railway and road construction. These features will have some impact on the choice of research method in the literature. Unless otherwise noted, the data drawn on comes from the *China Statistical Yearbook*.

First, infrastructure investment in the late 1990s turned from weak to strong. Similar to the developmental trend of China's fixed asset investment (see Figure 6.1), the proportion of China's transportation and communications infrastructure investment in gross domestic product (GDP) gradually fell year-by-year from the beginning of "reform and opening" to 1991. If we include irrigation and electrical infrastructure investment, then there are only figures for the most recent few years. Data before that is less comparable due to the frequent changes in the statistical coverage of the *China Statistical Yearbook*. After 1991, there is a

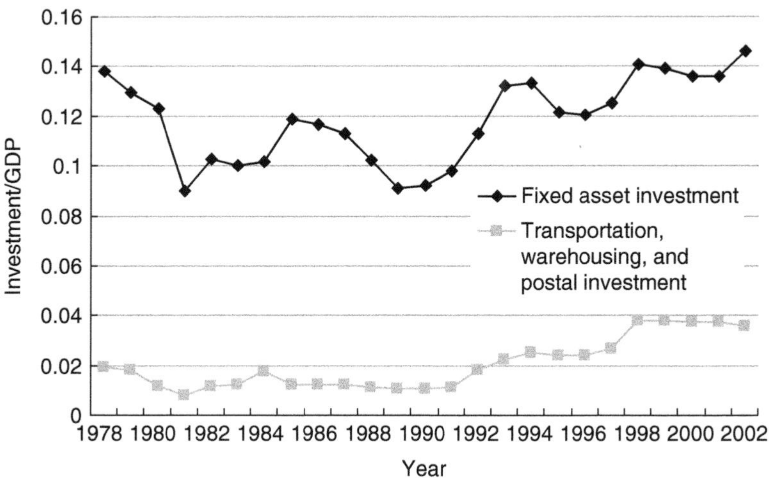

Figure 6.1 Fixed asset investment and transportation, warehousing, and postal investment proportion of China's GDP.

Note: The infrastructure investment portion of the social fixed asset investment in the *China Statistical Yearbook*. Figures after 2004 are not included due to the report's change in statistical coverage.

structural change: fixed asset and infrastructure investment's proportion of GDP began to increase.

Second, China's recent scale of infrastructure investment is significantly higher than that of other countries. As shown in Figure 6.2, in 1994 and 2002, infrastructure investment accounted for about 1 percent of the US GDP, while in

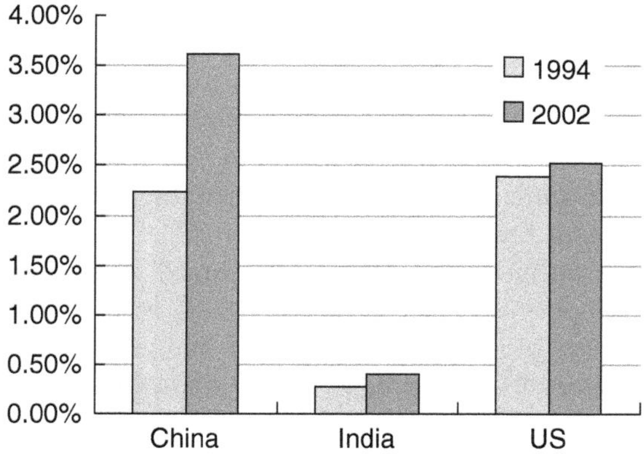

Figure 6.2 Transportation infrastructure investment proportion of GDP: China, India and US.[2]

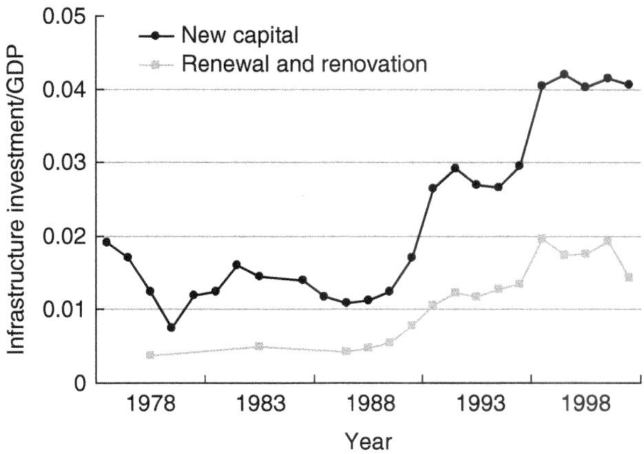

Figure 6.3 Transportation, warehousing and postal new facility investment and upgrade investment proportion of GDP.

1994, China's infrastructure investment accounted for 2.2 percent of GDP, rising to about 3.6 percent in 2002. India's figures only include the central government investment portion, which is around 0.3–0.4 percent and has grown with the passage of time.

Third, China's infrastructure investment mainly comes from new construction, not the maintenance or rebuilding of the original facilities. Figure 6.3 shows transportation, warehousing and postal new facility and upgrade investment as a proportion of GDP. Starting in the 1990s, the growth rate of new investment is markedly higher than that of upgrade investment.

Fourth, China's transportation infrastructure investment post-"reform and opening" was mainly concentrated on roads, while growth in investment on railways was rather slow. Figure 6.4 gives the log values of the length of roads,

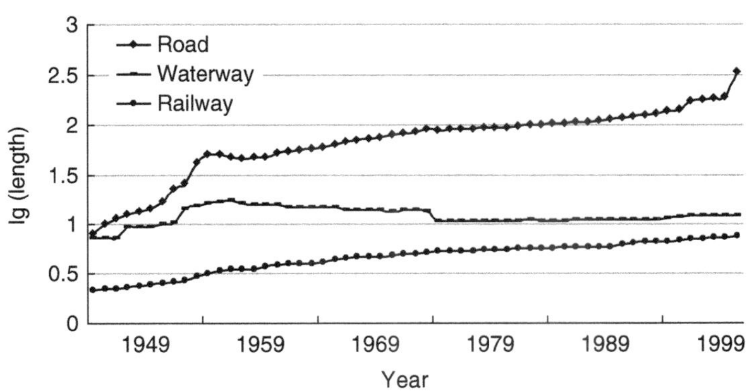

Figure 6.4 Road, railway and waterway length (log values).

Table 6.2 All types of transportation proportion of total fixed assets (%)

Year	*1985*	*1990*	*1995*	*2000*	*2006*
Share of railway transportation	6.4	3.4	4.8	3.8	2.1
Share of road transportation	2	4.2	4.1	7.9	6.9
Share of waterway transportation	2.6	2	0.8	0.4	1.1
Share of airway transportation	1.3	0.5	1.2	1.3	0.5

Data source: *China Statistical Yearbook*, corresponding years.

railways, and waterways post-Liberation. Roads trump railways whether in length or in growth rate.[3] The dotted line represents inland waterways. Since inland transportation employs natural navigation routes, investment is low, and thus received attention in the early years after the founding of the People's Republic of China and consequently, developed rapidly. Entering the 1960s, due to the decline in investment and the increase in dams, navigable mileage kept decreasing until the 1980s, when it gradually started to increase again. Table 6.2 provides the fixed asset investment amount for all types of transportation in each year.

Fifth, the financing structure of infrastructure (other than railways) trends toward regionalization. On the whole, before "reform and opening," China's transportation investment had an investment and management apparatus centrally planned by the central government.[4]

After "reform and opening," the central government's financing for transportation infrastructure investments declined year-by-year. The investment structure for different modes of transportation also varied largely, as the railways were mainly central government investments, accounting for around 90 percent in recent years, while road transportation was mainly local, with local investment

Table 6.3 2004–2008 Transportation, warehousing and postal actual fixed asset investment (unit: hundred million yuan)

	2004		*2008*	
	Central	*Local*	*Central*	*Local*
Transportation, warehousing and postal services	1,371.5 (19.3%)*	5,720.01 (80.7%)	4,544 (28.9%)	11,156.5 (71.1%)
Railway transportation	752.73 (88.9%)	93.57 (11.1%)	3,694.8 (90.7%)	378.4 (9.3%)
Road transportation	200.69 (4.3%)	4,464.84 (95.7%)	311.3 (4.2%)	7,100.2 (95.8%)
Water transportation	106.58 (19.9%)	428.05 (80.1%)	164.5 (13.7%)	1,039.6 (86.3%)
Electricity and heat generating	1,699 (35%)	3,155 (65%)	0	0

Data source: *Yearbook of China Transportation & Communications*, corresponding years.

usually around 95 percent (Table 6.3). This may have a large impact on investment efficiency, which we will elaborate upon later. The investment structure of waterway transportation went through major changes, but local investment is maintained at about 80–90 percent – a dominant position. Bai and Qian (2010) have a detailed narrative on the change in the roles of the central and local government in infrastructure investment.

6.3 Channels through which transportation infrastructure investment impacts on economic growth

Transportation infrastructure investment may influence economic growth through all sorts of channels. First is transportation cost-savings. When the quality of roads is higher or the distance is shorter, transportation costs will decline. Current research mostly considers the monetary costs of transporting goods (Fogel, 1964). Another major cost-saving comes from transport time cost-savings, which is reflected in a reduction of the time goods spend en route. This can accelerate the turnover of funds occupied by inventory, while the time savings from passenger transport gives passengers more time to engage in other activities, creating more value for society. The decrease in unit transport costs will lead to further enhancement of market integration, further expanding both domestic markets and the consequent economies of scale, facilitating overall economic growth (Lu and Chen, 2009).

The second channel through which transportation infrastructure investment may impact the economy is by raising firm labor productivity. One example is when railway networks are more developed, firms need not keep as much inventory in reserve, which lowers inventory costs, increasing productivity (Shirley and Winston, 2004; Li and Li, 2009).

Third, road and railway network construction may influence Chinese regional economic disposition. For example, due to high transportation costs, industry may originally have been equally distributed nationwide. After the transportation network develops, many firms may relocate to the coastal regions, which has efficiency implications for the overall economy. Research in this field is still non-existent.

Transportation infrastructure investment may have many other influencing channels. Through studying central-to-local fiscal transfer payments, Fan (2011) demonstrated that government investment in infrastructure may lead to an increase in corruption. In addition, roads and railways can impact on the property market; an increase in transportation volumes could bring about more accidents and economic losses.

6.4 Empirical analysis on the impact of infrastructure construction on the national economy

This section summarizes the empirical evidence for the different channels through which infrastructure impacts on the overall economy. Similarly, the emphasis of our discussion will be in terms of transportation infrastructure investment.

6.4.1 Measurement issues

How should infrastructure be measured? Two types of method are commonly used: one is measurement in terms of investment amount. Early researchers mostly employed this approach, such as Barro (1990), Holtz-Eakin (1988), Shirley and Winston (2004), Fan and Bai (2004) and Zhang (2007). The upside to this approach is its ability to reflect both the quantity and quality of transportation infrastructure investment. But "since when the perpetual inventory approach is used to estimate capital stock, corresponding assumptions should be made for age and depreciation of asset in use, meanwhile an assumption must be made for the initial period's capital stock, for different types of infrastructure, these are all difficult to scientifically estimate,"[5] so measurement errors may be large.

Another method is to use physical forms to indicate the stock of infrastructure. This is mostly seen in micro-level studies, such as Fleisher and Chen (1997), Wang and Wang (2006), Zong and Li (2006), Li and Li (2009), who employed the mileage of all types of transportation infrastructure as an indicator. Liu et al. (2010) employed railway density, road density and their rank to substitute for the level of transportation infrastructure;[6] there have also been academics who have attempted to design comprehensive indicators that can reflect infrastructure stock, Démurger (2001) calculated a transportation density indicator that included railways, roads and waterways. Zhang et al. (2007) employed primary composition analysis to establish a comprehensive indicator.[7]

As discussed above, Chinese transportation infrastructure investment is mainly in new facilities, so it is feasible to apply mileage empirically. Measurement errors may also be relatively small.

6.4.2 The relationship between infrastructure construction investment and economic growth

In previous literature, studies on the impact of infrastructure on the economy mainly employed macro-econometrics. Initially, time-series models were used. Recently, the panel-data method was widely applied. For example, Démurger (2001) employed provincial level panel data from 1985 to 1998 and numerous control variables to conduct close analysis and found that the relationship between transportation infrastructure and regional growth is most evident, and communications infrastructure is also somewhat correlated. Fan and Zhang (2004) arrived at similar findings.

A major problem with literature in this field is that similar methods could reach drastically different conclusions. For example, the oft-cited Fan and Bai (2004) and Wang and Wang (2006) both employed time-series methods to analyze the relationship between Chinese annual investments in infrastructure and output. Although the main variables in the two studies are similar, since the actual data employed by them come from different sources with large variations, obvious disparities exist between the regression results. Fan and Bai (2004) found that returns on Chinese transportation infrastructure investment far surpass the US.

However, Wang and Wang (2006) found that returns on Chinese transportation infrastructure investment are lower than the US. This is the issue that the current study needs to carefully examine.

In addition, although macro-econometric results mostly prove that Chinese infrastructure construction is positively correlated with Chinese economic development, this does not reflect causality, that is, whether infrastructure construction impacts China's economy is still unclear. This is because in terms of econometric methodology, infrastructure investment is endogenously decided, which may create bias for regression results. Moreover, the quality of Chinese data is mixed (e.g., the two studies cited above employ vastly differing data on capital), and figures from different sources may possibly be very different, which will also impact on regression results. Another drawback to employing macro-econometrics is its inability to tell us the channels through which infrastructure investment impacts the economy.

6.4.3 Channels through which infrastructure investment impacts on the economy

Recently, more studies are employing micro-econometrics in order to attempt to solve the above-mentioned endogeneity issue and seek channels through which infrastructure investment impacts on the economy. The results are summarized below.

Evidence on transport cost-savings is fairly clear. Li and Chen (2012) studied the impact of China's 1994 double-track construction of the Lanxin Railway on transport cost-savings and market integration. Since there is no any direct information on transport costs, the study used the price difference between the same goods in Urumqi and Lanzhou to reflect changes in the actual transport costs. The study found that double-track construction caused goods leaving Xinjiang to save 30 percent on transportation, generating a social return of over 10 percent annually. These transport cost-savings mostly came from reduced congestion. Since economic growth exceeded the pace of infrastructure investment, China's transportation network was very congested in the 1980s and 1990s, generating high transport costs. Infrastructure investment reduced these situations to a large extent, lowering transport costs (Park et al., 2002).

On the other hand, theoretically speaking, transportation infrastructure investment may reduce labor transport costs (e.g. time costs), thereby generating more labor reallocation, e.g., rural labor working in the city. But there is still a lack of empirical evidence to show whether transportation investment will cause more people to work in the city. Rozelle et al. (1999) conducted a rigorous study on the factors that lead to labor reallocation and they did not find evidence proving that the situation of transportation had any significant impact on migrant labor. Of course, whether the results of such a study reflect the general circumstances in China is still worth exploring.

Research regarding the impact of transportation construction on enhancing Chinese firms' productivity is still in its nascence. Li and Li (2009) provided some evidence by studying the impact of road construction on Chinese firms' inventory. At the start of "reform and opening," Chinese inventory levels were high; about 80 percent of annual sales in the retail sector. After "reform and opening" Chinese inventory levels fell drastically and they have already declined to about 15 percent in the retail sector, equivalent to the level seen in developed countries. There are many reasons for this decline, a major one being China's road investments, which can explain half of the decline in the inventory-sales ratio in the past decade. Lower inventory costs save the capital from occupation, thereby generating an enhancement of firm productivity.

There is also the question of whether improvements in transportation infrastructure networks impact on industrial agglomeration or the geographical distribution of industry. Lu and Chen (2006) and Jin et al.'s (2006) studies discovered that roads and communications facilities have a positive effect on agglomeration. Faber's (2009) study showed that Chinese road construction indeed has widely varying impacts on different regions; positive impacts on developed regions and possibly negative impacts on remote regions. From the perspective of development, this may be bad news, as one of the objectives for building roads is to increase the development level of remote regions, but this may actually cause resources and economic activity in remote regions to agglomerate toward developed regions, effectively creating a negative impact on remote regions. However, in terms of the nation's overall efficiency, the redeployment of industry brought by construction of roads will enhance the agglomeration effect and overall economic productivity.

6.4.4 Investment efficiency and financing structure of transportation infrastructure

The issue discussed above is whether infrastructure investment has any impact on the economy. A more important question is: Is China's infrastructure investment efficient? Answering this question requires estimating the long-term and short-term consequences for all channels of infrastructure investment. Given that China's current research is still in its infancy, research results cannot yet provide reliable answers. Nevertheless, existing evidence can provide some helpful information to answer this question. Specifically speaking, we can make conjectures on investment efficiency from three aspects: first, by comparing China's road and railway density with other countries; second by estimating and comparing China's socioeconomic return on infrastructure investment with other countries;[8] third, by studying the trend of China's infrastructure investment return as time passes. One conclusion from combining evidence in these three aspects is that China's current infrastructure investment efficiency is rather low. The specifics regarding the studies are discussed below.

Wang et al. (2000) calculated China's road and railway density and compared it to the UK, the US and several other countries. In accordance with this approach, this chapter combines updated data and performs a similar calculation (see Table 6.4). The main finding is: whether in terms of population or geographical

Table 6.4 Comparisons of transportation infrastructure density between China, India and the US

	Railway per capita (kilometer/10,000 persons)	*Road per capita (kilometer/10,000 persons)*	*Railway density (kilometer/100 square kilometers)*	*Road density (kilometer/100 square kilometers)*
China (2003)	5.6	140	0.76	18.85
India (1985)	8	208	2.08	51.96
US (1988)	80.8	2455	2.19	66.5

Data source: Wang et al. (2000) and the *China Statistical Yearbook*, 2004.

density, China's road and railway investment in 2003 was still lower than India's in 1985 and much lower than the US in 1988. We must admit that an approach comparing density must assume that the quality of each country's transportation infrastructure is consistent. This assumption may not hold and that will impact on our conclusion. If a study could calculate density adjusted for infrastructure quality, it would be a significant contribution.

According to Li and Li's (2013) research results on the relationship between roads and inventory, for every yuan invested in roads in late 1990s China, inventories could be reduced by about 0.02 yuan. As a comparison, Shirley and Winston (2004) found that in the US, in the 1970s, each dollar invested could lower inventories by $0.07; in the 1980s, each dollar invested could lower inventories by $0.02; in the 1990s, each dollar invested could lower inventories by less than $0.01. The marginal rate of return exhibits a distinct decline. Thus, though the density of road transportation networks in the US during the 1970s and 1980s was already much higher than that of China, the returns on road investment (in terms of inventory) is still not lower than China's current returns on road investment. If Chinese and American findings are comparable, then the above conclusion shows that China's road investment efficiency is rather low. For the two to be comparable, it needs to be assumed that the industrial structure of the two countries is similar.

As time passes, what will the future look like? Theoretically speaking, if China's demand for transportation does not change structurally, its investment rate of return will decline. This is because past road and railway construction had the major economic effect of reducing interregional transportation congestion. Congestion has been radically reduced now and further investment will result in fewer gains in this aspect. Moreover, due to massive recent investment, roads that connect major cities in China are already close to a straight line. If more investments are to be made to narrow transportation distances, the cost will be much higher than in the past, so investment rates of return will decline (assuming demand for transportation does not significantly increase).

In fact, Li and Li's (2013) study has already discovered that China's road investments have declining returns. This study's data sample is medium to large industrial firms from 1998 to 2007. They found that, before 2002, China's road investments had a significant impact on the decline of firms' inventory: for every yuan invested, inventory would fall by 0.02–0.03 yuan. But after 2002, road investment basically had no further impact on inventory declines. Thus, in a relatively short time period, external returns for China's road investment seemed to have dropped precipitously. Interestingly, Bai and Qian's (2010) study provided the average (private) rate of return on capital for roads. They discovered that the rate of return from 1985 to 2000 exhibited a downtrend overall, but the rate of return after 1998 did not decline and actually rose slightly. Bai and Qian (2010) also calculated the average (private) rate of return on capital for electricity and heat generating industries and found a similar trend; rates of return exhibited a downtrend from 1985 to 2000, but rose significantly after 2003. In comparison, the private rate of return on railways only declined in the late 1980s and was stable thereafter.

Why is Chinese infrastructure investment inefficient? One possible factor is that the financing structure does not fit the infrastructure's externalities. In Li and Li's (2013) study on inventory, they found that the reason roads had such a strong impact on inventory is that most basic materials rely on interprovincial transportation and road construction mainly effects non-local firms. In other words, Chinese road investment may have large interprovincial externalities. Since Chinese road investment mainly comes from local government and local government does not put much thought into the impact of its investment decisions on other regions, road projects with high investment returns may not receive attention from local investors (e.g. local government), thereby causing investment efficiency to be at the low end. Another possibility is the combination of China's unique "upwardly accountable" political system and fiscal decentralization, which causes local government officials to compete through yardsticks (political achievements), strengthening their incentives for attracting capital and investing in infrastructure (Zhang et al., 2007). The result is that local infrastructure projects obtain support even if they lack efficiency, thus creating overinvestment.

6.5 Conclusion

Research on the effectiveness of Chinese infrastructure investment is still in its nascence and many important issues need to be explored. The current available evidence shows that infrastructure investment does indeed have positive effects on enhancing economic efficiency. Specifically, in terms of transportation infrastructure, its impact on the economy may go through channels such as reducing congestion, integrating regional markets, lowering firms' inventory costs, etc. Such effects differ among regions: development of interregional transportation infrastructure may lead to firms leaving underdeveloped regions and agglomerating in developed regions, thus developed regions may gain more in terms of economic aggregate than underdeveloped regions.

In terms of investment efficiency, although the density of China's infrastructure investment is lower than developed countries, the social rate of return on investments may be lower than developed countries and is still falling rapidly. A potential reason is infrastructure financing's dependence on local funding. Since some types of infrastructure (such as road networks) have strong interregional externalities and local investment decisions do not take them into consideration, road projects with high returns may not be built. Another possibility is the incentive mechanism for local government officials leading to their investment in low-return local infrastructure.

Notes

1 Xi Liu is thanked for his outstanding assistance with this project.
2 Figures on China come from the data in the *China Statistical Yearbook* (1996 and 2003) on transportation industry's fixed asset investment. India's figures come from its Ministry of Finance's Economic Survey (1997–1998 and 2006–2007). US data comes from Table A-3 in CBO's (Congressional Budget Office) article "Trends in Public Spending on Transportation and Water Infrastructure,1956 to 2004."
3 In 2006, due to the inclusion of village paths in the calculations of road mileage, the total length of roads increased dramatically.
4 During the Great Leap Forward, local governments became the main source of financing. For more on the financing of Chinese transportation infrastructure investment, Gao (2005) has a full and comprehensive review.
5 Wang and Wang (2006) have discussed this issue in depth.
6 Specifically speaking, Liu et al. (2010) employed an "operating railway mileage per square kilometer" indicator for railway density; "road mileage per square kilometer" was used to indicate road density. Other than overall road density, roads were divided into six categories, namely, highway, first tier, second tier, third tier, fourth tier and unranked, according to road surface quality and ease of passage.
7 Zhang et al. (2007) selected four major types of infrastructure for measurement: transportation, energy, communications and city, while taking into consideration the disparity in measurement units, and employed primary composition analysis to construct an index that reflects overall infrastructure, in which kilometer mileage (10,000 kilometers) was selected for transportation infrastructure.
8 Gramlich (1990) and Holtz-Eakin (1992) pointed out that if the discounted net profits are positive, then transportation infrastructure investments are worthwhile. The direction of future infrastructure investments can be determined by different rates of return on capital.

References

In English

American Congressional Budget Office, 2007, *Trends in Public Spending on Transportation and Water Infrastructure, 1956 to 2004*, August.

Bai, Chong-En, Yingyi Qian, 2010, "Infrastructure Development in China: the Cases of Electricity, Highways, and Railways," *Journal of Comparative Economics*, 38, pp. 34–51.

Barro, Robert J, 1990, "Government Spending in a Simple Model of Endogenous Growth," *Journal of Political Economy*, 98(5), pp. 103–125.

Démurger, Sylvie, 2001, "Infrastructure Development and Economic Growth: an Explanation for Regional Disparities in China?" *Journal of Comparative Economics*, 29(1), pp. 95–117.

Faber, Benjamin, 2009, "Market Integration and the Periphery: The Unintended Effects of New Highways in a Developing Country," London School of Economics, Mimeo.

Fan, Shenggen, Zhang, Xiaobo, 2004, "Infrastructure and Regional Economic Development in Rural China," *China Economic Review*, 15(2), pp. 203–214.

Fleisher, Belton M., and Chen, Jian, 1997, "The Coast–Noncoast Income Gap, Productivity and Regional Economic Policy in China," *Journal of Comparative Economics*, 25(2), pp. 220–236.

Fogel, William Robert, 1964, *Railroads and American Economic Growth: Essays in Econometric History*. Baltimore: The Johns Hopkins Press.

Gramlich, Edward M, 1994, "Infrastructure Investment: a Review Essay," *Journal of Economic Literature*, 32(3), pp. 1176–1196.

Holtz-Eakin, Douglas, 1988, "Private Output, Government Capital, and the Infrastructure Crisis," *Discussion Paper No. 394*, Columbia University.

Li, Han and Zhigang Li, 2013, Road Investments and Inventory Reduction: Firm Level Evidence from China, *Journal of Urban Economics*, pp. 43–52.

Li, Zhigang and Chen Yu, 2012, Estimating the Social Return to Transport Infrastructure: A Price-Difference Approach Applied to a Quasi-Experiment, (October 2012). *Journal of Comparative Economics*.

Maddison, Angus, 1998, *Chinese Economic Performance in the Long Run*, Paris: OECD.

Park, Albert, Hehui Jin, Scott Rozelle, and Jikun Huang, 2002, "Market Emergence and Transition: Arbitrage, Transaction Costs, and Autarky in China's Grain Markets," *American Journal of Agricultural Economics*, 84(1).

Rozelle, Scott; Taylor, J. Edward; DeBrauw, Alan, 1999, "Migration, Remittances, and Agricultural Productivity in China," *American Economic Review*, 89(2), pp. 287–291.

Shirley, Chad and Clifford Winston, 2004, "Firm Inventory Behavior and the Returns from Highway Infrastructure Investments," *Journal of Urban Economics*, 55(2), pp. 398–415.

In Chinese

Bai, Shouyi, 1987, *The History of Transportation in China*, Henan: Henan People's Publishing House.

Cheng, Mi Ru, 1980, *Imperialism and China's Railways*, Shanghai: Shanghai People's Publishing House.

Fan, Jiuli and Baoli Bai, 2004, "The Effect of Infrastructure Capital on Economic Growth," *Economic Tribune*, 10–12, p. 11.

Fan, Ziying, 2011, "Transfer Payment, Infrastructure and Corruption," Huazhong University of Science and Technology, *Working Paper*.

Gao, Feng, 2005, *Transportation Infrastructure Investment and Economic Growth*, Beijing: China's Financial and Economic Publishing House.

Jin, Yu, Zhao Chen, and Ming Lu, 2006, "Industry Agglomeration in China: Economic Geography, New Economic Geography and Policy," *Economic Research Journal*, 4, pp. 79–89.

Li, Han, and Zhigang Li, 2009, "The effect of Transportation Infrastructure Investment on Businesses Inventory: An Empirical Research Based on Panel Data of Manufacturing Enterprise," *Management World*, 8, pp. 73–80.

Liu, Binglian, Peng Wu, and Yuhai Liu, 2010, "Transportation Infrastructure and Total Factor Productivity Growth in China," *China Industrial Economics*, 3, pp. 54–64.

Lu, Ming, and Zhao Chen, 2006, *Market Integration and Industry Agglomeration in China's Regional Development*, Shanghai: Shanghai People's Publishing House.

National Bureau of Statistics of China, various years, *China Statistical Yearbook*, Beijing: China Statistics Press.

The Editorial Committee of Chinese Roads History, 1999, *The History of Chinese Roads*, Beijing: China Transportation Press.

The Editorial Committee of Railways' Built History in China, 2003, *The History of Railway Construction in China*, Beijing: China Railways Publishing House.

Wang, Huijiong, Boqi Li, and Shantong Li, 2000, *Sustainable Development and Transportation*, Beijing: China Railway Publishing House.

Wang, Renfei, and Jingjie Wang, 2006, "The Output Elasticity and Optimum Scale of Chinese Infrastructure: A Study Based on the Aggregate Production Function Model," *Economic Science*, 2, pp. 99–111.

Zhang, Guangnan, Xiaoying Li, and Guanghan Chen, 2010, "Employment, Output and Investment Effects in China's Infrastructure," *Management World*, 4, pp. 5–13.

Zhang, Jun, Yuan Gao, Yong Fu, and Hong Zhang, 2007, "Why Does China Enjoy So Much Better Physical Infrastructure," *Economic Research Journal*, 3, pp. 4–19.

Zhang, Xueliang, 2007, "Regional Comparative Analysis on the Relationship between Transport Infrastructure and Economic Growth in China," *Journal of Finance and Economics*, 8, pp. 51–63.

Zong, Jiafeng, and Jing Li, 2006, "The Experimental Analysis of Infrastructure Development and Economic Growth in China," *Statistical Research*, 18–21, p. 7.

Part IV

Agglomeration and balance

7 The trends in geographical agglomeration of Chinese manufacturing industries

Canfei He and Fenghua Pan

7.1 Introduction

Since "reform and opening," as market reforms progressed and China integrated into the world economy, the geographical disposition of Chinese manufacturing changed dramatically. In macro-terms, industry gradually agglomerated toward the eastern coastal regions, accompanied by gradually declining manufacturing proportions in the central and western regions, the decline of old industrial regions represented by the northeastern provinces being especially evident (Fan and Scott, 2003; Wen, 2004a,b; He et al., 2007a; He et al., 2008a; He, 2008; Lu and Tao, 2009; He et al., 2010a). At the same time, numerous industrial clusters formed in many districts, counties, and even townships. These industrial clusters are often composed of hundreds if not thousands of same-industry firms and export large amounts of their products to foreign markets (Wang, 2001, 2010). Meanwhile, each level of government objectively facilitates the geographical agglomeration of industries by setting up development zones at the national level, provincial level, municipal level, and county level. Whether on the macro-scale or micro-scale, industrial agglomeration is pervasive in China.

Theoretically, location theory, trade theory and economic geography models can explain geographical agglomeration of industry. Classical trade theory believes that two countries (regions) should each produce goods that have a comparative advantage, thereby realizing maximum welfare. Neoclassical trade theory believes that industry location is determined by exogenous resource endowments such as technology, labor and natural resources, industry agglomerates in regions with comparative advantage (Ohlin, 1957). Each region participates in the division of labor according to comparative advantage and lowering trade barriers will increase regional specialization and geographical concentration of industry. Market integration will facilitate the geographical agglomeration of industry. Neoclassical trade models may explain the geographical disposition of industry to a certain extent, but comparative advantage is not the only explanation for industry specialization and geographical concentration. Classical trade theory assumes perfect competition and constant returns to scale and equilibrium in factor returns is reached through trade. However, traditional theory cannot explain the pattern of trade between developed regions and countries, where large amounts of trade occur within industries or even companies. New trade theory and new economic geography employed economies of scale and monopolistic competition assumptions, breaking through the limitations of traditional trade theory, and discovered that economies of scale is an important factor that impacts industry agglomeration, as firms tend to agglomerate in regions with large market potential (Krugman, 1980). At the same time, inclusion of transportation costs through the iceberg model assumption leads to the discovery of the inverted U relationship between industrial agglomeration and transportation costs, that is, when transportation costs are high, industrial agglomeration is low; as transportation costs fall, industrial agglomeration increases; once transportation costs fall to a certain level, industrial agglomeration declines again. In new economic geography models, the geographical location of industry is entirely internalized (Krugman, 1991; Venables, 1996). The geographical agglomeration of industry is determined by the mutual effect of transportation costs and economies of scale. However, new economic geography models do not deny the importance of traditional geographical factors (Jin et al., 2006; He et al., 2010b). In fact, some traditional geographical factors become primary driving forces for the geographical agglomeration of industry according to the new economic geography theory. Such a purely geographical factor leads to the initial agglomeration of industry and the geographical agglomeration of industry is further strengthened through new economic geography factors. No one factor can explain the industrial location phenomenon in the real world, natural advantage and economies of agglomeration jointly determine industrial location (Krugman, 1991).

In transitional economies, the market mechanism that industrial agglomeration relies on is incomplete, institutional and policy factors play a critical role in the geographical layout of industry. Research shows that institutional changes that have accompanied "reform and opening" are an important perspective in understanding China's geographical disposition of industry (He et al., 2010a). On the one hand, transitioning from a planned economy to a socialist market economy implies that the market mechanism becomes the fundamental means through which resources are allocated, thus comparative advantage and locational advantage can be gradually introduced to China's industrial location; meanwhile, under the context of economic globalization, participating in international trade and introducing foreign direct investment can enhance the impact of comparative advantage and competitive advantage on industrial location, further facilitating the agglomeration of industry toward the coastal regions that are better positioned geographically (Ge, 2009; He and Xie, 2006). On the other hand, decentralization of economic powers, especially fiscal decentralization, greatly enhanced the autonomous decision-making abilities of local governments, creating fierce regional competition. Local governments have strong regional protectionist tendencies and emulate each other's industrial development strategies, which, to a certain extent, lead to duplicated construction, convergence of industry structure and dispersed industrial disposition (Young, 2000; Bai et al., 2004a; Poncet, 2005). The geographical disposition of Chinese manufacturing forms and continuously adjusts under the mutual effect of such agglomeration and dispersion forces.

Currently, industrial agglomeration has become a focal point for academia and the policymaking community. On the one hand, industrial agglomeration is believed to be an important means through which local economic development and industry upgrading can be realized; on the other hand, widespread controversies exist concerning the long-term impact of industrial agglomeration on regional development disparities This chapter will examine the reasons for and trends in agglomeration of manufacturing since "reform and opening" from a macro-scale. The second section in this chapter will summarize research on the factors that influence the agglomeration of Chinese manufacturing. The third section will analyze the present situation and trend of Chinese manufacturing agglomeration. The fourth section concludes and attempts to peer into the future.

7.2 Agglomeration of Chinese manufacturing industries under economic transition

China's economic transition can be summarized as the process of marketization, globalization and decentralization (He et al., 2008a). Since "reform and opening," Chinese industry achieved spatial restructuring under the background of such economic transition. Mainstream economic theory presumes a perfect market environment when explaining industrial agglomeration. China's marketization provided the conditions for comparative advantage and agglomeration economies becoming the driving force for industrial agglomeration, of which traditional location factors such as transportation costs, resource input obviously impact the agglomeration of Chinese industry. For example, He et al.'s (2007b) study discovered that industries with high input of agricultural goods are rather dispersed, while industries with high input of metallic minerals are more agglomerated. Wang and Wei (2007) found that the degree of labor intensity and the extent to which industry is agglomerated are significantly negatively correlated and believe that traditional comparative advantages in fields such as labor are important factors that led to a decrease in the geographical concentration of Chinese manufacturing. Lu and Tao (2007) also discovered that transport costs and natural endowments are important factors that impact an industry's agglomeration as well. He and Zhu's (2010) study on Chinese resource intensive industries found that resource endowment, historical foundations, convenience of transportation, market scale, etc. all have significant impact on the distribution of resource intensive industries. He et al. (2010b) observed the regional and industry differences of Chinese industrial agglomeration and introduced location features and industry characteristics to explain the geographical agglomeration of Chinese industry, verifying the importance of agricultural factor input and labor input in industrial agglomeration, meanwhile also discovering the importance of new economic geography factors and institutions.

In recent years, academics cited new economic geography models to explain the agglomeration of Chinese industry. For example, Jin, Chen, and Lu (2006) employed the new economic geography analytic framework to discuss the impact of factors such as economic geography and economic policy on Chinese industry agglomeration, and used provincial level panel data from 1987 to 2001, to study the factors that impact Chinese regional industrial agglomeration. They found that: (1) opening of the economy promoted industry agglomeration, while opening of the economy is related to geographical and historical factors; (2) market capacity, urbanization, the improvement of infrastructure and weakening of government's role are all conducive to industry agglomeration; (3) coastal regions have a geographical advantage when it comes to industry agglomeration. Other than the role played by economic geography, policy is another important factor that causes industrial agglomeration. Lin and Wang (2006) also employed the economic geography analytic framework, discovering that transport cost differences form the locational advantage of manufacturing in coastal regions. Huang and Li (2006) found that traditional comparative advantage theory and new economic geography have some degree of explanatory power for the distribution of Chinese industry, e.g. regional natural resource endowment and market scale both have significant impacts on industry agglomeration. He et al. (2010b) found that only in industries with high degrees of marketization does new economic geography factors have significant facilitating effects on the agglomeration of industry.

However, the geographical agglomeration of Chinese manufacturing cannot be understood without China's unique transitional context. China's "reform and opening" is spatially and temporally gradual, which creates different policy environments for different industries in different regions, and since the way and extent regions and industries react differ as well, this eventually leads to differences in the development achievements and growth modes for different regions and industries. Much research is directed toward China's special transitional background, studying the impact these factors have on the agglomeration of Chinese manufacturing. These factors mainly include globalization and decentralization aspects.

First is economic globalization. Globalization is undoubtedly a critical impetus for China's becoming a world factory. For manufacturing, participating in international trade and employing foreign capital are doubtlessly two of the most important aspects of globalization. Trade liberalization that accompanies economic transition can give full play to China's comparative advantages, increasing industry specialization. Studies find that exports have a significant impetus on the spatial agglomeration of Chinese manufacturing (Chen et al., 2008). Large amounts of foreign direct investment entering China also facilitated the geographical agglomeration of Chinese manufacturing to a great extent (He and Wang, 2010). Ge (2009) studied the relationship between globalization and the agglomeration of Chinese industry and discovered that industries that are highly reliant on exports or foreign capital agglomerate in regions where foreign markets are readily accessible, industries that are export-oriented and have high proportions of foreign investment have higher degrees of agglomeration than other industries. He et al. (2007b) employed data from China's 2004 First Economic Census and proved industries with high degrees of foreign capital utilization and international trade participation are more agglomerated. As China's openness to the outside world deepens, the impact of FDI and foreign trade on the disposition of China's industry and their impetus on industrial agglomeration becomes stronger and more significant (Xian and Wen, 2006). The entry of foreign capital plays a major role in the development of China's manufacturing and has become a significant component of China's manufacturing. Thus, the location choices by foreign firms have a significant impact on industrial agglomeration. Some studies examined what affects location choices made by foreign firms, e.g. Zhang and Chen (2006) estimated the impact of the degree of industrial agglomeration, the ownership structure and other traditional regional characteristics on the geographical location choices of foreign firms and discovered that a highly significant agglomeration effect exists; Zhao and Zhang (2007) used the logical connection between spatial agglomeration and manufacturing growth as a premise and empirically studied the foreign capital factor in Chinese manufacturing's spatial agglomeration from three aspects, finding that the industry spatial agglomeration effect is evident in foreign capital; based on new economic geography theory, Amiti and Javorcik (2008) studied the location choices of foreign firms in China from 1998 to 2001 and found that market and supplier accessibility at the provincial level is the most important factor that influences foreign firms in their location choices.

Second is regional decentralization. China's economic transition is accompanied by the decentralization of economic decision-making powers and fiscal powers. Decentralization of power triggered fierce interregional competition, which caused local governments to adopt a strategy of emulating each other when formulating industrial policy (Thun, 2004). A local government official performance review system based on economic development achievements, moderate local autonomy, fiscal incentive system, and hard budgetary constraints jointly caused local governments to follow the leader in terms of industrial development, developing similar industries, thereby accelerating regional economic growth and creating China's dispersed industrial layout (He et al., 2007b). Fiscal decentralization further motivates the regional protectionist policies of provincial governments (Young, 2000; Bai et al., 2004b). Local governments tend to protect high value-added, high profit margin and high tax revenue-generating industries, such as tobacco, food, pharmaceuticals, beverages, transportation equipment, machinery, etc. (State Council Center for Development Studies, 2004). In short, regional decentralization causes regional market segmentation and distortion in the allocation of productive factors, lowering the geographical concentration and degree of specialization of Chinese industry (Bai et al., 2004b; He et al., 2007b). Regional decentralization enables local governments to play a larger role in the development of the local economy, but decentralization often turns into an anti-market force. Decentralization creates local protectionism, which is unconducive to industrial specialization, inhibits interregional competition, and may facilitate competition between the diversification and localization of regional industry development. Bai et al., (2004b) employed provincial level data and found instead that industries that have a high proportion of state owned enterprises and high profit–tax rates are more spatially dispersed. Huang and Li (2006) found that the impact of regional protectionism was limited to the inland regions in the 1990s. Lu and Tao (2007) also found that regional protectionism restricted the regional agglomeration of Chinese industry to a large extent. He et al.'s (2007b) empirical study found that regional protectionism at the provincial level may significantly impact industrial geographical location, while it is difficult for such protectionism to have a large impact at the county level due to resource and market scale limitations.

On the whole, under an economic transition background, market forces, globalization forces as well as local forces interweave and jointly impact Chinese industrial location. Market forces motivate firms to conduct locational layout in accordance with comparative advantage and economies of scale, thereby promoting the geographical agglomeration of industry. Participating in globalization can give full play to China's comparative advantages, facilitating agglomeration of Chinese industry in the macro-scale. Local forces may facilitate the dispersion of industry at the macro-level, but at the local level, construction of industrial parks and industrial cluster zones of all sorts by local government may enhance the level of industrial agglomeration.

7.3 The current situation and trend of the geographical agglomeration of Chinese manufacturing

Currently, there is a large amount of literature that examines the degree of spatial agglomeration of Chinese manufacturing and its evolving trend. These studies usually employ the Gini coefficient or EG index to measure agglomeration, of which the Gini coefficient usually adopts industry data while the EG index adopts firm data (see Table 7.1). Wen (2004a,b) employed the Second and Third Industrial Census data to study the regional agglomeration of Chinese industry and found that up to 1995, many Chinese manufacturing industries were highly agglomerated in a few coastal provinces. Comparative analyses on the agglomeration of industries in 1980, 1985, and 1995 illustrate that since "reform and opening," Chinese industry has become more concentrated in regional terms. Fan's (2004) study found that since "reform and opening," the interregional level of specialization and market integration has been enhanced and the layout of industries has been fundamentally changed, with most industries already having undergone, or currently undergoing, relocation to the eastern coastal regions; further discussions that take into account international experience suggest that China's current phase is still in the "high industrial agglomeration of industries, low regional specialization" condition, in which the level of domestic market integration is still low overall and lagging behind the level of integration shown toward foreign markets. This causes manufacturing to concentrate in the eastern coastal regions. Luo and Cao (2005) adopted the EG index (Ellison and Glaeser, 1997) and a customized five province degree of concentration to measure the degree of agglomeration for 20 Chinese manufacturing industries in 1993, 1997, 2002, and 2003. They found that industrial agglomeration declined during 1993–1997, while most industries displayed an increase during 1997–2003. Technology intensive industries have the highest agglomeration, seconded by capital intensive industries; labor intensive industries are the most dispersed. Regional distribution of industry is highly unbalanced, with Jiangsu, Guangdong, Shandong, Zhejiang and Shanghai taking up a large

Table 7.1 Representative papers that study the measurement and influencing factors of Chinese industrial agglomeration

Author (year)	*Precision of data, agglomeration index, geographical scale*	*Time period (year)*	*Main variables affecting agglomeration*
Wen (2004a,b)	Two-digit manufacturing, Gini coefficient, Province	1980, 1985, 1995	Market scale, transportation cost
Luo and Cao (2005)	Two-digit manufacturing, EG index, Province	1993, 1997, 2002, 2003	–
Lu and Tao (2006)	Firms, EG index, Province, prefectural city and county	1998–2003	–
He and Xie (2006)	Two-digit manufacturing, Gini coefficient, Province	1980–2003	Economic globalization, comparative advantage and economies of scale
Huang and Li (2006)	Two-digit manufacturing, Gini coefficient, Province	1980, 1985, 1990, 1997	Regional features, industry features and interaction term between the two
Jin, Chen, and Lu (2006)	Industry, Proportion of Industry, Province	1987–2001	Economic geography, new economic geography, economic policy
He, Pan and Sun (2007)	Two-digit, three-digit and four-digit manufacturing, Gini coefficient, Province, prefectural municipal and county	2004	Comparative advantage, globalization and institutions, agglomeration economics
Wang and Wei (2007)	Two-digit manufacturing, Gini coefficient, SP index, MHHI index, Province	1980–2003	Labor intensity, technology intensity, economies of scale, market scale, industry correlations
Lu and Tao (2007)	Girms, EG index, Province, prefectural municipal and county	1998–2003	Regional protectionism, spillover effect, transport cost and natural endowment
Ge (2009)	Two-digit manufacturing, Gini coefficient, Province; Firms, EG index, Province	1985, 1990, 1994, 1999, 1998–2005	Market potential, globalization factor, resource input
He, Xie and Pan (2008)	Two-digit manufacturing, Gini coefficient, Province	1980–2004	Policy and institution factor, labor quality and cost, economies of scale, natural resources and location accessibility
He, Zhu and Zhu (2010)	Two-digit manufacturing, Gini coefficient, Province	1980–2004	Location features, industry features, comparative advantage, new economic geography factor

Data source: Assembled by authors.

proportion of total industry, while remote regions in the west lag way behind. Polarization is severe. Overall, the agglomeration of manufacturing demonstrates strong positive correlation with industrial growth.

Lu and Tao (2006, 2007) used the EG index to calculate a set of indicators for the clustering and co-agglomeration[1] in industrial regions, studied the trend of industrial agglomeration in Chinese manufacturing from 1998 to 2003 and made international comparisons, finding that the regional agglomeration of Chinese industries is still in an ascending phase. Whether in terms of regional agglomeration of industries or regional co-agglomeration of industries, China is still at a level lower than that of western developed countries in recent times. Huang and Li's (2006) study found that the unbalanced distribution of industry declined slightly in the 1980s, whereas the unevenness and degree of concentration in distribution of industry showed a marked acceleration in the 1990s. He and Xie (2006) elongated the time period under study, used figures on two-digit industries in each province from 1980–2003 and found that Chinese manufacturing has become more and more concentrated spatially. Specifically speaking, most industries tended toward dispersion in the 1980s but inclined even stronger toward concentration in the 1990s. Ge (2009) calculated the EG index of industrial agglomeration and found that the level of agglomeration in Chinese industry drastically increased from 1985 to 2005. Based on the 2004 First Economic Census data, He et al. (2007b) calculated the Gini coefficient and Moran's I coefficient for distribution of manufacturing industries under different geographical scales and found that Chinese manufacturing was highly agglomerated in the Pearl Delta, Yangtze Delta and Bohai Rim region, with some continuous strands in North China, the Northeastern provinces, Sichuan, Hubei and Hunan; the smaller the spatial scale used and the narrower the division of industries, the more concentrated manufacturing is spatially. Also, the correlation coefficients of geographical agglomeration of industries at the provincial, municipal and county level scale are high.

These studies span across different time periods, covering the early years of "reform and opening" to 2005 and overall find that the agglomeration of Chinese industry shows a gradual uptrend. However, there was, to a certain extent, a downtrend in the 1980s and industrial agglomeration increased only after the 1980s.

However, these studies generally have the drawbacks of too short a time frame and poor continuity. In addition, since its ascension to the WTO in 2001, China has further integrated into the world economy, and growth, whether in terms of foreign direct investment or export trade, has been significant. In recent years, the appreciation of the Chinese yuan, the implementation of new labor laws, ever more rigorous management of land supply, increasing labor costs, especially in coastal regions, evident increases in overall production costs, more stress on the environment, etc. have led some industries to begin relocating and even group relocation has appeared (Wang, 2010). The "Grand Western Development Program", "Revitalization of Northeast-China Old Industrial Bases," "Rise of Central China," etc. regional balanced development policies may have a significant impact on the restructuring of Chinese industry's geographical disposition.

Then, under the new circumstances, will the trend in Chinese industry's degree of agglomeration show new changes? To this end, this chapter will employ more complete and newer datasets to calculate and analyze the status quo and trends in the degree of agglomeration of Chinese industry.

7.3.1 Data source and research method

This chapter studies the geographical concentration of Chinese two-digit manufacturing at the provincial level from 1980–2008 in order to reflect the characteristics and trends in the spatial distribution pattern of Chinese manufacturing. Since the "China Industry Economic Statistical Yearbook" after 1998 only publishes figures for 20 two-digit manufacturing industries by province, and the classification standards and codes for manufacturing industries were adjusted during this period, in order to guarantee the continuity and comparability of data we merged a portion of industry data and obtained 19 two-digit manufacturing industries. The food processing industry includes food processing and food manufacturing, and the machinery industry includes general equipment manufacturing and special equipment manufacturing. Since Hainan became a separate province from Guangdong in 1988 and Chongqing separated from Sichuan and became directly administered, in order to maintain the continuity and comparability of results data for Hainan in all years is absorbed in Guangdong, and Chongqing's data in all years is absorbed in Sichuan, so this leaves us with 29 spatial units.[2]

Figures for 1980, 1984 and 1985 come from "PRC 1985 Industrial Census Data" (Vol. 4, 29 provinces); 1988–1994 and 1997 data, respectively come from 1988–1995 and 1998 "China Industry Economic Statistical Yearbook;" figures for 1995 come from "PRC 1995 Third National Industrial Survey Compendium (Regional Volume);" 1998–2008 figures come from 1998–2009 "China Industry Economic Statistical Yearbook;" 2004 figures come from 2004 Economic Census data. Data for some years was supplemented by historical industrial census database figures. The 1989–1992 non-ferrous metals industry data comes from the "Yearbook on Ferrous Metals in China." Unless otherwise noted, the figures for the graphs and tables in this chapter all come from the above data or are based on calculations from these figures.

There are many ways to measure the geographical agglomeration and concentration of industry, of which the Gini coefficient is a generally used method (He and Pan, 2007). This study will mainly use the Gini coefficient to measure the degree of geographical agglomeration of industry. Gini coefficients were first used to measure unevenness and the geographical agglomeration of industry is an uneven phenomenon as well. Gini coefficients range from 0 to 1. A higher reading indicates a higher geographical agglomeration for an industry. The formula for the Gini coefficient of geographical industry agglomeration is as follows:

$$\mathrm{AG}_i = \frac{1}{2\mathrm{N}^2\mu}\sum_j\sum_k\left|\frac{x_{ij}}{X_i}-\frac{x_{ik}}{X_i}\right| \quad (1)$$

In the equation, x_{ij} or x_{ik} is the output or employment of industry i in province j or k. X_i is the total national output or employment of industry i, while μ is the average share of industry i in each province and N is number of provinces.

In order to test whether manufacturing is concentrated in neighboring spatial units and whether spatial autocorrelation exists in distribution, this chapter calculated the Moran's I coefficient for industries at the provincial level as follows:

$$I = \frac{n\sum_{i}\sum_{j\neq i} d_{ij}\left(x_i - \bar{x}\right)\left(x_j - \bar{x}\right)}{\left(\sum_{i}\sum_{j\neq i} d_{ij}\right)\sum_{i}\left(x_i - \bar{x}\right)^2} \quad (2)$$

In the equation, when province i and j are neighboring, d_{ij} equals 1, otherwise it is 0. x_i or x_j is i or j province's proportion of output or employment in a certain industry, $\bar{x}$ represents the average of an industry's proportion of industrial output or employment in each province, n is for number of provinces. The lowest Moran's I value is −1 and the highest is 1. A higher absolute value means stronger correlation. A positive Moran's I value means that industry distribution is positively spatially autocorrelated, that is, industries display an obvious trend of being distributed in neighboring provinces.

7.3.2 Current situation and trend of spatial distribution of Chinese manufacturing

7.3.2.1 Current situation of the geographical agglomeration of manufacturing

Based on industrial output,[3] this chapter calculated the 2008 provincial Gini coefficient of 19 major manufacturing industries, the concentration ratio of the top four provinces (CR4), the proportion of the eastern regions, and spatial autocorrelation coefficient Moran's I in order to compare the overall agglomeration trend for different industries (see Table 7.2).

First, industrial agglomeration is significant. Gini coefficients for industries are generally high. Among the 19 industries, chemical fibers manufacturing has a 0.793 Gini coefficient, electronics and communications equipment's Gini coefficient reaches 0.783, and only a few industries have Gini coefficients below 0.5. At the same time, we can observe a high degree of industry agglomeration from the CR4 index. There are ten industries that have CR4 readings over 50 percent, among which electronics and communications equipment, apparel and other fiber products, and chemical fibers manufacturing have the highest CR4 readings.

Second, disparity between industries is wide. Chemical fiber manufacturing, electronics and communications equipment, apparel and other fiber products, and textiles are the most agglomerated, with a Gini coefficient above 0.7 for all of them; beverages, nonferrous metal metallurgy, pharmaceuticals, oil refining and tobacco processing are more dispersed, with Gini coefficients below 0.5. On the whole, technology and capital intensive industries are relatively agglomerated and resource dependent industries have lower degrees of agglomeration.

Table 7.2 Current situation of the geographical agglomeration of Chinese manufacturing (2008)

Industry	*Gini coefficient*		*Proportion of top four provinces*		*Proportion of eastern regions (%)*	*Moran's I coefficient*
	Output	*Employment*	*Province*	*CR4 ratio (%)*		
Food processing	0.538	0.514	Shandong, Henan, Guangdong, Liaoning	46	61	0.1369*
Beverages	0.464	0.424	Sichuan, Shandong, Guangdong, Henan	40	50	0.0741
Tobacco	0.499	0.479	Yunnan, Hunan, Shanghai, Jiangsu	42	40	0.065
Textiles	0.742	0.692	Jiangsu, Zhejiang, Shandong, Guangdong	73	83	0.2483**
Apparel and fiber products	0.746	0.746	Jiangsu, Guangdong, Zhejiang, Shandong	67	90	0.1704*
Paper and paper products	0.656	0.591	Shandong, Guangdong, Jiangsu, Zhejiang	60	76	0.0641
Oil refining	0.493	0.496	Shandong, Liaoning, Guangdong, Shanxi	43	63	–0.1391
Chemicals	0.574	0.471	Jiangsu, Shandong, Guangdong, Zhejiang	54	71	0.2389**
Pharmaceuticals	0.489	0.43	Shandong, Jiangsu, Zhejiang, Sichuan	40	60	0.2083**
Chemical fiber	0.793	0.667	Zhejiang, Jiangsu, Fujian, Guangdong	81	89	0.2007**
Non-metallic minerals	0.57	0.504	Shandong, Henan, Guangdong, Jiangsu	49	64	0.1371*
Ferrous metals metallurgy	0.505	0.453	Hebei, Jiangsu, Shandong, Liaoning	47	68	0.2738**
Non-ferrous metals metallurgy	0.484	0.407	Henan, Jiangsu, Shandong, Guangdong	40	47	0.0477
Metals products	0.669	0.678	Guangdong, Jiangsu, Zhejiang, Shandong	60	85	0.033
Machinery	0.617	0.588	Jiangsu, Shandong, Zhejiang, Liaoning	51	76	0.3411***
Transportation equipment	0.548	0.53	Jiangsu, Guangdong, Shandong, Sichuan	39	65	0.1181
Electrical equipment	0.681	0.719	Guangdong, Jiangsu, Zhejiang, Shandong	65	83	0.0298
Electronics and communications equipment	0.783	0.776	Guangdong, Jiangsu, Shanghai, Shandong	75	94	–0.0309
Instruments and office supplies machinery	0.714	0.702	Guangdong, Jiangsu, Zhejiang, Shanghai	67	86	–0.0129

Note: *, ** and ***, respectively, show that the spatial autocorrelation coefficient Moran's *I* value is significant at the 10%, 5% and 1% level.

Third, industries show an evident trend toward agglomerating in the eastern regions, with over 80 percent of seven industries in eastern regions; high proportions are in Jiangsu, Guangdong, Shandong and Zhejiang, etc. eastern coastal provinces. The industries with the highest proportion in eastern regions are electronics and communications equipment, apparel and other fiber products, chemical fibers manufacturing and metal products.

Fourth, the distribution of some industries displayed strong spatial autocorrelation. Distribution of the machinery industry had the highest spatial autocorrelation, followed by ferrous metals metallurgy and textiles. The Moran's *I* coefficient for machinery reached 0.34.

In addition, we calculated the Gini coefficient for each industry based on employment and found that the employment Gini coefficient for most industries was lower than the output Gini coefficient.

Finally, judging from the distribution of manufacturing output by province, eastern coastal provinces have an obvious advantage, with Guangdong, Jiangsu, Zhejiang, Shandong, Liaoning, and Shanghai being where manufacturing is mostly agglomerated, while the scale of manufacturing is relatively small in the western provinces other than Inner Mongolia and Sichuan (see Figure 7.1).

Since "reform and opening," Chinese industry has become ever more agglomerated in the coastal provinces and many specialized towns or industrial clusters have formed within provinces. Under the assistance of local governments and trade associations, these industrial clusters significantly enhanced the international competitiveness of Chinese industry through deep supply chain labor division (Wang, 2010). These industrial clusters are often agglomerated in small

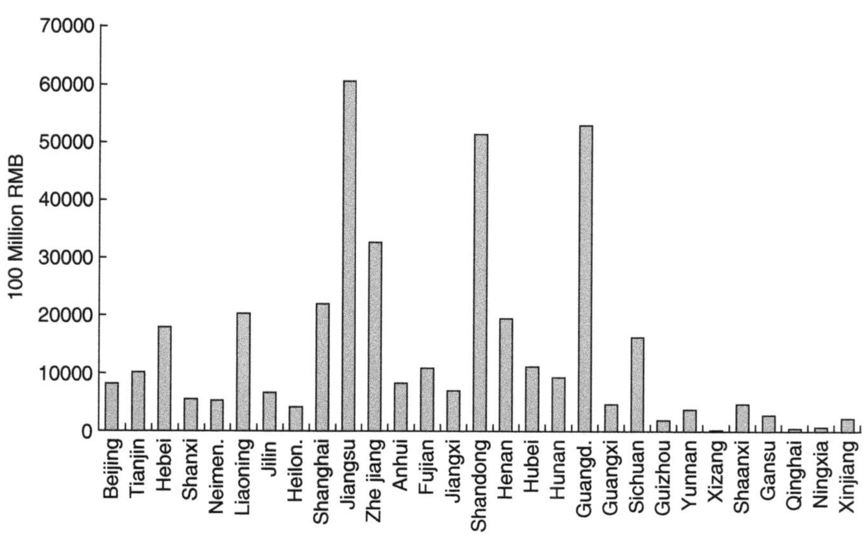

Figure 7.1 Provincial distribution of total Chinese manufacturing output value (2008).

spatial ranges, but their foreign and domestic market share is usually shockingly large. Table 7.3 lists pertinent information for 27 national level specialty industry bases in Wenzhou, Zhejiang.

These specialty industrial bases are mostly specialized in one or two industries, but there are thousands of firms concentrated in each of them, which participate in division of labor within the cluster but mutually compete as well and occupy a significant domestic and foreign market share. For example, as a shoe capital famous nationwide, Wenzhou has over 5,000 shoemaking firms with over 25 percent market share domestically. Leqing is the famous capital of electrical appliances with over 3,000 firms and a market share reaching 50 percent. Lucheng's lighter production base goes even further with 90 percent of the foreign market and its eyeglasses production base dominates 80 percent of the domestic market. The competitiveness of these industries comes from the deep division of labor in these industry clusters, which significantly reduces production and transaction costs.

Wenzhou is only an epitome of the development of industry clusters in eastern coastal regions. One basic experience from the development of industry in coastal provinces is the construction of industrial cluster zones and the development of industry clusters. Jiangsu and Zhejiang's industrial cluster zones are the main carriers of industry development spatially, as each industrial cluster zone has one or more specialized industries. For example, according to Wang (2010), Taizhou, Zhejiang, is China's auto parts production base, capital of Chinese festival lanterns, China's filter cloth city, capital of pumps and valves, capital of gifts, hometown of water pumps, etc. Ningbo, Zhejiang is the China's hometown of apparel, famous knitwear city, hometown of lamps, hometown of moulds and stationery production base. Jiaxing, Zhejiang is a famous city for export apparel manufacturing, chemical fibers, "static flocking," woollen sweaters, "warp knitting," cloth craft, etc. Nantong, Jiangsu is famous for textile embroidery, textile production base, dyed-yarn weaving, etc. Changzhou is a production base for apparel manufacturing, new paints, furniture, and the Three Medicines, as well as famous for fabric manufacturing. Yangzhou is the capital of electronic devices, toys and toothbrushes. Specialty townships in Guangdong are also a world-famous industry agglomeration phenomenon (Wang, 2010). For example, Shunde District, Foshan concentrated industry clusters in fields such as flowers, furniture manufacturing, household electrical appliances, minor ironware, plastic products, etc., and developed many specialized markets on this basis. There are specialized industry clusters in pottery, stainless steel materials, knitwear, etc. in Foshan's municipal district.

7.3.2.2 Spatial autocorrelation in the distribution of Chinese manufacturing

Due to the existence of common inputs and markets or in order to obtain economies of agglomeration, firms in the same industry have a tendency to be neighboring and agglomerated. Due to industry ties, the geographical agglomeration of some industries may surpass administrative zones. Agglomeration of industry to

Table 7.3 27 national level specialty industry bases in Wenzhou, Zhejiang

Name	*Location*	*No. of firms*	*Domestic market share*	*Representative firm or brand*
Capital of shoes	Wenzhou	5,500	25%	Aokang, Kangnai, Red Dragonfly, Jierda, etc.
Capital of electric appliances	Leqing	3,200	5%	Zhengtai, Delixi, Tianzheng, Changcheng, etc.
Apparel	Wenzhou	3000	8%	Fapai, Zhuangji, Baoxiniao, etc.
Casual wear	Wenzhou	425	–	Metersbonwe, Senma, Gaobang, etc.
Leather capital	Pingyang	550	–	–
Hometown of zippers	Yongjia	200	8%	Changcheng Group, Baiteli Zippers
Shaver production base	Lucheng	100	6% (2003)	Feike, Dingling, Rifeng, etc.
Printing	Cangnan	1,600	2% (2003)	Xinya, Shuguang, Fukang
Lighter production base	Lucheng	500	9% (2003) 7% (Foreign)	Dahu
Pen capital	Lucheng, Longwan	200	Water colored brush 9%; mechanical pencil, ball-point pen 3%	Aihao, Tianjiao, Huanqiu, Weitai, etc.
Lock capital	Lucheng	400	65% (23)	–
Casual shoes production base	Ruian	230	92%	Zhejiang Bangsai Shoes
Plastic film production base	Ruian	32	1%	–
Packaging and medical equipment production base	Ruian		–	–

National Torch Program smart electrical appliances production base	Leqing		–	–
Drills (construction) production base	Leqing	100	66%	–
Electronic devices and components production base	Leqing	2,500	33%	–
Precision moulds production base	Leqing	3,000	–	–
Circuit breaker production base	Leqing	140	6%	–
Explosion-proof electronic devices production base	Leqing	180	6%	–
Stainless steel pipes production base	Longwan	170	7%	–
Metal cleaning equipment capital	Longwan	825	5%	–
Commercial gifts production base	Cangnan, Pingyang	2,000	–	–
Auto parts capital	Ruian	1,200	–	–
Eyeglasses production base	Lucheng	800	8% (2003)	Dolphin sunglasses
Plastic woven products hometown	Pingyang	500	5%	–
Synthetic leather capital	Longwan	80	7% (2003)	–
Pump and valve hometown	Yongjia, Ouhai	300	–	–

Data source: Wang (2010).

a certain extent will cause diseconomies of agglomeration and industry may disperse toward neighboring regions. In addition, neighboring regions may emulate and learn from each other's industrial development policies. Thus, spatial autocorrelation may exist in the spatial distribution of industry. As China's market reforms deepen and the forces of globalization become ever stronger, the degree of spatial autocorrelation in the distribution of industry may change as well. This chapter selected figures from 1980, 1990, 2000, and 2008 and calculated the Moran's *I* coefficient for the distribution of industries at the provincial level (see Table 7.4).

From 1980 to 2008, the spatial autocorrelation of the distribution of Chinese manufacturing showed a general decline. In 1980, many industries displayed typical positive spatial autocorrelation, with 17 out of 19 industries having significantly positive Moran's *I* coefficients. The spatial autocorrelation Moran's *I* coefficient for textiles reached 0.4526 and the spatial Moran's *I* coefficient for all industries in aggregate was 0.3267 as well. But, by 2008, only nine industries had a positive Moran's *I* coefficient, and the Moran's *I* coefficient for all industries in aggregate declined to 0.1179. Why was there a downtrend in the degree of spatial

Table 7.4 Spatial autocorrelation Moran's *I* coefficient of distribution of Chinese manufacturing

Industry	*1980*	*1990*	*2000*	*2008*
Food processing	0.2038**	0.1157	0.1035	0.1369*
Beverages	0.3244***	0.1126	0.0151	0.0741
Tobacco	0.2259**	0.0832	0.0652	0.065
Textiles	0.4526***	0.4353***	0.239**	0.2483**
Apparel and fiber products	0.3384***	0.1448*	0.0492	0.1704*
Paper and paper products	0.2717**	0.1703*	0.0436	0.0641
Oil refining	–0.1063	–0.0962	–0.1365	–0.1391
Chemicals	0.3247***	0.298	0.1777**	0.2389**
Pharmaceuticals	0.2515**	0.0101	–0.0175	0.2083**
Chemical fiber	0.1148**	0.2982**	0.5178***	0.2007**
Non-metallic minerals	0.2823**	0.1587*	0.0252	0.1371*
Ferrous metals processing	0.095*	0.1708**	0.3478***	0.2738**
Non-ferrous metals processing	–0.1774*	–0.1967*	0.0016	0.0477
Metals products	0.2269**	0.1918**	–0.0069	0.033
Machinery	0.2883**	0.3785***	0.4258***	0.3411***
Transportation equipment	0.1475*	0.1237*	0.1697	0.1181
Electrical equipment	0.1789**	0.0202	0.0035	0.0298
Electronics and communications equipment	0.3559***	0.1238*	–0.0536	–0.0309
Instruments and office supplies machinery	0.3276***	0.4396***	–0.0565	–0.0129
All manufacturing	0.3267***	0.2552**	0.0725	0.1179*

Note: *, **, and ***, respectively, mean significance at the 10%, 5%, and 1% level.

autocorrelation in industry layout? One possible reason may be the strong planned economy characteristic of Chinese industry layout before "reform and opening," as each province pursued industrial development plans that thought "large and all inclusive." Since endowments for neighboring provinces are rather similar, statistics show that the distribution of many industries is concentrated in neighboring provinces. After "reform and opening," the distribution of industry was more affected by market forces, development of industry further concentrated in provinces with location and comparative advantage, smashing the old pattern. At the same time, protectionist policies by the local government incentivize more the concentration of related industries within a province and not clustering across provinces.

7.3.2.3 Typical spatial distribution of industry and its changes

Though common features exist for the spatial distribution and trend of manufacturing industries, due to industry differences, significant disparities still exist in the spatial pattern of different industries. Below, we will use textiles, electronics and communications equipment, ferrous metals metallurgy and transportation equipment industries as representatives and analyze the change in spatial distribution of typical industries.

In the case of the textiles industry, in 2008, Jiangsu, Zhejiang, and Shandong became the provinces where textiles were mainly concentrated in, as the output of each province accounted for over 20 percent of the national output and the three combined approached nearly 65 percent of the national output. Compared with 1980, Zhejiang's proportion increased the most, while Shandong and Guangdong's proportion saw large increases as well; Shanghai, Liaoning, Hebei and Sichuan saw evident declines from 1980 levels (see Figure 7.2 and Table 7.5). Textiles are a typical labor intensive industry. The export proportion of this industry is high and the trend toward agglomeration in the eastern coastal provinces is quite apparent.

In the case of the electronics and communications equipment industry, in 2008, this industry mostly agglomerated in Guangdong, Jiangsu, Shanghai, Beijing and Shandong, which are the core regions of the Yangtze Delta, Pearl Delta, and Bohai Rim region (see Figure 7.3 and Table 7.6). Compared with 1980, Guangdong's proportion increased the most and Shandong's proportion also saw a large increase; while Liaoning, Shanghai, Sichuan and Tianjin saw evident declines from 1980 levels. Quite typical features of this industry include a high proportion of foreign capital and a high proportion of products exported; in addition, this industry has high technical and human capital requirements. Therefore, the coastal disposition feature of this industry is obvious; meanwhile, this industry tends to agglomerate toward core cities abundant in talent and technology resources, e.g. Shanghai, Beijing, etc.

In the case of the ferrous metals metallurgy industry, in 2008 this industry was mostly agglomerated in the Bohai Rim region, with large proportions in Hebei, Tianjin, Liaoning and Shandong, and Jiangsu as well (see Figure 7.4

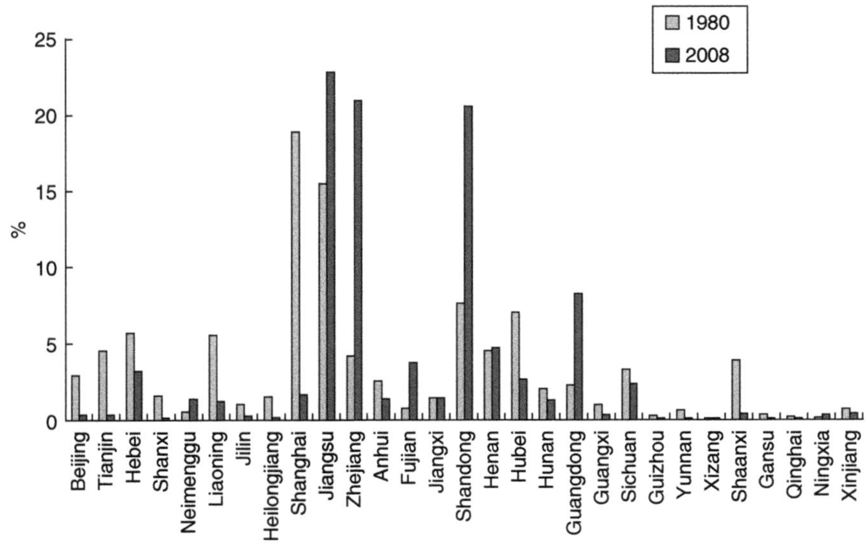

Figure 7.2 Proportion of total textiles output value by province (1980 and 2008).

and Table 7.7). Compared with 1980, Hebei's proportion saw the largest increase, with Shougang's migration to Caofeidian, perhaps the main reason and Jiangsu's proportion saw a large increase as well; while Shanghai, Sichuan and Beijing saw apparent declines from 1980 levels. This industry has a high degree of dependence on steel resources and iron ore resources are relatively abundant in the Bohai

Table 7.5 Proportion of total textiles output value by province (1980 and 2008)

Province	*1980*	*2008*	*Province*	*1980*	*2008*
Beijing	2.89%	0.30%	Henan	4.52%	4.65%
Tianjin	4.51%	0.34%	Hubei	6.99%	2.60%
Hebei	5.71%	3.16%	Hunan	1.97%	1.29%
Shanxi	1.56%	0.09%	Guangdong	2.21%	8.18%
Inner Mongolia	0.52%	1.34%	Guangxi	0.93%	0.36%
Liaoning	5.58%	1.20%	Sichuan	3.23%	2.34%
Jilin	1.04%	0.24%	Guizhou	0.26%	0.02%
Heilongjiang	1.53%	0.15%	Yunnan	0.63%	0.06%
Shanghai	18.82%	1.62%	Tibet	0.01%	0.00%
Jiangsu	15.50%	22.81%	Shaanxi	3.88%	0.40%
Zhejiang	4.18%	20.95%	Gansu	0.33%	0.06%
Anhui	2.52%	1.34%	Qinghai	0.11%	0.04%
Fujian	0.76%	3.72%	Ningxia	0.10%	0.29%
Jiangxi	1.44%	1.42%	Xinjiang	0.65%	0.40%
Shandong	7.61%	20.61%			

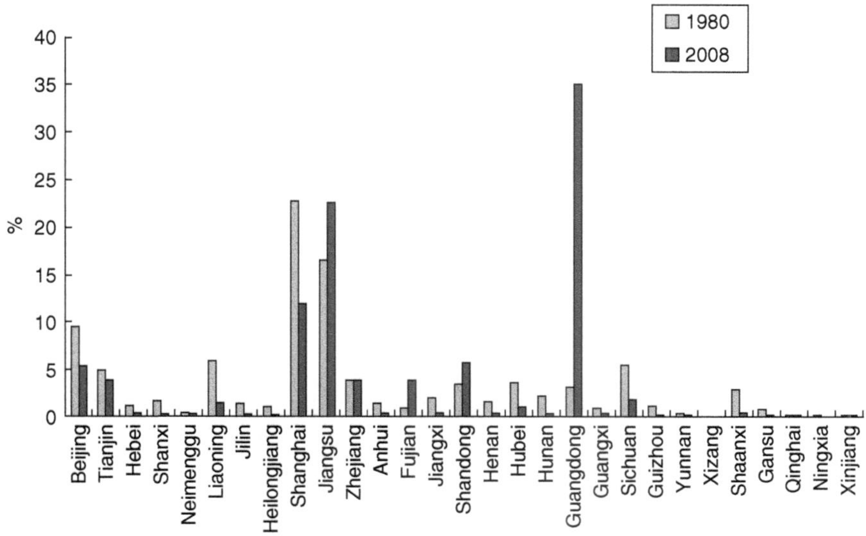

Figure 7.3 Proportion of total electronics and communications equipment output value by province (1980 and 2008).

Rim region. At the same time, this industry needs to import large amounts of iron ore, thus its coastal disposition feature is also quite significant.

Compared with the other industries, transportation equipment industry's distribution at the provincial level is the most dispersed. In 2008, there were nine provinces with a proportion exceeding 5 percent and no province's proportion of

Table 7.6 Proportion of total electronics and communications equipment output value by province (1980 and 2008)

Province	*1980*	*2008*	*Province*	*1980*	*2008*
Beijing	9.54%	5.43%	Henan	1.64%	0.32%
Tianjin	5.03%	3.84%	Hubei	3.69%	1.12%
Hebei	1.16%	0.35%	Hunan	2.20%	0.34%
Shanxi	1.63%	0.23%	Guangdong	3.18%	35.03%
Inner Mongolia	0.25%	0.21%	Guangxi	1.02%	0.27%
Liaoning	5.92%	1.40%	Sichuan	5.56%	1.82%
Jilin	1.41%	0.12%	Guizhou	1.19%	0.07%
Heilongjiang	1.03%	0.04%	Yunnan	0.35%	0.03%
Shanghai	22.70%	12%	Tibet	0.00%	0.00%
Jiangsu	16.54%	22.61%	Shaanxi	3.01%	0.44%
Zhejiang	3.88%	3.88%	Gansu	0.90%	0.03%
Anhui	1.42%	0.37%	Qinghai	0.12%	0.00%
Fujian	0.97%	3.91%	Ningxia	0.01%	0.00%
Jiangxi	2.00%	0.38%	Xinjiang	0.08%	0.03%
Shandong	3.58%	5.72%			

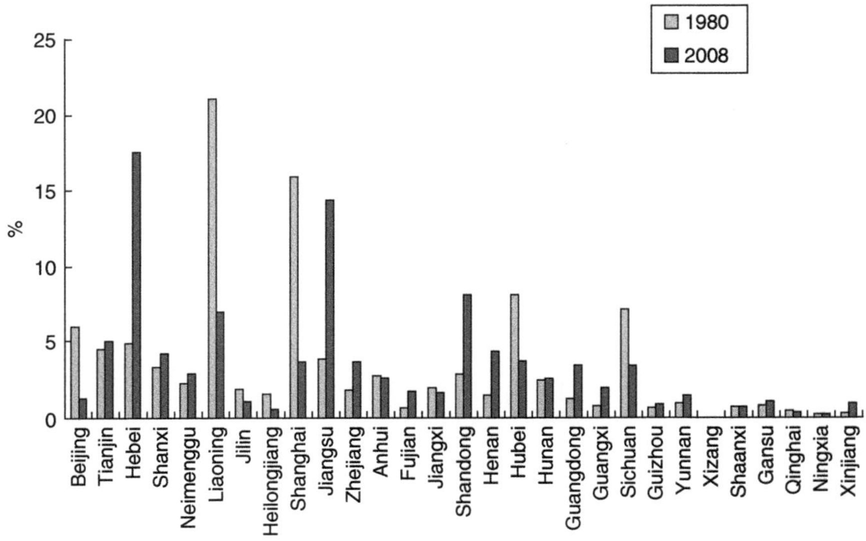

Figure 7.4 Proportion of total ferrous metals metallurgy output value by province (1980 and 2008).

output value exceeded 15 percent. At the same time, compared with 1980, the degree of change in the spatial pattern of the industry is lowest (see Figure 7.5 and Table 7.8). In 1980, there were eight provinces with a proportion of over 5 percent, which changed to nine in 2008, of which seven were the same. Beijing's proportion saw an apparent decline and Liaoning and Sichuan's proportion fell as

Table 7.7 Proportion of total ferrous metals metallurgy output value by province (1980 and 2008)

Province	*1980*	*2008*	*Province*	*1980*	*2008*
Beijing	5.95%	1.33%	Henan	1.43%	4.28%
Tianjin	4.50%	5.08%	Hubei	8.07%	3.77%
Hebei	4.90%	17.50%	Hunan	2.51%	2.52%
Shanxi	3.34%	4.25%	Guangdong	1.26%	3.37%
Inner Mongolia	2.20%	2.87%	Guangxi	0.73%	1.90%
Liaoning	21%	6.95%	Sichuan	7.09%	3.41%
Jilin	1.83%	1.07%	Guizhou	0.60%	0.81%
Heilongjiang	1.58%	0.51%	Yunnan	0.88%	1.45%
Shanghai	15.88	3.66%	Tibet	0.00%	0.00%
Jiangsu	3.88%	14.35%	Shaanxi	0.70%	0.66%
Zhejiang	1.80%	3.68%	Gansu	0.77%	1.09%
Anhui	2.74%	2.62%	Qinghai	0.42%	0.34%
Fujian	0.67%	1.69%	Ningxia	0.20%	0.20%
Jiangxi	1.94%	1.66%	Xinjiang	0.27%	0.91%
Shandong	2.86%	8.06%			

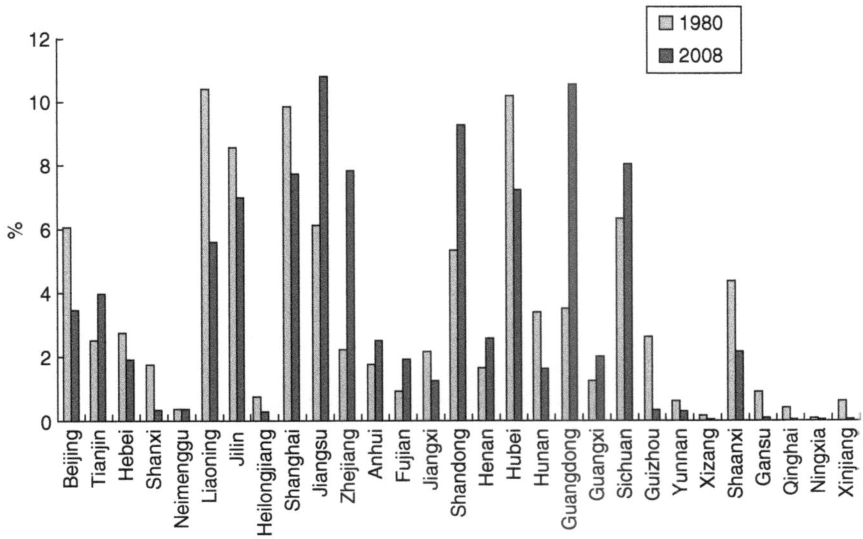

Figure 7.5 Proportion of total transportation equipment output value by province (1980 and 2008).

Table 7.8 Proportion of total transportation equipment output value by province (1980 and 2008)

Province	*1980*	*2008*	*Province*	*1980*	*2008*
Beijing	6.08%	3.45%	Henan	1.63%	2.59%
Tianjin	2.54%	3.97%	Hubei	10.21%	7.26%
Hebei	2.76%	1.94%	Hunan	3.39%	1.61%
Shanxi	1.78%	0.31%	Guangdong	3.54%	10.56%
Inner Mongolia	0.36%	0.37%	Guangxi	1.27%	2.03%
Liaoning	10.41%	5.60%	Sichuan	6.34%	8.04%
Jilin	8.57%	6.97%	Guizhou	2.65%	0.33%
Heilongjiang	2.91%	0.98%	Yunnan	0.64%	0.31%
Shanghai	9.86%	7.70%	Tibet	0.15%	0.00%
Jiangsu	6.15%	10.83%	Shaanxi	4.36%	2.17%
Zhejiang	2.23%	7.86%	Gansu	0.89%	0.08%
Anhui	1.75%	2.52%	Qinghai	0.40%	0.01%
Fujian	0.91%	1.94%	Ningxia	0.08%	0.00%
Jiangxi	2.17%	1.27%	Xinjiang	0.62%	0.03%
Shandong	5.33%	9.28%			

well, though their proportions are still high; Guangdong's rise is notable while Zhejiang's proportion rose evidently as well; this industry displays a trend toward agglomerating in the eastern regions, with seven out of the nine regions exceeding 5 percent in the eastern coastal regions. The spatial pattern of this industry is mainly influenced by a few factors. First, influence from state regulations is large, especially the auto industry. For example, foreign auto firms must joint venture with domestic firms in order to enter the Chinese market and the location choice must depend on the original firm. Second, the industry pattern before "reform and opening" has a deep influence, as this industry's investment barriers are very high and require strength in capital and technology, thus regions without any previous industry fundamentals can rarely develop rapidly from scratch. Third, since the auto industry holds the highest proportion in the transportation equipment industry and market demand from the developed eastern regions is large, thus this industry's coastal disposition feature is quite significant. Fourth, since the auto industry contributes greatly to local economic development and government revenues, it is strongly protected by local governments. Regions vie to attract auto firms and attempt to make it a dominant industry, thereby causing a dispersed disposition in the auto industry.

7.3.3 The trend in the geographical pattern of Chinese manufacturing (1980–2008)

7.3.3.1 Change in geographical agglomeration of Chinese manufacturing

After "reform and opening," the aggregate output of Chinese manufacturing rose spectacularly while industry became increasingly concentrated spatially. This chapter has calculated the Gini coefficients for each industry at the provincial level from 1990–2008, thereby quantitatively analyzing the trend in geographical agglomeration of each industry.

First, the trend in agglomeration of Chinese industry has obvious phases. Figure 7.6 displays the weighted Gini coefficient average of industrial output value, and 1990, 1997, and 2003 could more or less be viewed as boundaries. Before 1990, the overall degree of agglomeration trended downwards; this was followed by an apparent ascending period, and mild changes thereafter; but after 1997, a new wave of increases began, reaching its climax in 2003; after which point, the degree of industrial agglomeration began to fall again. The trend in the degree of manufacturing agglomeration by industry is very similar to that of the weighted average of all industries. Most industries followed the trajectory of an initial decrease, then an increase, finally decreasing again. However, from 1980 to 2008, the overall trend of the degree of industrial agglomeration was still upwards. If a regression is performed on the Gini coefficients of each industry against time, an overwhelming majority of regression coefficients would be positive (see Table 7.9), among which apparel and other fiber products, paper and paper products, instruments and office supplies machinery and electronics and communications equipment have the largest coefficients, which means that the rate of increase in agglomeration for these four industries is the fastest. The trend in

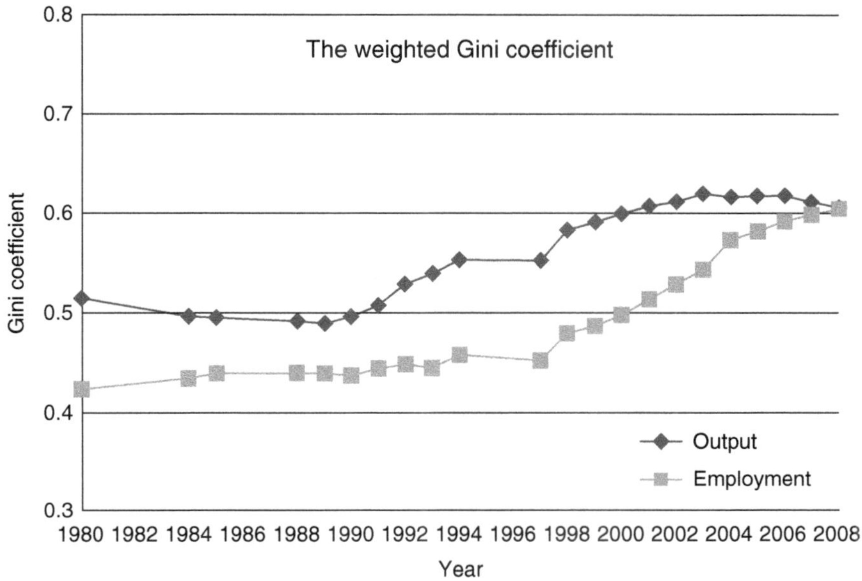

Figure 7.6 Trend in the Gini coefficient of Chinese manufacturing (1990–2008).

Table 7.9 Trends in Chinese manufacturing Gini coefficients (1980–2008)

Industry	*Regression coefficient of Gini coefficient on time*
Food processing	0.008***
Beverages	0.003***
Tobacco	0.001
Textiles	0.008***
Apparel and fiber products	0.013***
Paper and paper products	0.012***
Oil refining	–0.007***
Chemicals	0.006***
Pharmaceuticals	0.001**
Chemical fiber	0.005***
Non-metallic minerals	0.007***
Ferrous metals metallurgy	–0.002***
Non-ferrous metals metallurgy	–0.001
Metals products	0.011***
Machinery	0.009***
Transportation equipment	0.004***
Electrical equipment	0.009***
Electronics and communications equipment	0.009***
Instruments and office supplies machinery	0.010***

Note: (1) From 1980 to 2008, there are 23 years with data; 1980 is given the value 1 while other years are given the value T=1+Year–1980, e.g. 2008's value would be 29; (2) *, **, and ***, respectively, mean significance at the 10%, 5%, and 1% level.

geographical agglomeration of industry is consistent with China's gradualist regional opening policy. Since the 1980s, the regional and institutional advantages of coastal regions attracted a large number of firms, especially foreign firms; since the 1990s, agglomeration of industry in the coastal regions has further strengthened, thereby gradually enhancing the overall level of agglomeration in Chinese industry.

Second, the geographical agglomeration of most industries peaked in around 2003–2005 and maintained that level or began to decline. Out of 19 industries, six saw their degree of agglomeration peak in 2003; two in 2005; two in 2006; three in 2007; while three others peaked in 1980 and two in 1994 (see Table 7.10 and Figure 7.7). Thus, in general, we can determine that change in agglomeration of manufacturing is entering a turning point, as the degree of agglomeration for most industries reached their peak around 2004 and maintained that level or declined. In addition, only oil refining saw its lowest value in 2005 while the others were all before 1997, which proves that most industries became more agglomerated after "reform and opening."

Third, compared with 1980, most industries were more agglomerated in 2008 (see Table 7.11 and Figure 7.7). Apparel and other fiber products and paper and

Table 7.10 Extreme and average values for Gini coefficients of Chinese manufacturing

Industry	*Average*	*Highest value and year*		*Lowest value and year*	
		Highest value	*Year*	*Lowest value*	*Year*
Food processing	0.473	0.551	2005	0.365	1980
Beverages	0.47	0.506	2003	0.393	1980
Tobacco	0.537	0.606	1994	0.485	1988
Textiles	0.651	0.742	2007	0.555	1988
Apparel and fiber products	0.666	0.769	2003	0.469	1980
Paper and paper products	0.535	0.666	2007	0.415	1985
Oil refining	0.562	0.702	1980	0.493	2005
Chemicals	0.501	0.583	2006	0.425	1988
Pharmaceuticals	0.465	0.49	1994	0.44	1989
Chemical fiber	0.707	0.8	2006	0.618	1989
Non-metallic minerals	0.499	0.577	2007	0.41	1980
Ferrous metals metallurgy	0.518	0.583	1980	0.497	1995
Non-ferrous metals metallurgy	0.423	0.54	1980	0.355	1997
Metals products	0.602	0.712	2003	0.478	1984
Machinery	0.556	0.63	2001	0.454	1984
Transportation equipment	0.523	0.563	2003	0.476	1985
Electrical equipment	0.626	0.71	2003	0.513	1984
Electronics and communications equipment	0.699	0.791	2005	0.576	1989
Instruments and office supplies machinery	0.651	0.754	2003	0.518	1990

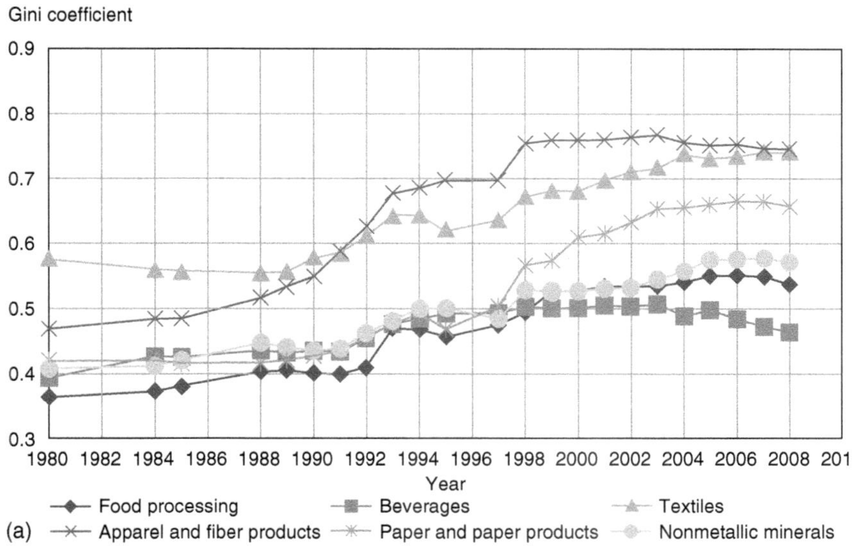

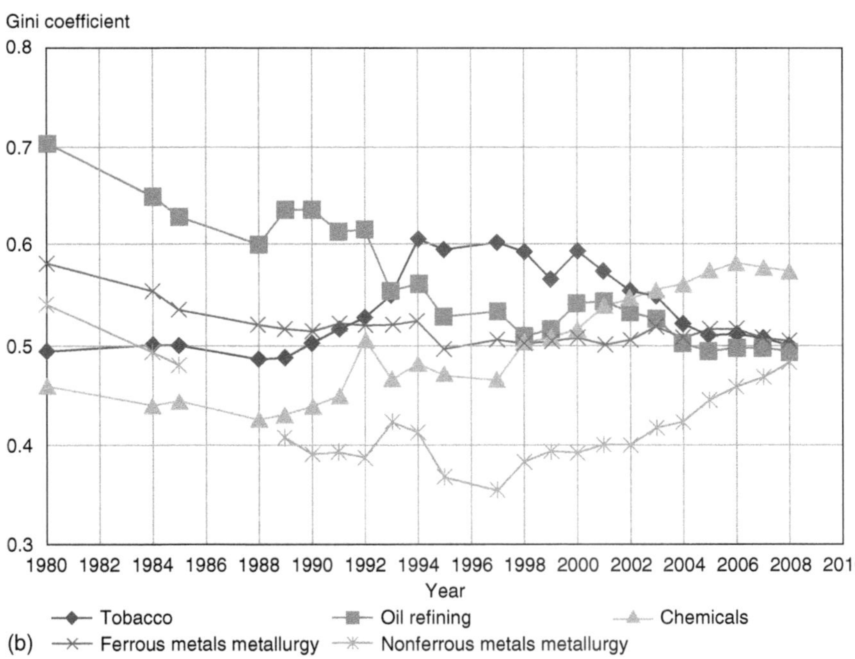

Figure 7.7 Trend in geographical agglomeration of different industries (1980–2008). (a) labor intensive industries; (b) resource intensive industries; (c) capital and technology intensive industries.

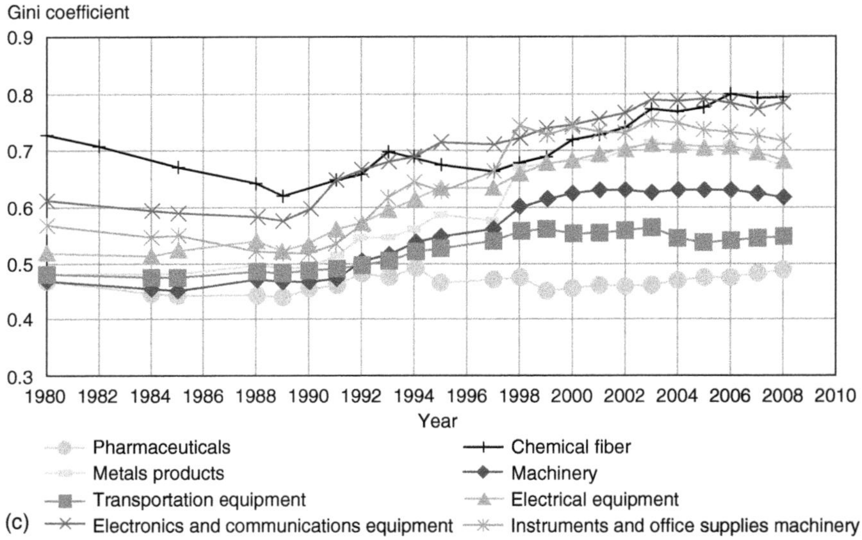

(c)

Figure 7.7 Continued

Table 7.11 Gini coefficient and change of manufacturing output value by industry

Industry	*Gini coefficient*				*Change in Gini coefficient (1980–2008)*
	1980	*1990*	*2000*	*2008*	
Food processing	0.365	0.4	0.526	0.538	0.172
Beverages	0.393	0.435	0.501	0.464	0.071
Tobacco	0.494	0.503	0.595	0.499	0.005
Textiles	0.577	0.577	0.681	0.742	0.165
Apparel and fiber products	0.469	0.55	0.759	0.746	0.277
Paper and paper products	0.419	0.425	0.609	0.656	0.237
Oil refining	0.702	0.638	0.543	0.493	–0.209
Chemicals	0.459	0.438	0.517	0.574	0.115
Pharmaceuticals	0.469	0.455	0.456	0.489	0.02
Chemical fiber	0.729	0.632	0.72	0.793	0.064
Non-metallic minerals	0.41	0.435	0.527	0.57	0.16
Ferrous metals metallurgy	0.583	0.514	0.507	0.505	–0.078
Non-ferrous metals metallurgy	0.54	0.39	0.392	0.484	–0.056
Metals products	0.485	0.498	0.681	0.669	0.184
Machinery	0.47	0.468	0.625	0.617	0.147
Transportation equipment	0.481	0.488	0.553	0.548	0.066
Electrical equipment	0.519	0.536	0.685	0.681	0.162
Electronics and communications equipment	0.611	0.596	0.743	0.783	0.172
Instruments and office supplies machinery	0.566	0.518	0.741	0.714	0.148

paper products saw the largest increase in agglomeration as they both rose from low-agglomeration industries to become high-agglomeration industries. In 19 industries, only three saw a decrease in Gini coefficients, which are oil refining, ferrous metals metallurgy and nonferrous metals metallurgy respectively, all of which are typical resource industries. Among them, oil refining went from high-agglomeration to low-agglomeration, while ferrous metals metallurgy and non-ferrous metals metallurgy were not highly agglomerated in the first place, the former's Gini coefficient continuously declined while the latter rebounded after experiencing a decline. Pharmaceuticals and transportation equipment, which occupy important positions in modern manufacturing, showed little change in degree of agglomeration and were still low-agglomeration industries by 2008. According to a survey by the State Council Center for Developmental Studies, both of these industries are protected by local governments and have high value-add[4] and profit-tax rates. Regions compete to develop them thereby lowering the industry's geographical agglomeration.

However, it needs to be pointed out that Gini coefficients calculated using employment to measure industrial agglomeration show different characteristics. Judging from the trend in weighted average value of all industries, industry agglomeration has constantly increased after "reform and opening" but the magnitude of the increase was small until the rapid ascension phase after 1997, which persisted until 2008, that is, there were no apparent turning points in the trend, though the upward trend did slow down after 2004. The industry agglomeration Gini coefficient calculated with employment according to industry shows similar changes, the overall trend is similar to that of the Gini coefficient calculated with output value. However, no evident turning point has appeared in many industries, there has only been a decrease in the rate of increase of agglomeration.

Finally, industries that have different factor intensities display significant differences in the trend of geographical agglomeration (see Figure 7.7). No apparent dispersion trend appeared in labor intensive industries in the 1980s, as they have generally became more spatially concentrated since the 1980s. In the mid-1990s, labor intensive industries accelerated in their agglomeration. Development strategies dependent on exports by labor intensive industries facilitated the agglomeration of these industries toward coastal regions, thereby bringing them closer to international markets. An evident trend toward balance across regions existed in the 1980s for resource intensive industries, as the degree of geographical agglomeration fell for many industries. Since the 1990s, chemicals and nonferrous metals metallurgy continuously agglomerated spatially; other industries such as tobacco, ferrous metals metallurgy and oil refining tended toward spatial dispersion. On average, resource intensive industries are more dispersed than labor intensive industries and capital/technology intensive industries. Capital/technology intensive industries underwent a structural adjustment spatially in the 1980s. During the planned economy era, large numbers of capital/technology intensive industries were dispositioned in the inland regions, such as Sichuan, Hubei, Shaanxi, Jilin, Heilongjiang, etc. Since "reform and opening," while the coastal provinces were enhancing labor intensive industries, capital/technology intensive industries were developing under the drive of foreign capital and domestic demand. But since the mid-1990s, some industries such as pharmaceuticals, transportation equipment, and machinery, due to their long industrial chain and broad industrial connections, were developed in competition by each region in order to create industry clusters and lengthen their industrial chains. Thus, these industries did not further agglomerate spatially. Other capital/technology intensive industries dominated by foreign capital, such as electronics and communications equipment, instruments and office supplies machinery, chemical fibers, etc. further concentrated toward the coastal regions. On the one hand, foreign firms export heavily and need to be close to international markets; on the other hand, in order to reduce risk and production costs, foreign firms are inclined to follow other firms that have made previous investments.

7.3.3.2 Changes in geographical distribution of Chinese manufacturing: comparisons between 2008 and 1990

Chinese industry trends toward spatial agglomeration overall, but different regions display different features in change. We compared the geographical distribution of manufacturing in the initial and final year of the period in question. On the whole, compared with 1980, 2008 Hubei, Sichuan, and Heilongjiang saw the largest declines in their proportion of nationwide manufacturing while Guangdong, Zhejiang and Inner Mongolia experienced distinct increases (see Figure 7.1 and Figure 7.8). The decline in the status of old industrial bases and the national strategy of prioritizing development of eastern coastal regions after

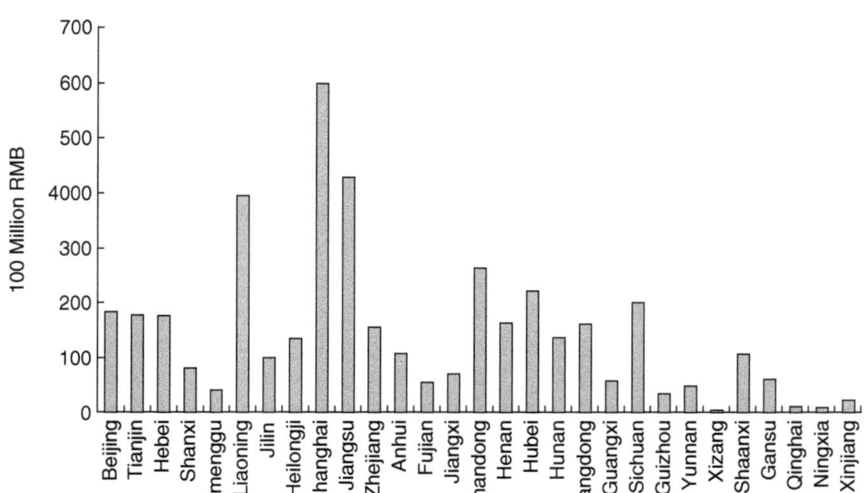

Figure 7.8 Distribution of Chinese manufacturing output value by province (1980).

"reform and opening" is somewhat connected, whereas the rise of Guangdong and Zhejiang is the result of developing export-oriented and private economies: Guangdong attracted huge amounts of foreign capital due to its proximity to Hong Kong and Macau, meanwhile obtaining export markets for large amounts of manufactured goods; Zhejiang's private firms rose rapidly after "reform and opening," meanwhile, just like Guangdong, massive exports provided the condition for growth in manufacturing. A prominent feature is that both provinces developed traditional industry clusters that are competitive on an international scale (Wang, 2001).

Looking at the change in the top four provinces where manufacturing is distributed, Shanghai and Liaoning's status distinctly declined and Guangdong and Zhejiang's elevation is most prominent (see Table 7.12). At the beginning of "reform and opening," Shanghai as a city alone was able to lead the provinces, which illustrates the low industrial development level in other regions nationwide. The decline in Liaoning's status reflects in spades the relative backwardness of the northeastern regions during the process of "reform and opening." The rise of Guangdong and Zhejiang is the result of globalization and marketization forces. Since the early years of "reform and opening" to the present day, Jiangsu has occupied a decisive position in many industries, creating prosperity in the Yangtze Delta together with Shanghai and Zhejiang. The national status of Shandong's manufacturing rose gradually as it has both resource and coastal location advantages, and at the same time, it has a large population and there is a lot of room for growth in manufacturing. Some industries are highly agglomerated in a few provinces, e.g., electronics and communications equipment is agglomerated in Guangdong, chemical fibers and textiles are agglomerated in Jiangsu and Zhejiang, and apparel is agglomerated in Jiangsu and Guangdong. Viewing the trend in the eastern, central and western regions distribution of manufacturing industries, from 1980 to 2008, 15 out of 19 industries saw a marked increase in their eastern regions, while only four declined; on the contrary, only two industries increased their proportion in the central regions and only four industries increased their proportion in the western regions. In the northeastern regions, the proportion of all industries decreased.

The gradual decline of the northeast's old industrial bases after "reform and opening" was especially evident (see Table 7.13).

7.4 Conclusion and prospects

After "reform and opening," China experienced marketization, globalization, and regional decentralization, which led to significant changes in the institutional environment for the development of industry as firms became autonomous decision-making entities, while facing more severe market competition. Under the joint effects of market forces, global forces, and local forces, the geographical disposition of Chinese industry underwent the process of dispersion to concentration. A review of the literature shows that traditional trade theory, the new economic geography theory and agglomeration economics are important perspectives

Table 7.12 Top four provinces in each manufacturing industry and corresponding changes

Industry	*1980*		*2008*		*Change (%)*
	Top four provinces	*(%)*	*Top four provinces*	*(%)*	
Food processing	Jiangsu, Heilongjiang, Guangdong, Shandong	29	Shandong, Henan, Guangdong, Liaoning	46	17
Beverages	Shandong, Sichuan, Zhejiang, Jiangsu	34	Sichuan, Shandong, Guangdong, Henan	40	6
Tobacco	Henan, Shandong, Shanghai, Yunnan	42	Yunnan, Hunan, Shanghai, Jiangsu	42	0
Textiles	Shanghai, Jiangsu, Shandong, Hubei	49	Jiangsu, Zhejiang, Shandong, Guangdong	73	24
Apparel and fiber products	Shanghai, Jiangsu, Liaoning, Beijing	38	Jiangsu, Guangdong, Zhejiang, Shandong	67	29
Paper and paper products	Shanghai, Liaoning, Shandong, Sichuan	31	Shandong, Guangdong, Jiangsu, Zhejiang	60	29
Oil refining	Liaoning, Heilongjiang, Shandong, Guangdong	57	Shandong, Liaoning, Guangdong, Shanxi	43	–14
Chemicals	Shanghai, Jiangsu, Beijing, Liaoning	38	Jiangsu, Shandong, Guangdong, Zhejiang	54	16
Pharmaceuticals	Shanghai, Jiangsu, Liaoning, Sichuan	38	Shandong, Jiangsu, Zhejiang, Sichuan	40	2
Chemical fiber	Shanghai, Liaoning, Jiangsu, Beijing	68	Zhejiang, Jiangsu, Fujian, Guangdong	81	13
Non-metallic minerals	Jiangsu, Liaoning, Shandong, Hebei	34	Shandong, Henan, Guangdong, Jiangsu	49	15
Ferrous metals metallurgy	Liaoning, Shanghai, Hubei, Sichuan	52	Hebei, Jiangsu, Shandong, Liaoning	47	–5
Non-ferrous metals metallurgy	Shanghai, Liaoning, Gansu, Hunan	46	Henan, Jiangsu, Shandong, Guangdong	40	–6
Metals products	Shanghai, Jiangsu, Liaoning, Tianjin	40	Guangdong, Jiangsu, Zhejiang, Shandong	60	20

Continued

Table 7.12 Continued

Industry	*1980*		*2008*		*Change (%)*
	Top four provinces	*(%)*	*Top four provinces*	*(%)*	
Machinery	Shanghai, Liaoning, Jiangsu, Shandong	41	Jiangsu, Shandong, Zhejiang, Liaoning	51	10
Transportation equipment	Liaoning, Hubei, Shanghai, Jilin	39	Jiangsu, Guangdong, Shandong, Sichuan	39	0
Electrical equipment	Shanghai, Liaoning, Jiangsu, Guangdong	44	Guangdong, Jiangsu, Zhejiang, Shandong	65	21
Electronics and communications equipment	Shanghai, Jiangsu, Beijing, Liaoning	55	Guangdong, Jiangsu, Shanghai, Shandong	75	20
Instruments and office supplies machinery	Shanghai, Jiangsu, Beijing, Sichuan	48	Guangdong, Jiangsu, Zhejiang, Shanghai	67	19

through which the agglomeration of Chinese industry can be understood. However, under the special institutional environment of China's transitional economy, globalization and local decentralization have important impacts on the agglomeration and dispersion of Chinese manufacturing.

Based on statistical data and literature review, this chapter systematically depicted and analyzed the current situation and trends of Chinese manufacturing agglomeration since "reform and opening." On the whole, the geographical agglomeration of Chinese industry is high at the current stage and displays a trend toward agglomerating in the eastern coastal regions. Significant industry differences exist in the geographical agglomeration of Chinese manufacturing. Industries dependent on specific natural resource inputs have relatively lower degrees of geographical agglomeration, while capital/technology intensive industries that rely heavily on intermediate inputs have high degrees of geographical agglomeration. Since labor intensive industries are dominated by foreign capital and are mainly export-oriented, they are highly concentrated in coastal provinces. From "reform and opening" to the present day, the geographical agglomeration of Chinese manufacturing has increased significantly. The trend in Chinese industry agglomeration exhibits apparent phases. From the early 1990s, geographical agglomeration of industry entered an acceleration phase, and the degree of geographical agglomeration reached a peak around 2004. Compared with the early years of "reform and opening," old industrial bases such as Hubei, Sichuan, Heilongjiang, etc. saw their proportion of national manufacturing output fall significantly, while eastern coastal provinces such as Guangdong and Zhejiang's proportions rose markedly.

Table 7.13 Regional distribution and change of manufacturing output value (unit: %)

Industry	*Eastern regions*		*Central regions*		*Western regions*		*Northeastern regions*	
	2008	*Compared with 1980*	*2008*	*Compared with 1980*	*2008*	*Compared with 1980*	*2008*	*Compared with 1980*
Food processing	61	7	30	–3	9	–4	12	–3
Beverages	50	–2	28	–4	21	6	9	–3
Tobacco	40	–5	29	–9	31	14	3	–4
Textiles	83	15	13	–9	4	–6	2	–7
Apparel and fiber products	90	24	9	–13	1	–11	5	–8
Paper and paper products	76	16	19	–11	5	–5	3	–16
Oil refining	63	–8	22	–2	15	9	17	–23
Chemicals	71	8	19	–4	9	–4	6	–7
Pharmaceuticals	60	–4	27	3	13	2	10	–3
Chemical fiber	89	7	8	–7	3	0	4	–11
Non-metallic minerals	64	5	27	–2	9	–3	8	–8
Ferrous metals metallurgy	68	4	24	–2	9	–2	9	–16
Non-ferrous metals metallurgy	47	0	37	8	16	–9	4	–10
Metals products	85	18	10	–12	4	–6	7	–8
Machinery	76	13	17	–8	7	–6	11	–6
Transportation equipment	65	14	24	–9	11	–5	14	–8
Electrical equipment	83	16	12	–9	5	–7	4	–11
Electronics and communications equipment	94	21	3	–12	2	–9	2	–7
Instruments and office supplies machinery	86	18	9	–8	5	–11	3	–9

The rise of the new economic geography drew the attention of domestic and foreign academic and policymaking communities. The impact of economic integration on industry agglomeration is especially noteworthy, as unbalanced regional development, namely the formation of a core-periphery structure, may follow. Thus, for a China with significant regional disparities, industry agglomeration is both a theoretical and a policy issue that involves the enhancement of industry competitiveness and balanced regional development. At the same time, the impact of China's special transitional economy background on industry agglomeration should continue to be followed. As China's economic transition deepens and its position in the global economy adjusts, how global forces and local forces further impact the spatial distribution of industry is worth exploring further.

Notes

1 Co-agglomeration refers to the degree of agglomeration of two or more industries in one region.
2 For simplicity, this chapter will use province to refer to provincial level administrative unit, including province, directly administered municipality and autonomous region.
3 Unless otherwise mentioned, all indices and indicators are calculated on the basis of total industrial output.
4 Refers to the share of value-added in total industrial output value.

References

In English

Amiti, M., and B. S. Javorcik, 2008, "Trade Costs and Location of Foreign Firms in China," *Journal of Development Economics*, 85(1), pp. 129–149.

Bai, C., Y. Du, Z. Tao, and S. Tong, 2004a, "Local Protectionism and Regional Specialization: Evidence from China's Industries," *Journal of International Economics*, 63, pp. 397–417.

Chen, Z., M. Lu, and Y. Jin, 2008, "Economic Opening and Industrial Agglomeration in China," In *Economic Integration in East Asia, Perspectives from Spatial and Neoclassical Economics*, ed. M. Fujita, S. Kumagai and K. Nishikimi, 276–315. New York: Edward Elgar.

Ellison, G., and E. Glaeser, 1997, "Geographic Concentration in U.S. Manufacturing Industries: a Dartboard Approach," *Journal of Political Economy*, 105(5), pp. 889–927.

Fan, C., and A. Scott, 2003, "Industrial Agglomeration and Development: a Survey of Spatial Economic Issues in East Asia and a Statistical Analysis of Chinese Regions," *Economic Geography*, 79(3), pp. 295–319.

Ge, Ying, 2009, "Globalization and Industrial Agglomeration in China," *World Development,* 37(3), pp. 550–559.

He, C., and W. Junsong, 2010, "Geographical Agglomeration and Co-agglomeration of Foreign and Domestic Enterprises in China," *Post-Communist Economies*, 22(3), pp. 323–343.

He, C., W. Yehua, and P. Fenghua, 2007, "Geographical Concentration of Industries in China: The Importance of Spatial and Industrial Scale," *Eurasian Geography and Economics,* 48(5), pp. 603–625.

He, C., W. Yehua, and X. Xiuzhen, 2008, "Globalization, Institutional Change and Industrial Location: Economic Transition and Industrial Concentration in China," *Regional Studies*, 42(7), pp. 923–945.

Krugman, P., 1980, "Scale Economies, Product Differentiation, and the Pattern of Trade," *American Economic Review*, 70(5), pp. 950–959.

Krugman, P., 1991, "Increasing Returns and Economic Geography," *Journal of Political Economy*, 99(3), pp. 483–499.

Lu, Jiangyong, and Zhigang Tao, 2009, "Trends and Determinants of China's Industrial Agglomeration," *Journal of Urban Economics*, 65(2), pp. 167–180.

Ohlin, B., 1957, *Interregional and International Trade*. Cambridge: Harvard University Press.

Poncet, S., 2005, "A Fragmented China: Measure and Determinants of Chinese Domestic Market Disintegration," *Review of International Economics*, 13(3), pp. 409–4301.

Thun, E., 2004, "Keeping up with the Jones: Decentralization, Policy Imitation and Industrial Development in China," *World Development*, 32(8), pp. 1289–1308.

Venables, A., 1996, "Equilibrium Locations of Vertically Linked Industries," *International Economic Review*, 37(2), pp. 341–359.

Wen, M., 2004a, "Relocation and Agglomeration of Chinese Industry," *Journal of Development Economics*, 73(1), pp. 329–347.

Young, A., 2000, "The Razor's Edge: Distortions and Incremental Reform in the People's Republic of China," *Quarterly Journal of Economics*, 115(4), pp. 1091–1135.

In Chinese

Bai Chong'en, Du Yingjuan, Tao Zhigang et al., 2004b, "Local Protectionism and Industrial Concentration in China: Overall Trend and Important Factors," *Economic Research Journal*, 4, pp. 29–40.

Fan Jianyong, 2004, "Market Integration, Regional Specialization and Tendency of Industrial Agglomeration: An Implication for Regional Disparity," *Social Science in China,* 6, pp. 39–51.

He Canfei, Zhu Shengjun, Wang Junsong, and Pan Fenghua, et al., 2010a, *Geographical Location of China's Manufacturing: Regional and Industrial Differences*. Beijing: Science Press.

He Canfei, 2008, *Geographical Concentration and Agglomeration of China's Manufacturing*. Beijing: Science Press.

He Canfei, and Pan Fenghua, 2007, "Geographical Concentration and Agglomeration of Industries and Industrial Clusters: Measurement and Identification," *Progress in Geography*, 26(2), pp. 1–13.

He Canfei, and Pan Fenghua, 2009, "Economic Transition, Dynamic Externalities and City Industry Growth in China," *Geographical Research,* 28(3), pp. 726–737.

He Canfei, Pan Fenghua, and Sun Lei, 2007, "Geographical Concentration of Manufacturing Industries in China," *Acta Geographica Sinica*, 62(12), pp. 1253–1264.

He Canfei, and Xie Xiuzhen, 2006, "Geographical Concentration and Provincial Specialization of Chinese Manufacturing Industries," *Acta Geographica Sinica,* 61(2), pp. 212–222.

He Canfei, Xie Xiuzhen, and Pan Fenghua, 2008, "Locational Studies of Chinese Manufacturing Industries," *Geographical Research*, 27(3), pp. 623–635.

He Canfei, Zhu Yangang, and Zhu Shengjun, 2010b, "Industrial Attributes, Provincial Characteristics and Industrial Agglomeration in China," *Acta Geographica Sinica*, 65(10), pp. 1218–1228.

He Canfei, and Zhu Yangang, 2010, "An Empirical Study on the Geographical Distribution of Resource-based Industries in China – A Case Study of Oil Processing and Coking Industry and Ferrous Metal Smelting and Rolling Processing Industry," *Journal of Natural Resources*, 25(3), pp. 488–501.

Huang Jiuli, and Li Kunwang, 2006, "Foreign Trade, Local Protectionism and Industrial Location in China," *China Economic Quarterly*, 5(3), pp. 733–760.

Jin Yu, Chen Zhao, and Lu Ming, 2006, "Industry Agglomeration in China: Economic Geography, New Economic Geography and Policy," *Economic Research Journal,* 4, pp. 79–89.

Lin Lisheng, and Wang Yeqian, 2006, "Transport Cost, Labor Mobility and the Spatial Distribution of Manufacturing Industries," *Economic Research Journal,* 3, pp. 115–125.

Lu Jiangyong, and Tao Zhigang, 2006, "Industrial Agglomeration and Co-Agglomeration in China's Manufacturing Industries: with International Comparison," *Economic Research Journal*, 3, pp. 103–114.

Lu Jiangyong, and Tao Zhigang, 2007, "Determinants of Industrial Agglomeration in China: Evidence from Panel Data," *China Economic Quarterly*, 6(3), pp. 801–816.

Luo Yong, and Cao Lili, 2005, "A Positive Research on Fluctuation Trend of China's Manufacturing Industrial Agglomeration Degree," *Economic Research Journal*, 8, pp. 106–127.

Research Group of the "Building up a Uniform National Market in China" in Development Research Center of the State Council, 2004, "The report of the local protection in China: A preliminary analysis based on the sampling without firms," *Review of Economic Research*, 18, pp. 31–38.

Wang Jici, 2001, *Innovative Space: Industrial Cluster and Regional Development*. Beijing: Peking University Press.

Wang Jici, 2010, *Beyond Clusters: A Theoretical Exploration of China' Industrial Clusters*. Beijing: Science Press.

Wang Yeqiang, and Wei Houkai, 2007, "Characteristics of Industries, Competition for Space and the Geographic Concentration in Manufacture," *Management World*, 4, pp. 68–77.

Wen Mei, 2004b, "Relocation and Agglomeration of Chinese Industry," *Economic Research Journal*, 2, pp. 84–94.

Xian Guoming, and Wen Dongwei, 2006, "FDI, Regional Specialization and Industrial Agglomeration," *Management World*, 12, pp. 18–31.

Zhang Junni, and Chen Yuyu, 2006, "Agglomeration Effect, Ownership Structure and Location Choice: Evidence from Foreign Direct Investment in China," *China Economic Quarterly*, 5(4), pp. 1091–1108.

Zhao Wei, and Zhang Cui, 2007, "FDI and Manufacturing Agglomeration in China: Evidence of 20 Industries," *Economic Research Journal,* 11, pp. 82–90.

8 The impact of spatial agglomeration on Chinese manufacturing

Jianyong Fan and Fangwen Li

8.1 Introduction

Intuitively, industry agglomeration includes two types of economic phenomena. First, viewed on a large regional scale, fragmentation is evident in the spatial distribution of non-agricultural industries (especially tradable manufactured goods). For example, some regions abound with non-agricultural industries, while economic activities and population are sparse in most regions. If observing from afar, the distribution of human economic activity could be seen to be concentrated in just a few regions of North America, the EU, and North-east Asia. In China, since 1978, the coastal regions have become the place where manufacturing is concentrated. Second, viewed on a small regional scale, agglomeration is reflected in the differences and efficiency gaps between city and countryside, large cities and small cities. Based on these economic phenomena, this chapter will divide industry agglomeration into two categories: large geographical scale industry and small geographical scale industry – and, to the authors' knowledge, such a classification has never been made before. Another reason to make such a classification is the fact that the theoretical foundation of these two types of industry agglomeration is different. The basis for large geographical scale industry agglomeration is *New Economic Geography* theory, which generates pecuniary externalities (Fujita and Thisse, 2002). Opinion on this theory has more or less reached a consensus. The basis of small geographical scale industry agglomeration is urban economics, which generates technological externalities (Fujita and Thisse, 2002). However, opinions on its micro-level fundamentals are far from unanimous, and may remain in a "much to be said on both sides" situation long into the future.

Since there is a clear dividing line in industry agglomeration, the objective of this chapter is to classify and comment on relevant domestic empirical studies. Specifically, we discuss the status quo of both large and small geographical scale industry agglomeration, as well as their impact on productivity. As no consensus has been reached on the micro-level theoretical foundation for small geographical scale industry agglomeration, we will not review the corresponding empirical literature. In fact, such literature is hard to come by domestically. When conducting literature reviews, the aim of this chapter is to enunciate the current phase of Chinese industry agglomeration and its macro-economic mechanism. The chapter tries to tell the story of China; to understand the status quo and the impact of Chinese industry agglomeration, and not just use data or models to prove that it exists.

Based on the above-mentioned considerations, the structure of this chapter is as follows: the second section will descriptively analyze the circumstances of large geographical scale industry agglomeration and its impact on interprovincial *per capita* GDP gaps; the third section will lay out the empirical analysis model of large geographical scale industry agglomeration; the fourth section will summarize domestic empirical literature on large geographical scale industry agglomeration and the outlook for present and future research; the fifth section is descriptive evidence on small geographical scale industry agglomeration and the sixth section is the empirical analytic framework and literature review of small geographical scale industry agglomeration. The final section concludes.

8.2 Large geographical scale industry agglomeration and interprovincial *per capita* GDP gaps

8.2.1 Descriptive evidence on large geographical scale industry agglomeration

We will first depict the regional and provincial level spatial agglomeration and relocation of manufacturing over the past decade, then link industry agglomeration and the Gini coefficients of interprovincial *per capita* GDP and observe whether or not industry agglomeration contributed to changes in the Gini coefficients of interprovincial *per capita* GDP. Circumstances that need to be explained and made clear beforehand are as follows:

1. We divide China into the following regions: northeastern region (Heilongjiang, Jilin, Liaoning); Jingjin region (Beijing and Tianjin); northern coastal region (Shandong and Hebei); eastern coastal region (Jiangsu, Shanghai, Zhejiang); southern coastal region (Guangdong, Fujian, Hainan); central region (Shanxi, Anhui, Jiangxi, Henan, Hunan, Hubei); northwestern region (Inner Mongolia, Shaanxi, Ningxia, Gansu, Tibet, Xinjiang, Qinghai); and southwestern region (Sichuan, Chongqing, Guangxi, Yunnan Guizhou). For details on the basis of this demarcation, refer to the National Information Center (2005).
2. In our choice of time points, we selected 2004 as the turning point, as we believe that both the degree of industry agglomeration and interprovincial *per capita* GDP gaps deepened in the period between the start of "reform and opening" and 2004, whereas industry dispersed spatially and interprovincial *per capita* GDP gaps narrowed from 2004 to the present. Such a demarcation is based on the results of our data analysis.
3. We have calculated all indicators and figures by ourselves. The reason for this is: first, our calculations reached similar results to others; second, the most recent figures come from 2007 or 2008 and can appropriately reflect the latest progress in industry agglomeration and dispersion.

4. GDP figures for the three industries in each province come from the "China Compendium of Statistics 1949–2008," while manufacturing data comes from the National Bureau of Statistics' recently declassified "Micro-level database for large-scale industrial firms."
5. The analysis methods here are as follows: when analyzing the industry agglomeration in each region or province, each region or province's proportion of industry and the Gini coefficient indicator will be adopted; when analyzing interprovincial *per capita* GDP gaps, the Gini coefficient indicator will be used; when analyzing the source of changes in the Gini coefficient of interprovincial *per capita* GDP gaps, it will be dissected into the concentration effect produced by industry agglomeration and structural effect reflected by the change in proportion of industry output value. Introductions on the above methods can be viewed in this chapter's appendix, below.

This chapter will focus on describing the spatial agglomeration and dispersion of manufacturing, respectively. A major point of this chapter's narrative is 2004, which was a turning point for industry agglomeration and dispersion in coastal regions. Before 2004, endogenous mechanisms for coastal regions becoming priority spatial locations for industry agglomeration were nothing more than: policy support for coastal regions in the first 20 years of "reform and opening;" superior geographical location situated closer to high-income foreign markets (Jin, Chen, and Lu, 2006); high population density (Fan, 2004a); enhanced market scale from central and western regions' labor migration (Fan, Wang, and Shen, 2004); and inflow of capital from central and western regions (Guo et al., 2003). Combining these factors, an accumulation cycle mechanism in the *New Economic Geography* sense enabled the market scale and spatial efficiency of coastal regions to exhibit a "snowball" type uptrend, spatial distribution of industry to display a typical "core-periphery" structure, and even the spatial distribution of the urban system to exhibit a "core-periphery" structure (Xu, Chen, and Lu, 2010).

But since 2004, a reversal has appeared in the trend toward industry agglomeration in coastal regions. Although academia has not reached any unanimously accepted empirical conclusions, we believe the following factors play a critical role: (1) once industry agglomeration reaches a certain level, the price of non-tradable goods, especially immobile factors such as land, rises naturally, which is reflected in the dramatic increase of the property prices in coastal regions over the last decade; (2) farmland protection policies implemented since 1998 have gradually become more rigorous, at the same time, interprovincial exchange in non-agricultural construction-use land indicators is prohibited, which greatly restricts the supply of land for coastal regions, especially large cities in the coastal regions, usable for the development of non-agricultural industries, which forces land prices in the coastal regions to appreciate rapidly. As to the second factor, Fan and Shao (2011) found that property prices differed greatly between coastal and inland regions, large cities and small and mid-sized cities, which directly propelled the dispersion of manufacturing toward inland regions or small and mid-sized cities.[1]

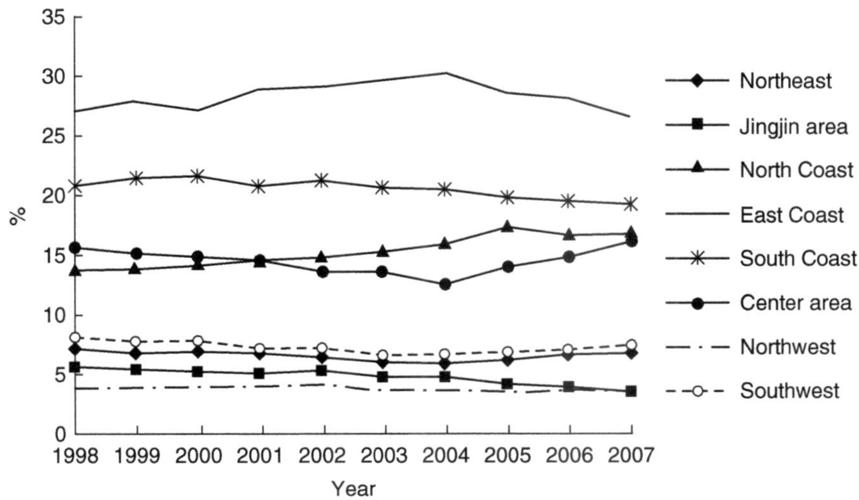

Figure 8.1 Evolution of eight regions' industry share (1998–2007).

Data source: Authors' calculations based on "Micro-level database on above-scale Chinese industrial firms" (National Bureau of Statistics, historical data).

Under the above narrative context, representative descriptive evidence is provided on industry agglomeration and dispersion during 30 years of "reform and opening." The chapter starts from the shift in industry agglomeration around 2004 and the use of value-added in the micro-level database on above-scale industrial firms from 1998–2007, as the main object of analysis. Judging from the results (see Figure 8.1, Table 8.1, and Figure 8.2), the eastern coastal region's proportion of industry was highest throughout the studied period, accounting for 26.7–30.3 percent of national output, followed by the southern coastal region, which accounts for 19.2–21.5 percent of national output, the central region and northern coastal region in turn; the other four regions' (southwestern region, northeastern region, Jingjin region and northwestern region) proportion of industry are the lowest, with each of them accounting for less than 7.4 percent. It should be pointed out that the eastern coastal, southern coastal and northern coastal regions' aggregate proportion of industry reached 62–67 percent during 1998–2007. The percentage was 62 percent, 67 percent, and 63 percent at the time points 1998, 2004, and 2007, respectively. Thus, these three regions are, to a certain extent, still the core of China's manufacturing

However, the above-mentioned "core-periphery" spatial distribution structure of industry agglomeration changed in 2004, as manufacturing began to disperse toward the northern coastal and central regions. This is mainly reflected in the eastern coastal region's proportion of industry rapidly declining to only 26.7 percent in 2007 after peaking at 30.3 percent in 2004; whereas the southern coastal region's proportion of manufacturing has steadily declined since 2000 from

Table 8.1 Difference of each region and province's proportion of industry at major time points (1998–2007)

	Difference between 2004 and 1998 value	*Difference between 2007 and 2004 value*	*Difference between 2007 and 1998 value*
Northeastern region	(0.0110)	0.0071	(0.0039)
Beijing-Tianjin region	(0.0086)	(0.0112)	(0.0198)
Northern coastal	0.0225	0.0083	0.0308
Eastern coastal	0.0315	(0.0361)	(0.0045)
Southern coastal	(0.0026)	(0.0129)	(0.0154)
Central region	(0.0316)	0.0355	0.0039
Northwestern region	(0.0023)	0.0008	(0.0015)
Southwestern region	(0.0159)	0.0084	(0.0075)
Heilongjiang	(0.0070)	(0.0020)	(0.0090)
Liaoning	(0.0045)	0.0088	0.0043
Jilin	0.0004	0.0003	0.0007
Beijing	(0.0060)	(0.0074)	(0.0134)
Tianjin	(0.0026)	(0.0038)	(0.0064)
Shandong	0.0288	0.0096	0.0384
Hebei	(0.0063)	(0.0013)	(0.0076)
Shanghai	(0.0261)	(0.0186)	(0.0448)
Jiangsu	0.0237	(0.0115)	0.0123
Zhejiang	0.0317	(0.0060)	0.0257
Fujian	0.0057	(0.0027)	0.0030
Guangdong	(0.0089)	(0.0108)	(0.0198)
Hainan	(0.0007)	0.0008	0.0001
Hubei	(0.0213)	0.0009	(0.0204)
Anhui	(0.0011)	0.0017	0.0006
Jiangxi	(0.0015)	0.005	0.0035
Hunan	0.0007	0.009	0.0097
Henan	(0.0076)	0.0194	0.0117
Shanxi	(0.0008)	(0.0002)	(0.0009)
Inner Mongolia	0.003	0.0033	0.0062
Tibet	(0.0002)	0	(0.0002)
Ningxia	(0.0005))	(0.0000)	(0.0005)
Xinjiang	(0.0007)	(0.0010)	(0.0017)
Gansu	(0.0016)	(0.0013)	(0.0029)
Qinghai	(0.0002)	0.0003	0.0001
Shaanxi	(0.0016)	0.0003	(0.0013)
Yunnan	(0.0070)	(0.0019)	(0.0090)
Guizhou	(0.0021)	(0.0002)	(0.0024)
Guangxi	(0.0045)	0.0031	(0.0014)
Chongqing	(0.0017)	0.0015	(0.0002)
Sichuan	(0.0006)	0.0062	0.0056

Note: Values in parenthesis are negative.

Data source: Author's calculations based on "Micro-level database for above-scale Chinese industrial firms" (National Bureau of Statistics, historical data).

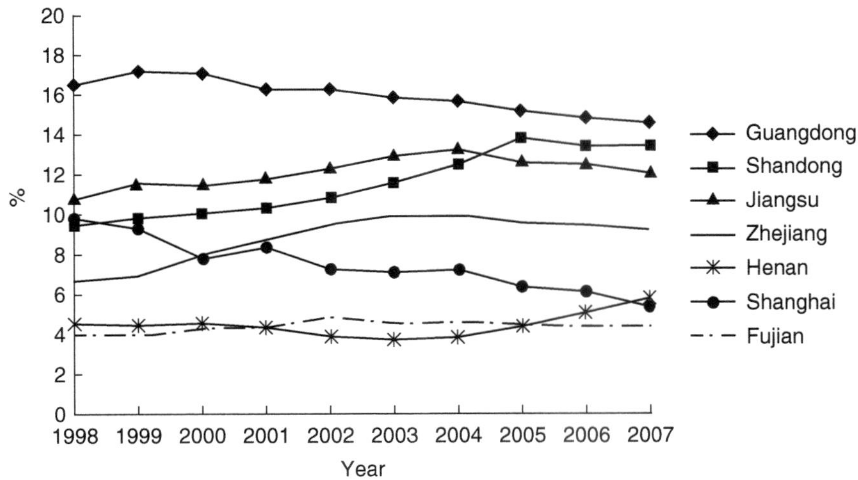

Figure 8.2 Evolution of the seven most agglomerated provinces' industry share (1998–2007).
Data source: Author's calculations based on "Micro-level database for above-scale Chinese industrial firms" (National Bureau of Statistics, historical data).

21.5 percent to 19.2 percent in 2007. Conversely, as peripheral regions to the eastern coastal and southern coastal regions, the central region and northern coastal region caught a portion of the manufacturing that relocated out of the eastern coastal and southern coastal regions, e.g. the northern coastal region's proportion rose from 13.6 percent in 1998 to 17.2 percent in 2005, maintaining that level thereafter, and slightly declining to 16.7 percent in 2007; while the central region's manufacturing faced net outward relocation before 2004, declining from 15.6 percent in 1998 to 12.5 percent in 2004, but its proportion of industry has been in a steady uptrend since 2004, reaching 16.0 percent by 2007. At the same time, the southwestern and northeastern regions' proportion of industry increased by a little after 2004, with the southwestern region increasing by 0.84 percent and the northeastern region increasing by 0.71 percent by 2007.

We then depict on the provinces level of the eight major regions' trend of industry agglomeration or dispersion, and the results are shown in Table 8.1. In terms of the eight major regions, from 1998–2004, only the eastern coastal and northern coastal regions saw their proportion of industry rise, and at the provincial level, Zhejiang, Shandong and Jiangsu's proportion of industry rose by 3.17 percent, 2.88 percent and 2.37 percent, respectively, while among the other provinces, only Hunan, Inner Mongolia, Fujian and Jilin saw their proportion of industry increase, the magnitude of which was uniformly minute. From 2004–2007, regions where industry dispersed include the Jingjin, eastern coastal and southern coastal region.[2] If we set aside the Jingjin region, the eastern coastal region saw the largest decline in its proportion, especially Shanghai and Jiangsu which experienced 1.86 percent and 1.15 percent declines respectively, while Zhejiang only lost 0.6 percent to outward relocation; in the southern coastal region, Guangdong was the main loser, losing 1.08 percent to outward relocation. In terms of provinces experiencing inward relocation of industry, the central region is most prominent with a 3.55 percent increase, of which Henan accounts for 1.9 percent, Hunan accounts for 0.9 percent, while other provinces do not stand out. The northern coastal region's share of manufacturing saw significant gains, reaching 0.83 percent, of which Shandong accounts for 0.96 percent.

Let us take a look at the seven major provinces where manufacturing is most concentrated, as shown in Figure 8.2. Among those provinces, Guangdong and Shanghai's proportion of industry is in a "constantly decreasing" trend; Jiangsu and Zhejiang's proportion is in a "first increasing, then decreasing" trend, of which the turning point is around 2004 for both; Shandong and Fujian's proportion is in a "first increasing then constant" trend, in which Shandong's proportion of manufacturing increased from 9.6 percent in 1998 to 13.8 percent in 2005; Henan's proportion of manufacturing is in "first declining then increasing" trend, with the turning point in 2004, rising from 3.8 percent to 5.7 percent in 2007.

Up to now, judging from the perspective of the major regions and provinces, 2004 is the turning point of the change of manufacturing's spatial distribution during 1998–2007. During 1998–2004, the increase in Zhejiang, Jiangsu and Shandong's proportion of manufacturing caused manufacturing to exhibit a trend toward agglomeration overall, but during 2004–2007, due to the decline in Guangdong, Jiangsu and Shanghai's proportion of industry, manufacturing overall exhibited dispersion and relocation features.

8.2.2 *Evolution of manufacturing spatial agglomeration and interprovincial* **per capita** *GDP gaps*

What endogenous mechanisms exist between manufacturing spatial agglomeration and interprovincial *per capita* GDP gaps? In an intuitive sense, agglomeration of non-agricultural industries in the coastal regions means that the distribution of non-agricultural industries in other regions is relatively sparse, while non-agricultural industries imply relatively high labor productivity under China's fundamental situation of lots of people and little land. From this perspective, a high degree of industry agglomeration in coastal regions means that their *per capita* GDP will be higher than other regions. In terms of *New Economic Geography* mechanisms, a core-periphery industry distribution implies that the core region has relatively high labor productivity and wage levels. But a precondition for the formation of interregional wage differentials is restricted interregional mobility of low-skilled labor and relative unrestricted interregional mobility of skilled labor. This is because if low-skilled labor mobility is to reach ideal unrestricted conditions, then a slight difference in real interregional wage levels will induce interregional migration of low-skilled labor. At the same time, the inflow of skilled labor to coastal regions generated human capital externalities,[3] further exacerbating interregional income gaps. Thus, China's current spatial agglomeration and interprovincial *per capita* GDP gaps are closely linked and this relationship is precisely caused by the dual segmentation of the coastal regions' labor market.

So, how to analyze the relationship between industry agglomeration and interregional income gaps? Here, we will link the unequal distribution of the secondary industry with the Gini coefficient of interprovincial *per capita* GDP, which will be accomplished by dissecting the Gini coefficient of interprovincial *per capita* GDP (for details, see Appendix, below), while the spatial agglomeration of the secondary industry will be measured with the secondary industry's Gini coefficients as well. The sequence and objective here are as follows: first we will present the Gini coefficient of interprovincial *per capita* GDP during 1978–2008 and the contribution of each industry to the *per capita* GDP Gini coefficient, in order to observe whether the secondary industry contributes significantly to the *per capita* GDP Gini coefficient; next, we will link annual dynamic changes in the *per capita* GDP Gini coefficient with the unbalanced distribution and output share of each industry (mainly the secondary industry), in order to examine whether the unbalanced distribution of the secondary industry will have any critical or dominant guiding effect on the expansion or narrowing of *per capita* GDP Gini coefficient. If we can achieve the above two goals, we can say that the spatial agglomeration of the secondary industry is a critical impetus for interregional development gaps.

Since the central government implemented a regional development policy supportive of coastal regions before 2004, much manufacturing relocated and agglomerated in that region. Under the current conditions where mobility of low-skilled labor is restricted and mobility of skilled labor is relatively unrestricted, such a tendency for location choice that leads to industry agglomeration will facilitate continuous increases in interregional *per capita* GDP gaps. Thus, from Deng Xiaoping's Southern Talk in 1992 to 2004, the interprovincial *per capita* GDP Gini coefficient consistently rose, but after 2004, there emerged a clear trend toward a portion of manufacturing in the coastal regions relocating to the central regions, especially Henan, whereas interprovincial *per capita* GDP gaps began to reverse as well (see Figure 8.3).

How should the composition of the interprovincial *per capita* GDP Gini coefficient be viewed? Especially since the secondary industry's share of GDP is high and its spatial distribution is uneven, how much does this contribute to interprovincial *per capita* GDP gaps? Viewed from the composition of the Gini coefficient, it is mostly the sum of the product of each industry's share of output value and the Gini coefficient by industry (see Appendix, below). We therefore calculated the contribution of each industry to the interprovincial *per capita* GDP Gini coefficient (see Figure 8.4) and found that the secondary industry's contribution is largest, reaching 65–72 percent during the whole period under study. At the same time, judging from the output value, the secondary industry's share has maintained at a high level (51–67 percent) and as time goes by, its share of output value trends toward increasing, which precisely reflects the reality of local governments pursuing GDP growth under a fiscally decentralized system.

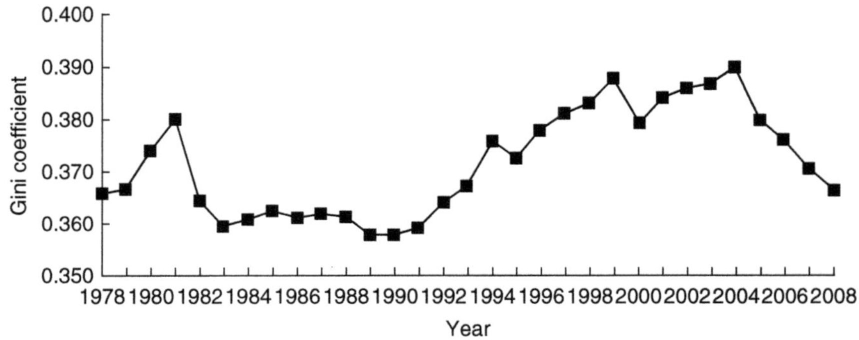

Figure 8.3 Trend of interprovincial *per capita* GDP Gini coefficient from 1978 to 2008.
Data source: Historical issues of the *China Statistical Yearbook.*

Although the secondary industry's Gini coefficient trends toward declining after 2004, what impact does the composition of manufacturing output value and its uneven spatial distribution have on dynamic changes in the interprovincial *per capita* GDP Gini coefficient? We subtracted each year's *per capita* GDP Gini coefficient with the previous year's coefficient and dissected the change into two sources: the first is the "structural effect" caused by the change in each industry's output value; the second is the "concentration effect" caused by the uneven spatial distribution of the various industries. Having considered both the theory explained in this chapter and the real world context, the secondary industry is the "main factor" that leads to changes in the Gini coefficient. However, what we care

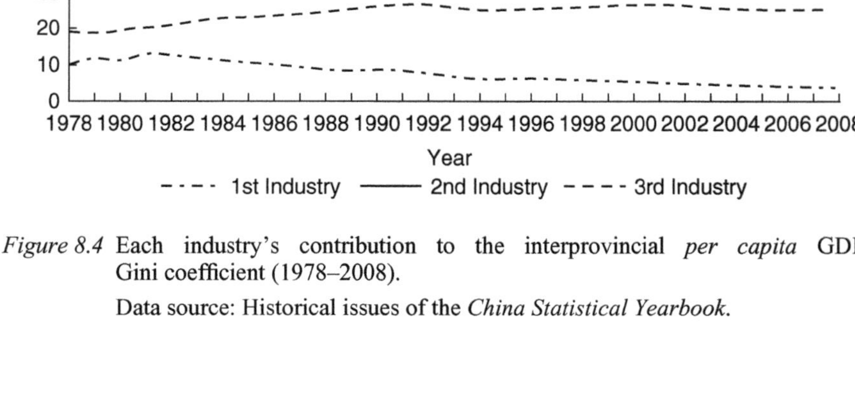

Figure 8.4 Each industry's contribution to the interprovincial *per capita* GDP Gini coefficient (1978–2008).

Data source: Historical issues of the *China Statistical Yearbook.*

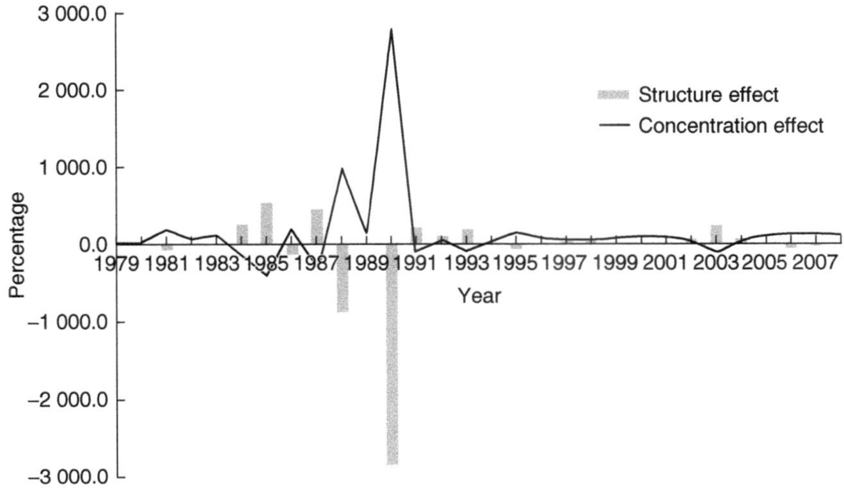

Figure 8.5 Structural dissection of 31-province *per capita* GDP Gini coefficient changes from 1978 to 2008.

Data source: Historical issues of the *China Statistical Yearbook* and authors' calculations.

about and anticipate more is whether the impact of uneven spatial distribution has a larger impact than the share of output value on changes in the Gini coefficient, that is, does the concentration effect exceed the structural effect? Figure 8.5 presents the answer to this question. In most years, the concentration effect exceeds the structural effect. The two periods in which the Gini coefficient respectively rose before 2004 and declined after 2004 both reflect this characteristic.

So far, through the above three-part description of data, we can basically reach the following fundamental conclusions: (1) 2004 was an evident turning point for industry agglomeration, as industry concentration was dominant before 2004 and industry dispersion dominant after 2004. (2) Such an industry concentration and dispersion phenomenon has an important impact on the change of interprovincial *per capita* GDP Gini coefficients and greatly dominates the trend in regional development gaps. Then, we have to ask further: what are the endogenous mechanisms for the impact of such large geographical scale industry agglomeration on interregional development gaps? This is the question the next section will endeavor to answer.

8.3 Empirical analytic framework for large geographical scale industry agglomeration and interregional *per capita* GDP gaps

Continuing the discussion in the previous section on the mechanisms that led to the impact of large geographical scale industry agglomeration on interregional income gaps, this section will include the following relationships: first, before entering the formal expression of the model, the relationship between large geographical scale industry agglomeration and interregional income should be expressed in an easy-to-understand manner; second, other than simply using wages to measure interregional income, what indicator should generally be used to measure large geographical scale industry agglomeration? The above two aspects form the main content of this section and the entrance point for the discussion.

8.3.1 Expression of the relationship between large geographical scale industry agglomeration and interregional income gaps

Large geographical scale industry agglomeration generally refers to the uneven distribution of non-agricultural industries (especially manufacturing) on a large geographical scale. Its impact on regional income levels takes effect through pecuniary externalities generated by such uneven distribution. Generally speaking, the size of pecuniary externalities is determined by the density and frequency of transactions between suppliers and buyers and transaction cost savings, while the latter is determined by tangible factors such as geographical spatial location, state of infrastructure, etc. and intangible factors such as institutions, culture, customs, etc.

The starting point of the *New Economic Geography* adopts the assumption of increasing returns to scale (Fujita, Krugman, and Venables, 1999, Ch. 4; Helpman and Krugman, 1985, Ch. 6). It has implications on two levels: first, increasing returns to scale at the firm level, assuming that a manufacturer only produces a differentiated variety under a monopolistically competitive market structure; second, increasing returns to scale at the regional level, which is a combination of assumption of increasing returns to scale at firm level and assumption of transport costs (see below). The more types of manufactured goods agglomerated in a region, the larger its market scale and increasing returns to scale are more evident. Another main assumption of New Economic Geography is the existence of transport costs for interregional mobility of manufactured goods, which is usually depicted as "iceberg costs" (Samuelson, 1954). If one unit of a good is transported from region r to region j, then only $\frac{1}{T_{rj}}$ units arrive (T_{rj} is larger than 1). Under these two assumptions, geographical concentration of manufacturers with increasing returns to scale spatially generates such a mechanism: when interregional transport costs decline to a certain level, interregional mobility of skilled labor in advanced sectors such as manufacturing becomes an important factor for industry agglomeration (Krugman, 1991 and see below). Under such a mechanism, the market scale of a region (namely, the increasing returns to scale at the regional level) is in fact endogenously determined by increasing returns at the firm level, transport costs for interregional mobility of manufactured goods and interregional mobility of labor (Fujita et al., 1999, Ch. 4).

We will now describe the mechanism through which mobility of skilled labor generates industry agglomeration (Fujita et al., 1999, Ch. 4). Assume there exist two regions with similar resource endowments and preferences and labor in the manufacturing sector can flow across regions. Due to historical accidental factors,

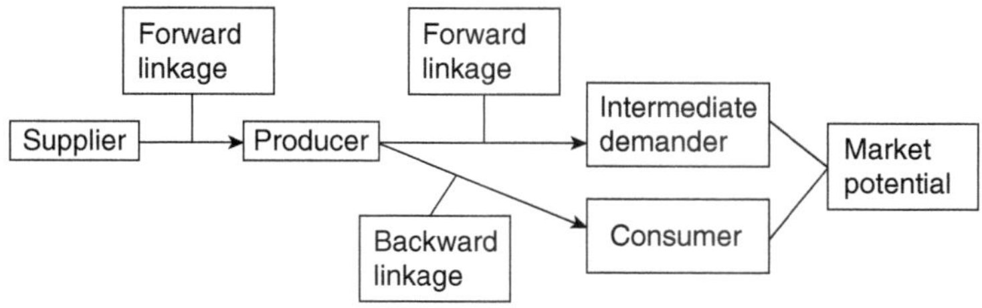

Figure 8.6 Endogenous mechanism for large geographical scale industry agglomeration.

at one point coastal regions slightly lead inland regions in manufacturing. As time passes, there exist the following two forces that propel manufacturing to agglomerate in the coastal regions (see Figure 8.6): first, the price index effect generated from forward linkages from manufacturing. In layman's terms, the existence of this type of effect can be determined by observing whether "matching industries" are complete; second, the *Home Market Effect* generated by backward linkages from manufacturing, commonly referred to as "market scale effect" or "increasing returns to scale at the regional level". We will first look at the price index effect. If manufacturing industries with upstream and downstream linkages agglomerate in the same region, then there would be benefits such as reduced shrinkage in transit and transport costs for intermediate inputs, shared knowledge spillovers, etc., thereby lowering the price for intermediate inputs, and then lowering the overall factory price for manufactured goods, increasing production efficiency. If the coastal regions initially lead the inland regions in manufacturing, then inland firms may anticipate the existence of the price index effect in coastal regions, and inland firms will successively relocate to coastal regions and invest there. At the same time, since the price index for manufactured goods in coastal regions is low and the degree of differentiation in manufactured goods is strong, real incomes for workers will be higher than those in inland regions. Then inland labor will migrate toward the coastal regions, thereby increasing the market scale of coastal regions, which is known as the "Home Market Effect" or "market scale effect." Under these two effects, two regions that were not much different initially, through the impact of the above-mentioned agglomeration forces, will respectively experience contraction in inland manufacturing and expansion in coastal manufacturing. At the same time, the *New Economic Geography* believes that the price index effect is caused by manufacturing forward linkages and the market scale effect is caused by manufacturing backward linkages.

Through the above agglomeration mechanisms, we can see that whether a region's advanced sectors (manufacturing, etc.) can agglomerate is determined by the strength of the agglomeration forces, and the latter is determined by factors such as mobility of firms and skilled labor, etc. The relatively stronger "matching industry capabilities," and relatively larger "market scales" a region has are exactly the pecuniary externalities this chapter is talking about.

So, how do pecuniary externalities impact regional income levels? Coastal regions, where pecuniary externalities are relatively higher, contain manufacturing with lower price indexes, abundant differentiated goods, and strong specialized division of labor. If property prices in coastal regions are not considered, then the real income level and welfare of skilled labor or workers are both higher than inland regions. This implies that pecuniary externalities positively push forward the increase in regional income levels. We now consider the relationship between interregional income gaps and large geographical scale industry agglomeration under the following two situations[4]: first, barriers to the inflow of inland skilled labor to coastal regions are small, while there are barriers to the inflow of low-skilled labor to coastal regions. This situation is quite close to China's reality. At this moment, relatively high pecuniary externalities only benefit local workers in the coastal regions and non-local skilled workers that have migrated into the coastal regions, as their real wage levels including social security are higher, while non-local low-skilled labor cannot equally enjoy social security benefits such as retirement and health, etc. At this point, interregional income gaps expand; second, there are no barriers at all to the interregional mobility of low-skilled labor. Under this ideal condition, with even a slight difference in real wage levels including social security between regions, labor in regions with lower real wage levels will erase this difference through interregional migration, which will narrow interregional income gaps. This is to say, originally existing interregional pecuniary externality differences can be narrowed through the migration of low-skilled labor, and then narrowing interregional income level gaps (for details, see below).

Furthermore, through what kind of mechanism do pecuniary externalities influence wage levels? Through what channels do labor mobility impact pecuniary externalities? That is to say, through what kinds of mechanism do labor mobility and pecuniary externalities influence wage levels? The question can be answered by constructing a real market potential (RMP in short) indicator (see next section for details).

8.3.2 Model of relationship between large geographical scale industry agglomeration and interregional income GDP gaps

Here we will describe a theoretical framework from the perspective of demand and supply. (Readers unfamiliar with mathematical notation can skip this section.)

8.3.2.1 Demand perspective

Here, we use the Dixit–Stiglitz–Krugman monopolistic competition model (Fujita et al., 1999, Ch. 4). In this theoretical model, it is assumed that the consumer utility function is double-layered in the Cobb–Douglas form: $U = M^{\mu} A^{1-\mu}$, where M represents manufactured goods; A represents agricultural goods; and μ represents the expenditure share of manufactured goods. Assume E_j is the consumption expenditure of region j on a typical manufacturing industry (e.g. automobiles).

For differentiated manufactured goods, consumers choose all sorts of differentiated varieties, the elasticity of substitution between different varieties is fixed and represented with σ. This coefficient is usually larger than 1 and the closer to 1 it is, the more differentiated manufacturing goods are. The expenditure for a consumer in region *j* on a typical manufactured variety produced in region *i* is:

$$p_{ij}x_{ij} = \frac{p_{ij}^{1-\sigma}}{\sum_k n_k p_{kj}^{1-\sigma}} E_j \tag{8.1}$$

where p_{ij} is the price a consumer in region *j* pays for a manufactured good produced in region *i*, which is the product between region *i*'s factory price p_i and T_{ij}, the transport cost between region *i* and *j*, n_k is the number of differentiated varieties in the representative industry imported from region *k*. If the representative industries are expanded to all varieties of that industry, assume the number of varieties in that industry is n_i, then the amount of trade between regions *i* and *j* for that industry is:

$$n_i p_{ij} x_{ij} = n_i p_i^{1-\sigma} T_{ij}^{1-\sigma} E_j G_j^{\sigma-1} \tag{8.2}$$

where, the price index for manufactured goods in region *j* is $G_j = [\sum_{k=1}^{R} n_k p_{kj}^{1-\sigma}]^{\frac{1}{1-\sigma}}$, at the same time, assume all major manufacturing industries are symmetric, then the price index for all manufactured goods in region *j* is also $G_j = [\sum_{k=1}^{R} n_k p_{kj}^{1-\sigma}]^{\frac{1}{1-\sigma}}$.

Starting from Equation (8.1), for a representative firm in region *i*, the demand it faces is the product between the amount demanded by all consumers in region *j* and transport cost T_{ij}, and adding up all *j* regions that conduct trade with it:

$$x_i = \sum_{k=1}^{R} x_{ij} T_{ij} = \sum_{k=1}^{R} (p_{ij} T_{ij})^{-\sigma} E_j G_j^{\sigma-1} T_{ij} = p_i^{-\sigma} RMP_i \tag{8.3}$$

Where RMP_i equals $\sum_{j=1}^{R} T_{ij}^{1-\sigma} E_j G_j^{\sigma-1}$, that is, in terms of the demand for the major categories of the industry's goods, the sum of the demand from all regions *j* for region *i*'s products forms the real market potential of that industry in region *i*. The real market potential for region *i* includes two components: first, the interregional transport cost $T_{ij}^{1-\sigma}$, which reflects the geographical distance or artificial trade barriers between regions; second, the market capacity $E_j G_j^{\sigma-1}$, which reflects the purchasing power E_j and manufactured goods price index $G_j^{\sigma-1}$ of all *j* regions, $G_j^{\sigma-1}$ is then closely related to the differentiation of manufactured goods σ and interregional transport costs. Therefore, real market potential actually reflects the market size of region *i* including indicators such as geographical factors and elasticity of substitution. It differs from the nominal market potential in the Harris (1954) sense. The latter is only the weighted sums of purchasing power E_j and inversed geographical distance, which do not reflect the manufactured goods price index $G_j^{\sigma-1}$ that has real *New Economic Geography* implications.

8.3.2.2 Supply perspective

Based on the assumption of increasing returns to scale for individual firms, from the firms' supply perspective, a typical region *i* firm's profit function is:

$$\pi_i = p_i x_i - w_i \left[F + c_i x_i \right] \tag{8.4}$$

Where $p_i x_i$ represents a typical firm's income level, of which x_i is the firm's output level. Below, we will focus on elaborating the firm's production function. Due to the assumption of increasing returns to scale at the firm level, establishment of any factory requires a fixed initial input of labor, set as F (here we only consider the skilled labor factor input, as we assume low-skilled labor cannot move across regions). When x_i units of goods are produced, a cost of $w_i \left[F + c_i x_i \right]$ occurs.

According to the optimal pricing strategy for monopolistically competitive firms $p_i = w_i c_i \dfrac{\sigma}{\sigma - 1}$, and since monopolistically competitive firms have zero economic profits [let Equation (8.4) be equal to 0], we can obtain the equilibrium output level:

$$x_i^* = F \frac{\sigma - 1}{c_i} \tag{8.5}$$

Combining the firm's optimal pricing strategy, equilibrium output level [Equation (8.5)] and the demand the firm in region *i* faces [Equation (8.3)], we can obtain the wages a firm is willing to pay at equilibrium:

$$w_i = \frac{\sigma - 1}{c_i \sigma} \left[RMP_i \frac{c_i}{F(\sigma - 1)} \right]^{\frac{1}{\sigma}} \tag{8.6}$$

The above equation shows the wage a region's worker can receive at equilibrium is affected by the real market potential on the right side of the equation. Thus, we have established the theoretical relationship between real market potential and wages.[5] Current research on the relationship between large geographical scale industry agglomeration and wages all originate from Equation (8.6). For example, Fan and Zhang (2009) and Liu et al. (2007, 2008).

In the above theoretical model, we perceive pecuniary externalities as the size of real market potential, and this is how they affect wage levels. It still needs to be explained in detail what the relationship between mobility of skilled labor, mobility of low-skilled labor and real market potential is. Again, we will make a theoretical explanation for two cases:

First, mobility of skilled labor is unrestricted and mobility of low-skilled labor is restricted. The restricted mobility of low-skilled labor here is relative, and only means that relative to the mobility of low-skilled labor, the mobility of skilled labor is not as sensitive to welfare such as pensions, healthcare, offspring education etc. If inland skilled labor and low-skilled labor both flow into coastal regions, then in terms of the composition of RMP, inflow of skilled labor more effectively increases the level of expenditures E relative to low-skilled labor, thereby quickly enhancing the RMP of coastal regions; if we take one step backwards and consider a more realistic situation in which the inflow of low-skilled labor is constrained by interregional labor market segmentations, then more of the coastal regions' real market potential spillover will be enjoyed by local workers, and the interregional wage level and other forms of income level gaps will all expand. This is exactly China's reality and is dubbed "price adjustment of the labor factor" in theory (Head and Mayer, 2006).

Second, mobility of skilled and low-skilled labor is unrestricted for both. We will focus on the case of unrestricted low-skilled labor mobility, which is to say, low-skilled labor is perfectly elastic and highly sensitive to interregional wage gaps. Here, interregional wage and RMP gaps could be eliminated through the mobility of low-skilled labor, interregional income gaps will be narrowed to the greatest extent. If we consider the equation for RMP, inflow of low-skilled labor to the coastal region will cause the price index for manufactured goods in that region G_i to decline rapidly (Fujita et al., 1999), effectively cancelling out any increment in expenditures E_i that are relatively slower to change. This is known in theory as "quantitative adjustment" (Head and Mayer, 2006). Its real world implication is that coastal region urban labor market discrimination and segmentation should be eliminated.

8.4 Large geographical scale industry agglomeration and interregional wage gaps: comprehensive review based on empirical research

8.4.1 Regional differences in real market potential

By employing Equation (8.3) and the data on 1997 interregional trade volumes, we can obtain the average real market potential for all regions by calculating the market potential for each prefectural level municipality (see Table 8.2). Combined with the previous section's industry distribution, we can more readily understand the regional differences in real market potential: the average real market potential of eastern coastal and southern coastal regions is evidently higher than that of other regions, respectively reaching 0.072 and 0.055; the second level is Jingjin and northern coastal regions, respectively 0.032 and 0.028; the third level is the central region at 0.024; the fourth level is the northeastern, northwestern, and southwestern regions at around 0.019. At the same time, according to the source of real market potential, it can be divided into intraregional internal urban demand, intraregional demand from other cities, demand from other domestic regions, and foreign demand. In terms of absolute value and proportion, other cities in the local region account for most of the region's real market potential.

Table 8.2 1997 RMP average value and composition for eight major regions

Region	*RMP*	*Composition of RMP (absolute value)*				*Share of composition of RMP (%)*			
		Internal	*Intraregional*	*Other regions*	*Foreign*	*Internal*	*Intraregional*	*Other regions*	*Foreign*
National	0.03252	0.00689	0.02025	0.00354	0.00179	21.2	62.3	10.9	5.5
Northeastern	0.01947	0.00442	0.01228	0.00194	0.00083	18.7	65.6	10.8	4.9
Jingjin	0.03194	0.01921	0.00616	0.00321	0.00336	60	19.4	10.1	10.5
Northern coastal	0.02869	0.00721	0.01508	0.00311	0.0033	23.3	53.4	11.4	12
Eastern coastal	0.07249	0.01848	0.04841	0.00244	0.00315	21.3	69.9	3.9	4.9
Southern coastal	0.05547	0.01299	0.03745	0.00206	0.00296	20.2	68.9	4.5	6.4
Central	0.02376	0.00437	0.01547	0.00315	0.00076	17.3	65.6	13.8	3.3
Southwestern	0.01763	0.00454	0.0098	0.00256	0.00073	23	57.1	15.5	4.4
Northwestern	0.0192	0.00676	0.00929	0.00235	0.0008	29.2	51.1	14.5	5.2

Data source: Estimated with data from 1997 "China Interregional Input Output Model" (National Information Center, 2005). For details see Fan, Gao, and Zhang (2010).

In Table 8.2, judging from the aggregate values, there is an obvious division among the eight major domestic regions: the first level is the eastern coastal and southern coastal regions, where ample real market potential is induced by demand from intraregional core cities and other cities in the region, which forms a significant agglomeration effect in these two coastal regions. The second level is northern coastal and Jingjin region. As for the Jingjin region, Beijing is still the political and cultural capital of China, while Tianjin had not yet shown itself as a northern economic center in 1997; at the same time, market potential induced by other cities within the region in the northern coastal region was too small at only 0.015, significantly lower than the 0.04 level of eastern coastal or southern coastal regions. Thus, the agglomeration effect reflected as division of labor, coordination and matching had not yet formed among prefectural level cities in this region. The third level is the central region, slightly lower than northern coastal and Jingjin regions but higher than the western and northeastern regions. Market potential induced by demand from cities themselves is lowest in this region, only 0.00437, a proportion of 17.3 percent, which is also the lowest. Thus the large cities within this region are seriously underdeveloped; whereas the market potential induced by demand from other cities in the region, which best reflects agglomeration effects, is also significantly lower than eastern coastal and southern coastal regions, but is level with the northern coastal regions. The fourth level is the northeastern, northwestern and southwestern regions, the pecuniary externalities of which are between 0.017 and 0.019, market potential induced by demand from the developmental level of large cities themselves is at a low level as well; meanwhile, the measure of the agglomeration effect within a region—market potential induced by demand from other cities within a region is at around 0.009–0.012, the lowest nationwide.

8.4.2 Real market potential and interregional wage gaps

The previous section of this chapter was mainly based on the authors' past research, which narrated the descriptive evidence and generation mechanism for large geographical scale industry agglomeration and its impact on interregional income gaps. From such a narrative, we can observe that although there has been interprovincial spatial dispersion of industry, starting in 2004, the coastal regions are still the core region where industry is distributed; meanwhile, we divided labor into the interregional mobility of skilled labor and low-skilled labor and illustrated the different influencing mechanisms through which industry agglomeration impacts interregional income gaps created by the difference in their mobility. Here we will continue the aforementioned descriptive evidence and theoretical mechanisms and will continue to provide empirical evidence of industry agglomeration on interregional income levels through a narrative. The course and main content of the narrative will include: first comprehensively reviewing existing *New Economic Geography* literature through such aspects as definition of market potential, econometric methods, the magnitude of econometric results, etc., and commenting on existing literature and proposing outlooks on present and future research.

8.4.2.1 Different definitions of market potential

According to a literature review, only the following four domestic studies have tried applying Equation (8.6) to conduct empirical analysis, Fan and Zhang (2009), Liu, He, and Yin (2007), Liu and Yin (2008), and Hering and Poncet (2010), respectively (see Table 8.3 for details). Of these studies, Fan and Zhang (2009) and Hering and Poncet (2010) used Redding and Venables' (2004) approach as a source of reference, estimating the real market potential of each city on the basis of the trade gravity model. Whereas Liu et al. (2007, 2008) estimated nominal market potential using Harris's (1954) definition to represent the degree of large geographical scale industry agglomeration.[6] Real market potential and nominal market potential differ in two aspects: first, the distance index as defined in nominal market potential is −1, whereas the distance index as defined in real market potential is obtained through a trade gravity model regression, normally ranging between −0.5 and −0.95; second, nominal market potential cannot include regional price indices and substitution elasticities, whereas real market potential can be rigorously derived from the trade gravity model, including regional price indices and something similar to price substitution elasticity coefficients among between products, thus the nominal market potential equation is intuitive and does not have a solid theoretical foundation.

Here, we need to compare and explain the real market potential calculation method by Fan and Zhang (2009) and Hering and Poncet (2010). Although both of these studies use Redding and Venables (2004) as their source of reference, significant differences remain.

First, data source difference: Fan and Zhang's trade figures come from the "1997 interregional input output model" published in 2005, which divides China into eight major regions and 17 industries. The trade figures are divided by "industry × region", which makes them bidirectional. Hering and Poncet (2010) used trade data for 23 provinces in 1997, the drawback of which is the data being one-way, with no trade data by industry. At the same time, there are no figures on trade volumes from each province to other provinces in the data. They employed Wei's (1996) approach: intraprovincial trade data is obtained by subtracting a province's total exports (including exports overseas and exports beyond the province) from its total output, while data on exports beyond the province is indirectly estimated from relevant unpublished figures from the Ministry of Foreign Trade and Economic Cooperation. Given that most of the figures used by Hering and Poncet are estimated, errors are more likely to occur.

Second, real market potential differences obtained from the trade gravity model. The basis for calculating real market potential is the estimators for distance and frontier effects. The frontier effects obtained by Hering and Poncet (2010) are equivalent to a 54 percent implied tariff rate between provinces. Such a level is equivalent to that of tariffs between early EU member countries, thus they propose that there is a risk China is heading toward "disintegration" internally. The frontier effect obtained by Fan and Zhang is equivalent to an implied tariff rate of 28 percent, far lower than the former.

Table 8.3 List of empirical studies on large geographical scale industry agglomeration

Study	*Variables and econometric method*			*Data and level of research*	*Main conclusions*
	Dependent variable	*Independent variable*	*Econometric method*		
Fan and Zhang (2009)	1998 and 1999 prefectural level municipality employee wage	1997 real market potential (trade gravity model)	Wage variable lagged 1–2 years; regional fixed effects; check for robustness according to real market potential in different groups	Prefectural level city; "1997 China interregional input output model," "China City Statistical Yearbook"	Pecuniary externalities: +, elasticity coefficient of real market potential at 0.22–0.32
Liu, He and Yin (2007)	Prefectural level wages	Nominal market potential	Sum of distance inversed as instrument variable, 2SLS	Prefectural level city, "China City Statistical Yearbook," panel data	Pecuniary externalities: +, elasticity coefficient of nominal market potential 0.61
Liu and Yin (2008)	Prefectural level wages	Nominal market potential	System GMM, first order autoregression	Prefectural level city, "China City Statistical Yearbook," panel data	Pecuniary externalities: +, elasticity coefficient of nominal market potential 0.9
Li and Huang (2006)	TFP for each province	Nominal market potential	OLS, annual fixed effects	Provincial level data for time points 1982,1990, and 1998	Pecuniary externalities: insignificant
Hering and Poncet (2010)	CHIP wages	Municipality-level real market potential (trade gravity model)	Sum of distance inversed as instrument variable, 2SLS	Wages at household level, CHIP data; municipal level real market potential	Pecuniary externalities: +, elasticity coefficient of real market potential 0.06

8.4.2.2 Different econometric methods

Given that simultaneity or omitted variable endogeneity exists between market potential and wage levels, errors in the market potential coefficient are hard to avoid. The aforementioned studies have all considered this issue and employed different methods to deal with it. For example, Liu et al. (2007) and Hering and Poncet (2010) both employed instrument variables, which were the sum of inversed distances from each city to other cities, as the sum of inversed distances for each city is exogenous relative to the city's wage level, while relative to the city's market potential, it implies intrinsic geographical factors. It needs to be explained that Hering and Poncet's (2010) approach to dealing with distance is more rigorous. They divided the whole world into 11,700 squares, one of the conditions being that only cities with more than two persons per square kilometer are enlisted into "other cites." Liu and Yin (2008) employed another method to control the endogeneity issue. They used a dynamic first order autoregression to perform a two-step system GMM estimation. Fan and Zhang (2009) did not use instrument variables and instead adopted the measure of lagging real market potential by 1–2 years, or respectively testing real market potential according to its source, or controlling for province fixed effects.

8.4.2.3 Different econometric results

The four aforementioned representative studies obtained largely varying market potential coefficients. The coefficient obtained for nominal market potential ranged between 0.6 and 0.9 (Liu et al., 2007, 2008), while Fan and Zhang (2009) obtained real market potential coefficients ranging between 0.22 and 0.32. Hering and Poncet (2010) obtained coefficients that only ranged from 0.05 and 0.10. We have no means by which to comment on which result is better or worse, but Redding and Venable's econometric result for 101 countries ranged from 0.15–0.25. We believe that the variation in the four results is mainly closely related to the choice of nominal market potential and real market potential as coefficients for real market potential are apparently lower than that of nominal market potential. Although Liu et al. employed GMM methods to perform regressions, which can achieve more consistent estimations, they still only obtain the impact of nominal market potential on wages. If the coefficient estimation induced by the choice of explanatory variables errs is on the high side, it cannot be corrected by using the GMM method.

8.4.3 Outlook on the study of large geographical scale industry agglomeration and interregional income gaps

As Liang and Qian (2007) put it, research on the endogenous interactive relationship between pecuniary externalities and industry agglomeration has relatively mature theoretical foundations, and a number of good empirical studies have emerged. Most empirical studies are based on the classic *New Economic*

Geography wage equation [Equation (8.6) here], and due to the application of different econometric methods, the market potential coefficients obtained differ as well. Thus, we believe that empirical research on large geographical scale industry agglomeration may go further in the following several directions:

1. Extending *New Economic Geography* theory to new trade theory and new-new trade theory, applying abundant Chinese interregional trade data or other data to empirically test relevant statements. For example, Fan and Xie (2010) applied the trade volume data from the Chinese interregional input output model for each industry to test for existence of new trade theory's Home Market Effects. We believe that, new–new trade theory could totally be used to test the validity of the relationship between firms' self-selection and survival of the fittest abilities and regional productivity. Such research could also delve deeper.
2. A question that is more closely related to this chapter is: does large geographical scale industry agglomeration only impact on wages and not the total factor productivity of the region? Does this statement only suit China's circumstances, not foreign circumstances? Since judging from the relevant foreign literature, higher productivity is often reflected in compensation for the labor factor—wages are higher, so interregional income gaps are also closely related to productivity (or total factor productivity). However, China's circumstances are unique as the economy at the county level is developed under a fiscally decentralized system, county-level governments are relatively strong, and each local government endeavors to attract business and capital to develop manufacturing in pursuit of GDP growth, to the extent that the industrial structure of most country-level economies are mainly composed of manufacturing. Similarly, in the county-level economies of coastal regions, each county-level economy has a large market potential, but due to deficient economies of scale and regional protectionism factors, drawbacks such as low production efficiency and environmental degradation are exhibited. Thus, Li, and Huang (2006) also proved that nominal market potential does not have positive facilitating effects on the total factor productivity in each province. In this sense, there is still a long way to go in the current stage in transforming the mode of economic growth and pursuing scientific development.
3. How does large geographical scale industry agglomeration research experience better serve policy research? For example, can interregional balanced development and major function-oriented zone planning be linked to large geographical scale industry agglomeration? Fan, Gao, and Zhang (2010) equated real market potential with spatial efficiency and found that the spatial efficiency of the eight major domestic regions varied significantly, further pointing out that the current regional balance policy with balanced regional development as its main content may lose accumulated spatial efficiency. However, some sort of relationship must exist between major function-oriented zone planning and large geographical scale industry agglomeration. The mechanism that connects the two awaits deeper research.

8.5 Descriptive evidence on small geographical scale industry agglomeration

The description here on small geographical scale industry agglomeration is mainly used for application toward the Theil index at the prefectural municipality level and application toward the industry EG index and industry Gini coefficient of county-level economies (see Appendix for composition of indicators). All data comes from the micro-level database on above-scale industrial firms collected and edited by the National Bureau of Statistics. The indicator under calculation is firm value-add and all cited calculation results here were obtained by the authors themselves.

8.5.1 Theil index

We employ the value-added indicator from the micro-level database on above-scale Chinese industrial firms. First, we calculate the national average Theil index value at the prefectural municipality level, and then we dissect the prefectural municipality level Theil index into two parts: interprovincial Theil index and intraprovincial Theil index for each city (see Table 8.4 for calculation results). Third, we eliminate the coastal regions' prefectural level municipalities and focus only on the distribution of manufacturing in cities within the central and western regions in order to compare the relative inequity of manufacturing distribution between cities in coastal regions and cities in central and western regions. Finally, in order to draw on international experience as a reference, we list the Theil index values of the distribution of manufacturing across cities in France at three time points, of which 1930 could roughly be thought to be equivalent to China's current mid-industrialization phase.

We can observe the following characteristics: (1) The Theil index between nationwide prefectural level cities is at a relatively low level overall, with a 0.43 average between 1998 and 2007. In comparison, the Theil index for French manufacturing distribution was 0.93 during mid-industrialization in 1930 and 0.50 during post-industrialization in 2000. (2) Dissecting nationwide prefectural level cities' Theil index into unequal distribution between interprovincial and intraprovincial prefectural cities produces interesting phenomenon: the intraprovincial Theil index is always lower than the interprovincial Theil index, with an average of only 0.20, accounting for 47.1 percent of the overall national Theil index. As a comparison, the French intraprovincial Theil index in 1930 and 2000 was respectively 0.62 and 0.33, and its corresponding contribution to the overall Theil index 67.7 percent and 66 percent, respectively. (3) If non-coastal prefectural level and above cities are separately listed, although their Theil index only averages at 0.37, it clearly contrasts with the national level Theil index in that the internal Theil index (Tw) for non-coastal regions, whether in absolute value terms or contribution share terms, is always larger than the nationwide intraprovincial Theil index, averaging 0.22 and 59.22 percent, respectively. This implies that the distribution between cities within the non-coastal regions is even more varied, whereas a

Table 8.4 Evolution of manufacturing distribution at prefectural level and above municipality during 1998–2008 (Theil index)

Year	*T*	*Tb*	*Tw*	*Tb (100%)*	*Tw (100%)*
Nationwide prefectural level and above cities					
1998	0.415	0.232	0.183	55.9	44.1
1999	0.414	0.206	0.208	49.8	50.2
2000	0.428	0.22	0.208	51.4	48.6
2001	0.446	0.238	0.208	53.4	46.6
2002	0.435	0.226	0.209	52	48
2003	0.449	0.239	0.21	53.2	46.8
2004	0.464	0.248	0.216	53.4	46.6
2005	0.439	0.234	0.205	53.3	46.7
2006	0.419	0.226	0.194	53.9	46.1
2007	0.393	0.206	0.187	52.4	47.6
Average	0.43	0.2275	0.2	52.9	47.1
Non-coastal prefectural level and above cities					
1998	0.362	0.141	0.222	38.8	61.2
1999	0.358	0.142	0.216	39.7	60.3
2000	0.387	0.153	0.234	39.5	60.5
2001	0.379	0.157	0.223	41.3	58.7
2002	0.375	0.153	0.222	40.7	59.3
2003	0.371	0.149	0.222	40.2	59.8
2004	0.38	0.163	0.216	43	57
2005	0.357	0.147	0.21	41.1	58.9
2006	0.345	0.145	0.2	42	58
2007	0.344	0.143	0.201	41.5	58.5
Average	0.37	0.15	0.22	40.78	59.22
Between French cities					
1860	0.6	0.29	0.4	48.3	51.7
1930	0.93	0.3	0.62	32.3	67.7
2000	0.5	0.17	0.33	34	66

Note: Theil index calculation results and equations for French manufacturing all come from Combes et al. (2008). Tb represents interprovincial Theil index between cities and Tw represents intraprovincial Theil index between cities.

Data source: Author's calculations based on "Micro-level data on above-scale Chinese industrial firms" (National Bureau of Statistics, historical data).

flattening characteristic is evident in the coastal regions. Therefore, we believe that China's manufacturing, relative to France in the same development phase, is rather equal in its distribution between prefectural level cities, especially among prefectural level cities within provinces in the coastal regions.

8.5.2 EG index

We will use the EG index (see Appendix for details) here to analyze the unequal distribution of manufacturing at the county-level economy. The calculation results

Table 8.5 Weighted average county-level EG index's trend of change (1998–2007)

	Two-digit manufacturing industries and county-level	*Four-digit manufacturing industries and county-level*
1998	0.0021	0.0087
1999	0.0021	0.0077
2000	0.0026	0.0088
2001	0.0028	0.009
2002	0.0031	0.0106
2003	0.0042	0.0158
2004	0.0038	0.0125
2005	0.0038	0.0121
2006	0.0036	0.0125
2007	0.0031	0.0119

Note: Weights equal each industry's proportion of national industrial value-add, the method for weight averaging EG indices, see Lu and Tao (2009).
Data source: Author's calculations based on "Micro-level data on above-scale Chinese industrial firms" (National Bureau of Statistics, historical data).

are in Table 8.5 and Table 8.6. It can be clearly observed that the level of manufacturing agglomeration in country-level economies is rather low. Generally speaking, for four-digit manufacturing industries, an EG value below 0.02 at the county-level is thought to be a low agglomeration level (Elisson and Glaeser, 1997; Lu and Tao, 2009). In our study period, the weighted average EG index value for four-digit manufacturing at the county level did not exceed 0.02, the highest value being 0.0158 in 2003. Next, viewing the time trends changed for the EG index for four-digit manufacturing at the county level, 2003 is an obvious turning point; from 1998–2003, the EG index gradually increased at all levels, showing that the degree of regional agglomeration gradually strengthened for manufacturing during 1998–2003; but after 2003, the EG index's trend reversed.

In order to make international comparisons more convenient, we calculated the percentage of low, medium and high agglomeration industries for four-digit manufacturing industries at county-level (Table 8.6) and made comparisons with existing literature. The basic conclusion still is, relative to foreign developed countries, the degree of agglomeration for Chinese manufacturing at the county-level is still obviously at the low end, which is wholly consistent with Lu and Tao's (2009) conclusion. Of course, direct comparisons may be improper, as the following factors may be come into play: first, the EG index used to measure manufacturing distribution in international literature varies, e.g. Maurel and Sedillot (1999) and Devereux et al. (2004) employed an agglomeration index different from the EG index created by Ellison and Glaeser (1997); Lu and Tao (2009) as well as this text employed the EG index in Ellison and Glaeser (1997). Next, due to differences in the division of data according to year, industry and region, even if it is an agglomeration indicator for Chinese manufacturing, the one used in this text has slightly different industry classifications than that in Lu and Tao (2009).

Table 8.6 Comparison of EG index of county-level, four-digit manufacturing industries and values from existing studies

Study	*Country*	*Year*	*Industry*	*Region*	*Calculated object*	*Proportion of low agglomeration industries (%)*	*Proportion of medium agglomeration industries (%)*	*Proportion of high agglomeration industries (%)*
This Chapter	China	1998	478 4-digit industries	2,921 counties (districts)	Industrial value-add	80.13	13.18	6.69
	China	1999	481 4-digit industries	2,932 counties (districts)	Industrial value-add	82.95	11.23	5.82
	China	2000	482 4-digit industries	2,895 counties (districts)	Industrial value-add	81.57	10.14	8.28
	China	2001	472 4-digit industries	2,876 counties (districts)	Industrial value-add	80.08	10.38	9.53
	China	2002	482 4-digit industries	2,806 counties (districts)	Industrial value-add	81.12	10.37	8.51
	China	2003	482 4-digit industries	2,852 counties (districts)	Industrial value-add	78.22	13.90	7.88
	China	2004	482 4-digit industries	2,745 counties (districts)	Industrial value-add	76.14	15.35	8.51
	China	2005	482 4-digit industries	2,767 counties (districts)	Industrial value-add	76.56	15.35	8.09
	China	2006	482 4-digit industries	2,802 counties (districts)	Industrial value-add	75.31	14.52	10.17
	China	2007	482 4-digit industries	2,837 counties (districts)	Industrial value-add	73.86	16.60	9.54
Lu and Tao (2009)	China	2003	539 4-digit industries	3,142 counties (districts)	Employed persons	78.48	13.17	8.35
Ellison and Glaeser (1997)	US	1987	459 4-digit industries	3,000 counties	Employed persons	10.00	65.00	25.00
Maurel and Sedillot (1999)	France	1993	273 4-digit industries	95 counties	Employed persons	50.00	23.00	27.00
Devereux et al. (2004)	UK	1992	211 4-digit industries	113 postal zones	Employed persons	65.00	19.00	16.00

Low, medium, and high agglomeration industries, respectively, refer to industries with $EG<0.02$, $0.02 \leq EG<0.05$ and $EG \geq 0.05$ (Ellison and Glaeser, 1997); this text refers to Lu and Tao (2009).

8.5.3 Gini coefficient

From the large regional scale perspective, even though in 2004 a turning point and a trend toward dispersion to the central regions emerged in manufacturing location distribution, manufacturing is quite unbalanced in its distribution overall and the advantages for concentrating in the coastal regions are still evident (Wang et al., 2010). Then, if the region under study shifts from the provincial level to the county level, what will the location distribution of manufacturing look like? We calculated the Gini coefficients for two-digit and four-digit manufacturing industries at the county level and weight averaged the coefficients according to each industry's share of total value-add by all industries (see Table 8.7). Looking at the calculation results: (1) county-level Gini coefficients are at a high level, the Gini coefficient for two-digit and four-digit industries reaching 0.81 and 0.91 respectively, which reflects the fact that among 2,800 counties nationwide, the distribution of manufacturing industries is highly unbalanced and most industries may be concentrated in very few counties; (2) looking at the static trend, there has been no obvious trend in the county-level Gini coefficient and no turning point has appeared in any year, which differs from the 2004 turning point observed in large regional or provincial level industry agglomeration; however, there is an exception: the Gini coefficient was significantly lower in 2007 than in 2006 as well as the years before, as the two-digit industry coefficient fell from 0.80 in 2006 to 0.78 and the four-digit industry coefficient fell from 0.91 in 2006 to 0.82. (3) Relevant to the findings here, the results in Table 8.4 and Fan and Shao (2011) both found that in terms of the location distribution reflected by the aggregate output of all prefectural municipalities and manufacturing industries, the distribution of manufacturing between prefectural cities is rather equal, its Theil index value averaging 0.43 between 1998–2007; this reminds us that if we add up the output of all manufacturing industries and then look at its spatial distribution, distribution of manufacturing at the county level should be rather equal, resulting in the flattening of urban systems (Fan and Shao, 2011). Combined with the results above, and given that county level is a rather low regional level, we can infer that specialized production in manufacturing is at a rather high level in county-level economies.

If we consider the Gini coefficients in Table 8.7 in each two-digit industry, we get the results shown in Table 8.8. On the whole, the Gini coefficient for most industries is between 0.70 and 0.80, proving again the unbalanced distribution of manufacturing at the county level, and to a certain extent implies that the degree of specialization is rather high at the county level. Whereas only food processing industry and nonmetallic minerals industry have Gini coefficients below 0.7, as the location of these two industries severely rely on the local supply of agricultural products or nonmetallic minerals and the inputs are only suitable for short distance transportation. Industries with Gini coefficients above 0.9 include tobacco, chemical fiber, communications, computer and other electronic equipment, and waste management.

Table 8.7 Weighted average of county-level industry Gini coefficient (1998–2007)

	1998	*1999*	*2000*	*2001*	*2002*	*2003*	*2004*	*2005*	*2006*	*2007*	*Average of all years*
Weighted average for 2-digit industries	0.821	0.817	0.82	0.825	0.821	0.824	0.819	0.809	0.803	0.784	0.814
Weighted average for 4-digit industries	0.943	0.927	0.928	0.87	0.927	0.928	0.918	0.915	0.912	0.818	0.909

Note: Weights for calculating the weighted average Gini coefficient for all industries equal each industry's proportion of national industrial value-add.
Data source: Author's calculations based on "Micro-level data on above-scale Chinese industrial firms" (National Bureau of Statistics, historical data).

Table 8.8 Two-digit industry county-level Gini coefficient and changes (1998–2007)

Industry	*1998*	*1999*	*2000*	*2001*	*2002*	*2003*	*2004*	*2005*	*2006*	*2007*
Food processing	0.609	0.618	0.602	0.615	0.619	0.62	0.614	0.606	0.599	0.59
Food manufacturing	0.749	0.741	0.748	0.747	0.745	0.742	0.725	0.724	0.709	0.69
Beverages	0.745	0.742	0.746	0.751	0.759	0.76	0.738	0.738	0.716	0.688
Tobacco	0.972	0.971	0.971	0.975	0.974	0.974	0.976	0.978	0.981	0.984
Textiles	0.791	0.783	0.777	0.788	0.786	0.78	0.79	0.782	0.78	0.765
Apparel and fiber products	0.868	0.859	0.859	0.862	0.855	0.86	0.862	0.856	0.857	0.831
Leather, fur and feather products	0.859	0.865	0.866	0.876	0.869	0.872	0.863	0.857	0.857	0.842
Wood processing and related products	0.792	0.784	0.784	0.776	0.75	0.742	0.711	0.692	0.684	0.669
Furniture	0.89	0.877	0.876	0.881	0.872	0.88	0.879	0.877	0.874	0.853
Paper and paper products	0.734	0.741	0.746	0.759	0.755	0.766	0.759	0.761	0.765	0.748
Printing and packaging	0.82	0.821	0.831	0.829	0.823	0.824	0.83	0.817	0.818	0.796
Sports and cultural equipment	0.941	0.933	0.929	0.932	0.921	0.919	0.918	0.912	0.908	0.882
Oil refining	0.945	0.942	0.943	0.935	0.926	0.915	0.88	0.863	0.861	0.85
Chemicals	0.718	0.709	0.726	0.725	0.72	0.732	0.737	0.715	0.71	0.695
Pharmaceuticals	0.8	0.784	0.781	0.769	0.762	0.752	0.74	0.733	0.725	0.706
Chemical fiber	0.947	0.944	0.94	0.925	0.921	0.932	0.924	0.923	0.926	0.928
Rubber products	0.88	0.865	0.86	0.867	0.863	0.868	0.869	0.869	0.861	0.844
Plastics	0.837	0.836	0.841	0.84	0.839	0.835	0.837	0.821	0.816	0.795
Non-metallic minerals	0.633	0.627	0.625	0.64	0.618	0.62	0.638	0.636	0.631	0.622
Ferrous metals metallurgy	0.883	0.885	0.88	0.874	0.865	0.868	0.84	0.836	0.828	0.811
Non-ferrous metals metallurgy	0.835	0.816	0.821	0.858	0.794	0.791	0.762	0.761	0.752	0.72
Metals products	0.82	0.821	0.817	0.82	0.817	0.825	0.828	0.816	0.812	0.796
General equipment manufacturing	0.799	0.796	0.792	0.799	0.793	0.801	0.806	0.796	0.788	0.778
Specialty equipment manufacturing	0.783	0.782	0.783	0.796	0.778	0.785	0.802	0.791	0.786	0.778
Transportation equipment	0.864	0.854	0.848	0.857	0.859	0.864	0.845	0.834	0.831	0.827
Electrical equipment	0.864	0.863	0.87	0.874	0.872	0.869	0.876	0.869	0.864	0.841
Communications, computer and other electronic equipment	0.948	0.94	0.943	0.944	0.943	0.949	0.951	0.952	0.95	0.929
Instruments and office supplies machinery	0.929	0.917	0.92	0.916	0.912	0.921	0.917	0.911	0.911	0.881
Handicraft	0.829	0.824	0.823	0.833	0.825	0.834	0.83	0.818	0.816	0.805
Waste management	0.999	0.999	0.997	0.996	0.995	0.983	0.962	0.953	0.95	0.934

Data source: Author's calculations based on "Micro-level database for above-scale Chinese industrial firms" (National Bureau of Statistics, historical data).

Comprehensively, manufacturing distribution measured at the prefectural municipality level with the Theil index is rather equal, and measured at the county level with the EG index is rather equal as well, but manufacturing distribution measured with the Gini coefficient at the county level is very unbalanced, which actually realistically measure agglomeration from multiple angles for all manufacturing industries in small geographical scales. We believe that the conclusions from the three indices above are not contradictory. The results from Theil index aggregate the output of all manufacturing industries at prefecture level, while the results of the EG index at county level deducted the size of individual firms.

8.6 Impact of small geographical scale industry agglomeration: empirical analytic framework and literature review

8.6.1 Empirical analytic framework

How can we describe the impact of technological externalities produced by small geographical scale agglomeration at low regional levels on economic growth and production efficiency? Considering China's realities, the current extensive mode of economic growth and economic structure adjustment are both closely related to the technological externalities produced by small geographical scale industry agglomeration, thus empirical research on technological externalities has stronger policy implications relative to the pecuniary externalities produced by large geographical scale industry agglomeration. In neoclassical growth models, technological progress is like a black box, whereas technological externalities are an important path to uncovering this black box at a rather low regional level.

We define technological externalities as a technological shift in the firm production function. Under the Hicks neutrality assumption,[7] the firm production function can be written as $y_j{=}g(A_j)f(x_j)$, where x_j is the factor input vector, A_j depicts the external environment faced by firms, $g(A_j)$ is the impact of an agglomerated environment on firm production output. Related theory on technological externalities states that the external environment faced by firms is the sum of all individual externalities caused by the interaction of large numbers of firms when they agglomerate. The agglomeration externalities which a firm can receive and make use of depends on the firm itself and its ability to interact with other firms. All things being equal, the technological externalities produced by the interaction between any two firms j and k is determined by the geographical distance E_{jk}^{G}, industrial frontier distance E_{jk}^{I}, and time gap E_{jk}^{T} between the two. The aggregate of such external economies from agglomeration can be measured by $a(E_{jk}^{G},E_{jk}^{I},E_{jk}^{T})$. At the same time, the efficiency firm j obtains from interacting with firm k is determined by the degree to which firm j and k interact. The larger x_j and x_k, the stronger the degree of interaction. Such efficiency can be expressed as $q(x_j, x_k)$. Based on considerations of these two aspects, the total agglomeration economies (i.e. technological externalities) firm j obtains from interaction with all other firms K is:

$$A_j=\sum\nolimits_{k\in K} q(x_j,x_k)a(E_{jk}^{G},E_{jk}^{I},E_{jk}^{T}) \tag{8.7}$$

The firm's production function is:

$$y_j = g\{\sum_{k \in K} q(x_j, x_k) a(E^G_{jk}, E^I_{jk}, E^T_{jk})\} f(x_j) \tag{8.8}$$

Given that the regional level of research is at the city level or even lower, at the same time differing from the abstractness of macroeconomic models, the technological externalities here are intuitive and accessible. Technological externalities are usually analyzed from the perspective of industry externalities, geographical externalities and temporal externalities (Rosenthal and Strange, 2004), of which geographical externalities set out from employment density and temporal externalities set out from dynamism. Here we will focus on illustrating industry externalities, which have the widest application.

For a firm at a low regional level, the industry externalities it enjoys are actually only different industry level choices of economies of scale. If the industry externalities a firm enjoys come from the economies of scale of the industry the firm belongs to, and is caused by the agglomeration of many firms within the same industry in a certain city, facilitating technology and knowledge spillovers between firms within the industry, then such types of industry externalities are known as "localization economies" and its dynamic form is known as "MAR externalities" (Marshall, 1920; Arrow, 1962; Romer, 1986). If the industry externalities a firm faces come from the economies of scale of all industries or the number of industries in a city, which is to say, knowledge complementarity, or spillovers between industries creates large returns and positive impacts for firms, then such types of industry externalities are known as "diversification economies" and its dynamic form is known as "Jacob externalities" (Jacobs, 1969).

Judging from past research and international urban development experience, industry externalities of localization economies are often reflected at the regional level of mid-sized and small cities and relatively mature manufacturing (Henderson, 1986; Henderson et al., 1995); whereas industry externalities of diversification economies are often reflected at the regional level of large cities or high-tech industries (e.g. Glaeser et al., 1992). Can such a general empirical rule be applied to test the realities of Chinese intercity industry distribution? This is one of the objectives of this chapter's review.

8.6.2 Literature review

So, how should we conduct a review of existing literature? Combining the definition of small geographical scale agglomeration and general rules unveiled by relevant foreign literature, we have assembled the following threads:

1. Is the regional level choice prefectural level municipality or even county-level economy?
2. Is the choice of industry level appropriate for the measurement of localization or diversification economies? The above two points actually form the premise for the appropriateness of empirical research. The bottleneck constraints

on current domestic empirical research are precisely reflected in its inability to reach these two preconditions.

3. The focal point of technological externalities is firm production efficiency or production efficiency at a relatively low regional level and relatively narrow industry level, the most simple and direct measurement indicator of which is factor productivity, but such a choice may produce a technological bias toward a certain factor, thus in this sense, total factor productivity is most appropriate.
4. Since the dependent variables in this type of empirical study are usually labor productivity or total factor productivity etc. indicators, while independent variables are small geographical scale agglomeration variables—specialization and diversification indicators, explanatory variables and explained variables often interact as both cause and effect, and a tough issue in empirical research is how to solve endogeneity issues, since the application of fixed effects, instrument variables or lags of the explanatory variable all more or less exist estimation errors to different degrees, thus the choice of econometric method is often the key to such empirical research.
5. Due to the existence of innate flaws in the aforementioned econometric indicators' construction and technical means, on the issue of whether the magnitude of econometric results are uniform, we are currently far from a consensus on the quantitative conclusions on technological externalities, and more reliable and robust conclusions will depend on the overcoming of the abovementioned flaws.

Here, we will use these five points as a benchmark for comprehensively reviewing existing relevant domestic empirical research.

8.6.2.1 Choice of regional level

Looking at the definition of small geographical scale agglomeration, relatively lower regional levels are the suitable level to conduct research on technological externalities. This has already been mentioned in He and Pan (2009). Empirical studies abroad have already met this requirement (Glaeser et al., 1992; Henderson et al., 1995). The underlying reason is, if the regional level is too high, the localization or diversification economies indicators used to measure industry externalities cannot accurately reflect objective reality, since concepts such as localization economies are formed strongly on the basis of small regional scale industry. If this benchmark is used to observe relevant domestic empirical literature (Table 8.9), on the whole, most studies are at the provincial level (He and Pan, 2009; Li and Song, 2008), some studies have reached the prefectural level municipality or even district level in major cities (Fan, 2006; Liu, 2009; Chen and Yang, 2008), of which Chen and Yang's (2008) object of study is the production efficiency of eight major regions within Beijing. Calculating technological externalities at the provincial level is unreasonable since most Chinese provinces are rather large and have a rather complete assortment of industries, which means the specialization

Table 8.9 List of relevant representative studies on technological externalities

Study	*Variables and econometric method*				*Econometric method*	*Econometric level and data source*	*Main conclusions*
	Dependent variable	*Localization economies*	*Urbanized economies*	*Other critical variables*			
Chen and Yang (2008)	Industry labor productivity	Industry output level	Output level of other industries in region		Fixed provincial effects	Panel data on 8 two-digit manufacturing industries by province; "China Industry Economy Statistical Yearbook"	Urbanization economies exist for 5 industries; Localization economies exist for 5 industries; Specialization and urbanization economies exist for 3 industries
Fan and Shi (2009)	Four-digit industry labor productivity	Number of employment or firms in same four-digit industries represent agglomeration within industry	Number of employment or firms in other four-digit industries under the same two-digit industries represent agglomeration in related industries		Four-year lags of explained variable to reduce impact of endogeneity	Four-digit manufacturing at province level; "China Markets Yearbook"	Both exist, but agglomeration within industry effect is higher than agglomeration of related industries effect
Zhang, Zhan and Zhou (2007)	Labor productivity	Relative specialization index	Industry co-agglomeration index	EG index for agglomeration in industry	Fixed effects and GLS	Three-digit manufacturing industry at provincial level; Guoyan website manufacturing data	Localization economies are insignificant; Agglomeration with industry index and co-agglomeration index both positively impact labor productivity

Batisse (2002)	Each province's two-digit industry value-add growth rate	Relative specialization index	Relative diversification index (inverse HHI)		Industry-province panel data, industry fixed effects	30 two-digit manufacturing industries in 29 provinces "China Industry Economy Statistical Yearbook" (1988–1997)	Localization economies do not exist, urbanization economies exist
Bo (2007)	Industry output value growth rate	Relative specialization index	Diversification index (HHI)		One lag of diversification index; Hausman test	Panel data on 25 two-digit manufacturing industries in 29 provinces between 1994–2003; "China Industry Economy Statistical Yearbook"	Localization economies do not exist, urbanization economies exist, but are non-linear
Li and Song (2008)	Urban regional domestic product share of total output of all cities in that year	Relative specialization index, measured by largest industry share of employment in city	Diversification index (inverse HHI minus national value)		Fixed effects; GLS	2003–2005, 284 Prefectural level city data; "China City Statistical Yearbook"	Urbanization economies exist, elasticity coefficient of 0.01–0.022; localization economies do not exist
He and Pan (2009)	Industry growth rates of each city	Relative specialization index	Diversification index (inverse HHI)	Indicator measuring competition: Firm/employed persons	Fixed industry effects	Prefectural level city two-digit manufacturing data from 2000–2005; China Annual Census of Industrial Enterprises	Both are non-linear

Continued

Table 8.9 Continued

Study	*Variables and econometric method*				*Econometric method*	*Econometric level and data source*	*Main conclusions*
	Dependent variable	*Localization economies*	*Urbanized economies*	*Other critical variables*			
Fan (2006)	Urban non-farm labor productivity			Density of non-farm employment	Urban land area as instrument variable for employment density	2004 Prefectural level city and sub-provincial city data; "China City Statistical Yearbook"	Elasticity coefficient of non-farm employment density around 0.088
Liu (2009)	Urban non-farm labor productivity	Relative specialization index (industry with largest location quotient in a city)	Relative diversification index	Density of non-farm employment	Whether said region had railways passing through in 1933 as instrument variable for non-farm employment density	2003–2006 Prefectural level city, non-agricultural industries; "China City Statistical Yearbook"	Elasticity coefficient of non-farm employment density around 0.17; Localization economies exist, urbanization economies do not exist
Chen and Yang (2008)	Wage levels for each neighborhood in Beijing as proxy variable for labor productivity			Industrial output per unit of land (output density) Employed persons per unit of land (employment density)	2000 employment density and neighborhood area as instrument variable for non-farm employment density	Neighborhood level for eight major districts in Beijing; "Beijing 2004 Economic Census Data"	Elasticity coefficient of output density 0.118; elasticity coefficient of employment density 0.162

Note: The equation for the often used relative specialization index in the table is: $S_{sp} = \frac{\frac{VA_{sp}}{VA_p}}{\frac{VA_{sn}}{VA_n}}$, *s* represents an industry, *p* represents a province, *n* is the national level, *VA* is value-add or total output; the often used relative index equation is

$$\mathrm{DIV}_{sp} = \frac{\frac{1}{\sum_{s' \neq s}^{s} \left[\frac{VA_{s'p}}{VA_p - VA_{sp}} \right]^2}}{\frac{1}{\sum_{s' \neq s}^{s} \left[\frac{VA_{s'n}}{VA_n - VA_{sn}} \right]^2}}$$

, which is effectively the inverse HHI.

Localization economies promote growth in the low initial phase and inhibit growth after surpassing a certain phase; urbanization economies are negative at the initial phase and promote industry growth after surpassing a certain phase.

economies indices calculated will necessarily be rather low, e.g. two-digit industry specialization indicators for Zhejiang province are mostly low, but at the county level, the specialization feature of each county is extraordinarily apparent (also known as cluster economies).

Studying the impact of technological externalities on production efficiency at the provincial level is mostly out of consideration for the accessibility of data, but from the perspective of scientific academic research and the intension of technological externalities, the narrower the choice of regional level under study the more suitable it is, e.g. Rosenthal and Strange (2003), Henderson (2002) employed data at the zip code level; Arzaghi and Henderson (2006) employed 100 m × 100 m grids of Manhattan, New York, as their geographical unit. Thus, we believe that it is suitable for present and future studies on small geographical scale agglomeration to be conducted on a relatively low regional level.

8.6.2.2 Choice of industry level

In terms of the intuitive meaning of technological externalities, a relatively low industry level would be suitable. Viewing domestic literature, due to troubles with data accessibility, most literature is based on two-digit industries with only very few studies conducting empirical analysis on three-digit or even four-digit industries, e.g. Fan and Shi (2009) and Zhang et al. (2007). Why is a narrower choice of industry better? We believe that the narrower industry choice is, the more accurately an industry's production efficiency and technological externalities indicators can be measured, thus the more controllable the industry features are, therefore the impact of technological externalities on production efficiency can be accurately measured. At the same time, two-digit industry is still a wide range and includes many four-digit industries with significant variations, thus, it would be ideal for research on technological externalities to choose four-digit industries and below.

8.6.2.3 Indicators measuring technological externalities

The static indicators of technological externalities are specialization economies and diversification economies. The dynamic indicators are MAR externalities and Jacob externalities. Since the implications of these indicators are straightforward, their usage is uniform in domestic and foreign literature. The indicators can usually be classified into absolute indicators and relative indicators. Absolute indicators, e.g. Chen and Yang (2008) employed the output level of one industry and the output level of other industries to respectively represent specialization economies and diversification economies; Fan and Shi (2009) employed number of employed persons or firms of four-digit industries as an indicator for specialization economies, and some academics employed largest industry share of employment in city as a specialization economies indicator (Li and Song, 2008; Liu, 2009); whereas for diversification economies, most academics directly applied the inverse HHI, e.g. Bo (2007), et al.

As far as specialization economies are concerned, the basic meaning of relative indicators is an industry's proportion in a region relative to the national average for that industry, which is effectively a location quotient, a specialization economies indicator measured in Zhang et al. (2007), Batisse (2002), Bo (2007), He and Pan (2009), etc. As far as diversification economies are concerned, most studies adopt the average of inverse HHI of a region relative to the inverse national HHI, e.g. Batisse (2002), Li and Song (2008), He and Pan (2009), and Liu (2009).

8.6.2.4 Production efficiency indicator choice

Technological externalities impact industry production efficiency. From an intuitive sense, such production efficiency could be labor productivity or total factor productivity. Most studies employ labor productivity and not total factor productivity; while there are studies (Chen and Yang, 2008) that use wages to substitute for labor productivity. We believe that adopting labor productivity and not total factor productivity, under China's current industry structure which is mainly composed of labor-intensive industries and assembling manufacturing, may generate an estimate that underestimates efficiency; whereas using wages for estimation may generate even more severe underestimates, since labor market competition currently exists in China's urban sector, the wage level of the industrial sector is actually determined by the average production efficiency of the agricultural sector.

We believe total factor productivity is more suitable as a production efficiency indicator choice. At the same time, the direction of present and future research should be the reaction of each component within total factor productivity (technological efficiency improvements, technological changes, factor reallocation, economies of scale) toward technological externalities. Since at the urban level, can technological externalities be reflected in the impact on total factor productivity, or even further, reflected in the impact on a component of total factor productivity?

8.6.2.5 Econometric method choice

An unavoidable issue when analyzing technological externalities and production efficiency is endogeneity, that is, is it actually technological externalities that generate improvements in production efficiency, or high production efficiency levels that attract constant inflow of non-local factors that increases regional specialization economies or diversification economies? A general overview of existing literature shows that the general solution is taking a few years of lagged values or introducing instrument variables or adopting fixed effects, e.g. Bo (2007) and Fan and Shi (2007) both referred to the Henderson et al.'s (1995) approach, lagging the diversification economies indicator or non-farm employment density used to measure technological externalities by one to four years; Liu (2009) and Fan (2006) employed whether or not railways passed through in 1933 and urban land area as instrument variables for technological externalities. More studies employed industry fixed effects to solve this issue, e.g. Batisse (2002), Zhang et al. (2007), Li and Song (2008), and He and Pan (2009) et al.

As to the impact of technological externalities on production efficiency, we believe that the appropriate econometric method can be chosen in view of the accessibility of data, etc. and there are no rules set in stone.

8.6.2.6 Comparisons and conclusions of econometric results

Some studies found geographical externalities (measured by non-farm employment density) having a positive impact on production efficiency (an elasticity coefficient around 10 percent), and most studies analyzed the impact of specialization economies or diversification economies on production efficiency. Due to differences in the choice of regional levels, the conclusions differ widely as well. At the provincial level, most studies reached the conclusion that specialization economies have a negative impact on a province's economic growth, whereas diversification economies have a positive impact on economic growth, e.g. Batisse (2002), Bo (2007); but at the prefectural municipality level, most studies reached the conclusion that the Jacob externalities with diversification as its feature is more significant than MAR externalities with specialization as its feature, e.g. Zhang et al. (2007), Li and Song (2008). However, He and Pan (2009) discovered that specialization economies and diversification economies both show a nonlinear relationship with growth rates, though specialization economies initially facilitate industry growth and inhibit industry growth after surpassing a certain phase, while conversely, diversification economies initially inhibit industry growth, but facilitate growth after surpassing a certain phase.

The above-mentioned empirical conclusions have not reached a consensus. This chapter explains differences in the econometric results of technological externalities with different selections of regional level. At the provincial level, due to its large economic aggregate and wide assortment of industries, diversification economies facilitate production efficiency and increase in economic growth; conversely, if a province's tendency toward specialization is evident, then its industry structure will be monotonous and growth potential will be limited. But at the city level, due to the relatively large reduction in economic aggregate and types of industry, all cities endeavor to develop manufacturing and the difference between city sizes is relatively smaller, specialization economies can actually facilitate efficiency improvement and economic growth. Thus, the above opinions to a certain extent support the economic results reached in the existing literature.

8.7 Conclusions

This chapter conducted a multi-industry, multi-indicator, multi-regional scale, and all-round narrative of Chinese manufacturing's location distribution. We found that: (1) from a large regional scale perspective, coastal regions overall have a rather apparent agglomeration advantage, although around 2004, a trend emerged when industry dispersed from eastern and southern coastal regions to central and northern coastal regions. The dispersion from Guangdong, Jiangsu, Shanghai, and Zhejiang to Henan, Shandong, etc. is especially evident; (2) based on the calculation results from small geographical scale at prefectural level and below and aggregated figures from all manufacturing industries, manufacturing distribution across prefectural cities is relatively equal and a flattening characteristic is significant in the urban system. However, at the county-level regional scale, the level of agglomeration in all manufacturing industries is still relatively high, which indirectly reflects the relatively high level of specialization at the county-level.

This chapter also reviewed the impact of pecuniary externalities and technological externalities (mainly industry externalities) on economic growth rates, production efficiency or income levels, and found that the impact of pecuniary externalities on income levels was significantly positive all along, but no consensus has been reached on technological externalities due to differing choices of regional levels, industry levels, etc.

Notes

1 It should be noted that to what extent property prices depend on the impact of local economic aggregate (or economic efficiency) and regulation of land use needs further research.

2 It should be noted that it cannot be discerned here whether a province's increase in proportion of industry is due to its attraction of dispersed industry in other provinces or only because its growth rate is higher than that of other provinces. It could only be believed that in general terms, an increase in a province's proportion of industry may include both of these factors.

3 "Human capital externalities" refers to the fact that an increase in a person's educational level not only increases his or her own income, but also the income of others. In other words, a person's income is not only related to his education, but also the education of others in the city where he lives. For more on "human capital externalities," see Moretti (2004).

4 Here we consider the relationship between the price of the labor factor and pecuniary externalities. A topic that requires further discussion is: what would the relationship be between the price of immobile land and pecuniary externalities? We believe that pecuniary externalities are actually a spillover indicator that measures the size of a regional market. Such a spillover will eventually be reflected in the price of the least mobile factor among the productive factors, such as land prices. In this sense, as the economic aggregate expands continuously, continuous appreciation in the level of property prices in coastal regions is totally compatible with economic theory.

5 Equation (9.6) is also the standard wage equation (Equation 4.27) in Fujita et al. (1999).

6 The formula for nominal market potential is $NMP_i = \sum_j \frac{Y_j}{D_{ij}}$, where Y_j is income level for region j and D_{ij} is the spatial distance between region i and j.

7 See Barro and Sala-i-Martion (1995, Ch. 2) for Hicks neutrality assumption. Generally speaking, technological progress will cause producers to obtain the same output with relatively less capital or labor input. These two cases are, respectively, named capital saving or labor saving technological improvements. If a technological improvement saves an identical amount of capital and labor input, then such an improvement is called a "neutral technological improvement."

References

In English

Anderson, G. and Ying Ge, 2005, "The Size Distribution of Chinese Cities," *Regional Science and Urban Economics*, 35(6), pp. 756–776.

Arrow, K., 1962, "The Economic Implications of Learning by Doing," *The Review of Economic Studies*, 29(3), pp. 155–173.

Arzaghi, M. and J. V. Henderson, 2006, "Networking off Madison Avenue," *Working Paper* No. 0515, Brown University.

Au Chun-chung and J. V. Henderson, 2006, "Are Chinese Cities too Small?" *The Review of Economic Studies*, 73(3), pp. 549–576.

Barro, R. and Xavier Sala-i-Martion, 1995, *Economic Growth*, New York: McGraw-Hill.

Ciccone, A. and R. E. Hall, 1996, "Productivity and the Density of Economic Activity," *American Economic Review*, 86(1), pp. 54–70.

Combes, P. P., 2000, "Economic Structure and Local Growth: France, 1984–1993," *Journal of Urban Economics,* 47(3), pp. 329–355.

Combes, P. P., M. Lafourcade, J. F. Thisse, and J. C. Toutain, 2008, "The Rise and Fall of Spatial Inequalities in France: a Long-run Perspective," *CEPR Discussion Paper*, No. DP7017.

Dekle, R. and J. Eaton, 1999, "Agglomeration and Land Rents: Evidence from the Prefectures," *Journal of Urban Economics,* 46(2), pp. 200–214.

Devereux, M. P., R. Griffith, and H. Simpson, 2004, "The Geographic Distribution of Production Activity in the UK," *Regional Science and Urban Economics*, 34(5), pp. 533–564.

Duranton, G. and H. G. Overman, 2005, "Testing for Localization Using Micro-geographic Data," *Review of Economic Studies*, 72(4), pp. 1077–1106.

Ellison, G. and E. Glaeser, 1997, "Geographic Concentration in U.S. Manufacturing Industries: A Dartboard Approach," *Journal of Political Economy*, 105(2), pp. 889–927.

Fujita, M. and D. Hu, 2001, "Regional Disparity in China 1985–1994: The Effects of Globalization and Economic Liberalization," *Annals of Regional Science*, 35(1), pp. 3–37.

Fujita, M. and J. Thisse, 2002, *The Economics of Agglomeration*, Cambridge: Cambridge University Press.

Fujita, M., P. Krugman, and A. J. Venables, 1999, T*he Spatial Economy: Cities, Regions, and International Trade*. Cambridge, MA: MIT Press.

Glaeser, E. L., H. D. Kallal, J. A. Scheinkman, and A. Shleifer, 1992, "Growth in Cities," *Journal of Political Economy,* 100(2), pp. 1126–1152.

Hanson, G., 1998, "Market Potential, Increasing Returns and Geographic Concentration," *NBER Working Paper*, No. 6429

Harris, C., 1954, "The Market as a Factor in the Localization of Industry in the United States," *Annals of the Association of American Geographers*, 64(1), pp. 315–348.

Head, K. and T. Mayer, 2006, "Regional Wage and Employment Responses to market potential in the EU," *Regional Science and Urban Economics*, 36(5), pp. 573–594.

Helpman, E. and P. R. Krugman, 1985, *Market Structure and Foreign Trade*, Cambridge, MA: MIT Press.

Henderson, J. V., 1986, "Efficiency of Resource Usage and City Size," *Journal of Urban Economics*, 19(1), pp. 47–70.

Henderson, J. V., 2002, "Marshall's Scale Economies," *Journal of Urban Economics*, 53(1), pp. 1–28.

Henderson J. V., A. Kuncoro, and M. Turner, 1995, "Industrial development in cities," *Journal of Political Economy*, 103(5), pp. 1067–1090.

Hering, L. and S. Poncet, 2010, "Market Access Impact on Individual Wages: Evidence form China," *Review of Economics and Statistics*, 92(1), pp. 145–159.

Hoppes, R. S., 1994, "Rejoinder: Industry-level Shift-Share Analysis," *Economic Development Quarterly*, 8(2), pp. 214–217.

Jacobs, J., 1969, *The Economy of Cities*, New York: Vintage.

Krugman, P. R., 1991, "Increasing Returns and Economic Geography," *Journal of Political Economy*, 99(4), pp. 483–99.

Lu, J. Y. and Z. G. Tao, 2009, "Trends and Determinants of China's Industrial Agglomeration," *Journal of Urban Economic*, 65(3), pp. 167–180.

Marshall, A. 1920, *Principles of Economics*, London: MacMillan.

Maurel, F. and B. Sedillot, 1999, "A Measure of the Geographic Concentration in French Manufacturing Industries," *Regional Science and Urban Economics*, 29(5), pp. 575–704.

Moomaw, R. L., 1981, "Productivity and City Size: a Critique of the Evidence," *Quarterly Journal of Economics*, 96(3), pp. 675–688.

Moretti, E., 2004, "Human Capital Externalities in Cities," In *Handbook of Regional and Urban Economics*, ed. J. V. Henderson and J. F. Thisse, Vol. IV: Cities and Geography. Amsterdam: North-Holland.

Nakamura, R. 1985, "Agglomeration Economies in Urban Manufacturing Industries: a Case of Japanese Cities," *Journal of Urban Economics*, 17(2), pp. 108–124.

Redding, S. and A. Venables, 2004, "Economic Geography and International Inequality," *Journal of International Economics*, 62(1), pp. 53–82.

Romer, P., 1986, "Increasing Returns and Long-rum Growth," *Journal of Political Economics*, 94(1), pp. 1002–1038.

Rosenthal, Stuart S. and William C. Strange, 2004, "Evidence on the Nature and Sources of Agglomeration Economies," In *Handbook of Regional and Urban Economics*, ed. J. V. Henderson and J. F. Thisse, Vol. I, V: Cities and Geography. Amsterdam: North-Holland.

Rosenthal, S. and W. C. Strange, 2003, "Geography, Industrial Organization, and Agglomeration," *Review of Economics and Statistics*, 85(2), pp. 377–393.

Samuelson, Paul A., 1954, "The Transfer Problem and Transport Costs, II: Analysis of Trade Impediments," *Economic Journal*, 64(2), pp. 264–289.

Scitovsky, T., 1954, "Two Concepts of External Economies," *Journal of Political Economy*, 62(3), pp. 143–51.

Stillwell, F. J. B., 1970, "Further Thoughts on the Shift and Share Approach," *Regional Studies*, 4(4), pp. 451–458.

Sveikauskas, L., 1975, "The Productivity of Cities," *Quarterly Journal of Economics*, 89(1), pp. 393–413.

Wei, Shang-jin, 1996, "Intra-national versus International Trade: How Stubborn Are Nations in Global Integration?" *NBER, Working Paper*, No. 5531.

In Chinese

Batisse, Cecile, 2002, "Specialization, Diversity and Chinese Growth," *World Economic Papers*, (4), pp. 49–62.

Bo Wen-guang, 2007, "Externalities and Industrial Economic Growth – Evidence from Chinese Provincial Panel Data," *Chinese Industrial Economy*, (1), pp. 37–44.

Chen Liang-Wen, Kai-Zhong Yang, 2008, "Industrial Agglomeration, Market Organization and Productivity – Empirical Research: Based on Provincial Panel Data of China's Manufacturing Industries," *Geographic Science*, 28(3), pp. 325–330.

Chen Liang-Wen, Kai-Zhong Yang, Ti-Yan Shen, and Wei Wang, 2008, "Economic Agglomeration Density and Labor Productivity: Based on Empirical Study on Beijing's Micro-data," *China Economic Quarterly*, 8(1), pp. 99–114.

Fan Jianyong, 2004a, "Industrial Agglomeration and Differential Regional Income: From the Chinese Evidence," *Chinese Social Sciences Review*, 1, pp. 56–71.

Fan Jianyong, 2004b, "Market Integration, Regional Specialization and Tendency of Industrial Agglomeration," *Chinese Social Sciences,* 6, pp. 39–52.

Fan Jianyong, Renyuan Gao and Yan Zhang, 2010, "Spatial Efficiency and the Strategy of Regional Harmony Development," *Journal of World Economy*, 2, pp. 104–119.

Fan Jianyong and Ting Shao, 2011, "Housing Price, Location of Diversified Product and Urban System," *Economic Research Journal*, 2, pp. 87–99.

Fan Jianyong and Lingyun Shi, 2009, "The Externality of Industries, the Competitive Environment of Enterprises, and Labor Productivity," *Management World*, 4, pp. 65–72.

Fan Jianyong, Lijun Wang and Linjie Shen, 2004, "Industrial Concentration and the Trans-regional Flow of Rural Labor Forces," *Management World*, 4, pp. 22–30.

Fan Jianyong and Qiangqiang Xie, 2010, "Home Market Effects and Spatial Distribution of Industries: Its Implication in Regional Coordinated Development," *Economic Research Journal*, 4, pp. 1077–119.

Fan Jianyong and Zhang Yan, 2009, "Economic Geography and the Differential of Regional Wages," *Economic Research Journal*, 8, pp. 73–84.

Fan Jianyong, 2008, *Research on Agglomeration and the Difference of Chinese Regional Income*, Gezhi Press, Shanghai: Shanghai People Press.

Fan Jianyong, 2006, "Industrial Agglomeration and the Difference of Regional Labor Productivity" *Economic Research Journal*, 8, pp. 73–84.

Guo Jinlong and Hongwei Wang, 2003, "Chinese Capital Flow across Regions and Growth Difference," *Management World*, 7, pp. 45–58.

National Bureau of Statistics, 2010, *China Compendium of Statistics 1949–2008*, Beijing: China Statistics Press.

The State Information Center, 2005, *China Interregional Input Output Model*, Beijing: Social Sciences Academic Press.

He Canfei and Fenghua Pan, 2009, "City Industry Growth: Perspectives of Dynamic Externalities and Economic Transition," *Geographical Research*, 28(3), pp. 32–40.

Jin Yu, Zhao Chen and Ming Lu, 2006, "Industry Agglomeration in China: Economic Geography, New Economic Geography and Policy," *Economic Research Journal*, 4, pp. 79–89.

Li Jinyan and Deyong Song, 2008, "Sepcialization, Diversity and Urban Agglomeration: based on Empirical Research of Panel Data on Cities," *Management World*, 2, pp. 25–34.

Li Kunwang and Jiuli Huang, 2006, "On the Difference of the Inter-Provincial Labor Output," *Nankai Journal (*Philosophy and Social Science Edition), 2, pp. 116–124.

Liang Qi and Xuefeng Qian, 2007, "Externality and Agglomeration," *Journal of World Economy*, 2, pp. 84–96.

Liu Xiuyan, 2009, "Industrial Agglomeration and Economic Growth: A Survey," *Industrial Economics Research*, 3, pp. 70–78.

Liu Xiuyan, Xiaohai He and Xingmin Yin, 2007, "Market Potential and Regional Wage Gap: An Empirical Study of China's Prefecture-level Panel Data," *Management World*, 9, pp. 48–55.

Xiuyan Liu and Xingmin Yin, "Spatial Externalities and Regional Wage Differences: A Dynamic Panel-Data Study," *China Economic Quarterly*, 8(1), pp. 77–98.

Wang Feian, Jue Wang, Tang Yun and Jianyong Fan, 2010, "Whether the Time Has Come for Manufacturing Dispersion," *Zhejiang Social Sciences*, 9, pp. 2–10.

Xu Zheng, Zhao Chen, Ming Lu, 2010, "Center-Periphery Model of China's Urban System—Empirical Research on Geography and Economic Growth," *Journal of World Economy*, 7, pp. 144–160.

Zhang Hui, Yubo Zhan and Kai Zhou, 2007, "Agglomeration, Diversity and Local Economic Growth: Demonstration Studies of Manufacturing Industries in China," *World Economic Papers*, 3, pp. 16–29.

Appendix

Regional industry share

In regional economics research, there are many indicators that measure industry spatial distribution characteristics. Regional share of an industry is one of them; this indicator is constructed as follows:

$$v_i = \frac{\sum_k \left(v_i^k\right)}{k}\text{，其中 } v_i^k = \frac{E_i^k}{\sum_i E_i^k} \tag{A.1}$$

where, k is number of industries, N is number of regions, v_i^k is industry k in region i's share of nationwide total employment of said industry, v_i expresses region i's industry share, which directly measures the average share of all industries in said region. It ranges between 0 and 1 and the closer it gets to 1, the higher the region's average share of manufacturing, thus the more developed its manufacturing.

Gini coefficient and its dissection

The simple calculation equation for Gini coefficient is as follows:

$$C_k = \frac{2}{n}\sum_{i=1}^{n} ix_i - \frac{n+1}{n}\text{，} x_i = \frac{y_i}{\sum_{i=1}^{n} y_i}\left(x_1 < x_2 < \ldots < x_n\right) \tag{A.2}$$

where, x_i is each region's *per capita* income's proportion of total income ordered from low to high, n is number of regions. Since the Gini coefficient can be dissected according to industry, thus the above equation can be used to respectively, solve for the Gini coefficient of each industry, then weighted to obtain the overall Gini coefficient. Through adding weights, the overall Gini coefficient could be expressed as:

$$G = \sum_k \left(\frac{\mu_k}{\mu}\right) C_k = \sum_k S_k C_k \tag{A.3}$$

where, G is the overall Gini coefficient, C_k is industry k's Gini coefficient, $\frac{\mu_k}{\mu}$ is each industry's output share in the three industries' aggregate output; S_kC_k/G represents industry k's contribution rate to the Gini coefficient.

As for how to structurally dissect changes in the Gini coefficient, we assume the rate of change for Gini coefficients of two neighboring periods is ΔG, therefore ΔG could be written in the following form:

$$\Delta G = \sum_k S_{k_{t+1}} C_{k_{t+1}} - \sum_k S_{k_t} C_{k_t} = \sum_k \left(S_{k_{t+1}} C_{k_{t+1}} - S_{k_t} C_{k_t} \right) \tag{A.4}$$

After reorganizing the equation we obtain:

$$\Delta G = \sum_k \Delta S_k C_{k_t} - \sum_k \Delta C_k S_{k_t} + \sum_k \left(\Delta S_k \Delta C_k \right) \tag{A.5}$$

where, $\Delta S_k = S_{k_{t+1}} - S_{k_t}$, $\Delta C_k = C_{k_{t+1}} - C_{k_t}$

$\sum_k \Delta S_k C_{k_t}$ is the overall Gini coefficient change caused by structural changes in industry k's output, also known as the "structural effect"; $\sum_k \Delta C_k S_{k_t}$ is the overall Gini coefficient change caused by the degree of concentration in industry k's output, also known as the "concentration effect"; $\sum_k (\Delta S_k \Delta C_k)$ is the overall Gini coefficient change caused by the comprehensive effect of structural changes in and concentration changes of industry k's revenue, and is known as the "comprehensive effect."

Theil index

The Theil index is an index that measures unevenness, its most important quality and advantage is its resolvability. In economics, the Theil index is often used to measure regional gaps, employing *per capita* GDP, GDP, population, industrial output, industrial value-add, etc. as variables to measure. In this chapter, the Theil index was used to measure the uneven distribution of manufacturing between prefectural level cities. At the same time, according to its resolvability, we divided the unevenness of manufacturing between prefectural level cities into the sum of interprovincial unevenness and unevenness between cities within a province (Combes et al., 2008):

$$T = \sum_{d=1}^{D} \frac{A_d}{A} log \frac{A_d}{\frac{A}{D}}$$

$$T = T_w + T_b \tag{A.6}$$

$$T_b = \sum_{r=1}^{R} \frac{A_r}{A} log \frac{\frac{A_r}{D_r}}{\frac{A}{D}}$$

In the above equation, A_d represents manufacturing value-add in prefectural city *d*, *A* represents national manufacturing value-add, *D* represents the number of prefectural cities nationwide. A_r represents value-add of province *r*, D_r represents the number of prefectural level cities in province *r*. The Theil Index (T) can be dissected into the intraprovincial Theil index (T_w) and interprovincial Theil index (T_b). The larger the index reading is, the higher the degree of concentration. Two extreme cases are: if value-add in all regions are equally distributed, $A_d = \frac{A}{D}$, then T=0; if value-add is concentrated in one region, then T=log$D$.

EG index

The EG index used in this text employs the form in Ellison and Glaeser (1997). Assume there are R regions, the formula for calculating the EG index for industry *s* is:

$$r_s = \frac{G_s - \left(1 - \sum_r \lambda_r^2\right) H_s}{\left(1 - \sum_r \lambda_r^2\right)\left(1 - H_s\right)} \tag{A.7}$$

Where G_s is the coefficient of industry *s* in R regions, $G_s = \sum_r \left(\lambda_r^s - \lambda_r\right)^2$, λ_r^s is the regional share of industry *s* in region *r*, λ_r is the ratio of region *r*'s industrial output of all industries to the nationwide industrial output of all industries. When $\lambda_r^s = \lambda_r$, that is an industry's distribution in region *r* is the same as the distribution of all industries in region *r*, $G_i = 0$, and industry *s* is evenly distributed. The larger the gap between λ_r^s and λ_r and the larger the coefficient G_s is, the higher an industry's degree of agglomeration. Assume there are *i* firms in industry *s*, $H_s = \sum_i z_i^2$, H_s is the HH coefficient of industry *s*, of which z_i is the ratio of firm *i*'s industrial value-add to the whole industry's industrial value-add. It can be seen from the formula that the EG index takes into account the internal structure of industries.

9 Urban spatial structure

Housing, jobs, and related urban issues

Siqi Zheng

9.1 Introduction

Agglomeration economies are the driving force behind the formation and development of cities. The relative forces of positive externalities brought by agglomeration economies and the possible negative externalities (congestion effect) determine the optimal city size. So, if we look into a specific city, how are economic activities distributed and how is space allocated as an economic resource? These are the issues this chapter will discuss.

It can be intuitively observed that land and property prices, population density, height and density of buildings, display distinct spatial variances in different locations within a city. Office buildings with dozens and even over a hundred stories are concentrated in the central business district, whereas low-storied residential buildings and industrial plants can often be seen in the suburbs. In many American cities, the income level of suburban residents is often relatively high, while the inner city is relatively poor with high crime and unemployment rates; however, in many European cities with a long history, such as Paris, high income individuals prefer to live in the downtown area (Brueckner et al., 1999). Studies show that in major Chinese cities, downtown residents have a higher income level than suburb residents (Zheng et al., 2006). It could also be observed that urban area is constantly expanding and farmland at the city margins is gradually transformed into land for urban usage. These phenomenon are what urban spatial structure theory attempts to explain—how spatial resources are allocated between two major economic entities, firms and households. The two core endogenous variables, "jobs" and "housing" have important impacts on the spatial distribution of productivity, wages, commuting and property (as well as land) prices in cities. At the same time, these factors in turn impact the spatial interactive relationship between jobs and housing.

The study of "urban spatial structure"[1] involves multiple fields, mainly including urban economies, urban geography, urban planning, regional science etc. This chapter's analysis will basically employ the perspective of urban economics while absorbing useful opinions and methods from neighboring fields.

This chapter is divided into five sections. The second section will display the urban spatial distributions of factors such as housing prices, land prices, population and employment and discuss the explanatory power of monocentric and polycentric models on the spatial distribution of these factors. The third section, focuses on the spatial relationship between housing and jobs and study the inside economic mechanisms. "Jobs and housing imbalance" creates large demand for transportation which may induce traffic congestion and environmental pollution, so should such a balance be pursued? The discussions in this chapter will illustrate that the relative forces of agglomeration economies' "adhesion" and commuting costs' "friction" will determine this spatial relationship. If "adhesion" far exceeds "friction," cities will trend toward a monocentric form; the stronger "friction" is, the higher the degree of mixture between jobs and housing. In Chinese cities, the increase in the importance of agglomeration economies and the great improvement of transportation infrastructure enables the degree of jobs–housing separation to gradually grow larger, so a biased pursuit of "balance between housing and jobs" is unrealistic. The fourth section will discuss several relevant urban issues and public policies regarding the spatial relationship between housing and jobs, including employment barriers to and housing affordability for the disadvantaged, traffic congestion and environmental pollution. This section also introduces an integrated study and policy design framework that comprehensively takes land use, transportation and the environment into consideration. The basic line of thought goes as follows: institutional barriers to firms' and households' location choices should be eliminated and the externalities of location choice and transportation activities should be correctly priced, in order to enhance the Pareto efficiency of urban spatial resource allocation, at the same time, an appropriate public policy design can achieve better welfare distribution effects. The fifth section concludes.

9.2 Spatial distributions of housing prices, land prices, population, and employment

9.2.1 Starting from the classic monocentric model

Since the housing reform began, China's urban real estate development and residential construction market have been very active. From 1998 to 2009, nationwide city and township residential housing constructed area totaled 14.91 billion square meters, accounting for over 90 percent of the total housing stock.[2] Such a large sample size provides an excellent opportunity to observe the spatial distribution of housing prices in cities. Figure 9.1 plots the spatial distribution of 2006–2009 Beijing commodity housing projects on Geography Information System's electronic map,[3] with the size of the circles representing average sale price. It can be observed that housing prices trend toward gradually decreasing from the city center on outwards.

If a simple OLS regression is performed, one can more clearly observe the existence of a significantly negative spatial gradient in housing prices. For every kilometer further outward, property prices decrease by 2.32 percent [see Equation (9.1)]. Defining the city center of Beijing as Tiananmen—from the perspective of urban historical development and road network construction, defining the city center in this manner is quite appropriate. Of course, some believe that

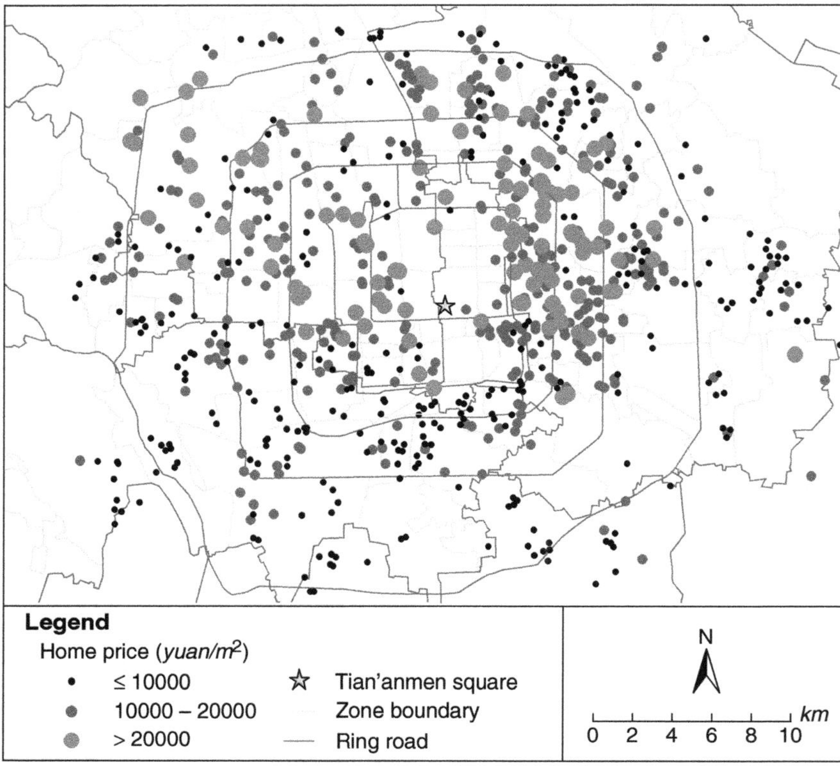

Figure 9.1 Spatial distribution of Beijing commodity housing projects.

Data source: Beijing Real Estate Transaction Data (constructed on the basis of Beijing Real Estate Transaction Net).

Beijing's CBD—outside Jianguomen—is the center of economic activity in Beijing, under such a situation, significantly negative spatial gradient could be obtained as well, the magnitude of which is similar to the former [see Equation (9.2)]. In Equation (9.1) and Equation (9.2), the analysis unit is the commodity housing project and year dummies are controlled for:

$$\begin{aligned}&\ln(\text{Price}) = 9.256 - 0.02321 \times \text{distance to Tiananmen}\\&(612.40^{***})\ (-45.22^{***})\\&+ \text{Annual dummy variable} \qquad (9.1)\\&R^2 = 0.342,\ \text{sample size} = 4805\end{aligned}$$

$$\begin{aligned}&\ln(\text{Price}) = 9.249 - 0.0233 \times \text{distance to CBD}\\&(617.07^{***})\ (-45.44^{***})\\&+ \text{year dummies} \qquad (9.2)\\&R^2 = 0.344,\ \text{sample size} = 4805\end{aligned}$$

*** significant at 1% level.

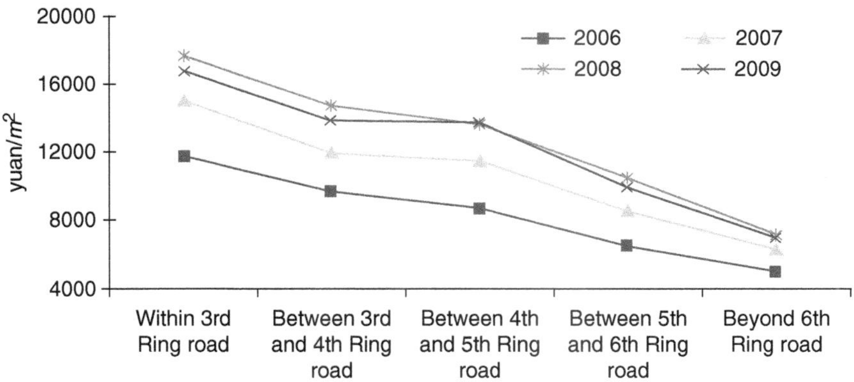

Figure 9.2 Lines showing spatial distribution of Beijing commodity housing prices.

Figure 9.2 reflects such a spatial distribution pattern in housing prices more intuitively. The housing prices in every point in the city increased with time, but in the same time frame, the negative spatial gradient is always maintained consistently.

The above-mentioned spatial pattern in the distribution of Beijing housing prices is not unique and exists in many small and mid-sized Chinese cities. Figure 9.3 is the spatial price distribution graph for 2005–2009 Chengdu newly constructed commodity housing projects, in which similar patterns can be observed. Employing the prices of every traded commodity housing unit as a sample, using Chengdu's city center (Tianfu Square) as a benchmark, OLS regressions can similarly obtain a spatial gradient for housing prices of 4.3 percent.

$$\begin{aligned}&\ln(\text{Price}) = 8.432 - 0.043 \times \text{distance to city center}\\&(6380.36^{***})\ (-280.42^{***})\\&+ \text{year dummies} \qquad (9.3)\\&R^2 = 0.392,\ \text{sample size} = 463561\end{aligned}$$

*** significant at 1% level.

The above seemingly-simple pattern is exactly the origin of modern urban spatial structure theory's development. In the 1960/70s, three urban economists Alonso, Muth and Mills proposed a monocentric city model (Alonso, 1964; Muth, 1969; Mills, 1972). In the following more than 40 years since, this highly abstract theoretical model has always given strong explanations for urban spatial structure, even though many cities are no longer viewed as monocentric cities. The monocentric city model is rich in content and its major contribution lies in providing an effective theoretical framework for the study of general equilibrium of urban space and its adjustment. It can also empirically measure and compare the level of urban centralization and can be easily extended as well.

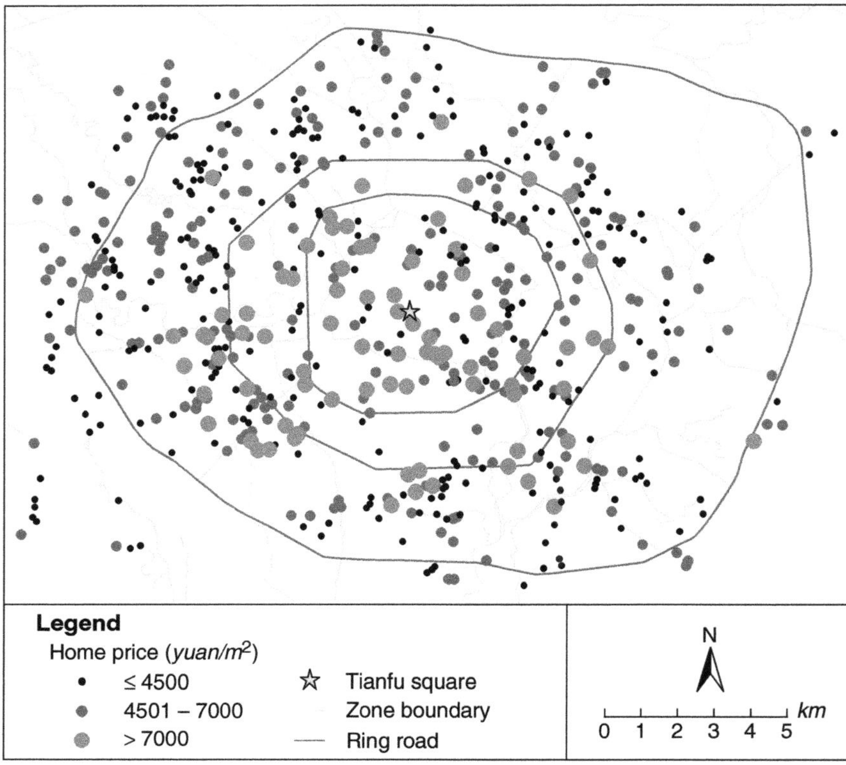

Figure 9.3 Spatial distribution of Chengdu commodity housing prices.

Data source: Chengdu Real Estate Transaction Data (constructed on the basis of Chengdu Urban and Rural Housing Administration Bureau's database).

The monocentric city model simplifies cities into homogeneous circle areas with only one employment center, the size of which is ignored. In this city, every household has one employed person and all workers are homogeneous. They all need to commute to the CBD to work and earn income. Employees allocate their income between housing expenditures, consumption of other goods and commuting costs under a budget constraint and pursue the maximization of the former two items' utility.

Under such assumptions, we can obtain the following five basic inferences.

9.2.1.1 Housing rent decreases with an increase of distance to CBD

Housing rent decreases with an increase of distance to CBD, that is, negative spatial gradient exists for housing rent (for details, see Appendix).

This is because when residents choose residential locations, they make the trade-off between commuting and housing costs. The farther away a location is from the CBD, the higher the costs of commuting to and from work and the lower the rent residents are willing to pay. The curve that depicts the spatial change of residents' willingness to pay rent is called the "bid-rent curve" or "bid-rent function." If different resident groups have different bid-rent curves, then according to the principle of "going to the highest bidder," the group with the highest bid-rent will occupy the location in any location. Eventually, the rent curve will envelope these bid-rent curves. In the simplest monocentric model, there is only one group of people, thus the bid-rent curve is the final rent curve.

Capitalizing the rents of future years and you get the current price of property. If we assume that the capitalization rate of rent does not change spatially across the city, then property prices and rent will have the same spatial distribution characteristics. Of course, one could also consider the spatial difference of capitalization rates. For some hotspot locations (e.g., locations near the downtown area), people expected there would be a high increase in the future rent, so the capitalization rate will be on the low end, which is to say, the price-to-rent ratio will be relatively high. Here, the spatial distribution curve for property prices will be much steeper than the curve for rent, though the negative gradient trend will be the same. The spatial distribution curve of historical annual housing prices in Beijing in Figure 9.2 and the spatial distribution curve of historical annual housing prices in Chengdu in Figure 9.4 are consistent with this inference of the monocentric model. At the same time, we can see that, on the time dimension, the spatial distribution curve of property prices is constantly shifting upwards. This is the comprehensive result of two effects: first, over the past several years, macroeconomic factors and supply and demand in China's urban housing market caused overall urban housing prices to rise fast, thereby leading to an increase in the housing prices of each location; second, even if we do not consider the former factor, urban population growth and spatial expansion alone will bring increases in the housing prices of every location within a city.

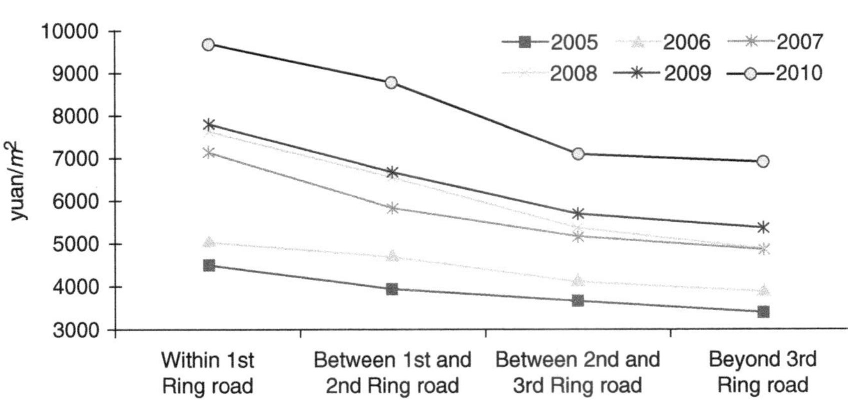

Figure 9.4 Price distribution curve of Chengdu commodity housing projects.

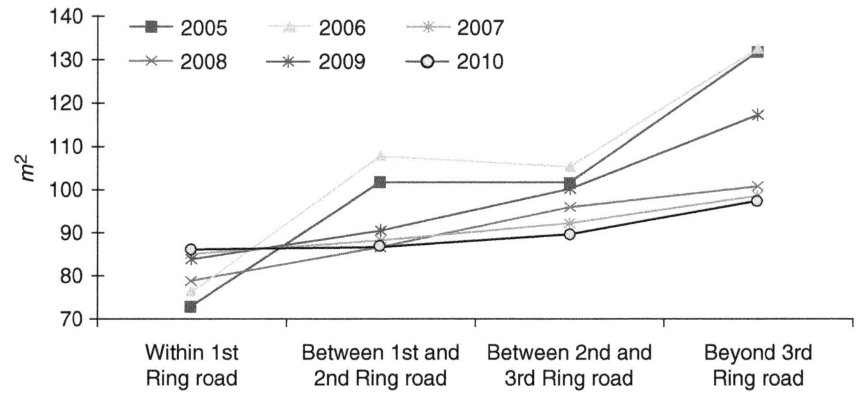

Figure 9.5 Spatial distribution curve for an average area of Chengdu newly constructed commodity housing units.

9.2.1.2 Consumption of housing increases with the distance to the CBD

From the above inferences, it could be seen that the optimal utility of residents in the monocentric model is undifferentiated across different locations, reaching a spatial equilibrium. Since the price of other consumption goods does not change spatially, then while satisfying budgetary constraints, a substitutive relationship exists between the consumption of housing and its price, i.e. in locations near the downtown area where property prices are high, housing rents (price per unit) are high for residents, thereby causing consumption of housing to be on the low end and vice versa.

Does this inference hold in Chinese cities? Figure 9.5 provides the spatial distribution curve for average area of Chengdu newly constructed commodity housing unit—it can be observed that this pattern exists as the simple OLS regression beneath the Figure also evidences the existence of a significantly positive gradient. But this Figure only reflects a small portion of the housing stock. In Chinese cities, about 1/3–1/2 of the housing stock is currently composed of houses constructed before the housing reform, which were later sold at low subsidized prices by work units (*danwei*) to their employees, also known as "*fanggai* housing". Since the *fanggai* housing was constructed at an earlier period, their area was small and a high proportion was situated in the inner city. If this portion of the housing stock is taken into consideration, then the positive gradient of the housing consumption curve in Figure 9.5 will be even more evident.

$$\begin{aligned}&\ln(\text{Area}) = -0.216 + 0.026 \times \text{Distance to city center}\\&(-114.18^{***})\ (121.94^{***})\\&+ \text{year dummies} \qquad (9.4)\\&R^2 = 0.054,\ \text{sample size} = 463561\end{aligned}$$

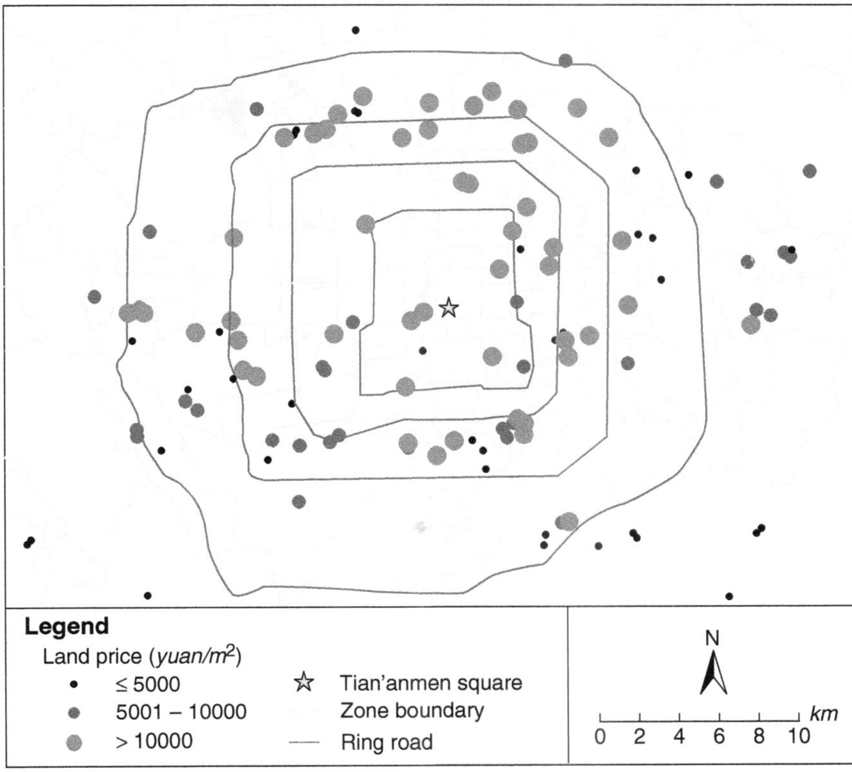

Figure 9.6 Spatial distribution of Beijing land sales.

Data source: Beijing land database (constructed on the basis of Beijing Land Coordination and Reservation Center data).

9.2.1.3 Land rent (land price) decreases with increase in distance to CBD

The rent of land is the difference between housing rent and construction cost. Construction cost does not shift with location, so the distribution of land rent is spatially consistent with housing rent. By employing the sale price of tracts of land from bidding and auctions in Beijing from 2005 to 2008, the existence of the inference in Beijing can be tested for. Figure 9.6 displays the spatial distribution of these tracts of land and Figure 9.7 is the spatial distribution curve of the sale price of these land tracts—the pattern of gradually declining prices from the city center on outward is very apparent as well. The equation below the Figure shows the validity of the negative gradient at 1 percent significance.

$$\begin{aligned}&\ln(\text{Price}) = 8.990 - 0.036 \times \text{distance to city center}\\&(54.16^{***})\ (-12.05^{***})\\&+ \text{year dummies}\end{aligned} \tag{9.5}$$

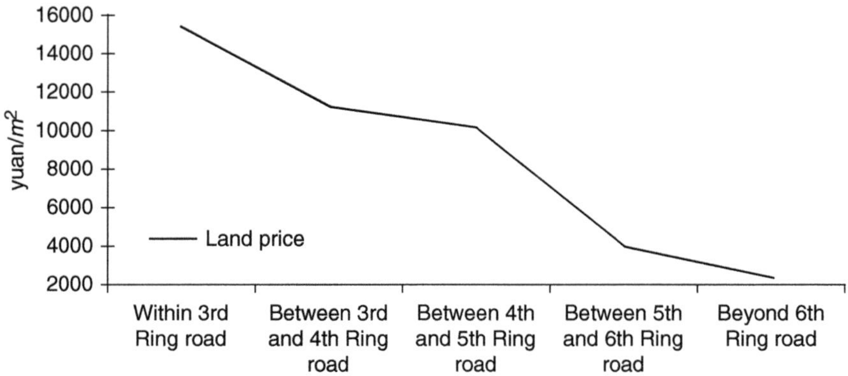

Figure 9.7 Spatial distribution curve of Beijing land sale prices.

$R^2 = 0.387$, sample size = 367
*** significant at the 1% level.

9.2.1.4 The density of buildings decreases with the increase of distance to CBD

From the perspective of property developers, there exists a substitution effect between capital and land. The price of capital does not change spatially across cities, thus in the city center where land prices are high, real estate developers will tend to use more capital to substitute for land, and more houses will be built on the same area of land. Generally speaking, the floor-to-area ratio (FAR) can be one reflection of building density. Does spatially negative gradient exist for this indicator? Figure 9.8 and the simple OLS regression below show that a significant

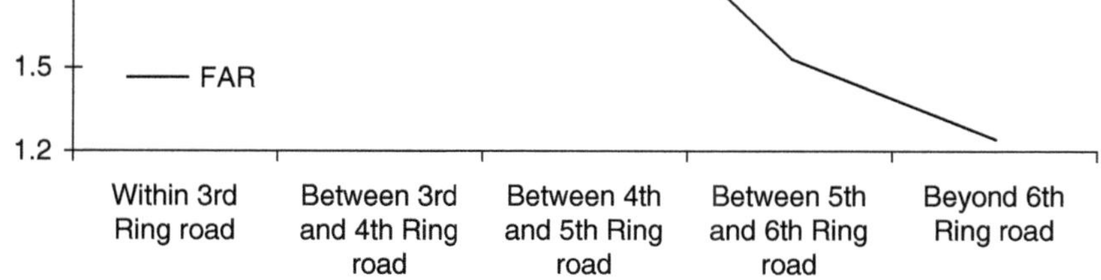

Figure 9.8 Spatial distribution curve of Beijing land sales floor-to-area ratio.

negative gradient exists. In fact, we can intuitively observe in daily life tall office buildings crowded in the downtown's CBD with a high building density, whereas houses in the suburbs are relatively lower and dispersed.

$$\begin{aligned}&\ln(\text{floor-to-area ratio}) = 0.713 - 0.010 \times \text{distance to city center}\\&(7.35^{***})\ (-5.76^{***})\\&+\text{year dummies} \qquad (9.6)\\&R^2 = 0.198,\ \text{sample size} = 367\\&{}^{***}\ \text{significant at the 1\% level.}\end{aligned}$$

9.2.1.5 Population density decreases as distance to CBD increases

From the city center outward, building density gradually declines and *per capita* housing consumption gradually increases, which causes population density to steadily decrease. In fact, population density is one of the variables paid most attention to when urban economists study urban spatial structure. In the next section, we will examine the spatial distribution of population density in detail.

9.2.2 Population spatial distribution

Population density is the amount of population per unit area of land and is an important indicator in measuring the spatial distribution of urban population, reflecting the intensity of urban economic activity and land use. It is noteworthy that the population figures used for population density calculations are gathered in accordance with the residence of urban population. Intuitively speaking, urban residents have to go home and sleep at night, so urban population density is expressed as the distribution characteristics of urban population at night from 12 a.m. midnight to 6 a.m. dawn (Ding, 2007).

Figure 9.9 depicts a three-dimensional distribution graph of urban population in seven world cities, including Shanghai, China. It can be observed that other than Moscow, spatial distribution of population density in the other six cities show astonishing similarity—the steady spatial decline in population density, which is in accordance with the 5th inference of the monocentric city model, the only difference being the different rates at which this decline takes place (Bertaud, 2001). The population density in downtown Shanghai is much higher than that in London and New York and the spatial rate of decline in Shanghai's population density is also high. As the subsequent text will discuss, in many large Chinese cities (including Shanghai), due to historical path dependence and the lagged provision of public goods, urban public goods (especially high quality public goods) are still highly concentrated in the inner city, which causes the population density of the inner city to be overly high and the degree of suburbanization to be low, displaying a steep gradient in the decline of population density—Shanghai's population is around 69 percent of New York's population, but its constructed area is less than 10 percent of New York's (Ding, 2007).

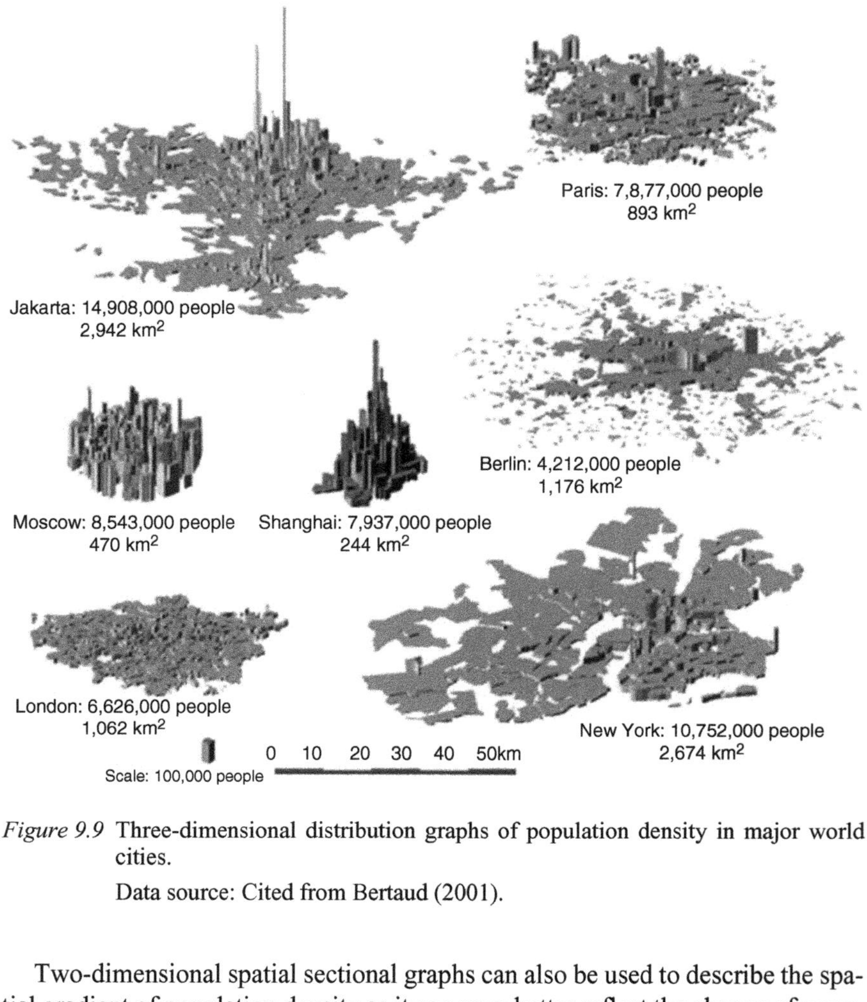

Figure 9.9 Three-dimensional distribution graphs of population density in major world cities.

Data source: Cited from Bertaud (2001).

Two-dimensional spatial sectional graphs can also be used to describe the spatial gradient of population density as it can even better reflect the change of population density as distance to city center changes. Figure 9.10 provides the two-dimensional spatial sectional graph for population density in several famous metropolises. Judging from the big picture, the feature of steady spatial declines in population density exists in these cities, which is exactly the 5th inference of the monocentric city model. In some cities, the downtown area does not have the highest population density, which may be due to the existence of historical building protections, restrictions on building height, etc.

In a statistical sense, the spatial gradient of population density can be estimated with a population density function. Since Clark's (1951) study, many academics have endeavored to estimate the population density function for different cities and study its change over time. According to McDonald's (1989) review, a large number of results from empirical research on cities all follow two laws: first,

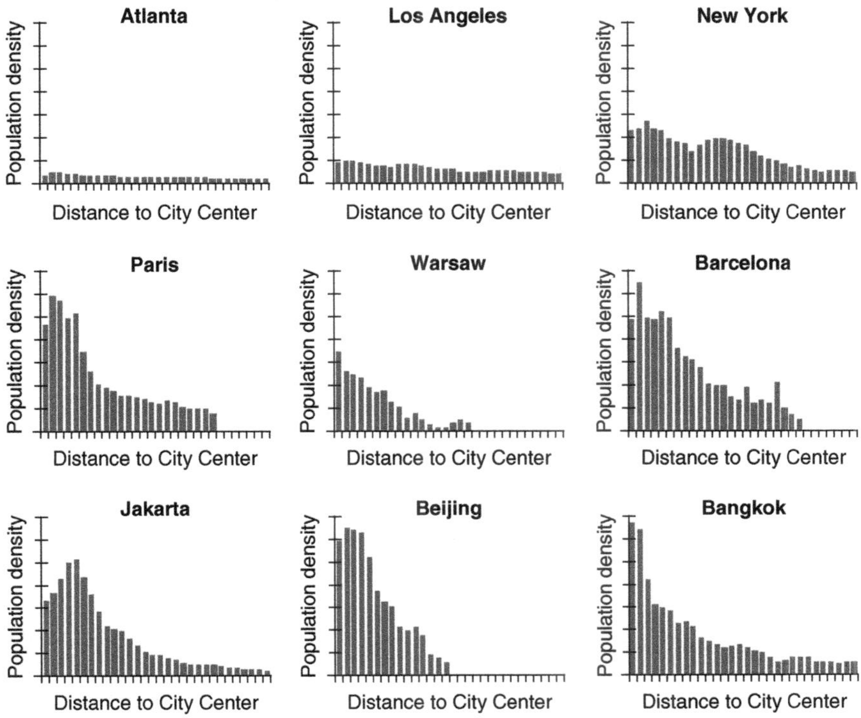

Figure 9.10 Two-dimensional distribution graph of population density in major cities.
Data source: Cited from Bertaud (2004).

positive density gradients—density decreases as the distance to city center increases; second, the density gradient decreases with time, displaying a suburbanization pattern. The population density function and the spatial gradient equation of property prices are similar. By performing a single variable OLS regression on the log value of population density against the distance to city center, the coefficient before distance shows the percentage decrease in population density for every kilometer away from the city center. By employing 2000 Census Beijing neighborhood population figures, the below simple regression could be performed.

$$\text{Ln(population density)} = 10.484 - 0.119 \times \text{distance to city center} \quad (9.7)$$
$$(8.91^{***})\ (-8.28^{***})$$
$$R^2 = 0.426, \text{ sample size} = 129 \text{ zones}$$
*** significant at the 1% level.

The above highly parsimonious model can explain 43 percent of the variation in spatial population density. The coefficient before distance is –0.119, which means for every kilometer away from the city center, population density decreases

Table 9.1 Estimates of population density gradient for several cities

City	*Year*	*Density gradient (unit: km^{-1})*	*City*	*Year*	*Density gradient (unit: km^{-1})*
London	1801	0.79	New York City	1900	0.20
	1841	0.58		1940	0.13
	1901	0.23		1950	0.11
	1931	0.17	Chicago	1880	0.48
	1939	0.14		1900	0.25
	1961	0.09		1940	0.13
Paris	1817	1.47		1956	0.11
	1856	0.59	Boston	1900	0.53
	1896	0.50		1940	0.19
	1931	0.48	Sydney	1911	0.30
	1946	0.21		1954	0.16
Frankfurt	1890	1.17	Christchurch	1911	1.01
	1933	0.58		1951	0.84
Birmingham, UK	1921	0.50	Yangon	1931	0.73
	1938	0.29		1951	0.34
Los Angeles	1940	0.17			

Data source: Clark (1967, pp. 349–351).

by 11.9 percent. This gradient value is roughly twice that of the average population density spatial gradient (–0.048) for US cities in 2000 (Baum-Snow and Kahn, 2005). Table 9.1 lists some figures for the change in population density with time around the world and it is not hard to see that Beijing's population density gradient is only half of the average gradient level of these cities around the 1950s. At the same time, the population density gradient of these cities gradually eased in their rate of change, which reflects the suburbanization of urban residence.

9.2.3 Cluster and dispersion of employment

The monocentric model was rapidly expanded. The employment was no longer only concentrated at the city center, with the land occupied by other industries taken into consideration. Following a similar line of thinking, firm location choice is a process of trading-off locational advantages and costs (rent). For households in the monocentric model, locational advantage is mainly convenience in getting to work and home; for firms, locational advantages may include many aspects. Before road transportation (especially highways) had developed, the long distance transportation of goods mainly relied on railroads and waterways, so early cities mostly developed around ports or railway stations. At this point, the closer a place was to the city center's port or railway station, the lower the transport cost and the higher the rent. With the rise of highway construction and air transportation, the transport cost of goods places an increasingly small restriction on firm location choice. There is massive land supply for the entrance or exits of numerous highways in the suburbs, so the transportation conditions are convenient. At the same time, since manufacturing often requires large tracts of low-storied plants to accommodate the production lines, the high price of land in the city center seems uneconomical. The combined effect of these factors jointly promotes the suburbanization of manufacturing (Anas et al., 1998).

The advent of the tertiary industries, especially the rapid development of technology intensive industries such as finance, insurance, consulting, legal services, high tech, etc. also enabled the transport cost of goods to no longer be a crucial cost factor. These industries need to be agglomerated even more, as they rely on social networks and face-to-face communication. Though modern communication methods—such as the internet, video phone, etc.—mean that remote contact is no longer an obstacle, the fact is that entrepreneurs and technical development personnel sitting in a meeting or congregating informally in a coffee shop or restaurant is more conducive to generating inspirations and creating business opportunities (Glaeser, 2007), thereby increasing productivity and helping firms operate more efficiently. Such face-to-face communication may be between similar firms (e.g. information sharing), or between firms and their suppliers (e.g. vertically integrated information), or between firms and their clients (e.g. marketing). Thus, even today when modern communications are highly developed, firms in these industries are still willing to pay high rents and agglomerate in the tall and clustered office buildings in the city center. Many manufacturing firms also set up their company headquarters in the CBD, leasing a little space to accommodate the company's management, research, marketing and business negotiation personnel, while locating the production function in the suburbs.

Spatial data (especially official statistics) on employment distribution within cities is harder to access than population distribution, and this is even more so in China, so quantitative research in this field is extremely sparse. Differing with the nighttime population distribution reflected by population density, employment density could be thought of as the daytime urban population distribution. Here, we employ basic unit census and economic census employment data and explore the pattern of employment spatial distribution. The 2004 national economic census figures for Beijing show the employment density for Beijing as 7,000 persons per square km and the employment density around 14,700 persons per square km in the four inner city districts. Whereas in 1995 Manhattan, New York had an average employment population density of 33,700 persons per square km and Tokyo's four central districts had an average employment density of 47,000 persons per square km. It could be noted that compared with Manhattan and Tokyo's four central districts, the agglomeration of employment opportunities in inner Beijing is not high.

Let us then compare the spatial gradient of employment density and population density. The 2001 national basic unit census data (Beijing sample) gave the number of employed persons per neighborhood and industry, which could also be converted into employment density. First, we will take a look at the employment density spatial gradient of all industries:

$$\ln(\text{employment density}) = 1.558 - 0.204 \times \text{distance to city center}$$
$$(9.76^{***})\ (-15.2^{***}) \qquad (9.8)$$

$R^2 = 0.641$, sample size = 132
*** significant at 1% level.

The very simple model in Equation 9.8 can explain 64 percent of the difference in spatial employment density. The spatial gradient of employment density is –0.204 and its absolute value is apparently larger than the spatial gradient of population density, which is –0.119 [see Equation (9.7)]. This is actually a common characteristic of many cities—employment distribution is much more compact than population distribution—in other words, employment is more clustered (Ding, 2007). This is easy to understand, as industry requires agglomeration economies more than daily life.

$$\ln(\text{employment density}) = 0.749 - 0.159 \times \text{distance to city center} \quad (9.9)$$
(4.52***) (–11.4***)
$R^2 = 0.506$, sample size = 129
*** significant at 1% level.

Then we employ the 2004 national economic census Beijing sample to perform the same regression. Comparing the results of the two equations, we find that the spatial gradient of employment density becomes flatter, which reflects the suburbanization of urban employment to a certain extent. Miezkowski and Mills' (1993) research also points out that the density gradient for employment is larger than that for population but it declines more rapidly with time.

So, in different industries, does the spatial distribution of employment differ? According to theory, technology intensive industries have a stronger preference for agglomeration economies and are willing to pay a higher rent for city center locations (i.e. a rather steep bid-rent curve), thereby occupying locations near the city center, and the gradient (absolute value) of employment density will be relatively high. Conversely, manufacturing and other labor intensive industries will have relatively milder employment density gradients. If finance and insurance, business consulting, real estate, research and development, and high technology industries are defined as technology intensive industries and other industries are defined as labor intensive, and a spatial gradient equation is performed on both respectively, it could obviously be observed that high technology industries have a steeper spatial gradient and are more clustered:[4]

Technology intensive industries

$$\ln(\text{employment density for technology intensive types}) = 8.706 - 0.217 \times \text{distance to city center} \quad (9.10)$$
(17.2***) (–11.13***)
$R^2 = 0.500$, sample size = 126

Labor intensive industries

$$\ln(\text{employment density for labor intensive types}) = 10.123 - 0.172 \times \text{distance to city center} \quad (9.11)$$

(33.7***) (–14.84***)
R^2 = 0.640, sample size = 126
*** significant at 1% level.

The reader may be puzzled here. Can Beijing and Chengdu (or other Chinese cities) really be viewed as monocentric cities? Their employment is not concentrated in the city center, but spread all over the city. This touches upon the question of how to comprehend the concept of a "monocentric city." First, we have to distinguish between abstract models and real cities. Although all employment centers are concentrated in a "point" with no size in the abstract monocentric city model, the relative degree of employment opportunity concentration is used to judge whether a city is closer to monocentric or polycentric (this is not an absolute question of "yes or no" but a question of degree). A rather consistent criteria used by American academics is, if a circular zone encompassing a 3-mile radius of the CBD as its center contains over 30 percent of the city's employment, then a monocentric model has rather good explanatory power for the urban spatial structure. By employing 2004 Chinese economic census Beijing figures, it can be calculated that 43 percent of employment opportunities are concentrated within the circle with Tiananmen as its center and a 3-mile (4.8 kilometer) radius, which clearly leans toward a monocentric city. At the same time, most of Beijing's public amenities are concentrated in the inner city. In this sense, Beijing could be viewed as close to a monocentric urban form. The spatial gradient analysis of property prices, land prices, population density and employment density above verify this point as well—the city center's leading role is still strong. It is also worth mentioning that the largest contribution of the monocentric model is its proposal of the main economic forces that drive urban spatial structure and basic analytic methods. These are still applicable in polycentric cities. Thus, discussions on the monocentric model are a natural starting point for the study of urban spatial structure. Of course, as the size of the city's main center expands continuously, the main center may divide into multiple subcenters. Below we will discuss issues relating to urban subcenters.

9.2.4 The rise of subcenters and their influence

9.2.4.1 Identification of subcenters and their spatial distribution

Ren et al. (2009) employed Beijing land sales figures from 1993 to 2004 and adopted a non-parametric method to fit the spatial distribution of Beijing land prices (Figure 9.11 is the contour line graph of land price spatial distribution; Figure 9.12 is a 3D graph). The results of the regression show that Beijing still displays an obvious monocentric urban spatial structure, with spatial development exhibiting asymmetricity: the eastern part is faster than the western part and the northern part is faster than the southern part. At the same time, the subcenter effect gradually emerges. The two places in the land price contour lines that stick out in Figure 9.11, respectively prove the two currently intuitively perceived

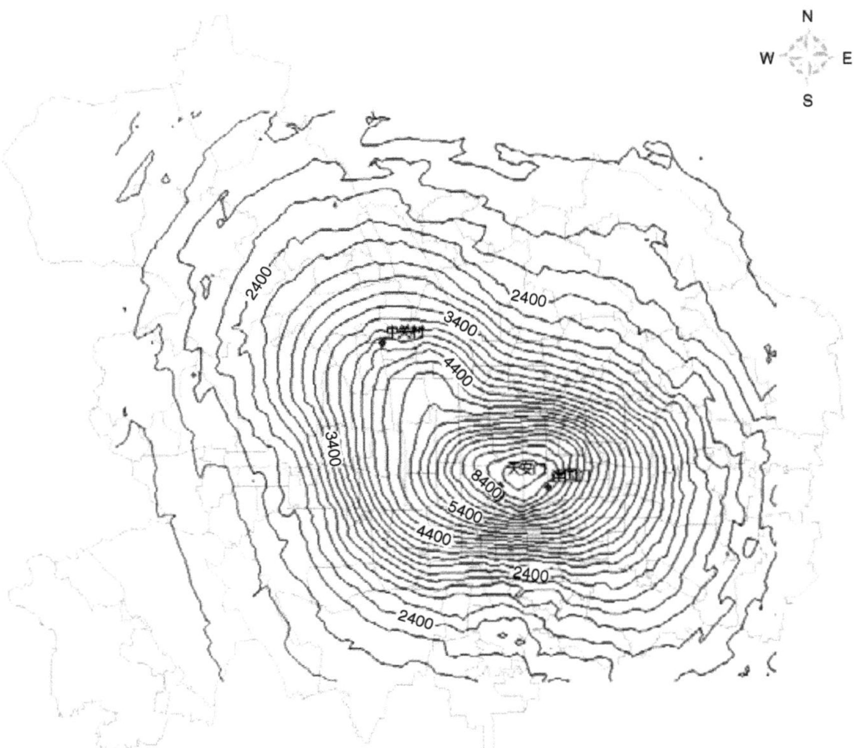

Figure 9.11 Contour line graph of Beijing land price spatial distribution.
Note: Isoline unit: yuan/m^2.

employment centers, that is, the main center CBD outside Jianguomen and the subcenter Zhongguancun area. Especially since the Zhongguancun area has a pulling effect on land prices as a subcenter, the land price contour line at the Zhongguancun area exhibits an obvious trend toward extension. In Figure 9.12, the land price surface peaks within the Second Ring, and a partial protrusion in the Zhongguancun area.

Some academics provided a more formal method for determining the employment center. For example, in the quantitative method provided by Giuliano and Small (1991), the whole city area needs to be divided into square grids (research on American cities generally sets the cells at 1/4 square mile, that is, 805 meters × 805 meters), and determines the employment center through the two following principles: (1) for a certain number of neighboring cells, the number of employment opportunities in each neighboring cell should exceed a lower limit D; (2) the overall employment opportunities in these cells should exceed a lower limit E. For example, Giuliano and Small (1991) set D to 10 persons/acre, roughly equal to 1,600 persons/cell, 2,500 persons/square km. E is generally set to

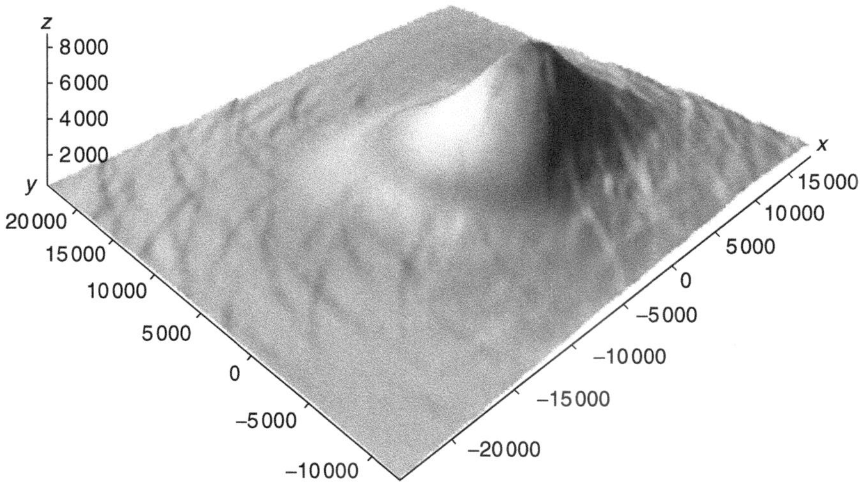

Figure 9.12 Three-dimensional Beijing land price simulation graph.

Note: Origin point is Tiananmen Square; x, y axis, units: meter; z axis represents land price, unit: yuan/m^2.

10,000 persons. In the employment centers selected through this manner, the one with the highest intensity is chosen as the main center. By employing the above principles, Giuliano and Small (1991) discovered 29 employment centers in 1980 Los Angeles; whereas Cervero and Wu (1998) determined 22 employment centers in 1990 San Francisco. Although this method is simple and convenient, drawbacks do exist. First, it is difficult for it to find centers in the suburbs with relatively low employment density and is not quite suitable for cities with rather high employment density gradients; next, the size of the analysis unit (tract of land) has a large impact on the result; third, it requires researchers to understand the local circumstances in order to determine the threshold values and "neighboring blocks of land" concept.

Another commonly used method is regression analysis. On the whole, this method is not only conducive to eliminating the impact of analysis unit size, through introducing objective statistical criteria, it also reduces inconsistent results generated by subjective differences in researchers' background knowledge, categorization criteria etc. Based on the assumption of monocentricity, McDonald (1987), McDonald and McMillen (1990) and McDonald and Prather (1994) fitted urban employment density functions and chose blocks of land with residuals between actual employment density values and fitted values significantly larger than zero as the employment center. Other studies employed nonparametric methods. McMillen (2001) used the locally weighted regression method to study six American cities, including Chicago. This method uses the employment density of neighboring land blocks to fit the employment density value of each land block, thereby choosing land blocks with residuals significantly larger than zero (0) as candidate centers. On the basis of these methods, Gordon, Richardson and Wong (1986) as well as McMillen and McDonald (1998) proposed a two stage method, that is, on the basis of finding the high value point of employment density within a region, further testing the candidate employment centers' explanatory power for the city's overall employment density function. The former found that out of 57 candidate centers in Los Angeles, only six have significant impact on the overall density function; the latter found that out of 20 candidate centers in Chicago, 17 influential centers could be distinguished.

Currently, figures for employment spatial distribution in Chinese cities are still not very refined (only reaching the zone, so-called *jiedao*, level. For instance, Beijing has about 120 zones) and there is not enough information to support refined analysis similar to those performed above. Gu et al. (2009) employed 2001 national basic unit census and 2004 national economic census figures to compile Beijing neighborhood level employment distribution figures (see Figure 9.13) and adopted a two stage method to preliminarily ascertain and analyze potentially existing employment centers in Beijing.

The first step is to find candidate employment centers. In view of the large analytic units and small sample sizes, the authors adopted direct comparison approaches to search for local employment population density high value points, listing analytic units with employment densities higher than 10 neighboring neighborhoods and townships as candidate centers. In the second step, the candidate centers' impact on the employment population density of the surrounding 10 neighborhoods and townships is tested, with the neighborhoods or townships that pass the test accepted as employment centers. In 2001, through the direct comparison approach, seven candidate employment centers were chosen, including Xuanwu District's Niujie neighborhood (employment population density at 90,193 persons/square kilometer; same unit is used for densities which follow); Chaoyang District's Jianguomen neighborhood (81,752); Guanzhuang neighborhood (53,720); Beijing International Airport area (5,468); Haidian District's Haidian neighborhood (33,839); Shangdi neighborhood (30,249) and Shijingshan district's Gucheng neighborhood (5,468). However, other than the Airport area, most candidate centers do not have significant impacts on the employment density of close neighborhoods or townships. In 2004, seven candidate employment centers were also found, but the members were not the same, respectively being Xicheng's Erlong Road neighborhood (represents the Financial Street, employment population density at 50,963 persons/square kilometers; same unit for the following); Chaoyang District's Jianguomen neighborhood (represents the CBD, 49,323); Beijing International Airport area (2,332); Haidian District's Shuangyushu neighborhood (represents Zhongguancun, 22,217); Shangdi neighborhood (22,884); Shijingshan District's Gucheng neighborhood (6,549) and Tongzhou District's Xinhua neighborhood (6,251), and discovered that several neighborhoods generated an impact on the employment density of nearby neighborhoods, which shows that some employment "subcenters" are growing. For some empirically verified employment centers such as CBD, Financial Street and

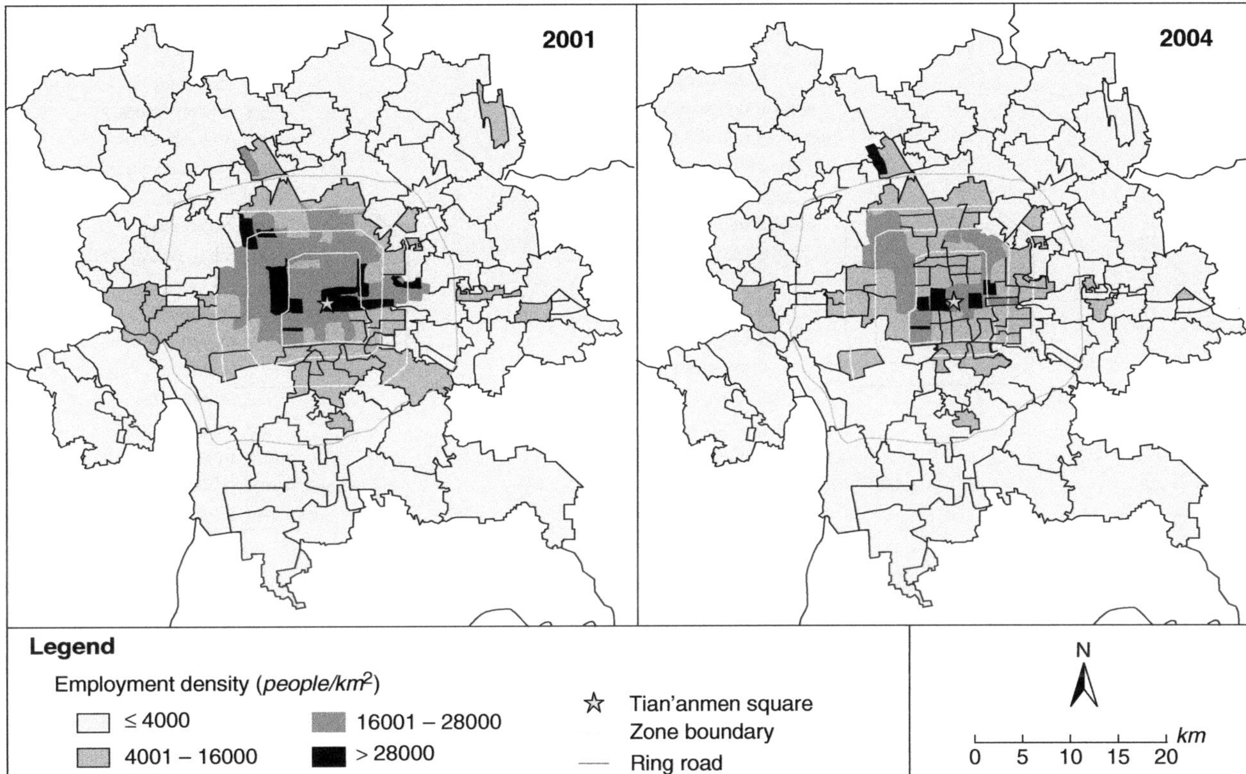

Figure 9.13 2001 and 2004 Beijing urban districts employment population distribution graph.

Data source: 2001 national basic unit census and 2004 national economic census Beijing figures.

Zhongguancun areas, it is exactly industrial agglomeration that leads to the increase in employment density, thus the employment density changes from Tiananmen outwards exhibit sharp changes in certain portions, proving the influence of these centers (see Figure 9.14). Also, the employment density gradient of the overall metropolitan area and beyond the Second Ring area is becoming more gradual, which is due to the suburban employment subcenters making their influence felt. These phenomenon all illustrate Beijing's trend toward a polycentric spatial structure.

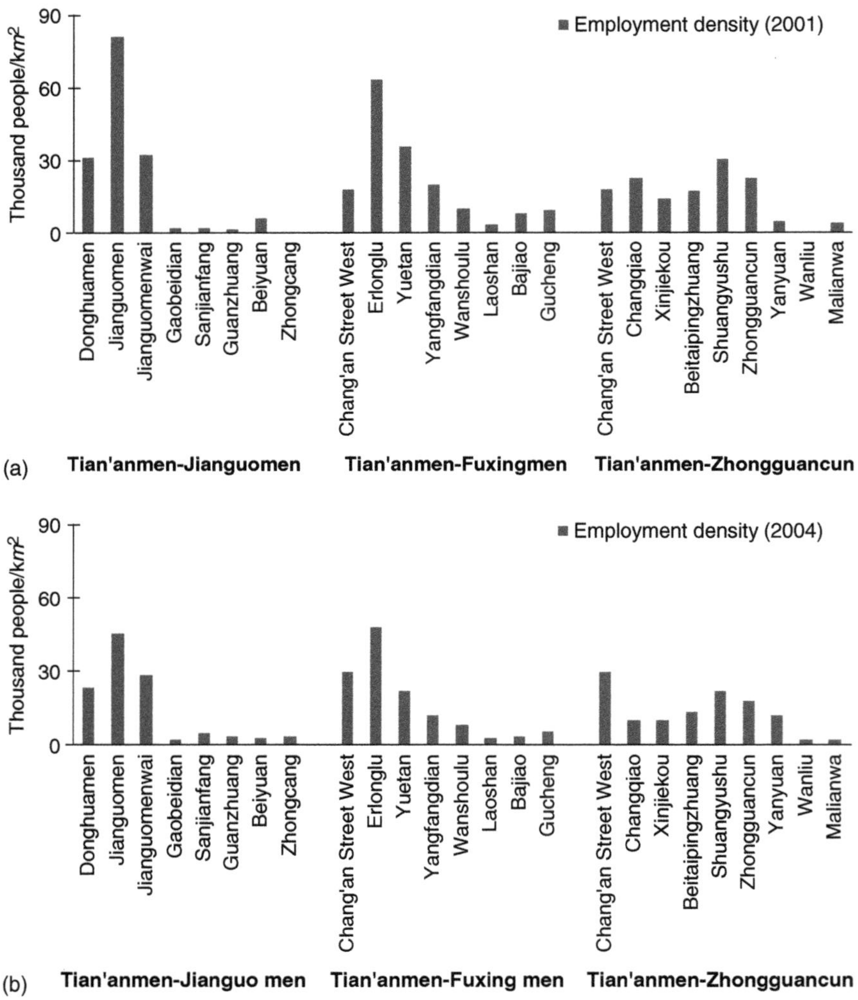

Figure 9.14 Graphs on employment density changes along certain Tiananmen directions. (a) 2001, (b) 2004.

9.2.4.2 Subcenters' formation mechanisms

The formation of employment centers is rooted in the demand of firms for agglomeration economies. Helsley and Sullivan (1991) proposed a simple model to explain how city centers (including main centers and subcenters) form and separate, through which the economic forces that propel the cluster and dispersion of employment opportunities in the urban space can be understood.

Figure 9.15 depicts how a firm's production costs change with the city center's size. The increasingly ascending curve represents the rise in wages. In large city centers, land is mainly occupied by firms and residential-use land is pushed toward more remote places, so the residential location of employees is far away from the firm's location. Hence, firms must pay higher wages to compensate for their employees' higher transportation costs. The wage curve will intersect with the vertical axis. The increasingly descending curve represents production costs other than wages. As the center's size increases, agglomeration economies have a stronger effect and can bring down production costs. This curve will necessarily intersect with the vertical axis (at A_0), but after that, it will gradually become parallel with the horizontal axis, an obvious nonlinear curve. The sum of these two curves is the total production cost. This curve will first decline, reaching its trough value, then rising as the effect of agglomeration economies marginally decreases (the curve becomes ever more gradual) and the increase in transportation costs leads to wage increases. The trough value can be used to represent the optimal size of this employment center. It could be observed that this train of thought is similar to that used to analyze the optimal city size—the trade-off between agglomeration economies and diseconomies.

An analysis more in tune with the real world follows. As a region develops, new firms enter the region and choose a location where production costs are

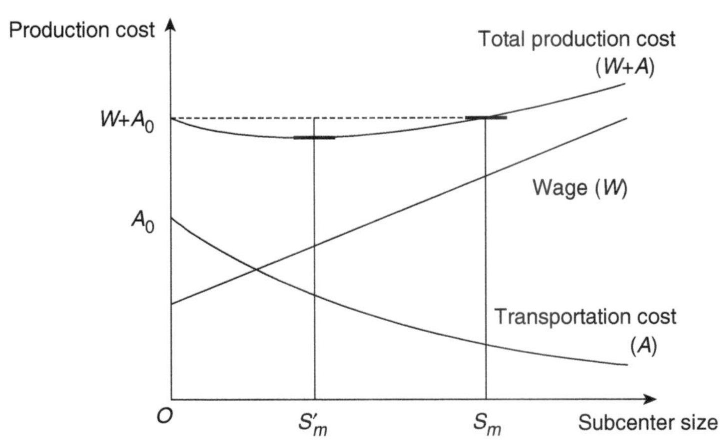

Figure 9.15 Subcenter size and firm costs.

Data source: Cited from Denise DiPasquale and William C. Wheaton (1996).

lowest and they invest in the construction of plant and equipment or facilities. After these investments become sunk costs, they will restrict the relocation of firms, even if production costs (wages and agglomeration costs) in another location are lower. At first, when the employment center is small, wages are low and agglomeration costs (A_0) are high (the place close to the origin in Figure 9.16). As this center expands, overall production costs will begin to decline, but a new center still will not form, as the overall cost there ($W + A_0$) will still be relatively high. Gradually, as this center reaches a certain optimal size (S_m), its overall production costs will increase to the same level as an isolated firm ($W + A_0$). Here, the next firm to arrive at this employment center will not benefit and growth in this center will end. As the city develops, the second center will begin to grow, new firms will be attracted to this center, and its development path will be similar to the first center. The production costs will first decline, then increase and always be lower than that of the first center (the first center's firm will not migrate to the new center with lower costs as migration requires investing in the construction of new plants). As the second center expands and reaches the size S_m, the third new subcenter will form and so forth. The eventual result will be multiple mature employment centers will appear after many years, each of which is roughly the size S_m, with one new on-going center smaller than S_m.

It is interesting that as modern communications technology develops, the costs of communication between firms decrease and the sensitivity to geographical distance is lower. If it is assumed that the firms' demand for agglomeration economies is constant, a small employment center size is enough to form agglomeration economies. The dotted line in Figure 9.16 reflects such changes. The overall production costs decline and become a more level U type, its low point close to the original low point. As such, for a city with the same number of firms, technological innovation will create more, relatively small-sized subcenters (with the size S'_m). This implies that as information costs decrease, firms that pursue the minimization of costs can better use the dispersed location to lower production costs (mainly wages).

9.2.4.3 Impacts of main and subcenters on factor spatial distribution

In summary, the empirical research conclusions of urban economists on the impact of main and subcenters on factor spatial distribution mainly include: first, main and subemployment centers can explain the distributions of employment, population and land (as well as housing) prices[5] in surrounding regions. Typical studies include Small and Song (1994). Gu et al.'s (2009) study also verifies that the impact of subcenters on distribution of employment in surrounding areas is gradually increasing in Beijing.

Second, the existence of multiple subcenters does not negate the dominant impact of main centers. As McMillen (1996) discovered, from 1836 to the present day, Chicago shifted from monocentric to polycentric, though the spatial distribution of urban land prices fluctuated, the basic trend is declining prices from the CBD on outward. The spatial gradient analysis on Beijing employment,

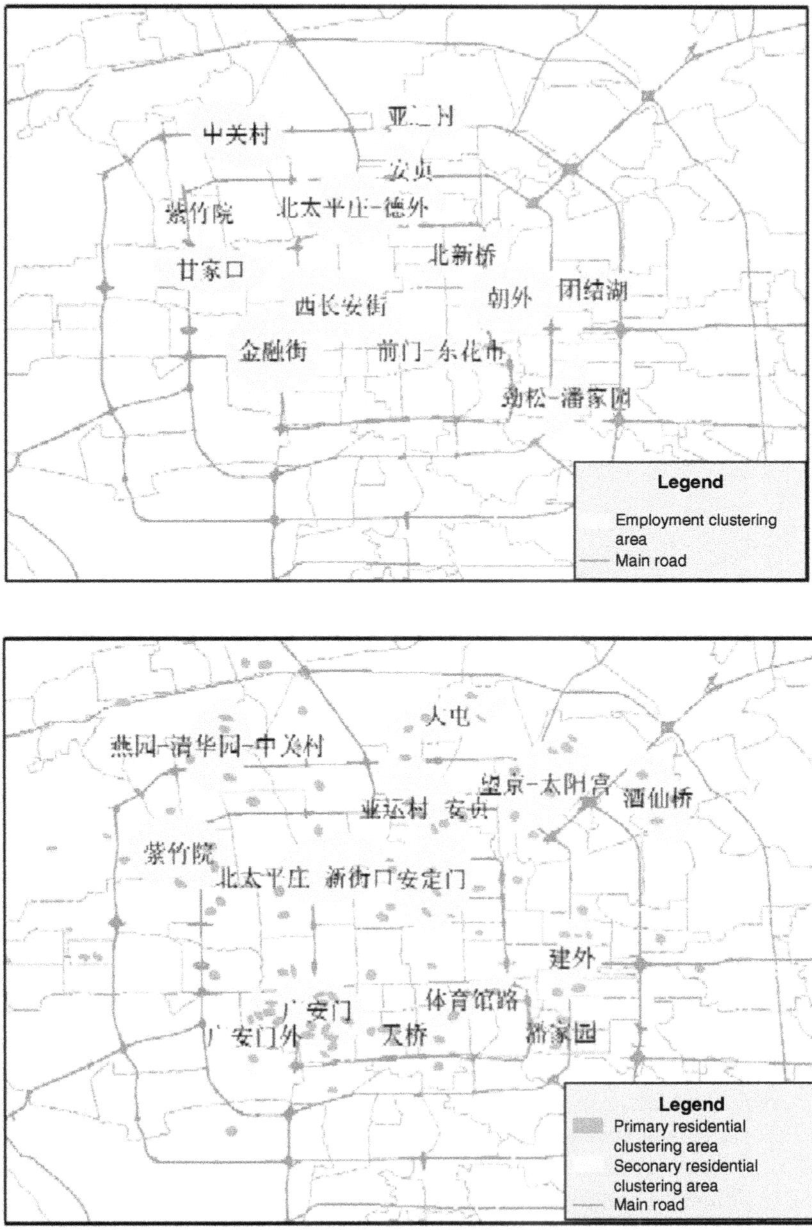

(a)

(b)

Figure 9.16 Residential and employment clustering area analysis. (a) Employment location. (b) Residence location. (c) Residential—employment agglomeration area difference analysis.

Data source: Cited from (Meng, 2009).

(c)

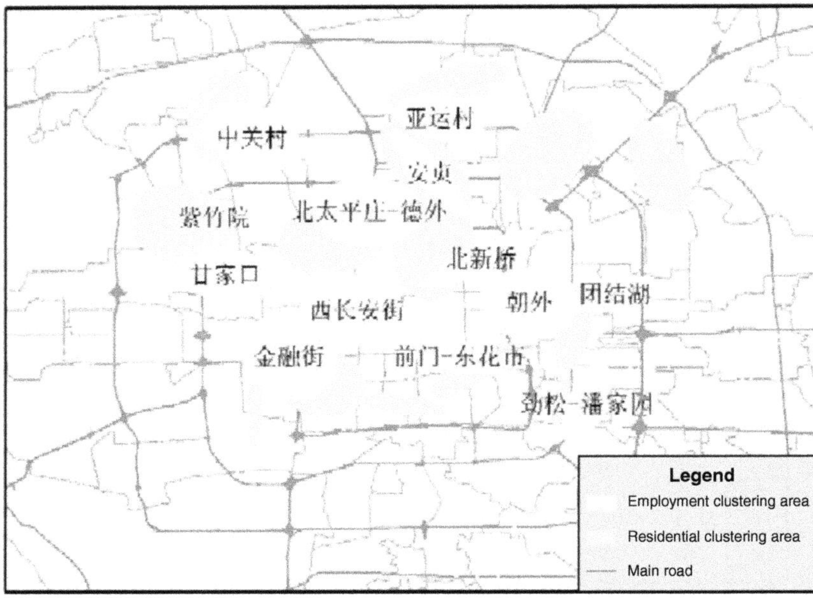

Figure 9.16 Continued

population, property and land prices performed before also proves this, with only the "distance to city center" variable, 40–60 percent of the factor spatial distribution can be explained. The main center's dominant effect is quite obvious.

Third, most jobs are distributed outside the employment center. In several typical American metropolises, around 50 percent of jobs are located outside the employment center (Song, 1994), thus making employment cluster and dispersion coexistent. In Beijing, if Jianguomen neighborhood, Jianwai neighborhood, Chaowai neighborhood, Donghuamen neighborhood, West Changan Road neighborhood, Financial Street neighborhood, and Zhongguancun neighborhood are defined as employment centers, they only contain 15.1 percent of all employment opportunities (according to 2004 Chinese economic census Beijing data).

Fourth, the actual transportation volume far exceeds the amount forecast by the traditional urban models (whether monocentric or polycentric). Hamilton's (1982) study is believed to be the source of these discussions as he proposed the issue of "excess commuting." Giuliano and Small (1993) followed-up afterwards. The traditional urban models have rather rigorous assumptions, including: commuting is the only reason for travel; people have consistent preferences for housing; each household has only one employed person; and fixed workplaces, etc. But subsequent research showed that the above assumptions cannot all be satisfied in reality. The heterogeneity of housing preferences, the need to travel to other urban amenities, households with two working family members who have different workplaces and future job changes, etc. are factors which may all lead to actual transportation volumes far exceeding those forecast by the traditional urban models.

9.3 Spatial relationship between residence and workplace: the "adhesion" of agglomeration economies and the "friction" of commuting costs

9.3.1 Manifestation of spatial relationship between residence and workplace

From the above analysis on the Beijing population density gradients and employment density gradients, the degree of agglomeration for employment is much higher than that for residence. In fact, with the development of urban transportation, the spatial separation of employment density and population density trends toward increasing (Ding, 2007). As aforementioned, employment density often reflects the daytime population density, while population (residential) density generally reflects the nighttime population distribution. Table 9.2 lists the spatial change of employment opportunities and housing from 1970 to 1990 for Tokyo's metropolitan area (with 1970 as 100), illustrating very well the trend toward separation between employment density and population density (Hiroka, 2000). Three districts near downtown (45 km^2) during this period saw a 37 percent increase in white collar workers, a 29 percent increase in daytime population (representing employment opportunities), whereas nighttime population decreased 35 percent; the inner eight districts (114 km^2) saw a 50 percent increase in white collar workers, a 25 percent increase in daytime population, while in the same period, nighttime population fell by 29 percent. The 23 Tokyo districts (621 km^2) saw an increase of 46 percent in white collar workers, an 8 percent increase in daytime population, and an 8 percent decrease in nighttime population in the same period.

The spatial separation of jobs and housing leads to overly high transportation needs and costs. Under the condition of insufficient supply of transportation facilities and low urban administration efficiency, this will cause transportation congestion, which has become a pervasive phenomenon in many large Chinese cities. For example, the average one-way commuting time in 2006 Beijing was 43 minutes (Horizon Research Consultancy, 2006), far exceeding major large cities in the US (Philadelphia the longest with 38.3 minutes) and Europe (UK leading with

Table 9.2 Spatial evolution of Tokyo employment and housing distributions

	1990		
	Daytime workers	*Daytime population*	*Nighttime population*
3 central districts	137	129	65
8 central districts	150	125	71
23 districts	146	108	92

Note: 1970 population is used as index value 100.
Data source: Hiroka (2000).

22.5 minutes) (United States Census Bureau, 2005; King and Leibling, 2003). Also, transportation congestion inevitably increases urban environmental pressure. Using Beijing as an example, motor vehicles account for 33 percent of inhalable particles, 64 percent of oxynitrides, and 51 percent of hydrocarbons in Beijing's air pollution. Motor vehicle exhaust gas has become Beijing's largest source of atmosphere pollution.[6] In order to alleviate these problems, some policymakers and scholars have proposed "jobs–housing balance", believing that residents should live as close as possible to their work places, in order to lower the volume of commuting and congestion, reducing transportation costs. "Jobs–housing balance" has always been a hotspot of academic and policy discussion. This concept could be traced back to Howard's (1902) proposal of a "garden city", which has a clear logic: assuming other factors are unchanged, an increase in the supply of housing around employment centers increases the proportion of residents that reside close to this employment center, as they will (or can) propose higher bids. The social impact is obvious too: such a mechanism can lower commuting demand, alleviating traffic congestion and air pollution, and also helping to reducing expenditures for medium and lower income households (Levine, 1998). Research by some academics show (Knaap et al., 2005) that the higher the mixture of different types of economic activities (or different types of land use), the easier it is for jobs and housing balance. Levine's (1998) study showed that whether a sufficient and affordable housing supply exists in close proximity to an employment center has a critical impact on the achievement of a good balance. But many academics believe the theoretical analysis and practical application of this concept is not yet mature, and the following text will further explore this issue. It is noteworthy that this balance relationship has also been used by academics to measure the degree of urban sprawl. It is generally believed that an overly low degree of jobs and housing balance is an important feature of urban sprawl, and there are some indicators that explain this, such as the "jobs–housing Gini coefficient" (Bento et al., 2003), number of employment opportunities in a certain region within 30 minutes' transportation (or a certain distance) (Ewing et al., 2002).

Many researchers launched quantitative research on the spatial relationship between jobs and housing in Chinese cities. Meng (2009) employed data from a questionnaire in 2005 Beijing (totaling 7,647 valid samples), in order to conduct a detailed statistical analysis on the commuting time and jobs–housing separation situation of employed workers. Data analysis shows that the average commuting time for Beijing employed workers is around 38 minutes, with commuting time within 30 minutes for only 35 percent of the total, and commuting time exceeding 40 minutes for 43.7 percent of total. Compared with the US, Beijing's employed persons have an overly high commuting time. According to the US Census Bureau's 2005 data, the average one-way commuting time for Americans is 25.1 minutes, of which Philadelphia leads with 38.3 minutes, followed by New York with 34.2 minutes; Washington comes in third with 33.4 minutes (United States Census Bureau, 2005). This may be due to the high degree of spatial separation between jobs and housing and may also be caused by

Table 9.3 Comparison of resident one-way commuting distance before and after moving (unit: kilometer)

	Average	*Standard deviation*
Before moving	7.51	6.43
After moving	11.95	5.41

Data source: Li and Li (2007).

over-congestion in traffic. Current Beijing commuting flows are still dominated by centripetal flows, though a certain proportion of centrifugal commuting exists. The author employed spatial cluster analysis to provide the main employment and residential clustering areas in Beijing (see Figure 9.16) and discovered a mismatch exists between the two. Detailed analysis shows that a few large residential areas that were key large-scale housing projects (e.g. Tiantongyuan and Huilongguan) have overly monotonous residential functions and the jobs–housing separation issue is especially prominent. Li and Li (2007) specially conducted a questionnaire on Tiantongyuan and Huilongguan. Although these two large residential areas are situated beyond the Fifth Ring Road within Changping District, the workplaces for 82 percent of the residents are concentrated within the Fifth Ring Road and 70 percent are even distributed within the Fourth Ring Road. The average one-way commuting time for the questionnaire samples is 54 minutes. After moving to Tiantongyuan and Huilongguan, the distance for outgoing residents increased significantly (see Table 9.3).

Zhou and Liu (2010) employed census data and survey data to analyze Guangzhou residents' residential and employment location choice and their spatial relationships from 1996 to 2007. They discovered that the neighborhoods formed under the planned economy have relatively stable residential and employment locations, but the new or renovated neighborhoods after market reforms have higher rates of residents moving or changing jobs. In those 10 years, the distance between residential and employment locations overall exhibited an uptrend, with commodity housing and low-income public housing the most evident. Liu et al. (2009) found a similar pattern in Beijing. The 600 or so questionnaire surveys they conducted showed that the average job–housing distance is 5.6 km, newly built residential communities and low-income public housing communities have the longest job–housing distances, 7.2 km and 10.1 km, respectively, with a commuting time of 40.4 minutes and 44.2 minutes, respectively. Employed workers that have recently moved have longer commuting distances, which shows that the degree of jobs–housing separation is increasing. The common trend of these studies is that under the joint impact of institutional transition and market forces, the degree of jobs–housing spatial separation in Chinese cities is becoming ever larger—the commuting distance and time increase significantly for residents living in new homes or those that have moved recently. These empirical findings do puzzle urban planners and administrators—should the concept of "jobs–housing balance" be pursued? Why is the trend in the real world always contrary to the concept? Should it be corrected?

In fact, although the "jobs–housing balance" concept is popular amongst the urban planning community, many economists believe the theoretical analysis and practical application of this concept is not yet mature. First, whether the two are balanced is highly sensitive to what scales the measurements take place at (Giuliano, 1991), e.g. in a small neighborhood or a larger range? Obviously, the smaller the scale, the harder it is to achieve balance (in the range of the entire city, it could be thought that jobs and housing are balanced, because in economics, city-wide scale is defined as an integrated labor market, labor demand and supply are basically equal). Crane (1996a) points out if work accessibility is enhanced, demand for transportation may actually increase as cost per trip declines. Giuliano (1991) and Hanson and Pratt (1988) believe that this concept is overly reliant on the "single worker households" and "commuting-dominant transportation demand" assumptions, which is not valid in the real world.

To sum up, although the jobs–housing balance pursued by urban planning academics may attain optimal transportation costs in theory, it is hard to realize this in reality. First, this inevitably sacrifices firms' benefits from agglomeration economies; second, some firms that have negative externalities (e.g. polluting firms) will severely impact the residential quality of surrounding residents; third, households with multiple working members will have dispersed working locations, and one residence cannot balance multiple employment locations; fourth, jobs–housing balance requires every firm to find suitable employees in the surrounding area and every worker to find a suitable job around his or her residence, which is hard to achieve in the labor market (Ding, 2007). Thus, "jobs–housing separation" is the inevitable rule of labor market and real estate market development. In fact, the increase in the importance of agglomeration economies brings ever more apparent jobs–housing separation, and the subsequent LRH model will elaborate on this point.

9.3.2 Theory and empirical findings on resident and firm location choice

In spatial general equilibrium, the spatial relationship between work and home is endogenously determined within the system under the individual choices of households and firms. Here, we will first take a look at the research findings of academics on residential location choice and firm location choice.

Research on residential location choice follows the research line from exogenous employment location to endogenous employment location, from monocentric model to polycentric model, from homogeneous households to heterogeneous households, gradually relaxing model assumptions and becoming more in touch with the real world. Residential location choice theory is based on consumer utility theory from microeconomics. The classic monocentric model assumes that all employment opportunities are concentrated in the city center, residents commute in a straight line to the city center from their homes and a downwardly convex bid-rent curve is obtained (Alonso, 1964; Muth, 1969; Mills, 1972). Zheng and

Zhang's (2007) analysis using Beijing micro-level data showed that when households make residential location choices, they indeed make the trade off between commuting costs and housing costs. On this basis, Yu, Zheng, and Liu (2008) also calculated the gradient of Beijing residential housing prices and its spatial variation to find that the price gradient in all spatial directions is closely related to commuting costs. However, discussions by Hamilton (1982), Small and Song (1992), etc. regarding "excess commuting" illustrates that the actual commuting volume in cities is much higher than the theoretical value from the monocentric model, even if polycentricity is taken into consideration, which demonstrates that residential location choice is not only influenced by employment, non-commuting travel, multiple family members working and moving costs all enhance the complexity of residential location choice. Brueckner et al. (1999) included the spatial distribution of urban amenities as an endogenous variable into the model and found that it has an important impact on residential location choice. Chen's (2008) theoretical model shows that differences in households' preference of urban amenities will lead to diverse residential location behavior, causing average urban commuting time to increase. Zheng, Fu, and Liu (2006) employed the ordinal Logit model to study the residential location choice behavior of households and their determinants in five Chinese cities and also proved the difference in residential location choices brought by difference in households' preference of urban amenities, while also empirically analyzing the market and institutional factors that prevent households from choosing freely, including the underdeveloped secondary market for housing, the imperfect housing finance system as well as insufficient supply of high density and small dwelling-size housing in the inner city. At the same time, academics also relaxed the definite and unchanged workplace assumption and studied optimal intertemporal residential location choice under uncertain future employment opportunities and the existence of moving costs (e.g. Crane, 1996b). Another important extension of residential location choice models is the inclusion of the supply of transportation facilities as an endogenous variable, which under the existence of congestion, is determined by residential location choice, transportation characteristics and transportation costs (Straszheim, 1998).

Firm location choice behavior research is mainly concentrated on the impact of agglomeration economies on location choice behavior. Theoretical research by academics shows that the mechanism through which agglomeration economies impact firm location choice is: the impetus for firms to agglomerate in a certain geographical location in the urban space is to obtain spillover economic benefits from spatial proximity with other firms, increasing their productivity, thereby influencing firms' willingness to pay (bid-rent) for different locations. While obtaining spatial agglomeration economic benefits, firms face costs from high land prices and high wages, and balancing the two impacts firm location choice decisions at the micro-level and impacts the formation and evolution of urban spatial structure at the city level. Wages and land prices have been used to test for the existence and intensity of agglomeration economies, but existing research on agglomeration economies mostly explore intercity migration and spatial agglomeration of different industries, especially manufacturing, whereas research (especially empirical) on agglomeration economies within cities and firm location choice is relatively deficient. Representative papers on the latter include Sivitanidou's (1996) empirical study on Los Angeles that found the degree of sensitivity of different firms toward agglomeration economies differ and has a non-negligible impact on the land market. Fuerst (2007) used the Manhattan office building market as an example, and through constructing hedonic price panel data models, found that the spatial proximity externalities and spillover effects of office buildings have a significantly positive influence on office building rent. Ren and Zheng (2008) studied the spatial structure characteristics of Beijing's commercial and residential land development through the dimensions of price gradient, development intensity, and development location. The study found that agglomeration economies play an important role in firm location choice in office buildings and its influence strengthens with time. Zheng et al. (2009) employed Beijing wages, commuting costs and employment density data to verify the profit motive of firm location choice (agglomeration economies) and cost motive (employee commuting costs), and found that compared to labor intensive industries, technology intensive industries have a stronger demand for agglomeration economies, thus the capitalization of employment density and employee commuting costs in wages is more evident.

9.3.3 Important determinants of the spatial relationship between residence and workplace

We will now analyze in depth the main determinants of the spatial relationship between jobs and housing. In the spatial general equilibrium, this spatial relationship is endogenously determined by the free choices of households and firms. In cities in the real world, the heterogeneity of residents' preferences and urban space, historical path dependence and intervention from institutions and policies of all sorts makes it hard for the aforementioned system to reach equilibrium in the short term. The interaction of multiple economic and non-economic forces causes the spatial dynamic between jobs and housing to be even more significant and complicated.

Zheng and Cao (2009) systematically discussed the determining mechanisms and influencing factors of the spatial relationship between jobs and housing in a city. The determinants can be summarized into three groups: the spatial distribution of job opportunities, housing opportunities, and urban amenities (see Figure 9.17). Job opportunities include the current location of the worker's and his or her spouse's job and expected location of future jobs; urban amenities include schools, parks, green space, hospitals, recreation centers, etc.; housing opportunities include the spatial disposition and quantity of housing supply and the area and cost of housing, especially the spatial disposition and accessibility of affordable housing. Different households may have different commuting costs, including time costs and monetary costs, e.g. high income individuals have high time costs and those who drive private vehicles will have high monetary costs. Based on their commuting costs and their demand and preferences for work,

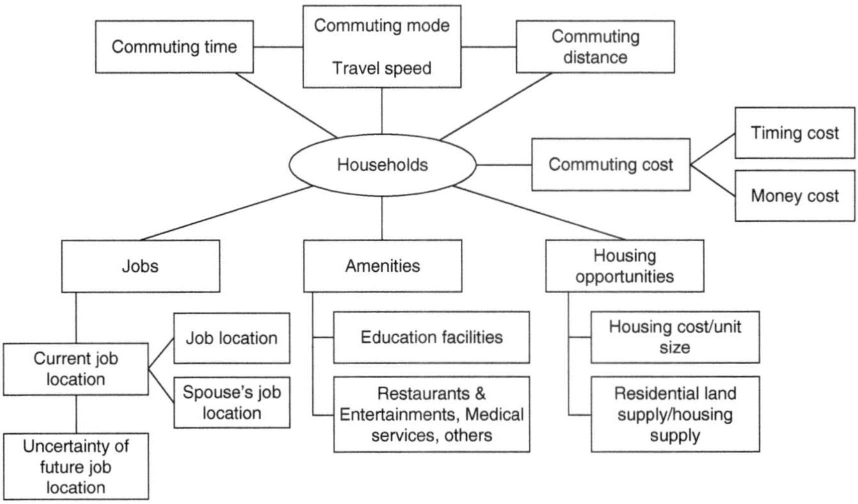

Figure 9.17 Theoretical analysis framework for the determining mechanisms of commuting time.

urban amenities and housing accessibility, households weigh costs and benefits and make a location choice decision, thereby determining the commuting time. Commuting time and distance usually have a similar pattern of change. Of course, the relationship between the two is affected by commuting vehicle and transportation speed.

Here, we can take a look at an empirical example (Zheng and Cao, 2009). This is a small sample size analysis, coming from a small survey on employed persons in Zhongguancun organized by the author in April 2007, with 288 effective observations. Since the employment location is set at Zhongguancun, the purpose of the survey is to understand where employed workers in such an urban subcenter choose to live. The shadowed area in Figure 9.18 is the residential location distribution of the sample and intensity is expressed through the shade of the color. It could be observed that the residence of these employed persons is dispersed throughout Beijing, but it is mainly contained in northwestern Beijing, where Zhongguancun is able to radiate its influence, and displays a feature of being distributed along the No. 13 subway line.

Empirical results show that when employment location is known, commuting cost is an important influencing factor of households' location choice. After controlling for other variables, high income individuals have high time costs and are inclined to choose closer locations to live in; if transportation costs can be reimbursed, then transportation costs can be significantly reduced and the spatial distance between home place and workplace could be lengthened. The residential and employment mobility of residents both impact residential location choice, thereby influencing commuting time. Compared to commodity housing,

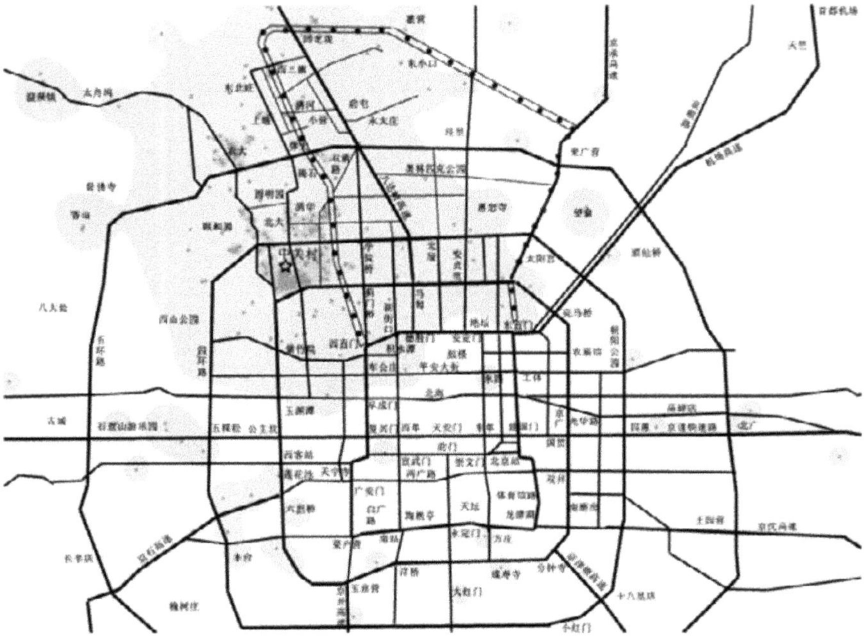

Figure 9.18 Residence distribution of Zhongguancun employee sample.

employees in rental housing have short commuting times. This is because the moving costs of those in rental housing are low and mobility is high, so employed workers can realize a better match between current employment location and residential location; whereas when homebuyers choose a residential location, they have to consider the possibility of a change in job location in the future, which increases the distance between residential location and current employment location. From the perspective of job mobility, the higher the probability that future employment will be in proximity to current employment, the closer the residential location will be to employment location. For example, in this sample, IT workers in Zhongguancun have shorter commuting times. This is because Zhongguancun is Beijing's main IT employment center, and even if IT workers change jobs in the future, they will probably remain in Zhongguancun. Also, the spouse's workplace will also impact the spatial distance between home and workplace. If the spouse's workplace is far from Zhongguancun, then the residential location choice will be the result of weighing the two workplace locations and the commuting time for both persons will be higher than if only one worked. Finally, due to historical path dependence, the *fanggai* housing units are mostly concentrated in the city center and close to employment opportunities, so commuting times are short. However, only urban residents who enjoyed the housing allocation welfare policy could obtain such *fanggai* housing units and the transaction frequency for these houses are still low, so although they have location advantages, they cannot be enjoyed by most people. This empirical analysis proved a number of theories regarding the spatial relationship between home and workplace and discovered the institutional factor's impact.

9.3.4 Main economic forces that determine employment agglomeration and dispersion—agglomeration economies and commuting costs

The use of urban land can be basically categorized into industrial land and residential land (a more refined categorization could include transportation land, public facility land, etc.). Therefore, in a more macro-sense, the spatial relationship between jobs and housing determines the basic feature of urban spatial structure—monocentric (completely separate of jobs and housing, employment totally concentrated in the city center), polycentric (employment clustered in several centers with better proximity to workers), and non-centric (employment is completely dispersed and fully mixed with homes).

The macro-manifestation of the abovementioned urban spatial structure is the result of the joint effect of micro-level location choice behavior by many firms and residents, so analysis should start from firm and household location choice behaviors. Lucas and Rossi-Hansberg successively published three papers (Lucas, 2001; Lucas and Rossi-Hansberg, 2002; Rossi-Hansberg, 2004), proposing an endogenous urban model based on externalities (LRH model in short). When analyzing urban spatial structure in equilibrium, this model relaxes the restrictive assumptions of the monocentric city model—employment activity is concentrated in the city center, and instead assumes that firms and households bid freely in different city locations; at the same time, based on agglomeration economies, it believes that firms can obtain externality benefits from spatial proximity to other firms, these externality benefits influence firm productivity thereby influencing their location choice decisions. Specifically speaking, when firms choose their location, they balance between agglomeration economies benefits, land costs and labor wage costs, pursuing maximum profits; households enter the model through the labor supply and their location choice balances between wage income, land costs and commuting costs, pursuing maximum utility. As such, firms and households form bid-rent curves and for every piece of land in the city, the highest bidder gets to own it, eventually forming a "jobs–housing" spatial distribution in the city. Here we will briefly introduce the core thoughts of the LRH model.

9.3.4.1 Model assumptions

A circular city with no differences in any direction. Economic activity within the city could be simply divided into two types: production and residence, which corresponds to commercial land and residential land in cities. For simplicity, this huge economic body produces one good, which is sold inside and outside the city, the price of which is exogenous. Land and labor are the two major inputs to produce this good and the productivity is influenced by technology—the stronger the agglomeration economies, the higher the technology. The supply elasticity of labor is determined by its utility, and its utility is influenced by the quantity of goods and residential land consumed. In order to attract labor, the wages firms pay need to compensate for commuting costs—the higher the degree of job–housing separation, the higher commuting costs and the corresponding wage costs will be.

9.3.4.2 Firm location choice

Firm output level is determined by land and labor inputs as well as production technology, which is a function of agglomeration economies, the two are positively correlated, and externalities enter the model through such a channel. The intensity of agglomeration economies is expressed as the density of surrounding firms—the more agglomerated firms are, the higher the density, and the higher each firm's technology and output is. The rent firms are willing to pay is the residual of revenues from sales minus labor and material costs, that is, economic profit is 0. Sales revenue is the product of number of goods sold and price. In an open economic system, price of goods, materials costs and value of capital are all exogenous variables (in the following equations, underlined variables are exogenous):

> Rent = Profit = Income – Costs
> = Numbers of goods sold × Unit <u>price of goods sold</u> – Labor costs – <u>Materials costs</u>
> Number of goods = g_1 (technology, labor, <u>capital</u>)
> Technology = g_2 (agglomeration economies)

From the above relationship, we can derive the bid-rent curve for firms, which is the city location function (since we are talking about a homogeneous, circular city, we can use distance to city center *d* to represent location):

> Rent firm is willing to pay rent at location *d* (bid-rent) = f_1 (agglomeration economies, wage costs)

The economic implications are: if firms cluster together (forming an employment center), then they will benefit more from agglomeration economies, but this will put them at a farther distance from labor (this is because residential land is "squeezed" to a farther area). When the intensity of agglomeration economies is very high, firms will be more inclined to stay in the city center and would rather pay high wages in order to compensate for their employees' long-distance commute costs; when the intensity of agglomeration economies is rather weak, firms will "follow" employees, in order to lower the wage costs for compensating commute costs.

9.3.4.3 Residential (worker) location choice

A worker allocates his income between housing (land) consumption and consumption of other goods, pursuing maximum utility:

> Wage income = Rent × Quantity of land consumed + Price of other goods × Quantity of other goods consumed + Commuting costs utility = g_3 (quantity of land consumed, quantity of other goods consumed)

From the above equation, we can derive the bid-rent function for labor, which is also a function of *d*. It should be noted that wage income here is the wage cost in the firm's bid-rent function.

> Rent household willing to pay at *d* (bid-rent) = f_2 (wage income, commuting costs)

9.3.4.4 Bid-rent conditions and constraint conditions

Obtain the aforementioned bid-rent function for firms and workers. In any city location, if the firm's bid-rent at location *d* is higher than the household's bid-rent, then location *d* will be occupied by a firm; if the firm's bid-rent at location *d* is lower than the household's bid-rent, then location *d* will be occupied by residents; if the two are equal, then the land will have a mixture of uses; at equilibrium, a worker cannot obtain a higher income by changing residential location.

9.3.4.5 Main model conclusions

By combining firm and worker's bid-rent functions, the LRH model infers the two main driving forces that determine urban spatial structure—agglomeration economies and commuting costs. In the model, the intensity of the two are expressed with two parameters, the agglomeration economies diminishing coefficient reflects the diminishing rate in agglomeration economies as the density of surrounding firms falls and the larger this coefficient is, the more inclined firms are to concentrate more tightly; the parameter for commuting costs is transportation costs per unit distance. Here, agglomeration economies and commuting costs could be vividly understood as the "adhesion force" and the "friction force." The directions of their effects are opposite. The simulated values from the model show that in cities with strong agglomeration economies and low (unit distance) commuting costs, firms are "adhered" together and are willing to pay high wage costs to employees for long-distance commutes. The equilibrium spatial structure here is a monocentric form with the highest commuting time; in cities with weak agglomeration economies and high commuting costs, the effect of "friction" becomes dominant and firms are inclined to be closer to employees to save on wage costs. The equilibrium spatial structure exhibits a total mixture of jobs and housing and commuting time is minimized. Multiple spatial structures between monocentric and total mixture will be derived from cases between these two extremes.

Based on the LRH model, we can further discuss the previously mentioned "jobs–housing balance" concept. Industrial agglomeration can bring economic efficiency, thus a "jobs–housing separation" is conducive to firms concentrating more effectively, enjoying the advantage of agglomeration economies, and increasing labor productivity. Relying on dispersed job opportunities to realize "jobs–housing balance" has the cost of sacrificing benefits from agglomeration economies, which is often hard to realize in an urban spatial structure dominated by market forces. The LRH model can also explain why after more convenient roads and track traffic are constructed, the separation of jobs–housing grows ever larger and the volume of traffic increases instead of decreases.

Interestingly, the evolution of China's urban spatial structure from the planned economy era to the market economy era does match the inferences of the LRH model quite well (Zheng et al., 2009). During the planned economy era, land resources were allocated according to central planing, each work unit constructed residential buildings on its own land (homes for its employees' family members). Employees lived in the work unit's area and usually only needed to walk or ride a bicycle to get to and from work and the commuting costs per unit distance were high. Firms engaged in productive activities according to commands and did not do business with one another, so there was no need for agglomeration economies—land in the city center did not necessarily have more of a locational advantage than land in the suburbs (of course, some traditional commercial activities were still relatively concentrated in the city center, such as Beijing's Wangfujing Street). Low agglomeration economies and high unit distance commuting costs were consistent with the "mixed job–housing" structural form. The development of the market economy since the 1980s has caused firms to be ever more closely connected with each other and the forces of agglomeration economies have gradually showed themselves. The development of the land market and property market also enable firms to obtain the most advantageous location by paying higher rent. Large scale road and track traffic construction, as well as development of the auto-industry, have lowered unit distance commuting costs. Under high agglomeration economies and low unit distance commuting costs, the locational advantage of city centers is all the more apparent and the "mixed jobs–housing" model was broken, and a "jobs–housing separation" spatial form gradually formed: technology intensive firms that require agglomeration economies are more concentrated in high density at the city center and a CBD forms. The main residential land is squeezed out of the city center and exhibits a trend toward suburbanization, with manufacturing moving further to the city's fringes. "Jobs–housing separation" brought about large transportation demand and even generated the issue of traffic congestion in some major cities. However, the benefits brought to the firm by agglomeration economies are so apparent that "mixed jobs–housing" becomes highly uneconomical.

The aforementioned evolutionary pattern of urban spatial structure implies that urban public policymakers should admit the inevitability of "jobs–housing separation" and endeavor to reduce the institutional constraints on firms' and workers' free choice of location, avoiding unnecessary sacrifices of economic efficiency. When designing urban planning and land supply policies, sufficient agglomeration of industrial land use should be promoted. At the same time, residential land should be provided at the rim of subway lines extended from employment centers to the urban periphery, or convenient high-speed transportation facilities should be provided between employment centers and the corresponding high-density residential areas. These are conducive to industrial agglomeration and reducing the commuting costs of residents.

9.3.5 Agglomeration economies displayed in urban spatial structure

Numerous researches on agglomeration economies are inter-city studies, which view cities as a single point. Controlling for other factors, a city's labor productivity (often represented using wages and firm output) is positively correlated with agglomeration economies (often represented using population density). Other chapters of this book introduced many such studies. Intra-city studies are relatively few. Rosenthal and Strange (2004) employed US data and performed an empirical study on agglomeration economies within cities and found that agglomeration economies decline to a low level 5 miles outward. Fu (2007) employed 1990 Massachusetts proprietary micro-level data to prove that agglomeration economies within cities only significantly exist when the distance between firms is very small and states that when testing for the four mechanisms of human capital spillovers at the census tract and block level, it is discovered that wages are high where employment density is high.

Zheng et al. (2009) employed data from a 2005 Beijing micro-level survey (around 6,000 effective samples) and studied whether Beijing firms balance between externalities from agglomeration economies and wage costs compensation for employee commuting costs as the LRH endogenous urban space model shows. The study found that after controlling for the heterogeneity of labor and dummies for residential location, Beijing firms indeed compensate for employees' commuting costs through wage premium. Firms do this to enjoy the externalities from agglomeration economies—at the same time wage premium exists in areas where employment density is high. In addition, the wage premium paid by skill intensive firms and the wage compensation for commuting costs are both significantly higher than labor intensive firms. This is because skill intensive firms are more dependent on agglomeration economies—face-to-face communication and knowledge spillover. These empirical findings illustrate that economic reform provides a condition for firms to benefit from agglomeration economies and as the degree to which firms and residents can freely choose location increases, agglomeration economies is already starting to shape the urban spatial structure in Chinese cities.

Ren et al. (2007) used office building transaction data on eight Beijing city districts from 1993–2004 and utilized the LRH model's line of thinking, constructing a model for the determination of land prices under agglomeration economies.

Their basic train of thought is, adding a "location potential" variable to the traditional hedonic pricing model in order to see if firms in office buildings are willing to pay a premium for this location potential variable. The method with which the location potential variable is constructed is similar to the measurement of agglomeration economies in the LRH model—weighted sum-of surrounding office building land, the weight being a negative exponential of the spatial distance to that particular piece of land, that is, as distance increases, it decreases exponentially. A higher location potential value implies a higher degree of agglomeration in this location's office buildings, and agglomeration economies are stronger. Their empirical results verify firms' preference for agglomeration economies as the location potential variable is significantly positive in the hedonic pricing model. At the same time, the elasticity of land prices to the location potential variable is rather larger in the latter phase of this period, which implies that as the market mechanism deepens in the allocation of land resources and the property market develops, the impact of agglomeration economies on land prices increases. They also found that different types of firms have different needs for agglomeration economies. Industries such as finance, insurance, management consulting etc. have higher requirements for agglomeration economies and are thereby more willing to pay high rents. In other words, in regions where industries such as finance, insurance, management consulting etc. are agglomerated, land prices have a high elasticity to the location potential variable.

9.4 Related urban issues and public policies

9.4.1 Employment barriers and housing affordability problem of the disadvantaged

The "spatial mismatch" between jobs and housing is also a hot issue in the labor market research. In Harvard researcher Kain's 1968 paper, with the situation in Chicago and Detroit as a starting point, the main reason for skill-deficient workers' high unemployment, low income, and high travelling time and costs in inner American cities was inferred to be that the many job opportunities originally within the city, especially blue collar production jobs, were moved to the suburbs; in the meantime, America's tradition of residential (racial) segregation caused African Americans to still be left in the downtown area. A "spatial mismatch" exists between job location and employee residence location, causing the demand side—the willingness of firms in the suburbs to hire workers in the inner city—declined; on the other hand, the supply side—the probability of low-skilled labor residing in the inner city finding a suitable job—declined as well (Kain, 1968). The proposal of this sharp issue initiated more and more social science academics to pay attention to employment and housing from the "spatial mismatch" perspective.

"Spatial mismatch" cannot be simply equated with "jobs–housing separation," but over-separation of the two caused by institutional constraints and market deficiencies. Due to differences in data and methodology, as well as different explanations toward empirical results, many debates currently still exist among academics regarding whether "spatial mismatch" is the true reason leading to employment barriers for the disadvantaged. For example, Ihlanfeldt and Sjoquist's (1998) study stated that spatial mismatch exists but varies widely across different regions; meanwhile measuring work accessibility at the individual level is still difficult. Brueckner and Zenou (2003) studied the impact of inequality toward African American workers in the housing market on wages and unemployment and found that the exclusivity of suburban housing (not easily accessible for African Americans) led to higher unemployment rates for African Americans in the downtown area compared to the city suburbs. However, Houston (2005) pointed out that deficiencies in some empirical methodologies will lead to the discovery of "false" spatial mismatches and believes that racial issues are not the real reason for spatial mismatches. Accompanying the development of China's urban residential suburbanization, issues such as "spatial mismatch" has also become a dilemma for low to middle-income individuals (especially people without local Hukous) in some major cities. Zhou and Liu's (2010) study state that since low-income public housing is often situated in the suburbs where sufficient job opportunities are lacking, the low to middle-income individuals that enjoy such housing have little room in choosing their jobs.

Associated with this issue is the affordability problem of housing for the disadvantaged. In urban space, the immobility of housing determines its locational relationship with workplace, schools, and other amenities, which induces corresponding transportation costs, becoming an important part of household living expenditures. Thus, to households, a seesaw relationship exists between housing cost and transportation cost which implies that the spatial relationship between jobs and housing is an important influencing factor for housing affordability. Data (Center for Housing Policy, 2006) shows that for every dollar in housing costs saved by American households (through moving to more remote areas, etc.), the transportation costs increase correspondingly by $0.77. As commute distances are further increased, the increase in household's transportation costs may even exceed the saving in housing cost. Zheng and Yang's (2007) empirical study on Beijing illustrated that if one-way commuting time is lowered by 1 minute, housing costs will rise by 0.6 percent. This implies that the spatial relationship between jobs and housing has also become an important influencing factor for households' housing affordability. In most relevant current research, the impact of households' transportation costs on housing affordability is generally neglected, while residential location choice by low-income groups is especially sensitive to this. The Center for Neighborhood Technology and the Center for Transit-Oriented Development in the US proposed an approach to housing affordability evaluation that simultaneously takes into account housing costs and commuting costs. The Center for Real Estate at MIT's Housing Affordability Initiative also considers jobs–housing spatial relationship when evaluating housing affordability.[7]

In China, the over-separation of jobs and housing has emerged in many cities. Large residential communities in the city edges have become "bedroom towns", bringing in large transportation pressures and social costs. Spatial opportunities for different social groups show rather high unevenness—many low-income households have to live in the city fringe for cheaper housing prices, but urban employment opportunities and public amenities are still concentrated in the inner city, so they require time-consuming and high-cost commutes, which increase living costs for low-income households. Middle to low-income residents (and other disadvantaged groups that have limited choices) face rather bigger hindrances in residential location and employment location, as they have to live very far away from the inner city and thus bear high commuting costs or lose job opportunities (or vice versa). Zheng et al. (2001) employed the traffic origination destination volume matrix, general cost matrix and value of time, and in combination with the actual situation of China's urban housing market and traffic system, design a transportation and housing affordability index (THAI), conduct index calculations from travelling and housing costs in 64 traffic tracts in eight Beijing districts and explore the distribution patterns in urban space and underlying economic and policy implications. They conclude that close attention should be paid to the comprehensive housing and transportation costs burdened by low-income groups. Low income subsidized housing should be constructed in locations with good accessibility (such as near subway stations). The government should also consider providing more affordable housing (such as allowing higher building density) in areas where employment is dense, providing middle- to low-income individuals with more housing options.

9.4.2 Urban transportation and environmental issues

9.4.2.1 Interactive relationship between transportation and land use

The transportation system is the link that ties together jobs and housing in the urban space, thus a close interactive relationship exists between land use and transportation, which has been a hot topic in recent years, discussed in urban planning, transportation planning and urban economics. Anas et al. (1998) believe that the evolution of the mode of transportation has caused the form and scale of urban spatial evolution to undergo tremendous changes. The wide use of passenger vehicles caused the scale of urban spatial expansion to increase significantly and polycentric, low-density manners of spatial expansion appeared. However, policies that develop urban public transportation, such as constructing metro lines, constructing transportation transfer hubs, etc. necessarily attracts large numbers of urban residents and firms to agglomerate near the new transportation facilities, thereby inducing urban space to spread out along a ray direction (i.e. the TOD model, transit oriented development).

The interactive relationship between transportation and land use can be briefly exhibited in Figure 9.19. On the one hand, the current mode of land use determines the spatial locations of homes, employment and urban amenities of all sorts, as well as determining commuting and non-commuting transportation demand and is the input end of urban transportation planning; on the other hand, the urban transportation system impacts the mode of land use (type and intensity

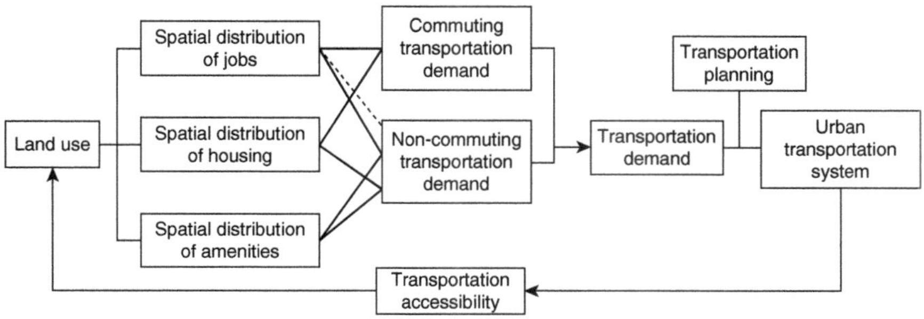

Figure 9.19 Interactive relationship between urban land use and transportation system.

of land use) through transportation accessibility. The key is in the cyclical and dynamic nature of this path of influence—the implementation of transportation plans will change future transportation demand through changing the future mode of land use. However, current transportation planning rarely considers the feedback impact of currently planned transportation infrastructure on land use (Garrett and Wachs, 1996).

Empirical studies on the impact of transportation on land use usually focus on how transportation accessibility affects surrounding property values and the intensity of land development. Voith (1993); Amstrong (1994); Benjamin and Sirmans (1996); McMillen and McDonald (2004); Cervero and Duncan (2002) and others, all discovered the locational advantage of being near a subway station can enhance residential and commercial property prices. Many Chinese researchers use data from major Chinese cities to verify the existence of such an impact, e.g. Wang et al. (2004); He and Zheng (2004); Zheng and Liu (2005); Cai et al. (2006); Liang et al. (2007); Zhang et al. (2007); Liu and Peng (2007); Gu and Jia (2008); Yang et al. (2008); Gu and Guo (2008); Yin and Tang (2008); Pan and Zhong (2008); Gu and Zheng (2010) and others. Gu and Zheng (2010) examine the "submarket effect" of subways, that is, the impact on suburban residential housing prices is larger than that on the downtown area's prices, while also finding that the intensity of land development surrounding subway stations increases significantly. Feng and Lu's (2010) study based on a natural experiment found that the quantity and quality differences of basic education in different areas in Shanghai have indeed already been capitalized into property prices.

9.4.2.2 Traffic congestion and environmental pollution

A tough issue major Chinese cities currently face is the rapid increase in private vehicles causing the urban transportation system to be overloaded. Urban planners and administrators lack consideration of future uncertain factors and planning passively follows urban development. The chaotic expansion of the city and mismatch of spatial utility makes the issue of traffic congestion more serious.

From 2001 to 2009, the number of motor vehicles owned rose from 73.98 million to 187 million,[8] with an average annual compounded growth rate of 12 percent. From 2001 to November 7 2010, the number of motor vehicles owned in Beijing rose to 4.634 million,[9] with the average growth rate over the past 10 years exceeding 10 percent. Using the transportation capacity of most Beijing Ring Roads as an example, if the Second, Third and Fourth Ring Roads are completely filled, they can only accommodate a maximum of 224, 000 vehicles, about 5 percent of the 4 million vehicles. A typical case is the evening four days before the 2010 Mid-Autumn Festival. A drizzle caused the most severe traffic jam in Beijing's history, with 143 jammed roads and the traffic of the whole city was in near paralysis. The traffic congestion issue quickly spread across the country from first-tier cities such as Beijing, Shanghai and Guangzhou to second-tier cities such as Jinan, Nanjing and Chengdu and even to several third-tier cities, where severe traffic jams successively appeared.[10]

Traffic congestion leads directly to environmental pollution. Slower speeds and low fuel efficiency both greatly increase urban transportation's energy consumption, air pollution and carbon emissions, making the environmental costs of urban transportation increasingly prominent. According to statistical figures, among Beijing's particle pollutants in the entire year 2008, over 50 percent came from the pollution generated by burning fuel, which mainly comes from exhaust gas from vehicles.[11] Under the context of rapidly increasing living standards and a booming automobile industry, the ownership rate of private vehicles inevitably increases rather quickly. Attempting to maintain low ownership rates of private vehicles to solve the traffic congestion and environmental issue is unrealistic. It needs to be explored which type of urban spatial structure is better for alleviating congestion and improving the environment in an "automobile society."

How do urban spatial structure characteristics (namely the spatial distribution characteristics of urban economic activity, especially the employment accessibility and urban amenities accessibility) eventually impact traffic congestion, energy consumption and environmental quality through influencing residents' travelling behavior? Empirical studies by many academics show that a compact urban form is often accompanied by a high spatial matching between jobs, housing and public amenities, which can lead to less transportation demand (including reducing ownership rates of private vehicles and frequency of private vehicle use) and will also encourage households to use highly efficient cars, eventually realizing lower urban transportation energy consumption and pollutant emissions (Newman and Kenworthy, 1999; Erling and Ingird, 2005; Ewing and Rong, 2008). By studying 66 US metropolitan areas, Glaeser and Kahn (2008) found that households residing in the city suburbs are more likely than those residing in the city center to drive a private vehicle and fuel consumption and pollutant emissions from private vehicles often increase due to the long distances between home place and workplace. Kahn's (2000) study also shows that for households with the same size and income level, the amount of driving for those living in the suburbs on average is 31 percent higher than those in the city center.

Compared with cities in western countries, Chinese ownership rate of private vehicles is low. However, as household incomes rise, the rapid increase in private vehicle ownership rates becomes an inevitable trend of development. Will the current trend of development for Chinese cities produce a result similar to western countries? Through studying the carbon emissions of Beijing residents' private vehicles, Huo et al. (2010) found that as the spatial distance between housing and job centers increases, the employment accessibility of households declines as well, which significantly increases the probability that they will purchase private vehicles. Zheng et al. (2010) analyzed transportation and travel carbon emissions from 74 Chinese cities and, after controlling for household characteristics at the micro-level, found that a city's level of economic development is significantly positively correlated with carbon emissions by private vehicles and believe that this may be related to rich cities often building more infrastructure such as roads etc. In addition, urban population density is significantly negatively correlated with *per capita* taxi carbon emissions and *per capita* bus carbon emissions, and for every additional 1,000 people per average square kilometer (sample standard deviation is roughly 19 percent), household taxi carbon emissions are reduced by 0.424 tons and bus carbon emissions are reduced by 0.837 tons. This may be due to shorter average travelling distances or a more efficient urban transportation system—in the case of the US, compact urban development contributes to less transportation carbon emissions, and high density big cities perform better in energy conservation and emissions reduction.

Here we give a detailed example, observing how urban spatial structure impacts private vehicle energy consumption and its carbon emissions from a minor angle—ownership of private vehicles and travel behaviors. Such an approach is applicable to the analysis of more complex issues. The rapid rise in the motor vehicle stock of Chinese cities is an objective reality. Using Beijing as an example, the motor vehicle stock reached 4 million in 2009. At the time of writing, it is still increasing at the rate of 1,300 per day, with private vehicles accounting for a proportion of around 80 percent. In other words, there is a private vehicle for every 1.75 households in Beijing. The rapid increase in the private vehicle stock, the slow speeds and low fuel efficiency caused by traffic congestion all greatly increase urban transportation's energy consumption, air pollution and carbon emissions, making the environmental cost of urban transportation increasingly more prominent. Under the context of swiftly rising living standards and a booming auto-industry, the ownership rate of private vehicles in Chinese households will necessarily rise quickly and it is hard to rely on administrative methods to control the growth of private vehicles to solve the congestion issue in the long run. But if we shift our angle, if we can improve the spatial distributions of jobs and housing within the city and provide reasonable transportation facilities, then we may be able to alleviate the traffic congestion and environmental issues brought by increasing incomes. When reaching an "automobile society", it is important to investigate what type of urban spatial structure has a better low-carbon effect.

Zheng and Huo (2010) employ a September 2009 survey conducted by Tsinghua University Institute of Real Estate Studies on Beijing households' "travelling energy consumption and residential environment" and explore the impact of urban spatial structure on transportation carbon emissions from the perspective

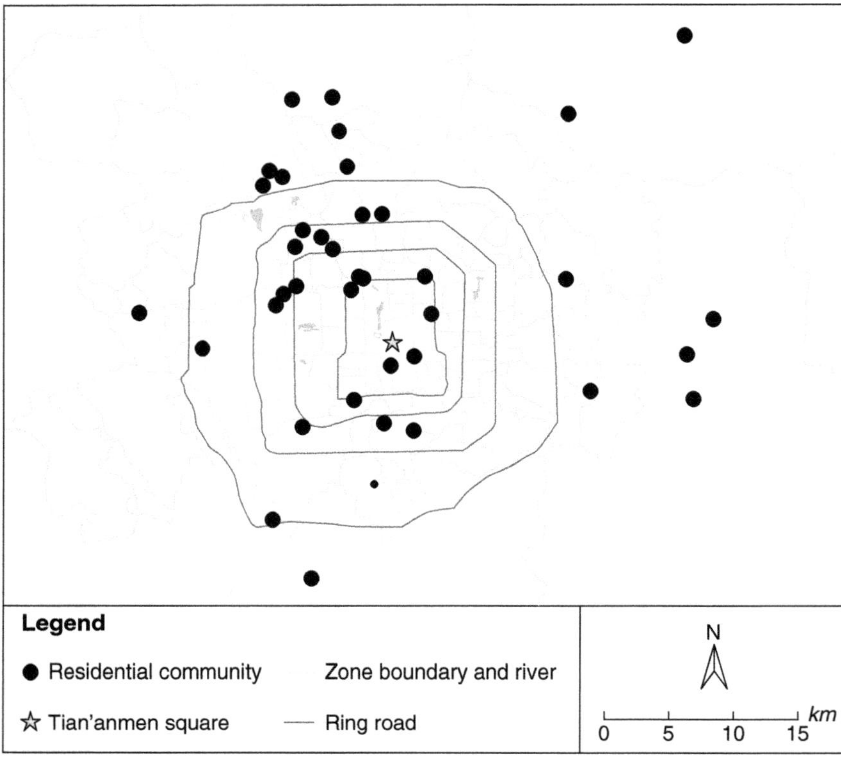

Figure 9.20 Graph of spatial distribution of residential communities.

Data source: Tsinghua University Institute of Real Estate Studies "Household travel energy consumption and residential environment" survey.

of private vehicle ownership and travel behaviors. In all, this survey involved 826 residential households in 38 Beijing communities (see Figure 9.20 for the spatial distribution of communities).

First, we use these micro-level sample data to estimate the relevant figures for 2009 Beijing private vehicle carbon emissions. Table 9.4 provides several statistics from the estimation results. It could be seen that 47.6 percent of Beijing

Table 9.4 Estimation results of Beijing private vehicle carbon emissions

Subcategory	*Sample size*	*Household daily life carbon emissions (ton/household)*			
		Average	*Standard deviation*	*Maximum value*	*Minimum value*
Private vehicles	393	4.104	3.655	29.489	0.084

households travel in private vehicles with an average carbon emission of 4.1 tons/household.

From the above calculations, we can see that the carbon emissions of private vehicles display a completely linear relationship with their amount of gasoline consumption. Thus, analyzing the influencing factors of private vehicle carbon emissions is in effect analyzing the influencing factors of private vehicle gasoline consumption (energy consumption). However, carbon emissions of private vehicles (energy consumption) do not have a direct linear relationship with mileage. When roads are rather congested (speed is low), the fuel consumption and carbon emissions per kilometer will be rather high (see Figure 9.21). Therefore, analysis on private vehicle carbon emissions that comprehensively takes into account both mileage and speed better reflects the level of energy consumption.

Through an econometric model, Zheng and Huo (2010) answer two questions: (1) what types of travelers are more likely to choose private vehicles as the main mode of transportation? (2) For travelers that choose private vehicles, what are the main determinants of carbon emissions? This is a typical case where a Heckman two-step regression econometric model needs to be used. It is discovered that, empirically, the higher income levels and population size are, the higher the probability residents will purchase cars, whereas the impact of age structure on residents' probability of car purchase displays an inverted U pattern, with the highest probability for heads of households purchasing cars at the age of 45. After controlling for these household characteristics, the better accessibility to employment centers and other urban amenities (public transportation, high quality education resources, etc.), the lower the probability of travelling in private vehicles. Given the probability of car purchase, the fuel consumption and carbon emissions of private vehicles are not impacted by income levels but are closely related with

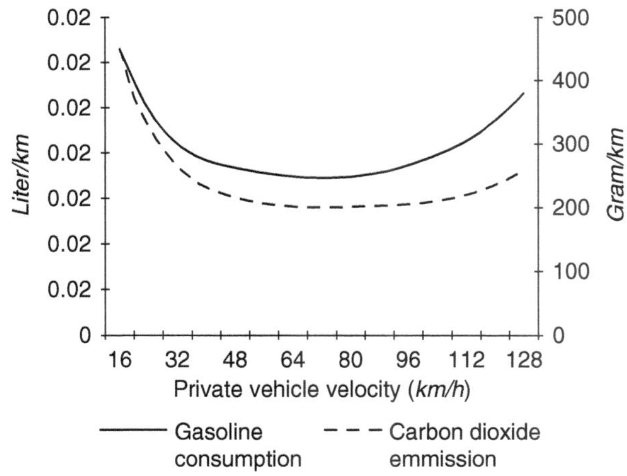

Figure 9.21 Relationship between private vehicle velocity and energy consumption per unit distance.

Data source: IPCC 2006 Guidelines for National Greenhouse Gas Inventories.

the cost of using private vehicles (mainly referring to whether gas expenditures are reimbursable). In addition, when a residence location's employment accessibility is relatively poor (reflected in long commute times) and traffic congestion is relatively severe, carbon emission levels for private vehicles will be raised.

Increasing the employment and public amenities accessibilities is crucial to reduce long-distance travelling demand, lowering incentives for driving private vehicles thereby lowering private vehicles' gas consumption and carbon emissions. However, if we take a more comprehensive perspective, jobs–housing separation in the urban space is the inevitable result of industrial agglomeration (Lucas and Rossi-Hansberg, 2002). The agglomeration of economic activities will bring positive externalities from agglomeration economies but also bring negative externalities such as congestion and environmental pollution (Kahn, 2006). Excessively pursuing "jobs–housing balance" in order to reduce commuting may sacrifice economic efficiency and is often hard to achieve in a market-oriented urban spatial structure. The key is how to reasonably balance between these two externalities. But the aforementioned problems do not exist for public amenities. If the spatial distribution of urban public amenities is unreasonable, it will lead to households' excess commuting and energy consumption in order to access these facilities, which is an extra environmental cost for cities. This part of energy consumption and carbon emissions should be lowered. Therefore, the reasonable and balanced spatial allocation of urban public goods (especially basic education and medical facilities) is important for reducing excessive transportation needs, energy consumption and carbon emissions and will facilitate the sustainable development of urban space. As a legacy of the planned economy, high quality public amenities are mostly concentrated in the city center, lagging behind the suburbanization of jobs and housing, therefore attention to this issue becomes especially important.

9.4.3 Land use, transportation, and environment integrated studies

9.4.3.1 Main approach of integrated studies

From the above discussions, it could be seen that the spatial relationship between jobs and housing gives rise to the spatial interaction between land use and transportation, while also producing corresponding environmental impacts. As environmental issues become more pronounced and with the rise of the sustainable development concept, the environmental impact of the interaction between land use and transportation gradually grew into a central research issue. Although land use itself has direct impacts on the environment, such as how locations where heavy industry and high-pollution industries are situated often have air, water, and solid waste pollution in the surrounding areas, while green fields and forestry have air purification and carbon fixation functions. However, the main focus here is the spatial distribution of economic activities and its interactive connection with transportation, the impact of which is concentrated in air pollution and carbon emissions.

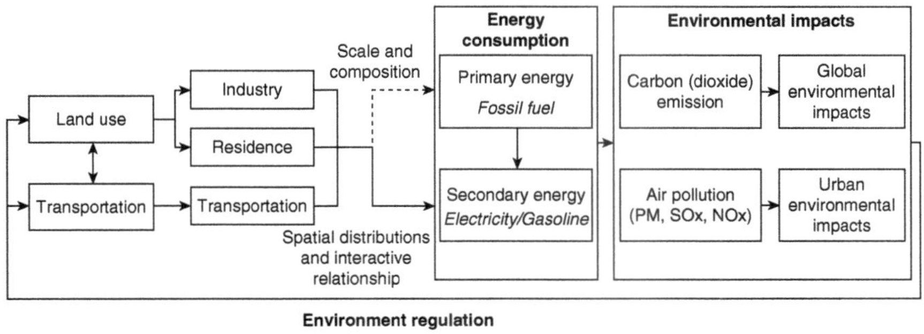

Figure 9.22 Paths through which land use and transportation produce environmental impact.

From the perspective of end-use, urban energy consumption could be divided into three major components: industrial, residential and transportation (Glaeser and Kahn, 2008). Figure 9.22 succinctly shows the path and feedback mechanism through which land use and transportation generate environmental impacts. Land provides space for industrial and residential activities, the two of which are connected through the transportation system. Industry, residence and transportation on the one hand directly impact energy consumption levels through the aspects of scale and composition (such as industry scale and the composition of secondary and tertiary industries, size and composition of population, total number of motor vehicles, etc.), on the other hand, their spatial distributions and interactive relationship (e.g. distance and intensity of commuting/non-commuting transportation, speed/congestion of traffic, suburban/urban area, high density/low density mode of urban expansion) also directly impact the level and structure of energy consumption. The environmental impact produced by energy consumption can be divided into two aspects, first of which is air pollution (e.g. particular matters, SO_2, oxynitrides, etc.), second of which is carbon dioxide emissions (carbon emissions in short). The degradation of environmental quality will lead to an increase in the public's environmental awareness and they will push the government to implement environment regulations, many of which are restrictions on land use and transportation. The feedback mechanism shown in Figure 9.22 illustrates the necessity to couple the interaction between "land use–transportation" and the environment.

If land use, transportation, and the environment are considered comprehensively, the depiction of the interactive relationship between land use and transportation in Figure 9.19 will be expanded into the following Figure 9.23.

The dynamic urban spatial model is a system of models composed of several interlinking sub-models. First, we need to choose and determine model characteristics and model construction techniques. Then we need to construct sub-models based on urban economics and transportation economics theories. Finally, we will connect the closely interlinked sub-models, enable them to operate collaboratively,

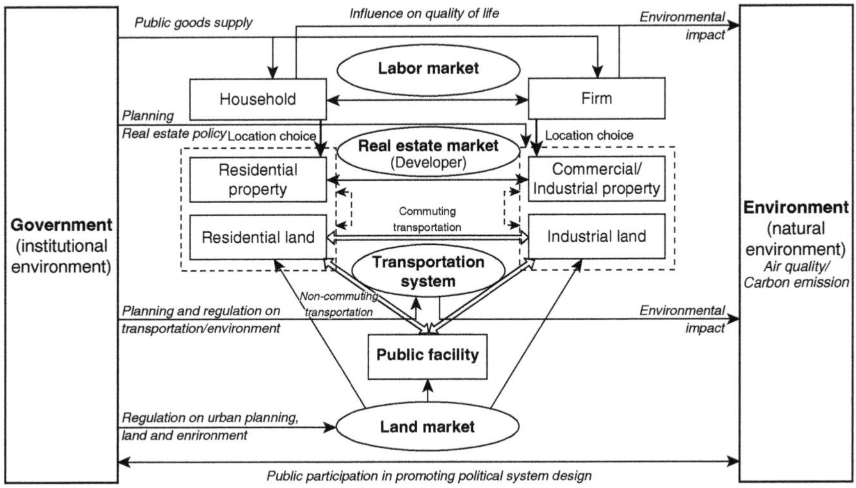

Figure 9.23 Conceptual framework of integrated studies on land use, transportation, and the environment.

Note: Dotted lines and arrows, respectively, represent transportation within the residential sector, transportation within the industrial sector, and transportation between industry and public amenities. These are not the focus of this chapter.

forming a general equilibrium model. Table 9.5 lists seven sub-models an integrated model should include. Each sub-model is independent of another yet they are interrelated. Other than these seven sub-models, the system requires two external modules: macroeconomic module and model presetting module. The former is mainly used to predict the macroeconomic conditions of future population, industry employment etc.; the latter provides specific preset conditions for user-customized models. The model control aggregate determined through macroeconomic models and the specific model presets entered by the user in accordance with specific cases jointly form the whole model's basic parameters. Through aggregate model adjustments, each model operates stepwise circularly according to the mechanism of its relationships with other models, forming a unified, closely interconnected system.

9.4.3.2 Designing integrated dynamic spatial model in practice

In order to form more direct and practical forecast and decision support instruments for urban planners and administrators, development of applied simulation models based on the "land use–transportation–environment" spatial interaction theory has gradually become more active. Especially beginning in the 1990s, as high performance computers became popular, analyzing and processing huge datasets became a reality and combined with the constantly maturing Geographic

Table 9.5 Sub-models of "land use–transportation–environment" integrated spatial model

Sub-model type	*Sub-model name*	*Sub-model introduction*
Behavioral models	(1) Firm relocation and location choice model	According to the profit maximization principle, firms consider benefits from agglomeration economies, wage costs and land costs, and make location choices decisions
	(2) Households relocation and location choice model	According to the utility maximization principle, households consider wages, land (housing) costs and transportation costs and make location choice decisions
	(3) Land and property price model	Firms' location choice and households' location choice each form a bid-rent curve, the rent-bidding behavior between the two forms land and property price distributions and determines the owner of each piece of land
	(4) Travel choice model	Under the conditions of job location and residential location choice, transportation accessibility, transportation costs (considering environmental and congestion externality costs) household members choose mode of travel, frequency of travel and time of travel
	(5) Land development model	According to the principle of the highest net present value (or real options method), in accordance with development costs and forecast sales price, the probability of development for each tract of land is determined
Physical models	(6) Transportation accessibility model	A suitable method for measuring accessibility is chosen, which impacts firms' and residents' demand and bid-rent for every location. Construction of transportation facilities will change each location's accessibility
	(7) Environmental impact and regulation model	Through the engineering relationships in environmental engineering, firm and household behavior are transformed into environmental impacts (such as air pollution or carbon emissions), realizing the embedding of environmental impact through the utility function, planning/ development restrictions, and general environment impact fees

Table 9.6 Currently mature urban spatial simulation models

Urban spatial simulation model	*Developer*	*Application status*
TRANUS 飡	Venezuela's Barra	Updated version: 2007/12; 2009/4; 2009/10, applied in multiple administrative levels, multiple planning fields; users across Europe, Americas, Asia
UrbanSim 飡	University of Washington Center for Urban Simulation and Policy Analysis	Latest version: 2009.11 (version 4.3), applied in practice to Eugene-Springfield, Oregon, Hawaii, Salt Lake City in the US and Taiwan, etc.
SLEUTH 飡	Keith CU	Applied in 2007 in San Francisco, Chicago and Japan's Tokyo metropolitan area
Others	CUF; CubeLand; DRAM/EMPAL; IRPUD; Metrosim, etc.	

Information System (GIS) technology, computer simulated urban spatial models have met with a great opportunity for development. Table 9.6 lists several currently rather mature simulation models and their application.

Using "Urbanism", developed by Professor Waddell from University of Washington Center for Urban Simulation and Policy Analysis (now UC Berkeley), as an example, this model has already completed the shift from experimental to application and is mainly used for urban growth planning, urban land zoning and transportation policy analysis. It uses the main sectors (household, commercial, development, government, etc.) in urban development as research subjects and year as unit of time, going from short-term to long-term quasi-dynamic simulation, with the goal of coordinating the relationship between land zoning, transportation planning and environmental protection, forecasting and simulating the direction of growth in urban space and potential problems that may arise. In applying the model to study Eugene-Springfield, Oregon, 271 traffic analytic units were analyzed and simulated in the COG (traffic model system). The studied areas were divided into 15,000 150 meter by 150 meter grid units to analyze residential location, employment location, property development and land prices, and transportation demand. The system was also used in the simulation of growth and evaluation of urban planning policy results in Salt Lake City, Seattle, Taipei, etc., the content of which includes: urban growth control, environmental restriction analysis, overall planning of land use, land-use density control; transportation infrastructure and policy, etc.

Although dynamic urban spatial modeling has a huge potential for application in Chinese cities, domestic research in this field is very lacking. Institutes such as the Beijing Municipal Institute of City Planning and Design and Tsinghua University have conducted relevant research work. It should be recognized that large variances exist between the complexity of China's urban spatial structural transition and institutional factors and Western, relatively mature, models. This implies that we cannot simply borrow Western models and must form independently pioneered theoretical systems and approaches to model designing. Thus for researchers in urban economics, urban planning and urban geography who wish to work in this field, this is both a very good research opportunity and not too small a challenge.

The author believes that for China to conduct research in this field, currently existing key points and difficulties are as follows. At the theoretical methodology level, on the one hand, innovations need to be made on existing international models, for example, how to better deal with endogeneity in models, equilibrium and dynamic issues, as well as externalities; on the other hand, how to fully take into account the uniqueness of Chinese cities and realize the localization of models, combining institutional transition and historical path dependence into urban spatial dynamic models, e.g. the dual structure of the land market, low liquidity of the housing market, high proportion of informal housing, rapid growth in ownership rates of motor vehicles, etc. At the data processing level, a sufficient balance between model accuracy and data accessibility needs to be attained. Even in major cities such as Beijing and Shenzhen, the accumulation of historical data is still unsatisfactory. When calibrating those models, only low resolution data can be used. How to best improve the accuracy of the model and the effectiveness of the predictions under such data quality is a real world issue that begs exploring.

9.5 Conclusions

The spatial structure of Chinese cities is experiencing rapid expansion and reconstruction. At the same time, historical path dependence exists due to the durability of urban infrastructure and buildings, and in addition to unique systems such as land, housing, and local public finances and their transitional features, multiple forces are combined together, increasing the complexity and uncertainty of urban spatial structure. However, China's current urban planning and the planning and administration policies of relevant departments lack consideration of such mutual dependence and uncertainty. During a period of rapid socioeconomic development and transition, planning passively follows urban development, forming many inefficiency and distortion issues in urban development. Thus, efficient urban planning and administration policies must be based on a deep understanding of the economic mechanisms and institutional constraints in urban spatial structure.

The spatial relationship between jobs and housing is precisely at the heart of urban spatial structure. Understanding the economic laws, interactive relationship and institution barriers of firm and household location choices is helpful to fully comprehending the interactive mechanisms between the urban land and real estate market, labor market and transportation system as well as exploring the roots and paths to alleviating high-profile "urban problems" such as traffic congestion, environmental pollution, employment barriers for the disadvantaged and housing issues.

This chapter displays the urban spatial distributions of factors such as housing prices, land prices, population and employment as well as the monocentric and polycentric models' explanatory power for the spatial distribution of these factors; subsequently, we focus on the spatial relationship between jobs and housing, discussing its outcome and behind economic mechanisms, the underlying fundamental economic issue of how to optimally make the trade-off between the agglomeration benefits brought by spatial proximity and the costs of congestion. The LRH model and relevant research tells us, the relative forces between agglomeration economies ("adhesion") and commuting costs ("friction") is the key that determines the spatial relationship between jobs and housing. As the importance of agglomeration economies in Chinese cities increases daily and with the constant improvement of transportation infrastructure conditions, the degree of "jobs–housing separation" will gradually increase, and a unilateral pursuit of "jobs–housing balance" is unrealistic and would harm urban economic efficiency. Then, how should potential "urban problems" such as traffic congestion and environmental pollution brought by the over-separation of employment and residence be mitigated? This chapter's analysis illustrates that the key is in designing appropriate institutional incentives, correctly "internalizing" the externalities of individual economic behaviors, which will help to achieve the social optimal jobs–housing relationship and spatial structure. Such institutions and policies will enhance urban efficiency and residents' quality of life, improve environment and facilitate the sustainable development of cities. This chapter finally discussed an important direction in the study of urban spatial structure—under a "land use–transportation–environment" spatial integrated research framework, establishing a dynamic urban spatial model, simulating and making scenario predictions for urban growth and spatial evolution, and simulating and evaluating the results of urban planning and administration policies. This will provide important support for the formulation of urban planning, transportation planning, and urban administration policies, as well as provide decision-making support for household and firm location choice and property development.

Notes

1 Bourne (1971) used systems theory vocabulary to rigorously express the concept of urban spatial structure. He proposed three core concepts that depict urban systems: (1) Urban form refers to the spatial distribution mode of all factors (including physical facilities, social groups, economic activity and public institutions); (2) Urban interaction refers to the interactive relationship between urban factors, which is integrated into several subsystems; (3) Urban spatial structure refers to the inside mechanism of urban factor spatial distribution and interaction, which integrates all the subsystems into an overall urban system entity.

2 Employing 2001–2006 *China Statistical Yearbook* actual residential housing area figures, using average annual growth rates to extrapolate for the 2009 residential housing stock.

3 This chapter's electronic maps are all drawn with ArcGIS Desktop.

4 We calculate the U statistic to test for whether significant differences in the statistical sense exist for these two spatial gradients:

$$U = \frac{g_{skill} - g_{labor}}{\sqrt{\frac{\sigma^2_{g_{skill}}}{n_{skill}} + \frac{\sigma^2_{g_{labor}}}{n_{labor}}}} = \frac{0.217 - 0.172}{\sqrt{\frac{0.019^2}{126} + \frac{0.012^2}{126}}} = 22.29 > U_{a=1\%} = 2.33$$

We can see that at the 1 percent significance level, technology intensive industries have a higher employment density gradient than labor intensive industries.

5 Urban spatial economics models usually first determine housing rent and land rent, the two of which convert through building density (capacity rate) and construction costs and have the same spatial change patterns (the gradients differ); then convert land and housing rent into land and housing prices through the capitalization rate and growth rate of rent, the rent and prices of which basically have the same patterns of change (the gradients differ).

6 See http://news.xinhuanet.com/legal/2009-01/31/content_10739115.htm.

7 Refer to http://web.mit.edu/cre/research/hai/index.html for details.

8 Figures from Ministry of Public Security website (www.mps.gov.cn/n16/n85753).

9 Figures from Beijing Transportation Administration Bureau website's (http://www.bjjtgl.gov.cn/) periodical updates.

10 See www.chinadaily.com.cn/dfpd/chongqing/2010-11-11/content_1187563.html.

11 *Data source*: http://news.xinhuanet.com/legal/2009拟01/31/content_10739115.htm.

References

In English

Alonso, W., 1964, *Location and Land Use*, Cambridge: Harvard University Press.

Amstrong, R., 1994, "Impacts of Commuter Rail Service as Reflected in Single-family Residential Property Values," *Transportation Research Record*, 1406, pp. 88–97.

Anas, A., R. Arnott, and K. A. Small, 1998, "Urban Spatial Structure," *Journal of Economic Literature*, 36(3), pp. 1426–1464.

Baum-Snow, N., and M. E. Kahn, 2005, "Effects of Urban Rail Transit Expansions: Evidence from Sixteen Cities, 1970–2000," *Brookings-Wharton Papers on Urban Affairs*, pp. 147–206.

Benjamin, J. D., and G. S. Sirmans, 1996, "Mass Transportation, Apartment Rent and Property Values," *Journal of Real Estate Research*, 12(1), pp. 1–8.

Bento, A. M., M. L. Cropper, A. M. Mobarak, and K. Vinha, 2003, "The Impact of Urban Spatial Structure on Travel Demand in the United States," *World Bank Policy Research Working Paper*, No. 3007.

Bertaud, A., 2001, *Metropolis: A Measure of the Spatial Organization of 7 Large Cities*, http://alain-bertaud.com.

Bertaud, A., 2004, "The Spatial Organization of Cities: Deliberate Outcome or Unforeseen Consequence?" *IURD Working Paper Series*. Paper No. WP-2004–WP-2001. Berkeley: Institute of Urban and Regional Development.

Bourne, L. S., 1971, *Internal Structure of the City*, New York: Oxford University Press.

Brueckner, K., F. Thisse, and Y. Zenou, 1999, "Why is Central Paris Rich and Downtown Detroit Poor? An Amenity-Based Theory," *European Economic Review*, 43(1), pp. 91–107.

Brueckner, K., and Y. Zenou, 2003, "Space and Unemployment: The Labor-Market Effects of Spatial Mismatch," *Journal of Labor Economics*, 21(1), pp. 242–266.

Center for Housing Policy, 2006, *A Heavy Load: The Combined Housing and Transportation Burdens of Working Families*, www.cnt.org/repository/heavy_load_10_06.pdf.

Cervero, R., and K. Wu, 1998, "Sub-centring and Commuting: Evidence from the San Francisco Bay Area," 1980–1990, *Urban Studies*, 35(7), pp. 1059–1076.

Cervero, R., and M. Duncan, 2002, "Transit's Value-Added Effects: Light and Commuter Rail Services and Commercial Land Values," *Transportation Research Record*, 1805, pp. 8–15.

Chen, F. N., 2008, "Commuting Distances in a Household Location Choice Model with Amenities," *Journal of Urban Economics*, 63, pp. 116–129.

Clark, C., 1951, "Urban Population Densities," *Journal of Royal Statistical Society*, A114(4), pp. 490–496.

Crane, R., 1996a, "Cars and Drivers in the New Suburbs: Linking Access to Travel in Neotraditional Planning," *Journal of the American Planning Association*, 62(1), pp. 51–65.

Crane, R., 1996b, "The Influence of Uncertain Job Location on Urban Form and the Journey to Work," *Journal of Urban Economics*, 39(3), pp. 342–356.

DiPasquale, D., and W. C. Wheaton, 1996, *Urban Economics and Real Estate Markets*, New Jersey: Prentice Hall.

Erling, H., and T. N. Ingrid, 2005, "Three Challenges for the Compact City as a Sustainable Urban Form: Household Consumption of Energy and Transport in Eight Residential Areas in the Greater Oslo Region," *Urban Studies*, 42(12), pp. 2145–2166.

Ewing, R., R. Pendall, and D. Chen, 2002, *Measuring Sprawl and Its Impact*, Washington, DC: Smart Growth America.

Ewing, R., and F. Rong, 2008, "The Impact of Urban Form on U.S. Residential Energy Use," *Housing Policy Debate*, 19(1), pp. 1–29.

Fu, S. H., 2007, "Smart Café Cities: Testing Human Capital Externalities in the Boston Metropolitan Area," *Journal of Urban Economics*, 61(1), pp. 86–111.

Fuerst, F., 2007, "Office Rent Determinants: a Hedonic Panel Analysis," *SSRN Working Paper*, http://ssrn.com/abstract=1022828.

Garrett, M., and M. Wachs, 1996, *Transportation Planning on Trial: The Clean Air Act and Travel Forecasting*, Thousand Oaks, CA: Sage.

Giuliano, G., 1991, "Is Job-Housing Balancing a Transportation Issue?" *Transportation Research Record*, 1305, pp. 305–312.

Giuliano, G., and K. A. Small, 1991, "Subcenters in the Los Angeles Region," *Regional Science and Urban Economics*, 21(2), pp. 163–182.

Giuliano, G., and K. A. Small, 1993, "Is the Journal to Work Explained by Urban Structure?" *Urban Studies*, 30(9), pp. 1485–1500.

Glaeser, E. L., 2007, "The Economics Approach to Cities," *NBER Working Paper,* w13696, http://www.nber.org/papers/w13696.

Glaeser, E. L., and M. E. Kahn, 2008, "The Greenness of Cities: Carbon Dioxide Emissions and Urban Development," *NBER Working Paper,* w14238, http://www.nber.org/papers/w14238.

Gordon, P., H. W. Richardson, and H. L. Wong, 1986, "The Distribution of Population and Employment in a Polycentric City: The Case of Los Angeles," *Environment and Planning* A, 18, pp. 161–173.

Hamilton, B. W., 1982, "Wasteful Commuting," *Journal of Political Economics*, 90(5), pp. 1035–1053.

Hanson, S. and G. Pratt, 1988, "Reconceptualizing the Links between Home and Work in Urban Geography," *Economic Geography*, 64(4), pp. 299–321.

Helsley, R. and A. Sullivan, 1991, "Urban Subcenter Formation," *Regional Science and Urban Economics*, 21(2), pp. 255–275.

Hiroka, H., 2000, "The Development of Tokyo's Rail Network," *Japan Railway & Transport Review*, 23(3), pp. 22–31.

Houston, S., 2005, "Methods to Test the Spatial Mismatch Hypothesis," *Economic Geography,* 81(4), pp. 407–435.

Howard, E., 1902, *Garden Cities of Tomorrow*, London: S. Sonnenschein.

Ihlanfeldt, R., and L. Sjoquist, 1998, "Spatial Mismatch Hypothesis: A Review on Recent Studies and Their Implications for Welfare Reform," *Housing Policy Debate*, 9, pp. 849–892.

Kahn, M. E., 2000, "The Environmental Impact of Suburbanization," *Journal of Policy Analysis and Management*, 19(4), pp. 569–586.

Kahn, M. E., 2006, *Green Cities: Urban Growth and the Environment*, Washington DC: Brookings Institution Press.

Kain, F., 1968, "Housing Segregation, Negro Employment, and Metropolitan Decentralization," *Quarterly Journal of Economics*, 82, pp. 175–197.

King, E., and D. Leibling, 2003, Commuting and travel choices, Presentation to the RAC Foundation, Railway Forum Conference.

Knaap, G. J., Y. Song, R. Ewing, and K. Clifton, 2005, "Seeing the Elephant: Multi-disciplinary Measures of Urban Sprawl," *Urban Studies and Planning Program*, University of Maryland, www.smartgrowth.umd.edu/research/pdf/KnaapSongEwingEtAl_Elephant_022305.pdf

Levine, J., 1998, "Rethinking Accessibility and Jobs-Housing Balance," *Journal of the American Planning Association*, 64(2), pp. 133–149.

Lucas, R. E., 2001, "Externalities and Cities," *Review of Economic Dynamics*, 4(2), pp. 245–274.

Lucas, R. E., and E. Rossi-Hansberg, 2002, "On the Internal Structure of Cities," *Econometrica*, 70(4), pp. 1445–1476.

McDonald, J. F., 1987, "The Identification of Urban Employment Subcenters," *Journal of Urban Economics*, 21(2), pp. 242–258.

McDonald, J. F., 1989, "Econometric Studies of Urban Population Density: A Survey," *Journal of Urban Economics*, 26(3), pp. 361–385.

McDonald, J. F., and D. P. McMillen, 1990, "Employment Subcenters and Land Values in a Polycentric Urban Area: The Case of Chicago," *Environment and Planning*, A22, pp. 1561–1574.

McDonald, J. F., and P. J. Prather, 1994, "Suburban Employment Centers: The Case of Chicago," *Urban Studies*, 31, pp. 201–218.

McMillen, D. P., 1996, "One Hundred Fifty Years of Land Values in Chicago: A Nonparametric Approach," *Journal of Urban Economics*, 40(1), pp. 100–124.

McMillen, D. P., and J. F. McDonald, 1998, "Suburban Subcenters and Employment Density in Metropolitan Chicago," *Journal of Urban Economics*, 43, pp. 157–180.

McMillen, D. P., 2001, "Nonparametric Employment Subcenter Identification," *Journal of Urban Economics*, 50(3), pp. 448–473.

McMillen, D. P., and J. McDonald, 2004, "Reaction of House Prices to a New Rapid Transit Line: Chicago's Midway Line, 1983–1999," *Real Estate Economics*, 32(3), pp. 463–486.

Mieszkowski, P., and E. S. Mills, 1993, "The Causes of Metropolitan Suburbanization," *Journal of Economic Perspectives*, 7(3), pp. 135–147.

Mills, E. S., 1972, *Studies in the Structure of the Urban Economy*, Baltimore, MD: Johns Hopkins Press.

Muth, R. F., 1969, *Cities and Housing*, Chicago: The University of Chicago Press.

Newman, P., and J. Kenworthy, 1999, "Costs of Automobile Dependence: Global Survey of Cities," *Transportation Research Record*, 1670, pp. 17–26.

Ren, R. R., Y. M. Fu, and H. Y. Liu, 2007, "Land Price Discovery in a City with Changing Land Uses: A Study of Spatial Interactions in Office Market in Beijing," The 12th Asian Real Estate Society (AsRES) International Conference, Macau, 2007.7 and

The 3rd International Symposium on Urban Development and Land Policy in China, Hangzhou, 2007.10.

Rosenthal, S. S., and W. C. Strange, 2004, "Evidence on the Nature and Sources of Agglomeration Economies," *Handbook of Urban and Regional Economics,* ed. J. V. Henderson and J.-F Thisse, 4, 2119–2172. Amsterdam: North-Holland.

Rossi-Hansberg, E, 2004, "Optimal Urban Land Use and Zoning," *Review of Economic Dynamics*, 7(1), pp. 69–106.

Sivitanidou, R., 1996, "Do Office-commercial Firms Value Access to Service Employment Centers? A Hedonic Value Analysis within Polycentric Los Angeles," *Journal of Urban Economics*, 40(2), pp. 125–149.

Small, K., and S. Song, 1992, "'Wasteful' Commuting: A Resolution," *Journal of Political Economy*, 100(4), pp. 888–898.

Small, K., and S. Song, 1994, "Population and Employment Densities: Structure and Change," *Journal of Urban Economics*, 36(3), pp. 292–313.

Song, S., 1994, "Modeling Worker Residence Distribution in the Los Angeles Region," *Urban Studies*, 31(9), pp. 1533–1544.

Straszheim, M., 1998, "The Theory of Urban Residential Location," In *Handbook of Regional and Urban Economics, Urban Economics*, ed. E. S. Mills, 717–757. Amsterdam: North Holland.

United States Census Bureau, 2005, *American Community Survey, Americans Spend More Than 100 Hours Commuting to Work Each Year*, Washington DC: United States Census Bureau.

Voith, R., 1993, "Changing Capitalization of CBD-Oriented Transportation Systems: Evidence from Philadelphia, 1970–1988," *Journal of Urban Economics*, 33(3), pp. 361–376.

Zheng, S. Q., R. B. Peiser, and W. Z. Zhang, 2009, "The Rise of External Economies in Beijing: Evidence from Intra-urban Wage Variation," *Regional Science and Urban Economics*, 49, pp. 449–459.

Zheng, S. Q., R. Wang, M. E. Kahn, and E. L. Glaeser, 2010, "The Greenness of China: Household Carbon Dioxide Emissions and Urban Development," *Journal of Economic Geography*, 10(6), pp. 1–32.

Zheng, S. Q., and Z. P. Yang, 2007, "Housing Price Gradient with Respect to True Commuting Time in Beijing: Empirical Estimation and Its Implications," *Proceedings of 2007 ICM Conference*, Wuhan, China.

In Chinese

Cai, W., Z. H. Hu, and X. F. Ye, 2006, "The Study of Action Principle and Influence Circle on Urban Rail Transit Development Benefit," *Journal of the China Railway Society*, 4, pp. 27–31.

Ding, C. R., 2007, *Urban Spatial Planning: Theory, Method and Practice*. Beijing: Higher Education Press.

Gu, J., and S. H. Jia, 2008, "The Effects of Expected Transport Improvements on Housing Prices and Price Spatial Distribution—Hangzhou-Based Research Evidence of Planning the Mass Transit Railway," *Economic Geography*, 6, pp. 1020–1024.

Gu, Y. Z., and R. Guo, 2008, "The Impacts of The Rail Transit on Property Values: Empirical Study in Batong Line of Beijing," *Economic Geography*, 3, pp. 411–414.

Gu, Y. Z., and S. Q. Zheng, "The Impacts of Rail Transit on Property Values and Land Development Intensity: The Case of No.13 Line in Beijing," *Acta Geographica Sinica*, 65(2), pp. 213–223.

Gu, Y. Z., S. Q. Zheng, and Y. Cao, 2009, "The Identification of Employment Centers in Beijing," *Urban Studies*, 16(9), pp. 118–124.

He, J. H., and S. Q. Zheng, 2004, "Can New Subway Improve Housing Price: Evidence from No.13 Subway Line in Beijing," *Urban Development*, 11, pp. 37–39.

Horizon Research Consultancy, 2006, *The 2006 Urban Mobility Report of China*, www.chinacity.org.cn/csph/csph/48106.html.

Huo, Y., S. Q. Zheng, and Z. Yang, 2010, "Low-Carbon Lifestyle and Its Determinants: An Empirical Analysis Based on Survey of Household Energy Consumption and Community Environment in Beijing," *Journal of Urban and Regional Planning*, 2, pp. 72–75.

Li, Q., and X. L. Li, 2007, "The Characteristics of Resident's Working-Trip in Inner-Suburb of Beijing," *Urban Problems*, 7, pp. 55–59.

Liang, W. K., L. Y. Kong, and W. B. Deng, 2007, "Impact of URT on real estate value: the case of Beijing Metro Line 13," *China Civil Engineering Journal*, 4, pp. 99–103.

Liu, G. W., and Y. Peng, 2007, "An Analysis on the Impacts of Urban Rail Traffic on Real Estate: Exemplified by Chongqing," *Urban Problems*, 1, pp. 65–69.

Liu, Z. L., Y. Zhang, and Y. W. Chai, 2009, "Home-Work Separation in the Context of Institutional and Spatial Transformation in Urban China: Evidence from Beijing Household Survey Data," *Urban Studies*, 7, pp. 110–117.

Meng, B., 2009, "The Spatial Organization of the Separation between Jobs and Residential Locations in Beijing," *Acta Geographica Sinica*, 12, pp. 1457–1466.

Niu, W. Y., 2010, *The China New-Approach Urbanization Report 2010*, Beijing: Science Press.

Pan, H. X., and B. H. Zhong, 2008, "The Impact of Metro on Property Price: A Case Study of Shanghai," *Urban Planning Forum*, 2, pp. 62–69.

Ren, R. R., and S. Q. Zheng, 2008, "Spatial Structure of Office and Residential Land Development: Price Gradient, Development Scale and Location Variation," *Progress in Geography*, 27(3), pp. 119–126.

Ren, R. R., S. Q. Zheng, and Y. J. Wang, 2009, "Spatial Distribution of Land Prices: A Nonparametric Approach," *Journal of Tsinghua University (Science and Technology)*, 49(3), pp. 325–328.

Wang, X., D. L. Zhu, and M. M. Zhang, 2004, "Analysis of the Influence of Rail Transit on the Distribution Layout of Real Estate Prices—A Case Study of Beijing Light Rail Line No.13," *Urban Problems*, 6, pp. 39–42.

Yang, G. W., L. Y. Kong, Q. H. Liang, and J. Zhang, 2008, "Analysis of Real Estate Value Increment Due to Beijing Metro Line Batong," *Journal of Beijing Jiaotong University*, 3, pp. 37–41.

Yin, A. Q., and Y. Tang, 2008, "The Impact on Real Estate Price by Urban Rail Transportation: Taking Nanjing Subway One for Example," *Urban Problems*, 2, pp. 29–34.

Yu, L., S. Q. Zheng, and H. Y. Liu, 2008, "The Spatial Variation and Affecting Factors of The Housing Price Gradients: The Case of Beijing," *Economic Geography*, 28(3), pp. 406–410.

Zhang, H., J. J. Ma, and H. L. Zhu, 2007, "Price Influence of Urban Mass Transit on Housing Projects Along the Line," *Journal of Beijing Jiaotong University*, 3, pp. 14–17.

Zheng, J. F., and H. Y. Liu, 2005, "The Impact of URRT on House Prices in Shenzhen," *Journal of The China Railway Society*, 10, pp. 11–18.

Zheng, S. Q., and Y. Cao, 2009, "The Determinants of Jobs-Housing Spatial Relationship in Beijing," *Urban Studies*, 16(6), pp. 29–35.

Zheng, S. Q., Y. M. Fu, and Liu, H.Y, 2006, "Spatial Structure and Hindrance to Housing Choice: Evidence from Matched Location and Location-Preference Data in Chinese Cities," *Journal of Urban Economics*, 60, pp. 535–557.

Zheng, S. Q., and Y. Huo, 2010, "Low-carbon Urban Spatial Structure: An Analysis on Private Car Traveling," *World Economic Forum*, 6, pp. 50–65.
Zheng, S. Q., K. J. Liu, and W. Z. Sun, 2011, "Affordability Index for Transportation and Housing: An Application in Beijing," *Urban Studies*, 2, pp. 54–61.
Zheng, S. Q., and W. Z. Zhang, 2007, "The Spatial Interaction of Housing Cost and Commuting Cost: Evidence from Beijing Market," *Progress in Geography*, 2, pp. 35–42.
Zhou, S. H., and Y. L. Liu, 2010, "The Situation and Transition of Jobs-housing Relocation in Guangzhou, China," *Acta Geographica Sinica*, 2, pp. 191–201.

Appendix

Theoretical derivation of the monocentric model

The monocentric model assumes the city is a homogeneous, flat circular area. All the employment activity is concentrated in the CBD, which is viewed as a dot. Assume that there are N homogeneous households in a city (there is 1 employed worker per household, so there are N homogeneous employed workers), the wage rate of employed workers is at y. The commuting cost of employed workers is directly proportional to the distance of their residence to the CBD. If unit distance commuting cost is t (including monetary and time cost, assuming t is a constant), then an employed worker living at a location distance x from the CBD has a commuting cost of tx. At the same time, the optimal consumption bundle for workers under the budget constraint is (q,c), realizing the maximization of utility function u(q,c). Of which, q is the consumption of housing services and c is the consumption of all other goods. Let the rent for housing distance x from the CBD be R(x), the price of other goods not changing with spatial location changes (their price could be unitized as 1), then the budget constraint condition for residents is:

$$R(x)q + c + tx = y \tag{A.1}$$

workers will choose the optimal consumption bundle (q,c) to realize the maximization of utility, that is

$$\max u(q, c) \tag{A.2}$$

From utility maximization theory in microeconomics, we know that:

$$\frac{\partial u / \partial q}{\partial u / \partial c} = R(x) \tag{A.3}$$

Let u_1 represent the partial derivative of u(q,c) for q, u_2 represent the partial derivative of u(q,c) for c. Then the above equation could be expressed as:

$$R(x) = \frac{u_1}{u_2} \tag{A.4}$$

At the same time, under the condition of spatial equilibrium, residents' optimal utility u(q,c) is indifferent in different locations, that is $\frac{du}{dx}=0$, and on this basis, the following derivations could be made:

$$\frac{\partial u}{\partial q} \bullet \frac{\partial q}{\partial x} + \frac{\partial u}{\partial c} \bullet \frac{\partial c}{\partial x} = 0$$

$$u_1 \bullet \frac{\partial q}{\partial x} + u_2 \frac{\partial (y - tx - Rq)}{\partial x} = 0$$

$$u_1 \bullet \frac{\partial q}{\partial x} + u_2 \bullet \left(-t - \frac{\partial R}{\partial x} \bullet q - \frac{\partial q}{\partial x} \bullet R \right) = 0 \tag{A.5}$$

Substitute (A.4) into (A.5), transpose terms and merge those of the same kind, obtaining:

$$\frac{\partial R(x)}{\partial x} = -\frac{t}{q} \tag{A.6}$$

The above equation shows that with an increase in distance to CBD, housing rents will decline and the absolute value of its spatial gradient is *–t/q*. This is because transportation costs constantly increase as distance to CBD increases, in order to guarantee the utility of urban households reach spatial equilibrium, residents near the city center need to bear higher housing rents then those far away from the city center. Therefore, each urban household needs to make the trade-off between housing costs and transportation costs.

10 The equalized intergovernmental transfer in China

Ziying Fan

10.1 Introduction

Pursuit of balanced regional development has been a main objective of every Chinese administration. Deng Xiaoping mentioned the eventual goal of balanced development in his "Two General Situations" theory.[1] If 30 years of "reform and opening" are divided into two phases, then it just so happens to correspond to the "Two General Situations." The first 20 years were spent practicing the first General Situation through market-oriented reforms, encouraging unbalanced development to spur economic take-off and the latter 10 years saw a start to facilitating regional balanced development through administrative means. In 1999, 2003, and 2004, programs aimed at supporting the western, northwestern and central regions were implemented, and special considerations were taken for these regions in aspects, such as preferential policies, direct investments by the central government and equalized transfer.[2] According to the statistics, the proportion of transfer obtained by the inland provinces rose from 68.1 percent in 1995 to 82.8 percent in 2007.

However, as pointed out in the "World Development Report 2009," there has been no precedent in achieving balanced growth objectives through governmental intervention. The past trajectory of development in China has displayed a trend toward agglomeration, with the western and central regions' proportion of national GDP constantly decreasing, from 20.24 percent and 29.62 percent in 1980 to 17.14 percent and 23.19 percent in 2006, respectively. However, at the beginning of the second 10 years of the "Western Development Program," policy at the central level still followed past modes, narrowing regional gaps by giving inland regions more support through governmental intervention.

With the tax sharing reform in 1994, decentralization of responsibilities and centralization of fiscal powers occurs at the same time. The central government controls over half of national fiscal revenue but is only responsible for a quarter of fiscal expenditures. It is exactly such vertical asymmetry in responsibilities and fiscal powers that enables the central government to link fiscal transfer and regional development, achieving certain national level goals through transfer, which includes the dilemma of balanced regional development. For example, in 2004, the subsidy to provincial, municipal and county governments from central government accounted for 54 percent of its total expenditures.

However, the impact of intergovernmental transfers for local governments is not quite so simple. On the one hand, fiscal transfer needs to equalize the public services; while on the other hand, it also has a significant impact on the behavior of local governments. Structural changes occurred in the tax efforts and expenditure behavior of local governments. Lower local tax efforts cause real tax rates to decouple from nominal tax rates (An, 2002; Qiao et al., 2006), whereas the asymmetric change in expenditure behavior further led to macroeconomic fluctuations (Guo and Jia, 2006; Li and Shen, 2009).

Based on the above understandings, this chapter will systematically review the evolution, impact and reform direction of Chinese transfer systems. As far as we know, there is no systematic review of Chinese transfer in the existing literature. Current Chinese transfer systems are linked with other specific systems, so policy evaluations and recommendations regarding the transfer system need to comprehensively consider the impact of other systems, such as China's regional development policies, taxation policies, industrial policies, etc. Even though much literature studies the impacts of China's transfer, few consider the constraints imposed on the transfer system by other systems.

The rest of this chapter proceeds as follows: the next section explores the substitution between factor mobility and governmental transfer under fiscal decentralization, as well as the rationale for the existence of fiscal transfer; the third section will review the institutional background of the previous adjustments in fiscal transfer, as well as the policy dilemmas each adjustment in transfer attempted to resolve; the fourth section evaluates the effects of transfer since the mid-1990s from several aspects: fiscal equalization, provision of public goods, economic growth, and intergovernmental relations; the fifth section will mainly evaluate the negative impacts of transfer on local economies and government behavior; the last section concludes and proposes prospects for future research.

10.2 The Tiebout model and the source of vertical transfer: a theoretical review

When discussing the relationship between central and local government, it is impossible to avoid the work of Tiebout (1956), which discoursed upon the necessity of decentralizing powers to local governments. Tiebout's model has two critical assumptions: the main objective of local governments is to provide public goods for residents within its jurisdiction and residents can freely move across regions. The former implies that local governments are accountable to a lower level and the latter implies that there is fully free factor mobility. In Tiebout's ideal world, residents move across regions at zero cost and the local tax burden and level of public goods are provided by a region impact residents' utility. Then residents with a preference for more public goods will eventually choose communities with high tax burdens with more public goods, and residents choosing low tax burden communities would have correspondingly lower preferences for public goods. Residents reveal their preference through choosing communities by "voting with their feet." As such, the "voting with their feet" mechanism guarantees the eventual choices of all residents are optimal and any change at this point would damage efficiency, while local governments design tax rates and public goods according to the preferences of local residents and attract as much labor as possible through adjusting this combination, which expands the government's tax base. In the expanded Tiebout–Hamilton–Oates model, the government's fiscal revenues are determined by property taxes, whereas property prices increase with the community's population, which implies that communities that provide more public goods, even if the average tax rates are not higher, will choose residents through the form of property prices (Hamilton, 1983). At the same time, regions compete with each other by adjusting the combination of tax rates and public goods. Such competition also guarantees that taxation costs are minimal for a certain level of public goods.[3]

Other than that, the advantage of local governments in providing public goods is also expressed in local informational advantage, lower agency costs, yardstick competition, and innovation incentives (Stiglitz and Dasgupta, 1971; Oates, 1972; Boadway, 2006). Therefore, many countries have re-emphasized the importance of decentralized governance (Rhode and Strumpf, 2003) and the Tiebout model has become a fundamental theory supporting the decentralization of power to local governments. If the Tiebout mechanism perfectly depicted the real world, then there would be no reason to transfer fiscal revenue from developed regions to backward regions, since under the "voting with their feet" mechanism, an area having relatively less fiscal revenues and public expenditures is the result of resident choice; such a low level of public goods provision already is an optimal choice, and any transfer would lower efficiency and reduce the utility of residents within a community (Gruber, 2005).

Then, the size of the gap between the Tiebout model and reality precisely illustrates the necessity of equalized transfer. There are at least three reasons to support intergovernmental transfer. The first is the failure of the Tiebout mechanism to take effect, e.g. residents cannot freely "vote with their feet" to reveal their preference[4] as some laws may restrict the free mobile of residents or the migration costs for residents are too high (such as national borders or institutional restrictions) causing residents with high preference for public goods to be restricted to regions with relatively few public goods. The second is the existence of externalities or neighborhood effects in public goods, the only solution of which is increasing conditional grants by an upper level government, since only a higher level of government can accurately calculate the marginal social return and cost of public goods and thereby determine the optimal level of public goods, especially when spillover effects exceed a jurisdiction's return, local governments may lose the incentive to produce such a public good. For example, a highway that passes through multiple provinces. The cost of producing such a highway may far exceed the local return which means local governments will not input any resources to that project. Also, for example primary education not only increases the local human resource level, but also reduces crime rates in the surrounding regions and facilitates economic growth in other regions. Local governments lack the corresponding incentives in this field as well. Hence, the central government could provide public goods through matching conditional grants, enabling local governments to undertake a proportion of costs that match its benefits (Breton, 1965; Gruber, 2005). Finally, there are the externalities of labor mobility. Labor mobility across different regions brings fiscal externalities and tax externalities. Regions competing to attract labor inflow through lowering tax rates may generate a "race to the bottom" equilibrium, causing regions with poor innate conditions to lack the ability to provide adequate public goods and cause populations to eventually become unevenly distributed across regions (Boadway and Flatters, 1982; Sato, 2000).

Thus, vertical transfer may possibly be the only approach that combines the superior qualities of decentralization while not violating the goal of equalization at the national level. At a practical level, local governments are often directly responsible for the provision of some local public goods, such as local roads, water supply, waste collection, etc., whereas some public goods with very large economies of scale are provided by the central government, such as national defense, diplomacy, etc. Public goods in between these two such as education, healthcare, regional roads, etc require input from both the central and local governments. Such public goods often have positive externalities on other regions and merely relying on central or local government to provide them will create the issue of asymmetric benefits and costs. The overall principle is that the economies of scale effect needs to be realized in the provision of public goods, and externalities need to be reduced, the different preferences of residents in each region should be satisfied as well, the best approach of which is a balance between the two (Oates, 1972). Theoretically, the demarcation of expenditure responsibility between different levels of government should be clear-cut, but the demarcation of revenue powers is often inconsistent and the demarcation of revenue powers and expenditure responsibility are often mismatched. For example, taxes that are highly mobile or distributive are better controlled by the central government since these taxes themselves are fair and the result of such taxation is relatively fair (Musgrave, 1983). For taxes that have more severe asymmetric information issues, a lower level of government should collect them (Shah, 1994). When mobility and redistributive effects are used as rules of taxation management, since these two types of taxes account for an overwhelming proportion of fiscal revenue, the central government will take up the majority of national fiscal revenues; at the same time, out of efficiency considerations, the responsibility for most expenditure should belong to local government. Such vertical imbalance leads to the central government transferring a portion of its fiscal surplus to the local government in order to compensate its deficit. Such a vertical imbalance is one of the main reasons for the emergence of fiscal transfer (Zeng, 2000).

Other than vertical imbalance, horizontal imbalance is another main reason for the emergence of fiscal transfer, namely, the equalization of public services. Due to differences in the tax base and tax rates, the ability of different local governments of the same level to raise fiscal revenues varies widely, while at the same time, most expenditure responsibility is similar, which causes the price (cost) of services provided by the government to differ widely across regions. In areas with low economic development, the government needs to set higher tax rates, while the quantity and quality of services is worse as well, which will further cause local residents to lack the necessary social and economic opportunities, e.g. deficient education and healthcare investment will lead to a shortage in future human capital. Different tax rates across regions will also cause physical capital and human capital to gradually escape from low-income, high-tax regions, and further increase economic disparities and poverty. Therefore, in a federalist government, intergovernmental transfer can equalize current government services or at least confer backward regions with enough ability to provide public services. This not only can increase future human capital, but due to low tax rates, it can also inhibit the outflow of local resources.

In summary, the main reasons for implementing fiscal transfer are three-fold. (1) Vertically unbalanced fiscal resources require the use of transfer to solve. In most countries, the central government controls the main tax base, e.g. the Japanese and Australian central government's proportion of national fiscal revenue is two-thirds, while the expenditure responsibility of local governments is large too, which requires the central government to transfer fiscal resources to the local government. (2) Horizontal imbalances require the implementation of fiscal transfer. Due to differences in initial endowment, even under the same taxation efforts, some regions may not be able to provide enough basic public services. If labor is unable to move freely, residents cannot equalize the enjoyment of basic public services through the "voting with feet" mechanism and fiscal transfer becomes a way to guarantee the basic rights of citizens. Other than economic efficiency considerations, equalizing transfer is also conducive to maintaining long-term political stability (Barro, 1999; Smart, 1998). (3) The existence of externalities requires fiscal transfer. For certain investments that have spillover effects, local governments lack motivation and require an upper level government to provide the necessary subsidy (Shah, 1994; Boadway and Hobson, 1993; Rosen, 1995).

Intergovernmental transfer can be categorized into four dimensions: (1) whether it is a categorical transfer or general transfer; (2) whether the transfer has a fixed formula or is allocated according to project; (3) whether the subsidy requires a lower level government's matching contribution (funds); (4) whether there are restrictions on the size of the subsidy (Fisher, 1996). These can be specifically divided into the forms displayed in Figure 10.1.

There are three major categories of transfer in China's current fiscal system: general transfer, tax rebates and earmarked grants. General transfer includes lump-sum transfer, minority region transfer, rural tax and fee reform transfer, etc.; tax rebates including consumption tax, value-added and income tax rebates; earmarked grants including specific subsidies and debt-issuance subsidies, the former includes various projects by central government. General transfer, correspond to the general grants in the standard categorization. Tax rebates correspond to revenue-sharing under general subsidy, while earmarked grants correspond to categorical grants. Most of China's earmarked grants have no amount limit.

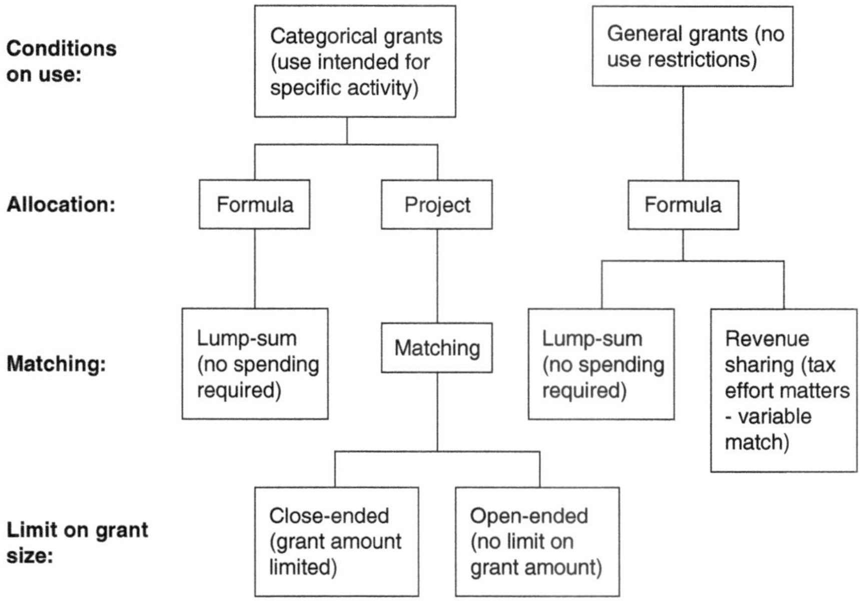

Figure 10.1 Categories of transfer.
Data source: Fishman (1996), p. 204.

10.3 Evolution of fiscal and taxation reforms and China's transfer system

There have been frequent changes in China's fiscal and taxation system and each fiscal and taxation reform was closely followed by adjustments in the transfer system. From Figure 10.2, it can be seen that meaningful fiscal transfer appeared after 1994, e.g. transfers in 1991 were only 6.45 billion RMB (renminbi), accounting for less than 4 percent of the total central expenditures and less than 3 percent of total local expenditures for that year. The impact on local government was small and transfer was mainly used to alleviate fiscal deficits in a very few backward regions and minority regions.

During the period from 1980–1993, China implemented a fiscal contracting system. Such a system endowed local governments with sufficient incentives for economic development, though due to the incredibility of the upper government, the central government's frequent adjustment of revenue-sharing ratios caused the local government to intentionally conceal fiscal revenues or transfer budget revenues to extra-budget revenues. The central government was often unable to make ends meet during this period and for many years, it had to ask the local government to "make contributions,"[5] with total transfer even reaching negative 5.57 billion RMB in 1993, thus leaving the central government with no further resources to conduct equalized transfer. In order to reverse the central

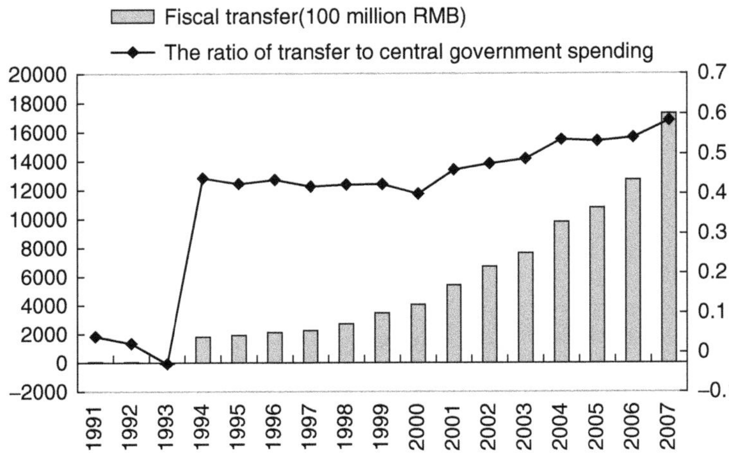

Figure 10.2 Historical transfer and proportion.
Data source: "Finance Yearbook of China" (2008, volume).

government's diminishing fiscal resources, the tax sharing system implemented in 1994 began to stipulate the center's share of revenue by law and change the previous revenue-sharing into tax-sharing.

The tax sharing reform changed central and local relationships in three ways. First, a unified tax rate and tax sharing mechanism guarantees the credibility of the central governments sharing proportion promise; next, the divided collection of national and local taxes lowered the incentive of local governments to conceal revenue; finally, large scale vertical transfer enabled the central government to conduct macroeconomic adjustments and purposefully balance regional economic disparities (Ma, 1997).[6] The 1994 tax sharing reform greatly improved both the degree of centralization and the fiscal status of the central government, causing both of the two proportions—fiscal revenue's percentage of GDP and central government's proportion of national fiscal revenue—to increase, among which the fiscal revenue's percentage of GDP rose from 10.8 percent in 1994 to 20.6 percent in 2007. The central government's proportion of fiscal revenue jumped in 1994 from 22 percent to 55.7 percent and more or less maintained a level of 50 percent thereafter. Meaningful fiscal transfer began to appear after 1994. The center's net transfer to the local increased from 181.9 billion RMB in 1994 to 1.2714 trillion RMB in 2006, averaging an annual growth rate of 17.6 percent, exceeding the center's fiscal revenue growth rate during the same period. The proportion of fiscal transfers in each year's central fiscal expenditures rose from 43.9 percent to 54.1 percent. Looking at the evolution over the years, the first jump point was 1994, during which transfer increased by 200 billion, but this was mostly through tax rebates as a compromise for the coastal provinces' smoothly carrying out the tax sharing reform. The second jump point was 1999, and a rapidly increasing trend was maintained afterwards, which is related to balanced regional development economic policies such as the "Western Development Program" (Wang, 2004).

From the perspective of fiscal revenue source, other than the tax sharing system significantly changing the original distribution pattern, the center made several major adjustments toward tax-sharing and tax categories after 2000 (see Table 10.1), the results of which further increased the fiscal centralization of the center, while at the same time weakening local fiscal resources. These adjustments were all accompanied by changes in the transfer system. If we count the return of two taxes as one type of transfer,[7] then this is the first time fiscal and taxation reforms matched transfer reforms. In addition, it is noteworthy that the original system for redistribution of revenue between center and local was retained as well. The central subsidies obtained before 1994 were distributed in the existing manner and the provinces that needed to contribute to the center under the contracting system continued to fulfill this responsibility and the subsidies and contributions of the original system persisted to this day. The implementation of the tax sharing system strengthened the center's fiscal resource to a certain extent. The central government officially introduced lump-sum transfer aimed at regional fiscal resource disparities in 1995. Such transfer not only gave minority regions preferential treatment, they also gave subsidies to regions with overly large fiscal deficits. Since they were in the pilot phase, the lump-sum transfer during this period was also known as transitional transfer. But due to their size being too small, they were not sufficient to reverse the trend toward increasing regional fiscal disparities. However, their proportion of central fiscal revenues rose from 0.64 percent in 1995 to 1.61 percent in 2001, which indirectly shows that fiscal balance gradually became the main objective of the central government's implementation of transfer. The tax and fee reforms starting in 2000 substituted administrative fees with regular taxes and merged extra-budget revenues into the budget, while lowering tax rates for specialty agricultural products and eliminating slaughter taxes, causing the tax revenue source of basic level government to fall sharply. The fiscal input into basic public services (e.g. education) fell and transfers based on local needs appeared to be urgent, such as earmarked grants aimed at education, healthcare, etc. Starting in 2001, the center added transfer for rural tax and fee reforms and provided subsidies aimed at provinces other than Beijing, Tianjin, Shanghai, Jiangsu, Zhejiang, Guangdong, etc. (Tsui, 2005; Yin, 2007). The central government began to promote the reduction and elimination of agricultural taxes in certain provinces starting in 2004. From 2006, it began to abolish the collection of agricultural taxes at the national level and aimed at the diminishing fiscal resources of the basic level governments, the center implemented matching subsidies for the abolishment of agriculture specialty taxes and lower agricultural tax rates. In 2005, it further implemented subsidies alleviating county and township fiscal difficulties. These fiscal subsidies basically sustained the functioning of basic level government. Unlike reforms that reduce basic level fiscal resources, the center implemented income tax sharing reforms in 2002, stipulating it will share 50 percent of income taxes, which originally entirely belonged to local government.[8] At one point, this caused the center's proportion of fiscal revenue to increase

Table 10.1 Revenue-sharing and transfer reforms since the 1990s

Year	*1994*			*2001*	*2002*	*2004*
Revenue reform	Tax sharing system			Tax and fee reform	Income tax sharing	Reduction and elimination of agricultural taxes
Year	*1994*	*1994*	*1995*	*2001*	*2002*	*2004*
New transfer project	Earmarked grants	(Subsidies from former system) Tax rebates, bond issuance subsidies, wage augmentation transfer	Lump-sum transfer	Minority region transfer	Rural tax and fee reform transfer	County and township rewards and subsidies[9]

by 3 percent. The center's increased fiscal resources were entirely used for lump-sum transfers to the inland regions. In 2002, narrowing regional fiscal disparities gradually became the main objective of central to local transfer.

We can basically categorize transfers according to whether or not their uses are designated. General transfer is usually for the assistance of local government fiscal deficits, adopting "formulas" to calculate each region's needs, and then allocating them according to a certain proportion. This is relatively objective and fair. For example, the lump-sum transfer aimed at balancing regional fiscal resource disparities that were officially introduced in 1995 adopted the following formula:

> Lump-sum transfer to a certain region = (Region's standard fiscal expenditures –Region's standard fiscal revenues) × Region's transfer coefficient

Where, standard fiscal revenues are local taxes plus other subsidies from the center, standard fiscal expenditures are the aggregate expenditures of all corresponding departments, and the transfer coefficient is based on the size of the center's fiscal surplus. As the center's fiscal revenues grew, the transfer coefficient rose from 4.2 percent in 1995 to 47.3 percent in 2005 (Li, 2006, p. 71) and a large rise in subsidies only began in 2002.

Another type is earmarked grants allocated according to "project," and compared to general transfer, earmarked grants have three characteristics. First, they require local governments to match contributions, for example, in the "two exemptions and one subsidy" *liangmianyibu* implemented in 2005 for compulsory education, the center undertakes at most 80 percent of expenditures and the local government is required to make room for the rest within the budget. Second, earmarked grants have designated uses and, strictly speaking, local governments are not allowed to change their uses and most are directed toward fields local

Table 10.2 2007 Center to local transfer

	Detailed categories	*Amount (hundreds of millions yuan)*	*Proportion (%)*
General transfer	Lump-sum transfer	2505	35.5
	Minority region transfer	173	2.4
	Rural tax and fee reform transfer	759	10.7
	Wage adjustment transfer	2234	31.5
	County and township rewards and subsidies transfer	339	4.8
	Other general transfer	1083	15.3
Earmarked grants	Education	391	5.7
	Science and technology	75	1.1
	Social security and employment	1961	28.4
	Healthcare	630	9.1
	Environmental protection	748	10.8
	Forestry and water conservancy	961	13.9
	Other specific transfer	2133	30.9

Note: Other general transfer includes rural compulsory education transfer, urban compulsory education transfer, resource depletion urban transfer, rural compulsory education debt subsidies, subsidies under former system, firm and public institution transition subsidies, year-end settlement, financial subsidies, etc. Other earmarked grants include subsidies in general public services, national defense, public security, culture, education and media, urban–rural community affairs, industrial, commercial, and financial affairs, transportation, etc.
Data source: Ministry of Finance, http://www.mof.gov.cn.

governments are unwilling to get involved in, such as agriculture, social security, environment, primary education etc. Finally, China's earmarked grants projects belong to different systems and there are many overlaps across projects, with unclear payment rules. For example, there are 239 earmarked grants projects allocated by the center's finances in 2005, among which 41 overlap, and 65 do not have regulations or have not publicized such regulations (National Audit Office of PRC, 2006).

From Table 10.2, it can be seen that, when not considering tax rebates, general transfer is almost equal with earmarked grants. Among general transfer, lump-sum l transfer is the most common, followed by wage adjustment transfer. It could be observed that narrowing regional disparities has become the main goal of general transfer. Whereas among earmarked grants, social security and employment is the most common, followed by forestry, water conservation and environmental protection, which shows that earmarked grants are mostly based on motivating local governments to increase the supply of local public goods.

Transfers from the center to the local are relatively transparent and disciplined, but fiscal arrangements and transfer at the provincial level and below are fuzzier and no provisions stipulating unified rules for arrangements below the provincial level exist, thereby giving provincial and municipal governments a lot of room to maneuver. From Figure 10.3, it could be observed that when counties are

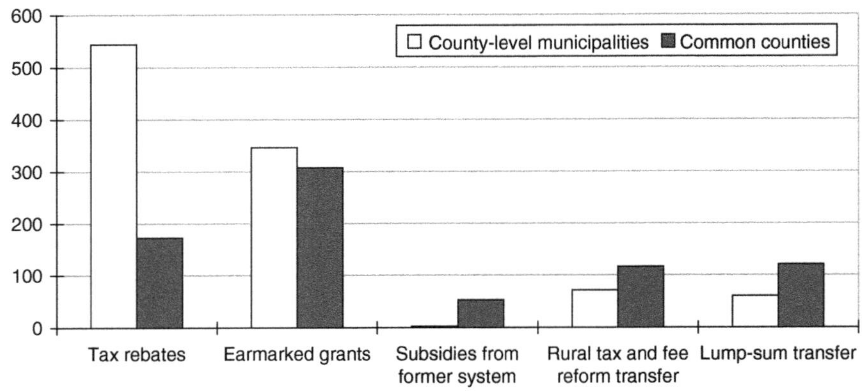

Figure 10.3 2002 County and county-level municipality transfer (billion RMB).
Data source: "2003 Statistics on National County-level Municipality Finances."

divided into county-level municipalities and common counties, common counties obtain more support in many types of transfer, other than earmarked grants, environmental protection and tax rebates, since the economic development level of county-level municipalities is twice that of common counties, making them satisfy the matching condition of earmarked grants better; general transfer, on the whole, tends to flow to counties will relatively poorer economies. But huge distributional differences exist within common counties. Transfer obtained by the common counties that have relatively poor economic development levels exhibit an inverse relationship with their own fiscal revenues, but in common counties with relatively developed economies, the two do not have any significant relationship; while in relatively economically developed county-level municipalities, fiscal transfer is actually positively correlated with local revenues. This phenomenon illustrates that common counties are more likely to receive transfer that balances gaps in fiscal resources, while county-level municipalities are more likely to receive earmarked grants. At the same time, relatively richer common counties and relatively poorer county-level municipalities are more likely to be systematically neglected by central and provincial governments (Yao, 2007).

10.4 Effectiveness of the Chinese transfer system

10.4.1 Does transfer narrow regional fiscal disparities?

Since the implementation of the tax sharing system in 1994, the center's fiscal resources were enhanced vertically, but horizontal disparities still exist. The tax sharing system protected regional vested interests in design by guaranteeing against a decline in coastal fiscal revenues from reform through the form of tax rebates. Here, subsidies from the former system, that is, institutional subsidies

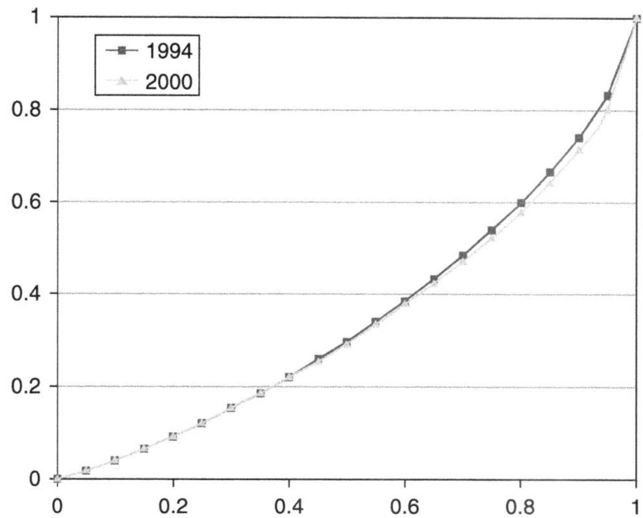

Figure 10.4 County level *per capita* fiscal expenditures Lorenz curve.
Data source: Tsui (2005).

by the center toward the local before the tax division system reform were used to balance regional fiscal disparities, but the amount of these subsidies are very small. Some provinces even eliminated former system subsidies to lower governments, so this did not inhibit fiscal disparities. Transitional transfer was introduced in 1995, namely solving the issue of expanding disparities in fiscal resources through the form of increased transfer to poor provinces. But as Figure 10.4 shows, transitional transfer was not able to alleviate existing disparities in fiscal resources. *Per capita* fiscal expenditure gaps actually increased in 2000 compared with 1994, and the Lorenz curve of *per capita* fiscal expenditures shows that the expenditure level of some counties is significantly higher than the national average.

Aimed at the issue of fiscal resource balance, Tsui (2005) employed data from over 2000 Chinese counties, adopting the Shorrocks decompose method and found that of all transfer projects, only former system subsidies were conducive to alleviating disparities in fiscal resources. In 2000, over 21 percent of disparities in fiscal resources were caused by tax rebates; in addition, the transitional transfer system had the goal of fiscal equalization in mind and allocates a certain amount of subsidies to regions with a fiscal deficit according to a fixed formula, but the actual result was expanded fiscal disparities, with 3 percent of fiscal disparities produced by transitional transfer. If a distinction is made between interprovincial disparities and within-provincial disparities, research shows that as time passes, the contribution of revenue source to interprovincial fiscal disparities increases, while its contribution to within-provincial fiscal disparities declines, but the former surpasses the latter, causing the contribution in the aggregate sense to be positive. The "Western Development Program" caused many fiscal resources to be inclined toward the western regions and the eastern and central regions often cannot obtain such transfer only because they are not in the west. But actually, intraregional fiscal disparities are much greater than interregional fiscal disparities, which indirectly illustrates that major issues still exist for allocating transfer through simple demarcations of regions into eastern, central and western.

Of all types of transfer, earmarked grants and tax rebates have the strongest inequality, since these two are not aimed at narrowing fiscal disparities (Shih and Zhang, 2007).[10] In 2003, regions with the strongest fiscal resources had *per capita* fiscal resources that were 37.4 times that of regions with the weakest fiscal resources and earmarked grants explains 17.7 percent of the difference (Yin, 2007). Some studies also found bargaining, personal favors and wide scattering in earmarked grants. In the conflict between upper and lower level governments, underdeveloped regions often lack voice and competitiveness, which results in most subsidies falling into the lap of rich regions, thus creating inequality (Jiang et al., 1999). Knight's (2002) research found that evident personal impacts exist in the process of project allocation. During the construction of highways in the US, states that have more members in the project's committee have a higher probability of obtaining a project. Our studies found a similar conclusion. Among the Party's 14th, 15th and 16th central committee members, the more members that had working experience in a certain province, the more transfer that province was able to obtain (Fan and Zhang, 2010a). In addition, transfer often requires local matching funds, which excludes the possibility of poor regions receiving subsidies and instead, enlarges fiscal disparities (Ahmad, 1998; Park et al., 1996). Even the factor approach transfer[11] aimed at solving fiscal disparities are unequal, since these transfers are often allocated according to population supported by the fiscal budget, so they may not narrow fiscal disparities in the *per capita* sense. As the state increases its input in balancing transfer and rules, regulating transfer payment systems become more standardized, the equalization effect of transfer is gradually exhibited after 2003 (Yin and Zhu, 2009).

Fiscal transfer is determined both by economic and political factors. Economic factors usually include income and urbanization levels. Regions with lower income obtain more transfer, whereas urbanization levels represent the necessary amount of public expenditures. Therefore, urbanization rates and transfer are positively correlated. Transfer according to economic factors is conducive to alleviating fiscal disparities, but in the actual formula for transfer, even for those aimed at narrowing regional fiscal disparities, they use local fiscal deficits as a standard, instead of being directly linked to level of economic development, which induces local governments (especially county level governments) to increase standard fiscal expenditures by expanding the size of government, thereby increasing fiscal deficits, inducing the center to transfer more fiscal resources to them, while out of administration efficiency and political stability considerations, the central government has to increase transfer to meet local deficits (Shih and Zhang, 2007). On the other hand, political factors are more important than economic factors in determining the allocation of transfer, as the US federal government gives more transfer to states that are more relevant to a president's re-election, which often causes economic and political factors to have a conflicting impact. The politically significant states often have high incomes, which results in higher incomes leading to more transfer (Wallis, 1996). Similar situations have also taken place in Russia and Germany. Russia gave politically unstable regions large transfer, while these regions often do not have the worst economy (Treisman, 1998). Although Germany reunified in 1990, every year after, the federal government transferred 5 percent of the former Federal Republic of Germany's output to make up for the disparity between the east and the west. The same took place in China. Out of political stability considerations, the center is more attentive to minority regions (Wang, 2004).

10.4.2 Does transfer increase the supply of public goods?

The center's fiscal subsidies to the local often have two objectives: one is to maintain the functioning of basic level government and the other is to equalize basic public services. According to the principles of cost–benefit, local public goods—that is, goods where all of the returns are enjoyed by local residents, such as urban trash collection, etc.—should be undertaken by the local government, and the central government should not subsidize it. But public goods with externalities, e.g. an increase in local education levels is conducive to lowering national crime rates, require subsidies from the central government, the standard of which is the equalizing of local benefits and costs (Oates, 1999; Besley and Coate, 2003). Conditional transfer could hence be used to motivate local governments to design their supply of public goods in accordance with the central government's standards, while achieving the center's objectives, motivating local governments to participate in the funding of such projects, on the one hand, utilizing the informational advantage of local governments and on the other hand, increasing the social return of public goods (Musgrave, 1997; Boadway, 2006). Studies on the US Aid to Families with Dependent Children show that for every 10 percent increase in the subsidy rate to low-income households, the *per capita* subsidies received increases by 1.5 percent, e.g. in 1970, the federal government paid 60 percent of the marginal cost and if the subsidy rate increased to 70 percent, *per capita* subsidies received increased by about $1 (Moffitt, 1984).

China indeed made use of earmarked grants with matching clauses to promote the supply of public goods. Center to local transfer has increased from 36.137 billion RMB in 1994 to 441.158 billion RMB in 2006; an average annual growth rate of 23.2 percent. These newly increased transfer funds are mostly expenditures in the agricultural support, education, science and culture, social security, etc. fields that are related to people's daily lives (Jia and Zhao, 2008). In terms of geographical distribution, over 40 percent of earmarked grants go to the western regions. For example, in the "two exemptions and one subsidy" for compulsory education implemented in 2005, the central government is responsible for 80 percent of the funding for tuition and other fees in western regions, 60 percent of the funding in central regions, while also being responsible for 50 percent of the central and western regions' student living expenses subsidies. The earmarked grants for western regions, begun in 1999, accounted for a rapidly increasing proportion of fiscal revenues, from 18 percent in 1995 to 76 percent in 2002, significantly improving the issue of inadequate expenditures on public goods in the western regions. Our study also found that for every 1 yuan increase in *per capita* earmarked grants, *per capita* investment in public goods will increase by 0.343 yuan for the locals.[12] *Per capita* earmarked grants reached 522 yuan in 2007, showing that investment in public goods provided by central government is 179 yuan per person (Fan and Zhang, 2010a). Relative to average fiscal subsidies, earmarked grants with matching conditions has a much more significant effect in solving the deficiency in supply of public goods. This shows that other than informal systems, in a relatively centralized country, the central government can cause the supply of public goods to reach a desirable level through formal systems (Tsai, 2007).[13]

Due to lack of data, research directed toward specific public goods is relatively hard to conduct, but some studies have tried to make progress in this field. Employing provincial level data, Zhang and Wang (2008) discovered that transfer by the central to provincial governments can significantly increase the completion rate of compulsory education. But studies employing micro-data cannot fully support this conclusion. Park and Shi's (2008) study found that the state's exemption and reduction of education fees has had almost no impact on elementary school enrollment rates, though the impact on secondary school enrollment rates is slightly higher, as every 10 percent decrease in education fees only increases school enrollment rates by 0.4 percent. Thus, for a special public good as education, since enrollment rates are already very high, the main effect of transfer is not increasing enrollment rates, but increasing education expenditures per student. However, if households spend money they would otherwise have spent on education on other things, after receiving education fee exemptions and reductions, then the effect of transfer is indifferent from normal household income subsidies. But if education fee exemptions and reductions do not fully crowd out education expenditures by households, then it is conducive for the increase in education quality. Shi (2008) employed Gansu survey data and found that for every 1 yuan increase in central education subsidies, household compulsory education expenditures will decrease by 0.613 yuan, while at the same time increasing household voluntary education expenditures by 0.651 yuan. This implies that central transfer did not fully squeeze out private education expenditures and transfers directed at education are conducive to increasing education investment per student.

10.4.3 Does transfer facilitate local economic growth?

In terms of long-term goals, whether central direct investments or indirect investments in local construction through transfer, the goal is to eventually facilitate economic growth in backward regions, enabling balanced growth in regional economies.[14] In 1985, due to previous rural reforms, regional disparities did slightly decrease at one point. Other than that year, regional disparities rose in every other year and regional disparities gradually became exhibited in club divergence between eastern regions and inland regions (Yao, 2000; Yao and Zhang, 2001). During the mid to late 1980s, disparities within inland provinces expanded as well, partially due to the then unfinished price reforms, as the double-track price system caused rich provinces to face even more severe price distortions, while out of political considerations, the central government's transfer (price subsidies) flowed to those relatively rich provinces. The investment of these provinces is artificially increased, thereby expanding the disparities within inland provinces. At the same time, such transfer lowers national overall investment efficiency (Raiser, 1998). Ma and Yu (2003) employed 1995–2000 Chinese provincial data and reached the conclusion that transfer did not facilitate regional economic convergence. They believe that the fiscal transfer system then included too many tax rebates, which actually further expanded regional disparities. In addition, transfer mainly flowed toward provinces with more minorities, e.g. there are 10 provinces with *per capita* GDPs lower than that of Xinjiang, but the *per capita* fiscal transfer received by Xinjiang is many times that of those ten provinces. The explanation for this is that central to local transfer includes too many objectives. Growth, balance and political stability are all included, while these objectives are often conflicting and the central government's transfer to provinces with serious social issues are even less, which illustrates to a certain degree that the central government intentionally uses fiscal transfer as a means of reward (Wang, 2004).

Purely in terms of the growth objective, the performance of vertical transfer has not been satisfactory. On the whole, the higher a province's proportion of central transfer is, the slower its growth (Chen and Lu, 2008). Our research found that transfer makes a positive contribution to local economic growth in the short run, since local government expenditures will therefore increase, thereby directly contributing to GDP growth, but in the long run, transfer may even produce negative impacts on local economic growth. We simulate the growth effect of transfer in Figure 10.5. The horizontal axis represents a 30-year study period, the vertical axis is the GDP growth rate (calculated in percentages). For every 1 percent increase in the proportion of transfer, the long term growth rate of a regional economy decreases by 0.03 percent. This type of inefficiency reaches 0.37 percent in the western regions (the real line in the diagram).[15] Such a result makes it worthwhile for us to ponder the structural changes brought by transfer. Strictly speaking, transfer is conflict with a decentralized structure and economic incentives for both outflow and inflow regions will decline. At the same time, overly high government expenditures will reduce development of the private economy and delay the construction of the market system (Fan and Zhang, 2010b).

10.5 Does transfer harmonize central–local relations?

Out of political stability considerations, fiscal authority in China is upwardly concentrated. In order to maintain the center's authority, the central government and provincial governments increase their control over lower level governments

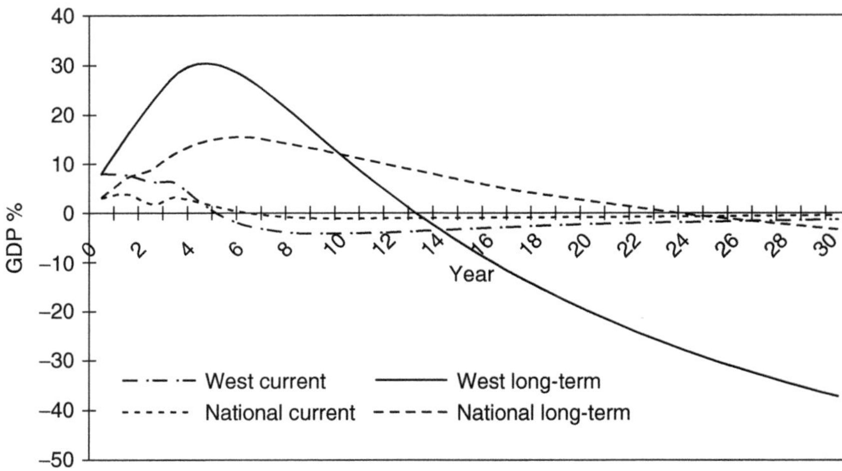

Figure 10.5 Lag and cumulative effect of national and western region transfer.
Data source: Fan and Zhang (2010b).

through fiscal transfer. This harmonizes intergovernmental relations to a certain extent, lowering the resistance of lower level governments to upper level government policy, indirectly facilitating market integration in the mid to late 1990s. Theoretically, China's decentralization reforms in the 1980s facilitated the growth of local economies, but using GDP as a performance indicator caused each region to "beggar-thy-neighbor," forming regional protectionism and vassal economies. Each region sought to restrict the outflow of local resources and inflow of nonlocal products and the whole country evolved into a "fragmented regional market" (Young, 2000), with border effects between provinces even larger than that of barriers between countries in the EU. Market segmentation becomes the main barrier restricting the domestic economy's development (Poncet, 2003; Wang et al., 2007). However, local governments adopt segmentation policies largely out of fiscal revenue concerns. Restricting the outflow of local resources and inflow of nonlocal products are both directed toward supporting the local economy, thereby obtaining more tax revenue in the current term or future periods. From this perspective, it is rational for local governments to engage in market segmentation. Certain backward regions may even reverse comparative advantages through such means and achieve faster economic growth in the future (Lu et al., 2004). Theoretically, conducting transfer to backward regions can cut the connection between market segmentation and fiscal revenues, reducing the segmentation actions of local governments (Lu et al., 2004, 2007). Local governments especially, will trade off the benefits of segmentation and direct central transfer. When the size of transfer enables backward regions to obtain a higher utility from participating in the division of labor than from segmenting markets, even under a fiscally decentralized system, backward regions will actively give up market segmentation, thereby increasing the market's scale effect.

On the basis of the "law of one price," the index calculated by the "price based approach" can show the level of market segmentation. The higher the index is, the more evident market segmentation is. We cite index values calculated by Gui et al. (2006) and Liu and Li (2008). Although the two indices were calculated using the same method, taking into account price changes of nine major categories of goods, the span of the data and the coverage of the calculations differ, the former only considering the impact of neighboring provinces whereas the latter takes into account the entire domestic market. From Figure 10.6, it could be observed that, although the two differ in absolute value, their time trends are completely identical. Market segmentation was relatively volatile before 1995 and the average level was rather high, while the index values began a significant, steady decline after 1995, with the level of market segmentation only a quarter of what it used to be. This is consistent with when fiscal and taxation reforms and central to provincial transfer increased. Our research shows a significantly negative correlation exists between vertical transfer and regional market segmentation. Such an effect is even more apparent in inland regions. Every 1 percent increase in transfer to inland regions can reduce its market segmentation by 4.3 percent from the current level. In the three major categories of transfer, earmarked grants contribute the most to market integration, while the effect of tax rebates is not apparent. This indirectly shows that the central government intends to use the uncertainty of earmarked grants to coordinate consistent behavior from local governments. From

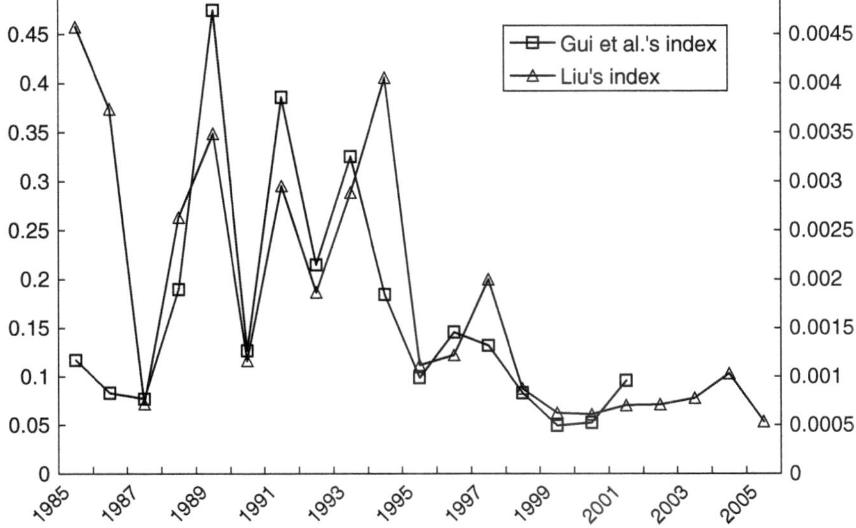

Figure 10.6 Trends in Chinese market segmentation.
Data source: Gui et al. (2006) and Liu and Li (2008).

the perspective of regional market integration, such a policy is relatively successful (Fan and Zhang, 2010c).

10.6 Drawbacks of the Chinese transfer system

10.6.1 Expansion of governmental expenditures and governmental size

Earmarked grants require local government behavior to change and general transfer that does not require local government behavior to change. However, local governments do not view general transfer equally with local revenues. General transfer will also change local government behavior and impact local economic growth and administrative efficiency. Early public finance theory was basically consistent with Wagner's law[16] stating that the main factor impacting a local government's size is the fiscal revenue constraint it faces, while the structure of revenue does not have any impact. In other words, local government treats transfer and local tax revenue as fiscal revenue in the same manner. Those provinces that receive transfer will lower effective tax rates at the same time and conversely, when transfer decreases, they will increase effective tax rates. Transfer from upper level governments only produces income effects, pushing the budgetary constraints of local government outwards, so the size of government will not change with fiscal revenue structure (Bradford and Oates, 1971), which implies that the central government's fiscal policy will not impact the overall size of government. However, empirical research finds that growth in the size of government far exceeds the limit explainable by Wagner's law and public finance theory. For every dollar increase in local revenues, fiscal expenditures only increase by \$0.02–0.05, while an identical amount of transfer causes fiscal expenditures to grow near or even exceed \$1, that is, in areas with the same fiscal revenue, those with a higher proportion of transfer will have larger governments. Such an "anomaly" is known as the "flypaper effect" (Hines and Thaler, 1995; Brennan and Pincus, 1996). There may be two reasons for the existence of the flypaper effect: one is the characteristics of the recipient of transfer such as the special institutional structure of local governments, uncertainty, fiscal illusion,[17] etc. (Bailey and Connolly, 1998). When local governments cannot ascertain the sustainability of transfer, they will be more inclined to use them for expenditures of the current period; the other factor is the giver of transfer, that is, the central government, may prohibit local governments from using transfer to pay for other expenditures and if supervision is achievable then the flypaper effect will be even stronger (Chubb, 1985).

We rank relative government size (expenditures/GDP) and *per capita* transfer in 1995 and 2007, and compare them after dividing them into three groups: increase, decrease, unchanged. We found that government size in most provinces has changed since 1995, with eight provinces experiencing an increase in their rank, nine decreasing and 13 basically unchanged. Among the eight coastal provinces, other than Jiangsu experiencing a small increase and Zhejiang unchanged, the other six provinces all experienced large declines, with Guangdong, Tianjin, and Fujian losing over seven ranks, respectively falling from 17th, 15th and 21st in 1995, to 26th, 23rd and 28th. The central and western provinces saw the largest increase, with Anhui and Sichuan, respectively, increasing by 11 ranks, and Heilongjiang and Shaanxi rising by five. It can be seen that the increase in government size since 1996 in China was not exhibited in abnormal growth in all provinces, but was mainly caused by growth in a few inland provinces. After ordering provinces according to *per capita* fiscal transfer (see Table 10.4), only Tibet did not change in 2007 relative to 1995. This is because Tibet has always received major support from the state. While 18 provinces experienced an increase in relative ranking, with all of them in the central and western regions; 11 provinces experienced a decline in their relative ranking; other than Yunnan and Hebei, the rest are all eastern coastal regions. Guangdong, Zhejiang and Jiangsu saw the largest declines, respectively from 10th, 12th, and 15th in 1995 to 30th, 27th, and 29th in 2007. Comparing Tables 10.3 and 10.4, we find that provinces with above-average growth in government size experienced different degrees of growth in transfer received, while the other provinces experienced declines in the transfer received. Through rigorous empirical research, we find that the flypaper effect in China is between 0.6 and 1.3, that is, every unit of transfer increases the level of government expenditures by 0.6 to 1.3 units, which is rather similar to most countries (Fan and Zhang, 2010d).

But the impact of transfer on government size is much larger as transfer is closely related to the issue of "governmental dead man." China's "upwardly accountable" political system has its unique points and the issue of redundancy in government has always been a focal point in institutional reforms. For example, the "three rewards and one subsidy" implemented by the central attempted to alleviate the local government's "Feeding Budge" dilemma.[18] Since 1982, China implemented six major downsize reforms but the effect of each reform was not

Table 10.3 Rank changes in relative government size (1995–2007)

Increase		*Decrease*		*Unchanged*	
Anhui	11	Guangdong	–9	Hebei	1
Sichuan	11	Tianjin	–8	Hunan	1
Heilongjiang	5	Fujian	–7	Hainan	1
Shaanxi	5	Inner Mongolia	–5	Xinjiang	1
Shanxi	3	Jilin	–5	Ningxia	1
Guizhou	3	Yunnan	–4	Qinghai	1
Jiangsu	3	Liaoning	–4	Gansu	–1
Hubei	2	Beijing	–3	Henan	–1
		Shandong	–2	Tibet	0
				Shanghai	0
				Guangxi	0
				Jiangxi	0
				Zhejiang	0

Note: Chongqing was established in 1997, so it is not included here.
Data source: Author's calculations according to statistical data.

Table 10.4 Rank changes in *per capita* fiscal transfer (1995–2007)

Increase		*Decrease*		*Unchanged*	
Shaanxi	9	Guangdong	–20	Tibet	0
Gansu	8	Zhejiang	–15		
Jilin	8	Jiangsu	–14		
Guizhou	8	Beijing	–12		
Hunan	7	Fujian	–10		
Jiangxi	7	Yunnan	–7		
Anhui	7	Shandong	–7		
Inner Mongolia	7	Tianjin	–6		
Hainan	6	Shanghai	–5		
Sichuan	6	Liaoning	–5		
Henan	5	Hebei	–2		
Ningxia	5				
Heilongjiang	5				
Xinjiang	4				
Qinghai	3				
Shanxi	3				
Guangxi	3				
Hubei	2				

Note: Chongqing was established in 1997, so it is not included here.
Data source: Author's calculations according to statistical data.

especially significant. The 1998 reform was the most vigorous, reducing the number of ministries in the State Council from 40 to 29, the number of divisions and bureaus by one-quarter, and the number of state bureaucrats from 33,000 to 16,000. In 1999, this reform was further extended to the local government and was only finally finished in 2002, during which it was stipulated that half of provincial government bureaucrats had to be cut and redundancies should be eliminated at the municipal, county and township level by an average of 20 percent. This reform caused administrative bureaucrats to fall from 7.39 million to 6.24 million nationwide and eliminated the most redundancies in all downsize reforms. Since 1995, government size exhibited a huge V shape, whether in terms of state departments or party departments, 2002–2003 was the trough and a sharp rise commenced afterwards, returning to pre-reform levels in 2007. But it could be seen in Figure 10.7, that the issue of redundancies appears more in inland regions and downsize reforms do not have much of an impact on them. Currently, governmental bureaucrats (*per capita*) in inland regions are twice those in eastern regions.

Yuan et al. (2008) employed county level panel data for China from 1994 to 2003 and discovered that the stronger a local government's dependence on transfer, the more bureaucrats there are sustained by its fiscal budget (see Figure 10.8). Their explanation for redundancies in underdeveloped regions is since underdeveloped regions are disadvantaged in economic development, when receiving fiscal transfer, they will tend to use them to expand the number of bureaucrats sustained by the fiscal budget in order to establish the local political support network and maintain local stability. However, our research showed that relative to

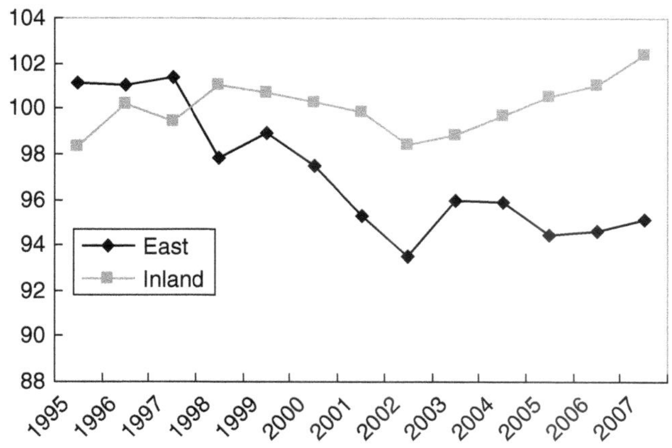

Figure 10.7 Number of governmental bureaucrats (per 10,000 people).

Data source: Author's calculations according to each year's "China Labor Statistical Yearbook".

fiscal subsidies, earmarked grants are more prone to induce redundancies in local government. For every 10,000 yuan increase in *per capita* earmarked grants, the bureaucrats per 10,000 people will increase by 98.6, equivalent to double the current level. The central government tolerates the existence of such a situation because they need to achieve the goal of supplying public goods through earmarked grants, and have no choice but to bear the expenditure and bureaucrats expansion brought by earmarked grants (Fan and Zhang, 2010a). The reason why earmarked grants lead to expansion in bureaucrats is because earmarked grants require higher skilled staff. After receiving earmarked grants local governments have to employ specialized people to operate projects, thereby causing government to increase in size (Shih and Zhang, 2007). Provincial and municipal governments may even encourage and induce county level governments to increase bureaucrats in order to obtain more fiscal transfer from the central government. Since the provinces and municipalities get to retain a portion of fiscal subsidies, they gain from that as well. Under a decentralized governance framework, the central government finds it hard to skip the provincial government and directly adjusts the size of county level governments (Shih et al., 2010).

10.6.2 Lower fiscal/tax efforts

The second negative impact of transfer is lower local government fiscal/tax efforts. Tax effort refers to the ratio between actual taxes raised and theoretical forecast. Theoretical tax level is usually calculated through statistical methods and then compared with actual taxes raised to obtain an index (Bahl, 1971). Since collecting taxes incurs costs, local governments are often prone to using

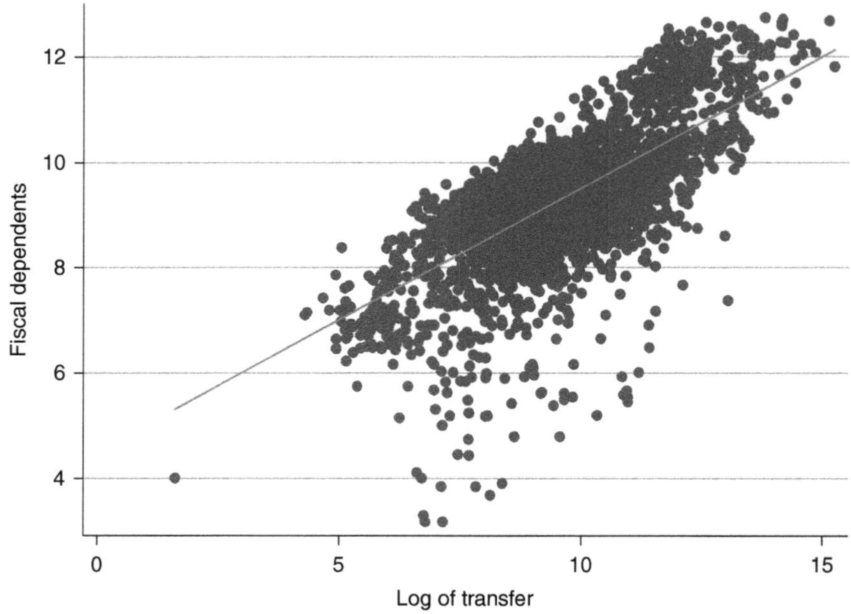

Figure 10.8 Number of people sustained by fiscal budget and fiscal transfer (2005).
Data source: "2006 National Prefecture, Municipality and County Fiscal Statistics".

transfer to substitute for local taxation, thus transfer lower local tax efforts. This effect is supported in some empirical studies, such as the study on Columbia which found that 96 percent of transfer projects lowered local tax efforts (Correa and Steiner, 1994). However, when the income effect of transfer is not very large, equalized transfer may actually lead to a higher equilibrium tax rate (Sam and Smart, 2006). A study on the US and Canada found that equalized transfer will not impact the local tax reaction function under certain assumptions (Leonzio, 2008). If the center employs a subsidy mode aimed at fiscal deficits, this will create an adverse incentive problem, that is, encouraging local governments to lower tax efforts while at the same time increaseing government expenditure, requesting more transfer from upper level governments through increasing fiscal deficits. Such a distortive effect will lower the fiscal independence of local governments (Chernick, 1979; Moffitt, 1992). In order to avoid the negative impact of transfer on tax effort, the center must perform the necessary improvements on the transfer system, such as increasing the weight of tax effort in the formula for transfer.

Most studies on China's transfer and tax effort find that the two are significantly negatively correlated. Qiao et al. (2006) found that tax rebates and aggregate transfer both inhibit local tax efforts while also finding that rich regions and poor regions react differently. The negative impact of transfer is mainly seen in rich regions and heavily populated provinces, while it has a positive effect in minority regions. Rich regions tend to lower taxation efforts to “leave wealth with the people” and lower the portion contributed to the central government. In Zhang and Chen’s (2007) study however, they found that tax rebates have a positive incentive on local tax efforts but general transfer and earmarked grants both produce negative incentives. However, in terms of regional disparities, Liu and Zhao (2009) found that the inhibitive effect of transfer on tax efforts mainly appears in inland regions, while the incentives are actually positive in coastal regions. Other than cost considerations, local governments reducing effective tax rates to compete for tax revenue is also a reason for lower tax efforts (Shen and Fu, 2006). Since reform and opening, China has always emphasized concentration of taxation power and unity of tax laws in taxation legislative power and taxation policy. The central government concentrated the legislative, explanatory and revision authorities for almost all taxes and local governments do not have legislative power over taxes. Even though each region does not have the power to adjust tax rates, a portion of tax revenue is collected by local government and the room for adjustment in tax efforts is large, causing effective tax rates to be far lower than nominal tax rates (An, 2002).[19]

The reason that different studies find different conclusion lies in different endowments and preferences in different regions. Wealthy regions have a relatively better tax base and tax collection costs are lower, so they are better able to reach the matching requirement for earmarked grants with their own fiscal resources, therefore increases in tax efforts and transfer are positively correlated. Poor regions have a weaker tax base and even if tax efforts are increased, the matching requirements for earmarked grants may not be reached, so they can only strive to obtain lump-sum transfer, reducing fiscal revenue at that level by lowering tax efforts, increasing the fiscal deficit and obtaining fiscal subsidies from the center. So for poor regions, tax efforts are negatively correlated with transfer, which illustrates the non-linearity of local governments’ reaction to transfer (Yao, 2007). The relationship between transfer and fiscal revenue for common counties is U-shaped. The lower the fiscal revenue on the left side of the U-shape, the more transfer obtained, and the opposite is true for the right side of the U-shape, which illustrates that the negative impact of transfer on tax efforts is mainly in those regions on the left side of the U-shape, while incentives for county-level municipalities on the right side of the U-shape are positive.

10.6.3 Asymmetric reactions of local revenue and expenditure

The third negative effect of transfer is asymmetric local government reactions, that is, when transfer to one region increases, the fiscal expenditure of that region increases accordingly, while once upper level governments reduce such transfer out of policy and economic considerations, the region’s fiscal expenditure will not significantly decrease and local governments will cope with reduced transfer through local taxation. During the 1970s and 1980s, the US federal government began to consider lowering the government deficit, thus reducing transfer to state governments, but at the same time, state governments correspondingly increased these specific expenditures (Forrester and Spindler, 1990; Stonecash, 1990; Stotsky, 1991). In a study on China, Li and Shen (2009) discovered that the revenue and expenditure decisions of local government show asymmetric reactions to vertical transfer. They also found that expenditure decisions are also asymmetric with an increase or decrease in transfer. With transfer decrease, local expenditure levels are maintained at a relatively stable level. Asymmetric reaction emphasizes full consideration of local government feedback and the long-term impact of such a transfer on local expenditure structure before upper level governments perform the transfer.

10.7 Conclusions and research prospects

China's circumstances are quite similar to those of most countries. The central government controls massive resources while also delegating responsibility for large amounts of expenditure to local governments. The phenomenon of asymmetric central fiscal powers and responsibilities exists in most countries. Fiscal revenue power is concentrated at the central level, perhaps out of efficiency considerations, for example avoiding duplication and omission in taxation and out of consideration for political stability, for example coordinating consistency in upper and lower level government behavior (Wedeman, 1999). While responsibilities are being decentralized, fiscal expenditure powers are being delegated as well and the central level makes up the gap between fiscal powers and responsibilities through vertical transfer. Strictly speaking, from the perspective of fiscal expenditure powers, asymmetries in fiscal powers and responsibilities do not exist at the central level; even if they do, they would not be too serious. On the contrary, asymmetries in fiscal powers and responsibilities really exist at the middle level, especially the provincial and municipal level. On the one hand, the tax sharing reform only divided the share between center and province, and taxes below the provincial level were handed to each province for it to deal with. Some provinces followed the tax sharing mode, while others continued the mode before the reform, or employed repeated consultations. Most provinces and municipalities are prone to over-concentrating middle and lower level governments' fiscal resources. However, most transfer goes through the center to the provinces and is then distributed from the provincial level downwards. Provincial governments have very strong incentives and room to retain part of the subsidy. In addition, provinces are prone to delegating expenditure responsibility to county level governments, causing county level governments to be unable to provide certain basic public services.

The main problem at the central level is lack of efficiency in transfer to lower level governments. From the perspective of the supply of public goods, the central government employing transfer to motivate local governments to increase the supply of public goods is the best option. Such a mode exists pervasively in an overwhelming majority of countries. For example, in 1990, federal subsidies obtained by states in the US account for 20 percent of their fiscal revenue, while that figure is 44 percent in Australia (Fisher, 1996). Our studies also find that transfer has a certain positive impact in China as a formal system. Transfer improved roads, basic education, social security etc. in underdeveloped regions, but from another perspective, the current transfer system may possibly be "captured" by local governments, as local government are inclined toward employing strengthened fiscal resources to expand the number of people sustained by the fiscal budget instead of constructive economic activity. Transfer has almost no impact on balancing local government fiscal deficits and may even intensify disparities among regions, as regions that are relatively developed, have relatively higher concentration of minorities and are situated in the west are more likely to receive transfer. From the long-term perspective, transfer does not facilitate local economic growth and alleviate economic disparities. Developmental levels for regions that obtain transfer may actually worsen.

When transfer attains a certain positive effect, the abovementioned negative impacts may not necessarily appear. First, for earmarked grants, although certain matching conditions should be taken to encourage the input of local governments, local fiscal and tax effort weights should also be added to the conditions, for example, stipulating that the local effective tax rate cannot be lower than a certain critical level, in order to prevent the negative impact of specific transfer on local taxation. At the same time, the current "administrative orders coming from multiple departments" situation needs to be changed, integrating identical or similar projects into the same department or concentrating authority over earmarked grants, getting to the root of the current chaotic situation, in order to establish a relatively unified and transparent payment mechanism and avoid rent-seeking activities. Next, for fiscal transfer, the effect of the factor based formula should be strengthened, though the design of more objective indicators should avoid indicators that can be manipulated by the local government, for example, substituting total population for bureaucrats sustained by fiscal budget as the factor for standard fiscal expenditures; avoiding policy inertia, changing the current method of transfer allocation which is divided according to east, central and west, directly linking transfer to equalization of fiscal resources.

Future studies on transfer can at least expand in the following few aspects. First, how the transfer is allocated. Although some literature conducted studies on this area, no study has yet classified different projects or differentiated between the different effects of economic and political factors in detail. On the one hand, some of the center's concrete policies are fuzzy. For example, in lump-sum transfer, there is a transfer coefficient controlled by the center, but for transfer at the provincial level and below there are even less concrete institutional regulations. On the other hand, due to a lack of detailed data, statistically testing for whether or not a certain transfer followed the rules becomes exceptionally difficult, and since earmarked grants involve different administrative departments, while at the same time, the process of allocation is mingled with strategic interaction between upper and lower level governments, the level of transparency is very low, and it is often hard for aggregated data to reflect the actual process of allocation.

Next, rent-seeking and corruption generated in the process of allocating transfer. Due to asymmetric information between the central and local government, the central government cannot fully differentiate the real fiscal resources of each region through a screening mechanism beforehand. Some matching conditions may only be partially implemented or not implemented at all, leading to these projects becoming "fishing projects" through which the local government asks the central government for money. A portion of earmarked grants do not even have concrete formulas and standards and are entirely dependent upon the subjective decisions by the ministries and committees of the central government, inducing the local government to conduct lobbying and bribery activities. Local governments need to lobby the central government to obtain central project funding and the countless Beijing liaison offices established in recent years is a reflection of such lobbying. Infrastructure projects often contain more rent-seeking and corruption opportunities (Mauro, 1998). There are still no studies in literature that directly link transfer and corruption in contemporary China, and exploration on the influencing mechanisms between these two are even more lacking.

Finally, there is the relationship between transfer and industrial relocation. The center increasing transfer to underdeveloped regions can alleviate the dependence of local fiscal expenditures on the economy, while lower fiscal and tax efforts by the local government in fact imply that the firms' effective tax rates are lower, which encourages firms to move from high tax burden regions to regions with lower tax burdens, that is, firms may move from the coastal regions to the inland regions. We have observed such a round of industrial relocation in practice, but we are not certain how big the impact of central fiscal transfer is on this issue and no studies that conduct research on the relationship between the two exist in the literature.

Notes

1 The first General Situation is: "coastal regions should accelerate opening to the outside world … thereby spurring the inland regions to develop better … the inland regions show consideration for this General Situation." The second General situation is: "after reaching a certain level of development, the coastal regions will be required to put in more effort to help the inland regions develop … the coastal regions at that point need to submit to this General Situation as well." Refer to the *Selected Works of Deng Xiaoping*, Vol. 3, pp. 277–278.

2 In 2000, the State Council officially promulgated the "Notification Regarding the Implementation of Various Policy Measures for the Western Development Program," pointing out that 12 provincial regions: Chongqing, Sichuan, Guizhou, Yunnan, Tibet, Shaanxi, Gansu, Ningxia, Qinghai, Xinjiang, Inner Mongolia and Guangxi would be heavily supported. One of the measures clearly proposed was increased fiscal transfer.

3 Here we simplify the economies of scale in provision of public goods as, if economies of scale are large enough, it will conversely require sufficiently free labor mobility.

4 When some studies discuss the applicability of the Tiebout model to China, they propose that China does not fulfil the basic assumptions of the Tiebout model: (1) sufficient factor mobility, although China is gradually relaxing the Hukou system, implicit restrictions still remain and is far from reaching free mobility; (2) government is downwardly accountable, while in China's current political system it is mainly upwardly accountable (Zhang, 2006).

5 For example, in 1980, due to fiscal difficulties, the central government borrowed 7 billion RMB from the local government; in 1982, it borrowed 4 billion. In 1983, the central government directly transformed the balance of the loans into a lower base in the local government's expenditure contract and correspondingly adjusted the local government's share of fiscal revenues and subsidies (Jia and Zhao, 2008, p. 29).

6 In the rules implementing the tax sharing reform, it used to clearly point out that one objective of the reform was to balance the fiscal resources of each region and through fiscal transfer, support the development of economically undeveloped regions and the transformation of old industrial bases. See "State Council Decision Regarding the Implementation of a Tax sharing Fiscal Management System" (Issued by the State Council [1993] No. 85).

7 In a rigorous sense, tax rebates are similar to factor-based transfer, that is, the distribution formula performs calculations in accordance with a certain amount of objective factors, since shared taxes are all collected by the central government, then transferred to the local government according to the 1993 tax base and a 30 percent growth rate; the procedure of which is the same with unconditional transfer.

8 The plan stipulates that the center's share in 2002 will be 50 percent and that will increase to 60 percent starting in 2003.

9 A certain amount is rewarded based on county and township downsizing.

10 Since earmarked grants provide assistance for designated projects, they become an effective means through which upper level governments can enhance political control over lower level governments.

11 Including lump-sum transfer, wage augmentation transfer, minority region transfer, difficult remote regions subsidies, rural tax and fee reform transfer.

12 The reason why it is below 1 is because the center's earmarked grants are not only aimed at the public goods sector, as much investment is directed toward other productive fields, such as agriculture and forestry.

13 It is usually believed that in an upwardly accountable country, the level of local public goods will be low, but research on China found that although the level of public goods is at the low end, it is still higher than theoretically predicted. Tsai's explanation is that China has a traditional clan system, which is inclusive and embeddable and can be mutually nested with the formal local government, inducing local government to increase investment in public goods. The underlying reason is that local officials pay attention to the prestige these organizations confer, which is conducive to their pursuit of personal objectives and the effective implementation of government policy. She employed 316 village level data on the Chinese countryside and discovered that areas with evident clan influence have elementary school buildings of higher quality.

14 For example, in the Western Development Program, the first goal is economic prosperity. See "State Council Notification Regarding the Implementation of Various Policy Measures for the Western Development Program".

15 Such a difference may reflect different reactions to transfer in different regions. Wealthy regions may input more into economic development, whereas underdeveloped regions lack incentives to develop their economy and are instead inclined to use transfer to expand bureaucrat, thus the negative impact of transfer on underdeveloped regions will be larger, see Yuan et al. (2007).

16 Wagner's law refers to an increase in the ratio of a country's government expenditures to GDP as an economy develops. This is because increased residents' demand for public services will cause a country to transit from laissez faire capitalism to a welfare state.

17 Fiscal illusion states that since taxpayers are not aware of the marginal price of public goods, they can only substitute the marginal price with average price, causing the eventual supply of public goods to exceed theoretical predict (Turnbull, 1992).

18 Stipulating that removal or merging of one township receives a 500,000 yuan reward, cutting down personnel by one person receives a 4,000 yuan reward. For personnel growth above the national average level, a fine of 500 yuan/person will be levied. See "2005 Central Fiscal Budget's Rewards and Subsidies To Assist Local Governments in Alleviating County and Township Fiscal Difficulties" (Finance Budget [2005] No. 77).

19 In the past decade, national fiscal revenue grew faster than GDP. A major reason is exactly the convergence of effective tax rates to nominal tax rates.

References

In English

Ahmad, Ehtisham, 1998, "The Reform of the Fiscal Transfer System," In *Taxation in Modern China*, ed. Brean, D. London: Routledge.

Bahl, Roy, 1971, "A Regression Approach to Tax Effort and Tax Ratio Analysis," *International Monetary Fund Staff Papers*, 18(3), pp. 570–612.

Bailey, Stephen J. and Stephen Connolly, 1998, "The Flypaper Effect: Identifying Areas for Further Research," *Public Choice*, 95, pp. 335–361.

Barro, Robert J., 1999, "Inequality, Growth, and Investment," *NBER Working Paper*.

Besley, Timothy and Stephen Coate, 2003, "Centralized versus Decentralized Provision of Local Public Goods: a Political Economy Analysis," *Journal of Public Economics*, 87(12), pp. 2611–2637.

Boadway, R. W., 2006, "Intergovernmental Redistributive Transfers: Efficiency and Equity," In *Handbook of Fiscal Federalism*, ed. Ahmad, Ehtisham and Giorgio Brosio. Cheltenham: Edward Elgar.

Boadway, R. W. and F. R. Flatters, 1982, "Efficiency and Equalization in a Federal System of Government: A Synthesis and Extension of Recent Results," *Canadian Journal of Economics*, 15, pp. 613–633.

Bradford, David F. and Wallace E. Oates, 1971, "The Analysis of Revenue Sharing in a New Approach to Collective Fiscal Decisions," *Quarterly Journal of Economics*, 85(3), pp. 416–439.

Brennan, G. and J. J. Pincus, 1996, "A Minimalist Model of Federal Grants and Flypaper Effects," *Journal of Public Economics*, 61, pp. 229–246.

Breton, Albert, 1965, "A Theory of Governmental Grants," *Canadian Journal of Economics and Political Science*, 31(2), pp. 175–187.

Broadway, Robin W. and Paul A. R. Hobson, 1993, "Intergovernmental Fiscal Relations in Canada," Canadian Tax Foundation, *Canadian Tax Paper* No.96.

Chen, Zhao and Ming Lu, 2008, "Is China Sacrificing Growth when Balancing Interregional and Urban-Rural Development?" In *Reshaping Economic Geography in East Asia*, ed. Huang, Yukon and Alessandro Magnoli Bocchi, 241–257. Washington DC: The World Bank.

Chernick, H., 1979, "An Economic Model of the Distribution of Project Grants," In *Fiscal Federalism and Grants-in Aid*, ed. Mieszkowski, P. and W. Oakland, 572–585. Washington DC: Urban Institute.

Chubb, John E., 1985, "The Political Economy of Federalism," *American Political Science Review*, 79, pp. 994–1015.

Correa, P. and R. Steiner, 1994, "Decentralization in Colombia: Recent Changes and Main Challenges," Paper prepared for Second Conference on the Colombian Economy, Lehigh University.

Fisher, Ronald C., 1996, *State and Local Public Finance*, 2nd edn. Chicago: Richard D. Irwin.

Forrester, John P. and Charles J. Spindler, 1990, "Managing Municipal Services in an Era of Declining Federal Assistance," *Policy Studies Review*, 10, pp. 63–84.

Gruber, Jonathan, 2005, *Public Finance and Public Policy*, New York: Worth.

Hamilton, B. W., 1983, "A Review: Is the Property Tax a Benefit Tax?" In *Local Provision of Public Services: The Tiebout Model after Twenty-Five Years*, ed. Zodrow, G. R., 85–108. New York: Academic Press.

Hines, James R. and Richard H. Thaler, 1995, "Anomalies: The Flypaper Effect," *Journal of Economic Perspectives*, 9(4), pp. 217–226.

Knight, B., 2002, "Endogenous Federal Grants and Crowd-out of State Government Spending: Theory and Evidence from the Federal Highway Aid Program," *American Economic Review*, 92(1), pp. 71–92.

Leonzio, Rizzo, 2008, "Local Government Responsiveness to Federal Transfers: Theory and Evidence," *International Tax and Public Finance*, 15(3), pp. 316–337.

Ma, Jun, 1997, *Intergovernmental Relations and Economic Management in China*, London: Macmillan Press.

Mauro, 1998, "Corruption and the Composition of Government Expenditure," *Journal of Public Economics*, 69, pp. 263–279.

Moffitt, R.A., 1984, "The Effects of Grants-in-aid on State and Local Expenditures: the Case of AFDC," *Journal of Public Economics*, 23, pp. 279–305.

Musgrave, Richard, 1983, "Who Should Tax, Where and What?" In *Tax Assignment in Federal Countries*, ed. Mclure, Jr. Canberra: Australian National University Press.

Oates, Wallace E., 1972, *Fiscal Federalism*. New York: Harcourt Brace Jovanovic.

Oates, Wallace E., 1999, "An Essay on Fiscal Federalism," *Journal of Economic Literature*, 37(3), pp. 1120–1149.

Park, Albert, Scott Rozelle, Christine Wong and Changqing Ren, 1996, "Distributional Consequences of Reforming Local Public Finance in China," *China Quarterly*, 147(9), pp. 751–778.

Park, Albert and Xinzheng Shi, 2008, "Impact of Education Fee Reductions on Enrollment in Gansu," Memo, University of Oxford and University of Michigan.

Poncet, Sandra, 2003, "Measuring Chinese Domestic and International Integration," *China Economic Review*, 14(1), pp. 1–21.

Raiser, Martin, 1998, "Subsidizing Inequality: Economic Reforms, Fiscal Transfers and Convergence across Chinese Provinces," *Journal of Development Studies*, 34(3), pp. 1–26.

Rhode, Paul W. and Koleman S. Strumph, 2003, "Assessing the Importance of Tiebout Sorting: Local Heterogeneity from 1850 to 1990," *American Economic Review*, 93(5), pp. 1648–1677.

Rosen, Harvey S., 1995, *Public Finance*. Illinois: Richard D. Irwin.

Sam, Bucovetsky and Michael Smart, 2006, "The Efficiency Consequences of Local Revenue Equalization: Tax Competition and Tax Distortions," *Journal of Public Economics Theory*, 8(1), pp. 119–144.

Sato, Motohiro, 2000, "Fiscal Externalities and Efficient Transfers in a Federation," *International Tax and Public Finance*, 7, pp. 119–139.

Shah, A., 1994, "The Reform of Intergovernmental Fiscal Relations in Developing and Emerging Market Economies," *Policy and Research Series No.23*, Washington DC: World Bank.

Shi, Xinzheng, 2008, "Does an Intra-household Flypaper Effect Exist? Evidence from the Education Fee Reduction Reform in Rural China," *Working Paper*, University of Michigan.

Shih, Victor and Qi Zhang, 2007, "Who Receives Subsidies: a Look at the County Level in Two Time Periods," In *Paying for Progress in China*, ed. Shue, Vivienne and Christine Wong. London: Routledge.

Shih, Victor, Qi Zhang and Mingxing Liu, 2010, "When the Autocrat Gives: Determinants of Fiscal Transfers in Authoritarian China," submitted to *World Politics*.

Smart, Michael, 1998, "Taxation and Deadweight Loss in a System of Intergovernmental Transfers," *Canadian Journal of Economics*, 31(1), pp. 189–206.

Stiglitz, J. E. and P. Dasgupta, 1971, "Differential Taxation, Public Goods and Economic Efficiency," *Review of Economic Studies*, 38, pp. 151–174.

Stonecash, Jeffrey M., 1990, "State Responses to Declining Federal Support: Behavior in the Post-1978 Era," *Policy Studies Journal*, 18, pp. 755–767.

Stotsky, Janet G., 1991, "State Fiscal Responses to Federal Government Grant," *Growth and Chang*, 23, pp. 17–31.

Tiebout, Charles, 1956, "A Pure Theory of Local Expenditure," *Journal of Political Economy*, 64, pp. 416–424.

Treisman, Deniel, 1998, "Russian's Taxing Problem," *Foreign Policy*, Fall, pp. 55–66.

Tsai, Lily, 2007, "Solidary Groups, Informal Accountability, and Local Public Goods Provision in Rural China," *American Political Science Review*, 101(2), pp. 355–372.

Tsui, K., 2005, "Local Tax System, Intergovernmental Transfers and China's Local Fiscal Disparities," *Journal of Comparative Economics*, 33, pp. 173–196.

Turnbull, Geoffrey K., 1992, "Fiscal Illusion, Uncertainty, and the Flypaper Effect," *Journal of Public Economics*, 48, pp. 207–223.

Wallis, J. J., 1996, "What Determines the Allocation of National Government Grants to the States?" *NBER Working Papers Series*: Historical Factors in Long Run Growth.

Wedeman, Andrew, 1999, "Agency and Fiscal Dependence in Central-provincial Relations in China," *Journal of Contemporary China*, 8 (20), pp. 103–122.

Yao, S., 2000, "Economic Development and Poverty Reduction in China over 20 Years of Reforms," *Economic Development and Culture Change*, 48(3), pp. 447–474.

Yao, S. and Z. Zhang, 2001, "Regional Growth in China under Economic Reforms," *Journal of Development Studies*, 38(2), pp. 167–186.

Yao, Yi, 2007, "Investigation the Equalization and Incentive Effect of Intergovernmental Grants in China," *Working Paper*, Cornell University.

Young, Alwyn, 2000, "The Razor's Edge: Distortions and Incremental Reform in the People's Republic of China," *Quarterly Journal of Economics*, 115, pp. 1091–1135.

Zhang, Xiaobo, 2006, "Fiscal Decentralization and Political Centralization in China: Implications for Growth and Inequality," *Journal of Comparative Economics*, 34, pp. 713–726.

In Chinese

An, Tifu, 2002, "How to Consider the Unexpected Increased Tax and Tax Cut," *Taxation Research Journal*, 8, pp. 10–17.

Fan, Ziying and Jun Zhang, 2010a, "Fiscal Transfer, Provision of Public Goods and the Expansion of Government's Size," *CCES Working Paper*, Fudan University.

Fan, Ziying and Jun Zhang, 2010b, "How did China Lose Efficiency for Equality?," *The Journal of World Economy*, 10, pp. 117–138.

Fan, Ziying and Jun Zhang, 2010c, "*Fiscal Decentralization*, Intergovernmental Transfer and Market Integration," *Economic Research Journal*, 3, pp. 53–64.

Fan, Ziying and Jun Zhang, 2010d, "Flypaper Effect: An Explanation of the Expansion of Governments' Size," *China Industrial Economics*, 12, pp. 5–15.

Guo, Qingwang and Junxue Jia, 2006, "The Behavior of Local Governments, the Impulse to Invest and Macroeconomic Stability," *Management World*, 5, pp. 19–25.

Gui, Qihan, Min Chen, Ming Lu and Zhao Chen, 2006, "Does the Domestic Goods Market of China Segregate or integrate? Based on Prices Measurement," *Journal of World Economy*, 2, pp. 20–30.

Jia, Kang and Quanhou Zhao, 2008, *Zhongguo Jingji Gaige Sanshinian*. Chongqing University Press.

Jiang, Xiaogan, Feng Wei and Shanghua Jiang, 1999, "An appropriate scale control of China's Fiscal Transfer," *Management World*, 3, pp. 51–61.

Li, Ping, 2006, *Zhongguo Zhengfujian Caizheng Guanxi Tujie*. Beijing: Zhongguo Caizheng Jingji Press.

Li, Yongyou and Yuping Shen, 2009, "Fiscal Transfer and the Decision of Revenue and Expenditure," *Management World*, 11, pp. 41–53.

Liu, Xiaoyong and Zhen Li, 2008, "Empirical Study on Fiscal Decentralization and Regional Market Segmentation," *Journal of Finance and Economics*, 2, pp. 88–98.

Liu, Yongzheng and Jianmei Zhao, 2009, "Intergovernmental Fiscal Transfers and the Differences of Local Fiscal Efforts under TSS Reform: Analysis of Alternative Dutch Disease Based on Multiple Classifications of Functions and Regions," *Journal of Finance and Economics*, 12, pp. 73–83.

Lu, Ming, Zhao Chen and Ji Yan, 2004, "Increasing Return, Development Strategy and Regional Economic Segmentation," *Economic Research Journal*, 1, pp. 54–63.

Lu, Ming, Zhao Chen and Zhenzhen Yang, 2007, "Equality and Growth Hand in Hand: Increasing Returns, Strategic Behavior and Efficiency Loss in the Division of Labor," *China Economic Quarterly*, 6(2), pp. 443–468.

Ma, Shuanyou and Hongxia Yu, 2003, "Inter-Governmental Transferment and Regional Economic Convergence in China," *Economic Research Journal*, 3, pp. 26–33.

National Audit Office of the People's Republic of China, 2006, *Guanyu 2005* Niandu Zhongyang Yusuan Zhixing Shenji Gongzuo Baogao.

Qiao, Baoyun, Jianyong Fan and Jiming Peng, 2006, "Intergovernmental Transfer and Tax Efforts," *Management World*, 3, pp. 50–56.

Shen, Kunrong and Wenlin Fu, 2006, "Tax Competition, Region Game and Their Efficiency of Growth," *Economic Research Journal*, 6, pp. 16–26.

Wang, Shaoguang, 2004, "Shunying Minxin De Bianhua," *Strategy and Management*, 2, pp. 51–60.

Wang, Yongqin, Yan Zhang, Yuan Zhang, Zhao Chen and Ming Lu, 2007, "On China's Development Model:The Costs and Benefits of China's Decentralization Approach to Transition", *Economic Research Journal*, 1, pp. 4–16.

Yin, Heng and Hong Zhu, 2009, "The Equal Effects of the China's Transfer in Counties," *Management World*, 4, pp. 37–46.

Yin, Heng, Linlin Kang and Lijuan Wang, 2007, "The Equal Effects of the China's Intergovernmental Transfer," *Management World*, 1, pp. 48–55.

Yuan, Fei, Ran Tao, Zhigang Xu and Minxing Liu, 2008, "Fiscal Transfers and Expansion of Fiscal Dependents in China's Fiscal Recentralization," *Economic Science*, 5, pp. 70–80.

Zeng, Junping, 2000, "The Equal Effects of China's Transfer," *Economic Research Journal*, 6, pp. 27–32.
Zhang, Henglong and Xian Chen, 2007, "The Effects of Intergovernmental Transfer on Tax Efforts and Equalization," *Economic Science*, 1, pp. 15–23.
Zhang, Lihua and Chong Wang, 2008, "Resolving System Deficiencies in the Financial Guarantee of Rural Compulsory Education—Central Transfer Payment System and the Powers of the Authority Structural Adjustment," *Economic Science*, 10, pp. 144–153.

Postscript

About a year ago, in the plan for this book, we wrote two sentences about its "origins": (1) It is time to comprehensively summarize research and experience on the development of Chinese regional economy; (2) China needs such a book, which performs empirical research on Chinese regional economy issues on the basis of reviewing existing literature, providing answers to major policy issues regarding Chinese regional and urban-rural development, while also acting in concert with the relevant education of graduate students. In retrospect, these objectives have mostly been attained.

The Fudan Lab for China Development Studies, Zhejiang University's Industrial and Spatial Economics Research Center and Zhongshan University Lingnan Academy's Industrial and Regional Research Center launched this collective research project. Our thoughts were to make the writing style of this book somewhere between the "World Bank Development Report" and "Handbook of Regional and Urban Economics," more focused on summarizing research than the former and more focused on concluding stylized facts and their corresponding policy implications than the latter.

In order to complete this task, we specially invited a group of domestic academics, who have done much research in relevant fields, to join us. They include Peking University's Canfei He, Tsinghua University's Siqi Zheng, Fudan University's Jianyong Fan, Nankai University's Jiuli Huang, Huazhong University of Science and Technology's Ziying Fan. Of course, this includes ourselves, namely, Zhongshan University's Xianxiang Xu, Zhejiang University's Xiwei Zhu and Fudan University's Zhao Chen, and Ming Lu affiliated with both Shanghai Jiao Tong University and Fudan. Over a year ago, Ming Lu met Zhigang Li at Hong Kong University and mentioned this collective project. Zhigang Li happily accepted the invitation and concluded research relating to infrastructure. We are especially honored that when Professor Jacques-François Thisse of Université catholique de Louvain (Belgium) learned of this project, he wrote the introduction for this book which elated us greatly. Therefore, as this book is about to become finished, as editors, we first thank all authors that worked on it. We also thank Fudan University's Allen Zhan for his translation and Fudan University's Haijun Ou and Fangwen Li and Shanghai Normal University's Xi Wu for their research assistance.

This collective project took a total of two years, but the accumulated knowledge it reflects far exceeds this. In September 2010, under the consideration of Southeast University School of Economics and Management's Dean Kangning Xu and Professor Qin Zhou and the organization of Xiuyan Liu and Jun Shao, the authors took the opportunity of the Young Economists Society congregation in Southeast University on regional economics to get together and fully study the progress of this book, while also reaching a consensus on major policy issues regarding China's regional and urban–rural development based on existing research. We hope this book can fill in the gap between regional and urban economics research and Chinese practice. The conclusion and assembly of research is a very complex task and over ten authors collectively accomplishing this task makes organizing the project even more difficult. We ask the reader to be generous with your criticism for the inaccuracies and omissions in this book.

The research in this book was assisted by funding from Fudan University "985 Project" towards the Fudan Lab for China Development Studies. At the same time, this project received the support of Zhejiang's Industrial and Spatial Economics Research Center and Zhongshan University Lingnan Academy's Industrial and Regional Research Center. The publication of this book received the support of Mr Yuanlong He and Mrs Na Li of Shanghai New Century Publishing Group's Truth & Wisdom Press, as well as Lindsey Hall (Taylor & Francis) and Ruchika Agarwal (Cenveo Publisher Services). We express our gratitude to all of them here.

The Editors
February 2013

Index

Introductory note

References such as "178–9" indicate (not necessarily continuous) discussion of a topic across a range of pages. Wherever possible in the case of topics with many references, these have either been divided into sub-topics or only the most significant discussions of the topic are listed. Because the entire work is about "China" and "regional development," the use of these terms (and certain others which occur constantly throughout the book) as an entry point has been restricted. Information will be found under the corresponding detailed topics.

For Product Safety Concerns and Information please contact our EU representative GPSR@taylorandfrancis.com
Taylor & Francis Verlag GmbH, Kaufingerstraße 24, 80331 München, Germany

www.ingramcontent.com/pod-product-compliance
Ingram Content Group UK Ltd.
Pitfield, Milton Keynes, MK11 3LW, UK
UKHW022006180926
475701UK00003B/230
9781138914810